THE
HISTORICAL ATLAS
OF
JUDAISM

A CARTOGRAPHICA PRESS BOOK

This book is produced by
Cartographica Press
6 Blundell St
London N7 9BH

Copyright © 2009 Cartographica Press

All rights reserved.
This book is protected by copyright.
No part of it may be reproduced, stored in a retrieval system,
or transmitted in any form or by any means, without the prior
permission in writing from the publisher, nor be otherwise
circulated in any form of binding or cover other than that in which
it is published and without a similar condition including this
condition being imposed on the subsequent publisher.

ISBN 10: 1-84573-413-0
ISBN 13: 978-1-84573-413-8

QUMHAOJ

Editorial & Design: Cartographica Press
Editor: Sarah Stubbs
Author: Dr Ian Barnes
Author: Josephine Bacon
Design: Vanessa Green and Louise Bolton
Layout: Cartographica Press
Production: Rohana Yusof
Fulfilment Assistant: Samantha Warrington

Cartography:
Cartographica

Printed in Singapore by
Star Standard Industries Pte Ltd.

THE HISTORICAL ATLAS

OF

JUDAISM

DR. IAN BARNES
EDITED BY: JOSEPHINE BACON

CARTOGRAPHICA

CONTENTS

CONTENTS ✳ 5

MAP LIST

INTRODUCTION

JEWS POSSESS A FOUR-THOUSAND-YEAR-OLD HISTORY DURING WHICH THEY HAVE CLUNG TO THEIR IDENTITY AND PHYSICALLY SURVIVED. THIS IS ALL THE MORE REMARKABLE SINCE THEY INITIALLY INHABITED ONE OF THE MOST WAR-TORN REGIONS OF THE WORLD.

The Near East has always been a transit area through which the old empires marched to war to compete with each other for land, people, and commerce – the Hittites, Egyptians and various Mesopotamian powers, the Persians, the Greeks and the Romans.

The Bible relates that the founder of the monotheistic religions, Abraham left Mesopotamia, moved to Haran and then into Canaan after God commanded him to do so. Canaan was promised to his descendants as their rightful territory forever. The story of the Egyptian captivity, the Exodus and renewed covenants with God and the foundation of Mosaic Law all feature in the early books of the Bible.

This historical atlas maps the history of Jews and Judaism, the movements of Jews in the Diaspora and their vicissitudes before the creation of a homeland and state in modern Israel. The Atlas is divided into six sections, based on chronology and events.

Under Origins, the early movements of the Patriarchs and the sojourn in Egypt of some of the Hebrew tribes; historians still debate the exact nature of the captivity by the Pharaoh. This period is placed within the broad context of ancient civilizations, their technology, style of warfare and international trade. The acquisition of Canaan is placed within the historical discussion of whether the seizure of Canaan was slow, a grinding attrition, or just a people gradually filtering into a region using both peace and war. The security of the Hebrews is placed within the framework of the activity of the Judges and Saul, the first king.

The Jewish Kingdoms maps the Davidic and Solomonic states, whose imperial status was created within a virtual international power vacuum. Israel's larger neighbours provided Jewish rulers with opportunities for aggrandisement and the development of commerce. The fragile nature of the state is shown by the split into the successor states of Israel and Judah, their histories, and their eventual destruction by Assyria and Babylon respectively.

Exile and Dispersal portrays the Babylonian exile, the homecoming of some of the Jews under Persian auspices, the conquest of the Ptolemaic empire by Alexander the Great, and the creation of a Hellenized Near East and Mesopotamia. The oppression of the Jews by Seleucid monarchs resulted in Jewish resistance and the birth of the Hasmonean state. Then there is the impact of Rome and how the harshness of Roman rule provoked two Jewish revolts, the destruction of the Second Temple and the further dispersal of Jews around the Mediterranean and beyond. The end of this chapter shows how Judaism partially shaped two new world monotheistic religions – Christianity and Islam.

Diaspora examines the condition of Jews under Islam and how Jews fared during the Middle Ages in various parts of Europe. The Christian demonization of the Jews is described in the Crusader excesses in their slaughter of Jewish communities along the River Rhine and in the Near East, especially the bloodbath following the capture of Jerusalem. This chapter also includes the fate of some Jewish communities in England at York, Lincoln and Oxford and their expulsion from England in 1290, events which do not often receive treatment in popular history books. The particular cruelty shown toward the Jews in Spain, part of the anti-Jewish and anti-Muslim crusade of the "Catholic Kings" features here as does ghettoisation, being forced to wear distinctive dress, the Cossack attacks and the spread of Jews around the world, particularly to the Americas.

The Jewish Diaspora created communities around the coasts of the Mediterranean and the Near East. For a variety of reasons, to seek new opportunities, or escape persecution, the Diaspora had continued over the last one thousand years. Above, a group of Jews go about their daily lives in an eastern European community, photographed toward the end of the nineteenth century. At this time, due to prevailing social conditions, many sought new homes in the New World, taking with them their many interpretations of Judaism and creating a truly global community.

Modern Jewish Experiences considers the Jewish experience in the nineteenth century and World War II. There are vignettes of the diverse and interesting communities in New York and London and the virulence of an anti-Semitism which rocked France during the Dreyfus Affair when human rights groups and anti-Semitic leagues engaged in street fighting while anti-Semitism was preached in the pulpit of many Roman Catholic churches in western France. The Affair, in part, led to the Theodore Herzl's conversion to Zionism and the consideration of the British Mandate of Palestine as a Jewish homeland, an area vaguely promised to both Jews and Arabs, one via the Balfour Declaration, the other through the MacMahon letter. The Holocaust is placed in the context of Jewish survival and Jewish resistance figures, both as partisans or serving in the ranks of Allied armies.

The Jewish Legacy examines aspects of the current situation. The creation of a series of Jewish settlements in Palestine preceded Israel's War of Independence and the continuing security needs of the new state receive treatment around the various wars which have been fought in the Near East. This situation is linked to the new phenomena of large-scale internationally implemented terrorism. Other contemporary issues, including the anti-Semitic extreme right wing and the anti-Semitic extreme left, are discussed, especially the perverse activities of Holocaust deniers.

The text of the atlas covers a number of other themes. These include Jewish sects – Samaritans, Pharisees, Sadducees and Karaites. The development of Jewish thought and culture is woven into the entire atlas. In sum, the atlas allows the reader to enjoy an understanding of the long and unusual history of the Jewish faith and its adherents.

ORIGINS

THE HEBREWS, OR ISRAELITES AS THEY WERE LATER KNOWN, WERE A
SEMITIC PEOPLE WHO PROBABLY MOVED NORTH FROM THE ARABIAN
PENINSULA IN AROUND 2000 BCE. A PROTO-SEMITIC LANGUAGE, FOR
WHICH THE ALPHABET WAS FIRST INVENTED, BECAME THE LINGUA
FRANCA OF THE MIDDLE EAST AT ABOUT THIS TIME.

Papyrus growing on the banks
of the Hula Lake. The Hula
was once a large swamp which
covered most of the Upper
Galilee. The pith from the
Papyrus plant was used to make
the "paper" for scrolls and
documents starting in around
4000 BCE.

During the Late Neolithic Period in Mesopotamia, there is evidence of a gradual move from subsistence hunting to village life based on agriculture and the domestication of animals. In Jericho's (Tell-es-Sultan) the lowest mound contains vestiges of a Neolithic culture prior to the invention of pottery. By the seventh and sixth millennia BCE, a town existed encircled by a strong wall of heavy stones. The houses were constructed from pounded earth, mud bricks and sometimes stone. There is evidence of worship of a mother-goddess, suggesting a fertility cult, with a triad of other gods – father, mother and son, a divine family. The inhabitants ate emmer wheat, barley, pulses, deer, wild cattle and boar. Jericho was the civilized world's trend-setter, approximately 5000 years before the time of Abraham.

Qal'at Jarmo, near Kirkuk, in Mesopotamia (Iraq), is the earliest known permanent village in the region. The lower levels of its mound display a Neolithic culture that could not make pottery. Jarmo's houses were built of adobe, sometimes on stone foundations. Archaeological evidence reveals various grains and the bones of sheep, goats, pigs and oxen, suggesting domestication of animals. The pre-pottery levels at Jarmo are as old as the corresponding levels in Jericho. Continuous occupation at Jarmo lasted 3000 years, contemporaneously with Catal Hüyük in Anatolia (Turkey). Other communities in Mesopotamia providing evidence of domesticated agriculture are Tell Abu Hureya and Zawi Chemi Shanidar in northern Iraq. Mureybet, Bouqras and Al Kosh were other early farming villages utilizing river-fed irrigation systems or rain. A Hassuna culture developed near Mosul, and Nineveh was first built at this time. In the Land of Canaan, communities similar to those at Jericho occurred in the Yarmuk Valley. There were similar Phoenicia and Syria early villages at Byblos, Ras Smara (Ugarit), and Tell Judeideh in Phoenicia (Lebanon) and Syria.

The semi-nomadic peoples of the Zagros Mountains moved from areas of wild rice growth into rain belts to cultivate crops. By the fourth millennium BCE, a three-temple religious site was developed at Tepe Gawra; one building was covered with vermillion-painted plaster. This is the oldest known example of such architecture. Mesopotamia was the site of the Obeid, Warka and Jemdet Nasr series of cultures. This period (c. 3500–2800 BCE) saw massive urban development and complex irrigation using dykes and canals; the slow drainage of Lower Mesopotamia resulted in the unlocking of rich, alluvial soil, ripe for agriculture and able to support a large population.

City-states developed, these societies using the wheel, oven-fired pottery and copper-smelting. Cylinder seals of great artistic merit were made, accompanied by the invention of writing. The Obeid Period saw the construction of rectangular mud-brick houses and courtyards separated by alleyways, with large spaces reserved for communal buildings, such as granaries. Religious sites were constructed using earth mounds as platforms such as at Eridu. Such temples were often fronted by a central square. The vast temple complex at Eridu on the mound known as Abu Shayhrayan, stood on the coast of the Persian Gulf at the mouth of the Euphrates, before the shoreline receded. The city also harboured a genesis myth involving Ziusudra in a Flood and Ship Flood epic, similar to Noah and his Ark.

The growth of urban settlements coincided with the discovery of copper and bronze. Copper was first smelted in the Middle East between 4500 and 3500 BCE, some 1000 years before its appearance in Europe. Bronze was an alloy of copper and tin. Copper was used in fourth millennium BCE in Mesopotamia and Egypt. Evidence suggests that it was mined in mountainous ore-bearing regions of the Caucasus, Armenia, Anatolia and at Timna in southern Negev. Tin was harder to find, being found chiefly in the Zagros Mountains though some was imported from Europe. Copper was widely used by 3000 BCE and was now imported from Cyprus. Evidence of the Early Bronze Age comes from Egyptian sources, along with archaeological finds at Beisan (Beit Shean), Megiddo and Jericho. Phoenician copper has been found at Ugarit and Byblos.

Semitic peoples moved into Mesopotamia, most historians now believing that they originated in the Arabian peninsula. Spreading out in a series of waves, they gradually encroached upon the early Sumerian peoples of Mesopotamia. Apparently, Sumerian-Semitic relations were harmonious as the Semites moved in from the desert margins. The Akkadians were one such Semitic-speaking group, becoming dominant before Sargon founded his dynasty in c. 2380–2223 BCE. In around 2000 BCE, a migratory wave from Arabia created Babylon from which a number of Semitic colonies emerged, developing into Assyria, the most successful military regime in the Ancient Near East. The Arameans, also Semites, founded states from the Euphrates to the Taurus Mountains and established kingdoms at Damascus and Nabatæa, occupying Edom, Moab and the Sinai Peninsula. A proto-semitic language became the lingua franca of the Near East. Jewish tradition maintains that the Hebrews were of Semitic origin (Genesis and Deuteronomy) and related to the Phoenicians and Canaanites. These Hebrews were also related to the Moabites and Edomites who also spoke a Semitic language.

THE ANCIENT NEAR EAST

IN THE LAND BETWEEN THE TWO GREAT CRADLES OF CIVILIZATION,
MESOPOTAMIA AND EGYPT, A UNIQUE SEMITIC CIVILIZATION
EMERGED OF WELL-FORTIFIED CITIES. THE INHABITANTS COULD
SMELT COPPER AND BRONZE AND THEY WORKED THE LAND AS
FARMERS, RETREATING TO THEIR CITIES AT NIGHT.

Human intervention created major changes to the landscape. Terracing is the best way to conserve water, as can be seen from this olive grove in southern Judea.

From the earliest historical period, Mesopotamia, the Land between Two Rivers, the Euphrates and the Tigris and Egypt with its Nile Valley, became cradles of civilization with dense populations. These regions were linked by the Fertile Crescent which also incorporated Canaan and Phoenicia.

Mesopotamia, under the Sumerians, consisted of a series of city-states. Unification was not achieved despite temporary dominance by one city or another. Eridu lost out to Kish which in turn was challenged by Lagash, Uruk, and Ur, and the kingdom of Mari in Syria. Ur became dominant by 2750 BCE under Kings Mesannepadda and Aannepadda, controlling large areas of southern Mesopotamia. Trade spread as far as the Indian Ocean. Mesopotamian seals have been unearthed in Egypt. The city of Ur was the legendary birth place of Biblical Abraham, sometimes known as Ur of the Chaldees.

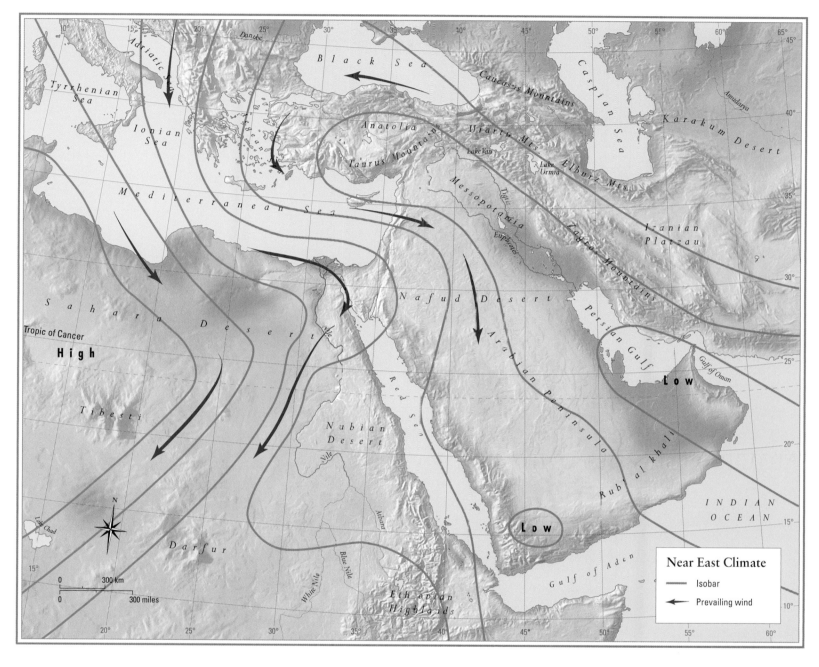

Cities with populations of 10,000 inhabitants or more were ruled by kings and priests. Their temples were brilliantly decorated and had ziggurats rising to the sky as a connection between earth and heaven. The pantheon of gods included Anu, the god of heaven, Enki, the water god and Enlil, the god of earth and storm. Sumerian temples were frequented by priests, scholars, teachers, mathematicians and astrologers, and became centres of learning in which cuneiform writing was invented. The many inscribed clay tablets found contain records of commercial transactions, as well as religious, literary and scientific works. In Uruk, tablets were found recounting the Epic of Gilgamesh. Temples were also food distribution points in times of famine. The gods were served and the rule of law maintained, using systems such as that of Ningirsu, designed to end the oppression of the poor. The Akkadians, a Semitic people living in Mesopotamia were also a sizeable component of population in northern Sumeria. They acquired Sumerian culture, used cuneiform script and adopted Sumerian gods. They developed an empire under Sargon (c. 2334–2279 BCE). He was reputably found floating in a rush basket, just like Moses. Sargon rose to power as cup-bearer to King Ur-Zababa of

Prevailing weather patterns over northeast Africa and the Middle East create conditions where the annual flooding of the Euphrates, Tigris and Nile provides an environment where consistent agriculture can thrive supporting large populations.

Kish. He declared his independence, built a capital at Agade and conquered Mesopotamia, Mari and Phoenicia. He reputably campaigned in the Zagros Mountains, in Elam, and allegedly sent a fleet to conquer Dilmun, a trading post which may have been modern Qatar, Bahrain or Oman. Trade eventually reached as far as the Indus Valley. The Akkadian Empire fell to the Gutians, invaders from the Zagros Mountains, who were succeeded by a new Sumerian dynasty.

Elsewhere, in Egypt, many cultural centres laid the foundations of civilizations based around a mixture of Hamitic and Semitic racial types. As in Mesopotamia, drainage and irrigation systems supported a society that could smelt copper. By the late fourth millennium BCE, two kingdoms developed, one in Upper and one in Lower Egypt, who used a hieroglyphic writing system. Eventually, Upper Egypt became dominant. King Narmer wore the white crown of the South, combined with the red crown of the North.

The Ancient Near East
in the Third Millennium

Akkadian ziggurat (stepped pyramid) of the type built at Ur. 32 ziggurats have been found in Mesopotamia, 28 in modern Iraq and four in Iran. They were constructed between the fourth millennium and the sixth century BCE.

The Third Dynasty (c. 2600) saw pyramid building. The Great Pyramid is 481 feet high with a base of 755 feet by 755 feet, consisting of 2,300,000 blocks of stone, each weighing 2.5 tons. Trading contacts existed throughout the region, including Canaan. Some Pharaohs mention military campaigns in Asia. Byblos, the port for Phoenician timber, became a virtual Egyptian colony and the Canaanites there created a syllabic script based on Egyptian hieroglyphs. The Egyptians possessed a large pantheon of gods, including Isis and Osiris.

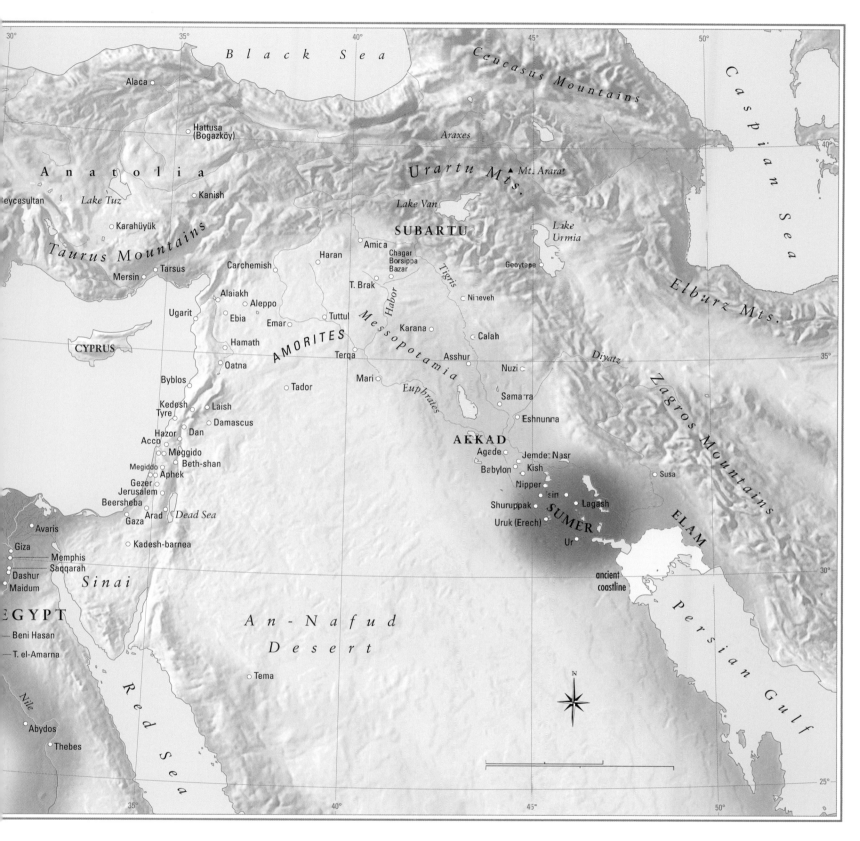

The land between Egypt and Mesopotamia at first failed to develop a sophisticated material culture but in the third millennium there was urban development, population increase and the foundation of solidly constructed, well-fortified cities, many of which are mentioned in the Bible, including Megiddo, Jericho, Bet Shean, Ai, Shechem, Gezer and Lachish. The population was essentially Canaanite and spoke a proto-Semitic language. The people were sedentary, tilling their fields during the day and retreating to their towns at night.

By the third millennium, powerful civilizations had become established in what was known as the 'Fertile Crescent.'

Genesis and the Patriarchs

The Bible Story of the Patriarchs has been confirmed over the years by archaeological finds from other parts of the Middle East.

The story of the proto-Israelites and their faith is shrouded in mystery, yet sufficient documentation has now been unearthed that describes historical events and characters. Nuzi texts, documents from Mari and Alalakh, Cappadocia and Boghazköy, Egyptian Execration tablets and the Amarna letters, all paint a picture that tends to support the Biblical narrative.

The patriarchs portrayed in the Bible were probably historical figures, who migrated with semi-nomadic peoples who gradually wandered westward from Mesopotamia to the Land of Canaan. They moved through marginal lands between settled areas and the desert using the ass as the favoured beast of burden. These progenitors of the Hebrews, who tended flocks of sheep and goats, were kin to the Moabites, Ammonites and Edomites, and Midianites. Additionally, Hebrews had powerful ties with Arameans, maybe because the latter were reputedly children of Shem, parallel in descent to Eber, the

The Ancient Near East in the Time of the Patriarchs 2000–1550 BCE

- Old Assyrian Kingdom
- Kingdom of Mari
- Old Babylonian Kingdom
- Egypt
- Egyptian influence

traditional ancestor of the Hebrews. Documents attest to the existence of a group of people known as the Habiru. This name describes a semi-nomadic people, a people from 'beyond' (ever). Semi-nomadic, occasionally sedentary, mercenaries or labourers on royal projects in Egypt, the Habiru have rightly or wrongly been identified with Hebrews; their life-style was certainly similar. It is interesting to note that a semi-nomadic life was possible throughout the Fertile Crescent from Mesopotamia to Egypt, suggesting a relatively peaceful period when people moved freely and trade flourished.

At the time of the Patriarchs, nomadic peoples frequently sought sustenance within powerful states in the region, especially in times of drought.

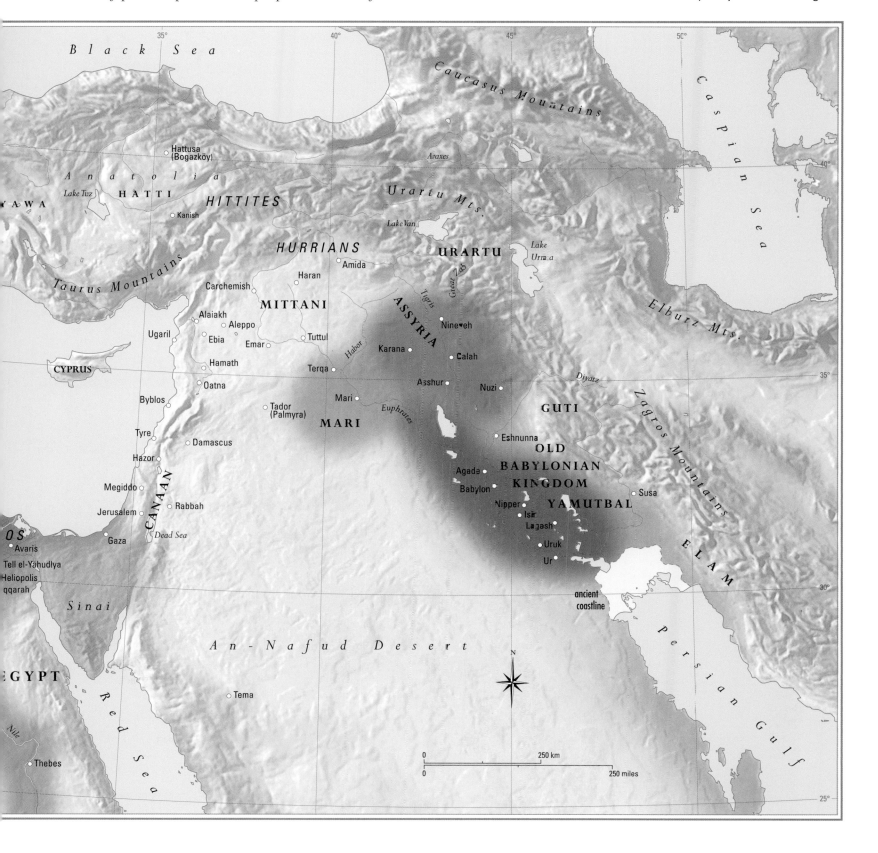

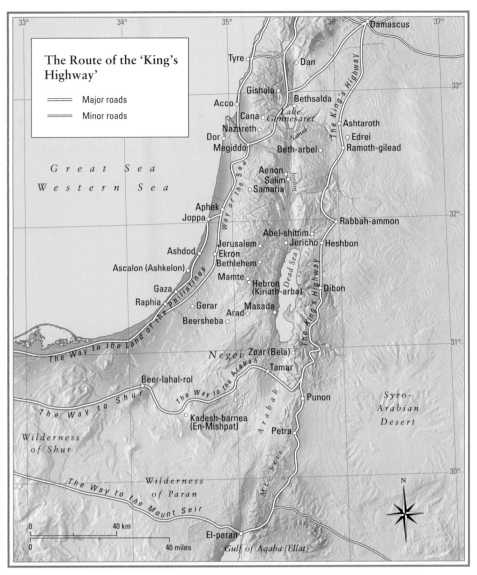

The Route of the 'King's Highway'

━━━ Major roads
━━━ Minor roads

Above: Major routes between Egypt in the west and Mesopotamia in the east pass through the bottleneck of Palestine. This territory proved to be of great interest to the superpowers of their day and would suffer repeated invasions.

Opposite: Major Old Testament sites, some locations are open to debate where modern archaeology does not provide an exact answer.

The early cities recorded the nature of the they imported such as gold, silver, precious stones, wine and aromatic perfumes, and spices. Gum arabic came from Sheba and copper was traded for tin originating east of Mesopotamia; tin and oil moved along trade routes as did luxury items. Cedarwood from Lebanon was a valuable commodity. Canaan constituted an important link on the two major trade routes that transited through the region. The Way of the Sea and the Way of the Philistines passed along the coastal plain from Egypt linking Raphia (Rafah) and Gaza to Tyre (Sur) where the route divided, with roads radiating north to Anatolia and Damascus. The other road, the King's Highway, led south from Damascus through the hills east of the Sea of Galilee and the Dead Sea. The road forked at one point, one branch leading west along the Way of Arabah and the Way of Shur to Beth-lahel-roi and Egypt; the other branch led south through Punon, Petra, and Eilat on the Gulf of Aqaba. Thus Africa, southern Arabia and Asia were linked via Canaan.

The Hebrews used these routes in their search for seasonal grazing in unsettled hill country and the Negev. The Canaanite cultural and urban region covered the Negev and Hills of Judaea north to Giscala, Bethsaida and Ashtaroth. Canaan comprises three areas: the long coastal plain stretching into modern Lebanon, eventually known as Phoenicia; Aram, the site of the Aramean city-states, spreading from the Horan south of Damascus to the last Hittite towns near the Euphrates; and Mount Lebanon to the west.

The Hebrew patriarchs wandered these routes for generations, avoiding violence but defending themselves when necessary. One of their number, the Biblical Joseph, found his way to Egypt, followed later by others, probably in search of new pastures when the traditional grazing lands suffered from drought. Some of these nomads were forced, like Habiru, to labour in the building of the great cities of Pithom and Raamses. The former can be found at Tel er-Retâbeh, west of Lake Timsah in northeastern Egypt; the latter became the Hyksos capital of Averis.

Following the Exodus, probably during the reign of Pharaoh Rameses II, the Hebrews fought in Canaan in the low hill country, known as the Shephelah and the hills of Judaea and Samaria, which became the region constituting the kingdoms of Israel and Judah. Thus, the scene has been set for the Hebrews to become a people, slaves in Egyptian bondage and escapees in an exodus to the conquest of Canaan.

Old Testament Sites
Numbered Sites:

1 Zemaraim
2 Geba-Gieah
3 Ramah
4 Gibeon
5 Beeroth
6 Azmaveth
7 Anathoth
8 Chepirah
9 Kiriath-Jearim
10 Mozah
11 Gibeah of Kiriath-Jearim
12 Waters of Nephtoah
13 Ananiah
14 As-shemesh
15 Nod(?)
16 Manahath
17 Chesalon

Damascus

S Y R I A

Ahlab
Tyre
Abel-beth-maacah
Kanah
Dan
Beth-anath
Taohnith
Yattir
Hammon
Kedesh
Rehob
Abel
Yiron
Merom
Abdon
Achzib
Beth-shemesh
Hazor
Lake Huleh
Naveh
Gath
Janoah
Karnaim
Beth-emek
Ramah
Acco
Neiel
Hukkok
Ashtaroth
Rehob
Jotban
Chinnereth
Sea of Chinnereth (Sea of Galilee)
Mishal
Aphek
Kabul
Kanah
Adamah
Shikmonah
Libnath
Hali
Rimmon
Rakkath
Aphek (?)
Golan (?)
Befen
Hannathon
Ruman
Hammath
Achshaph
Bethlehem
Aln
Daberath
Kedesh
Yarmuk
Kiriath-anab
Helkath
Shlimon
Japhla
Beth-yerah
Jokneam
Sarid
Kishion
Yenoam
Abel
En-dor
Dor
Ophrah
Shunem
Kamon
Megiddo
Jezreel
Hepharaim
Remeth
Edrei
Lo-debar (?)
Zephath
Aruna
Taanach
Beth-arbel
Beth-shean
Rogelim
Beth-haggan
Rehob
Ham
Ramoth-gilead
Borim
Ibleam
Gath
Dothan
Hepher
Bezek
Hammath
Jabesh-gilead
Abe-meholah
Socoh
Geba
Yazith
Siphtan (?)
Samaria
Tirzah
Jebel Um ed Daraj
Sepher
Hazeroth
Zaphon
Kozoh
Azzah
Shechem
Succoth
Mahanaim
Zarqa
Elmattan
Pirathon
Michmethath
Penuel
Taanath-shiloh
Aphek
Tappuah
Arumah
Janoah
Zarethan
Gath-rimmon
Bene-barak
Zaredah
Lebonah
Jokmeam
Ramath-mizpeh
Joppa
Jehud
Adam
Azor
Timmnath-serah
Geba
Gedor
Beth-dagon
Hadid
Neballat
Jeshanah
Jogbehah
Lod
Baal-hazor
Betonim
Gimzo
Beth-haran, Bethel
Ophra
Tyre of Toblah
Jazor
Rabbath-ammon
Mukhazi
lower upper 1
Ai
Eltekeh
Gittaim
Alath
Gilgal (?)
Shueb
Beth-nimrah
Jabneel
Gezer
Shaalbim
Mizpah
2
Naarah
Michmash
Jericho
Abel-keramim
Baalath
Aijalon
8 4 3
Alaon
Beth-arabah
Elealeh
Mephaath
Shikkeron
Timnah
Azekah
17 9
5 7 6
Almon
Hisban
Beth-haram
Heshbon
Ekron
Zorah
10 12 15
Jerusalem
Nebo
Bezer
Beth-shemesh
Eshtcol Zobah
11
Beth-hoglah
Beth-jeshimoth
Kiriathaim
Ashdod
Gath
Jarmuth
Bether
16 13 14
Medeba
Zanoah
Hushah
Secacah
Bath-baal-meon
Ashkelon
Achzib
Socoh
Etam
Bethlehem
City of Salt (?)
Nibshan
Almon-diblathaim
Libnah
Adullam
Netophah
Ether
Kellah
Gedor
Tekoa
Zereth-shahar
Lachish
Nazib
Beth-zur
Ataroth
Jahaz
Eglon
Beth-lephrah
Halhul
Beth-anoth
Keiloth
Kedemoth
Migdal-gad
Beth-tappuah
Hebron
Dibon
Beth-gamul
Gaza
Kein
Aroer
J U D A H
Dumah
Debir
Ziph
En-gedi
Mujib
Gerar
Ziklag
Anab
Carmel
M O A B
Sharuen
En-rimmon
Sucoh
Maon
Sansannah
Eshtemoa
Anim
Kerioth
Moladah
Kinah
Madmen
Beersheba
Jeshua (?)
Arad
City of Moab (?)
Hormah
Arad
Ramoth-negeb
Kir-hareseth
Aroer

Great Sea

Western Sea

Mt. Carmel

Mt. Gilboa

Harod

Jordan

Salt Sea (Dead Sea)

N e g e v

E D O M

Horonaim

Hasa

N

0 _____ 20 km
0 _____ 20 miles

ABRAHAM'S JOURNEYS

THE BIBLE TELLS THE STORY OF ABRAM, SON OF IDOL WORSHIPPER
TERAH WHO LIVED IN UR OF THE CHALDEES AND WHO
WANDERED WESTWARD TO THE PLAINS OF MAMRE AROUND
HEBRON, WEST OF THE RIVER JORDAN.

Abraham and the Three Angels
(God being disguised as an
angel) from the St. Louis Psalter.
Abraham, the founding father
of the Jewish people and of
Judaism, obeyed the divine
commandments without question,
as demonstrated by his willingness
to sacrifice his son, Isaac.

Terah, a descendant of Shem, dwelt in Ur, Mesopotamia, with his sons, Abram, Nachor and Aran. At God's command, Terah took Abram and his wife, Sarai (his half-sister), and Lot, son of the deceased Aran, to Haran in northern Mesopotamia where Terah died. Under divine inspiration, Abram travelled with his family and others to Sichem and Beth-el in Canaan where Abram built an altar. A famine broke out in Canaan, so Abram moved south to Egypt where he pretended that Sarah was his sister. When news of Sarai's beauty reached Pharaoh he placed her in his harem but when he discovered she was married to Abram, he returned her, rebuked Abram and expelled him from Egypt. After returning to Beth-el, Abram and Lot agreed to separate their respective clans lest they squabble over the limited grazing. Abram stayed in Canaan while Lot entered the Jordan Valley. When God informed Abram that all of the surrounding land would be given to his heirs, Abram moved his camp to the Plains of Mamre surrounding Hebron.

The rulers of the cities of Sodom and Gomorrah, south of Hebron, rebelled against their suzerain, Chedorlaomer, King of Elam. Eventually, the kings of nine northern cities fought each other, the Elamite ruler emerging victorious. Chedorlaomer then took Lot's clan and his livestock hostage. Abram immediately led 318 fighting men – an indication of how large his tribe had grown – in an attack to rescue his relatives.

Sarai, who was childless, gave Hagar, her Egyptian servant, as a concubine to Abram. The custom of the time required a childless wife to provide her husband with a woman. A son born of such a relationship could not be repudiated even if the official wife later gave birth. This explains Abram's problem in sending away both Hagar and Ishmael, the son she bore Abram. Some 13 years later, God visited Abram and promised him a son by Sarai; He symbolically changed Abram's name to Abraham and Sarai to Sarah. Later, God and two angels approached Abraham who was again promised a son, Isaac. Sarah, well past child-bearing age, laughed at this but was reprimanded by God. Abraham was told that the cities of Sodom and Gomorrah would be destroyed as punishment for their evil ways. Abraham beseeched God to spare the cities because Lot dwelt there, to which God agreed if Abraham could find ten honest men living in them. Abraham did not manage to do so and God destroyed the cities. There is proof today that some major disaster, probably an earthquake, eradicated the cities. Abraham's relatives, Lot and his two daughters escaped death by sheltering in a cave. There, the girls made Lot drunk and committed incest with him, in order to perpetuate their tribe. According to the Bible, the resulting children became the ancestors of the Moabites and Ammonites.

Witnessing the smoke and fire of the destroyed cities, Abraham moved south to Herar. Fearing its ruler, he again claimed that the beautiful Sarah was his sister. Abimelech, King of Gerar, seized Sarah but a dream revealed her true identity to him and she was returned to Abraham untouched. Abimlech and Abraham resolved their differences causing God to cure all of the barrenness in the King's household.

Sarah gave birth to Isaac who was circumcised on his eighth day in a covenant made by Abraham with God. Sarah was jealous of Ishmael and asked Abraham to exile Hagar and her son into the wilderness. God saved them from dying of thirst, promising Hagar that Ishmael would found a nation. Islamic tradition claims Ishmael as its ancestor.

Later, God ordered Abraham to sacrifice Isaac but he was saved from doing so at the last minute by an angel. A ram was killed instead, symbolizing the fact that human sacrifice was banned forthwith. Sarah died at Kiryat Arba (Hebron). Abraham then sent his servant to find a wife for Isaac. The servant saw Rebecca at the well and chose her for Isaac's wife. She was from the city of Nahor home of Abraham's brother, Nahor. So, Isaac married into the clan that had remained in Mesopotamian Haran. Abraham then married Keturah who bore him six sons. He died and was buried with Sarah in the cave of Machpelah in the Plains of Mamre. Isaac inherited all of Abraham's possessions.

Abraham left his home in Ur and migrated westward, eventually reaching Canaan. Archaeological finds confirm that Semitic shepherds lived a nomadic life migrating through this region.

Abraham's Journeys
c. 2000 BC
→ Abraham's migration to Egypt and return to Canaan
◄ - - Abraham's route of battle with enemy kings
← Military Route of the Kings from the north in Gen. 14

ISAAC, JACOB AND JOSEPH

THIS IS THE STORY OF THE SUBSEQUENT PATRIARCHS, JACOB WHO USURPED HIS BROTHER'S BIRTHRIGHT AND JOSEPH WHO WAS SOLD INTO EGYPT WHERE EVENTUALLY HE ROSE TO POWER AND EVENTUALLY FORGAVE HIS BROTHERS, THE FOUNDERS OF THE TWELVE TRIBES OF ISRAEL.

After Abraham's death, Isaac used an irrigation system to water his flocks and herds which became so numerous that Abimelech of Gerar drove Isaac away, being afraid of his wealth and power. Isaac settled at the oasis of Beersheba, where his son Jacob and mother Rebekkah conspired to deceive him into giving his blessing to the younger so, depriving the elder brother, Esau, of his birthright.

In revenge, Esau plotted to kill his younger twin, so Jacob fled north to his mother's Aramean relatives in Paddan-aram near Haran. During the journey, Jacob had a vision at Luz or Bethel where he saw a ladder ascending to God who informed him that his family and descendants would be very numerous. On arriving in Haran, he encountered his cousin Rachel who was watering her father's livestock. She ran to her father, Laban, who welcomed Jacob, offering him work and pay. Jacob said he would serve Laban for seven years if he could wed Rachel. At the eventual marriage ceremony, Laban deceived Jacob into marrying Rachel's older sister, Leah. Rachel's bride-price was another seven year's labour. While working for Laban, Jacob raised a family and became rich in flocks and herds. After 20 years dwelling in Haran, Jacob determined to return to Isaac in Canaan. He fled with his family and possessions but was overtaken by Laban in the Gilead hills. Arguments over ownership of the livestock were resolved.

Jacob journeyed to Mahanaim where he was told in a vision that he was now to be called Israel. Jacob and Esau met and made peace while Jacob made a home at Succoth but moved to Shalem in Shechem, buying land and erecting an altar named El-elohe-Israel. Unfortunately, Dinah, Jacob's daughter, was raped by Shechem, son of the Hivite Prince Hamor. Dinah's brothers, Simeon and Levi,

In this illustration from an American bible of the 1870s Joseph is being sold by his brothers

Opposite: Isaac lived his life in the Negev Desert. His son, Jacob, travelled through lands from Haran, near the Euphrates in the north, down to the Nile delta in the south. Jacob's youngest and favourite son, Joseph, set out from home to find his brothers. Jealous of their 'favourite' brother, they sold him into slavery.

presumably with assistance, killed Hamor, his son, and all the men of Shechem, destroying the city and capturing the livestock and women.

When Isaac died he was buried by his sons near Mamre. Jacob's own sons became the founders of the Twelve Tribes of Israel: Reuben, Simeon, Levi, Judah, Issaschar and Zebulon (Leah's children); Joseph and Benjamin (Rachel's children); Gad and Asher (children of Zilpah, Leah's handmaid); and Dan and Naphtali (children of Bilhah, Rachel's handmaid).

The story of Joseph and the coat of many colours given to him by his doting father is well-known. The events recounted probably occurred between 1720 and 1500 BCE when evidence suggests that various Semitic peoples were enslaved in Egypt. Joseph's arrogance enraged his brothers. so they sold him to itinerant Midianites. They deceived Jacob by smearing goat's blood on Joseph's coat, to persuade their father that his son had been killed by wild animals.

Joseph was sold to Potiphar, a Pharaonic official. Joseph earned promotion and ran the household but Potiphar's wife tried to seduce Joseph. His rejection of her enraged her so that she accused him of attempted rape, whereupon Potiphar had him imprisoned. While incarcerated, he interpreted dreams, especially those of Pharaoh's butler who was also in prison for a misdemeanour. When the butler was pardoned, he remembered Joseph when the Pharaoh had strange dreams. Joseph was released to interpret them and claimed that there would be seven years' of fruitful harvest followed by seven years' of famine. Joseph was made governor of Egypt to organize grain storage in preparation for the bad years he had predicted. His success allowed him to supply grain during the famine, not just for Egypt but as exports to other countries.

Canaan suffered food shortages so Jacob sent his ten older sons to Egypt to buy grain. Joseph recognized his brothers but they did not recognize him. He demanded that they bring Benjamin to him. He let his other brothers return home but kept Simeon as a hostage. On their return to Egypt with Benjamin, Joseph toyed with them threatening to keep Benjamin as a slave. He eventually revealed himself and forgave his brothers. Eventually, Jacob and his entire people settled in Egypt.

This painting by Frederich Overbeck shows Joseph's brothers dividing the money after successfully selling him into slavery. In the background (left) his coat is being dipped in goat's blood to deceive his father.

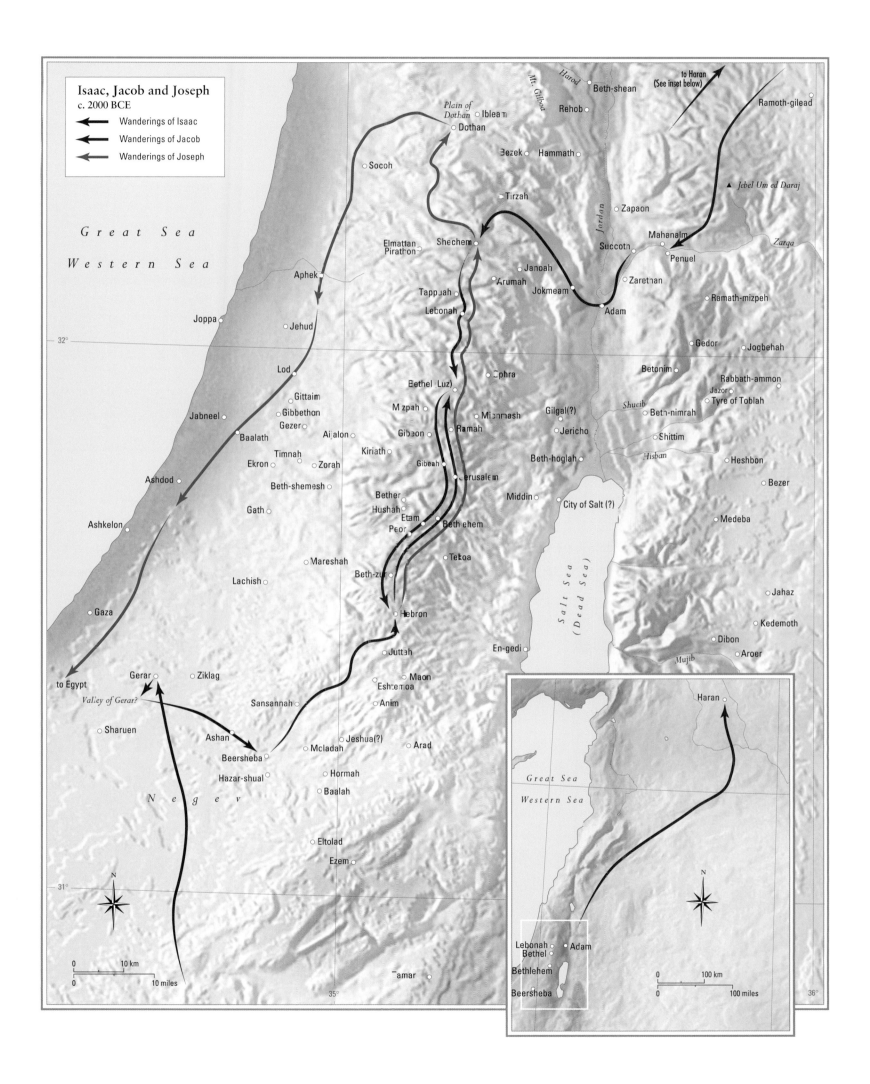

Isaac, Jacob and Joseph
c. 2000 BCE

→ Wanderings of Isaac
→ Wanderings of Jacob
→ Wanderings of Joseph

Great Sea

Western Sea

Joppa

Aphek

Jehud

32°

Lod

Gittaim

Jabneel

Gibbethon

Gezer

Baalath

Aijalon

Timnah

Ekron

Zorah

Beth-shemesh

Ashdod

Gath

Bether

Hushah

Gaza

Mareshah

Lachish

Beth-zur

Ashkelon

Juttah

Gerar

Ziklag

Valley of Gerar?

Maon

to Egypt

Eshtemoa

Sharuen

Sansannah

Anim

Ashan

Jeshua(?)

Arad

Mcladah

Beersheba

Hazar-shual

Hormah

Baalah

N e g e v

Eltolad

Ezem

N

31°

0   10 km

0   10 miles

Socoh

Plain of Dothan

Ibleam

Dothan

Bezek

Hammath

Tirzah

Elmattan
Pirathon

Shechem

Janoah

Arumah

Tappuah

Lebonah

Jokmeam

Bethel (Luz)

Ophra

Mizpah

Michmash

Gilgal(?)

Gibeon

Ramah

Jericho

Kiriath

Gibeah

Beth-hoglah

Jerusalem

Bethlehem

Etam

Peor

Tekoa

Hebron

Middin

City of Salt (?)

Mt. Gilboa

Harod

Beth-shean

Rehob

Jordan

Zapaon

Succoth

Mahanaim

Penuel

Zarethan

Adam

Janoah

to Haran
(See inset below)

Ramoth-gilead

▲ *Jebel Um ed Daraj*

Zarqa

Ramath-mizpeh

Gedor

Jogbehah

Betonim

Rabbath-ammon

Jazer

Tyre of Toblah

Shueib

Beth-nimrah

Shittim

Hisban

Heshbon

Bezer

Medeba

Jahaz

Kedemoth

*S a l t   S e a
(D e a d   S e a)*

En-gedi

Dibon

Aroer

Mujib

Tamar

35°

Great Sea

Western Sea

Haran

Lebonah
Bethel

Bethlehem

Beersheba

N

0   100 km

0   100 miles

36°

EGYPT AND ITS WORLD

THE EGYPTIAN PHARAOHS WHO REPLACED THE CRUEL HYKSOS TRIED TO MAKE PEACE WITH THEIR NEIGHBOURS AND PROTECT THE TRADE ROUTES. THE BATTLE OF KADESH MARKED A TURNING POINT, SINCE EGYPT COULD NO LONGER CONTROL THE REGION. THIS LEFT THE WAY OPEN FOR THE CONQUERING HEBREWS.

Ramses II c. 1290–1225 BCE. This limestone statue can be seen in Memphis today.

The Hyksos rulers of Egypt who enslaved Jacob's people were attacked by the vassal Amosis of Thebes who drove them into Gaza. The final Hyksos refuge at Sharuhen surrendered after a three-year siege. Pharaoh Tuthmosis III campaigned annually in Asia for nearly 20 years. Egypt was becoming a major power and as a result the Syrian cities united under the leadership of the King of Kadesh who marshalled his forces on the plain of Esdraelon under the walls of Megiddo. Tuthmosis outmanoeuvred these Canaanites and defeated them. Subsequent campaigns witnessed the capture of ports on the Phoenician coast, the city-state of Tunis, the invasion of Kadesh and the defeat of the Mitanni at Carchemish.

The hostility between the Mitanni and Egypt continued during the reign of Pharaoh Amenophis II who led two campaigns to crush revolts in Canaan. The reigns of the Pharaohs Amenophis III (1419–1379 BCE) Amenophis IV, also known as Akhenaten (1379–62 BCE), and Tutankhamun (1361–52 BCE), were peaceful rulers, however. A pact was concluded with the Hurrian-controlled Mitani state while diplomatic relations developed with Babylonia. The Amarna tablets indicate a new threat when the Hittite Kingdom conquered the Mitani, posing a danger to the Egyptian position in Canaan. Some Canaanite city-states formed a coalition that sought Hittite protection.

This weakening of Egyptian influence and prestige caused Pharaoh Setos I to reassert Egyptian power by campaigning in the Jordan Valley and along the Phoenician coast. He acquired coastal strongholds for a future campaign against the Hittites and also crushed an incursion into the Negev by the bedouin Sut (Shasu) tribe. Sethos continued the traditional Egyptian policy of protecting trade routes and maintaining the balance of power between his vassal Canaanite city-states. The Hittites disputed Egyptian control over Amurru, the Byblos hinterland and Sethos engaged Hittite forces at Kadesh, thereby regaining Amarru for Egypt. These border brawls were a virtual dress-rehearsal for the coming conflict between Seth's son, Rameses II, and Muwatalli the Hittite, a war over the control of the Orontes River.

In 1275 BCE, Rameses' army advanced to Byblos, in Amarru, to attack Kadesh. A major battle occurred there when the outmanoeuvred Egyptian brigades were ambushed while marching in a column. Rameses managed to extricate himself by virtue of skilled leadership and the arrival of reinforcements. Historians dispute the nature of the battle, some claiming that it was only fought with chariots, the infantry playing no part. There were heavy losses on both sides, however.

The ensuing military stalemate destroyed the regional balance of power in Syria and the land of Canaan. The Hittites regained their authority over the Amarru and invaded Upe. In retaliation, Rameses twice invaded the area reinforcing his authority over Canaan, the coastal ports and Amarru, while seizing several towns in the Orontes Valley from Hittite control. However, the Battle of Kadesh showed that neither power was strong enough to defeat the other while the Hittites were protected by their bastions at Aleppo and Carchemish which prevented an Egyptian incursion into northern Syria.

The virtual power vacuum in Canaan meant that the small city-states were in turmoil, creating such confusion that they ultimately found it difficult to resist subsequent Hebrew incursions. Mutawalli's son, Mursil III, was so inept that his uncle, Hattusil III, usurped him after seven years of his reign. Mursil fled to Egypt where Rameses refused to extradite him. Hittite war-mongering brought Rameses to Beth Shean in 1286 BCE. Meanwhile, the Assyrians under Adad-Nirari and Shalamaneser I (1275–46 BCE), were developing a powerful state in northern Mesopotamia. The Hittite client province of Hanigalbat was seized and Carchemish threatened. Not wanting war on two fronts, Hattusil and Rameses concluded a peace treaty in 1283 BC. Ties were further strengthened when Hattusil gave two daughters in marriage to Rameses (1270 BC). Rameses' long reign, and his domination of Canaan, brought numerous Semitic slaves, including the Hebrews, to an Avaris building project.

Egyptian policy sought to control Palestine creating defence in depth in front of its northeastern border.

The Egyptian Empire
c. 1600 BCE
Extent of the Egyptian Empire

EXODUS AND MOSES

THE EXODUS FROM EGYPT HAS BEEN CELEBRATED EVER SINCE BY THE FESTIVAL OF PASSOVER, THE FIRST TO BE MENTIONED IN THE BIBLE. THE GIVING OF THE LAW ON MOUNT SINAI MARKED THE FOUNDING OF THE HEBREW NATION INTO ONE NATION WITH A SINGLE GOD.

The Bible presents Moses as the adopted son of an Egyptian princess. As an adult, he killed an Egyptian who had murdered a Hebrew worker. This caused him to flee from Egypt and live as a shepherd with the Midianites in the Sinai Desert. The Midianites, who were descendants of Abraham through his second wife, worshipped the Hebrew God.

Under divine inspiration, Moses returned to Egypt, certain that God wished him to lead the Hebrews out of exile into the Promised Land. Exodus 7–12 describes the plagues inflicted upon the Egyptians, due to their refusal to release the Hebrews; they symbolize the battle between the Hebrew God and the Egyptian gods, who included Pharaoh Rameses himself.

Eventually, Moses led the Hebrews out of Egypt after the Passover, a rite that has become central to Judaism. Originally, it was a protective ritual for nomadic shepherds searching for pasture. The blood of a sacrificed lamb symbolized the life-giving power of the Deity and protected the shepherds against evil. The Passover meal reinforces the links between God and the Jews. The Exodus, added to the original Passover ritual, demonstrated God's victory over the Egyptian gods and his covenant with His people. Thereafter, all acts of deliverance in Jewish history can be seen as consequences of the Exodus and God's deliverance, and they have been celebrated as extensions of the Passover.

The passage of the Red Sea (actually the Sea of Reeds) in Exodus 14 probably symbolizes a crossing of the marshes near Lake Timsah and the Mediterranean coast. The pursuing Egyptian chariots floundered in the marsh and the Hebrews travelled southward to avoid the Egyptians and find Midianite help. Their wanderings in the wilderness are recorded as itinerary notes in Exodus, Numbers, Joshua, Leviticus and Deuteronomy. The route taken to Mount Sinai is unknown, as is

This detail from a fresco by Bartolo di Fredi (c.1330-1410) shows the Israelites crossing the Red Sea.

Opposite: Most probably the Hebrews crossed the marshy region to the east of the Nile delta. Their experiences on this journey through Sinai became the foundation of the nation's religion and identity.

even the location of the mountain and how long the wanderings lasted. Information is contradictory but it seems likely that Hebrew incursions into Canaan occurred on several occasions, the invaders moving into the land gradually on at least two different occasions. The first incursion was successful because it was helped by Hebrews living in southern Canaan who had not travelled to Egypt with Joseph and his brothers. The second met with resistance from the kingdoms in the Moabite plains east of the Dead Sea.

Fortified Canaanite cities in south Canaan were a barrier to the large Hebrew groups attempting to pass close to Kadesh-Barnea. The Hebrews were forced eastward to the ancient King's Highway. As regards the location of Mount Sinai, also referred to as Mount Horeb and Mount Paran, it was probably in the southern Sinai Desert. The tradition that the current mountain known as Mount Sinai was the true site must bear some weight. What matters most, however, is the covenant made with God at the sacred mountain from which the Hebrews derive their national identity and religious unity. The covenant granted the Promised Land to the Hebrews and commenced the worship of the God whose name is represented in the Tetragramnon YHWH, a term unknown outside the Hebrew writings. In Judges 5, YHWH is referred to as 'The One in Sinai'.

At Mount Sinai, laws were formulated that were accepted by the people. Jewish Written Law lays down the obligations to God and to each other as God's chosen people. The Ten Commandments (Exodus 20: 1–17 and Deuteronomy 5: 1–21), the first of 613 other commandments, are absolute and are unparalleled in ancient Near Eastern history. It is not known if the Hebrew god, YHWH, was worshipped before Moses. Some scholars claim that Moses learnt about him from Jethro, his father-in-law. Others think he was worshipped as the god of Moses' mother's clan. Exodus 15: 2 states: "The Lord is my strength and song, and He is become my salvation: He is my God, and I will prepare him an habitation; my father's God, and I will exalt him." At any event, the Law given at Mount Sinai constituted a new covenant linking the faith to the birth of a new nation.

This illustration from a medieval manuscript shows Moses releasing the waters of the Red Sea after the safe passage of his people.

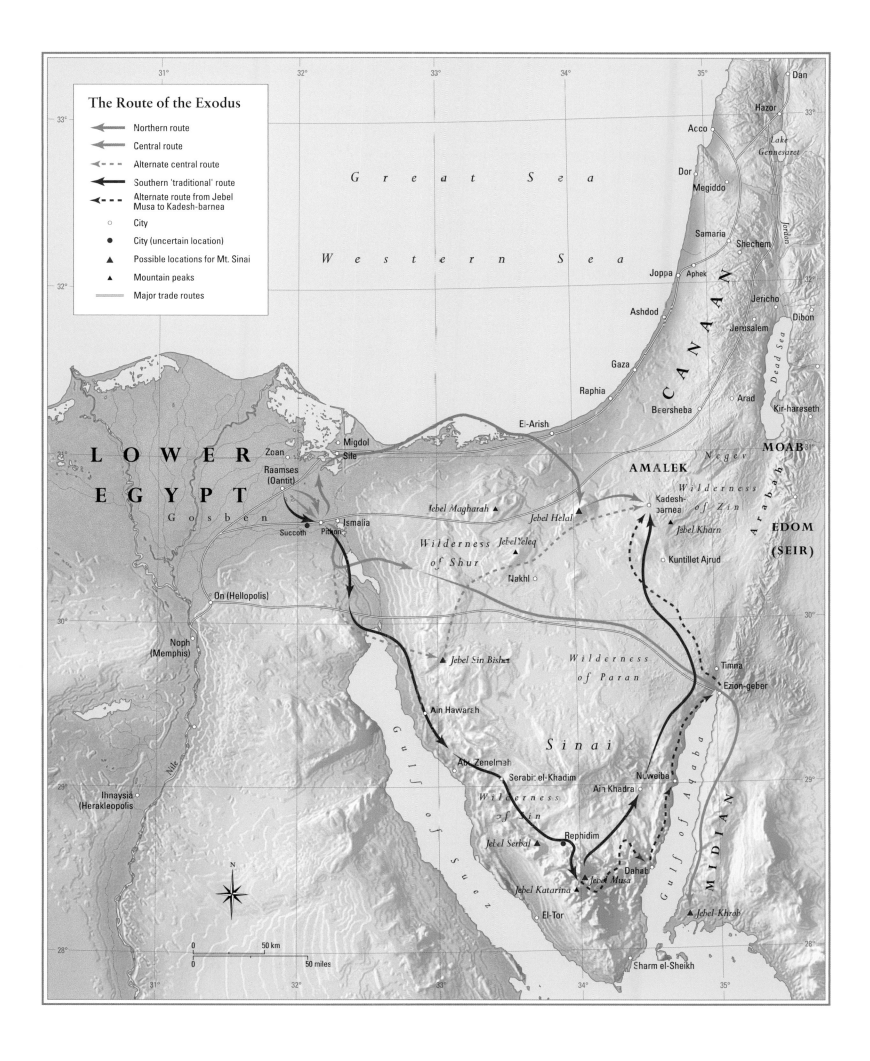

The Route of the Exodus

→	Northern route
→	Central route
◄---	Alternate central route
→	Southern 'traditional' route
◄---	Alternate route from Jebel Musa to Kadesh-barnea
○	City
●	City (uncertain location)
▲	Possible locations for Mt. Sinai
▲	Mountain peaks
══	Major trade routes

Dan

Hazor

Acco

Lake Gennesaret

Dor

Megiddo

Samaria

Shechem

Jordan

Joppa

Aphek

Jerusalem

Jericho

Dibon

Ashdod

Gaza

Dead Sea

Raphia

Beersheba

Arad

Kir-hareseth

El-Arish

MOAB

CANAAN

Negev

AMALEK

Wilderness of Zin

Kadesh-barnea

EDOM (SEIR)

Jebel Kharn

Arabah

G r e a t   S e a

Jebel Magharah ▲

Jebel Helal ▲

Kuntillet Ajrud

W e s t e r n   S e a

Jebel Yeleq ▲

Wilderness of Shur

Nakhl

Migdol

Sile

Zoan

LOWER EGYPT

Raamses (Qantir)

Goshen

Ismalia

Succoth

Pithom

On (Heliopolis)

Noph (Memphis)

Jebel Sin Bisher ▲

Wilderness of Paran

Timna

Ezion-geber

Ihnaysia (Herakleopolis)

Nile

Ain Hawarah

Gulf of Suez

Abu Zenelmah

Serabit el-Khadim

Sinai

Wilderness of Sin

Ain Khadra

Nuweiba

Gulf of Aqaba

MIDIAN

Jebel Serbal ▲

Rephidim

Dahab

Jebel Musa ▲

Jebel Khrob ▲

Jebel Katarina ▲

El-Tor

N

0   50 km

0   50 miles

Sharm el-Sheikh

CANAANITE CULTURE, RELIGION AND POLITICS

WHEN THE CHILDREN OF ISRAEL EMBARKED ON THEIR
CONQUEST OF THE PROMISED LAND THEY MET WITH FIERCE
OPPOSITION FROM THE TRIBES ALREADY SETTLED THERE,
ESPECIALLY THE CANAANITES BUT ALSO FROM THE PHILISTINES.

Before Israel entered the Promised Land, the region had developed in diverse political ways. The People from the Sea (almost certainly Cretans) who invaded Egypt and were repulsed, moved northward, settling along the Mediterranean coast and founding settlements at Gaza, Ashkelon, Ashdod, Gath and Ekron where they became known as the Philistines and were notionally vassals of Egypt.

The pre-Israelite population of the land were Canaanites or Amorites, although the Bible sometimes uses these names interchangeably. The Canaanites were a northwestern Semitic people who tended to settle on the coast and plains from Egypt in the south to Ugarit in the north, with a sparser population inland. By the time of the Israelite invasion, the Amorites had assimilated the language, social organization and culture of Canaan. Thus, the predominant population was racially and linguistically similar to that of the Children of Israel.

The Bible lists other races, such as the Hurrians who had arrived during the Hyksos era. Hittites, Hivites, Horites, Jebusites, Girgashites and Perizzites were probably non-Semitic. These might have all been Hurrian, with centres at Gibeon, Shechem and Lebanon. The Hittites were former subjects of the Hittite Empire and dwelt around Hebron. Whatever their origins, all groups were basically Canaanite in culture by the time of the invasion.

The Canaanite region had regular trading links with Egypt, Mesopotamia, Cyprus, Crete and Mycenean Greece. The Canaanites traded in wood from the forests of Lebanon and the highly-prized purple dye made from the murex, a shellfish. Trade was facilitated by the use of an alphabetic proto-Semitic script, the forerunner of the modern alphabetic scripts. The Canaanite religion was based upon pagan fertility rites. El was the father-god; the chief deity was Baal, the "Rider of the Clouds" or bull god. Goddesses included Astarte and Anat, the latter being Baal's wife. Portrayed as pregnant mothers or sacred whores, the goddesses also appear as war deities. The death and resurrection of Baal were re-enacted annually with rites including sacred prostitution, homosexuality and orgies, all a total anathema to the Children of Israel. Yet the Israelites adopted some of the Canaanites' rites and incorporated certain harvest festivals into their year. These became associated with the God of the Covenant in celebration of certain important events, such as the Giving of the Law.

Politically, Canaan was not united. It consisted of a multiplicity of city-states controlled by kings feudally subjected to rather corrupt Egyptian controlling agents. This political hotch-potch engaged in local power games and coalitions in a thoroughly chaotic manner. Being feudal, the kings were supported by chariot-driving aristocratic elites. Between the Amarna period and the Israelite invasion, the number of states doubled. East of the Jordan, the thinly populated lands were being settled by two peoples. The Edomites occupied the hills east of the Arabah between the southern tip of the Dead Sea and the Gulf of Aqabah. The Ammonites had also put down roots and two Amorite states existed one at Heshbon that controlled southern Gilead and the second along the Yarmuk River in Bashan.

Although Canaan had declined in wealth as a consequence of Egyptian misrule and the fact that Egyptian soldiers sometimes collected their pay arrears from the local population, the scattering of cities

Oilstone at Tel Hazor. The oil was pressed and trickled out through a small spout into a cup embedded in the ground.

were surprisingly well-constructed, fortified and often had their own drainage systems. Megiddo and Jerusalem had tunnels leading to water supplies for use during sieges.

Megiddo was a fortified hill dominating the coastal road where it left the Valley of Jezreel from a pass on the ridge of Mount Carmel. Strategically important, the city archeological excavations have revealed some 20 levels of occupation. The Canaanite King lived in a large fortified palace inside the city walls; a temple was also fortified. The major Canaanite city was Hazor which had a moat and defensive walls. There was a 15-acre upper city which had its own city walls. The city, which had a population of some 30,000 to 40,000, is mentioned several times in various records, and for the first time in Egyptian execration tablets dating from the nineteenth-century BCE. Hazor is also the only Canaanite city mentioned in an archive discovered in eighteenth century BCE Mari; Hazor's importance, wealth and wide-reaching commercial links are shown. The Egyptian Amarna archive (1st century BCE), refers to Hazor several times, as well being recorded in the military campaigns carried out by various Pharaohs in the fourteenth century BCE. This urban fortification was difficult to attack as Joshua's Israelites found out.

CANAAN CONQUERED

THE CONQUEST OF CANAAN WAS NOT ALWAYS BLOODTHIRSTY. SOME OF THE LOCAL INHABITANTS SIGNED TREATIES WITH THE ISRAELITES AND IN OTHER CASES THE SETTLEMENTS OCCUPIED BY THE NEWCOMERS HAD BEEN ABANDONED AT SOME TIME IN THE PAST.

As the Israelites approached Canaan, Moses sent out spies in advance including Joshua of Ephraim. Having gathered intelligence about possible invasion routes, Joshua and Moses moved the Israelites from Abel-Shittem in Moab to Gilgal. The story of the invasion is told in the Books of Joshua and the Judges and probably relate the combined experience of several invading groups over a period of decades. There is no doubt, that the Israelites fought fierce battles to gain control of Canaan but the epic campaigns are undoubtedly heavily embellished.

Extensive archeological excavations in Jericho reveal that the walled city had been destroyed some 300 years before the Israelite invasion. Tales of such an occasion may have been merged into the Biblical account. Ai, a settlement of some one thousand people, was captured and destroyed by a stratagem. Identified as Et-Tell near Bethel, archaeological digs show that it was uninhabited at the time of the Israelite conquest. However, Kirjath-Sepher and Lachish were vanquished, the former by fire, followed by a typical Israelite occupation. Eglon (Tell el-Hesi) and Hazor (Tell el-Qedah) were destroyed in the late thirteenth century BCE, according to the archaeological record, demonstrating the accuracy of the Biblical invasion epic.

One interesting episode of the invasion was the treaty made with the mixed-origin inhabitants of Shechem, a city dominating part of the hill country. The inhabitants may have been part of the folk movement that had brought Abraham to Canaan originally and this "kinship" fostered a mutual covenant. The Israelites traversed Shechemite land peacefully. The Hivites of Gibeon also entered into a treaty allowing Joshua and his invasion force right of passage into the Shephelah, the low hills bordering Philistia. The Hivites deceived Joshua by making him believe that they

The Israelites 'Crossing the River Jordan' by Badalocchio (1581–1647). The priests, directed by Joshua, are carrying the Ark of the Covenant through the miraculously dry bed of the River Jordan.

Opposite: The invasion of Canaan began with the crossing of the River Jordan. The army then concentrated and formed a base around the city of Gilgal, from there Jericho was captured. The campaign then developed into the central highlands and on towards Philistia.

were from a distant land and not his close enemies. Joshua eventually discovered the truth but did not wipe out the Hivites, instead making them "hewers of wood and drawers of water for the congregation and for the altar of the Lord", namely slaves. This can be contrasted with the slaughter of Hazor's population.

Joshua's campaign in central Canaan eventually split the land in two when his forces defeated and routed a coalition of the kings of Jerusalem, Hebron, Jarmuth, Lachish and Eglon. This success was followed by a swift advance to south of Azekah. Joshua continued on to attack Libnah, Lachish, Eglon, Hebron and Debir. In fact, Joshua himself may not have destroyed these cities since Caleb of Judah campaigned in the region after Joshua's death. Philistines or Egyptians may even responsible for their destruction.

Upper Galilee's fertile hills and forests were the next to suffer from the Israelite onslaught. As the Israelites encroached, maybe over years, gradually constricting Hazorite control, King Jabin of Hazor asked for help from his Canaanite allies. who assembled at the Waters of Meron while the Israelites camped in broken land and forests nearby. Chariots were totally unsuitable for this terrain and lightly armed, mobile Israelite soldiers routed their enemy and ensured that the Canaanites could not retreat to Hazor but were forced back to Sidon or the Valley of Mizpeh. Hazor's inhabitants were then butchered and the city torched. It was not resettled by the Children of Israel until the time of King Solomon.

The Book of Joshua describes the war which gave the Israelites a "land of milk and honey." The Canaanites were not destroyed however and skirmished continued. Small groups inhabiting the conquered land were often absorbed while Joshua 24 suggests that other people gave up their gods to join the Israelites in a covenant. Peoples such as the Kenites, who already believed in the One God, assimilated into the tribe of Judah. Thus, Israel was born of many strands.

Whoever was in power in Canaan, the region was for centuries under the shadow of Egypt. Here this heroic image of the Pharaoh is seen leading his troops against an Asian army.

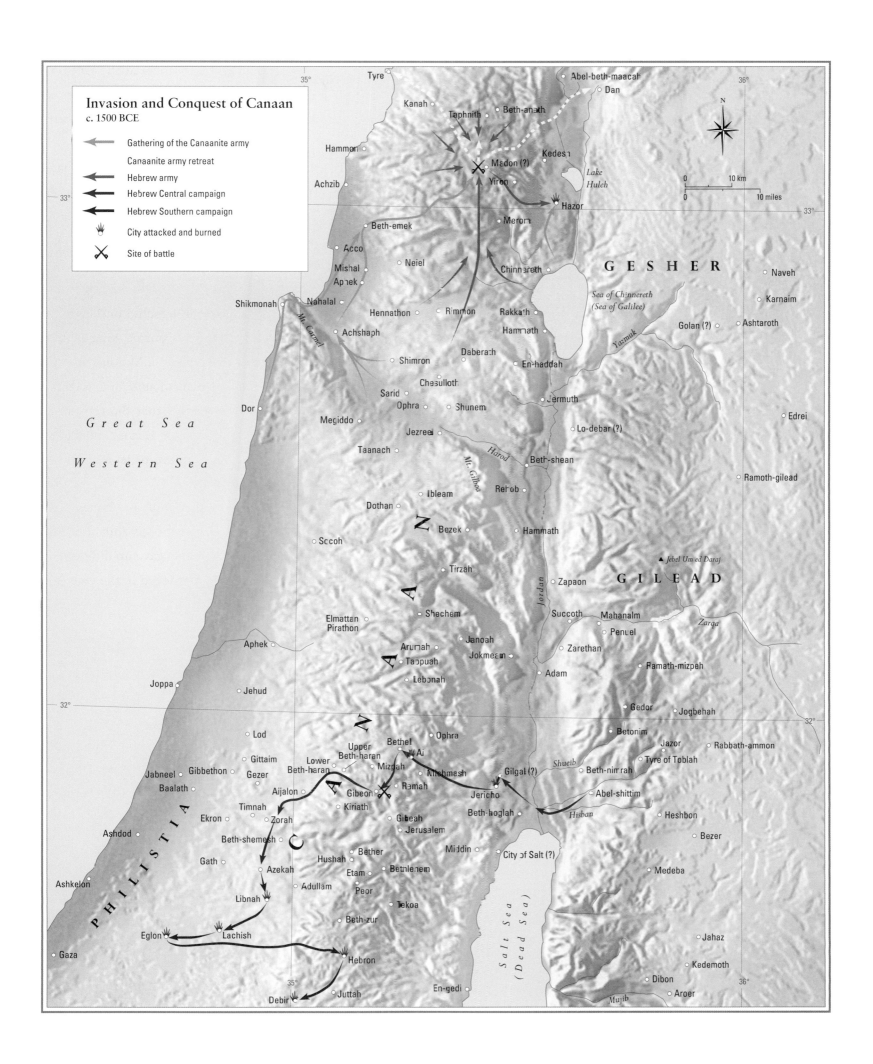

Invasion and Conquest of Canaan
c. 1500 BCE

→ Gathering of the Canaanite army
→ Canaanite army retreat
→ Hebrew army
← Hebrew Central campaign
◀ Hebrew Southern campaign
🖐 City attacked and burned
⚔ Site of battle

Great Sea

Western Sea

PHILISTIA

CANAAN

GESHER

GILEAD

Tyre
Abel-beth-maacah
Dan
Kanah
Taphnith
Beth-anath
Madon (?)
Kedesh
Lake Huleh
Hammon
Yiron
Hazor
Achzib
Meron
Beth-emek
Acco
Naveh
Mishal
Karnaim
Aphek
Neiel
Chinnereth
Golan (?)
Ashtaroth
Shikmonah
Nahalal
Achshaph
Hennathon
Rimmon
Rakkath
Hammath
Sea of Chinnereth (Sea of Galilee)
Yarmuk
Shimron
Daberath
Dor
Sarid
Ophra
Shunem
En-haddah
Jermuth
Edrei
Megiddo
Jezreel
Lo-debar (?)
Harod
Taanach
Beth-shean
Ramoth-gilead
Ibleam
Mt. Gilboa
Rehob
Dothan
Bezek
Hammath
Socoh
Jebel Um ed Daraj
Tirzah
Zapaon
GILEAD
Jordan
Succoth
Mahanaim
Zarqa
Shechem
Penuel
Elmattan
Pirathon
Janoah
Zarethan
Aphek
Arumah
Jokmeam
Ramath-mizpeh
Tappuah
Adam
Joppa
Jehud
Lebonah
Gedor
Jogbehah
Lod
Betonim
Gittaim
Upper Beth-haran
Bethel
Ophra
Jazer
Rabbath-ammon
Gezer
Lower Beth-haran
Mizpah
Ai
Gilgal (?)
Tyre of Toblah
Jabneel
Gibbethon
Aijalon
Michmash
Shueib
Beth-nimrah
Baalath
Gibeon
Ramah
Jericho
Abel-shittim
Timnah
Kiriath
Beth-hoglah
Heshbon
Ekron
Zorah
Gibeah
Hisban
Ashdod
Beth-shemesh
Jerusalem
Bezer
Gath
Hushah
Bether
Middin
City of Salt (?)
Azekah
Etam
Bethlehem
Medeba
Adullam
Peor
Libnah
Tekoa
Beth-zur
Jahaz
Eglon
Lachish
Hebron
Kedemoth
Gaza
Salt Sea (Dead Sea)
Dibon
En-gedi
Aroer
Debir
Juttah
Mujib

Mt. Carmel

N
0 — 10 km
0 — 10 miles

Israelite Settlement in The Promised Land

MANY OTHER TRIBES ASSIMILATED INTO THE CHILDREN OF ISRAEL, RECOGNIZING THE ONE GOD. TOGETHER THEY CREATED NEW SETTLEMENTS IN HITHERTO UNCULTIVATED REGIONS AND SETTLED DOWN TO BECOME ARABLE FARMERS.

As well as mingling with different peoples in Canaan, the Children of Israel who eventually came to the Promised Land incorporated various strains Moses' father-in-law, for instance, was a Midianite and the Book of Numbers states that his clan joined the wandering Israelites. Caleb, whose clan eventually colonized the Hebron area, was called a Kenizzite, an Edomite. Although not of the Tribe of Judah, the Calebites became known as Judahites. The tribe of Manasseh included the clans of Hepher, Tirzah and Shechem in Samaria. The first two are listed in Joshua as conquered Canaanite cities but Shechem was an Amorite city whose population in the time of the Judges was pagan, possessing a temple to the god Baal-Berith. These Canaanite cities were subsequently assimilated into the tribe of Manasseh. The southern part of the Promised Land was inhabited by Judah and Simeon but Samuel records Kenites, Kenizzites and Jerahmeelites who had probably infiltrated from the wilderness (desert) of Kadesh and were incorporated into Israel. There were instances of intermarriage with the local Canaanites as in the case of Judah's son, Shelah, who had a Canaanite mother.

Once in the Promised Land, the Israelites occupied tented encampments and created many settlements in the uninhabited and uncultivated hill regions. The Israelite settlers constructed four-roomed houses or took over the houses built around a courtyard in the Canaanite cities they destroyed or in the new towns and cities they built.

The gradual conquest and settlement of the Promised Land by the initial Twelve Tribes, shared the tradition that God had rescued them from Egypt and made a covenant with them as His Chosen People. The Exodus is therefore characterized in Jewish tradition as the supreme example of God's power. This was manifested in the Ark of the Covenant, Aaron's rod and the stone Tables of the Commandments.

The Exodus from Egypt is commemorated by Jews in Passover, the first festival to be mentioned in the Bible. The Covenant stretched back to before the Giving of the Law, to the time of Abraham. The Israelites believed they had been chosen by God to provide an example of righteousness to the world. This is the essence of Jewish belief, divine revelation and the vow to obey God's will, as symbolized in the "Shema", the Jewish confession of faith (Deuteronomy 6: 4–9, 11: 13–21 and Numbers 15: 37–41). A powerful link was thus forged between the history of the Children of Israel and their religion, something that has given Judaism its unique character. The First Commandment, as ordered in the Jewish Bible is "I am the Lord Thy God, who brought thee out of the Land of Egypt out of the House of Bondage (Slavery)."

When the Israelite tribes settled in the Promised Land, they had to learn to till the soil, a difficult and awesome task for nomad pastoralists. After the inhabitants had been conquered, the Israelites had to learn to grow wheat and barley, vines, fig trees and pomegranates. The tribes of Reuben, Gad, and half of Manasseh, maintained their pastoral life on the wide plains east of the River Jordan. Elsewhere, agricultural life became linked to the religious festivals and duties. In their new life, the Israelites operated within various social units. The family unit consisted of several generations – the patriarch and his wives, their issue and so on. The family probably married outside the extended family although Genesis and Samuel refer to marriage to a maternal first cousin. The family unit owned property, farmed the land and cared for the livestock. The clan was a wider social unit, of several extended families linked by marriage, who may have farmed the land communally. The elders dispensed justice depending upon social standing, wealth, prestige.

The Hebrew settlement of Canaan probably took many years to complete. At first only marginal land was occupied, later cities were captured, along with their surrounding farmlands.

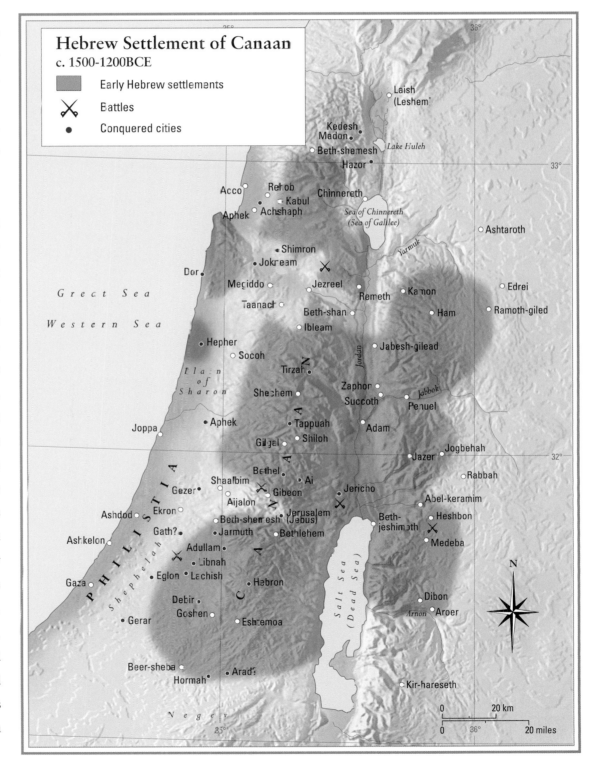

Hebrew Settlement of Canaan
c. 1500-1200BCE

- Early Hebrew settlements
- ✕ Battles
- • Conquered cities

TRIBAL DIVISIONS

THE PERIOD OF JOSHUA AND THE JUDGES WITNESSED MAJOR UPHEAVALS IN THE NEAR EAST. THE DOMINANT POWER, EGYPT, LOST MUCH OF ITS STRENGTH THROUGH HAVING TO FIGHT OFF INVADERS SUCH AS THE SEA PEOPLES AND THE ASSYRIANS.

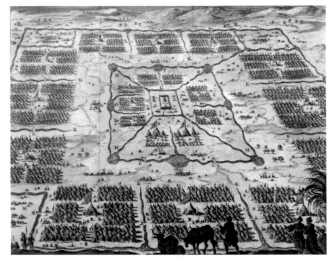

This illustration shows a gathering of the ancient Twelve Tribes of Israel.

Opposite: The tribal league seemed to have survived as a loose governmental form. All the tribes were still troubled by Canaanite enclaves remaining in their midst.

The territorial area of the Israelite tribes is difficult to pin down. In his old age, Joshua was ordered by God to divide the conquered land amongst the Israelites. However, much of Canaan remained outside Israelite control, especially the powerful cities of the plain which were in Philistine hands.

The Twelve Tribes traced their origins to the sons of Jacob. The people of Joseph had divided into two following his sons, Ephraim and Manasseh. Reuben, Gad, and half of Manasseh had been granted land east of the Jordan by Moses. Joshua had to apportion land west of the Jordan to Judah, Benjamin, Simeon, Zebulon, Issacher, Asher, Naphtali, Dan and the other half of Manasseh. The Levite tribe received no land, its members became a priestly caste and were given 48 cities and their pastures.

Tribal borders are difficult to plot because Joshua 13–19 contradicts Joshua 20–21. Borders were also subject to change as were the tribes. Simeon was an enclave in Judah and was absorbed. Dan failed to establish itself in its allotted territory and moved north to capture Laish which was renamed Dan. Then, Dan's original land was shared between Ephraim, Judah and the Philistines. Reuben ceased to exist fairly early on and other tribes and clans emerged, such as Mechir and Gilead.

The Israelite lands were not a coherent entity. The mountain areas were mainly in Israelite hands but the Israelites could not conquer the plains because they were unable to overcome the chariot forces of the coastal cities. The littoral and the Plain of Jezreel were outside Israelite control.

Israelites living there intermarried with Canaanites and alien enclaves were created, such as the Jebusite/Canaanite Jerusalem. Geography impacted upon tribal unity. The Galilean contingents were separated from their kin by Canaanite land in the Jezreel Valley. The Jordan Rift Valley divided the western and eastern tribes and the high ground was so isolated by defiles, valleys and scrubland that communities developed in isolation. Eventually northern and southern tribes regarded each other with suspicion. This weakened Israelite unity. Religious observance also changed on a local level, the Ark cult appearing less important to those geographically distant from it.

Canaan was overrun with invaders at this time and Egypt never recovered from the invasions of the Sea People and Libyans. Rameses III's temple at Medinut Habu contains depictions of a large sea-battle. His archers destroyed the Libyan army, some 4,000 being killed and captured, with the loss of 93 chariots. The Hittite Empire vanished under the onslaught of the Sea Peoples and the Phrygians. Assyria was weakened by the assassination of Tukulti-Ninurta I (c. 1197 BCE) and its renaissance under Tiglath-Pileser I (c. 1116–1078 BCE), who conquered Babylon, Armenia and northern Phoenicia. The next two centuries of Assyrian weakness can be explained by increasing pressure from the Arameans who invaded the Fertile Crescent during this period. Syria and Upper Mesopotamia became mainly Aramean with the growth of small city states such as Sham'al, Carchemish, Beth-eden and, particularly, Damascus. The Phoenicians recovered their strength and their renaissance witnessed the regeneration of Byblos and other ports as major trade centres.

When Joshua died, the Israelites lost their national leader and successful war general. The twelfth century BCE saw the Israelites desperately attempting to retain their conquests.

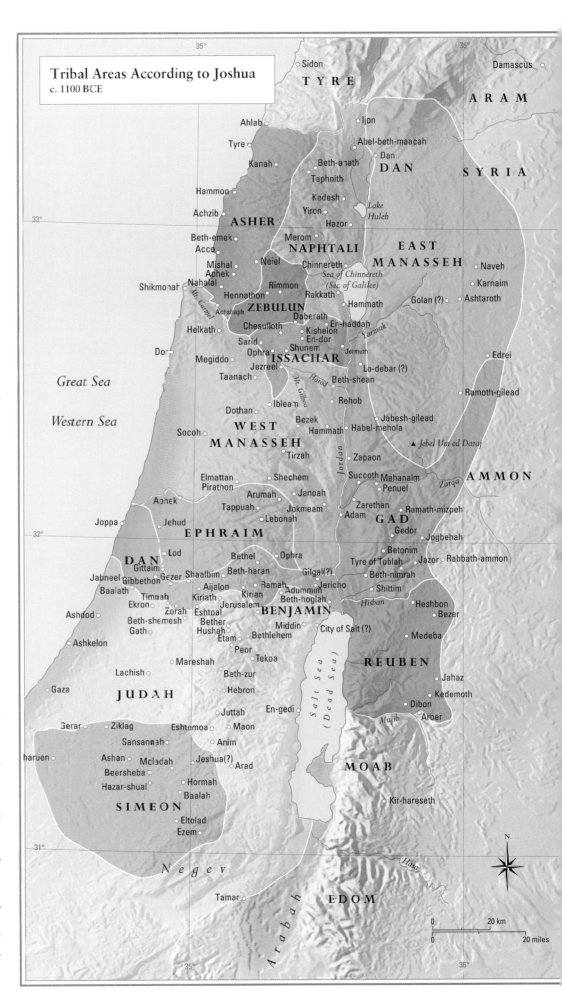

Tribal Areas According to Joshua
c. 1100 BCE

STRUGGLE OF THE JUDGES

THE ISRAELITES CONTINUED TO WORSHIP A VARIETY OF DEITIES AND IT WAS DIFFICULT FOR THE JUDGES, HOWEVER, CHARISMATIC, TO WEAN THEM AWAY FROM PAGAN RELIGIONS. THE PROBLEM WAS COMPOUNDED BY INTERMARRIAGE WITH LOCAL TRIBES.

Despite the fact that the Israelite tribes were supposedly worshippers of the one God, pagan cults continued to flourish among them. Some indulged in fertility cults, this being thought appropriate in an agricultural society. Others worshipped both Baal and God. The Book of Judges records this theological chaos and criticized their people for polluting themselves with pagan cults.

"Nevertheless the Lord raised up judges, which delivered them out of the hand of those that spoiled them. And yet they would not hearken unto their judges, but them went a-whoring after other gods, and bowed themselves unto them: they turned quickly out of the way which their fathers walked in obeying the commandments of the Lord; but they did not do so. And when the Lord raised them up judges, then the Lord was with the judge: for it repented the Lord because of their groanings by reason of them that oppressed them and vexed them." (Judges 2: 16–18)

Twelve judges emerged to deliver Israel from danger and apostasy; it is not sure when they ruled though the Bible probably places them in chronological order. The judges varied considerably in character and seem to act as champions in different locations helping local tribes. But all of the judges, male and female, were charismatic figures who could rally the tribes to rally and repulse Israel's enemies.

The Israelites had adapted from being a semi-nomadic people to settled farmers, making them more affluent. Their towns were not elaborate but they traded with the caravans that brought goods across the desert and as sea trade increased, certain tribes benefited (Judges 5: 17) and prospered. Hill towns learnt to line their water cisterns with lime plaster, enabling hill towns to

Deborah, the only female judge mentioned in the Bible, with Barak, her general.

sustain an increased population. Additional land was cleared and forests felled east and west of the River Jordan, creating more arable land.

Co-exisence with the Canaanites involved intermarriage and a confrontation with the Canaanite religion. Some Canaanites converted to worshipping God though their devotion may only have been superficial. Local fertility shrines on the hilltops remained cult centres and these preserved pagan rituals. As the Israelites became farmers, they often took on local agricultural deities regarding them as aspects of the true God. Agricultural religion was part of farming life and therefore it seemed natural to pray to fertility gods. Some people might have been so confused that they thought God and Ba'al were interchangeable.

So, the Israelites became the inheritors of Canaan, economically and culturally and as they became wealthier they became corrupted. As a primitive people, traumatized by living by the sword, they were seduced by the luxury of a more advanced culture. So, license, immorality and worshipping false gods took hold. "And the children of Israel dwelt among the Canaanites, Hittites, and Amorites, and Perizzites and Hivites, and Jebusites: And they took their daughters as wives, and gave their daughters to their sons and served their gods. And the children of Israel did evil in the sight of the Lord, and forgat the Lord their God, and served Baalim and the groves. Therefore the anger of the Lord was hot against Israel ..." (Judges 3: 5–8)

Othniel, the first judge mentioned in the Bible (Judges 3: 7–11) stopped an invasion by Cushan-Rishathaim from Aram-Naharaim (Babylonia). He resisted an Edomite attack which probably originated in northern Syria (Aram) since this area has a named area of Qusana-Ruma (Kûshân-Rum) which sounds similar.

Ehud prevailed against Moab (Judges 3: 12–30). In previous conflicts, Sihon, the Amorite, had seized Moabite land north of the River Arnon. Israel, recaptured this territory and the tribe of Reuben settled there. Apparently, Moab regained the region and pressured the tribe of Benjamin. Despite the Moabite repulse, the Bible does not say that the Moabites were ejected and the Israelites were forced to pay tribute to the Moabite King for 18 years, until Ehud killed him. Eighty years of peace ensued. Reuben was heavily damaged by this episode and ceased to be an effective tribe, eventually vanishing from sight.

Shamgar (Judges 3: 31) lived before the time of Deborah and apparently was not an Israelite though he defended Israelite territory from an attack of the Sea People, killing 600 of them. He was the ruler of Beth-Anath, a city in Galilee.

Deborah and Barak of the tribe of Naphtali (Judges 4–5) can be placed in history at approximately 1125 BCE. The Israelite settlements were divided in two by the Jezreel Valley. Alliances of Canaanites subjugated some of the Israelite clans. Deborah and Barak rallied six tribes from Benjamin to Galilee. They were helped by the heavy rains that caused their chariots to be bogged down in mud, enabling the Israelite infantry to massacre them.

Gideon of Manasseh was called in when Jezreel and the neighbouring hill country were attacked by camel-riding nomads. These raiders were Midianites, Amelkites and Bnei-Qedem. This is the first historical reference to domesticated camels, used here for seven years as a mobile, deadly strike force. Annual raids took place at harvest time, causing economic hardship and starvation. Gideon's victories gave him tremendous prestige and authority. His tribe wanted him to become a king but he utterly refused. His son, Abimelech, established himself as King of Shechem for a short while before being killed.

The story of Jephthah is a tragic example of how human sacrifice once again emerged in Israel despite the prohibition since the time of Isaac. Jephthah, a Gileadite, was leader of an outlaw band (Judges 11: 29). He was promised God's help if he sacrificed the next living thing that he met. Unfortunately, it was his unmarried daughter. The Ammonites, a tribe of wealthy caravan traders, wanted to move into Israelite-held Transjordan. They were repelled by Jephthah's men but he was forced to kill his daughter as his side of the bargain with God. "And she said unto her father, Let this thing be done for me: let me alone for two months, that I may go up and down upon the mountains, and bewail my virginity, I and my fellows. And he said, Go. And he sent her away for two months: and she went with her companions and bewailed her virginity upon the mountains. And it came to pass at the end of two months, that she returned unto her father, who did with her according to his vow which he had vowed and she knew no man. And it was a custom in Israel, that the daughters of Israel went yearly to lament the daughter of Jephthah the Gileadite four days in a year". (Judges 1: 27–40)

Samson's marital adventures and raids he conducted, the latter accurately reflecting the hostile situation on the borders of Philistia before full-scale war broke out. Samson's raids may have provoked the Philistines into taking this action against the Israelites.

Opposite: Some tribes possessed lands east of the River Jordan, granted to them by Moses. To the west of the river the land was allotted by Joshua. The exact location of borders and tribes remains one of the most difficult to resolve.

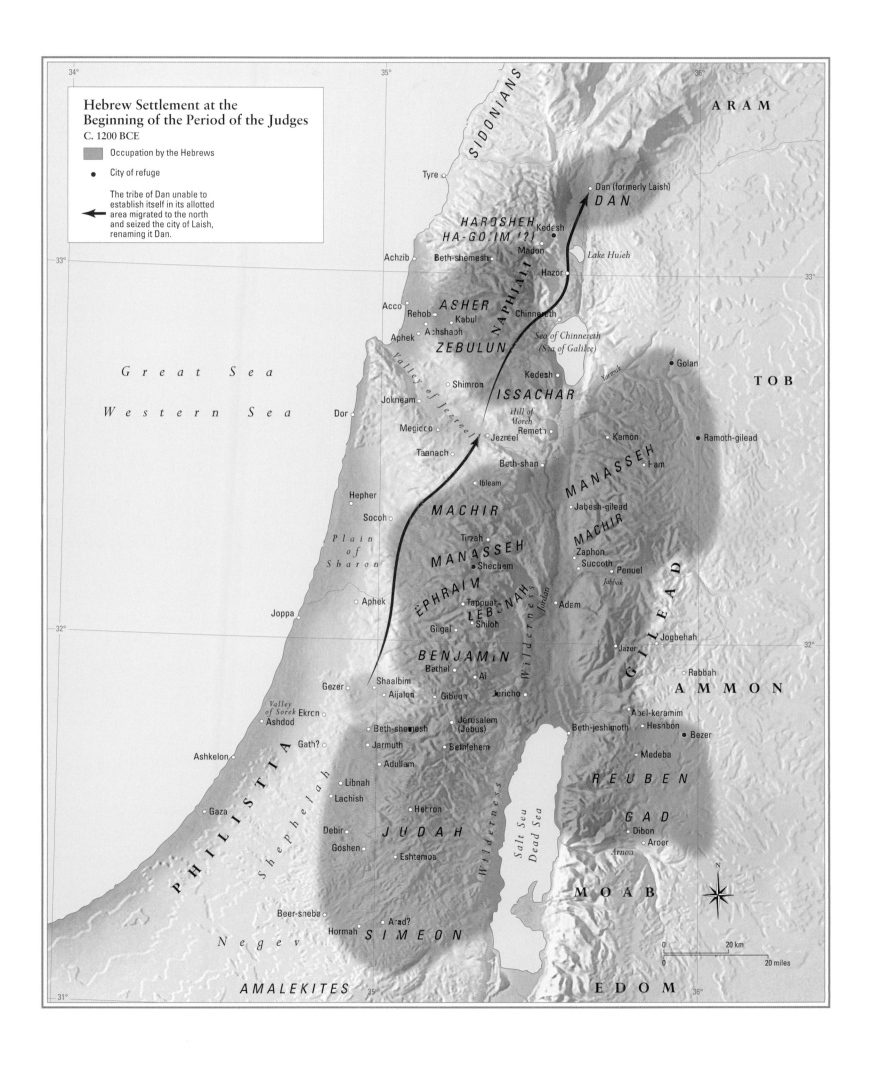

Hebrew Settlement at the
Beginning of the Period of the Judges
C. 1200 BCE

Occupation by the Hebrews

• City of refuge

The tribe of Dan unable to
establish itself in its allotted
area migrated to the north
and seized the city of Laish,
renaming it Dan.

ARAM

SIDONIANS

Tyre

Dan (formerly Laish)

DAN

HAROSHETH
HA-GOIM (?)
Kedesh

Achzib
Beth-shemesh
Madon

Lake Huleh

Hazor

Acco
ASHER

Rehob
Kabul
Chinnereth

Aphek
Achshaph

ZEBULUN
Sea of Chinnereth
(Sea of Galilee)

NAPHTALI

Kedesh
Golan

Shimron
ISSACHAR
TOB

Great   Sea

Jokneam
Valley of Jezreel
Yarmuk

Western   Sea
Dor

Hill of
Moreh
Remeth

Megiddo
Jezreel
Kamon
Ramoth-gilead

Taanach
Beth-shan

MANASSEH
Kamon

Ibleam
Jam

Hepher
Jabesh-gilead

Socoh
MACHIR
MACHIR

Plain
of
Sharon

Tirzah
Zaphon

MANASSEH
Shechem
Succoth
Penuel

Jabbok

EPHRAIM
Tappuah
Adam

Aphek
LEB-NAH

Joppa
Shiloh

Gilgal
GILEAD

BENJAMIN
Jazer
Jogbehah

Shaalbim
Bethel
Ai
Rabbah

Gezer
Aijalon
Gibeon
Jericho
AMMON

Valley
of Sorek
Ekron
Ashdod

Abel-keramim
Beth-shemesh
Jerusalem
(Jebus)
Heshbon

Gath?
Jarmuth
Beth-jeshimoth
Bezer

Ashkelon
Bethlehem

Medeba

Adullam

REUBEN

Libnah

Gaza
Lachish
GAD

Shephelah
Hebron
Dibon

Debir
Aroer

Goshen
JUDAH
Arnon

Eshtemoa
Salt Sea
Dead Sea

Beer-sheba
MOAB

Hormah
Arad?

Negev
SIMEON

AMALEKITES
EDOM

0   20 km
0   20 miles

THE ARK CAPTURED

THE PHILISTINES WERE FORMIDABLE ENEMIES, CONTROLLING THE COASTAL PLAINS AND BARRING ACCESS TO THE SEA. THEY WERE ALSO MORE TECHNOLOGICALLY ADVANCED.

A reconstruction of what the Ark of the Covenant may have looked like. At a battle fought near Ebenezer, the Philistines succeeded in capturing the Ark but after suffering various misfortunes, including afflictions with tumours, the Philistine leadership decided to send the Ark back. The Israelites happily received the Ark, taking it to Kiryat Yearim where it remained for approximately 20 years until King David removed it to his new capital, Jerusalem.

The Ark of the Covenant was the central shrine of the Twelve Tribes and generated a cult with its sacred rites and events and, most importantly, covenant law. This portable shrine originated in the desert and is described as being the tabernacle where God tented among His peoples and where He made His will known. The Ark was the focal point for the tribal league and its core institution. It was placed at Shiloh after the conquest of Canaan, being moved there from Gilgal.

When the Sea Peoples were defeated by Pharaoh Rameses III of Egypt, the Pelesata (Philistines) settled in the Promised Land as vassals or mercenaries to garrison Egyptian posts. These new migrants appeared in The Promised Land a few years before the Israelites and established themselves in the coastal region between the Shephelah, the coastal plain and the sea, part of which is now the Gaza Strip. The Philistines captured the Canaanite cities of Gaza, Ashkelon, Ashdod, Gath and Ekron. Gath and Ekron controlled the main coastal road from Egypt to Mesopotamia. The remainder guarded the route to Joppa (Jaffa) and Acre (Akko), the only sheltered harbour. Each Philistine city had its own king but they appointed a single leader in war. They were technologically more advanced than the Canaanites and Israelites and possessed iron weapons. This, together with their chariots and military discipline, made them formidable enemies. The Philistines advanced into the Negev and the Valley of Jezreel. The Canaanites and Israelites proved incapable of resisting them and the Philistines effectively ended Egyptian control and influence in the area. Even though they were never numerous, the Philistines acted as a military overlords ruling a Canaanite population.

The Philistines were intent on destroying any potential threat to the trade routes leading inland, so they destroyed the remaining Canaanite coastal cities and attacked other Sea Peoples such as the Tsikal. Dan moved northward to avoid attack. Border incidents, skirmishes and guerrilla warfare were used by the Israelites as evidenced by Samson's adventures.

In around 1050 BCE, the Philistines, under the leadership of the King of Gath, from his base at Aphek on the edge of the coastal plain, attacked the Israelites, who advanced with the Ark from Shiloh and were defeated at Ebenezer, losing some 4,000 men. A subsequent battle at Aphek is said to have resulted in some 30,000 Israelite deaths. Worst of all, the Ark was captured and its attendant priests, Phineas and Hophni, were killed. The Philistines then occupied Israelite land, seized Shiloh and destroyed the tent-shrine that housed the Ark, placing garrisons at strategic points. The Philistines prevented the manufacture of weapons and maintained their monopoly of iron-working, reducing the Israelites to dependence upon Philistine smiths for tool maintenance. The Philistines held much of the Negev, the central mountain range and the Valley of Jezreel, though they probably did not control Galilee and Transjordan. The garrisons could not maintain their hold on the central mountains and the Israelites gradually managed to arm themselves and develop resistance techniques and guerrilla warfare. On the other hand, the Israelites had no army, the symobls of its religion had been captured or destroyed and its priesthood murdered. They were in despair.

The Philistines carried the Ark to Ashdod, placing it in the temple of their god, Dagon. Dagon's idol was found fallen on its face. The idol was replaced but the next day was found decapitated with its hands severed. The people of Ashdod suffered a plague of hemorrhoids (I Samuel 5: 6). The Philistines next took the Ark to Gath and then to Ekron but the plague struck there and there was also an infestation of mice. After seven months, the Philistines relented and returned the Ark at Beth-Shemesh; the Israelites then carried it to Kiryat Yearim.

The Philistines attacked the Hebrews near the city of Aphek, the Hebrews were defeated and fell back. The Hebrews rallied and counter-attacked, this time taking the Ark into battle with them but again they were defeated, losing the Ark to the Philistines.

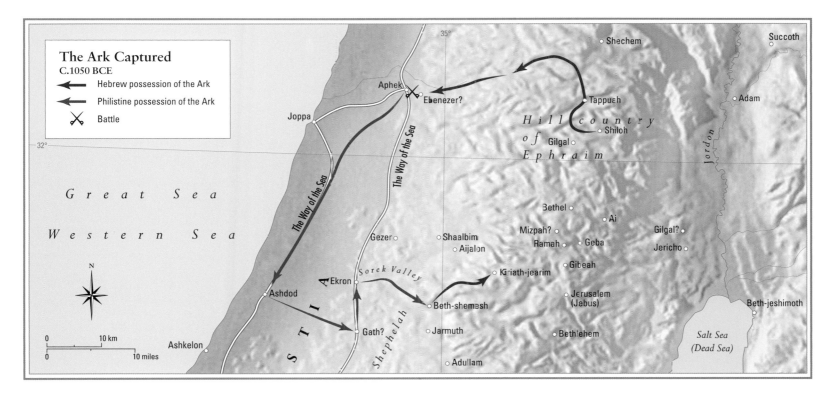

The Ark Captured
C.1050 BCE
⬅ Hebrew possession of the Ark
⬅ Philistine possession of the Ark
✕ Battle

The Phoenicians

ALTHOUGH THE PHOENICIANS LIVED IN THE AREA ROUGHLY
COVERED BY WESTERN SYRIA AND LEBANON TODAY, THEY ARE
SOMETIMES CREDITED WITH ORIGINATING IN THE ARABIAN
GULF. THEY WERE ACCOMPLISHED SEA-FARING TRADERS AND ARE
SAID TO HAVE INVENTED GLASS-MAKING.

Fortified temple of Rameses
III at Medinat Habu. The relief
shows Pharaoh leading the
captive Philistines whose
distinctive headdress is
reminiscent of the modern crew
cut or Mohican hairstyle.

The battles with the Philistines, who are said to have come from the island of Caphtor, modern Crete, lasted for two centuries in Cannan. Modern historians now claim that the Philistines were in fact from Anatolia, since Egyptian carvings identify southern Asia Minor as "Kefto". Whatever the case, they were one of a series of invaders known as the Sea Peoples and are also recorded in Egyptian documents.

They are mentioned extensively in the Bible – in Exodus, Joshua, Judges and Samuel. Their five capitals at Ashdod, Ashkelon, Ekron, Gath and Gaza were governed by kings and the communities became strong and wealthy from their iron-smelting and trade, helped by controlling the Way of the Sea. They adopted Canaanite speech and religion.

Their military strength is exemplified in the description of Goliath, a man covered in scales of bronze armour, greaves, a sword, an iron-tipped spear, whose shield was carried by a bearer. Their monopoly or iron-working is described in I Samuel 13: 19–22: "Now there was no smith found throughout the land of Israel: for the Philistines said, Lest the Israelites make themselves swords and spears. But all the Israelites went down to the Philistines, to sharpen, every man his share, and his coulter, and his axe, and his mattock." Consequently, the Israelites were soundly beaten at Ebenezer and Aphek by warriors with iron weapons.

Against King Saul, the Philistines met temporary defeat at Michmash, yet Saul fled to Gilboa. In two battles, David broke their power but the Philistines reasserted their independence after Solomon's death and continued their hostility toward Israel, as recorded in Amos and Joel. Eventually, the campaigning armies of Egypt and Assyria weakened them until they were absorbed by the Assyrians in the seventh century BCE. Cambyses, the Persian, described Philistia in 525 BCE as being Arab-controlled.

The Phoenicians, who lived further north, were a Semitic people based in a group of city kingdoms at Smyrna, Zarephath, Byblos, Jubeil, Arwad, Akko, Sidon, Tripoli, Tyre and Berytus. Tyre and Sidon tended to dominate the rest alternately. The Phoenicians arrived between 3,000–2,500 BCE. Certan historians place their origins in the Arabian Gulf.

Phoenicia was invaded and controlled by the Egyptians from about 1800 BCE, Byblos becoming an Egyptian port. In about 1400 BCE, Hittite competition with Egypt allowed Phoenicia to revolt and by 1100 BCE, it had won its independence. The Phoenicians became the finest ship-builders of their time. Their huge cargo ships are represented at the Egyptian tomb at Drah Abou'l Neggah which dates from c. 1500 BCE. The Phoenicians are also shown as manning the first biremes in two Assyrian reliefs of 70 BCE.

Phoenician fleets sailed the Mediterranean, founding many colonies. Their influence was extended over Dor and Ugarit in the Levant and they founded colonies at Utica and Carthage in north Africa. Their trade was originally based upon Tyrian purple, a dye made from the murex shellfish. The Tyrians established a second factory producing the dye at Mogador in what is now Morocco. Exports included cedar wood from Lebanon, pine, dyed linen, wine, metal goods, glass, glazed pottery, salt and dried fish. They transhipped silver from Spain and tin from Cornwall in Britain. According to Pliny, Hanno the Navigator sailed as far as the African Gulf of Guinea and even observed a volcanic eruption in the Cameroon Mountains. Pharaoh Necho II (606–593 BCE), according to Herodotus, sent a Phoenician fleet down the Red Sea which circumnavigated Africa, returning three years later through the Straits of Gibraltar.

The Phoenicians worshipped El, Baal and Astarte as well as gods from Egypt, Syria and Assyria. Relations with Israel were good in the time of King Solomon who sent Hiram of Tyre 440,000 bushels of wheat and barley and 340,000 gallons of oil (I Chronicles 2: 9) annually. In Ezekiel's time, Judah traded with Tyre sending wheat, honey and oil. Eventually, Phoenicia was conquered by Assyria, Persia and Alexander the Great, losing its identity under the Seleucids.

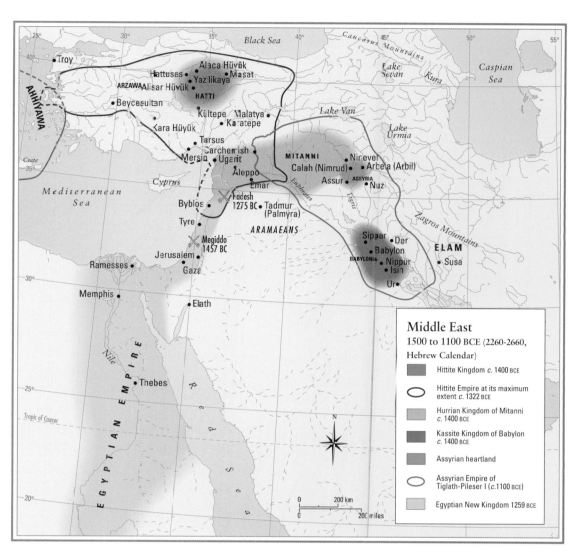

Phoenicia, a coastal area north of Tyre reaching up to Ugarit, was a small but influential civilization. Occasionally subject to the interests of Egypt, or the Hittites, they were at times fully independent and became amongst the finest shipbuilders in the Mediterranean, controlling trade and founding many colonies.

Samuel

THE PROPHET SAMUEL, WHO WAS ALSO A JUDGE, WAS EXHORTED BY THE PEOPLE TO FIND A KING AND, WITH GOD'S BLESSING, HE DID SO IN THE SHAPE OF SAUL. HIS FEAR THAT THIS MIGHT LEAD TO TYRANNY WAS EVENTUALLY JUSTIFIED.

The Bible represents Samuel as both judge and prophet, renowned for his role in creating an Israelite monarchy. His mother, Hannah, had been childless but after praying to God, she bore Samuel. In gratitude, Hannah dedicated the child to the service of the tabernacle at Shiloh. After he was weaned, Samuel was taken from Rameh, his birthplace and put in the care of Eli, Shiloh's chief priest.

Samuel was born during Israelite conflict with the Philistines and was contemporary with the disasters at Ebenezer and Aphek. When Eli died, Samuel inherited the mantle of spiritual leader of the Israelites. In his role as judge, Samuel toured the Israelite settlements every year but he lived at Rameh where he constructed an altar. Samuel believed that the Israelites could only be free and independent of the Philistines if they kept the covenant with God. So he summoned the Israelites to Mizpah where they were induced to confess their sins and put away false gods while Samuel prayed to God. The Philistines heard of the Israelite assembly and attacked Mizpah. "... But the Lord thundered with a great thunder on that day upon the Philistines, and discomfited them; and they were smitten before Israel." (I Samuel 7: 10) Despite this defeat, the Philistines soon returned in force at Geba, in a strong place dominating the main eastern approach through the Saddle of Benjamin into the Judaean hills. Eventually, the Israelites managed to eject them.

Intense border warfare continued in the hills and the Shephelah. Israelite resistance to the Philistine occupation was weakened by infighting and the Israelite guerrilla fighters were bedeviled by the lack of adequate weaponry against a well-equipped and disciplined enemy. Despite the violence, Samuel still managed to make his annual circuit of the settlements from Rameh to

Mizpah, Bethel, Naaran, Gilgal and Geba. Samuel mediated disputes and dispensed justice.

As Samuel grew old, he realized his sons, Joel and Abijah, would be unworthy to succeed him, being avaricious and corrupt. The Israelite elders were deeply concerned and visited Rameh to discuss the fact that no respected spiritual leader available. These elders considered that only centralized rule under a strong leader could adequately and decisively repel the Philistines. They desired a king and asked Samuel to find one. "... We will have a king over us; That we also may be like all other nations; and that our king may judge us, and go out before us, and fight our battles." (I Samuel 8: 19–20). Samuel objected to the idea of a monarchy fearing that it might result in despotism. However, he eventually yielded to God and public opinion.

Ultimately, the Bible states that Samuel's choice of king fell upon Saul of Gibeah, a well-known warrior with an experience of leadership. One of his virtues, in Samuel's eyes, was a lack of personal supporters with no power base for royal abuse. So, Saul of the tribe of Benjamin was anointed becoming King and leaving Samuel to retire from his leadership and return to Rameh. Samuel became prominent again when he rejected Saul for disobeying God and secretly anointed David as King in secrecy.

Saul had a hard task. He needed to motivate a national guerrilla movement that lacked effective weapons. The Israelites were also easily discouraged, as when the Ark was captured. An instant king demanded instant victory. Saul lacked the common touch with his men, however. He eventually proved to be an unlucky general and morale suffered following several military setbacks. Prior to this, Saul returned to Gibeah where fighting men joined him and received support from the people. Not all the Israelites supported Saul, however; some questioned his abilities. "But the children of Belial said, How shall this man save us. And they despised him, and brought him no presents." (I Samuel 10: 27)

The Calling of Samuel. An illustration of the much-loved Bible story. The child Samuel is shown with the priest Eli, who eventually realizes that the child had been called by God, in this picture from the John Brown Bible.

SAUL, KING OF ISRAEL

THE MAIN ENEMIES OF THE ISRAELITES, THE PHILISTINES, WERE SUBSEQUENTLY REPLACED BY THE AMMONITES, WHOM THE BIBLE STATES AS ORIGINATING FROM THE INCESTUOUS RELATIONSHIP BETWEEN LOT AND HIS DAUGHTERS. THE AMMONITES INHABITED WHAT IS NOW NORTHERN JORDAN.

Statue of a Philistine warrior in the Ashkelon Museum.

Opposite: The Philistine's efforts to expand their territory resulted in the unification of the Hebrews under Saul.

The Philistine occupation of parts of the land Israel, especially the Saddle of Benjamin, northeast of Gibeah, caused such a furore that the Israelite elders united in their demands for a king. The meeting convened at Mizpah by the judge and prophet Samuel, provides one version of events. However, there is another account of Saul's meeting with Samuel. Saul and a servant were sent by Saul's father into the hills of Ephraim to find some asses that had strayed from his father's land. Having failed in their mission, the two searchers reached Rameh where they decided to ask Samuel for help. Samuel welcomed Saul, predicted some future events in his life that later happened and subsequently anointed Saul with oil. "Then Samuel took a vial of oil, and poured in upon his head, and kissed him, and said, Is it not because the Lord hath annointed thee to be captain over his inheritance?" (I Samuel 10: 1)

Saul's task was to unite the tribes, keeping them bound together by their religious faith and the Israelite covenant with God. He had the mammoth task of defining a strategy with which to outwit the better armed and disciplined Philistines who had iron weapons and chariots. Saul's skill and determination were eventually to be tested – not against the People of the Sea but against the Ammonites. The Bible claims that these were the descendants of Lot by his drunken, incestuous relationship with one of his daughters. They lived east of the Jordan, their western border being the River Jabok where it flows south to north. The Moabites, the other descendants of Lot, probably lived south of the Ammonites. The Ammonite capital was Rabbath-Ammon (now Amman, capital of Jordan).

Nahash, the Ammonite leader, invaded Gilead and besieged the Israelite town of Jabesh-Gilead.

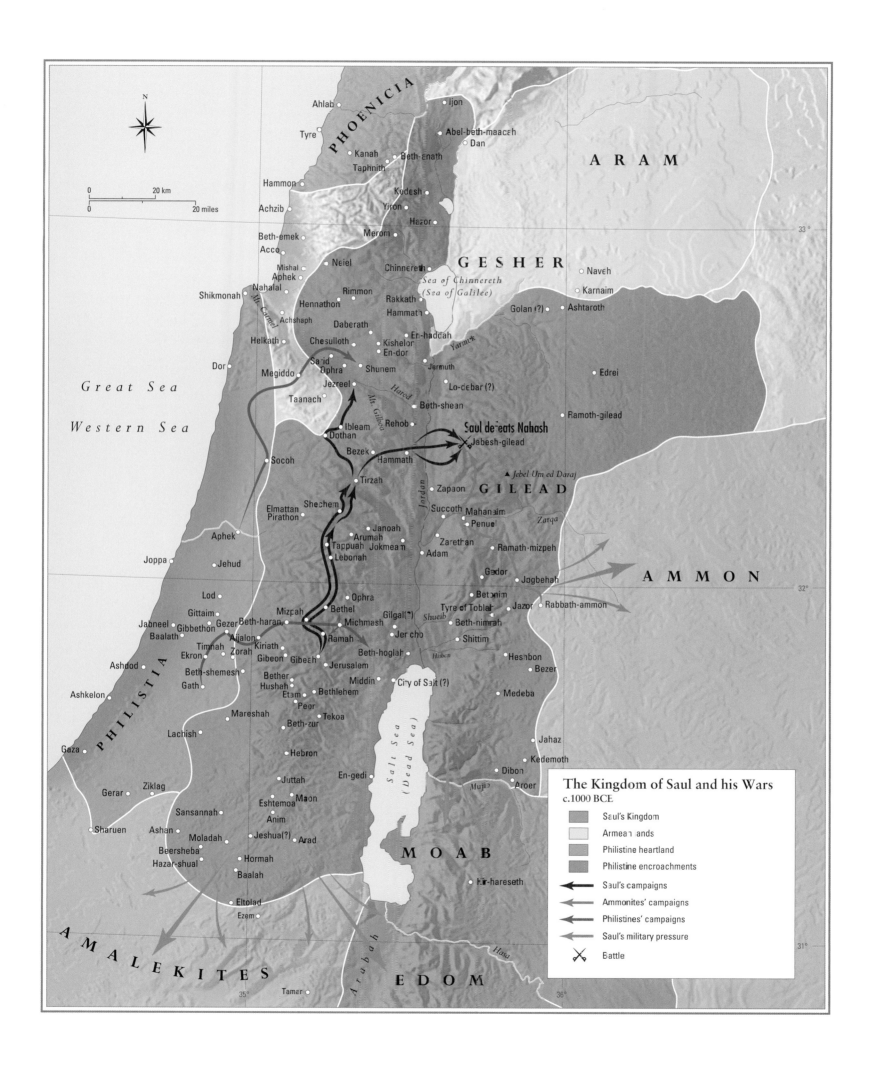

The Kingdom of Saul and his Wars
c.1000 BCE

- Saul's Kingdom
- Aramean lands
- Philistine heartland
- Philistine encroachments
- ← Saul's campaigns
- ← Ammonites' campaigns
- ← Philistines' campaigns
- ← Saul's military pressure
- ✕ Battle

The inhabitants promised to sign a treaty with Nahash, accepting his sovereignty but his condition for peace was the he put out the right eye of every male in the city. "On this condition will I make a covenant with you, that I may thrust out all your right eyes, and lay it for a reproach upon all Israel." (I Samuel 11: 2) As was normal under siege conditions, the elders agreed that if they were not relieved within a given time – in this case seven days – they would acquiesce.

The Jabeshites dispatched messengers requesting aid. Saul heard the news at Gibeah and summoned Israelite warriors to muster at Bezek, between Shechem and Beth-Shean. His demands were accompanied by pieces of a pair of oxen he had butchered: "Whoever cometh not forth after Saul and after Samuel, so shall it be done unto his oxen. And the fear of the Lord fell on the people, and they came with one consent" (I Samuel: 7). Saul displayed his mettle by leading his men in a forced march at night across the Jordan through the river bed of Wadi Yabis, below Jabesh-Gilead. At dawn, Saul sent three columns into the sleepy Ammonite camp, achieving total surprise. The slaughter commenced, continuing into daylight with the destruction and rout of the Ammonite army. Nahash was allegedly killed, although King David had dealings subsequently with an Ammonite named Nahash, so, either there were two kings named Nahash, or the besieger escaped. After the victory, Samuel led the Israelite army to Gilgal and Saul was re-affirmed as king. Samuel admonished the Israelites, reminding them of their past sins sins in worshipping Baalim and Ashtharoth (Baal and Astarte), and affirming that the true King of Israel was God.

"And when ye saw that Nahash the king of the children of Ammon came against you, ye said unto me, Nay; but a king shall reign over us: when the Lord your God was your king. Now therefore behold the king whom ye have chosen, and whom ye have desired! And, behold, the Lord hath set a king over you. If ye will fear the Lord, and serve him, and obey his voice, and not rebel against the commandment of the Lord, then shall both ye and also the king that reigneth over you continue following the Lord your God: But if ye will not obey the voice of the Lord, but rebel against the commandment of the Lord, then shall the hand of the Lord be against you, as it was against your fathers." (I Samuel 12: 12–15).

Meanwhile, some 14 miles westward, at Geba and Michmash, Philistine troops occupied the strategically important pass at the Saddle of Benjamin that controlled the Way of Beth-Horon into the Israelite highlands. Saul raised a brigade of 3,000 men, retaining 2,000 as he marched on Michmash and leaving the balance as a reserve with his son, Jonathan. That reckless prince assaulted Gibeah, however, surprising the Philistines in a victorious attack.

Saul broadcast news of the victory while the furious Philistines assembled their chariots, cavalry and infantry in large numbers and camped at Michmash, east of Beth-Aven. The Israelites fled in dismay, hiding in caves, woods and on hilltops though some reached Gad and Gilead east of the River Jordan. Witnessing the disintegration of his army, Saul retreated to Gilgal where he wanted to sacrifice to God and ask for help. He waited for Samuel to officiate but the prophet was delayed. Impatiently, Saul offered the sacrifice himself but Samuel arrived subsequently and was angry with Saul, denouncing him for usurping a priest's role. This spelled doom for Saul's kingdom. God would now seek a more suitable candidate for kingship. Samuel then abandoned Saul, leaving for Gibeah. Saul led his remaining 600 men to Gibeah, carefully avoiding three large companies of raiders dispatched from Michmash. Elsewhere, Jonathan and his armour-bearer surprised a Philistine outpost on a rocky prominence and killed its 20-man garrison. The Philistines at Michmash were shocked and panicked at this event. Seeing their confusion, Saul attacked routing the Philistines. Israelite deserters came from their hiding places and joined in the slaughter. The Philistines fled along the Way of Beth-Horon, passed Ayalon, to their own lands. The Israelite heartland was now secure, providing Saul with a base for future campaigns. Saul went on to campaign against all of the Israelites' enemies—Moab, Ammon, Edom, Zobah and Philistia. Samuel returned to tell Saul that God required the destruction of the Amalekites who had abused the Israelites, attempting to stop them at Rephidim but when finding it impossible, attacking the stragglers. Amalek, "smote the hindmost of thee, even all that were feeble behind thee, when thou wast faint and weary; and, they feared not God." (Deuteronomy 25: 18) Although enjoined to kill every living thing, Saul defeated some of the Amalekites, capturing their King, Agag, and butchering his followers but sparing the choicest flocks and oxen which he sent to Gilgal. Samuel condemned Saul for not killing everything as God had demanded, claiming that God rejected Saul yet again. Samuel hacked Agag to death with a sword and told Saul, "Thou hast rejected the word of the Lord, and the Lord hath rejected thee from being king over Israel." (I Samuel 15: 26). From then on, Samuel ignored Saul until the day Saul died.

View of modern Amman, showing archaeological remains from various periods. It is one of the oldest permanently-occupied cities in the world.

BIBLICAL WARFARE

THE HYKSOS AND THE HITTITES BOTH INVADED EGYPT AND BOTH WERE EVENTUALLY REPELLED. THE PHOENICIANS LEARNED TO USE SHIPS FOR FIGHTING, NOT JUST AS TROOP-CARRIERS, AND DESIGNED NEW TYPES OF POWERFUL SHIPS THAT DOMINATED THE TRADE ROUTES.

Relief at Akhmim in Egypt, showing a battle between the Egyptian and Hittite soldiers, 1274 BCE.

The Egyptian civilizations of the Old Kingdom (c. 3100–1990 BCE) and the Middle Kingdom (c. 1990–1680 BCE) were disrupted by the invading Hyksos. These earlier periods saw various enemies who sought to unify Upper and Lower Egypt. The troops used in the process wore a kilt, carried trunk-sized wooden shields and thrusting spears, and occasionally axes and maces, as depicted in Prince Emsah's grave at Asyut. The only enemy other than those of the unification wars were Nubian archers and spear-carriers who were eventually recruited into Upper Egypt's forces.

Heavy infantry with huge shields were introduced during the Middle Kingdom accompanied by a range of soldiers using javelins and poleaxes. Nubian archers continued to serve and spears were supplemented by daggers and light axes. Copper was being replaced by bronze but Egyptian smiths seemed incapable of casting solid bronze axe-heads and still used copper for arrowheads. A small standing army was supplemented by provincial militias. The only military action was directed against Nubians and desert nomads.

This primitive weaponry and army was confronted by the violence and speed of the Hyksos who invaded from Syria and Canaan. Their charioteers with composite bows swiftly captured Lower Egypt which was then once again separated from Upper Egypt. The Hyksos origins are unknown, though they are unlikely to have been a Semitic people. Did they conquer Egypt by force or did Egypt merely succumb to the threat of the fearsome Hyksos in their mail and helmets?

Whatever the case, the Hyksos ruled Lower Egypt for just over a century.

Meanwhile, Upper Egypt experienced a military revolution. The two-man chariot, driver and archer, was introduced, the latter wearing a leather jerkin with scale armor stitched to it. The composite bow now featured heavily, as did intelligence-gathering cavalry. War aimed at removing the Hyksos probably commenced under Kamose c. 1600 BCE. By 1570 BCE, the Hyksos had been driven back to Avaris, their capital, then expelled to the Gaza Strip. Experienced Egyptian troops were used by Tuthmosis III to secure his frontiers against the Libyans and Nubians. Canaan was then brought under control but fighting broke out with the Hittites, ending in the chariot battle at Kadesh (1298 BCE) that resulted in the division of Syria between the two empires.

In 1232 BCE, a confederation of Sea Peoples and Libyans invaded Egypt but was stopped by Pharaoh Merneptah's army. Egypt's last battles occurred under Rameses III who routed the Sea Peoples on land and sea, followed by a victory over the Libyans. Egypt entered a period of decline, however, and lost control of the land east of Sinai leaving a power vacuum that enabled the Israelites to build a state in Canaan.

In ancient warfare, ships were used only to transport soldiers. This was how the Pharaohs used their navy when advancing northward through Canaan. Guard ships were probably employed to protect ports and river mouths, such as the Nile Delta. The Egyptian temple at Medinet Habu provides wall illustrations of the "first" sea battle between Rameses III and the invading Sea Peoples who also used ships for transport rather than for fighting. The Egyptian war galleys measured 75 feet long with a 14-foot beam and were assembled on a keel. They were equipped with rams tipped with snarling animal heads. The galleys had 24 oarsmen and a complement of archers and spearmen who used fore and aft fighting platforms and a crow's nest/fighting top for a lookout or an archer. The Egyptians used their rams and composite bows to sweep enemy decks with arrows while manoeuvring to prevent the enemy boarding. The Sea Peoples were thwarted in their ambitions. Egyptian marine architecture declined and the Phoenicians became the major Levantine sea power, using bireme war galleys. These were eventually succeeded by Greek biremes and triremes in c. 500 BCE. They were 106 feet long and powered by 170 rowers.

The loosely constructed Hittite Empire north of Syria began to expand. Mussilis I (c. 1550–30 BCE) actually marched 500 miles from a base at Aleppo to Babylon which he captured, looted and destroyed. This raid relied on chains of depots in friendly and neutral states. After a period of weakness, King Suppiluliumas I (1380 BCE) came to the throne. His troops comprised a large chariot force supported by spearmen, swordsmen and axemen. By 1316 BCE, Hatti was an empire with secure borders and a battle-hardened army. King Muwatallis eventually clashed with the Egyptians at Kadesh. The battle was probably a chariot clash with competing squadrons in chaotic dog-fights. The Hittites were menaced by the Sea Peoples whom only the Egyptians were capable of defeating; the Hittites gradually lost their empire against this assault and another by Phrygians, leaving Hattusas and Ugarit burned to ashes. Caught between the powerful empires, the city states of Syria and Canaan relied on chariots and fortified cities for defense. Inter-city rivalry meant chariot clashes and sieges, often short-lived because attackers needed constant supplies. Offensive tactics consisted of the escalade, battering rams and undermining under walls. Only later did the Assyrians build furnace-hot fires against walls which melted stones into virtual roads of 'lava', still visible today.

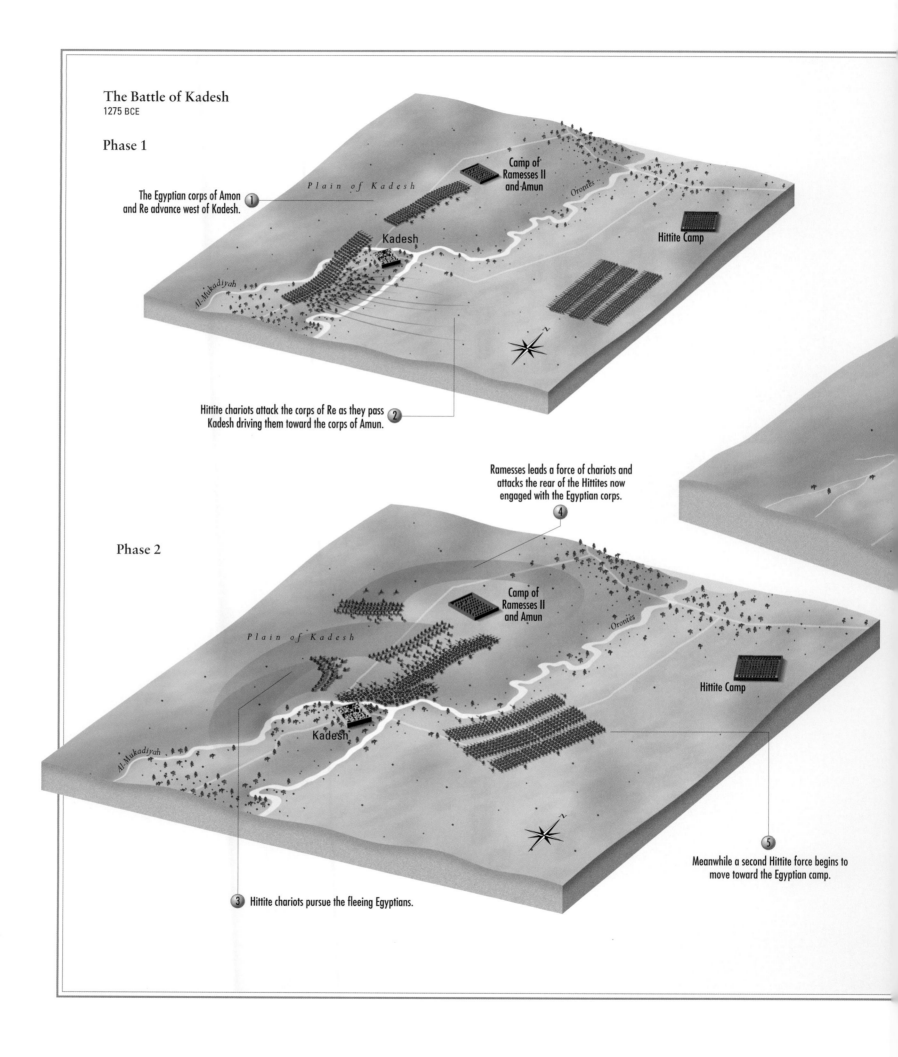

The Battle of Kadesh
1275 BCE

Phase 1

The Egyptian corps of Amon
and Re advance west of Kadesh. ①

Plain of Kadesh

Camp of
Ramesses II
and Amun

Orontes

Hittite Camp

Kadesh

Al-Mukadiyah

Hittite chariots attack the corps of Re as they pass ②
Kadesh driving them toward the corps of Amun.

Ramesses leads a force of chariots and
attacks the rear of the Hittites now
engaged with the Egyptian corps.
④

Phase 2

Camp of
Ramesses II
and Amun

Plain of Kadesh

Orontes

Hittite Camp

Kadesh

Al-Mukadiyah

Meanwhile a second Hittite force begins to
move toward the Egyptian camp.
⑤

Hittite chariots pursue the fleeing Egyptians. ③

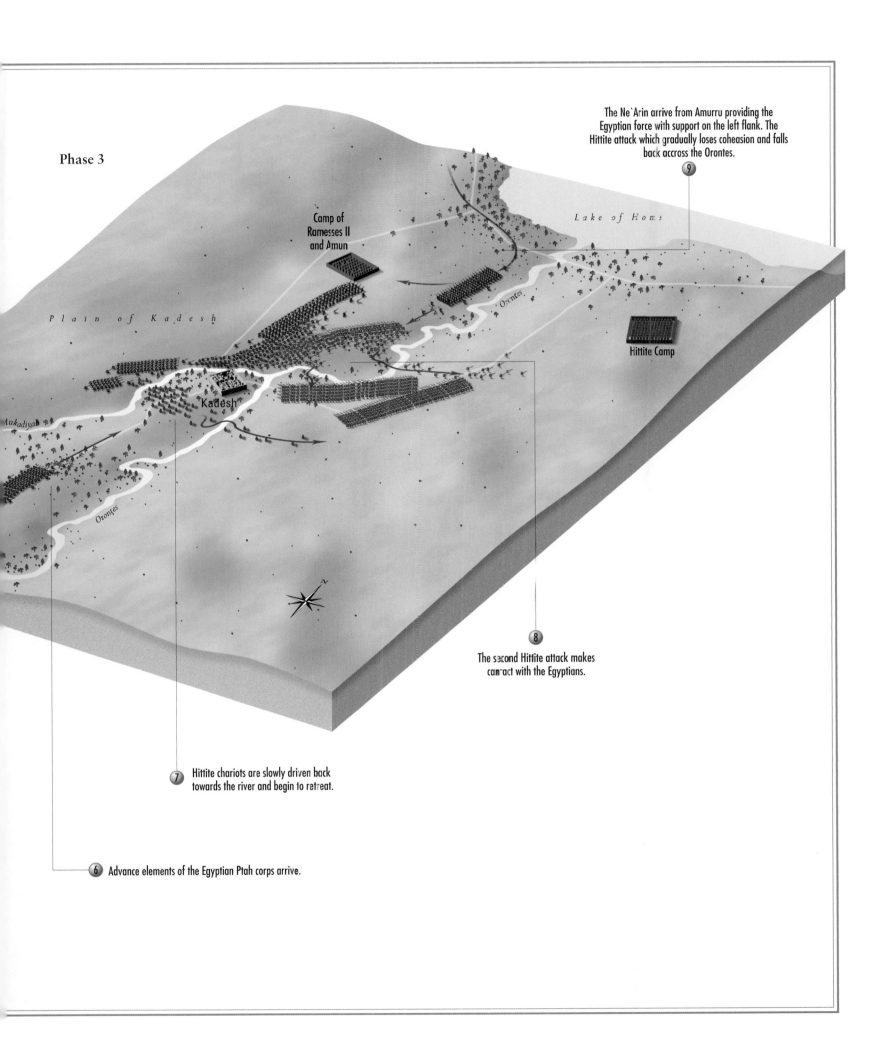

Phase 3

The Ne`Arin arrive from Amurru providing the Egyptian force with support on the left flank. The Hittite attack which gradually loses coheasion and falls back accross the Orontes.

9

Lake of Homs

Camp of Ramesses II and Amun

Plain of Kadesh

Orontes

Hittite Camp

Mukadiyah

Kadesh

Orontes

8

The second Hittite attack makes can-act with the Egyptians.

7 Hittite chariots are slowly driven back towards the river and begin to retreat.

6 Advance elements of the Egyptian Ptah corps arrive.

THE FAITH AND ITS HOLY PLACES

THE ARK OF THE COVENANT WAS AT FIRST A PORTABLE SHRINE OF THE TYPE MENTIONED IN UGARITIC TEXTS. AFTER IT WAS RETURNED BY THE PHILISTINES AND SHILOH WAS DESTROYED, KING DAVID GAVE IT A PERMANENT HOME IN JERUSALEM.

The Ark of the Covenant was the central shrine of the Twelve Ttribes, providing the Israelite God with a site for sacred rites and occasions. This tent-shrine originated in the desert, was portable and was sometimes known as the "tent of the meeting", in which God made His will known to His people. "And let them make me a sanctuary; that I may dwell among them." (Exodus 25: 8) This type of shrine is well-known, Ugaritic texts describe a similar, portable shrine to El and a Midianite tent-shrine has been found in the Timna mines.

God's home is portrayed as a tent in II Samuel 7: 6ff, the throne of a God-King. Thus the Israelits regarded the Ark as their central shrine although worship was allowed at other sites. After arriving in Canaan, the Israelites first camped at Gilgal, a retreat and mustering station, as well as a religious sanctuary and place of sacrifice (I Samuel 10: 8, 11: 15, and 15: 12). The shrine may first have been located at Shechem, then Bethel, but this is uncertain, despite there being a ceremony initiating the Israelite tribes at Shechem (Joshua 24) but Shechem was a Canaanite religious centre and, thus unlikely as a permanent site. Bethel possessed patriarchal links and is a possible site and Judges mentions the Ark's presence there (Judges 20: 26–28) but the Ark was also taken to Shiloh (Judges 21: 12).

Shiloh became a home for the Tabernacle (Joshua 18: 1), a religious centre for all the tribes and a place where land was apportioned to the seven landless tribes. Shiloh was administered by Eli the priest and his two sons Phinehas and Hophni (I Samuel 1: 24 and 3: 3). A priestly caste was not essential at the time however. The directions to build altars and the offering of sacrifices were addressed to the whole people, not a priest.

"And the Lord said unto Moses, Thus thou shall say unto the children of Israel, Ye have seen that I have talked with you from heaven. Ye shall not make me gods of silver, neither shall ye make unto you gods of gold. An altar of earth thou shalt make unto me, and shalt sacrifice thereon thy burnt offering, and thy peace offerings, thy sheep and thine oxen; in all places where I record my name I will come unto thee, and I will bless thee" (Exodus 20: 22–24).

The priesthood was not confined to the Levites at this time, as it eventually did, otherwise Samuel the Ephraimite would never have become priest of the sanctuary at Shiloh.

That the shrine was important is obvious but the Ark was vitally important not the city of Shiloh. When the Ark was captured by the Philistines, Shiloh was destroyed. When the Ark was returned to the Israelites, it was taken to the home of Abinadab at Kiryat Yearim; Abinadab's son, Eleazar, was appointed its guardian. Shiloh was destroyed and was later used as an example to Israel. "But go ye now unto my place which was in Shiloh, where I set my name at the first, and see what I did to it for the wickedness of my people Israel." (Jeremiah 7: 12) Jeremiah stood in the Temple berating Israel for its sins of theft, adultery, lies and worship of Baal, prophesying, "Therefore I will do unto this house, which is called by my name, wherein ye trust, and unto the place which I gave to you, and to your fathers, as I have done to Shiloh." (Jeremiah 7: 14). Eventually, King David moved the shrine to Jerusalem. Psalms 78: 68–70 states: "The Lord chose the tribe of Judah, the mount of Zion which he loved. And he built his sanctuary ... He chose David ..."

King David established his new capital city, Jerusalem, as the religious centre of the nation as well as its political focus, by relocating the Ark of the Covenant, the Hebrew portable shrine, there. His son, King Solomon, gave the Ark a permanent home in the form of a Temple built to a typical Canaanite pattern, The innermost sanctuary housed the Ark itself.

Canaanite temples contained a statue of the god but in the case of the Israelites, the sanctuary was empty. An outer, larger, sanctuary housed a small altar for offering incense, and other minor furnishings. The main altar for animal sacrifices stood before the Temple entrance in the courtyard. Only the priests could enter this area and the temple building; all of the people shared in the worship from outer courtyards.

Sacrifices were offered daily, with special rituals for the main festivals. Worship was a way of connecting the Israelites with the power shown by God at the escape from Egypt and the convenant made at Mount Sinai.

LEVANTINE TRADING NETWORKS

ARCHAEOLOGICAL EXCAVATIONS, ESPECIALLY THE EXPLORATION OF SHIPWRECKS USING MODERN DIVING TECHNIQUES HAVE REVEALED THE HUGE EXTENT OF EARLY INTERNATIONAL TRADE, WITH THE LEVANT AT ITS HEART.

The Levant and Mesopotamia have always been important posts on the trade route from the archipelago of Indonesia through the Mediterranean to Europe. The Assyrians (c. 3000 BCE) claimed the gods drank a wine made from sesame seeds on the night before they created the earth. Genetic evidence now suggests that sesame seeds originated in Indonesia and East Africa. The trade winds and prevailing currents enabled sailors to reach these distant shores even in prehistoric times.

The labourers constructing Cheops' pyramid were fed Asiatic spices and Sumerian evidence (c. 2400 BCE) points to the popularity of cloves from the Moluccas. The Egyptian Ebers papyrus (c. 1550 BCE) lists spices used as medicines and for embalming. Cassia, cinnamon, anise, marjoram and cumin were ingredients in the preparation used for washing the body cavities of corpses to be mummified. Cassia and cinnamon only grow in southeast Asia. About 1500 BCE, Queen Hatshepsut of Egypt sent ships to Punt, possibly Somaliland, southern Arabia, Zanzibar and the Dar-es-Salaam district, to acquire myrrh, ivory, ebony and monkeys. The voyage was successful, the ships returning with a cargo that included myrrh trees to plant in a temple to Amon-Ra in Thebes. The mummy of Rameses II, who died in 1213 BCE, has peppercorns in its nostrils, proving that trading in spices linked the Near East to Indonesia and Africa.

Copper, grain, lapis lazuli from Afghanistan, carnelian, obsidian, pearls from Dilmun, tin, lumber, ivory and textiles were traded through Anatolia and Mesopotamia. Ugarit and its port, Makhadu were key cities on this route, containing huge warehouses where goods arriving by ship or donkey from Egypt, Canaan, Mesopotamia, Cyprus, Crete, the Aegean islands and Greece Here, the textiles, ivory, metal, timber, ceramics and agricultural produce were transformed into manufactured goods for export. This Levantine kingdom, some 1,300 square miles in area, possessed a merchant fleet comprising several hundred vessels. Ugaritic texts and written records found in Ebla, Mari, Egypt and Hattushash, the Hittite capital, record the diverse nature of the goods shipped around the eastern Mediterranean. Marine archaeology has recovered Bronze Age ships off the coasts of Anatolia and Cyprus. Copper, tin, tools, glass ingots, glazed pottery, chemicals, amber beads (sourced from the Baltic or Sicily or Burma) ceramics from Canaan, Cyprus and Mycenae, elephant and hippopotamus tusks, jewellery, semi-precious stones, textiles, lumber, food and wooden furniture have been found as cargo. Ships also carried livestock – sheep, goats, oxen, donkeys, horses and geese. Ugarit had a significant population of foreign nationals: Hittites, Hurrians, Egyptians, Assyrians, Cretans and Cypriots, who were merchants or diplomats. The city was neutral ground, between the powerful states of Egypt and Hatti, but was tied to the latter as a vassal for much of the Bronze Age, paying tribute in gold, silver and purple-dyed wool.

Another shipwreck found off the coast of Libya attests to trade between Cyprus, Mycenae and Libya. Ivory trinkets and drinking cups made from ostrich egg shells in the Shaft Graves at Mycenae attest to relay trade with the Sudan. Trade also flourished with Malta, Sicily, Sardinia and the Etruscans of Italy. The Phoenicians, from their main port of Tyre, sailed to Britain, Spain and southern France. The agrarian societies of Europe sent cargoes of slaves, furs, honey and amber along the north-south river system and east-west along the Danube. Many goods reached the Near East through Anatolia or the city of Marseilles in France (founded 600 BCE).

Trade flowed between the empires and states of the ancient world carrying goods from East to West.

Eurasia in 1250 BCE
- ■ Important sites
- New Kingdom of Egypt
- Hittites
- Mitanni
- Elam
- Shang China
- Mycenaean civilisation
- Transition from hunting and gathering to agriculture
- Other urbanised regions

Major Bronze-using Regions
- Andronova steppe cultures
- Bronze Age Europe
- Mainland South-east Asia

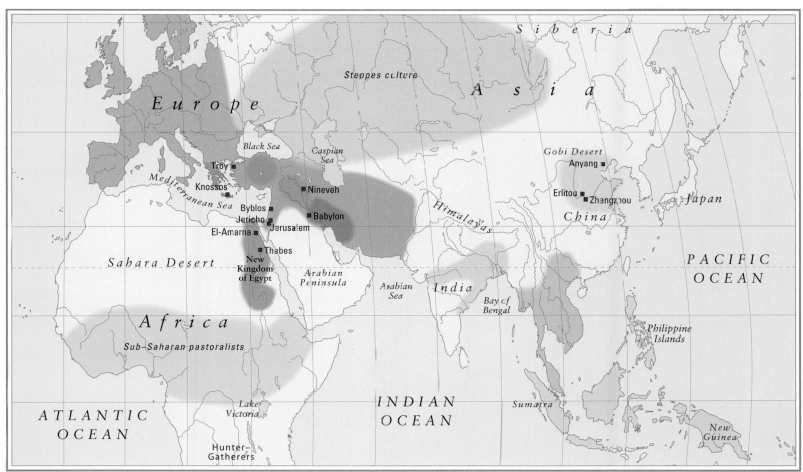

THE ASSYRIAN THREAT

THE BIBLE RECORDS THE ASSYRIANS AS FEARSOME ENEMIES OF THE ISRAELITES. FROM BEING VASSALS OF THE KASSITE RULERS OF BABYLONIA, THE ASSYRIANS WENT ON TO CONQUER LARGE PARTS OF THE MIDDLE EAST AND RULE THEIR ERSTWHILE MASTERS.

Walls and gate of Nineveh, just outside modern Mosul, Iraq. It is not known when the city was founded but this massive entrance and fortifications date from c. 600 BCE.

Assyria features prominently in Biblical history though there are few records concerning Assyria at the time of the Battle of Kadesh between the Egyptian and Hittite Empires Assyria, or Ashur as it is known in the Semitic languages, was conquered by King Hammurabi of Babylon. When the Kassites seized Babylon, Assyria became a vassal. In the fifteenth century BCE, the Mitanni sacked Assyria which then paid annual tribute to its new master until Mitanni power collapsed under pressure from the Hittites and rebellious Assyria.

Ashur-Uballit (c. 1365–1330 BCE) resolved to change Assyria's fortunes and expand its territories from the cities of Ashur, Nineveh, Arbil and Nimrud. Diplomatic contact was made with Egypt as recorded in the Tel Al-Amarna tablets, as follows:

"To Napkhoria (Akhenaten), Great King, King of Egypt, my brother, thus speaks Ashur-Uballit, King of Assyria, Great King, your brother: may well-being reign over you, your house and your land!

"I feel very pleased after having seen your envoy. This is felt, in truth ... before me. I have sent you a beautiful royal chariot, two white horses, an unfurnished chariot, and a beautiful stone seal as gifts. Of the Great King ... it is said: The gold is in your land like the dust; Why is there ... in your eyes? I have begun a new palace, and I want to have it ready soon. Send me as much gold as is required for its decoration and for what is needed.

"When my father, Ashur-Nadin-Ahe, sent his messengers to Egypt, they sent him twenty gold talents. And when the king of Khanigalbat [Mitanni] sent his messengers to your father [Amenhotep III] in Egypt, they sent twenty gold talents to him. See, to the King of Khanigalbat I am ... but to me you have sent only a little gold, which is not sufficient, in spite of the goings and comings of my messenger. If it is your intention that a sincere friendship exist send much gold! And you may send people on your part, and you will receive whatever you need."

The Assyrian's ambitions were enhanced when the Kassite King of Babylon asked for his daughter's hand in marriage. The union was disrupted when the Babylonian King was murdered. Ashur-Uballit sought revenge by attacking Babylon and establishing a new king there.

Assyria was rapidly becoming a great power. Ashur-Uballit's successor, Enlil-Nirari (c. 1330–21 BCE) defeated Kurigalzu and annexed the northern regions of Babylonia. His son, Arikdenilu (c. 1320–09 BCE) campaigned in the north and west and built Ashur, the royal capital. Interestingly, he was the first Assyrian King to keep military diaries. He was succeeded by Adad-Nirari (c. 1308–1276 BCE) and Shalmaneser I (c. 1275–46 BCE). The former defeated Kassite Babylonia and conquered Mitanni while the Egyptians and Hittites were jostling for control of northern Syria. After reaching the Euphrates, he adopted the title "king of everything". He built fortifications at Ashur, constructed new temples and restored existing ones. Shalmaneser continued his conquests. He fought in the far north against Uratu, a newcomer to the Near Eastern power struggle, crushed the Hurrians and their Hittite allies and reached Carchemich but went no further. Maybe, he recognized that the post-Kadesh treaty between Pharaoh Rameses II and Hattusilis III of the Hittites precluded further aggression. His son, Tukulti-Ninurta I (c 1245–09 BCE) conquered Kassite Babylon but he was assassinated by his son.

The Assyrian Empire steadily expanded toward the Hebrew Kingdoms. King Jehu of Israel, the northern kingdom, bought off the Assyrians with silver and gold. However, this gained only a temporary respite for the Hebrew Kingdoms.

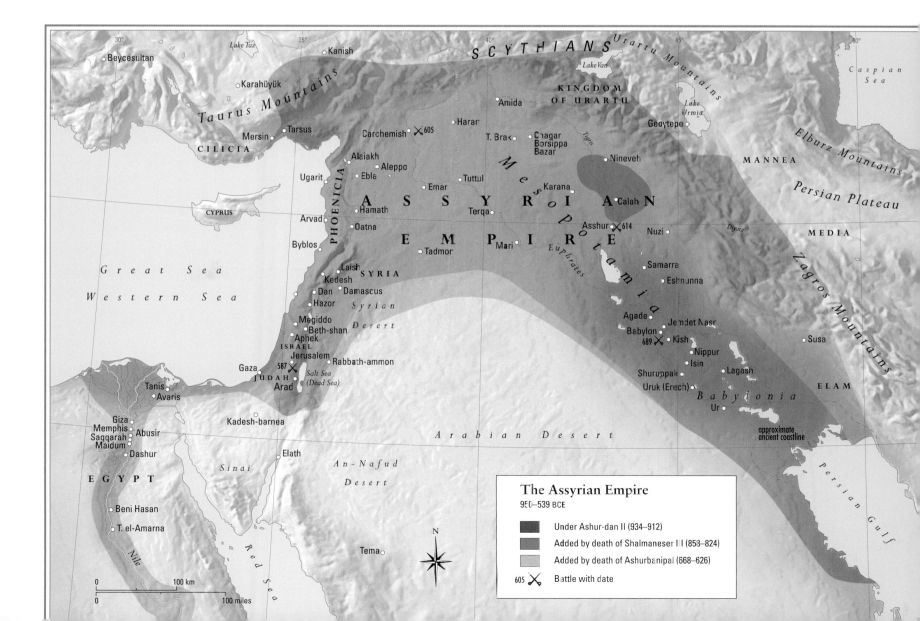

The Assyrian Empire
950–539 BCE

- Under Ashur-dan II (934–912)
- Added by death of Shalmaneser II (853–824)
- Added by death of Ashurbanipal (668–626)
- 605 ✗ Battle with date

THE JEWISH KINGDOMS

THE RIFT BETWEEN KING SOLOMON'S SONS AFTER HIS DEATH CAUSED THE JEWISH KINGDOM TO SPLIT INTO ISRAEL AND JUDAH. ISRAEL WAS THE LARGER AND MORE POWERFUL OF THE TWO, HAVING ACCESS TO THE MOST IMPORTANT TRADING ROUTES IN THE MIDDLE EAST.

Assyrian clay cylinders inscribed with an account of the campaigns and building operations of Tiglath-Pileser I, King of Assyria (c. 1100 BCE).

The history of the Jewish Kingdoms, commencing with David and Solomon, is recounted mainly in I Samuel, II Samuel, I Kings, II Kings and Chronicles. There are also references to the period in the books of Amos, Hosea, Micah, Isaiah and Jeremiah. Sources external to the Bible include a pylon in a Karnak temple reporting Pharaoh Sheshonk's raids into Canaan, Assyrian cuneiform records and Babylonian writings which establish a firm historical date for the capture of Jerusalem as March 597 BCE. Further information has been gleaned from ostraca, seals, seal impressions and an inscription in the Siloam Tunnel describing the tunnel's construction during King Hezekiah's reign (727–698 BCE). Archaeology provides evidence of town-planning, city walls, fortifications, pottery and water supply systems. Despite the mounting evidence, the chronologized framework of the kings remains unclear, since there are marked discrepancies between the Hebrew and external sources.

Kings David and Solomon created a secure and extensive empire, but the state collapsed after Solomon's death and split into two states, Israel and Judah. Israel was the more powerful kingdom owing to its size, proximity to the major trading routes and military resources. The Way of the Sea bypassed Judah but traversed Israel's hill country via the Mount Carmel ridge at Megiddo or went southeast through the Plain of Dothan. East–west commerce through Judah was insignificant because of the Dead Sea barrier. Israel benefited from the Dothan Plain and Shechem Pass which were major east–west trade routes. The Plains of Sharon and Jezreel, Galilee and northern Transjordan were also part of Israel, providing access to the Mediterranean, direct routes to Phoenicia and Damascus, and command of the north–south route through Transjordan. The northern state also possessed more cities than Judah. Militarily, Israel was always the more powerful, so much so that Judah made no serious attempts to confront Israel. When Amaziah of Judah (800–783 BCE) challenged Jehoash of Israel, Jehoash defeated Judah at Beth-Shemesh, invaded Jerusalem, looted the Temple and made Judah a client state (II Kings 14: 8–14).

Judah was ruled by the Davidic line – apart from a period of 300 years – thereby generating political stability. Israel had a more precarious leadership, since seven of its kings and one pretender were assassinated. Further political stresses in the northern kingdom resulted from the commercial self-interest of cosmopolitan cities and the diverse cultures that competed with the agricultural hill country, Transjordan, and Galilee. Israel also suffered from lying in the path of the main route through Syria and Canaan. Other states disputed control of the road and tensions between Egypt and the Mesopotamian powers of Assyria and Babylon dragged Israel into international politics, to its detriment. The north was also subject to political interference by prophets who wielded king-making and king-destroying authority.

The Jewish Kingdom split into two c. 925 BCE. Israel and Judah co-existed for about 200 years until 722 BCE when the Israelite capital of Samaria fell to the Assyrians. Judah survived for another 135 years until Jerusalem was destroyed by the Babylonians. Between 924–885 BCE, the two kingdoms were weak and hostile with effective rule probably shrinking down to the hill country west of the Jordan. Israel developed into a strong state in the Omrid Era (885–843 BCE), when it was even more prosperous than under King Solomon and it entered an alliance with Jehozophat's Judah.

The Jehu dynasty of Judah (843–745 BCE) heralded the attacks by kings Hazael and Ben-Hadad of Damascus. In Jeroboam's reign (843–745 BCE) both states recovered, but Tiglath-Pileser III (744–727 BCE) of Assyria controlled both Israel and Judah. Israel rebelled and Assyrian King destroyed it. Judah survived under Ashur-Banipal (668–627 BCE) while Assyria and Egypt established a détente. The Battle of Carchemish (605 BCE) made the Babylonians overlords of Syria and Canaan. Judah later rebelled and Jerusalem was destroyed in 586 BCE.

After the death of Solomon, the Kingdom split into two factions, Israel to the north and Judah to the south.

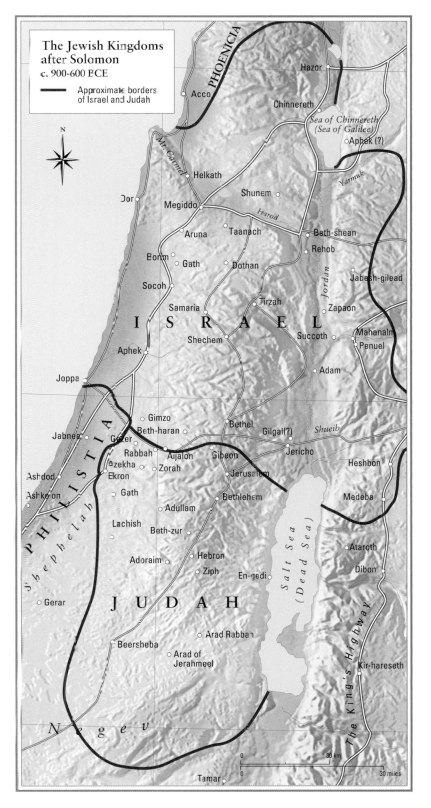

The Jewish Kingdoms
after Solomon
c. 900–600 BCE
—— Approximate borders
of Israel and Judah

DAVID'S RISE TO POWER

SAUL'S INSANE JEALOUSY OF DAVID CAUSED DAVID TO FLEE TO THE
SOUTH. SAUL GREATLY FEARED THE PHILISTINES WHO EVENTUALLY
CONQUERED HIS ARMY IN BATTLE, KILLING HIS BELOVED SONS
AND CAUSING HIM TO FALL ON HIS SWORD. THE PHILISTINES
DISPLAYED SAUL'S HEAD IN THEIR TEMPLE TO THEIR GOD, DAGON.

Tomb of King David on Mount
Zion, Jerusalem.

Opposite: The Philistines
fought and defeated King Saul,
rather than be captured, Saul
committed suicide. On hearing
the news, David marched north,
beginning a campaign to seize
the reins of power.

David came to Saul's notice owing to his skill as a musician and his slaughter of the giant Philistine warrior, Goliath. If the events in I Samuel 17: 32–51 are to be believed, David's victory against Goliath so sapped the morale of the Philistine army which was facing Saul's forces in the Valley of Elah that its soldiers fled back to Gath and Ekron. David became a famous warrior, won the hand of Michal, Saul's daughter and befriended his son, Jonathan.

Saul became jealous of David's success, thinking he planned to usurp his throne, causing David to flee from Gibeah in fear of his life. David sought Samuel's help and Jonathan's intercession; failing, he went to Nob to acquire food and Goliath's sword, formerly left in tribute there. He sought sanctuary in Gath but the Philistine King Achish believed him to be mad so he moved to Adullam in the Shephelah in disputed border lands. There, he gathered his brother's clan and those unhappy with Saul, creating an outlaw band of 400 men who moved to the Forest of Hereth while David's parents were sent for safety to the Moabite King.

After raising a Philistine siege of Keilah, David's presence was betrayed by the inhabitants. He was again forced to flee to escape Saul's pursuing force and hid near Horesh and then in the Wilderness of Ziph. The populace informed Saul who approached with 3,000 men forcing David south to the Wilderness of Maon. Fortunately for David, Saul had to return north to deal with a Philistine raid.

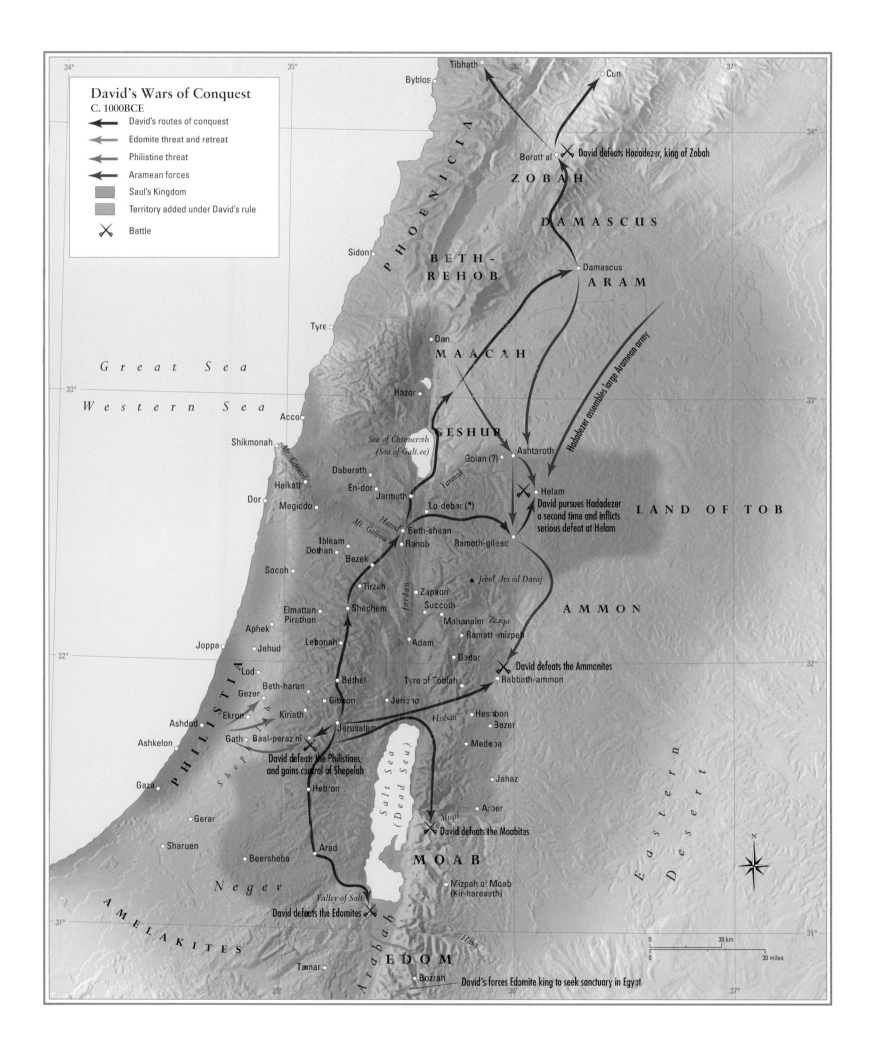

David's Wars of Conquest
C. 1000BCE

→ David's routes of conquest
→ Edomite threat and retreat
→ Philistine threat
→ Aramean forces
▬ Saul's Kingdom
▬ Territory added under David's rule
✗ Battle

Tibhath

Cun

Byblos

David defeats Hadadezer, king of Zobah

Berothal ✗

ZOBAH

PHOENICIA

DAMASCUS

BETH-
REHOB

Sidon

Damascus

ARAM

Tyre

Dan

MAACAH

Great Sea

Hadadezer assembles large Aramean army

Western Sea

Hazor

Acco

GESHUR

Shikmonah

Sea of Chinnereth
(Sea of Galilee)

Golan (?)

Ashtaroth

LAND OF TOB

Mt. Carmel

Daberath

Helkath

En-dor

Yarmuk

Golan (?)

Helam

Dor

Jermuth

Lo-debar (?)

David pursues Hadadezer
a second time and inflicts
serious defeat at Helam

Megiddo

Harod

Beth-shean

Ibleam

Mt. Gilboa

Rehob

Ramoth-gilead

Dothan

Bezek

▲ Jebel Jin ed Daraj

Socoh

Tirzah

Zapaon

Shechem

Succoth

AMMON

Elmattan
Pirathon

Jordan

Mahanaim

Zarqa

Aphek

Lebonah

Ramath-mizpeh

Joppa

Jehud

Adam

Lod

Gedor

David defeats the Ammonites

Beth-haran

Bethel

Tyre of Tobiah

Rabbath-ammon

Gibeon

Gezer

Kiriath

Jericho

Ekron

Ashdod

Jerusalem

Hisban

Heshbon

Bezer

Gath

Baal-perazim

PHILISTIA

David defeats the Philistines,
and gains control of Shepelah

Ashkelon

Medeba

Shephelah

Hebron

Salt Sea
(Dead Sea)

Gaza

Jahaz

Mujit

Aroer

David defeats the Moabites

Gerar

Sharuen

Arad

MOAB

Beersheba

Negev

Mizpah of Moab
(Kir-hareseth)

Valley of Salt

Eastern Desert

David defeats the Edomites

AMELAKITES

Arabah

EDOM

Tamar

Bozrah

David's forces Edomite king to seek sanctuary in Egypt

0 ——— 30 km
0 ——— 30 miles

Later, Saul again hunted David who proved to Saul that he could have killed him twice but had not done so because it was God's task to kill Saul. "The Lord forbid that I should stretch forth my hand against the Lord's anointed." (I Samuel 26: 11). David left the Wilderness and again sought sanctuary in Gath with his enlarged band of 600 men. Aware of Saul's hostility to David, Achish gave David the Philistine town of Ziklag in the Negev, to rule as its governor. Rather than attacking the Israelites in the Shephelah as Achish wanted, David assaulted the Amalekites, Geshurites and Gezrites, Israel's enemies, in the Negev while persuading Achish that he had raided southern Judea. When the Philistines raised a large army, mustering at Aphek prior to invading Israel, David was sent back to Ziklag because Achish remained uncertain as to his loyalty. Returning to the town, David found it burned down and looted by vengeful Amalekites; the families of his men and his two wives, Michal and Abigail, had been captured. He pursued the camel-mounted invaders into the Negev. Finding them feasting, his force killed all the men, rescued their own families and recovered all the booty acquired by the Amalekites in their recent raid. David shared the loot equally amongst the elders of southern Judah, thereby building a grateful and potential power base in that area.

Elsewhere, the Philistines marched from Aphek into the Jezreel Valley, eventually camping at Shunem at the foot of Mount Moreh. Saul's army collected at Mount Gilboa to the south, possibly near the mountain's springs. Saul was terrified at the prospect of fighting the huge Philistine host, so he visited the Witch of Endor, beseeching her to talk to Samuel's spirit. Samuel's ghost spoke: "Because thou obeyedst not the voice of the Lord, nor executedst his fierce wrath upon Amalek, therefore hath the Lord done this thing unto thee this day. Moreover the Lord will deliver Israel with thee into the hands of the Philistines: and tomorrow shalt thou and thy sons be with me: the Lord also shall deliver the host of Israel into the hand of the Philistines." (I Samuel 28: 18–19).

The hugely outnumbered Israelites occupied slopes unsuitable for Philistine chariot attacks but the Hebrews were still overrun by an infantry onslaught. The troops fled up Mount Gilboa where many were hunted down. Saul's sons, Jonathan, Abinadab and Malchishua were killed and Saul was wounded by an arrow. The King asked his armour-bearer to kill him. Upon his refusal, Saul fell on his sword. The Israelites on the other side of the valley fled their cities in fear. The victorious Philistines placed Saul's head in their temple to Dagon at Beth-Shean while his cadaver was hung from the city's walls. On learning this, warriors from Jabesh-Gilead, remembering how Saul had saved their city and eye-sight, secretly rescued his body and those of his sons and ritually interred them under a tree at Jabesh.

Israel had now lost the region adjacent to the Jezreel Valley. When news of the defeat reached David, he and his men bewailed their losses. Despite Saul's suspicious nature and his murder of 80 priests and their families at Nob for aiding David, Saul's military capabilities had prevented the Philistines from occupying much of Israel. David's now had to organize an Israelite counter-attack and liberate the occupied lands. The men of Judah anointed David at Hebron but the northern tribes were not loyal to him. Saul was succeeded by his son, Ish-bosheth, who reigned for two years in the north but was murdered by two of his officers who brought the King's head to David who had them executed. The northern tribes acknowledged David's kingship and their leaders went to Hebron to anoint him. David symbolised the unity his creation of a new capital captured from the Jebusites—Jerusalem.

King David by Pedro Berruguete.

JERUSALEM

THE CHOICE OF JERUSALEM, WHICH LAY IN A NEUTRAL AREA
BETWEEN THE NORTH AND SOUTH OF THE COUNTRY, AS THE
CAPITAL WAS A STROKE OF BRILLIANCE ON THE PART OF DAVID.
HE MOVED THE ARK THERE BUT WAS NOT ALLOWED TO BUILD A
TEMPLE TO THE ONE GOD.

View overlooking the Temple Mount. To the right of the Western Wall, the Kotel, in the centre of the picture, is the temporary covered wooden bridge connecting the Mugrabi Gate. to the Temple compound, enabling Muslims to attend prayers at Al Aqsa without having to pass through the Western Wall plaza.

After David was anointed King of Israel in Hebron, he directed his energies toward Jerusalem. The city stood on a small hill in a valley ringed by mountains and protected on three sides by ravines. It is first mentioned in Egyptian Execration Texts during the nineteenth and eighteenth centuries BCE and centuries later in the Amarna Tablets. During the Bronze Age, the inhabitants were the Jebusites, a Canaanite tribe controlling a segment of territory between the northern and southern Israelite tribes. Despite Joshua's defeat of the Jebusites and their allies in battle (Joshua 15: 63), it fell to David to capture Jerusalem (II Samuel 5).

The Bible suggests that a diversionary attack was mounted against Jerusalem's walls while a small force attacked and broke into the tunnel and vertical shaft leading to the Jebusite water supply. In reality, this was the most heavily fortified part of the walls and an unlikely target. Some other stratagem was probably employed. Jerusalem was a city that belonged to David but it was in neutral territory, neither part of the north nor the south, and had been captured by his personal troops. It was thus made the home of the Ark of the Covenant which was brought by ox cart from Kiryat Yearim. After a brief sojourn along the way in the home of Obed-Edom the Gittite, the Ark reached Jerusalem. This was the occasion for a great festival during which David danced virtually naked in the streets in praise of God. Michal, his wife, despised him for this adulation and was made barren by God as a punishment. Jerusalem now became the Holy City and central to Jewish tradition. It was also the capital, housing David's court and the administration. David did not build a Temple; instead, a tent-shrine was erected and two priests appointed to administer it. They were Abiathar of Shiloh's priestly line and Zadok, of unknown origin. The Ark tied the new state to God, the state being the patron and protector of the most sacred Hebrew artefact. David also showed that, compared with Saul, he neither neglected the Ark nor killed its priesthood. II Samuel 7 explains how Nathan the prophet asked God about a Temple and David learnt that it was his son who was to build the Temple while David retained the desert origins of God which was certainly pleasing to the conservative Nathan.

In Jerusalem, David gave pre-eminence to the Levites, thereby

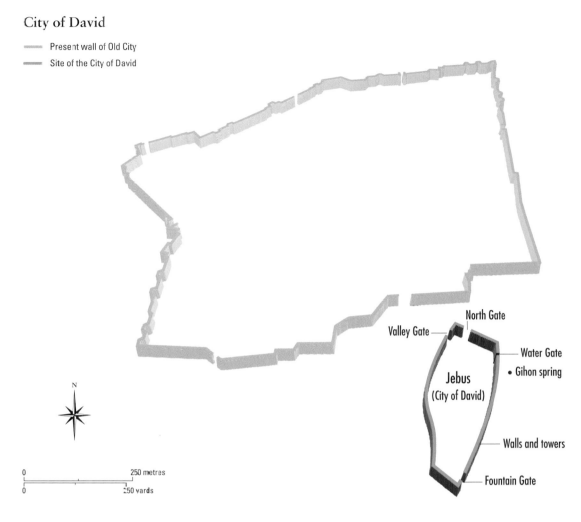

City of David

— Present wall of Old City
— Site of the City of David

North Gate
Valley Gate
Water Gate
• Gihon spring
Jebus (City of David)
Walls and towers
Fountain Gate

0   250 metres
0   250 yards

After David conquered Jerusalem, he made it his new capital. He also brought the Ark of the Covenant to Jerusalem.

inaugurating a Jerusalem–Judah linkage. The stronghold of the tribe of Judah was Bethlehem, David's home town, so they were particularly pro-Davidic, loyal and devoted. So supportive were they, that when Israel rebelled after Solomon's death, an important act of King Jeroboam I was to appoint new non-Levite priests (I Kings 12: 31). The Levites depended upon David for their living and became the civil administrators who helped him rule, especially the non-Israelite lands conquered by David.

The city was already known as Zion by the Jebusites and this term referring to a section of the city, has been used synonymously with Jerusalem. David strengthened the city's fortifications and had a palace built of cedar wood and stone by Phoenician craftsmen. However, the real beautification of Jerusalem was left to Solomon with his grandiose building projects of a palace and the first Temple in Jerusalem to house the Ark.

Jerusalem was important in another way. It was a typical Bronze Age city surviving into the Iron Age, carrying a culture of autocratic, hereditary rule. This heritage was common to other cities seized by David, such as Hazor, Megiddo and Shechem. This united the clans and villages of Israel and Judah. The Kingdom was no longer divided into city-states and tribal areas but had acquired a capital city, the centre of its religious worship and its administration and thus a kingdom in the modern sense. It also acquired the characteristics and culture of a Bronze Age Canaanite city especially since David permitted the indigenous Canaanite religious cults and their priests to remain in Jerusalem.

KING DAVID'S EMPIRE

AFTER SECURING HIS INTERNAL BORDERS AND INCORPORATING
OUTLYING NORTHERN REGIONS INTO HIS KINGDOM, DAVID
SET ABOUT MAKING INTERNATIONAL CONQUESTS. FAMILY FEUDS
RESULTED IN DAVID CHOOSING HIS SON, SOLOMON, BY BATHSHEBA
AS HIS HEIR AFTER THE REBELLION BY HIS ELDEST SON, ABSALOM.

As King of Judah, David welded together a diverse range of tribal elements into a new identity: Judah, the Simeonites, Calebites, Othnielites, Jerahmeelites and Kenites. Then David was proclaimed King over Israel in a covenant (II Samuel 5: 1–3). This union of north and south was fragile and acquiring Jerusalem, new to both tribal federations, was a shrewd move as was elevating this political center to a religious one by making it the home of the Ark of the Covenant.

Meanwhile, the Philistines attempted two attacks to relieve their garrisons in Judah, now threatened by David at Adullam. Defeated twice, the Philistines left the mountains and were presumably attacked in their cities on the coast. Although the Bible is unclear on this point, the five cities became tributaries and units of Philistine soldiers became mercenaries in David's pay. The King then consolidated his internal borders by taking the remaining Canaanite city-states north and south of Mount Carmel, in Jezreel and in Galilee. Although they contained some Israelite residents, they had never been under Israelite control. They may have fallen quickly if they had been Philistine vassals and no longer had their overlords' protection. They were incorporated into the state, becoming the King's subjects. Thus, the Kingdom grew from a tribal institution into a multi-cultural state.

David next set about securing Israel's borders by constructing an empire. The Bible is unclear about the chronology of events but not the outcome. The first Davidic war was waged against Ammon and its allies, the Aramean Kingdoms of Maaceh, Bethrehob and Zobah. Aramean intervention ended in battle and the Ammonites were beaten at Ramah. During the siege

Opposite: King David's Empire stretched way beyond the homelands of the Hebrew people and tested their ability to hold on to such diverse possessions.

there, David remained in Jerusalem, dallying with his mistress, Bathsheba, thereby earning a sharp admonition from the prophet, Nathan.

The conquest of Moab and Edom was certainly a brutal one. The Moabite troops were slaughtered and the Edomite royal family virtually exterminated, after which Edom was ruled as a conquered province. David went on to confront Hadadezer of Zobah in Syria, which provided Israel with copper mines and loot. The King of Hamath, a state north of Zobah on the Orontes River, tried to assuage David by sending him gifts. David subsequently negotiated a treaty with Hiram, King of Tyre.

This consolidated the small but complex empire which focused upon the personality of David of Judah and his Canaanite subjects, but not on the Israelites. Hence, power was very much centred on the crown, a situation rocked with the failed rebellion of David's son, Absalom, and a northern rebellion. The dispute was eventually resolved, when David chose Solomon. his third son, as his heir.

David's Kingdom

c. 1000–993 BCE

- Israelite territory
- Areas under Israelite rule
- Areas under vassal treaty
- Extent of David's Kingdom

SOLOMON, THE STATESMAN

SOLOMON'S DEMANDS FOR FUNDS AND LABOUR TO SERVICE
HIS ELABORATE BUILDING PROJECTS, ESPECIALLY THE TEMPLE
IN JERUSALEM, SOWED THE SEEDS OF SUBSEQUENT REBELLION
AMONG HIS SUBJECTS.

Artist's depiction of Solomon's
court (Ingobertus, c. 880 CE).

Solomon commenced his reign with murderous efficiency despatching his older brother, Adonijah, while David's general, Joab, was butchered while seeking sanctuary at an altar. All possible political opponents were thus eliminated leaving the Davidic line temporarily secure. Solomon sought to secure the position of the kingdom abroad by entering into careful alliances sealed by marriage to princesses from surrounding states and vassals. The most prominent of these was an Egyptian princess; the crown prince, Rehoboam, was the son of Naamah, an Ammonite (I Kings 14: 21). The most important alliance was the one with Tyre that had been initiated by David.

The Solomonic empire was to be held together by such alliances for the king was not a belligerant warrior, as his father had been. Nevertheless, Solomon left his kingdom with less territory than it had had at his accession. When David captured Edom, one of its princes, Hadad, sought asylum in Egypt. On the deaths of David and Joab, Hadad returned to Edom and rebelled, possibly organizing guerrilla raids on caravans, though the Bible is not specific as to his actions. Rezon, a soldier of Hadadezer, who captured Damascus and became king there, was more of a threat to the Jewish kingdom.

"And God stirred him up another adversary, Rezon, the son of Eliadah, which fled from his lord Hadadezer king of Zobah: And he gathered men unto him, and became captain over a band, when David slew them of Zobah: and they went to Damascus. And he was an adversary to Israel all the days of Solomon, beside the mischief that Hadad did: and he abhorred Israel and reigned over Syria." (I Kings 11: 23–25).

Solomon's power and authority was thus weakened in Aramean Syria. Israel's economy prospered under Solomon through royal monopolies, and the king's building projects employed many people, although there was much forced labour. Trade prospered, farming improved and one historian suggests that the native Israelite population doubled. Cities expanded, providing an impression of sustained growth but Solomon's wealth was insufficient to pay for all of his ambitious building projects, especially the Temple, as well as an expanded administration. The bureaucrats were so numerous that 550 alone were involved in supervising forced labour. David's regime had been based upon his personal income and tributes from foreign subjects to pay for a sparse administration. Solomon was no conqueror, however, so no new sources of tribute emerged. The budget was unbalanced creating a need for new modes of finance.

Solomon divided his realm into twelve administrative areas, each headed by a royal governor. These units roughly coincided with tribal areas but also included Canaanite city-states. Taxes were imposed while the diverse strands of the state were more closely integrated. The strains on society were immense; each area was required to pay for the upkeep of the court for one month. The old tribal alliances were thus weakened further.

The Queen of Sheba visiting Solomon, from an illuminated manuscript. French school, fourteenth century.

The king's demands for labour for his various projects culminated in the imposition of compulsory labour service and the Canaanite population was required to supply slaves. "And all the people that were left of the Amorites, Hittites, Perizzites, Hivites, and Jebusites, which were not of the children of Israel, Their children that were left after them in the land whom the children of Israel also were not able utterly to destroy, upon these did Solomon levy a tribute of bond-service unto this day." (I Kings 9: 20–21) Eventually, the system was introduced into Israel and labour gangs were rotated in Tyre to fell lumber. The numbers listed in the Bible may have been exaggerated for effect, however. "And king Solomon raised a levy out of all Israel; and the levy was thirty thousand men. And he sent them to Lebanon, ten thousand a month by courses: a month they were in Lebanon, and two months at home: and Adoniram was over the levy. And Solomon had three score and ten thousand that bare burdens, and four score thousand hewers in the mountains" (I Kings 5: 13–15).

Slaves were used at the Ezion-Geber refinery and in the Arabah copper mines. Naturally, this caused resentment. In the final years of Solomon's reign, Jeroboam, of the tribe of Joseph, rebelled with the encouragement of the prophet Ahijah, fleeing to Egypt when his plot failed. The northern tribes became totally hostile to Solomon. Rumours of his alleged apostasy, turning to the gods of his foreign wives, further damaged Solomon's reputation.

Tribal freedom and independence had ended, the concept of a shared religion inspiring common defense, all had ended. The Solomonic, autocratic state demanded obligations from subjects. The growth of the Temple cult generated problems and damaged old morality. The state sponsored the cult with God "dwelling in the Temple" giving Jerusalem an importance in Judaism that has never been abandoned. When the Temple was destroyed, did God vanish? To some the state had been blessed by God so state aims and God's aims were synonymous. The state became all, with religion apparently guaranteeing the state – a form of tyranny. Samuel's words of warning (I Samuel 8: 11–18) of the evils of kingship were now remembered.

SOLOMON'S TRADE

SOLOMON EXPANDED ISRAELITE TRADE FURTHER THAN EVER BEFORE, ALONG THE COASTS OF AFRICA AND NORTH TO ARAM (SYRIA).

Reconstruction of a Phoenician merchant ship.

Solomon engaged in considerable diplomatic activity and his alliance systems comprised a basis for Israel's commerce. The most important treaty was with Tyre, a link established by David. The Phoenicians held the Levantine coastline from Akko (Acre) northward. Under King Hiram I (c. 969–936 BCE), Tyre was expanding its maritime interests into Cyprus, Sicily, Sardinia, Spain and, possibly, North Africa. Sardinian copper mines were particularly important. Solomon himself controlled the Arabah copper mines just north of Ezion-geber (modern Eilat), at the head of the Gulf of Aqaba, where the largest copper refinery operated that was known in the ancient Near East. Solomon's fleet contained vessels designed to transport copper ingots. The mining industry and fleet were staffed and manned by Phoenicians. Solomon's copper supply was adequate for domestic use and there was even a surplus for export. The Phoenicians imported Israelite wheat and olive oil in return for the Lebanese hardwoods used in Solomon's building projects.

According to I Kings 9: 26–28, Solomon was inspired by the Phoenician traders and wished to expand Israel's trade through the Red Sea to the south. His fleet made regular journeys to Ophir. There have been many theories as to the location of this fabled land of wealth. Among the candidate are the Malabar Coast of India and the ruins of Zimbabwe, gold from whose mines may have been brought to Sofala on the coast. More likely, Ophir may have been on the African coast of the Red Sea or in the Arabian peninsula, in Yemen or Hadramaut, the purported home of the Queen of Sheba. The Bible reports imports to Israel from Ophir of gold, silver, almog wood, jewels, ivory, peacocks and monkeys.

Sheba, if located in the Hadhramaut, lay across the caravan routes leading to Mesopotamia and the Levant. This Arabian Kingdom dominated the spice and incense trade and may have had links to Ethiopia and Somalia after Egyptian influence weakened in that region. Possibly, Solomon's control of Ezion-Geber brought him into competition with the Sabean camel caravans. The Queen of Sheba may therefore have visited Solomon to negotiate a trade treaty. The fact that Solomon treated her with such respect suggests a successful agreement. Consequently, if I Kings 10: 15 is understood correctly, taxes and excise duties poured into the Israelite treasury as a result of this trade.

The Bible suggests (I Kings 10: 28 ff) that Solomon traded in horses from Cilicia and chariots from Egypt which may have required for the armed forces. This trade shows the importance of the geographical position of Israel. The Way of the Sea traversed the coastal plain through the Megiddo Pass where it met the main routes to Phoenicia, Damascus and Hamath. Israel's control of Megiddo, Gezer and Hazor meant that it controlled the route as it did the route over the Jordan. It could block or facilitate trade from Ezion-Geber to the Phoenician cities.

Hiram's provision of wood, craftsmen and sailors. Solomon owed Hiram so much money that he ceded territory in the Jezreel Valley as collateral or payment. "And it came to pass at the end of twenty years, when Solomon had built the two houses, the house of the Lord, and the King's house, (Now Hiram the King of Tyre had furnished Solomon with cedar trees and fir trees, and with gold, according to all his desire,) that then King Solomon gave Hiram twenty cities in the land of Galilee. And Hiram came out from Tyre to see the cities which Solomon had given him; and they pleased him not." (I Kings 9: 10–12).

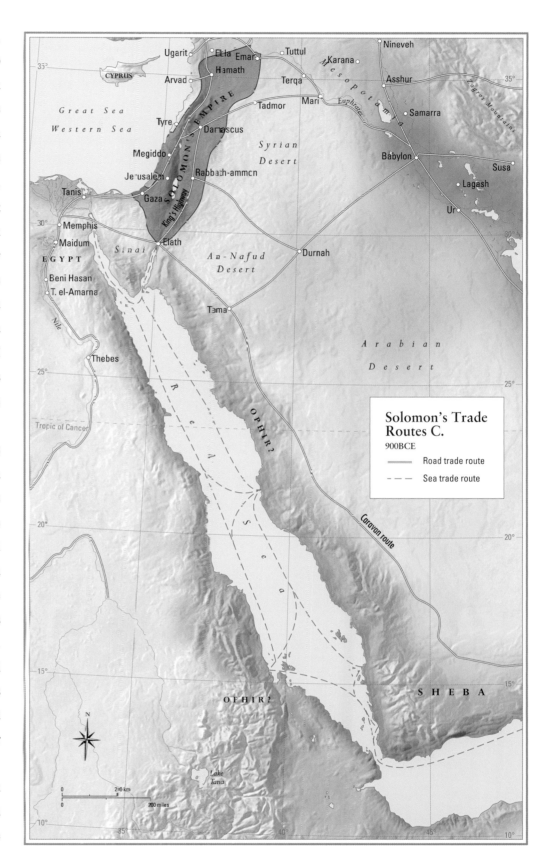

Solomon's trade routes indicating possible locations for Ophir. The city marked as Elath was the site of Ezion-Geber.

THE DIVIDED MONARCHY

WHEN THE KINGDOMS SPLIT, ISRAEL SET UP TWO SANCTUARIES, BETHEL IN THE SOUTH AND DAN IN THE NORTH, TO REPLACE THE TEMPLE IN JERUSALEM WHICH WAS NOW IN JUDAH. THESE SHRINES CONTAINED A GOLDEN BULL, ALLEGEDLY A SYMBOL OF GOD BUT DANGEROUSLY CLOSE TO PAGAN WORSHIP.

Jeroboam sacrificing to the Golden Bull, as depicted by Fragonard Jean-Honoré (1732–1806).

When Solomon died c. 931 BCE, the united Kingdom split into two, the northern and southern tribes dividing along the old demarcation line through the centre of Israel. The northern tribes formed the Kingdom of Israel, with Samaria as its capital, under Jeroboam, until conquered by the Assyrians in 721 BCE. The southern kingdom, Judah, with Jerusalem as its capital, was ruled by the descendants of David, commencing with Rehoboam, until it was eventually destroyed by the Babylonians in 587 BCE.

Such a division showed the fragility of the United Kingdom and its survival attests to the personal qualities of the first three kings. The split was caused by a range of economic and religious reasons that accentuated the traditional hostility and jealousy between the northern and southern tribes. The main reason for the rift, however, was the heavy taxation and forced labour needed for Solomon's building programme. Evidence suggests that the northern tribes were taxed more heavily than the south and the north was divided into 12 units to provide the monthly upkeep of the court. The southern tribes are not mentioned in relation to this financial burden. Despite the north being more prosperous than the south, the lack of equality in taxation boded ill for the survival of a united state.

The religious division occurred because many Hebrews preferred to remain loyal to the old nomadic concept of God rather than seeing Him incarcerated in a Temple. The old symbolism was associated with the sanctuaries at Bethel, Shiloh and Shechem rather than the new Temple in Jerusalem. The ancient priestly lines and organization of the old Covenant league had been replaced by a new line of priests in the Temple.

The Biblical accounts of the two Kingdoms were edited into their current form after Israel's destruction by the Assyrians. The accounts might were thus more favourable to Judah since they were written afterward. This bias favoured the southern Kingdom with its Davidic line so closely associated with the Jerusalem Temple cult. Histories of Israel after the Assyrian onslaught are not included in the Bible and readers are advised to look for them elsewhere. (2 Kings 8: 23 and 10: 34).

Jeroboam of Israel was a traitor who plotted against Solomon while administering the slave labour contingent for part of the north. His rebellion failed and he escaped to Egypt. When Solomon died, a delegation of northerners approached Rehoboam and were angry at his refusal to give them tax concessions while he threatened to increase their liabilities. Accordingly the northern tribes

The kingdoms of Israel and Judah at the time when they were first divided, in 796 BCE..

appointed Jeroboamas their King and fortified Shechem and Penuel. The prophets persuaded Rehoboam not to use his army against the rebels. Maybe, it was in their interest to favour the north against the power of Jerusalem-based kings with their Temple priests. During the long years of war between the two kingdoms, the stronger north prevailed.

The division between the two kingdoms was further accentuated by the two northern sanctuaries, Bethel, near the frontier with Judah and Dan in the far north. Both Bethel and Dan contained an image of a golden bull, a symbol of God, but dangerously similar to Baal and fertility rites. It is therefore unsurprising that the Bible condemns these two northern sanctuaries as pagan. The kingdoms were both threatened by the resurgent Egypt, under by Sheshonk I, the first Pharaoh of the 22nd Dynasty who conquered the road to Mesopotamia and the north as far as Phoenicia. Jerusalem was captured and the palace and Temple looted.

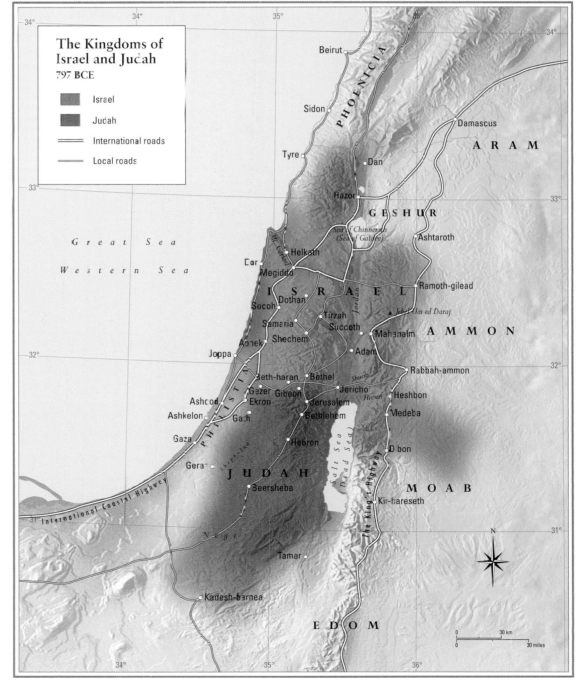

EGYPT INVADES

THE DEVASTATION WROUGHT BY THE EGYPTIAN INVASION UNDER THE PHARAOH SHISHAK (SHISHONK I) IN THE MID-NINTH CENTURY BCE WERE SEEN BY THE PROPHET SHEMAIAH, AS RECORDED IN CHRONICLES, AS A PUNISHMENT FOR REHOBOAM'S APOSTASY.

Collonade at the Karnak temple, built to commenorate Shishak's invasion of Israel and Judah (c. 926 –917 BCE).

Opposite: There was little Judah and Israel could do to prevent a determined military invasion. It was part of Egypt's foreign policy to maintain a strong influence in this small but important territory.

Shishak (Shoshenk I), first Pharaoh of the Twenty-second Dynasty, a usurping Libyan nobleman, ruled Egypt in the time of Solomon. Diplomatic relations were cordial at first, but the Solomonic state was an obstacle to Egyptian commercial and territorial ambitions since Israel controlled the major trade routes. When the kingdom divided, Shishak saw his opportunity to exploit the power vacuum created by to the division.

The Bible mentions an Egyptian invasion (I Kings 14: 24–26 and II Chronicles 12: 2–4) when the Pharaoh is reported to have captured 15 Judean fortresses and stolen the gold from Solomon's Temple and palace to be used as blackmail to spare Jerusalem. The Bible states that the Egyptian invasion force comprised 1,200 chariots and 60,000 cavalry, suggesting that the campaign was a very serious attempt to destroy the Hebrew successor states. Shishak had the story of his war inscribed into the Theban Temple of Amon at Karnak. The carvings list over 150 places he captured, showing that settlements in Judah, Israel, Transjordan and the Negev were attacked. Many of the names have become blurred through weathering so some information is missing. Archaeological evidence is plentiful, however, and supports the Egyptian version of the invasion. Settlements were burned down, marks of the fire being seen on gates and walls, while destroyed stores and dwellings demonstrate the consequences of the Egyptian attack. The Karnak carvings show the god Amon holding ropes tied to captured kings while other captives kneel before him.

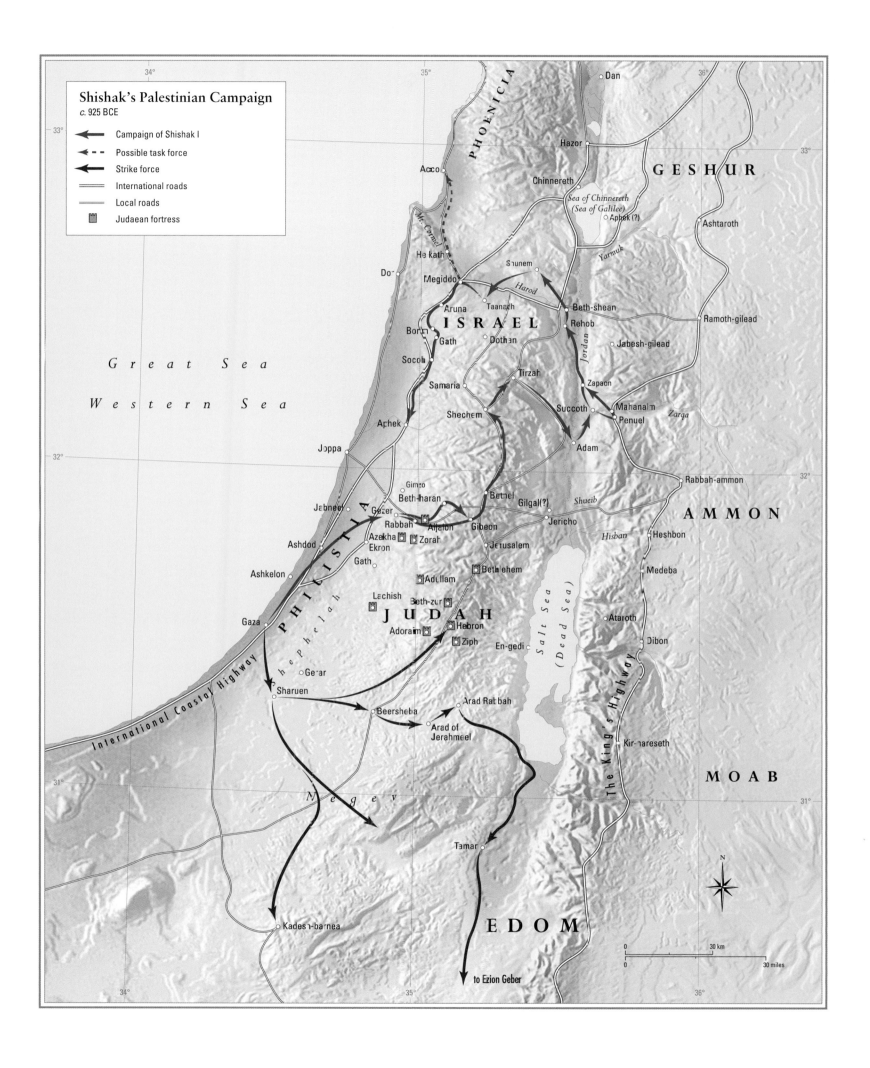

Shishak's Palestinian Campaign
c. 925 BCE

- Campaign of Shishak I
- Possible task force
- Strike force
- International roads
- Local roads
- Judaean fortress

The Egyptian army advanced along the Way of the Sea establishing its base at Gaza. The force divided there with one group attacking Sharuhen in the Negev. The inscriptions identified at Karnak list the captured settlements of Beersheba, Arad-Yerahmeel, Arad-Rabbah, Ramat Matred and Ezion-Geber. The Egyptians purged the entire Negev and archaeology shows that agricultural settlements established by Solomon were eradicated, suggesting that the Pharaoh wished to end Judean control of the area and its influence over Edom rather than settle it with Egyptians. Karnak lists 70 place-names from the Negev.

The other Egyptian force moved northward to Ashdod and Ekron in Philistia where a two-pronged attack was launched into Judah. One division of Shishak's army marched north, veering eastward through Beth-Horon, while a second division ripped into the central hill country eight miles south along the Way of Beth-Shemesh through Kiryat Yearim. The two forces met at Gibeon, six miles south of Jerusalem. According to the Bible, this is where Rehoboam came to ransom Jerusalem with the Temple's gold.

Pharaoh's force travelled along the central ridge road to enter the Kingdom of Israel. There were no defensive border fortifications because Judah was not considered to be a threat; Jeroboam regarded his exile in Egypt where he had been well-received as a defence but Shishak ignored the past. The invasion force blasted its way through all obstacles and Davidic and Solomonic fortifications posed little resistance to Egyptian might and military technology. The casement walls designed to resist battering-ram attacks were the latest inventions but were smashed and the new gatehouses were also destroyed as archaeological evidence at Gezer, Hazor and Megiddo shows. Shechem was probably destroyed and the Egyptians assaulted and damaged Israel's new capital at Tirzah. The Wadi Farah provided a road to the fords of Adam over the Jordan which was crossed. The Egyptians turned north to Succoth and through the Jabbok Valley to Mahanaim and Penuel, the latter being a Royal City of Israel. Shishak planned to destroy Israelite power across the Jordan.

Shishak retraced his steps down the Jabbok Valley and then moved north, annihilating Zaphon before re-crossing the Jordan and taking the route through the Jezreel Valley at Beth-Shean. The cities of Rehob, Beth-Shean and Shunem were captured. The southern edge of the Great Plain witnessed the burning of Ta'anach and five miles away, Solomon's great city and garrison of Megiddo was attacked, destroyed, then rebuilt as an Egyptian outpost guarding the Way of the Sea as it crossed the Carmel Ridge. There is evidence of Egyptian occupation in a fragment of a stele commemorating Shishak's victory. Egypt then re-opened its former links with Byblos.

The campaign was now over and Shishak returned to Egypt along the Way of the Sea, capturing towns on the way, including Aruna, Borim, Gath, Yaham and Socoh. He now controlled the trade routes not only in the northern valleys but in the Plain of Sharon and all the way down the Mediterranean coast to Philistia. The return itinerary is incomplete because the Karnak inscriptions break off at this point.

Shishak had succeeded in devastating Judah and Israel but was compelled to return to Egypt to quell insurrections there. Although Shishak ultimately failed to establish an empire in the Near East like his predecessor Thutmosis III, he ensured that Israel and Judah would not threaten his northern border for the near future. Egyptian records mention no battles so what happened to the impressive Solomonic chariot force? Presumably the troops were engaged in defense of cities during sieges.

The destruction layers found by archaeologists at many sites, such as at Gezer, Megiddo and Beth-

These relief wall carvings, dating from 1250 BCE, show the outcome of a successful Egyptian campaign. Egypt's enemies lie dead on the battlefield while the victorious chariots gallop by.

Shean, have been interpreted as being the result of Shishak's campaign but could an invasion force have managed to provision so many besieging forces? Whatever the case, Shishak had strengthened his strategic position, gained kudos for his dynasty, acquired much loot and showed Israel and Judah how vulnerable they were to a well organized invasion from a major power.

An interesting postscript is that the Chronicles saw the Egyptian invasion as a punishment for Rehoboam's apostasy. "Then came Shemaiah the prophet to Rehoboam, and to the princes of Judah, that were gathered together to Jerusalem because of Shishak, and said unto them, Thus saith the Lord, Ye have forsaken me, and therefore have I also left you in the hand of Shishak." (II Chronicles 12: 5)

Israel and Judah at War

DURING THE RECOVERY PERIOD FROM THE EGYPTIAN INVASION,
THERE WERE CONSTANT BORDER SKIRMISHES BETWEEN ISRAEL
AND JUDAH. WHEN KING OMRI ASCENDED THE THRONE
RELATIONS IMPROVED AND BOTH KINGDOMS PROSPERED BUT
THE OMRIDE DYNASTY WAS DESTINED TO SUFFER A CRUEL FATE.

The first 40 years after the Egyptian invasion saw constant border disputes between Israel and Judah, especially in Benjamite territory. Judah fought to secure buffer areas as a defense bastion for Jerusalem and succeeded. Rehoboam also built 15 fortified cities and dispersed his sons amongst them to secure his territory.

In Israel, Jereboam's son, Nadab, was assassinated and the throne usurped by Baasha who left his son Elah to reign after him. He was murdered in turn by chariot commander, Zimri who wiped out Baasha's entire family. Meanwhile, the Israelite army was engaged in battling the Philistines near Gibbethon. The troops proclaimed their leader, Omri, as King and he attacked Zimri's capital, Tirzah. The city fell and Zimri immolated himself in the palace's citadel. Omri founded a dynasty and introduced political and religious changes to Israel in his attempt to re-create a Solomonic state with Judah as a junior partner. Omri wanted peace and trade expansion. He forged an alliance with the Phoenicians when his crown Prince, Ahab, married Jezebel of Tyre and Sidon to seal the pact. Omri acquired some land for himself and built Samaria as his capital, using Phoenician architects. The Omride state grew in wealth, even rivaling that of Solomon.

Ahab succeeded his father in 869 BCE ensuring the continuation of existing policies. However, he made the mistake of isolating his Samaritan palace from the city by building a wall around it, separating the ruler from the people who had annointed him King. His Queen, Jezebel introduced the Baal cult causing consternation in traditional quarters. Ahab rebuilt Megiddo and Hazor, the former becoming a base for the Israelite chariot force, as evidenced by its large stable block. Hazor became a strong fortress with a water source that was made accessible by a miraculous feat of engineering.

These fortifications might have been in response to invasions by the Damascus Arameans. Ben-Hadad of Damascus was defeated in a siege at Samaria and his advance repelled next year on the Jordan. Each side wanted to command Aphek, a strategic point east of the Sea of Galilee, where an important path led up to the Bashan Plateau (the Golan Heights) on the road to Damascus. Ben-Hadad was defeated and surrendered. Under the terms of the truce, some Israelite cities were returned and the Israelites were allowed to trade in Damascus. Ben-Hadad was released from captivity. Ahab's transjordanian interests included retaining Gilead and controlling Ammon and Moab. Ammon however, retained its independence but Mesha, Moab's King, became a temporary vassal, when Israelite colonists settled in Moabite lands north of the River Arnon.

Elsewhere, Judah, under King Asa and his son Jehoshaphat, regained control of Edom along with land lost in Shishak's invasion and rebuilt Ezion-Geber. A merchant fleet was built on the Red Sea but proved incapable of revisiting Ophir. New communities were probably built west of Beersheba and the Wilderness of Judah was colonized in places such as the City of Salt. An attempt was even made at farming under the harsh conditions of the desert.

Both kingdoms again faced threats from abroad. In 859 BCE, Shalmaneser III succeeded to the Assyrian throne. He marched across the Euphrates into northern Syria and washed his weapons in the Mediterranean. Syria and Israel allied to resist this threat and fought Assyria at Qarqar, with Ahab supplying 2,000 chariots. Assyria was stopped. Ahab, with Judean help, then attacked Syria to improve his border security. Seeking to hold Gilead and take the Bashan Plateau, the hostile forces met at Ramoth-Gilead. Ahab was fatally wounded during the battle but remained on the field so his troops did not lose morale. Ahab died there and was buried in Samaria to be succeeded by his son Ahaziah who was killed in an accident. The throne passed to his brother Jehoram in 849 BCE.

Meanwhile, Mesha of Moab rebelled. Jehoram was joined by Jehoshaphat and tributary Edomites and fought Mesha at Horonim; Mesha retreated to Kir-Hareseth. Nevertheless, Israel had suffered the loss

Ahab and Jezebel confronted by the Prophet Elijah after stealing Naboth's vineyard. Jezebel, who introduced the cult of Baal again in Israel, is considered by the Bible to be the epitome of an evil woman.

of Ataroth and the fortified town of Jahaz while the tableland around Medeba and Heshbon and western lands as far as the Plains of Moab were lost. Next, Mesha, joined by Ammonites and Edomites, crossed the Dead Sea and took En-Gedi. The Judean forces stopped them in the Wilderness of Tekoa thereby breaking the enemy coalition. The Edomites were attacked by their erstwhile allies but still managed to stop Jehoram, Jehosaphat's son, near Zoar. Hence, the Edomites regained the copper mines of the Arabah and Ezion-geber. Meanwhile, Jehoram of Israel re-engaged in battle against the Syrians. Being wounded, he took refuge in his summer palace at Jezreel where he was joined by his nephew Ahaziah, now King of Judah. Events now conspired to end the Omride dynasty in a bloodbath of violence.

ASSYRIAN DANGER

THE ASSYRIANS REPEATEDLY ATTACKED THEIR NEIGHBOURS, UNTIL EVENTUALLY, UNDER KING SHALMANEZER V (727–722 BCE), CAPITAL OF THE KINGDOM OF ISRAEL, SAMARIA, WAS CAPTURED AND ITS POPULATION SENT INTO EXILE INTO THE ASSYRIAN EMPIRE. THIS MARKED THE END OF THE KINGDOM OF ISRAEL.

Siege of a city under the Assyrian King Tiglath-Pileser II (745–727 BCE).

The records of the military campaigns of the Assyrian kings are preserved on clay tablet. Archaeologists have thus been able to piece together the tale of Assyrian expansion westwards, resulting in the ultimate collapse of Israel. King Ashurnasirpal II (883–859 BCE) consolidated the conquests of his father, Tukulti-Ninurta II. He quelled rebellions, re-organized his provinces and encouraged the acquiescence of his subjects by publicly flaying the rebel governor of Nishtun at Arbela. He devastated Armenia, pacified the Arameans and exacted tribute from the strong state of Bit-Adini. He crossed the Euphrates and campaigned ss far as the Mediterranean via Carchemish and the Orontes, gaining tributes from cities such as Tyre, Sidon, Byblos and Arvad.

Shalmaneser III (858–824 BCE) reached the Mediterranean in the first year of his reign. Every state in northern Syria was forced to pay him tribute. In response, the small states of the former Canaan, led by Hamath and Damascus, allied to resist Assyrian incursions. In 853 BCE, Shalmaneser returned westward and found himself confronted with a coalition of twelve states at Qarqar, including Hadadezer of Damascus and Ahab of Israel. The Assyrians claimed victory in the battle, even though they did not succeed in acquiring Aramaea and the Levant.

In 841 BCE, Shalamaneser campaigned westward but failed to capture Damascus. Nevertheless, Tyre, Sidon and Jehu of Israel paid him tribute. The Black Obelisk of Nimrod, now in the British Museum, shows where 'Jehu, son of Omri' bowed before Shalmaneser. In 837 BCE, the Assyrian King embarked on his last expedition westward, receiving tribute from Damascus, Tyre,

Sidon and Byblos. Assyria was then forced to fight the constant incursions by mountain tribes on its eastern and northern borders. Cilicia was captured and expeditions were mounted against Sardur I, King of Urartu (Van). Meanwhile, Damascus waged war against Israel and Judah.

Shalamaneser's grandson, Adad-Nirari III (811–783 BCE) also led campaigns, receiving tribute from Tyre, Sidon, Damascus, Israel, Edom and the Philistines. A succession of Assyrian kings were replaced by a general known as Tiglath-Pileser III (744–727 BCE). He reduced the independence of governors and campaigned in Azerbaidjan to split the Medes and Urartuans. The latter formed an alliance with the Syrian city of Arpad. Urartu (Ararat) was defeated and Arpad wiped out of history. A northern Syrian alliance was crushed leaving all of the rulers from Damascus through eastern Anatolia paying tribute. In 735 BCE, an expedition to Urartu was partially successful. These achievements, as well as better military equipment restored Assyria's strength. As far as the Levant was concerned, in 743 BCE, Tiglath-Pileser marched to the Lebanese mountains and King Azariah of Judah paid tribute. Afterward, the annual Assyrian western campaigns changed as Tiglath-Pileser III changed tactics, no longer accepting tribute but moving the

The Near East in the time of Assyrian ascendancy (eighth and seventh centuries BCE). Israel, Judah and the Canaanite cities are referred to here as the Levantine States.

elites of conquered peoples to other parts of his Empire. In 734 BCE, he attacked the Brook of Egypt. Next year, Israel was attacked. Megiddo and Hazor were flattened and Israel's territory beyond the Jordan, Galilee, and the coastal plain became the Assyrian provinces of Gal'aza (Gilead), Magidu (Megiddo) and Du'ru (Dor). In 732 BCE, King Ahaz of Judea asked Tiglath-Pileser for help against Damascus. This city was destroyed and the land divided into four Assyrian provinces. The population was exiled. Samaria was spared since its people killed their rebellious King Pekah. In 724 BCE, Shalmaneser V captured Hoshea, King of Israel. In 721 BCE, Israel was annihilated by Sargon II who captured Samaria and exiled the population to Assyria and Media.

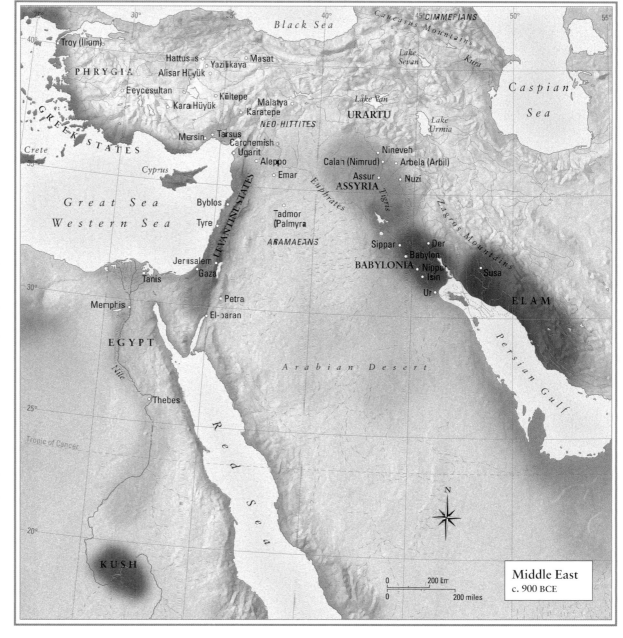

ASSYRIAN WARFARE

"THE ASSYRIAN CAME DOWN LIKE THE WOLF ON THE FOLD,

AND HIS COHORTS WERE GLEAMING IN PURPLE AND GOLD:

AND THE SHEEN OF THEIR SPEARS WAS LIKE STARS ON THE SEA

WHEN THE BLUE WAVE ROLLS NIGHTLY ON DEEP GALILEE."

(LORD GEORGE BYRON, 1788–1824)

Close combat. This detail, from a relief carving from the palace of Ashurbanipal at Nineveh, shows an Assyrian infantryman equipped with a spear attacking an Elamite archer.

Byron, the poet, encapsulated the view of savage Assyrians massacring innocent civilians in their cities, like wolves attacking sheep. This imagery, however, ignores the Assyrian scientific application of all aspects of military technology and weaponry when campaigning against rebels or conquering foreign lands. The Assyrians were brilliant at classic pitched battles in open country but that was not enough. After a victory in the field, the enemy were subjected to hot pursuit until they sought refuge in a city. Then, the Assyrians would demonstrate their skill at siege warfare, by escalade or normal siege, for years if necessary. The Assyrians thus developed a technique of flexible warfare, combining combat and siege in all the major campaigns waged between 1270 and 648 BCE, from Shalmaneser I (1274–1246 BCE) to Assurbanipal (669–c. 627 BCE). Military activity was bolstered by physical and psychological terror and the unusual treatment afforded to defeated peoples, the deportation of their elites into parts of the empire.

Assyrian military power began with the construction of standing armies under Tiglath-Pileser III (745–728 BCE). Before his reign, Assyrian success had been dependent upon a national military levy imposed by provincial governors. Thus, an army consisted of local troops, armed and equipped according to their culture and led by their governors. Different regions specialized in distinctive roles: heavy and light infantry, archers, lancers and spearmen.

When re-organized, Assyrian army units were constituted on a decimal basis with the 200-man kisri being amalgamated into super-divisions of some 15,000 men. Armies were commanded by the King or his two marshals, the turtan. The armies consisted of mutually supporting troops of all types with a special emphasis on infantry backed up by cavalry and chariots. Infantry were divided into missile units of archers and slingshot infantry, chariots were mobile archer platforms, while cavalry were either archers or lancers.

The army also contained logistics units capable of carrying military equipment and basic foods on pack-donkeys and ox-carts. Armoured battering rams, siege machines and materials used to make siege engines at the point of conflict would be transported. The standing army of professional soldiers lived in garrisons in the major cities which were known as ekal masharti (mustering palaces). They contained parade grounds for military manoeuvres, barracks and storerooms for provisions and equipment. Eventually, armour and equipment were manufactured and standardized by the state.

The heavy archer was clad in scaled armour covering body and head with a helmet added. Armed with a composite bow and sword, he was protected by a shield-bearer who also carried arrow quivers. Medium archers had no head cover while the unarmoured light archers were mobile and used for skirmishing. These troops could be compared with British musketeers in regiments of the line in the Napoleonic Wars with their light companies and the skirmishing rifle regiments. Slingshot fighters wore both helmet and brigandine. The major shock-troops were armoured spearmen who carried swords and large shields. Light spearmen wore no helmets.

The Assyrians were renowned for their use of chariots. Two-wheeled and highly mobile, these vehicles carried a driver, archer and two shield-bearers. The chariot was manoeuvrable and could deliver missiles in hit-and-run nuisance attacks but if it ran into infantry who stood firm, a chariot's crew were easy prey. The sheer psychological threat of ranks of chariots was a weapon in itself. The prophet Isaiah 2: 7 remarked, "Their land also is full of silver and gold, neither is there any end of their treasures; their land is also full of horses, neither is there any end of their chariots." However, at the Battle of Qarqar, Shalmaneser III claimed victory in a drawn battle of contending chariot forces.

The cavalry arm developed over time. Like European dragoons, Assyrian cavalry initially consisted of mounted archers aided by a mounted shield-bearer for protection when the archer dismounted to shoot. Eventually, the cavalry became a reconnaissance force but was also used to fire composite bows from the saddle. Like chariots, cavalry would then be mobile fire-power which could thin enemy ranks, keep enemy skirmishers at bay and discourage enemy attacks. However, these archers remained linked to infantry providing mutual support unlike later Mongol armies in which they were essentially mounted archers with a reflex bow The lancers were important when harrying a defeated foe fleeing to the nearest city for sanctuary.

When implementing a siege, the Assyrians would encircle a city and attempt to cut off any water supply or access for a relief forces. Then a target area on a wall would be selected for making a breach. The ground would be leveled so siege-engines could approach and all necessary roads, ramps, bridges or causeways would be constructed. Towers, higher than the walls, with archers on top, would keep the defenders at bay while the ram would batter sections out of the wall or pick at interstices until chunks could be prised out. Miners might dig under the wall to destroy foundations. Scaling

Next page: Assyrian armies were skilled on the open battlefield and had developed siege craft to a fine art. Following the occupation of a conquered territory Assyrian exploitation was equally ruthless.

ladders would be massed against the walls to storm the ramparts defended by archers. Sometimes cities would be starved into submission as in Babylon in 648 BCE.

The audience halls of the Assyrian palaces' were decorated with bas-reliefs depicting Assyrian military glories. Other forms of pressure were the cutting off hands, burning alive, putting out eyes and slicing off ears and noses, special punishments for those who had rebelled. Defeated peoples were deported to ensure political stability and to populate undeveloped territories. Deportees were nurtured by the state until they could provide for themselves with the state aiding irrigation projects. Ethnic communities and families were not separated and were allowed to speak their own language and pursue their own faiths. Cultural mixing produced a multi-cultural and multi-linguistic court whose new ideas were assimilated into Assyrian life.

However mighty the Assyrians, their armies could be defeated by disease as described in II Kings 19: 35–36 when King Sennacherib besieged Jerusalem in 701 BCE. "And it came to pass that night, that the angel of the Lord went out, and smote in the camp of the Assyrians an hundred fourscore and five thousand: and when they arose early in the morning, behold, they were all dead corpses."

"For the Angel of Death spread his wings on the blast,
And breathed in the face of the foe as he passed;
And the eyes of the sleepers waxed deadly and chill,
And their hearts but once heaved, and for ever grew still.

"… And the widows of Ashur are loud in their wail,
And the idols are broke in the temple of Baal;
And the might of the Gentile, unsmote by the sword,
Hath melted like snow in the glance of the Lord!"

(Lord George Byron, 1788–1824).

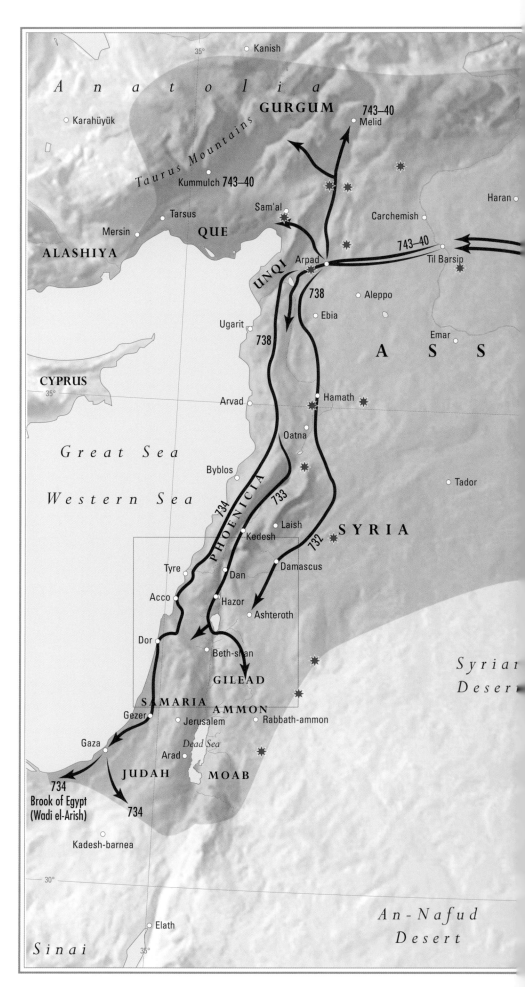

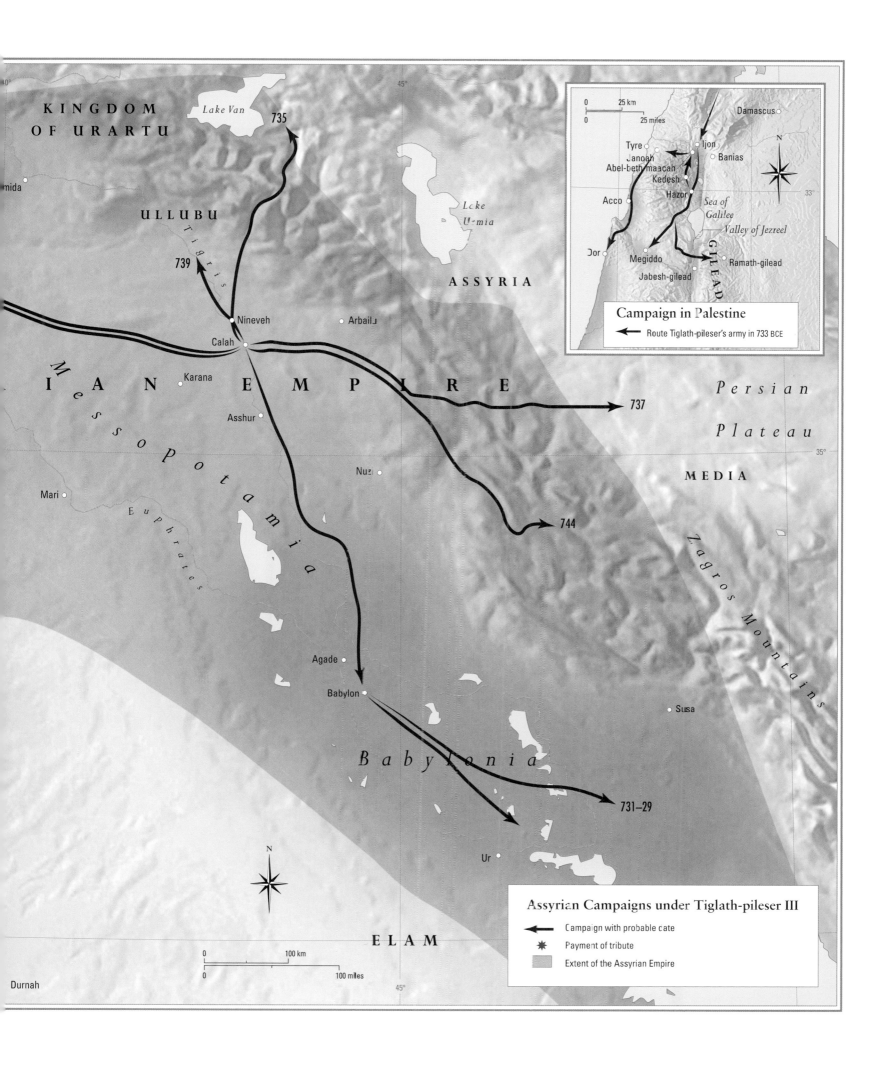

KINGDOM
OF URARTU

Lake Van

735

ULLUBU

Tigris

739

Nineveh

Calah

Karana

I A N   E M P I R E

Asshur

Messopotamia

Mari

Euphrates

Nuzi

Arbail

ASSYRIA

*Lake
Urmia*

737

Persian

Plateau

744

MEDIA

35°

Zagros Mountains

Agade

Babylon

Susa

Babylonia

731–29

Ur

ELAM

0   100 km

0   100 miles

Durnah

45°

Campaign in Palestine

25 km

25 miles

Damascus

Tyre
Janoah
Abel-beth-maacah
Kedesh
Acco
Hazor
Dor
Megiddo
Jabesh-gilead
Ijon
Banias
*Sea of
Galilee*
Valley of Jezreel
Ramath-gilead
GILEAD
N
33°

→ Route Tiglath-pileser's army in 733 BCE

Assyrian Campaigns under Tiglath-pileser III

→ Campaign with probable date

✳ Payment of tribute

Extent of the Assyrian Empire

THE PROPHET ELIJAH

THE FATE OF THE HOUSE OF OMRI WAS SEALED BY JEZEBEL, WHO MARRIED HIS SON, AHAB. SHE ATTEMPTED NOT ONLY TO INTRODUCE THE WORSHIP OF BAAL BUT TO ERADICATE WORSHIP OF THE ONE GOD, CAUSING HUGE RESENTMENT. ATALIAH OF JUDAH KILLED HER WHOLE FAMILY IN ORDER TO SEIZE POWER.

When Ahab succeeded Omri as King of Israel, his wife Jezebel attempted to replace worship of the One God with the worship of Baal, her Phoenician deity. Several hundred priests of Baal and Asherah were brought into the country and resisters of the foreign cult might be murdered. God's places of worship were attacked and altars to God destroyed. The prophet Elijah offered resistance to Jezebel and fled for his life, recruiting a helper, Elisha, to carry on his work to bring Israel back from the brink of apostasy. This new prophet continued Elijah's work of purging the kingship of Israel and Syria. In Damascus, Elisha helped the sick King Ben-Hadad but told the King's servant, Hazael, to seize the throne. Hazael smothered his master and usurped the throne. When King Jehoram was wounded in battle with the Syrians at Ramoth-Gilead, he returned to his palace at Jezreel to recover and was visited by his nephew, Ahaziah, who had just become King of Judah. Elisha sent a minor prophet to the Israelite army commander, Jehu, to anoint him King with orders to eradicate the Omride line.

Meanwhile, the House of Omri had become unpopular. The gap between rich and poor was widening, despite the economic boom in Israel. The poor were often forced to mortgage their land for their children to survive and a drought caused many to lose their farms. Jezebel aroused religious fury; conservative groups like Rechabites, a Kenite clan, were keen to wipe out the evil in their midst. Later, this group swore not to drink wine, nor to own vineyards, nor to plough land, nor to build houses, but to live in tents like their ancestors. They clung to old nomadic, democratic ways reminiscent of the tribal covenant. Interestingly, in 1835, in England, an Independent Order of Rechabites was established whose members pledged to forswear alcohol, each branch of the movement being called a "Tent."

Jehu's annointing was acclaimed by his soldiers and adherents of traditional nationalism and by a soldiery sick of mismanaged warfare against the Syrians or hostile to the conspicuous consumption, corruption and apostasy of the governing elites. Revolution was nigh. Jehu travelled by chariot to Jezreel and was met by Jehoram and Ahaziah. Jehu shot Jehoram with an arrow and the fleeing Ahaziah was wounded after a chase and died in Megiddo.

Jehu then purged Israel of the pagan religion. Jezebel was thrown from her palace window, trampled by horses and eaten by dogs until only her skull, feet and palms of her hands remained, thereby fulfilling one of Elijah's prophecies. Jehu next mocked the elders of Samaria, challenging them to select one of Ahab's 70 sons to fight him. Instead, they sent him the heads of all the sons. Advancing on Samaria, Jehu killed more of Ahab's kin and upon arrival killed priests and followers of Baal in an orgy of butchery.

Jehu's dynasty survived for nearly a century. He eradicated paganism at the cost

Elijah Receiving Bread and Water from an Angel, c. 1626–28, by Peter Paul Rubens. Musee Bonnat, Bayonne, France.

of wiping out the kingdom's elite. "So Jehu slew all that remained of the house of Ahab in Jezreel, and all his great men, and his kinfolks, and his priests, until he left him none remaining." (II Kings 10: 11) The state failed to function properly without administrators, so that society's ills were not eradicated. Later prophets, such as Amos, pointed out the social and economic inequalities and Hosea remarked that pagan rites continued to be practised. The murder of Jezebel ended friendly relations with Phoenician Tyre and killing Ahaziah destroyed the alliance with Judah.

Israel's military strength suffered. Unable to resist Shalmaneser III of Assyria, Jehu paid tribute. When the Assyrian turned north to fight Urartu, Hazael of Damascus struck and Israel lost all of the land east of the Jordan as far as Moab. Jehoahaz (815–802 BCE), his son was defeated and Israel lost the Valley of Jezreel, the coast and Galilee to Aramean domination, becoming a Damascene dependency. The Queen Mother, Athaliah, Ahab's daughter, seized the throne of Judah, killing all except Joash, the infant son of Ahaziah. The chief priest and royal guard crowned the child when he reached the age of seven and executed the protesting Athaliah. Joash was welcomed by his people; the temple to Baal was destroyed.

ISRAEL AND JUDAH RESURGENT

KING UZZIAH IN JUDAH AND JEROBOAM II IN ISRAEL BOTH REIGNED OVER PROSPEROUS KINGDOMS. THERE WERE TECHNOLOGICAL ADVANCES IN AGRICULTURE AND DEFENCE, BUT THE GAP BETWEEN RICH AND POOR WAS GROWING, TO THE DISTRESS OF THE PROPHETS WHO FORESAW THAT THIS WOULD END BADLY.

The kingships of Jeraboam over Israel and Uziah over Judah were periods of relative prosperity. The expansion of Syria to the north had overwhelmed the kingdoms enemies, leaving them in peace for around 40 years, until the death of Jeraboam in 746 BCE.

When Joash became King of Judah, he ensured its survival by sending the invading Hazael of Damascus some Temple treasure as tribute. In 800 BCE, Joash was assassinated. His son, Amaziah, seeing the Assyrians threatening Damascus, used this breathing space to defeat the Edomites in the Valley of Salt thus gaining control of the copper deposits there. Amaziah had used Israelite mercenaries who had been sent home before his victory. With no booty, these men looted some of the cities of Judah and this became a casus belli between the two Hebrew states. They fought at Beth-Shemesh where Amaziah was captured. Jerusalem fell and the Temple was plundered. A section of the city wall was torn down.

Jehoash, King of Israel, continued his victories. The sick Elisha urged him to wage war against Damascus and the strategic area of Aphek was captured which Jehoash's son, Jeroboam II used as a springboard to invade Aram and seize Damascus. Meanwhile, Amaziah was murdered leaving his throne to Uzziah in 783 BCE.

The Assyrians were then diverted from their attacks on the Hebrew kingdoms by a rebellious Babylonian vassal and pressure from Urartu. Nevertheless, Adad-Nirari III (811–784 BCE) captured Damascus and exacted much tribute. Syria then became embroiled in conflict with Hamath. Jeroboam II of Israel and Uzziah of Judah found themselves in a favourable position in this international power vacuum.

Uzziah wanted to develop his country. New wells were dug and cisterns created to allow large flocks and herds in an upgrade of agriculture. Soil types were tested to find the most suitable plants for different micro-climates. Grain was planted in the valleys and plains and vineyards on the

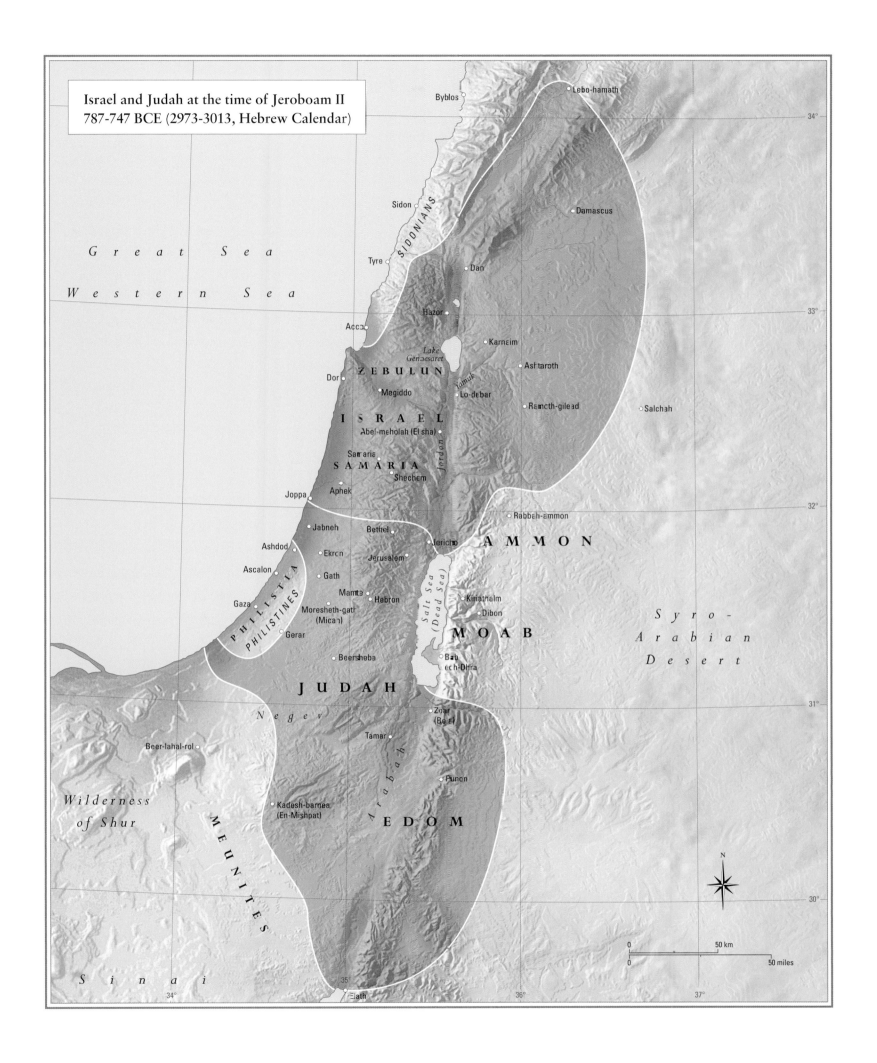

Israel and Judah at the time of Jeroboam II
787-747 BCE (2973-3013, Hebrew Calendar)

Lebo-hamath

Byblos

Damascus

Sidon

SIDONIANS

Great Sea

Western Sea

Tyre

Dan

Hazor

Acco

Karnaim

Lake
Gennesaret

Ashtaroth

Dor

ZEBULUN

Megiddo

Lo-debar

Ramoth-gilead

Salchah

ISRAEL

Abel-meholah (Elisha)

Samaria

SAMARIA

Shechem

Jordan

Joppa

Aphek

Rabbah-ammon

Jabneh

Bethel

Jericho

AMMON

Ashdod

Ekron

Jerusalem

Ascalon

Gath

Syro-
Arabian
Desert

Mamre

Kiriathaim

Gaza

PHILISTIA

Moresheth-gath
(Micah)

Hebron

Dibon

PHILISTINES

Gerar

MOAB

Salt Sea
(Dead Sea)

Beersheba

Bab
ech-Dhra

JUDAH

Negev

Zoar
(Bela)

Beer-lahai-roi

Tamar

Arabah

Punon

Wilderness
of Shur

Kadesh-barnea
(En-Mishpat)

EDOM

MEUNITES

Sinai

Elath

N

0   50 km

0   50 miles

hillsides. He built military-agricultural settlements in the Negev in order to command and police trade routes allowing control of much of the Arabian traffic. Standard fortifications were constructed with casement walls and a minimum of eight towers to guard crossroads and strategic points. Agricultural settlements were created at many of these forts. Such tower fortifications have been found by archaeologists at Beer-Sheba, Hormah, and Arad, Other towers were erected: "... Also be built towers in the desert and digged many wells." (II Chronicles 26: 10).

Uzziah also improved Jerusalem's fortifications, installing wooden shields on the walls to protect defenders and he built engines to fire bolts and throw large stones and rocks. The Bible claims he had over 300,000 soldiers with an elite strike force similar to David's personal guard. War was waged against Edom with the capture of land as far as Ezion-Geber which was rebuilt as a fortified port. Judah's position along the trade routes was further secured by dominating the north-western Arab tribes in Gurbaal and the Meunites in the Edom desert. The northern stretches of the King's Highway were held by the tribute-paying Ammonites. Uzziah secured the Shephelah and invaded Philistia. He built a fort at Azekah and demolished the defenses of Gath, Ashdod, and Jabneh. Gath and Jabneh were assimilated by Judah as was some of Ashdod's territory. Joppa (Jaffa) was captured, bringing all western invasion routes into Judah under Uzziah's control. Judean cities were constructed amongst the Philistine population. In sum, Uzziah enhanced his reputation, gained access to the Mediterranean, and regained all of the southern land of Solomon's Kingdom.

In Israel, Jeroboam II laid the foundations of economic prosperity. He used Aphek for an attack on Syria, seizing control of the plateau around Lodebar and capturing Ramoth-Gilead. There is some evidence that he attacked Karnaim. His campaign led through through Aram, to Damascus and northward to Lebo-Hamath, to the furthest extent of David's and Solomon's lands. Jeroboam was able to control both Damascus and Hamath. Evidence suggests that Israel annexed lands across the Jordan north of the Yarmuk River and reached a border point on the Dead Sea. However, it is unclear whether Jeroboam constrained the Moabites or actually conquered them, since Amos 6: 14 and Isaiah 15: 7 provide conflicting accounts.

Israel now benefited from the rich agricultural land of Gilead and exacted tribute from the defeated peoples. The affluence encouraged conspicuous consumption and evidence exists of extravagance criticized by the prophets. The existing cities became too small for the expanding population. At Megiddo many public buildings and high grade stone houses have been found. Pottery fragments, known as ostraca, list produce stored in the royal warehouse at Samaria, including "aged wine" and "purified oil." When these items were delivered, they were recorded on a shard before becoming a ledger entry.

Excavations at Hazor show examples of the finest houses dating from Jeroboam's reign. Stores, workshops, and houses were built during this renaissance. The two-story homes were so well built that stairs remain after 2700 years. Material goods reached a high standard. One find is an ivory cosmetic spoon, its handle beautifully carved in an inverted palmette design, common in the Near East at this time. The back of the spoon bowl is sculpted in the shape of a woman's head, with two doves entangled in the woman's hair. A tower measuring 33 x 23 feet (10 x 7 metres) was added to the north-western corner of the city, possibly an extra defence against a future Assyrian attack.

The excavations at Tel Hazor. The city of Hazor was greatly expanded and improved under Jeroboam II, with stone houses and additional fortifications.

The wealth of Israel was not spread equally and economic disparities incensed Amos the prophet who recognized that God loved all His people, not just the wealthy. Perpetrators of conspicuous consumption would be punished.

"Ye that put away the evil day, and cause the seat of violence to come near; That lie upon beds of ivory, and stretch themselves upon couches, and eat the lambs out of the flock, and calves out of the midst of the stall; That chant to the sound of the viol and invent to themselves instruments of musick, like David; That drink wine in bowls, and anoint themselves with the chief ointments: but they are not grieved for the affliction of Joseph. Therefore now they shall go captive with the first that go captive, and the banquet of them that stretched themselves shall be removed." (Amos 6: 3–7).

The state ignored the poor and poor farmers were in the thrall of money-lenders. If their crops were ruined by drought or pestilence, this could lead to foreclosure, eviction, and even being sold into slavery. The homogenous equality of the old tribal league with society upholding covenant law had been destroyed by the monarchy, business interests, and the absorption of alien cultures, such as the Canaanites and worshippers of Baal. Traditional customs and morality were seriously compromised.

The prophet Hosea foresaw Israel in danger of destruction. "Woe unto them! For they have fled from me: destruction unto them! Because they have transgressed against me: though I have redeemed them, yet they have spoken lies against me." (Hosea 7 13) And, "My God will cast them away, because they did not harken unto him: and they shall be wanderers among the nations." (Hosea 9: 17) Amos fulminated against moral decline, exploitation, drunkenness, injustice, and apostasy while Hosea foresaw the perils of Assyria.

"An east wind shall come up from the wilderness, and his spring shall become dry, and his fountain shall be dried up: he shall spoil the treasure of all pleasant vessels. Samaria shall become desolate: for she hath rebelled against God: they shall fall by the sword: their infants shall be dashed in pieces, and their children with child shall be ripped up." (Hosea 14: 15–16).

COLLAPSE OF THE KINGDOMS

ISRAEL AND JUDAH WERE NOW ATTACKED ON ALL SIDES. THE ASSYRIANS IN THE NORTH TARGETED ISRAEL WHILE THE PHILISTINES IN THE SOUTH REGAINED THEIR POWER, RECOVERED TERRITORY CAPTURED BY JUDAH, AND ATTACKED SETTLEMENTS IN THE NEGEV AND THE ARABAH.

Israel's prosperity ended when Jeroboam died in 746 BCE. His son, Zechariah, ruled for six months before being murdered at Ibleam. The murderer, Shallum, seized the throne but ruled for only one month before being killed by Menahem, a brutal man whose troops slaughtered pregnant women at the sack of Tappuah and who devastated its hinterland because the people rejected him as King.

Meanwhile, Assyria had decided to change its policy of restricting its border to the Euphrates with subservient vassal states across the river. Assyria felt threatened by the westward-expanding Urartu (Ararat) that had created an alliance with the north Syrian states. This coalition threatened Assyrian trade routes. On ascending the throne, Tiglath-Pileser III attacked the Urartu alliance in 743 BCE, defeating the Urartu forces and capturing Arpad by siege. He then marched on Unqi at the northern end of the Orontes, seizing its capital, Kullania, in 738 BCE. New Assyrian provinces were created in Simirra (Sumuru) and Khatarikka and tribute was received from Rezin of Damascus, Menahem of Israel, and the Kings of Tyre, Gubla, and Hamath. The land conquered was incorporated into the Assyrian Empire as new provinces. Enemy elites were deported there while depopulated areas were settled with peoples from other parts of the empire.

The tribute paid by Menahem was recouped from Israel's population. The taxation produced great anger and resentment but it gave Menahem seven years' grace. His son, Pekahiah, had just ascended the throne when he was murdered by Pekah, leader of a Gileadite coup d'état.

Elsewhere, Tiglath-Pileser challenged Urartu's influence. In 739 BCE in Ullubu (the Dohuk-Zakhno area of north Iraq), in 737 BCE in the Median area of northeast Persia, and in 735 BCE when he marched on Urartu itself. In 734 BCE, Tiglath-Pileser attacked Philistia, taking Gaza and reaching the Brook of Egypt. The nomadic tribes were defeated and he appointed an Arab tribal chief as his Warden in Sinai. Diplomatic relations were extended to other Arab rulers in northern Arabia and eastern transjordan. Then, Pekah of Israel and Rezin of Damascus created another anti-Assyrian coalition, including Tyre, Ashkelon and some of the tribes in northern Arabia and transjordan. They sought to include Jotham of Judah but he refused as did his son, Ahaz, who ascended the throne in 735 BCE. Pekah and Rezin planned to attack Judah and replace Ahaz with someone who would join in their schemes.

Ahaz was dismayed at the plot against him. Judah lost lands in transjordan and Rezin sent troops southwards and acquired Ezion-Geber. Rezin also joined Pekah in an attack on Judah. Jerusalem was besieged, causing Ahaz to contemplate requesting aid from Assyria but the prophet Isaiah persuaded him to rely on God. Meanwhile, the prophet Oded was stirring up trouble for Pekah in Israel.

The Israel-Damascus coalition encouraged other enemies of Judah to take their revenge. Edom grabbed its independence and seized the entire mineral-rich Arabah down to Ezion-Geber, as well as launching raids into the Negev. The Philistines recovered territories acquired by Uzziah and captured the cities of Beth-Shemesh, Socoh, Timnah, Ayyinalon and Gimzo. Two key invasion routes were now open to the heart of Judah, the Ways of Beth-Horon and Beth-Shemesh. To make matters worse, the Philistines captured Gederoth and attacked the Negev, destroying Uzziah's network of agricultural-military communities. Ahaz begged the Assyrians for help, sending Temple treasure as a gift. This period demonstrates the political and dynastic instability in Israel. Hosea pronounced Israel's doom when Menahem seized power.

Despite its reputation for aridity the Negev was home to valuable flocks of goats and sheep, here the Negev blooms after winter rains.

THE END OF ISRAEL

KING AHAZ OF JUDAH WAS RESOUNDINGLY DEFEATED BY ASSYRIA
TO WHICH HE HAD ORIGINALLY APPEALED FOR PROTECTION
AGAINST DAMASCUS. HE WAS FORCED TO ABASE HIMSELF BEFORE
THE ASSYRIAN KING, AND TO THE HORROR OF THE PROPHETS
ISAIAH, HOSEA AND MICAH, ADOPTED THE ASSYRIAN RELIGION.

Ahaz's appeal to Tiglath-Pileser III had an immediate impact. The Assyrian king already planned to acquire Syria and make it an Assyrian province He realized that Egypt might object to an upset to the balance of power and planned to neutralize any southern threat that might isolate Damascus before it was destroyed. That Israel was allied to Rezin of Damascus meant that Israel was in danger too, far more so than Pekah realised. Tiglath-Pileser implemented three consecutive campaigns which left Israel in dire straits.

In 734 BCE, the Assyrian army marched down the Mediterranean coast along the Way of the Sea toward the Brook of Egypt. South of Akko (Acre), the Assyrians refused to use the route between Mount Carmel and the sea, instead turning inland. They crossed into the mountains at Yokneam and emerged east of Dor where the army rejoined the Way of the Sea. In this fashion, the Assyrians bypassed the Israelite strongholds, avoiding the delays associated with sieges. However, at some point, Tiglath-Pileser attacked Gezer, a potential threat to his strung-out communications and logistics. Archaeologist have found evidence that Gezer was burned down and its foritifed gate-house destroyed. Tiglath-Pileser's Nimrod palace contains a bas-relief providing evidence of the siege and seizure of Gazru (Gezer). The Assyrians captured Gaza and marched to the Brook of Egypt where they held off the Egyptian forces and isolated the north from Egyptian influence. In 733 BCE, Tiglath-Pileser attacked Israel outright, possibly to capture Gilead and Galilee and isolate Damascus from the west and south.

King Pekah was now to reap the reward for his ill-conceived alliance with Rezin. The Assyrian forces streamed from passes between the Lebanese mountain chains and entered the Rift Valley near the Israelite fortresses of Ijon and Abel-Beth-Macaah which were easily taken. The campaign route stuck to the Galilee's foothills owing to the swamps of Lake Huleh. However, to progress further, the Assyrians needed to capture Hazor which guarded the way south. This fortified city sat upon a 130-foot high mound, a commanding position. Archaeological evidence shows that the Assyrians burst into the citadel from the eastern side of the mound which was easier to scale. Only the foundations remain. Hazor was destroyed then razed to the ground, leaving a three-foot deep layer of ash over the mound. Such severe treatment has not been found in any other archaeological dig in the region.

Tiglath-Pileser divided his forces to deliver a three-pronged attack against Israel. One division was despatched to Kadesh and Upper Galilee to Janoah. The force then moved to Akko and then down the Way of the Sea between Mount Carmel and the coast to Dor where records of its progress end. This division may have then been used to reinforce garrisons against Egypt or joined the siege of Megiddo after marching up the Wadi Ara.

The second and third divisions approached the Sea of Galilee where they went their separate ways. One marched to Pehel and Jabesh-Gilead, a smaller unit taking Mahanaim before entering Gilead. The final division climbed out of the Rift Valley at Adamah and marched westward through

The fearsome Assyrian war machine in action. This bas-relief shows a city under siege.

Lower Galilee, devastating the cities of Rumah, Kanah, Jotbah and Hanathon. From there, the force crossed the plain to reach Megiddo. This key administrative center of northern Israel possessed state-of-the-art fortifications. The inset-outset walls allowed flanking fire and the city was thought to be a major obstacle to any invasion force, but then Hazor had the same reputation. Megiddo was captured but the destruction cannot easily be ascertained because the city was entirely rebuilt subsequently in a grid pattern, entirely unlike Israelite Megiddo. The new Assyrian city was named Magiddu, and was made the capital of a new Assyrian province. The coast south of Mount Carmel as far as Kanah became another province. All of the captives were deported to Assyria.

In the Israelite capital, Samaria, Hoshea murdered Pekah and became the last king of Israel. Assyrian evidence suggests Hoshea was aided by Assyria. This usurpation gave Israel a chance to survive. Assyria had stolen half of Israel's lands west of the Jordan and of Gilead. The truncated state also had to pay tribute from its sparse remaining resources. Israel was surrounded by Assyria on three sides.

In 732 BCE, Tiglath-Pileser seized Damascus and deployed southwards to acquire Syrian Bashan. There were mass deportations to Assyria. Syria was then carved up into the Assyrian provinces of Damascus, Karnaim, and Hauron Ammon. Edom and Moab were kept loosely in the Assyrian orbit and paid tribute, in return for Assyrian protection from nomadic raids from the east and south. Meanwhile, Ahaz of Judah had sent Tiglath-Pileser his tribute of Temple and palace treasures. He was summoned to Damascus to prostrate himself before his rescuer from the designs of Israel. "And Tiglath-Pileser King of Assyria came unto him, and distressed him, but strengthened him not." (II Chronicles 28: 19) At Damascus, Ahaz saw an altar of his rescuer's god and had a copy made which was placed in the Temple in Jerusalem, a pure act of servility. He even moved God's altar to a less prominent position. "And he brought also the brazen altar, which was before the Lord, from the forefront of the house, from between the altar and the house of the Lord, and put it one the north side of the altar." (II Kings 16: 14).

In 727 BCE, Tiglath-Pileser III died and was succeeded by Shalmaneser V. When a powerful king died, his distant lands would rebel. Hoshea was no different. He sought aid from Egypt and received assurances, but these were empty words. Hosea was taken prisoner. Samaria was filled with refugees as the Assyrians attacked the city which was was well-fortified and difficult to capture. The siege lasted three years. Assyrian persistence even survived the death of their king. In 721 BCE, Samaria's walls were breached, marking the end of the Kingdom of Israel. The new King, Sargon, claimed to have deported 27,290 captives to Mesopotamia and Media. New peoples were imported into Samaria who merged with the remnants of Israel. This admixture is, according to some, the origin of the Samaritans. Sargon's records mention revolts in Hamath, Damascus, Samaria (the old province of Dor with the rump of Israel) and Gaza. An Egyptian army sent to relieve the Gazan rebels was defeated and Sargon marched on to take Raphia. He deported 9000 inhabitants after tearing down its walls. Egypt again supported a rebellion in Ashdod. Judah, Edom and Moab were involved but soon withdrew. The Judaean King Hezekiah waited for the inevitable punishment. Ashdod and its port, Gath, Ekron, and Gibbethon were captured as was Azekah, which commanded the Way of Beth-Shemesh was also seized. The road to Jerusalem was now open.

After conquering the region, Syria set about imposing its own system of administration and tax collection. New borders were drawn up under which the region's diverse population lived.

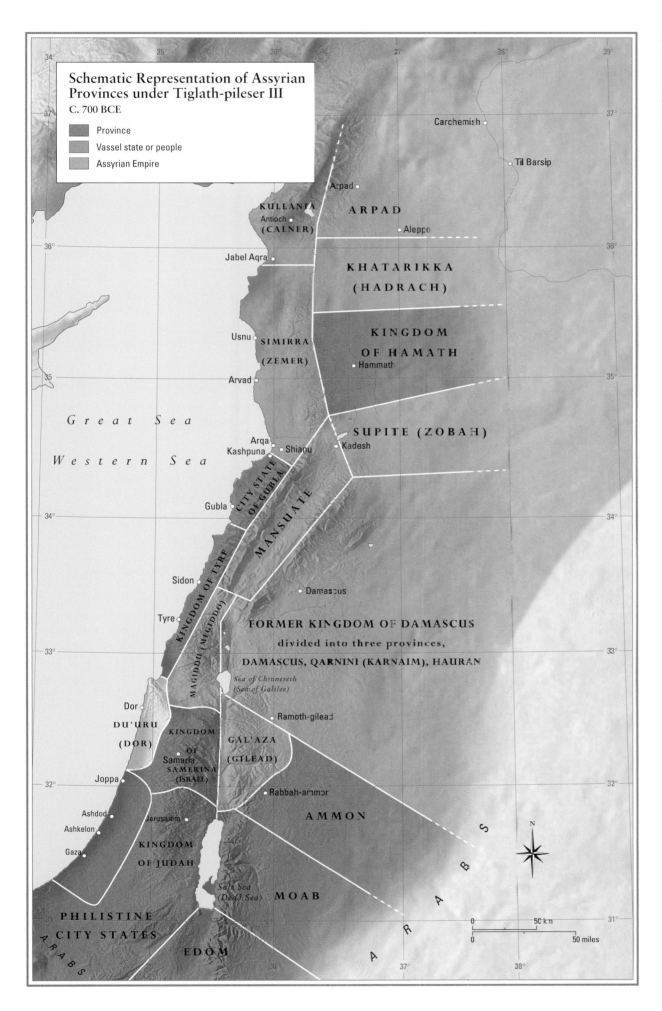

Schematic Representation of Assyrian Provinces under Tiglath-pileser III

C. 700 BCE

- Province
- Vassal state or people
- Assyrian Empire

Carchemish

Til Barsip

Arpad

KULLANIA
Antioch (CALNER)

ARPAD

Aleppo

Jabel Aqra

KHATARIKKA
(HADRACH)

Usnu

SIMIRRA
(ZEMER)

KINGDOM
OF HAMATH

Hammath

Arvad

Great Sea

Western Sea

Arqa
Kashpuna Shiaou

SUPITE (ZOBAH)

Kadesh

CITY STATE OF GUBLA

Gubla

MANSUATE

Sidon

Damascus

Tyre

KINGDOM OF TYRE

MAGIDDU (MEGIDDO)

FORMER KINGDOM OF DAMASCUS

divided into three provinces,

DAMASCUS, QARNINI (KARNAIM), HAURAN

Sea of Chinnereth (Sea of Galilee)

Dor

Ramoth-gilead

DU'URU
(DOR)

KINGDOM
OF
Samaria
SAMERINA
(ISRAEL)

GAL'AZA
(GILEAD)

Joppa

Rabbah-ammon

Ashdod

Ashkelon

Jerusalem

AMMON

KINGDOM
OF JUDAH

Gaza

Salt Sea (Dead Sea)

MOAB

PHILISTINE

CITY STATES

EDOM

ARABS

N

0   50 km
0   50 miles

HEZEKIAH AND SENNACHERIB

HEZEKIAH DID MUCH TO FORTIFY JUDAH AGAINST THE ASSYRIANS BUT IN VAIN. WHEN HE REBELLED AGAINST THEM, THEY TOOK TERRIBLE REVENGE, DESTROYING MOST OF THE COUNTRY. THEY WOULD HAVE BESIEGED JERUSALEM HAD THEY NOT BEEN STRUCK DOWN WITH DISEASE. BUT THE WAR WAS NOT OVER.

Hezekiah at prayer, a woodcut from a 1929 German Bible.

Soon after the end of Israel, Sargon II had to deal with rebellion in Babylonia. A Chaldean prince called Merodach-Baladan seized independence and it took twelve years to pacify the region. To quell the rebellion, Sargon was forced to thin out his garrisons in conquered territory, including Samaria. The new Levantine provinces were at risk. In 720 BCE. Hezekiah of Judah wanted to reverse his father's pro-Assyrian policies and therefore briefly joined the rebellion in 713–12 BCE. Sargon quashed all the rebellions throughout his vast domains, leaving them to the mercy of his less able son, Sennacherib, who ascended the throne in 704 BCE. This monarch seemed to prefer the less taxing occupation of prettifying his capital at Nineveh.

Exploiting this peaceful interlude, Hezekiah refused to pay tribute, prepared for war, and redeveloped Jerusalem's defences. One brilliant feat of engineering was to drive a water tunnel under the city from the Gihon Spring in the Kidron Valley to fill the Pool of Siloam in Jerusalem. The 1750-foot tunnel was hacked out of solid rock. It was between 3 and 11 feet wide and 4 to 16 feet high. Simultaneously, the King sought to plug the few springs in the hills surrounding his capital or was prepared to contaminate them. His tunnel can still be seen.

Recognizing that the Assyrians were unlikely to attack Judah through the Negev or the eastern deserts, Hezekiah built fortifications in the Shephelah as bastions to his capital. He knew that the Way of Beth-Shemesh was a strategic weakness, so he fortified it and upgraded the northern fortresses constructed by Rehoboam. Sennacherib claimed to have captured 46 cities and forts in Judah so it can be assumed that Hezekiah turned Judah into a defensive hedgehog. Judah itself became a fort. Hezekiah protected his southern borders by forays into Edom, standardised military equipment, and stockpiled missiles and shields. The King's religious reforms were intended to encourage Samaria and Galilee to join in the rebellion but they did not.

Hezekiah also hoped for support from his fellow rebel, Merodach-Baladan of Babylon. The Philistines faced a difficult situation. Ashdod and Gaza had been badly hurt by Assyria before and remained quiescent. King Sidqa of Ashkelon allied with Hezekiah but Padi of Ekron remained loyal to Sennacherib. His people arrested him and sent

Sennacherib drives his chariot in a royal procession.

him to Hezekiah who threw him in prison. Ammon, Moab, and Edom appeared not to be involved or backed off from the potential war. Enter Egypt. Pharaoh Shabako promised military help and an Egyptian–Judah alliance was signed much to the anger of the prophet Isaiah who thought God alone was sufficient defense.

"Woe to the rebellious children, saith the Lord, that take counsel, but not of me; and that cover with a covering, but not of my spirit, that they may add sin to sin That walk to go down into Egypt, and have not asked at my mouth; to strengthen themselves in the strength of Pharaoh, and to trust to the shadow of Egypt! Therefore shall the strength of Egypt be your shame, and the trust in the shadow of Egypt your confusion." (Isaiah 30: 1–3).

By 702 BCE, Sennacherib again controlled Babylonia and immediately sought vengeance against his southern vassals and tributaries. A large army invaded Phoenicia causing King Luli of Tyre to flee to Cyprus while his city and its environs were so devastated that Tyre never regained its commercial importance though its colonies, such as Carthage, prospered. The Assyrians moved quickly into Philistia and western Judah. Joppa was crushed. Then Sennacherib faced the Egyptians at Eltekeh and defeated them. Next, Timnah and Ekron fell.

The Assyrians used a two-pronged attack fighting along the Way of Beth-Horon, coursing through Bethel, Aiath, Michmash, Geba, Anathoth, and Nob. Part of this first force captured Ramah, thereby isolating the bypassed Mizpah. Evidently, the city was so strong that isolation was preferable to assault. Sennacherib then surrounded Jerusalem. The second Assyrian force besieged Lachish, then set fire to the city. Simultaneously, Libnah, Moresheth-Gath, Mareshah, and Adullam were attacked as the Shephelah was systematically laid waste.

Fortunately, the Assyrians were devastated by plague when they attempted to besiege and they withdrew, leaving Judah with cities sacked and burned and a ruined countryside. Sennacherib boasted of deporting 200,150 people. Later, Hezekiah sent tribute to Sennacherib, including his own daughters and concubines, or so the Assyrians claimed.

THE PROPHETS

THE JEWISH PROPHETS WOULD MAKE PREDICTIONS BUT THEIR
ROLE ALSO INCLUDED ACTING AS SOME SORT OF LEADER OF THE
OPPOSITION. THEY CONSTANTLY WARNED THE KINGS AND THE
PEOPLE AGAINST STRAYING FROM THE PATH OF ORTHODOXY AND
WORSHIPPING THE FALSE GODS OF BAAL, MARDUK. AND ASTARTE.

Prophets have existed in all faiths in the Near East and Mediterranean. As portrayed in the Bible these representatives of God's word dare to argue with kings, something unheard of in other societies, and can persuade the populace of the need for change socio-economic and political change, in line with God's will. When Solomon's kingdom split into Israel and Judah, Ahijah of Shiloh was important in establishing Israel and Shemaiah managed to obtain an uneasy truce between the two states for a while. The stories of Elijah and Elisha invoke the supernatural, especially when Elijah was translated into heaven. Over time, prophets became so numerous that the people would consult them like oracles. Eventually, such prophets fell out of favor particularly under Assyrian dominance.

Under international threat, a new body of prophets emerged who were well versed in social analysis and international politics as well as a desire to get back to basics in a religious sense. This particular group preached against inequality, desired social justice and wanted a return to the moral demands made by God under the Covenant. Ritual conformity was not as important as morality. These prophets stated that if the people did not renounce all other gods and if they did not respect their fellows, then Israel and Judah were doomed, but for a tiny remnant who would survive. These key prophets were Amos and Hosea in Israel and Micah and Isaiah in Judah. Another group of prophets emerged just before Judah's collapse, the most important being Zephaniah and Jeremiah.

The prophets were at their most influential in times of moral crisis and national emergency. Amos criticized corrupt practices such as tampering with weights and measures and condemned judges for taking bribes. He condemned the worship of foreign gods. Hosea described the Covenant as a marriage, with God the husband and Israel the wife. Joining the Baal cult was adultery, which would result in divorce. Micah's prophesies foresaw Jerusalem and the Temple as a heap of ruins but out of this Judah would be ruled by a prince from Bethlehem of David's line. Isaiah, in Hezekiah's time, attacked reliance on Egypt, inveighed against godless leadership, and finally claimed God would destroy Assyria. After the death by disease of the force besieging Jerusalem, Isaiah fades from sight.

All of the prophets affirmed that moral decay and spiritual sickness would result from idolatry and apostasy. Baal and Astarte (Ashtoreth) were the true enemies. Baal was a major Canaanite deity often represented as a bull. An open-air shrine excavated in northeastern Samaria has revealed a bronze bull. Was this misuse of the shrine similar to that of Jeroboam who erected such bulls in the temples of Dan and Bethel? Altars to Baal were often replaced by altars to God, and this may have caused confusion in the minds of some. Groves of holy trees (Asherah) were also worshipped.

Astarte (Ashtoreth) is represented in the Bible as Baal's consort and is considered to be a fertility goddess. The bare-breasted statuettes of her show tend to be more erotic rather maternal and this goddess was connected with prostitution, both male and female, in the Bible. "And he brake down the houses of the sodomites, that were by the house of the Lord, where the women wove hangings for the grove." (II Kings 23: 7) It is strange that the worship of the One God also included the seraphim and cherubim, of which images were placed in the Temple. A cherub, karibu or genie in Akkadian, was a winged figure with a lion's body and female head. This sphinx-like creation is common in Syrian-Phoenician iconography and is often found incised in ivory panels from Samaria.

This mid-nineteenth century picture shows the Prophet Ezra preaching to his Jewish audience.

JOSIAH

KING JOSIAH ATTEMPTED TO INTRODUCE RELIGIOUS REFORMS
INTO JUDAH WHICH HAD BECOME CONTAMINATED WITH
PAGAN CULTS. HE BANISHED IDOLS AND DESTROYED THE PAGAN
SHRINES. HE EVEN CONTRIVED FOR A NEW BOOK OF THE BIBLE
TO BE DISCOVERED, THE BOOK OF DEUTERONOMY.

Hezekiah was succeeded by his son, Manasseh (687/6–642 BCE), who became totally subservient to Assyria and its gods. He undid his father's work and turned back the clock to the policies of Ahaz. Altars to Assyrian deities were placed inside the Temple, sacred prostitution was permitted within its precincts, and even human sacrifice took place. Arguably the worst King to occupy the Davidic throne, Manasseh was cursed by the prophet Jeremiah (Jeremiah 15: 1–4) Amon, his son, followed his father (642–640 BCE) but was murdered leaving the succession to his eight-year-old son Josiah (640–609 BCE).

These events coincided with the last days of the Assyrian Empire. Babylon was its usual hotbed of dissent, aided by Elam to the east. Egypt could no longer be controlled and Pharaoh Psammetichus I (663–609 BCE) refused to pay tribute and created the twenty-sixth Saite Dynasty. The northern frontier was overrun by Cimmerians and Scythians, Indo-Aryan tribes, who were repelled by Sargon II. King Asshurbanipal was faced with Babylonian and Elamite rebellion and the Arab tribes that overran Edom, Moab and Syria. The Assyrian king reasserted his authority and wiped out the Elamite state.

Nabopolassar founded a new Babylonian state and sought an alliance with the Indo–Aryan Medes and Persians. The Babylonian–Median alliance eventually triumphed over the Assyrian-Egyptian pact and by 609 BCE, Nineveh had been destroyed and Assyria annihilated.

Judah prospered during this time of international flux. Josiah initiated a period of religious reform. The Assyrian gods were cast out of the Temple and the building purified. Josiah also exercised his authority in provinces in which Assyria had lost effective control, especially in the former Israel.

While the Temple was being repaired and cleansed, a "book of the law" was conveniently found by the prophetess Hulda. It appears to have been a copy of Deuteronomy. Josiah feared that Judah's failure to observe God's law would bring divine wrath upon him and his country. Chapter 13 of Deuteronomy denounces idolatry as a capital crime, a view very much in line with those of Josiah. The pagan priests and prostitutes of both sexes in the Temple were

Sixteenth-century engraving of the Dutch School, showing the last kings of Judah, Manasseh (697–642 BCE), Amon (642–640 BCE), and Josiah (640–609 BCE). Musee des Beaux-Arts, Rennes, France.

executed. Josiah regarded the shrines, or high places, from Bethel in Samaria to Beer-sheba in the Negev as idolatrous. The temple at Bethel was desecrated and its priests butchered. All the outlying shrines in Judah were closed down and their priests being brought to Jerusalem where financial provision made for them. These priests of the high places were not given the equality granted them in Deuteronomy, probably due to professional jealousy by the Temple priests.

The reforms can be considered as an aspect of nationalism whereby Judah claimed its independence from Assyrian religious domination. The true faith was proclaimed again with Zion at its heart and acceptance of a new book of Holy Writ. Hezekiah's values were reasserted and this strengthened the monarchy during a time of international crisis. The prophets supported Josiah. Zephaniah and Jeremiah harked back to the values of Isaiah and the Code of Moses. God had brought Israel out of Egypt and made Israel God's chosen people. "The remnant of Israel shall not do iniquity, nor speak lies; neither shall a deceitful tongue be found in their mouth: for they shall feed and lie down, and none shall make them afraid." (Zephaniah 3: 13).

If II Kings 22–23 and II Chronicles 34–35 are to be believed, Josiah apparently ruled not only Judah but former Israelite territory such as the provinces of Megiddo and Samaria and parts of Gilead. His territories thus lay astride the Way of the Sea. At this point, international events touched upon Judah and Josiah. As Assyria collapsed, the Syrian and Levantine region became a prize to be fought over between the Babylonians and Egyptians. Pharaoh Necho II (610–595 BCE) marched north with his armies to aid the remnants of the Assyrian forces. Josiah sought to stop him at Megiddo. Josiah was defeated and killed and Judah became part of the Egyptian Empire between 609–605 BCE.

BABYLONIA

THE EVIL ASSYRIANS WERE DESTROYED AND NINEVEH FELL. BUT THEY WERE SUCCEEDED BY THE BABYLONIANS WHO RANSACKED THE TEMPLE IN JERUSALEM AND USED THE SACRED VESSELS IN THEIR FEASTS. THEY WERE OVERTHROWN BY THE MEDES AND PERSIANS, JUST AS THE WRITING ON THE WALL HAD PREDICTED.

Belshazzar's Feast as depicted by Rembrandt. The "writing on the wall" is, in this case, meaningless as Rembrandt knew no Hebrew and merely selected letters from the alphabet at random.

The Aramean Chaldeans of Babylon had never been decisively defeated by the Assyrians and were in constant rebellion. Around 630 BCE, Nabopolassar crowned himself King of Babylon, drove the Assyrians out of Uruk, and commenced rebuilding his kingdom. Canals and cities were refurbished while he trained Crown Prince Nebuchadrezzar in the skills and duties of kingship.

Elsewhere, the Medes conducted raids from their Persian stronghold, even attacking Nineveh. In 615 BCE, they conquered Arrapkha (Kirkuk) and next year utterly destroyed the former Assyrian capital of Ashur. Cyaxares, the Median King, then forged an alliance with Nabopolassar with the intent of destroying Assyria and dividing its Empire. In 612 BCE, Kalakh and Nineveh were captured. The Assyrian commander of the western empire then assumed the Assyrian kingship under the name of Ashuruballit II (611–609 BCE) and was crowned in Haran. The allied Medes and Babylonians attacked; Assyria was finally destroyed in 609 BCE. It was at this time that the prophet Nahum commented upon the fall of Nineveh: "There is no healing of thy bruise; thy wound is grievous: all that hear the bruit of thee shall clap the hands over thee: for upon whom hath not thy wickedness passed continually?" (Nahum 3: 19)

In 605 BCE, the Babylonian King Nebechadrezzar led his armies to victory over the Egyptians under Pharaoh Necho II at the Battle of Carchemish. The Babylonians then stormed through Syria and the Levant. In 605 BCE, on his father's death, the Crown Prince returned to Babylon for his coronation. The new King now had the task of pacifying his newly acquired territories. In 604 BCE, he captured Ashkelon and attempted to invade Egypt but was stopped in a long campaign. Elsewhere,

Babylon raided the Syrian Arabs and moved against a rebellious Judah in 598 BCE. Jerusalem was captured in March 597 BCE and 3,000 of its inhabitants, including King Joiakin, were deported to Mesopotamia. When Judah rebelled again in response to an Egyptian force reaching Sidon, Nebuchadrezzar reacted by besieging Jerusalem for eighteen months. The capture of the city destroyed the Kingdom of Judah and most of the population were sent into Babylonian exile.

The Babylonians and Medes remained at peace after their alliance had succeeded in its aim, Median ambitions being aimed at Lydia. They also consolidated their gains in Armenia and northern Persia. This neo-Babylonian Empire was remarkably short-lived, however, ending in 539 BCE. It had an efficient civil service but a heavy taxation system to sustain Nebuchadrezzar's armies which had to be rebuilt after one hard war against the Egyptians and the various building projects. Babylonia was redeveloped, relieving it from the poverty it had endured under harsh Assyrian rule. Trade routes were redirected through Babylon which became a large, well-designed city. The irrigation system was repaired and many minor canals were added to increase the agricultural economy which blossomed.

The Babylonian Empire commenced its decline with the death of Nebuchadrezzar. His son, Evil-Merodach ruled two years (561–560 BCE) but was murdered by his brother-in-law, Neriglissar (559–556 BCE) who campaigned by both land and sea in Cilicia. His son, Labashi-Maruk was killed and usurped by an Aramaean, Nabonidus. This enigmatic figure was a devotee of the moon-goddess, Sin, his mother being her high priestess. The priests of the local god Marduk were highly displeased. In foreign adventures, Nabobidus presided over a raid into Cilicia and the capture of Haran, his mother's city, and he allied with Astyages of the Medes against the Persians who were growing in power under their leader, King Cyrus II.

The Israelite exiles in Babylonia despised Nabonidus as did King Cyrus who deposed him. The priests of Marduk resented him for supporting Sin. For some obscure reason Nabonidus decided to reside in the oasis of Taima in Arabia, where he built a palace complex. He lived there for ten years leaving the administration of the empire to his son, Belaharusur, known as Belshazzar in the Book of Daniel. This prince refused the ritual duty of performing New Year rites associated with Marduk. The priests of Marduk promised Cyrus that they would give him Babylon without a fight if he kept their privileges. In 539 BCE, Cyrus attacked northern Babylon, fighting a battle at Opis whose inhabitants he slaughtered. Other cities then opened their gates, as did Babylon. Nabonidus surrendered and was pensioned off with a parcel of territory in Persia. The rapid and peaceful submission of Babylonia ensured its survival as a cultural unit in the new Persian Empire which was based upon patience, tolerance, and negotiation.

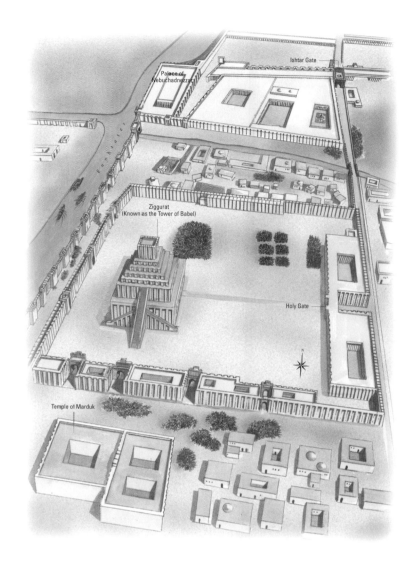

Central Babylon after its rebuilding under Nebuchadrezzar, c. 550 BCE.

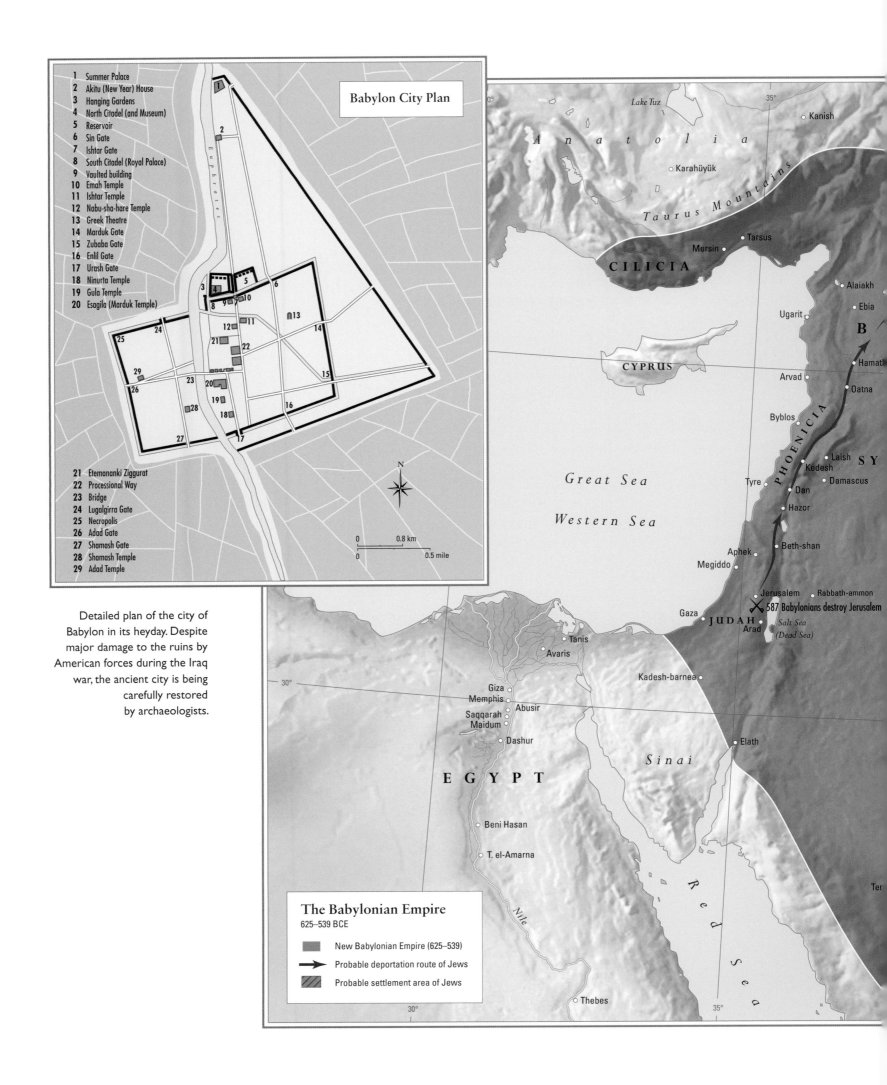

Babylon City Plan

1 Summer Palace
2 Akitu (New Year) House
3 Hanging Gardens
4 North Citadel (and Museum)
5 Reservoir
6 Sin Gate
7 Ishtar Gate
8 South Citadel (Royal Palace)
9 Vaulted building
10 Emah Temple
11 Ishtar Temple
12 Nabu-sha-hare Temple
13 Greek Theatre
14 Marduk Gate
15 Zubaba Gate
16 Enlil Gate
17 Urash Gate
18 Ninurta Temple
19 Gula Temple
20 Esagila (Marduk Temple)

21 Etemananki Ziggurat
22 Processional Way
23 Bridge
24 Lugalgirra Gate
25 Necropolis
26 Adad Gate
27 Shamash Gate
28 Shamash Temple
29 Adad Temple

Detailed plan of the city of
Babylon in its heyday. Despite
major damage to the ruins by
American forces during the Iraq
war, the ancient city is being
carefully restored
by archaeologists.

587 Babylonians destroy Jerusalem

The Babylonian Empire
625–539 BCE

◼ New Babylonian Empire (625–539)

→ Probable deportation route of Jews

▨ Probable settlement area of Jews

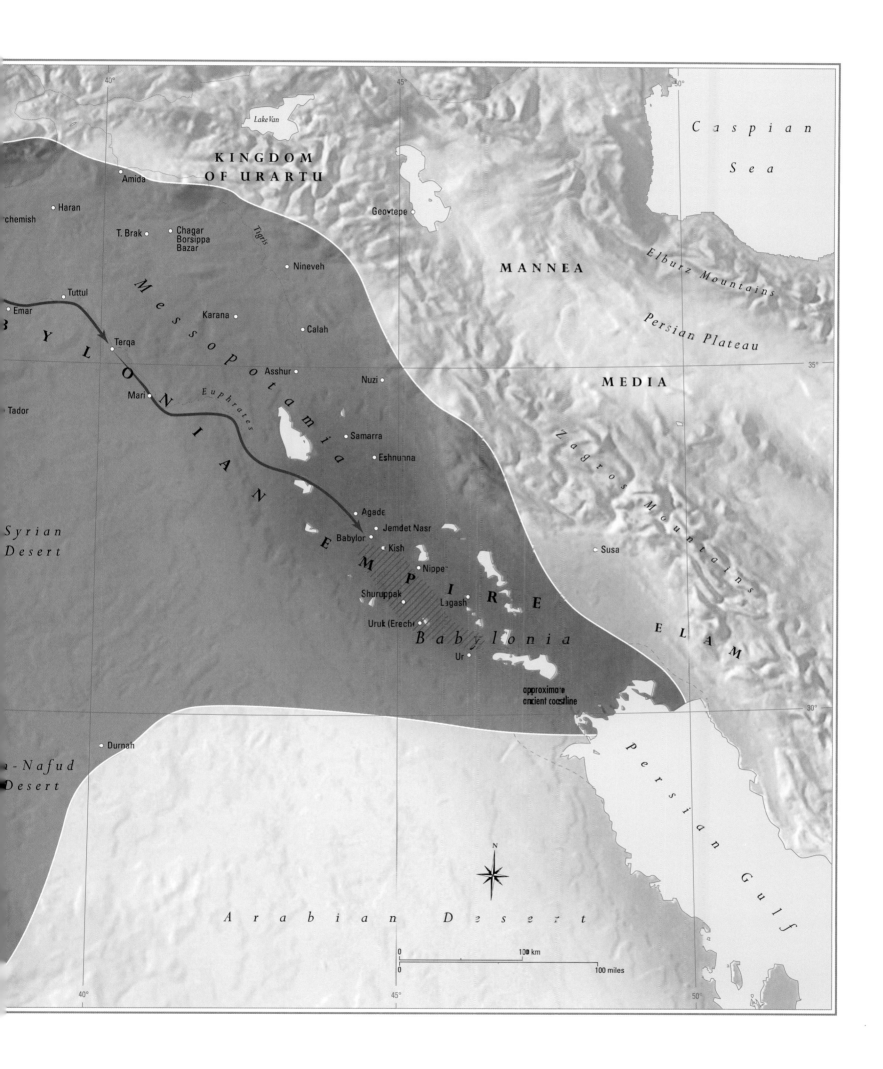

Lake Van

KINGDOM OF URARTU

Geovtepe

Caspian Sea

Amida

Haran

rchemish

T. Brak

Chagar
Borsippa
Bazar

Tigris

Nineveh

MANNEA

Elburz Mountains

Persian Plateau

Tuttul

Emar

B

A

B

Y

L

O

N

I

A

N

Karana

Terqa

M e s s o p o t a m i a

Calah

MEDIA

Tador

Mari

Euphrates

Asshur

Nuzi

35°

Samarra

Eshnunna

Z a g r o s   M o u n t a i n s

*Syrian
Desert*

E

M

P

I

R

E

Agade

Babylor

Jemdet Nasr

Kish

Nippe

Susa

E

L

A

M

Shuruppak

Lagash

Uruk (Erecht

B a b y l o n i a

Ur

approximate
ancient coastline

30°

a-Nafud
Desert

Durnah

P e r s i a n   G u l f

N

A r a b i a n   D e s e r t

0   100 km
0   100 miles

40°

45°

50°

DEPORTATION AND DESTRUCTION OF JUDAH

GEDALIAH, A JEW, GOVERNED JUDAH UNDER BABYLONIAN RULE, BUT HIS ASSASSINATION CAUSED THE DISAPPEARANCE OF JUDAH.

The main gate of the City of Babylon. The glazed brick frieze of animals, whose brilliance survives as if it were new, is typical of the later Persian decoration.

Jehoahaz succeeded to Josiah's throne but Pharaoh Necho II deposed him in favor of his brother, Jehoiakim. A heavy tribute was exacted from Judah by taxing all free citizens. In 605 BCE, Nebuchadrezzar of Babylon attacked, defeating the Egyptians at Carchemish. Hot pursuit found the retreating enemy at Hamath where they were trounced yet again. Next year, the Babylonian advance continued into Philistia where Ashkelon was destroyed. Jehoiakim switched allegiance to Babylon (603 BCE) and Judah was saved. In 601 BCE, Nebuchadrezzar fought a battle near the Egyptian border, both sides being severely damaged. The Babylonians went home to reorganise and rebuild their army. Jehoiakim chose this opportunity to rebel.

Nebuchadrezzar responded by sending Babylonian troops with guerrilla units of Arameans, Moabites, and Ammonites to raid Judah and keep Jehoiakim guessing as to Babylonian intentions. At this time Judah was experiencing a moral crisis. All of the recent religious reforms had collapsed, immorality, and corruption, and peculation were widespread. Such was the lack of respect for those who had financed the Egyptian tribute that the King enlarged his royal palace at Ramat Rachel using forced labor. The prophet Jeremiah condemned Jehoiakim inveighing against the red-painted stones used at the palace. In 598 BCE, the Babylonians marched south and Jehoiakim died, possibly assassinated for his misdeeds.

Jeremiah said of Jehoiakim, "Therefore thus sayeth the Lord concerning Jehoiakim the son of Josiah King of Judah; they shall not lament for him, saying, Ah my brother! Or, Ah sister! They shall not lament for him, saying, Ah lord, Or, Ah his glory. He shall be buried with the burial of an ass, drawn and cast forth beyond the gates of Jerusalem." (Jeremiah 22: 18–19).

Jehoiachin, the eighteen-year-old son of Jehoiakim, became king and within three months

Jerusalem had surrendered. Lachish and Debir may have been stormed at this time. The Judaean king, his mother, elders, nobles and the anti-Babylonian group of politicians were deported to Babylon, accompanied by much loot. The King's uncle, Mattaniah, was enthroned as a Babylonian puppet, taking the name of Zedekiah. Judah was shorn of some territory losing the Shephelah and the Negev. Zedekiah was a spineless character who failed to stand up to his nobles, themselves inferior to those who had been deported. In 595–94 BCE, a rebellion occurred in Babylonia and Jerusalem immediately started negotiations with Edom, Moab, Ammon, Tyre and Sidon. Some of the deported Israelites were stirred up by prophets with promise of a return to Judah. Some of these prophets were executed for treason, but reports of their activity fueled rebellion in Judah. Jeremiah denounced the lies circulating amongst the exiles and suggested they prepare for a long stay. The plot was not backed by the Egyptians and came to nought. Zedekiah sent emissaries to Nebuchadrezzar (Jeremiah 29: 3 ff) assuring him of his loyalty.

Incapable of dealing with his nobles, Zedekiah eventually came out in open revolt. Ammon might have joined in but records show that, apart from Tyre, still under siege from the last rebellion, Zedekiah received no other support, Edom supporting Babylon. Nebuchadrezzar's response was swift. The Babylonians laid siege to Jerusalem by surrounding it and then set about destroying Gibeah, Arad, Eglon, and En-Gedi. Archaeological excavations at Lachish, Beth-shemesh, Debir, Beth-Zur, and Ramat Rachel show how thorough was the destruction. The ruins at Lachish show the fury of the Babylonians. Fires were set against the walls with the heat melting the mortar between the stones which then ran down the entrance roads in streams. Jerusalem remained unbeaten but an Egyptian relief forces was stopped somewhere near Gaza.

The siege continued into 587 BCE. Jeremiah's Lamentations depict the horrors of the experience. Eventually, supplies ran out, and the Babylonians breached the walls. Zedekiah fled to Rabat-Ammon but was pursued, captured, and taken to Nebuchadrezzar at Riblah. There, he was forced to watch his sons being killed before his eyes were put out and his deportation to Babylon followed. Some leading priests, soldiers, and administrators were executed. Nebuzarandan, commander of the Babylonian King's guard, rounded up thousands for exile to Babylon leaving only the poorest to tend the vines and plow the land. Jerusalem was then torched. "This is the people who Nebuchadrezzar carried away captive: in the seventh year three thousand Jews and three and twenty: In the eighteenth year of Nebuchadrezzar he carried away captive from Jerusalem eight hundred thirty and two persons: In the three and twentieth year of Nebuchadrezzar Nebuzar-adan the captain of the guard carried away captive of the Jews seven hundred forty and five persons: all the persons were four thousand and six hundred." (Jeremiah 52: 28–30). Since only men were counted, but were accompanied by their wives and children, this number can be easily quadrupled.

Judah was organised into the provincial system of Babylonia and placed under Gedaliah, a Judean aristocrat whose father, Ahikim, had once saved Jeremiah's life and whose grandfather, Shaphan, had been Josiah's secretary. The administration center was at Mizpah. Gedaliah was murdered by Ishmael, a member of the royal house. Gedaliah's friends fled to Egypt, taking a reluctant Jeremiah with them. Judah faced a third deportation in 582 BCE and was then incorporated into the province of Samaria. Judah was no more.

EXILE AND DISPERSAL

THE WHOLE OF THE HOLY LAND WAS NOW GOVERNED BY
FOREIGN POWERS AND THIS WAS A POWERFUL INCENTIVE
FOR JEWS TO LEAVE. LARGE COMMUNITIES WERE FORMED IN
THE MEDITERRANEAN BASIN, ESPECIALLY EGYPT, AND THE
COMMUNITY LEFT BEHIND IN BABYLON ALSO FLOURISHED.

Daniel, cast into a den of lions
by the Babylonia King Darius.
This famous story is depicted in
this ninth-century Irish carving.

The period between the collapse of the kingdoms of Israel and Judah and the occupation of the Near East by the Roman Empire was marked by the gradual dispersal and forced exile of the Jews. This may have been state policy as in the case of the Assyrians and Babylonians or as the consequence of the two Jewish revolts against Rome. Jews gradually began to move out of the Holy Land, and settled around the Mediterranean, especially in the hellenized regions created by Alexander the Great, such as Cyprus, with very large communities in Egypt and Babylonia (Mesopotamia).

King Sargon II (722–705 BCE) of Assyria had destroyed the kingdom of Israel and deported much of the population which settled at Halah and on the Habor, the river of Gozan, and in the cities of the Medes. Samaria was repopulated with deportees from other parts of the Assyrian Empire—Babylon, Hamath, Syrian Sepharvaim (Sibriam), and Arabs after 716 BCE.

The Bible provides two accounts of the Judean revolt against the Babylonians, the end of Jerusalem, and the deportation of the Judeans. II Kings 24: 18 to 25: 21 and Jeremiah 52: 1–30 agree in most respects but differ as to the number of Jews sent into exile. Whatever the discrepancy in figures, large numbers were sent by Nebuchadrezzar into Babylonian exile, especially the nobles and craftsmen. The deportations may have benefited the Judeans remaining because these lower classes could occupy deportees' lands. Other Judeans fled to Moab, Edom and Ammon but some returned and placed themselves under the authority of the "puppet king" Gedaliah, the ruler appointed by the Babylonians. After the murder of Gedaliah, some Judeans fled to Egypt and they joined existing Jewish communities there. Isaiah (11: 11) refers to Judeans inhabiting various areas along the Nile and Jeremiah 44: 1 addresses Jewish communities in Egypt at Migdol, Tahpanhes (Daphnae), Memphis, and Pathros in Upper Egypt. Some Jewish soldiers and their families lived at Elephantine, guarding Egypt's southern border. Jewish mercenaries were sent to Egypt under Pharaoh Psammetichus I or II and Judean troops are mentioned as being taken to Egypt in ships in Deuteronomy 26: 68. Others settled in Egypt during the reign of the Judean King Manasseh (687–642 BCE). When the Persians seized the Babylonian Empire, state policy toward the exiles changed. Jews were allowed to return to Jerusalem to rebuild the Temple and city and the Persian province of Judah was established.

The Jews of Babylonia were an active community, codifying parts of the Bible and firming up the notion of the Law. The Diaspora really began in earnest after Alexander the Great defeated the Persian Empire (332–323 BCE). The Alexandrine Empire linked the Mediterranean and the Fertile Crescent as far as India into one political entity, imbued with Hellenistic culture and with Greek as a lingua franca. The Levant remained a theater of war, even after Alexander's death. As the Jewish population grew, there was pressure to cultivate the less fertile soil in the hills around Jerusalem. Many Jews left the Holy Land, moving to Greek cities founded by Alexander's successors while others continued the tradition of acting as mercenaries, particularly those who served the Ptolemies of Egypt. In the second century BCE, the Jewish leader, the priest Onias, was allowed to construct a temple at Leontopolis which began to rival the Temple of Jerusalem and lasted for some three centuries. In some ways, this temple competitor became a magnet for refugees from Seleucid oppression, even before the Maccabean revolt.

Jews also became engaged in long distance trade, helped by the existence of Jewish communities elsewhere in the Mediterranean. This Diaspora was augmented by Jews captured during the Judean revolts of AD 66–70 and AD 132. Jewish slaves and freemen spread around the western Mediterranean where they could be found by the third and fourth centuries CE. The numbers involved are uncertain but the Jewish philosopher, Philo of Alexandria (20 BCE–50 CE), claimed there were a million Jews in Egypt. Other evidence can be found in the New Testament, especially the Acts of the Apostles, which refers to Jews in Syria, Asia Minor and Greece. Josephus, the Jewish historian who fought the Romans in the first Jewish revolt, lived in Rome, but was in contact with Jews in Egypt and Cyrene. Evidence can be found in the Roman catacombs and the political importance of the Alexandrine Jewish community is recorded on many papyri.

The Diaspora Jews obeyed the Law, the dietary laws and the Sabbath. After the Destruction of the Temple, synagogues were built which were not only centers of prayer but seats of community administration. This autonomy was accepted by the host countries. However, the apparent independence of a closed community with its own identity often generated anti-Semitism especially amongst Alexandrine Greeks who resented Jewish attempts to become full citizens of the city while refusing to join in the city's pagan cults. Hostility flared into revolt between CE 117–119 in Egypt, Cyrene, and Cyprus after which these communities were exterminated. Josephus also recounts that, for no apparent reason, eighteen thousand Jews were slaughtered in Damascus.

BABYLONIAN EXILE

THE BABYLONIAN EXILE WAS NOT THE TERRIBLE HARDSHIP THAT THE BIBLE PORTRAYS, WHICH IS WHY SO MANY JEWS REMAINED BEHIND WHEN THEY WERE FINALLY ALLOWED TO RETURN TO JERUSALEM UNDER THE PERSIANS. THOSE LEFT IN JUDAH TURNED LARGELY TO PAGAN WORSHIP DURING THE BABYLONIAN EXILE.

Although the elite families of Judah were exiled to Babylon, a rump Israelite population remained in Samaria, Galilee, and transjordan, some of whom joined the worship of God centered on Jerusalem, though most were unaffected by Josiah's reforms. These areas had been under alien rule for 150 years and practiced a syncretic form of Judaism, according to the prophet Hosea. Many pagans had also had settled there, deported by the Assyrian kings from other parts of the empire.

The Jews who lived in Babylon must be recognised as representing not just the elite of Judah and the worship of God but the future of the faith. The exiles lived mainly in towns and cities along the irrigation channel known as the River Chebar. These waters of Babylon ran through the middle of lower Mesopotamia from Babylon to Erech, a distance of more than 100 miles. The exiles were permitted to create their own communities and allowed to farm and engage in other occupations. Some became wealthy and prospered through careers in the court and administration. Hence, the exile was not dangerous or punitive, indeed it was rather benevolent. Jews were allowed to meet and pursue some kind of community life (Ezekiel 8: 1). There is also evidence that Jehoiachin became a state pensioner and was called the King of Judah. He was later suspected of sedition, however, and imprisoned.

Jeremiah wrote from Jerusalem: "Build ye houses, and dwell in them; and plant gardens, and eat the fruit of them; Take ye wives, and beget sons and daughters; and take wives for your sons, and give your daughters to husbands, that they may bear sons and daughters; that ye may be increased there, and not diminished." (Jeremiah 29: 5–6) Indeed, Babylon might well have provided extra opportunities for Jews. Many entered commerce, benefiting from the trade routes running through Babylon.

Jeremiah and other contemporary prophets thought that the exile was God's punishment on his wayward people but they should not despair. Nevertheless, some exiles pined for Jerusalem and considered themselves in bondage, albeit with velvet chains. The famous Psalm 137 expresses the pain. "By the rivers of Babylon, there we sat down, yea we wept, when we remembered Zion. We hanged our harps upon the willows in the midst thereof. For they that carried us away captive required of us a song; and they that wasted us required of us mirth, saying, Sing us one of the songs of Zion.

"How shall we sing the Lord's song in a strange land?

If I forget thee, O Jerusalem, let my right hand forget her cunning.

If I do not remember thee, let my tongue cleave to the roof of my mouth; if I prefer not Jerusalem above my chief joy." (Psalm 137: 1–6)

The greatest danger facing the Jews was the shock suffered to their religious beliefs. Their state and cult and claimed Jerusalem as God's eternal choice of home and the Davidic dynasty of rulers which would never end. The Assyrians had destroyed that theology. Additionally, the easy life experienced in Babylon meant that many Jews forgot their homeland and merged with the local population. Jews also faced new experiences in the biggest city in the known world whose diverse cultures showed up Jerusalem as a backwater in a micro-state. For others, the Exile was a deserved punishment and a purge prior to a new beginning. To survive with their faith intact, Jews needed to preserve their identity by following a set of religious observances

The Sabbath became a test of obedience because it distinguished Jews from others, as did the ritual of circumcision. Jews ended the old ceremonial rites of religious conformity and instead strictly observed these two tests. Ritual cleanliness also became important, especially in an "unclean," pagan land. Literary activity became important; the records and traditions of the past were rewritten, rethought, and codified. The Law was explained and commented upon and the Deuteronomy stories edited. The Pentateuch provided a theological history of the world starting with the Creation and ending with the Laws handed down at Sinai, the eternal truth for the past and for the future.

Some exiles dreamed a return to Zion and the recreation of a Davidic state and this school of thought was encouraged when Evil-Merodach released Jehoiachin from prison. The prophet Ezekiel had visions of a return to the homeland (Ezekiel, 40–48) based upon the twelve tribes in a purified tribal league. The line of Zadok would preside over a theocratic state with a secular prince taking a subordinate role to the priests. Everything foreign and unclean would be excluded. The center of this renaissance was to be the Temple. Eventually, under the Medes, Ezra the Scribe was allowed to return to Jerusalem taking the Law with him.

Opposite: The modern reconstruction of the Ishtar Gate at Babylon. The gate was covered with blue enameled bricks with reliefs of dragons and bulls, a reflection of the importance of this once powerful city.

BABYLON

ALTHOUGH THE BIBLE TRIES TO PORTRAY THE TOWER OF BABEL IN A NEGATIVE LIGHT, THE MIXING OF LANGUAGES AND CULTURES WAS A POSITIVE ASPECT OF THE BABYLONIAN EMPIRE, CREATING A COSMOPOLITAN SOCIETY. THE TOWER AND THE HANGING GARDENS MUST HAVE BOTH BEEN AN IMPRESSIVE SIGHT.

Babylon became a city in the twenty-third century BCE, a provincial capital ruled by the kings of Ur. In late nineteenth century BCE, the Amorite King Sumuabum creating the first Babylonian kingdom. Babylon was developed and enlarged by his successors, especially Hammurabi who expanded the Babylonian kingdom and built the first ziggurat, a stepped pyramid. The city became a focal point for the conflicts between the Assyrian, Aramean and Chaldean peoples and was eventually destroyed by the Assyrian King Sennacherib. It was rebuilt by his son but badly damaged again by fire in 648 BCE during hostilities between the Assyrian King Ashurbanipal and his brother who ruled the client Kingdom of Babylonia.

When the Assyrian Empire fell before the onslaught of the Babylonians and their Median allies, the Chaldean leader Nabopolassar and his son Nebuchadrezzar commenced rebuilding the city. Palaces and temples were built or restored and the Processional Way, the Ishtar Gate and the ziggurat known as the Temple of Babel became important. The Ishtar Gate, the main entrance to the city, was decorated with blue enameled brick reliefs depicting bulls and dragons. Lions, too, were a favorite motif as symbols of royal power, used to decorate processional routes.

Nebuchadrezzar's palace contained more than 600 rooms whose brick walls proclaimed the King as protector of Babylonia. Decorations included gold and lapis lazuli-coated sculptures and carvings created by the most skilled cratsmen of the day. Another palace, known as the Museum Palace, contained antiquities from all parts of the Empire. Herodotus claimed that Babylon was more splendid than any other city in the known world. He stated that the outer walls were 56 miles long, 80 feet thick, and almost 330 feet high. The city was surrounded by a moat 164 feet wide. Modern archaeologists are more conservative. The moat was 39 feet wide and there were three fortified walls around the city, the outer wall being 23 feet thick. The inner wall was reinforced by towers at 59-foot intervals. The Euphrates ran through the city with 1,179 temples and shrines dispersed throughout the city, the most important, such as the Esagila temple to Marduk the dragon-god, stood on the river bank.

The city was designed on a grid pattern with roads built parallel or at right-angles to the Euphrates. The Processional Way was 69 feet wide and led from the Ishtar Gate to the ziggurat and temple of Marduk. It was constructed from stones 39-inch square, lined with red and white bricks, with drainage channels on each side. During the annual New Year festival an image of Marduk was conveyed through the city along this road, led by Nebuchadrezzar himself.

This was the home of the legendary Hanging Gardens of Babylon. A story says the Nebuchadrezzar's Median wife, Amytis, missed the trees, fragrant plants and hills of her northern homeland. According to the Greek historians Strabo and Diodorus, the gardens consisted of a series of irrigated terraces. Water was raised from the Euphrates to a holding pool on the top terrace and then gradually released downward. Archaeologists have so far failed to locate this Second Wonder of the Ancient World. The ziggurat of Etemenanki, known as the Tower of Babel, was a temple dedicated to Marduk, built on seven levels connected by stairways, so that to reach the top required one complete circuit of the ziggurat. Each level was probably a different color, an assumption based on Babylonian practice, with a temple at the top. Nebuchadrezzar recounted how the outside of the shrine was covered with blue glazed tiles and the interior had a cedar roof. The walls were lined with gold, alabaster, and lapis lazuli. A gold Marduk was seated on a golden throne. The Babylonians established a labor pool for the building projects. Clay tablets show that food supplied to workers, drawn from all parts of the empire, was sufficient for a healthy and fit life.

Babylon seen from the north, looking south, in Nebuchadrezzar's time, with the Ishtar Gate in the foreground.

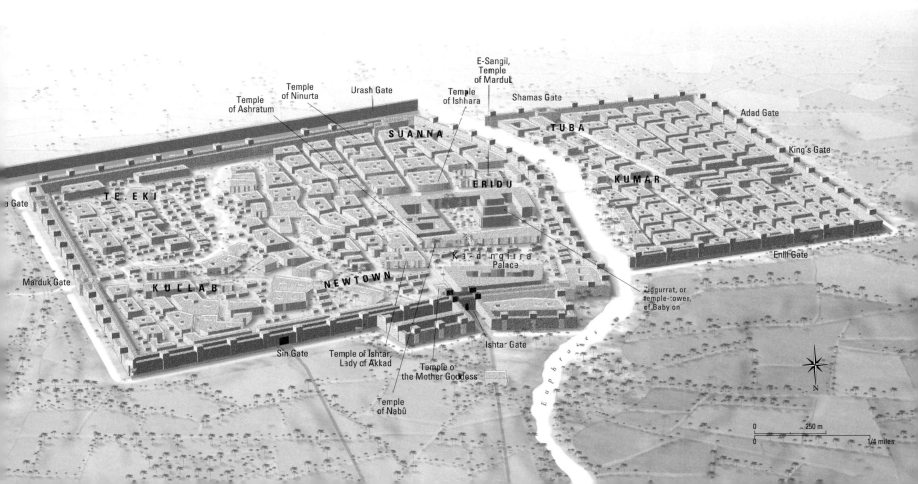

RISE OF PERSIA

ALTHOUGH CYRUS WAS DEFEATED IN BATTLE, THIS WAS AGAINST ENEMIES OUTSIDE HIS KINGDOM. HIS REIGN WAS PEACEFUL OWING TO HIS SHREWD POLICY OF TOLERANCE, ALLOWING HIS SUBJECTS TO PURSUE THEIR OWN CUSTOMS AND RELIGIONS, AS LONG AS THEY PAID HIM TRIBUTE AND SERVED IN HIS ARMY.

Relief in the Tryptilon (dining-hall) at Persepolis, depicting King Darius (c. 589–486 BCE). The site was begun by Darius and building continued under his successors.

The Persian Empire was the greatest empire that the world had yet seen. The King's authority extended from central Asia to Libya and from the western shores of the Black Sea to the River Indus, spanning the continents of Africa and Asia and for some time spreading into Europe via Thrace, as the Greeks fell under its thrall.

The Greek historian, Herodotus (c. 484–425 BCE), recorded that the Persian King Cyrus the Great ascended the throne in 559 BCE, and commenced his reign by uniting all of the tribes of Persia and southwestern Iran. He was the vassal of Astyages of Media, the Medes being another Persian people who ruled Anatolia westward to the Halys River and may also have controlled parts of Syria and northern Mesopotamia. Herodotus stated that Cyrus rebelled against his Median overlord; a battle in 550 BCE resolved the conflict when most of the Medes joined Cyrus. The Medes became close allies of the Persians to such an extent that few Greeks distinguished between these masters of the Iranian plateau.

Croesus, King of Lydia, in Asia Minor, which also controlled all the Greek cities on its coast made an alliance with Sparta, Babylon and Egypt and invaded the Persian province of Cappadocia. Cyrus responded rapidly and cleverly. When winter approached, Croesus sent his non-Lydian troops home asking them to return in spring. Cyrus continued his advance through the snow, however, and besieged Sardis, the Lydian capital. The walls were scaled and the citadel captured along with Croesus and his fabled wealth. Miletus paid tribute but Cyrus'

Median General, Harpagus, was left to mop up the Ionian Greek cities making the Persians the lords of Asia Minor.

Little is known about the years after the conquest of Lydia but it is assumed that Cyrus extended the frontiers of his kingdom to the River Indus in the east and the River Oxus in the northeast. In 539 BCE, Cyrus invaded Babylonia and slaughtered the population of Opis. Babylon then opened its gates and the Persians entered unopposed, probably supported by a priestly fifth column. Another version claims that Cyrus diverted the waters of the Euphrates and entered the city via the riverbed. Cyrus was clever enough to perform all of the royal rites associated with the god Marduk, took the Babylonian royal title, and returned all of the statues and effigies of gods that Nabonidus of Babylon had seized and locked away in Babylon. The rest of Babylonia passed swiftly into Persian hands.

Cyrus was so successful because he was a great general who could outwit his enemies as in the Lydian campaign. His troops were well-trained and their officers came from their own tribes. Unlike the Assyrians and Babylonians, Cyrus did not expect the defeated peoples to change their customs and gods in favor of the victorious nation. The conquered peoples of the Babylonian Empire were allowed to return home. Cyrus' son, Cambyses, was eventually installed in Babylon as its king. In 538 BCE, Cyrus promulgated the decree that allowed the Jews to return to Judah and rebuild their Temple. This is recorded in Ezra 1: 1–4. This enlightened rule was, in fact, a practical policy designed to prevent unrest. As long as taxes and tribute were paid, and army service performed, the people were left to their own devices. During Cyrus' reign there were no rebellions though fighting continued on the borders. Herodotus states that Cyrus was killed in a campaign against the Massagetae, who lived north of the Oxus in Central Asia and were similar to the Scythians. According to legend, their queen turned Cyrus' skull into a drinking vessel.

Cambyses II succeeded his father, apparently murdering his brother, Bardiya, to avoid any succession disputes. Although accused of being mad and brutal, Cambyses was a skillful military campaigner and continued his father's policies of tolerance. He turned his attention to Egypt which was then allied to Polycrates, tyrant of Samos. Pharaoh Amasis made extensive use of Greek mercenaries led by Phanes of Halicarnassus, who deserted to the Persians. He apparently liaised with Bedouin who supplied water to the Persians as they marched down the Way of the Sea. When Amasis died, his less capable son, Psammetichus III, was defeated at Pelusium. Egypt was conquered and organised as a Persian satrapy. The Greeks of Libya, Cyrene and Barca submitted to Cambyses as did the island of Cyprus. Cambyses failed in his attempts to capture Ethiopia or the Oasis of Ammon and dreams of a campaign against Carthage were shelved. However, another report states that Nubia was tributary to Persia under Darius I. Cambyses won Egypt partly because of Phanes' defection with the Egyptian defence plan. Polycrates joined him as did the Egyptian admiral which enabled the Persians to supply their advancing army by sea.

On Cambyses death, Darius, a member of the royal family, seized the kingship and spent the first two years quelling rebellions all over the Empire, especially in Media and Parthia. He defeated the usurper Gaumata and prevented unity amongst the rebels who tended to be on the periphery of the Empire. He then sought to expand his dominions.

In the east, Darius conquered Sind and most of the Punjab thereby bringing the Indus Valley under his control. He campaigned against the Scythians in southern Russia and acquired Thrace and a strip of land in the Balkans along the Black Sea to the Danube.

A revolt by the Ionian cities was helped by mainland Greek city states. Once the rebellion had been crushed, an expedition to Greece was planned. Many Greek states submitted but Athens and Sparta rebelled and defeated the Persians at Marathon in 490 BCE. Revenge against the Greeks had to wait until the campaigns of Darius' son, Xerxes.

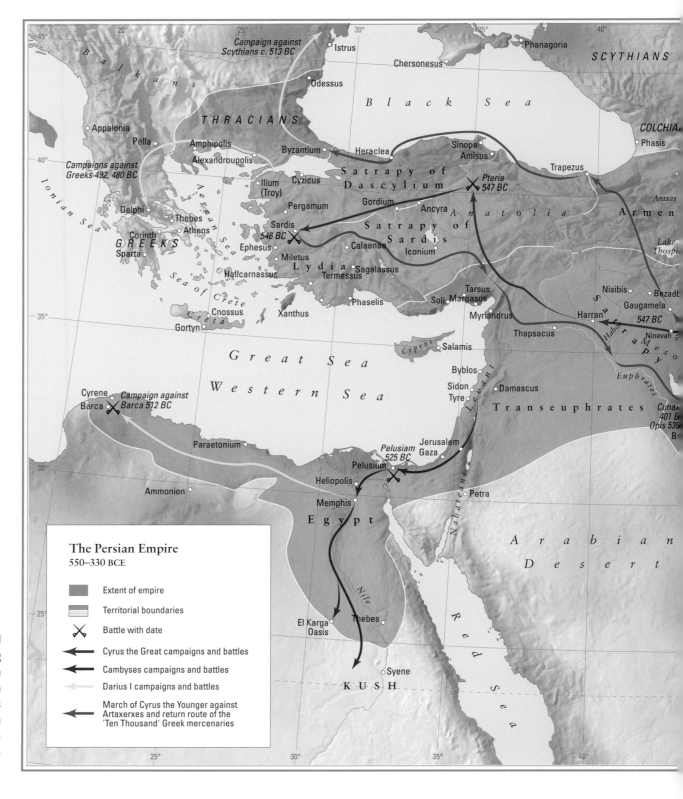

The Persian Empire expanded rapidly, eventually becoming a vast, multi-ethnic state. The Persians adopted a more benign approach to the various religions under their rule, the Jews were amongst several exiled peoples granted permission to return to their homelands.

The Persian Empire reached its zenith under Darius. The Nile and Red Sea were joined by a canal, an extensive road system linked the Empire, legal reforms were introduced and the coinage was standardised to facilitate trade. The Empire was divided into 20 satrapies, each ruled by a semi-autonomous Median or Persian nobleman. Each satrap also had a local military commander who was answerable to the King. Travelling inspectors audited the satrapies. Aramaic became the lingua franca of the Empire. The Persian religion was monotheistic. Its god was Ahura Mazda, who fought against the forces of evil for the benefit of his devotees.

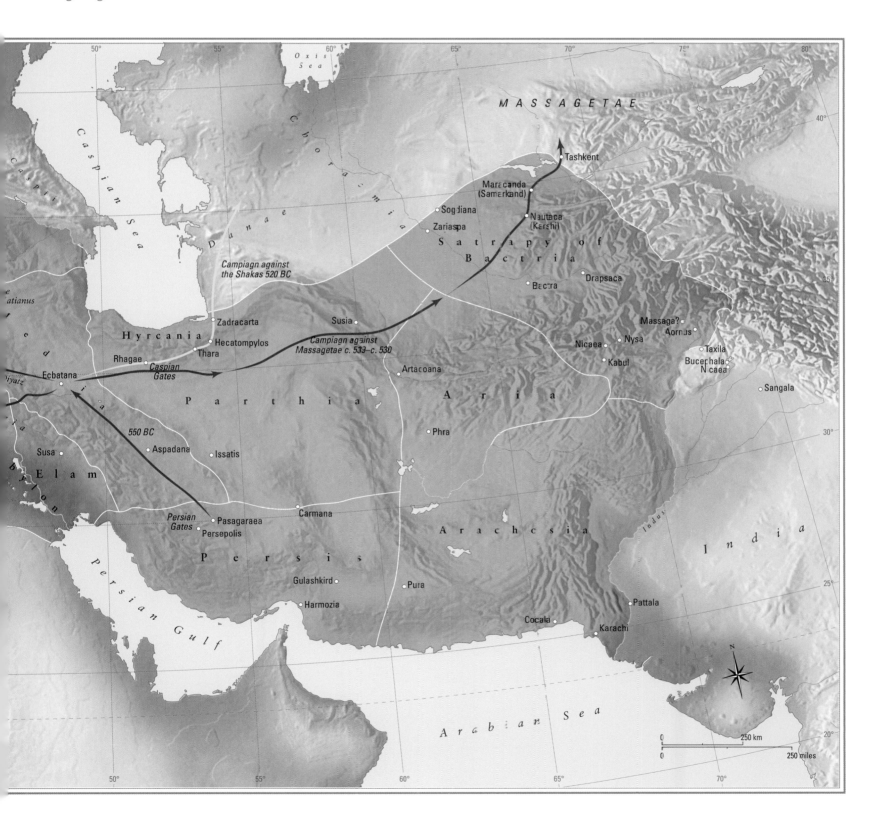

HOMECOMING

ONLY A SMALL MINORITY OF JEWS RETURNED TO JUDAH, AND THEY

FOUND CONDITIONS HARSH AND DIFFICULT. THEY MANAGED

TO BUILD A SMALL TEMPLE, NOTHING LIKE THE GRAND EDIFICE

OF KING SOLOMON'S TIME. THEY WERE DISHEARTENED AND

DISGRUNTLED, UNTIL NEHEMIAH BECAME GOVERNOR OF YAHUD.

The Jews returned to a devastated land, even the city of Jerusalem lay in ruins, it was not until Nehemiah became governor that the city was rebuilt. Above, the archeological remains of the city of David.

In 538 BCE, the Jewish exiles in Persia received an edict allowing them to return to Judah and restore the Temple. An Aramaic text of one of Cyrus' decrees states:

"In the first year of Cyrus the king the same Cyrus the king made a decree concerning the house of God at Jerusalem, Let the house be builded, the place where they offered sacrifices, and let the foundations thereof be strongly laid; the height thereof threescore cubits, and the breadth thereof threescore cubits; With three rows of great stones and a row of new timber: and let the expenses be given out of the king's house; And also let the golden and silver vessels of the house of God, which Nebuchadnezzar took forth out of the temple which is at Jerusalem and brought unto Babylon, be restored, and brought again unto the temple which is at Jerusalem, every one to his place, and place them in the house of God." (Ezra 6: 3–5)

Ezra chapter 1 states that the Jews allowed to return would be those working on the Temple and others remaining in Persia could help to finance the work. There was no decree allowing a general return of Jews to Judah. A mass movement was probably not envisaged because the Persians had not yet moved large forces into Syria and the Levant and would not do so until the campaign against Egypt. Conditions were thus not suitable for a mass return. Many Jews were happy to remain in Persia and the Books of Haggai and Zechariah do not mention large numbers of returnees. The small numbers of Jews who did return to Judah were probably joined by others over time, eager to leave Persia when Cambyses died and Babylon rose in revolt at the beginning of the reign of Darius I.

A group of exiles, led by Sheshbazzar, a prince of Judah, journeyed to Jerusalem from the

Nippur region of Babylonia. On arrival in Judah, they found the region to be impoverished and backward. Judah (Yehud) was a region within the Persian province of Abar-nahara. Evidence from Ezra and Nehemiah suggests that it extended from just north of Bethel to south of Beth-Zur and from the Jordan to just west of Emmaus and Azekah, an area of some eight hundred square miles.

Jerusalem was ruined, testament to the brutal Babylonian attack. Some poor Jews left behind at the exile remained living on the hilltops. As the new owners of the land; they resented the returnees, as did the resident Edomites forced from their own lands to create room for Arab tribes. The Samaritans also disliked the exiles, especially after

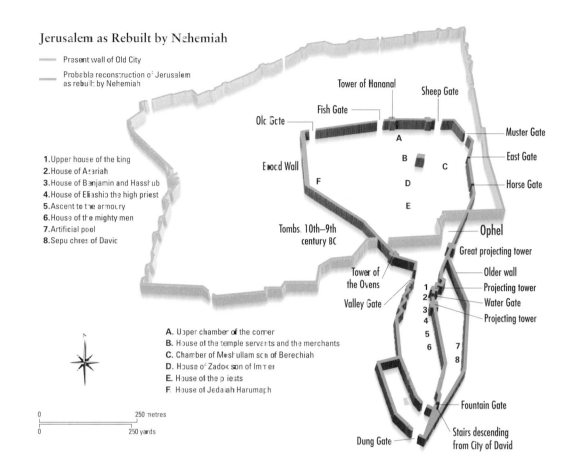

Jerusalem as Rebuilt by Nehemiah

— Present wall of Old City
— Probable reconstruction of Jerusalem as rebuilt by Nehemiah

1. Upper house of the king
2. House of Azariah
3. House of Benjamin and Hasshub
4. House of Eliashib the high priest
5. Ascent to the armoury
6. House of the mighty men
7. Artificial pool
8. Sepulchres of David

A. Upper chamber of the corner
B. House of the temple servants and the merchants
C. Chamber of Meshullam son of Berechiah
D. House of Zadok son of Immer
E. House of the priests
F. House of Jedaiah Harumaph

0 ——— 250 metres
0 ——— 250 yards

As shown in this map, Nehemiah's Jerusalem was larger than the City of David, which it covered, but smaller than the present Old City. The City was roughly the same shape during the Roman Empire which makes it easy to see how the Church of the Holy Sepulcher, marking the place of the crucifixion of Jesus, lay outside the city walls at the time.

their offer of help to rebuild the city was rejected because they were considered to be syncretistic in their faith. The exiles found life hard and crop failure left them debilitated and incapable of doing much rebuilding.

The initial returnees were given a new lease of life when a second wave of Babylonian Jews arrived in Jerusalem, led by Zerubbabel, Sheshbazzar' nephew, and Jeshua, who eventually became High Priest. Zerubbabel became the civil governor and the returnees were inspired by the arrival of the two prophets, Haggai and Zechariah. Realizing that the Babylonian Jews were resented and in potential danger, Zerubbabel decided to again fortify Jerusalem.

Tattenai, the governor of Abar-Nahara, complained to Darius about the fortifications. A search was made of the archives and Cyrus' decree found. Tattenai was told to allow the building and help it with finance from royal revenues. In 515 BCE, the Temple was re-consecrated. It was small and totally unlike the Solomonic Temple. This Second Temple was not the center of a new nation but the focus of a religious community based upon Deuteronomic Law. After the Temple was completed, the community fell apart because there was no project to unify it. Religious life deteriorated, and mixed marriages occurred. Nevertheless, the religious community existed and more Jews drifted into Judah. Tekoa, Beth-Zur and Keilah were repopulated. Jewish society in Judah was on the verge of disintegration, however. Eventually the harsh condition of the Jews in Yehud came to the notice of Nehemiah in Susa, cupbearer to the King of Persia. He asked to be allowed to go to Jerusalem and continue to rebuild its fortifications. The king consented and Nehemiah was made governor over Judah.

NEHEMIAH AND EZRA

THE CONTRIBUTIONS TO JUDAISM OF NEHEMIAH THE PROPHET AND EZRA THE SCRIBE CANNOT BE UNDERESTIMATED. THEY BROUGHT MATERIAL AND SPIRITUAL SUCCOR TO THE JEWS OF YEHUD AND HELPED SHAPE JEWISH OBSERVANCE AND THE MODERN PRACTICE OF THE RELIGION.

The walls of Jerusalem were rebuilt under the supervision of the Prophet Nehemiah. This illustration of the rebuilding comes from the John Brown Bible.

There was a total reorganisation of the Jewish community in Yehud in the fifth century BCE. This clarified its status, preserved its religious and physical identity, and re-established the observance of the Law which continues to this day. Nehemiah and Ezra were responsible for these achievements. Nehemiaht gained political status for the Jewish community and introduced administrative reforms, and Ezra systematically reorganised and reaffirmed the community's spiritual life.

Yehud was quite important to the Persian kings since its geopolitical position was astride communications and logistics lines to Egypt where a rebellion was led by Megabyzus, a Persian general who threatened the military road and its depots. A submissive Levant and Syria would prevent disorder from spreading; hence, there was a need to terminate Samaritan hostility toward the Jews. Nehemiah's mission thus served both Jewish and Persian interests.

Political conditions in Abar-Nahara, the Persian satrapy that covered the Levant, were evolving, especially trade with Greece. Phoenicia dominated the coast from Akko to Gaza, its ports, including Dor, now settled by colonies of Greek traders. Remnants of Attic pottery provide evidence of Greek imports at Akko, Gaza and Ashdod. Gaza had become a royal Persian fortress. The Arabs had infiltrated from north Arabia into Edom, the Negev and southern Syria and were to develop into the important trading community known as the Nabateans. The evicted Edomites established themselve in Yehud, in the desert south of Beersheba and Hebro and became known to the Romans as Idumeans. Transjordan was administered by Tobiah, Governor of Ammon; he had family connections with the High Priest in Jerusalem. Samaria, under Governor Sanballat was angry that Judah had been sculpted out of Samaria and given to Nehemiah. When Nehemiah arrived in Yehud, he found a despondent and divided people with Samaritans and Jews at loggerheads, each believing they worshipped the one true God.

Nehemiah decided that the walls should be constructed immediately. Labour was levied from all Yehud, each group of builders being given a section of wall to finish. However, the build was hindered by Tobiah, Sanballat, and Geshem, the Arab leader of the desert peoples. The first two men used their friends and relations in Jerusalem to delay the construction. Arabs, Ammonites and Ashdodites terrorized Jewish villages, and Josephus, the historian, claims many Jews were killed. In response, Nehemiah split his labor gangs in two; one group was armed with spears, shields, bows and coats of mail, mounting guard in shifts while the others worked with swords belted at their waists. Jews were attracted to Jerusalem from the countryside to secure the city and themselves. Evidently, the walls were raised in fifty-two days but all the architectural buttressing, revetments, battlements and other elements took another two years and four months to complete. Once Nehemiah had completed his mission, he returned to Susa after twelve years but managed to gain another term governing Yehud.

Ezra the Scribe was commanded by Artaxerxes I to restore Jewish law. His most important contribution was the codification of the first four books of the Bible. These, together with Deuteronomy, make up the Torah, the Five Books of Moses.

Nehemiah's second term in office witnessed: a series of uncoordinated religious reforms. He had to find funding for the Temple and its priests through the exaction of tithes; he enforced Sabbath observance; and he opposed mixed marriages, even to the extent of assaulting offenders. To prevent trading on the Sabbath, he decreed the city gates closed on that day, and when he saw market stalls erected outside the gates, he threatened the stall-holders with arrest. He was infuriated to find children of mixed marriages who were incapable of speaking Hebrew. When he learned that a grandson of High Priest Eliashib had married the daughter of Sanballat, the Samaritan, he drove him from the land. Nehemiah failed to establish a lasting religious policy. but he saved the Jewish community of Yehud, built an honest administration, kept the Temple running and provided political stability and physical security, all this in the face of considerable opposition.

The Scribe, Ezra, secured royal authority over religious affairs in Abar-Nahara. He rode to Jerusalem carrying donations from Babylonian Jews, gold from the king, and the Scrolls of the Law which he was determined to enforce. A virtual religious sheriff, Ezra had the right to force all Jews to order their affairs in accordance with the Law. This Law was read out in public in several languages. His deputies helped him but Ezra's main concern was mixed marriages where Jewishness could be lost and the religious community diminished in numbers.

Ezra confessed the congregation's sins before the Temple and his people acknowledged their misdeeds. A voluntary covenant was made by which men divorced their foreign wives and their children were put aside. A commission was established to investigate marriages and after a three-month session all mixed marriages were dissolved. (Ezra 10: 14–44)

Ezra's rule was of outstanding importance. If Moses had founded Israel, Ezra reconstituted the people of Israel and restored their faith to the Jews in a form that would survive throughout the ages. Ezra the Scribe aided the Jews in defining their identity based upon the Law as a religious constitution.

ALEXANDER THE GREAT

WHEN THE PRIESTS FEARED THAT ALEXANDER THE GREAT WOULD ATTACK THE TEMPLE, THEY CAME OUT TO MEET HIM. ACCORDING TO THE STORY, HE DISMOUNTED AND BOWED TO THEM, AN ACTION UNHEARD OF FOR THE GREAT CONQUEROR. TO THIS DAY, ALEXANDER IS A FAVOURITE JEWISH FORENAME.

Alexander the Great ascended the throne of Macedonia after his father's murder in 336 BCE. He immediately executed all those accused of his father's assassination, together with any possible rivals and opponents. He was utterly ruthless, not a trait expected in a pupil of Aristotle. He embarked on a series of conquests, advancing to the Danube to kill and burn out the Getae, then crushing an Illyrian invasion and moving south to stamp out revolts in Thebes, Athens, Arcadia, Elis and Aetolia. Thebes was razed to the ground, with thousands being killed, and the rest sold into slavery. The other rebels submitted and accepted Macedonian garrisons.

In 334 BCE, leaving Antipater behind as governor in Greece, Alexander crossed the Hellespont with 35,000 infantry, 5,000 cavalry and 160 ships in support. Memnon of Rhodes, commander of Darius' Greek mercenaries, wanted to retreat using a scorched earth policy but the satraps intended to preserve their provinces and forced him to face Alexander at the River Grannicus. Alexander attacked the mercenaries and Persians, defeating them with few Macedonian losses. He refused to take on the Persian fleet, however, and decided to defeat it by occupying all coastal ports and cities in the Persian Empire. Therefore, after conquering Lycian and Pisian hill tribes in western Asia Minor, he advanced southward and soon met Darius and the main Persian army which moved onto the plain at Issus in northeastern Syria (333 BCE). Macedonian pikemen drove a hole through the Persian forces who were savaged by Alexander's cavalry. Darius offered Alexander 10,000 talents of gold and all his lands west of the Euphrates if he stopped fighting but Alexander wanted unconditional surrender.

Alexander captured Darius' family who were treated with respect, and then progressed south to Syria and Phoenicia. Only Tyre refused to submit and was captured after a seven-month siege. Egypt was the next target and its submission ensured strategic control of the eastern Mediterranean coastline. The city of Alexandria was founded at the mouth of the Nile and became a major trading center and place of learning. The campaign moved north to attack Babylon. After crossing the Tigris and Euphrates, Alexander fought Darius at Gaugamela (331 BCE) and, victorious, advanced to Arbela where he took much Persian treasure. Babylonia and Susa surrendered but Persepolis resisted and was burned down, either for resisting or as revenge for the burning of the Acropolis in 480 BCE.

Darius was pursued into Media where he was murdered by the satrap Bessus. Alexander could now legitimately claim to be the Great King, only needing the satraps' submission. His empire extended beyond the Caspian Sea to the Oxus (Afghanistan and Baluchistan) and northward to Bactria and Sogdiana. Alexander decided to conquer the rest of the Persian Empire and crossed the Indus to capture the Punjabi Kingdom of Porus on the Hydaspes. His troops now refused to go any further, so Alexander followed the Indus to the sea, arriving back in Babylon in 323 BCE, where he died of fever in the summer of that year. Alexander had acquired a great Empire but failed entirely to organise it or provide for its future after he died.

Alexander the Great inherited Macedonia and its Greek possessions from his father Philip II. Through his own determination and military talent, he extended this inheritance from northern Greece to the River Indus.

Alexander founded twenty-five cities, thus spreading Hellenistic influence. Simultaneously, Alexander had began to adopt Persian dress and married the Sogdian noblewoman, Roxana. He became convinced of his own divinity and ordered the Greek states of the Hellenic League to recognise him as the son of Zeus Ammon. Upon his death, Alexander's generals wished to make the posthumous child of Alexander and Roxana king but the soldiery preferred the Macedonian half-wit Philip III Arrhidaeus, son of Philip II. When Alexander IV was born to Roxana, a joint rule was created under a regency, Roxana and her son being protected by Alexander's mother Olympias. Cassander, Antipater's son eventually murdered Olympias, Roxana, Alexander IV and Philip III Arrhidaeus. The sprawling Empire disintegrated.

Alexander's death caused his generals to wage war against each other. The northwest provinces broke free but retained some Greek influence. Antigonus, the most powerful general, initially seized power but was challenged by his most determined rival, Seleucus I. After twenty years of fighting, Seleucus acquired the lion's share of the Empire.

The most successful general was probably Ptolemy who seized and ruled Egypt, founding a dynasty administered by Greeks and Macedonians. Cleopatra, the last of the dynasty, was reputedly the first to learn the Egyptian language. In 276 BCE, Antigonus Gonatus founded a dynasty in Macedonia. which lasted until Macedonia was conquered by Rome in 168 BCE.

The Seleucid Empire was the largest successor state, reaching its zenith under Antiochus III who seized Armenia and invaded Parthia which had grown into a realm of the nomadic Parni under Arsaces I. He then made an alliance with the Greco-Bactrian state created by Diodotus I. Eventually, he controlled southern Asia Minor, Syria and all points south to Egypt though there

Alexander the Great on his restless campaign of conquest destroyed the Persian Empire and established Greek civilization to the bounds of the known world.

were some territorial exchanges with Egypt due to continued hostilities. Antiochus III meddled in Macedonian affairs and came into conflict with Rome. His fleet was defeated at Myonnesus (190 BCE), while he and his army were beaten at Magnesia (190 BCE) in Asia Minor. The resultant Peace of Apameia forced Antiochus to hand over Asia Minor west of the Taurus Mountains. The land was

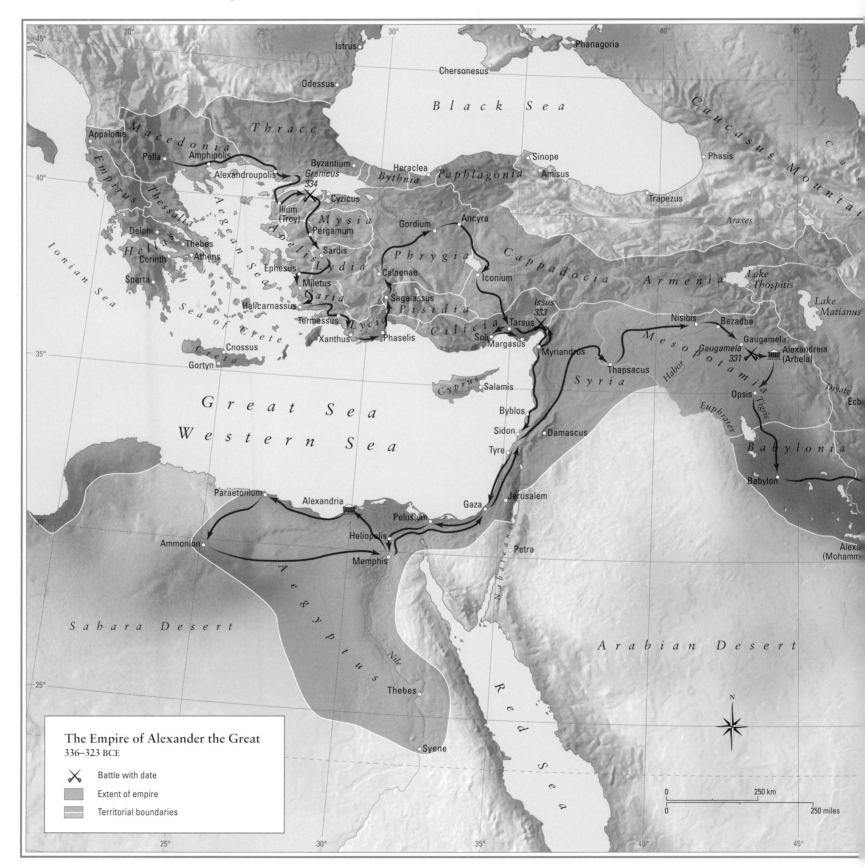

The Empire of Alexander the Great
336–323 BCE

✕   Battle with date

    Extent of empire

    Territorial boundaries

divided between Rhodes and Pergamon. When Antiochus died, the Seleucid state was weakened by wars against Egypt and Parthia. At this time, the Jews under Judas Maccabeus rebelled and created the Hasmonean state that was eventually annexed by Rome. In 64 BCE, Pompey the Roman made Syria, the Seleucid rump, into a Roman province.

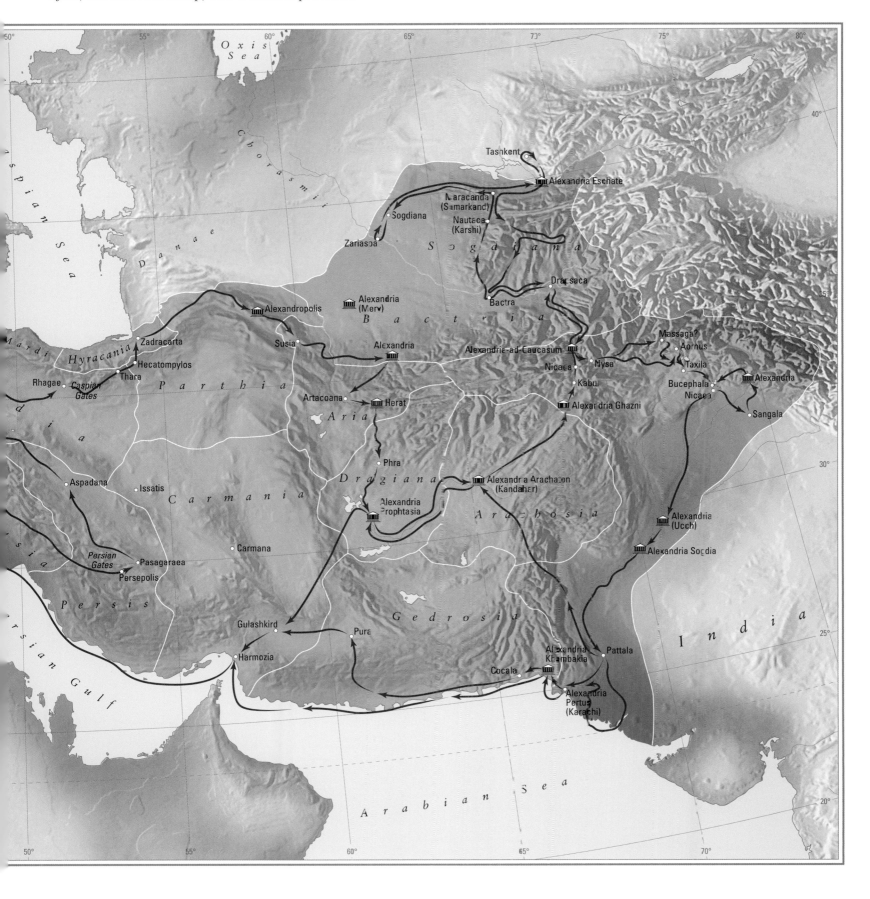

The Seleucid Boot

THE SELEUCIDS WERE TOTALLY UNLIKE ALEXANDER AND HIS PREDECESSORS THE PERSIANS, IN THAT THEY WERE TOTALLY INTOLERANT OF OTHER RELIGIONS, PARTICULARLY ANTIOCHUS IV WHO CONSIDERED HIMSELF A GOD, AND INSISTED THAT HIS SUBJECTS WORSHIP HIM.

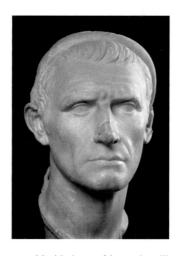

Marble bust of Antiochus III (223–187 BCE) replica of an original from the third century BCE. Louvre, Museum, Paris.

Under the Ptolemies, the Jews enjoyed considerable religious freedom. They had had an established presence in Egypt since the fall of Israel and Judah. A number of books of the Bible reached their final drafts during this period when Jewish scholarship flourished. Unfortunately, hostilities between the Egyptian and Seleucid empires led Antiochus III (223–187 BCE) to vanquish the Ptolemies at the battle of Paneoin. The Seleucid border was now pushed south of Raphah in a slightly crooked line to reach the Dead Sea, The Jews now had to deal with a new ruler who was utterly ignorant of religious toleration and demanded sacrifice to himself as god.

Antiochus dreamt of recreating the former Alexandrine Empire. He pursued territorial ambitions in Macedonia but was suddenly faced by Rome which trounced him militarily at Magnesia in 190 BCE in western Asia Minor with a naval defeat following at Myonnesus the same year. The peace terms included the payment of an indemnity for twelve years and the loss of Asia Minor. This apparent Seleucid weakness caused Armenia and Bactria to claim independence. Hostages were taken including a Seleucid son who later became Antiochus IV. Seleucid support of Hannibal aroused hostility from Rome. Seleucid dreams were now blocked in the West so the Seleucids sought expansion elsewhere but could not finance such adventures. The Syrian monarch needed cash for the Roman indemnity and to pay for his mercenary troops and he attempted to raise money by looting wealthy temples. His son and successor, Seleucis IV (187–175 BCE) attempted to claim the wealth of the Jewish Temple in Jerusalem as property of the state but failed. The former hostage, his brother, Antiochus (175–164 BCE) heightened Jewish and Hellene antipathy by using violence as a political tool.

Antiochus IV (known as Antiochus Epiphanes ("the godhead"), which his enemies distorted into

Antiochus Epimanes ("the mad") wanted a uniform, conformist empire and sought to eradicate any non-Hellene and therefore rebellious faith, including Judaism. The Seleucids wanted to spread and consolidate Hellenism and Judah was an enclave of religious dissent. In 174 BCE, Antiochus deposed the High Priest, Onias, replacing him with Jason, one of his brothers. This new High Priest commenced building a gymnasium, an icon of hellenization. Jews began to adopt Greek dress and the broad-brimmed hat, the petasos, the headgear of Hermes, the god of the gymnasium. Jews were forced to use this institution where all went naked, so they could not hide their circumcision and were punished for it. Some Jewish men had operations to reverse circumcision but nakedness revealed their apostasy. Short Greek tunics were equally reviled, as they left the legs bare. The Greek obsession with the perfection of the human body and its physique was a totally new concept to Jewish thought.

"Now such was the height of Greek fashions, and increase of heathenish manners, through the exceeding profaneness of Jason, that ungodly wretch, and no high priest; That the priests had no courage to serve anymore at the altar, but despising the temple, and neglecting the sacrifices, hastened to be partakers of the unlawful allowance in the place of exercise, after the game of Discus called them forth: Not setting by the honors of their fathers, but liking the glory of the Grecians best of all." (II Maccabees 4: 13–15).

The Jews considered Hellenism to be a type of pantheism, a continuation of Canaanite religion with Antiochus as the new Baal embodying Canaanite god-qualities of hate, lust, anger, greed and envy. The Greek worldview was in total opposition to that of Israel, the requirement to building a structured society that was ruled by God's law, love and justice, not by greed and aggression. Jason confined himself to cultural affairs, but Antiochus deposed him in favor of Menelaus thereby generating confusion and conflict between the supporters of three High Priests—Onias, Jason, and Menelaus.

Antiochus began to indulge in new foreign policy fantasies believing that Rome in the West and Parthia in the East were neither obstacles nor a threat. In 174 BCE, he campaigned against Egypt and despite early successes was compelled to retreat when a Roman fleet arrived unexpectedly in the Nile Delta. His prestige damaged, Antiochus turned against Judah in a fit of pique. Jason deposed Menelaus but the Seleucid monarch reversed this action and robbed the Temple's treasures, looted and burned parts of Jerusalem, and established a citadel, the Accra, on a hill overlooking the Temple (167 BCE), as a symbol of Seleucid domination. Antiochus then attempted to enforce Hellenism upon Judah. The Temple at Jerusalem was consecrated to Olympian Zeus and the Samaritan sanctuary of Mount Gerizim was dedicated to Zeus.

Temple sacrifices were banned, Sabbath observance and circumcision were prohibited upon pain of death. Pagan altars were erected throughout Judah and unclean animals sacrificed on them. Jews were forced to eat pork or be killed. Opposition came from the scribes in particular, one of whom, Eleazar, preferring death to desecration, became an example to all Judah with his love of the faith (II Maccabees 6: 18–19).

"Now the fifteenth day of the month of Casleu, in the hundred forty and fifth year, they set up the abomination of desolation upon the altar, and builded idols throughout the cities of Juda on every side; and burned incense at the doors of their houses, and in the streets. And when they had rent in pieces the books of the law which they found, they burned them with fire... They put to death certain women, that had caused their children to be circumcised. And they hanged the infants about their necks, and rifled their houses, and slew them that had circumcized them." (I Maccabees 1: 54–56; 60–61).

THE MACCABEAN REBELLION

THE TRIUMPH OF THE MACCABEES AND REDEDICATION OF THE TEMPLE AFTER ITS DESECRATION BY THE SELEUCIDS IS MARKED BY THE ONLY JEWISH FESTIVAL, HANNUKAH, THAT IS NOT BASED ON A BIBLICAL EVENT.

Judas Maccabeus rededicates the altar of the Temple, following his defeat of the Syrians and occupation of Jerusalem in 164 BCE. The Hasmoneans, whom Maccabeus led, were at the forefront of Jewish resistance to Seleucid occupation.

The inevitable Jewish rebellion broke out in the town of Modi'in in the center of Israel, when a Syrian official and a Jew made to offer a sacrifice on a pagan altar. This apostasy so incensed Mattathias, of a priestly line that he killed the Syrian and the apostate, and fled with his five sons into the Judean wilderness, where they could survive attacks mounted by Seleucid forces occupying the urban centers on the plains. Guerrilla warfare began against the Syrians and Hellenised Jews.

More and more Jews fled into the hills including many of the sages. Some of the rebels were pursued into this rough terrain, but being caught on the Sabbath did not resist, and some one thousand died. This uncompromising adherence to the Law was not practical militarily. The Jews reconsidered the Law and decided that they were able to defend themselves on the Sabbath. "At that time therefore they decreed, saying, Whosoever shall come to make battle with us on the sabbath day, we will fight against him; neither will we die all, as our brethren that were murdered in the secret places." (I Maccabees 1: 41)

In 166 BCE, Mattathias died and his son, Judas, known as Maccabeus ("the hammer") assumed the leadership of the revolt, his family becoming known as the Maccabees. Judas' military campaigns lasted for six years. At this time, most of the Seleucid forces were busy quelling the Parthians or guarding borders against possible Roman incursions and consequently saw the Judean revolt as a mere local affair of little significance. Judas waged guerrilla warfare with night attacks on towns and cities, killing and driving out Seleucid troops, executing apostates and traitors, while destroying pagan altars. His successes caused his band of guerrillas to grow into a small army. Appollonius, the Seleucid governor of Samaria, attacked Judas' army but was defeated and killed, his sword being used by Judas afterwards. Victory brought loot, captured weapons and recruits. This pushed Seron, the governor of Coele-Syria, to march against Judas with an army that included many hellenised Jewish traitors. Judas won battles at Beth-Horon, where Seron and eight hundred of his men were killed, Mizpah and, Beth-Zur. Learning of these defeats Apollonius divided his forces rather than engaging Parthia and gave half his troops to Lysias, his chief minister, to quel Judah. "Moreover, he delivered unto him the half of his forces, and the elephants, and gave him charge of all things that he would have done, as also concerning them that dwelt in Juda and Jerusalem: To wit, that he should send an army against them, to destroy and root out the strength of Israel, and the remnant of Jerusalem, and to take away their memorial from that place; And that he should place strangers in all their quarters, and divide their land by lot." (I Maccabees 1: 34–36)

Lysias despatched Ptolemy, Nicanor and Gorgias with some forty thousand infantry, seven thousand cavalry, and war elephants into Judah, where they pitched camp near Emmaus. Even traders joined the camp, expecting to buy Jewish prisoners of war as slaves. Judas and his brothers masssed their forces at Mizpah, prayed, and marched against the Seleucids. Meanwhile, Gorgias led a night column of five thousand infantry and one thousand cavalry hoping to surprise the Jewish camp, but found no-one there.

At dawn, Judas attacked Emmaus with three thousand men, defeated the Syrians, plundered their camp, and burned it. When Gorgias returned, seeing the smoke and the Jews in battle array, he fled to Philistia, leaving Judas to complete his looting. Next year Lysias assembled sixty thousand infantry and five thousand cavalry and marched into Idumea, camping at Beth-Zur. The Judean army of ten thousand men under Judas attacked the Seleucids and killed five thousand of them, leaving Lysias to retreat to Antioch where he planned a new mercenary army to campaign next year. The road to Jerusalem was now clear, allowing Judas to find priests to purify and rededicate the Temple (164 BCE). This Temple cleansing is celebrated by the Feast of Hanukkah when candles are lit. Mount Zion was fortified, as was Beth-Zur, but the Seleucid Accra in Jerusalem was not captured.

Judah was now blessed with a two-year period of peace and Judas used this respite from Syrian attack to combat the tribes that were persecuting Jewish minorities as a response to the re-dedication of the Temple. The Idumeans were attacked at Acrabatene, as were the Ammonites in transjordan. Simon, Judas' brother, campaigned in Galilee, while Judas and his brother Jonathan marched through in Gilead. The Jewish minorities were transported to Judah thereby increasing its population and the strength of the Maccabean army.

In 164 BCE, Antiochus IV died, leaving a minor, Antiochus V, under the vice-regency of Lysias. The latter invaded Judea, stormed Beth-Zur, defeated Judas at Beth-Zechariah, and forced the Jews back to Jerusalem. One Maccabee brother, Eleazar, was trampled to death by an elephant he killed. The Jews sued for peace which Lysias was forced to grant owing to murderous strife amongst the Seleucid royal family. The Jews were granted religious freedom but the Temple fortifications had been destroyed. The peace did not last long. Alcinus, a renegade leader of the Hellenised Jews, journeyed to Antioch to meet the new Seleucid king, Demetrius I (162–150 BCE) and offer him allegiance.

Gerasa was one of the numerous Hellenistic cities founded in Palestine. It was a member of a group of self-governing cities in the Decapolis. It was these Greek foundations that increasingly influenced many in Jewish society.

Opposite: The Seleucid rulers of Palestine promoted their own Greek culture and religion at the expense of others. This would prove too much for many Jews.

General Bacchides was sent with a large Syrian army to Judea to protect Alcinus and capture the Maccabee brothers. Alcinus killed many Jews and rebellion flared again. A large Syrian army, led by Nicanor, was defeated in a great victory at Beth-Horon. Nevertheless, many Jews despaired at the constant Syrian attacks and deserted Judas who fought his final battle with his remaining eight hundred men at Elasa against Bacchides. Judas managed to put the enemy right-wing to flight but fell in battle. Jonathan and Simon Maccabee buried him secretly at the family sepulcher at Modi'in. "Moreover they bewailed him, and all Israel made great lamentation for him, and mourned many days, saying, How is the valiant man fallen, that delivered Israel!" (I Maccabees 9: 20–21)

In 159 BCE, Alcinus died, thus weakening the hellenised faction of the Jews. The Seleucid kingship was disputed by two factions, both claimants seeking support from Jonathan, acknowledging him as leader of all of the Jews and appointing him High Priest. Jonathan and Simon strengthened their position, ostensibly while supporting one contender, Alexander Balas. Beth-Zur and Joppa were given Jewish garrisons and Gaza was captured. The other Syrian contender, Demetrius II, was defeated near the Sea of Galilee. Jonathan commenced re-fortifying Jerusalem and other Judean fortresses. Trypho, Balas' guardian, feared the growing independence of the Jews, especially with their new port at Joppa. He managed to capture Jonathan and his sons at Ptolemais and murdered them. Simon took on the Jewish leadership, finished fortifying Jerusalem, seized and fortified Gazara, and captured the Accra in Jerusalem. Judea was virtually independent but the recent victories had been fought by mercenaries, rather than Jewish soldiery. Simon re-established relations with Rome (1 Maccabees 12: 17–32) and Sparta (1 Maccabees 12: 5–23), and negotiated away the tribute owing to Demetrius II.

Simon began rebuilding the Jewish state. The Accra was strengthened, becoming Simon's home and his son, Johanan, became commander of the Judean forces. Agriculture and trade flourished again. The links with Rome and Sparta were renewed. Simon remained ruler and High Priest. The Jews were now sovereign in both religion and politics.

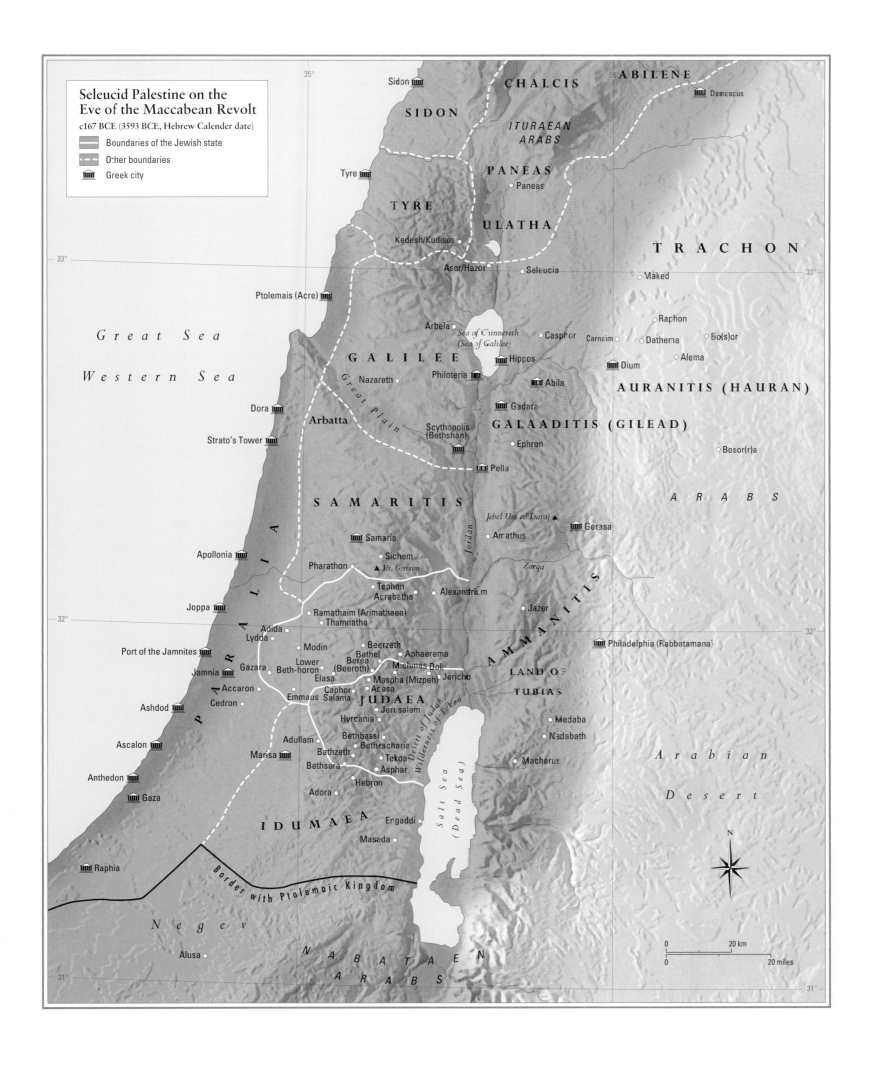

Seleucid Palestine on the
Eve of the Maccabean Revolt

c167 BCE (3593 BCE, Hebrew Calender date)

Boundaries of the Jewish state
Other boundaries
Greek city

CHALCIS

ABILENE

Sidon

Damascus

SIDON

ITURAEAN
ARABS

Tyre

PANEAS

Paneas

TYRE

ULATHA

Kedesh/Kudisos

TRACHON

Asor/Hazor

Seleucia

Maked

Ptolemais (Acre)

Arbela

Sea of Chinnereth
(Sea of Galilee)

Casphor

Carnaim

Raphon

Dathema

Bo(s)or

Great Sea

GALILEE

Nazareth

Philoteria

Hippos

Abila

Alema

Western Sea

Dora

Arbatta

Gadara

AURANITIS (HAURAN)

GALAADITIS (GILEAD)

Strato's Tower

Scythopolis
(Bethshan)

Ephron

Bosor(r)a

Pella

Jebel Um ed Daraj ▲

SAMARITIS

Gerasa

ARABS

Samaria

Arrathus

Apollonia

Sichem

▲ Mt. Gerizim

Zarqa

Jordan

Pharathon

Tephon
Acrabatha

Alexandrium

Jazer

Joppa

Ramathaim (Arimathaea)

Thamnatha

AMMANITIS

Adida

Lydda

Modin

Beerzeth

Bethel

Aphaerema

Philadelphia (Rabbatamana)

Port of the Jamnites

Berea
(Beeroth)

Michmas

Dok

Jamnia

Gazara

Lower
Beth-horon

Maspha (Mizpeh)

Jericho

LAND OF
TUBIAS

Accaron

Elasa

Caphor
Salama

Acesa

Emmaus

JUDAEA

Cedron

Jerusalem

Ashdod

Hyrcania

Medaba

Ascalon

Adullam

Bethbassi

Bethzacharia

Nadabath

Marisa

Bathzeth

Tekoa

Desert of Judah
Wilderness of Tekoa

Anthedon

Bethsura

Asphar

Macherus

Arabian

Gaza

Hebron

Adora

Salt Sea
(Dead Sea)

Desert

IDUMAEA

Ergaddi

Masada

Raphia

Border with Ptolemaic Kingdom

Negev

Alusa

NABATAEN
ARABS

N

0   20 km
0   20 miles

THE HASMONEANS

DESPITE BEING THE DESCENDANTS OF THE VALIANT MACCABEES, THE HASMONEANS WERE UNWORTHY AND UNSUITABLE MONARCHS, DISPLAYING MENTAL INSTABILITY, EXTRAVAGANCE AND DISREGARD FOR THEIR SUBJECTS. THE FORCIBLE CONVERSION TO JUDAISM OF SUBJECT PEOPLES SOWED THE SEEDS OF THE JUDAEA'S DOWNFALL.

Gold earring from the Hasmonean Period found in the excavations in the City of David, just south of the present city walls of Jerusalem.

The ruling family of the Maccabee line were known as the Hasmoneans. After Simon the Maccabee was murdered with two of his sons, his third son, John Hyrcanus (134–104 BCE), moved to Jerusalem where he was acknowledged as Simon's successor. Rome's interference stopped the murderer, Abubus, Simon's son-in-law, from seizing Jerusalem with Syrian allies. John eventually raised a large army and surprisingly helped the Seleucid Antiochus VII in a campaign against Parthia in a plan to regain Mesopotamia. The Seleucids were defeated. John repudiated any allegiance to the Seleucids and rebuilt Jerusalem's walls that Antiochus had reduced in the recent siege. John strengthened his position by renewing the treaty of friendship with Rome. After 129 BCE, John Hyrcanus ruled the independent state of Judaea, as shown in the coins of the period.

John implemented a series of attacks against weaker neighbours in order to expand his territories. Samaria and Shechem were key targets. These fortresses contained Samaritan worshippers who made sacrifices at a temple on Mount Gezerim. This Samaritan temple cult was an abomination to the priests in Jerusalem and both cities were destroyed. Galilee, inhabited by Aramaic-speaking pagans, was captured and Hyrcanus forcibly Judaised these Ituraeans including circumcision of all males. The same brutal fate was meted out to the inhabitants of Idumaea (Edom). A further conquest was the settlement at Medeba, east of the Dead Sea, threatening Nabatean trade routes to the north. The cities of the northern frontier—Pella, Dion, Gadera and Hippos, all east of the Jordan—joined in a league with Philadelphia and Gerasa, known as the Decapolis (Greek for "ten cities"). These Greek cities were not forcibly converted to Judaism but paid tribute to Judaea. The

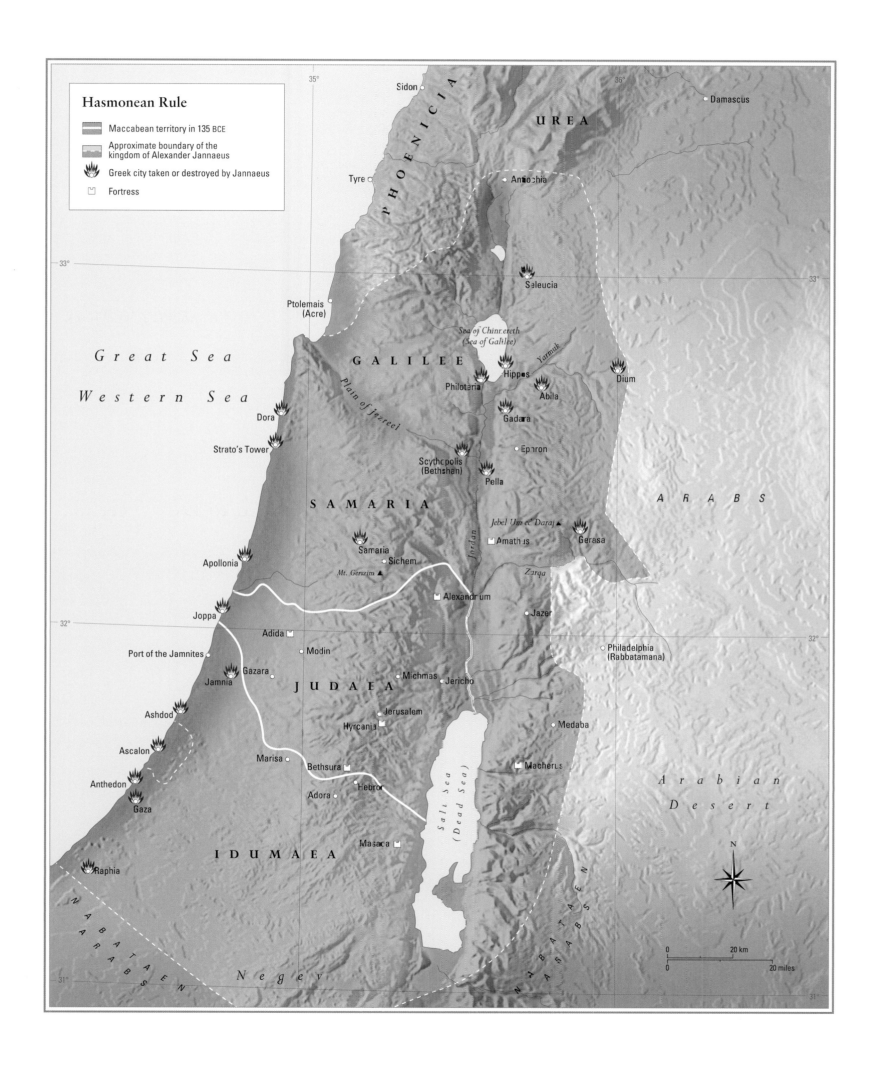

Hasmonean Rule

Maccabean territory in 135 BCE

Approximate boundary of the kingdom of Alexander Jannaeus

Greek city taken or destroyed by Jannaeus

Fortress

Sidon

Damascus

UREA

PHOENICIA

Tyre

Antiochia

Seleucia

Ptolemais (Acre)

Sea of Chinnereth (Sea of Galilee)

Great Sea

GALILEE

Western Sea

Hippos

Philoteria

Yarmuk

Dium

Abila

Gadara

Dora

Ephron

Strato's Tower

Scythopolis (Bethshan)

Pella

Plain of Jezreel

ARABS

SAMARIA

Jebel Um ec' Daraj ▲

Gerasa

Samaria

Amathus

Jordan

Apollonia

Sichem

Mt. Gerizim ▲

Zarqa

Joppa

Alexandrium

Jazer

Adida

Philadelphia (Rabbatamana)

Port of the Jamnites

Modin

Gazara

Michmas

Jericho

Jamnia

JUDAEA

Ashdod

Jerusalem

Hyrcania

Medaba

Ascalon

Marisa

Bethsura

Macherus

Antheon

Adora

Hebron

Gaza

Salt Sea (Dead Sea)

Arabian Desert

IDUMAEA

Masada

Raphia

NABATAEN ARABS

Negev

N

NABATAEN ARABS

0   20 km

0   20 miles

Opposite: Differing factions within the Jewish state fought bitter battles between themselves, eventually both sides appealed to the Romans to restore order.

Hasmonean state reached a kind of compromise between Judaism and Hellenism; John's sons were given Greek names.

Hyrcanus died in 104 BCE and was succeeded by his son Aristobulos I, a paranoid ruler who imprisoned most of his brothers and mother. His favorite brother was mistakenly killed by a royal bodyguard which hastened the King's further decline into madness and death after vomiting blood. A surviving brother, Alexander Janneus (Yannai) (103–76 BCE) was released from prison and made king, as shown in the coinage of the period.

Alexander attempted to expand his lands. An attack on Ptolemais failed but all other port cities of the Levant were captured, Gaza being seized with extreme brutality. Good relations were enjoyed with the Egyptian queen, Cleopatra, who, if angered, could have summoned Roman help. Other Hasmonean successes were the seizure of towns in Galceitis, Gaulantis, and Syria. The Nabateans remained a thorny problem, however, continuing their raids and threats to Judaea and sometimes interfering in Hasmonean family feuds. The security of the southern and eastern borders was aided by the forts at Hyrcania, Masada, and Macherus. These were linked to other fortifications at Beth-Zur, Gezer, Alexandrium, and Dok.

Alexander Janneus used mercenaries in his campaigns and seemed uninterested in the feelings of his Jewish subjects. The religiously orthodox Pharisees developed a party that was in conflict with the state. The Pharisees scorned the pomp, power, and prestige of the monarchy in their devotion to the Law. Alexander, as the High Priest, even failed to observe the Law. At the Feast of the Tabernacles (Sukkot) Alexander was bombarded with citrons, which led to him to massacre his opponents. He is alleged to have crucified eight hundred rebels in Jerusalem; the historian Josephus maintains that the victims' wives and children were butchered before the eyes of the dying men.

Alexander died from a war wound but before doing so, advised his wife, Alexandra Salome (76–67 BCE), to seek a rapprochement with the Pharisees. She became Queen rather than allowing her son to succeed to the throne. The older son, Hyrcanus, was passed over, possibly because he was mentally impaired. The next son, Aristobulos, was not proposed lest there be strife or even civil war. Instead, Hyrcanus was appointed High Priest by Alexandra Salome, a move that pleased the Pharisees. The Queen, as woman, was not allowed to preside over the Sanhedrin, the Jewish parliament, and placed her brother in this position. Alexandra Salome felt secure in her pact with the neighboring Ptolemies and now that the Seleucids were weak. Her accommodation with the Pharisees was popular. She filled vacancies in the Sanhedrin with Pharisees rather than Sadducees, an extremely conservative group who adhered strictly to the precepts of the Torah. When the Queen died in 67 BCE, the Pharisees backed Hyrcanus II as King and High Priest while the Sceducees supported Aristobulos who already controlled some parts of Judea. The latter usurped the monarchy after defeating his brother. Alexander Janneus had appointed a local governor whose son, Antipater, became an adviser to Hyrcannus and persuaded him to regain his crown. The two escaped to Petra, capital of Nabatea. The Nabatean ruler, Aretas, was easily persuaded to help Hyrcannus. Judaea was now fought over by Hyrcanus, Antipater, and the Nabataeans, who besieged Jerusalem.

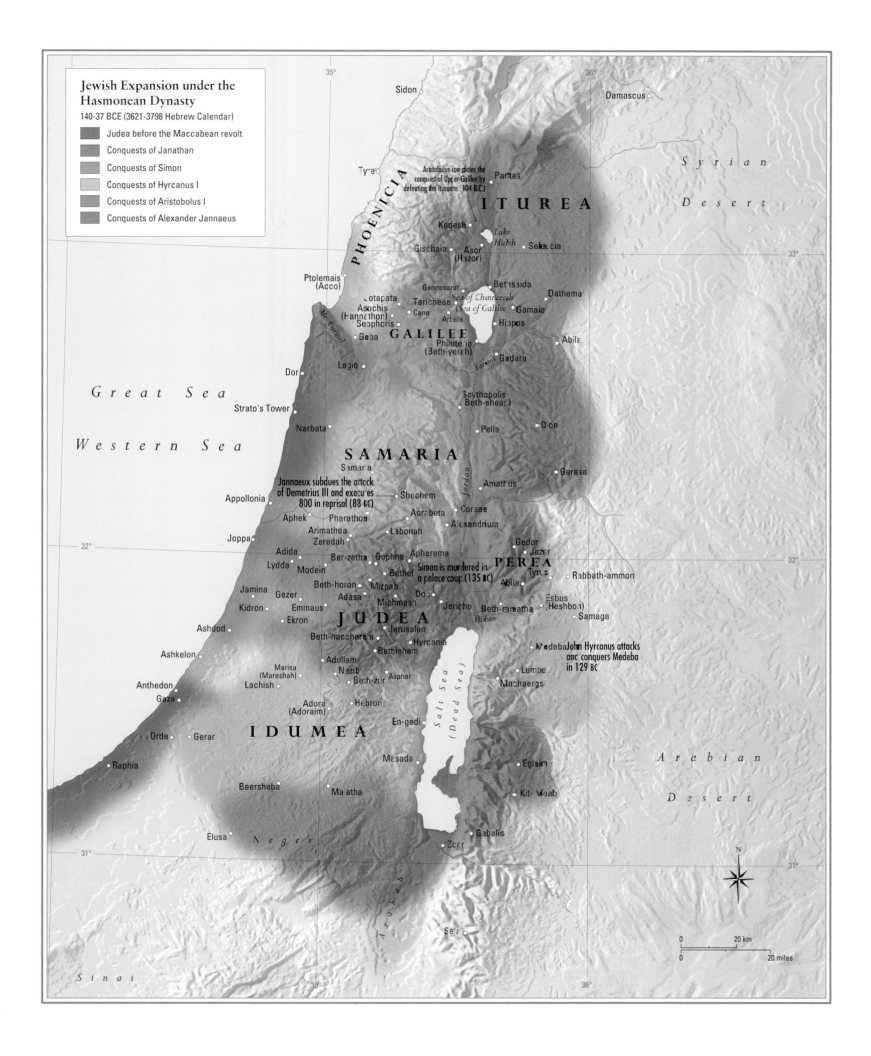

Jewish Expansion under the Hasmonean Dynasty

140-37 BCE (3621-3798 Hebrew Calendar)

- Judea before the Maccabean revolt
- Conquests of Janathan
- Conquests of Simon
- Conquests of Hyrcanus I
- Conquests of Aristobolus I
- Conquests of Alexander Jannaeus

Sidon

Damascus

S y r i a n

D e s e r t

Tyre

Aristobulus completes the
conquest of Upper Galilee by
defeating the Itureans 104 B.C.

Partas

ITUREA

Kedesh

*Lake
Hulsh*

Seleucia

Gischaia

Asor
(Hazor)

PHOENICIA

Ptolemais
(Acco)

Jotapata

Gennesaret

*Sea of Chinnereth
(Sea of Galilee)*

Bethsaida

Dathema

Asochis
(Hannathon)

Taricheae

Cana

Gamala

Seophoris

Artela

Hippos

Mt. Carmel

Geba

GALILEE

Philoteria
(Beth-yereh)

Abile

Dor

Legio

Gadara

Yarmuk

Strato's Tower

Scythopolis
(Beth-shear)

G r e a t   S e a

Narbata

Pella

D on

Gerasa

W e s t e r n   S e a

SAMARIA

Samaria

Jannaeux subdues the attack
of Demetrius III and executes
800 in reprisal (88 BC)

Shechem

Amathus

Appollonia

Acrabeta

Coraea

Aphek

Pharathon

Alexandrium

Joppa

Arimathea

Lebonah

Zeredah

Gedor

Jazer

Adida

Ber-zetha

Gophna

Apherema

PEREA

Lydda

Modein

Bethel

Simon is murdered in
a palace coup (135 BC)

Tyrus

Rabbath-ammon

Beth-horon

Mizpah

Abila

Jamina

Gezer

Adasa

Doc

Jericho

Esbus
(Heshbon)

Kidron

Emmaus

Michmash

Beth-ramatha

Hisban

Samaga

Ekron

JUDEA

Jerusalem

Ashdod

Beth-haccherem

Hyrcania

MedebaJohn Hyrcanus attacks
and conquers Medeba
in 129 BC

Ashkelon

Bethlehem

Marisa
(Mareshah)

Adullam

Nazib

Lemba

Anthedon

Lachish

Beth-zur

Asphar

Machaerus

Gaza

Adora
(Adoraim)

Hebron

*Salt Sea
(Dead Sea)*

Orda

Gerar

IDUMEA

En-gedi

Raphia

Masada

Eglaim

Beersheba

Ma atha

Kit- Moab

A r a b i a n

D e s e r t

Elusa

N e g e v

Gabalis

Zoer

Arabah

Sela

N

S i n a i

| 0 | | 20 km |
| 0 | | 20 miles |

THE ROMAN EMPIRE

THE ROMAN EMPIRE EXPANDED FROM ROME OVER THE ENTIRE MEDITERRANEAN IN THE SPACE OF THREE HUNDRED AND FIFTY YEARS. MANY CLIENT STATES YIELDED TO IT WITHOUT A FIGHT BUT THE POWERFUL GENERAL POMPEY SET OUT TO CONQUER ASIA MINOR AND OTHER STATES NOT YET IN THE THRALL OF ROME.

Panels from the altar at Pergamon, now in the Berlin Museum.

Rome was founded in 735 BCE and was under Etruscan domination for two hundred and fifty years. It controlled a strategic ford over the River Tiber and managed to bring neighboring tribes under its domination before overthrowing the Etruscans, establishing a republic and conquering Etruria. Through a combination of warfare and diplomacy, Rome defeated the Samnites and by 266 BCE ruled all of Italy south of the Rubicon. Rome then intervened by invitation into the political maneuverings of Messina in Sicily, suddenly confronting the Carthaginian Empire in North Africa, the most important seafaring and trading land in the Mediterranean. The first Punic War followed in 238 BCE with the victorious Rome acquiring Sicily, Corsica, and Sardinia.

Roman hegemony in the Mediterranean forced the Carthaginian armies under Hannibal in the Second Punic War (218–201 BCE), to move overland through Spain and cross the Alps into Italy. Sixteen years of war ensued, ending with Scipio's victory at Zama in 202 BCE. Rome now acquired most of Spain but found it difficult to hold out against hostile Lusitanians and Celtiberians. The Roman victory in the final Punic War (149–146 BCE) resulted in the complete destruction of the city of Carthage and the Carthaginian Empire, with Rome gaining control of North Africa. Simultaneously, in 191 BCE, the Romans conquered Cisalpine Gaul in Northern Italy after defeating the Celts at Telamon. When Rome defeated its enemies in the Italian peninsula, the land acquired was shared among Roman citizens who established semi-autonomous colonies or individual land-holdings. Some conquered cities became "Roman" or were coerced into an alliance with Rome. Rome's territorial gains during the Punic Wars became provinces ruled by magistrates sent by the Roman Senate to administer the territory and collect tribute.

Roman expansion fueled ambitions. During the second Punic War, Philip V of Macedon forged an alliance with Hannibal. Two wars, in 214 and 200 BCE, crushed Macedon, and a third in 168 BCE saw Macedon reduced to the status of a Roman province. This was the fate of the rest of Greece in 146 BCE. Rome also supported the Asian state of Pergamon against Seleucid ambitions. Antiochus III of Syria had concluded a secret pact with Philip V of Macedon. The Seleucid fleet was beaten at Myonnesus (191 BCE) and Antiochus himself was defeated at Magnesia (190 BCE) in Asia Minor. The resulting Peace of Apameia forced the Seleucid king to surrender Asia Minor west of the Taurus Mountains, which was then divided between the Roman allies of Pergamon and Rhodes. The Seleucids were also required to pay a huge war indemnity, burn their fleet, and kill their war elephants. These last two terms were only partially implemented and Seleucid power was merely dented. In 166 BCE, Antiochus Epiphanes mustered a fifty thousand-strong army at Antioch; Antiochus Sidetes led a larger army against the Parthians in 130 BCE.

Seleucid decline in the Near East may have been less due to the Romans and more the result of internecine conflict in the Seleucid royal family and Parthian incursions into Babylonia. Nevertheless, the defeats by Rome caused Armenia, under Artaxias, and Bactria to break away from the Seleucid Empire. The relationship between Rome and Pergamon was an unusual one. Successive rulers of the Hellenised kingdom fell under the influence of Rome, a security measure to deter aggressive neighbors. King Attalus died in 133 BCE and in his will he bequeathed his state to Rome, together with his treasury. Elsewhere, Rome conquered southern Gaul, providing a land bridge between Italy and Spain, supporting the Via Domitiana. In 118 BCE, the first Roman colony in France was founded at Narbo Martius (Narbonne). In North Africa, Jugurtha of Numidia was defeated (105 BCE) while Mauretania became a protected kingdom and friendly Leptis Magna hosted a Roman garrison.

In 101 BCE, Roman forces invaded Cilicia, burning out its pirates' nests and making the area a province. In 96 BCE, Ptolemaeus Physkon, King of Cyrene, willed his state to the people of Rome, thereby allowing Rome to make further inroads into Libya. In fact, geopolitically, Rome was projecting its power eastward along the Mediterranean's southern and northern shores.

During the last century BCE, the Roman Republic became increasingly dictatorial in its domestic policies. Generals Marius and Sulla became all-powerful. The latter was just one of the generals fighting three wars against Mithridates VI Eupator of Pontus. He invaded the province of Asia and butchered between 30,000–100,000 Romans and other Italians. In 63 BCE, the Pontine ruler committed suicide, thus ending the war followed. During these conflicts, the young general Gnaeus Pompeius Magnus (Pompey), came to the fore. Pompey's career in the East (67–61 BCE) commenced a campaign against Aegean pirates, helped by the young senator C. Julius Caesar. Backed by an army of twenty legions and five hundred ships with the Lex Gabinia granting Pompey three years' command over all seas and coastal areas as far as 60 miles inland from the Straits of Gibraltar to the Bosphorus. Rome and Italy were placed under Pompey's sole military authority for an unlimited

Next page: The Roman Empire sought to increase its influence in the east, Pompey developed a policy of weakening regional powers, while bolstering smaller client states.

period by the lex Manilia which also awarded him the power to make treaties and alliances.

Pompey continued the Roman policy of weakening strong powers in the East while bolstering small states. At this time, Asia Minor comprised Bithynia, Pontus, and Cappadocia which were still ruled by Iranian princes, the remnants of the satraps who held power under the Persian Achaemenids. After Mithridates was defeated, his relation, Tigranes of Armenia, surrendered to Rome. He was deprived of his recent conquests and was fined six thousand talents. Pompey felt free to consolidate Rome's eastern territories and establish a series of buffer client-states. He created four provinces, Asia, which remained intact; Bithynia-Pontus (excluding eastern Pontus); Cilicia, including Pamphylia and Isauria; and Syria, the area around Antioch. The client kingdoms consisted of eastern Pontus, Cappadocia, Galatia (under King Deitarus), Lycia, and Judaea. The buffer states, friends (*amici*) or allies (*socii*) of Rome were a barrier against Parthia. In northern Mesopotamia, some lands were given to Tigranes. In the south, a Jewish Judea remained, as did Arab Chalcis (Ituraea) and Nabatea.

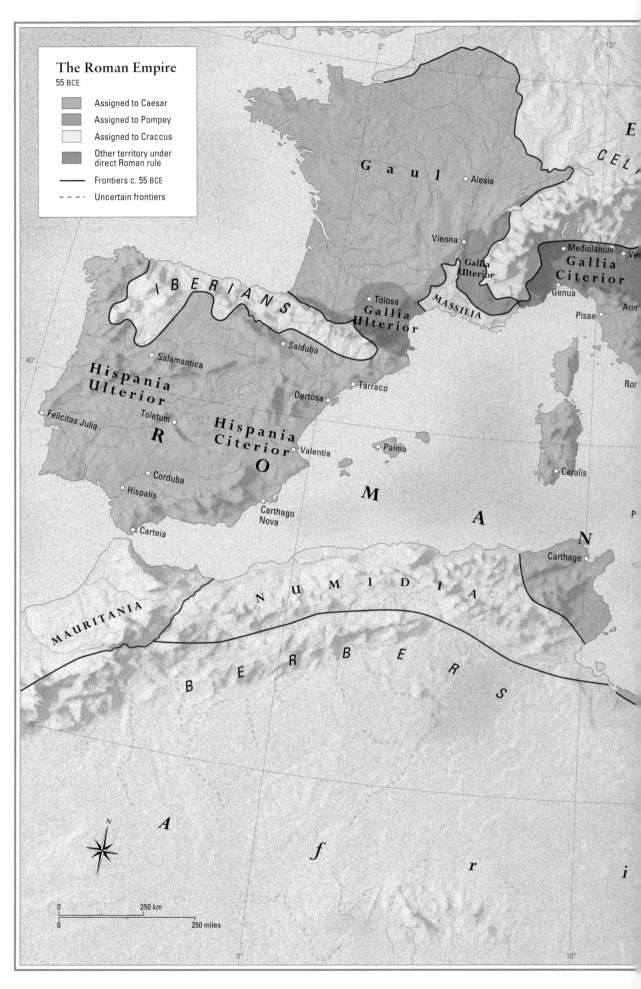

ROMAN DOMINATION

POMPEY, THE WICKED GENERAL WHO SACKED THE TEMPLE IS IN
STARK CONTRAST TO HIS FATHER-IN-LAW, JULIUS CAESAR. CAESAR
WAS GRATEFUL FOR THE SUPPORT OF THE JEWS EARLY IN HIS
CAREER AND GRANTED THEM RELIGIOUS FREEDOM DURING HIS
RULE OF JUDAEA. JULIUS IS STILL A FAVOURITE JEWISH FIRST NAME.

Gnaeus Pompeius Magnus
(Pompey) (106–48 BCE)
the powerful general who
conquered Asia Minor and
eventually Judaea.

Opposite: The Roman general
Pompey launched his campaign
entering Jerusalem in 63 BCE.
This brought about an end to a
period of Jewish independence
that had lasted less than a
hundred years.

The survival of Judaea and the Arabic-speaking Nabateans depended upon the several embassies that the Levantine states had despatched to Pompey. The Jerusalem delegations were mutually hostile. Hyrcanus II and Antipater were supported by the Pharisees, whereas the Sadducees maintained that Aristobulos was the more effective of the two brothers and should be King. Some militant Pharisees begged Pompey to abolish the Judaean kingdom and re-establish a theocratic state as had existed under Ezra and the Maccabees but Pompey supported Hyrcanus and he returned to Jerusalem as King (64 BCE). The Nabateans were ordered to quit Judaea.

Pompey intimidated the Nabateans by marching two legions south (63 BCE). While Aretas engaged the Romans at Petra, Aristobulos tried to seize the throne. Pompey quickly returned to Jerusalem and besieged the Temple precinct in which the usurper's supporters sought refuge. The three-month siege

Pompey's Campaign Against Jerusalem
63 BCE

Jewish state 64–65 BCE

Pompey's campaign

Siege of Jerusalem

Damascus

SYRIA

ITURAEA

Mt. Hermon

Panias

PHOENICIA

Kedesh

Lake Huleh

Seleucia

Gush Halav

Ptolemais

Gennesaret

Bethsaida

Sea of Chinnereth
(Sea of Galilee)

Gamala

Jotapata

Great Sea

Mt. Carmel

Sepphoris

GALILEE

Hippus

Abila

Western Sea

Mt. Tabor

Gadara

Dor

DECAPOLIS

Scythopolis
(Beth-shan)

Pella

Dion

SAMARIA

Jebel Um ed Daraj

Gerasa (Jerash)

Samaria

Tirzah

Mt. Ebal

Amathus

Shechem

Zarqa

Mt. Gerizim

Apollonia

Coreae

GILEAD

Alexandrium

Jordan

Joppa

Gedor (Gadara)

PERAEA

Philadelphia
(Ammon)

Doc

Jericho

Esbus

Pompey captures Jerusalem in 63 BC
bringing Roman control to Palestine

Heshbon

Jerusalem

Mt. Nebo

JUDAEA

Ascalon
(Ashkelon)

Herodium

Medaba

MOABITIS

N

Gaza

Salt
Sea
(Dead Sea)

0   20 km
0   20 miles

Masada

IDUMAEA

Under the rule of the Maccabees the independent Jewish state entered in to a defensive alliance with Rome, however, when this state collapsed and civil war broke out both sides called for Rome to restore peace. As a result from 56 BCE Palestine fell under the rule of Rome who appointed local kings under a Roman governor.

ended with the walls being breached and the rebels killed. Aristobulos was sent to Rome and Hyrcanus re-established as High Priest. Pompey reinforced his personal authority by violating Temple protocols by entering the Holy of Holies that was reserved for the High Priest. Even the Seleucid Kings had observed such Temple niceties but Pompey had defiled the Temple and trampled over Jewish sensibilities; his behaviour damned him forever in Jewish eyes and he was loathed.

Jewish spirits were dashed further when Pompey decided to reduce the size of the Judaean state and abolish the monarchy. The Judaean state of Alexander Janneus was pruned. The Greek city states in the northeast were placed outside Jewish control in a league known as the Decapolis. The coastal cities from Dor, south to Gaza were given limited autonomy. Some northern territories were ceded to Ituraea and Ptolemais. These two areas were placed under the loose jurisdiction of the new Roman province of Syria. A statelet was created for the Samaritans around Shechem and Mount Gezerim. Hyrcanus II retained the title of High Priest but received the lower title of Ethnarch rather than king, to indicate to the Jews that they now inhabited a client-state, and their leader only existed at the whim of Rome.

Antipater continued as Hyrcanus' advisor for some twenty years, ensuring he played his part in religious and secular duties. The historian Josephus states that Marcus Crassus stole 2000 talents of gold from the Temple to fund his anti-Parthian expedition, but Antipater and Hyrcanus prevented a Jewish revolt in outrage. Aristobulos was away in Rome but he became a pawn in the contest for power between Julius Caesar and Pompey. In 27 BCE Octavian, Caesar's nephew and heir, received the title "Augustus" with extraordinary constitutional powers and control over the most important armies and provinces. Rome had gained an Emperor.

The Pompey-Caesar conflict developed into an alliance between Brutus and Cassius against Octavian and Mark Antony. Hyrcanus and Antipater played political musical chairs with the ethnarch becoming a client of Pompey, then Julius Caesar, of Cassius, and then Octavian and Mark Antony. Antipater consolidated his power by moving his two oldest sons, Phasael and Herod, into important political positions. Antipater died in 43 BCE leaving the Sadducees and other opponents to Hyrcanus II to find an alternative Hasmonean candidate in Antigonus II, the surviving son of Aristobulos and nephew of Hyrcanus. He and his followers were driven from Jerusalem. Herod married Mariamne, the grand-daughter of Aristobulos. Antigonus recruited Parthian backing during the Roman civil war because Parthia wanted to seize any opportunity to weaken Rome. Furthermore, support for Antigonus might have won over overt support from the hundreds of thousands of Jews of Mesopotamia which the Parthians had conquered in 140 BCE.

The Parthians moved into Jerusalem, killed Phasael and arrested Hyrcanus. Josephus claims that Antigonus sliced off Hyrcanus' ears, thus making him unfit to serve as High Priest and sent him to Babylon. Herod fled to Rome via Arabia and Egypt. In 39 BCE, the Senate declared Herod King of Judaea. He was despatched with mercenaries and a Roman force under Sosius to Judaea which he captured, seizing Antigonus in 37 BCE and killing him. Herod brought Hyrcanus back to Jerusalem. Octavian confirmed Herod as client-king in 31 BCE. Hyrcanus eventually plotted against Herod, was found guilty, and executed in 30 BCE. The same year saw Herod ruling Judaea (with Idumaea), Samaria, Galilee and Peraea. He was also given sovereignty over Greek cities in Samaria (Hippos and Gadara) and all of the coastal cities save Ashkelon (Ascalon).

Pompey's Settlement of the Hasmonean Jewish State
64–40 BCE

— Hasmonaean state before Pompey's settlement

▮ Jewish state after Pompey's settlement

▮ Jewish territories ceded to Ituraea and Ptolemais

▮ Samaritan state

□ Large towns within the borders of non-Jewish states

△ Gabinius' synedria

⌂ Fortress of Jannaeus

▭ Other political boundary

CEDED TO ITURAEA

CEDED TO PTOLEMAIS

Panias

Lake Huleh

GALILEE

Sea of Chinnereth (Sea of Galilee)

Sepphoris

Hippus

Dium

Geba

Gadara

Dora

ESDRAELON

Great Sea

Western Sea

Strato's Tower

Scythopolis

DECAPOLIS

Pella

Samaria

Gerasa

Shechem
Mt Gerizim

SAMARIA

Zarqa

Apollonia

Alexandrium

Arethusa

Joppa

Gedor

PERAEA

Philadelphia

JUDAEA

Shueib

Jamnia

Jericho

Azotus

Hierosolyma (Jerusalem)

Hisbon

Esbus

Hyrcania

Medeba

Ascalon

Betogabris

Salt Sea (Dead Sea)

Gaza

Machaerus

Adora

IDUMAEA

Mujib

Masada

N

NABATAEA

0   20 km
0   20 miles

Hasa

HEROD'S KINGDOM

THE TYRANT HEROD, WHO MARRIED TEN WIVES, DID MUCH TO BEAUTIFY JERUSALEM BUT AT HUGE EXPENSE. HIS MASSIVE BUILDING PROJECTS ALL OVER THE COUNTRY WERE FINANCED BY FORCED LABOUR AND HEAVY TAXATION. AFTER HIS DEATH, THE KINGDOM FELL APART THROUGH THE GREED OF HIS SUCCESSORS.

The taking of Jerusalem by Herod the Great, 36 BC, by Jean Fouquet, late fifteenth century.

Herod the Great ruled Judaea on behalf of Rome from 40 BCE and his family remained prominent for the next one hundred and fifty years. This Idumean used force to stabilize his unruly kingdom but is mainly remembered for his building program. Herod constructed new cities and provided buildings for every type of public usage, from baths, theaters and gymnasia, to a temple for emperor worship, a port and the rebuilding of the Temple on a magnificent and grandiose scale.

Jerusalem was restored with improved walls, four great towers and a huge new fortress, the Antonia. The steep slopes on which the city stood were faced on three sides with smooth stones to deter attackers. Herod gave Jerusalem a theater and a hippodrome and an amphitheater was erected on flat land outside the city at which musical concerts and athletic events could be staged. Herod also built himself a magnificent new royal palace decorated with rare stone as a backdrop to silver and gold artefacts. The palace incorporated circular cloisters, long walks and gardens bordered by ornamental canals and pools.

In 27 BCE, Herod rebuilt an enlarged Samaria as another military fortress to intimidate the surrounding countryside, as well as being a refuge in times of disturbance and war. The city was surrounded by a two-mile long wall and possessed a new Corinthian-style temple with a statue of the

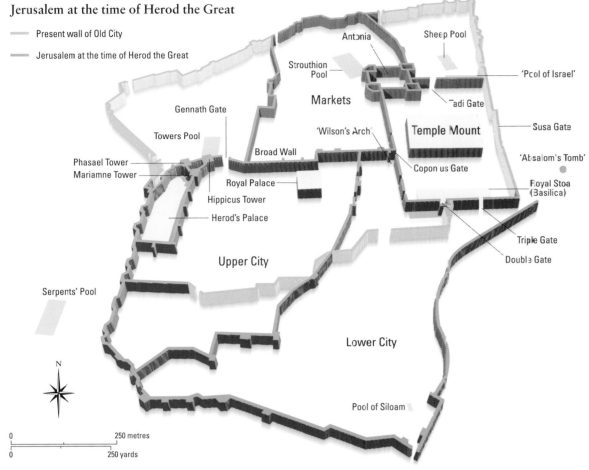

Jerusalem at the time of Herod the Great

— Present wall of Old City
— Jerusalem at the time of Herod the Great

Antonia
Sheep Pool
Strouthion Pool
'Pool of Israel'
Markets
Gennath Gate
Wadi Gate
'Wilson's Arch'
Temple Mount
Towers Pool
Susa Gate
Broad Wall
Phasael Tower
'Absalom's Tomb'
Mariamne Tower
Coponus Gate
Royal Palace
Royal Stoa (Basilica)
Hippicus Tower
Herod's Palace
Triple Gate
Upper City
Double Gate
Serpents' Pool
Lower City
N
Pool of Siloam

0 — 250 metres
0 — 250 yards

Herod the Great took the city by conquest in 37 BCE. It had already been devastated by Roman armies in 63 and 54 BCE and plundered by a Parthian army fourteen years later. Herod rebuilt the city's walls and towers, the Temple Mount and the Antonia Fortress with its great towers.

emperor at its entrance. The city was renamed Sebaste, the Greek word for Augustus to whom it was dedicated. An entirely new port-city was built at Caesarea. A 200 foot-wide breakwater protected the harbor and there was a large dockyard enclosed by a semi-circular sea wall. The city was designed on a grid system with a temple to Augustus, an amphitheater, a Roman forum and an aqueduct that brought water from Mount Carmel, some thirteen miles away. The sewerage system was cleansed by tides and sea currents. Like all other building projects, forced labour and heavy taxation paid for the program.

Elsewhere, Herod overhauled the fortresses at Alexandrium, Hyrcania, and the palaces of Masada. New fortresses were erected at Herodium and Jericho. A new city was built north of Jericho and named Phasaelis after Herod's murdered brother. A shrine was built to cover the cave of Machpelah in which the Patriarchs are interred. Herod's projects are best remembered by his Temple which took eighty-four years to complete. This lavish building incorporated 162 Corinthian columns, the tallest being 100-foot high.

Herod ran a virtual police state. Repression was normal and even extended to his own family. He had his Hasmonean princess wife executed, as well as three of his sons. Other family members were banished. Herod's family tree is difficult to plot since he married ten times, two wives having the same name. Herodias, a granddaughter of Herod and Mariamne I, married Herod Boethus, a son of Herod I's third marriage, and later Herod Antipas, a son of the fourth marriage. Salome, a daughter of Herodias and Herod Boethus, and therefore both a granddaughter and great granddaughter of Herod I, married Philip, a son of the fifth marriage. Herod is reputed to have ordered the death

This reconstruction shows Herod's Palace, built on the Wadi Qelt, just south of Jericho.

of baby boys at the time of Jesus' birth but there is very little evidence to support this. He died in 4 BCE and was given a sumptuous funeral, despite his unpopularity.

Herod's will divided the kingdom into three parts, the tetrarchies. Archelaus was to be King over Judea, Idumaea and Samaria, a region incorporating the cities of Sebaste and Caesarea. Herod Antipas was created tetrarch of Galilee and Peraea, territories separated by the Decapolis. His half-brother Philip was made tetrarch of the mainly gentile areas north and east of the Sea of Galilee. Salome, Herod's sister, was given Azotus, Jamnia, Phasaelis, and Herod's palace in the city of Ascalon. The cities of Gaza, Gadera, and Hippus were placed under the authority of the governor of Syria. The tetrarchs argued over their prizes, even going to Rome to plead their cases. In the tetrarchies, violence broke out against Archelaus; the troops slaughtered rioters and drove others led by Herod's cousin, Achiab, into the hills. Varus, the governor of Syria, brought in Roman troops to pacify the area but palaces were burned at Jericho, Beth-Ramatha, and Amathus. Varus returned from Syria with two legions and a cavalry force loaned by Aretas IV of Nabatea. The Sepphoris rebels were captured and sold as slaves. The Romans and their allies pacified the region leaving the brothers to rule.

Archelaus ruled as ethnarch for ten years, until Jews and Samaritans complained about his harshness. He was summoned to Rome, deposed, and exiled to Gaul. Samaria, Judea and Idumaea became the Roman province of Judaea (CE 6). In Galilee and Peraea, Antipas ruled for forty-three years. bringing peace and prosperity. He rebuilt the destroyed cities and founded Tiberias, famous for its warm springs. Antipas divorced his first wife, the daughter of Aretas IV and married Herodias. The Nabateans won the ensuing war. John the Baptist criticised the marriage for which he was beheaded. Eventually, Antipas, responding to his nagging wife, went to see the Emperor Caligula to seek elevation to kingship. Caligula deposed him, exiling him to Lugdunum (Lyons) in Gaul. Antipas is the Herod to whom Pontius Pilate, procurator of Judaea, sent Jesus (Luke 23: 7–15). Philip then ruled the rump of Judaea with his wife Salome. He expanded Paneas as his capital and renamed it Caesarea Philippi. Bethsaida was turned from a fishing village into a town.

Antipas and Philip established a peace lasting through the first three Roman governors. Caesarea Maritima became the capital, downgrading Jerusalem. Judaea was policed by 3000 auxiliaries drawn from non-Jewish Sebaste and Caesarea. Eventually, Valerius Gratus, appointed by the Emperor Tiberias, came to Judaea in CE 15. He deposed the High Priest, Ananaias, the position eventually going to his son-in-law Joseph Caiaphas. This High Priest co-operated with Pontius Pilate, a character who totally failed to understand the national pride and religious beliefs of Jews.

Under Roman governorship Herod was the first king to be appointed under the new political arrangements

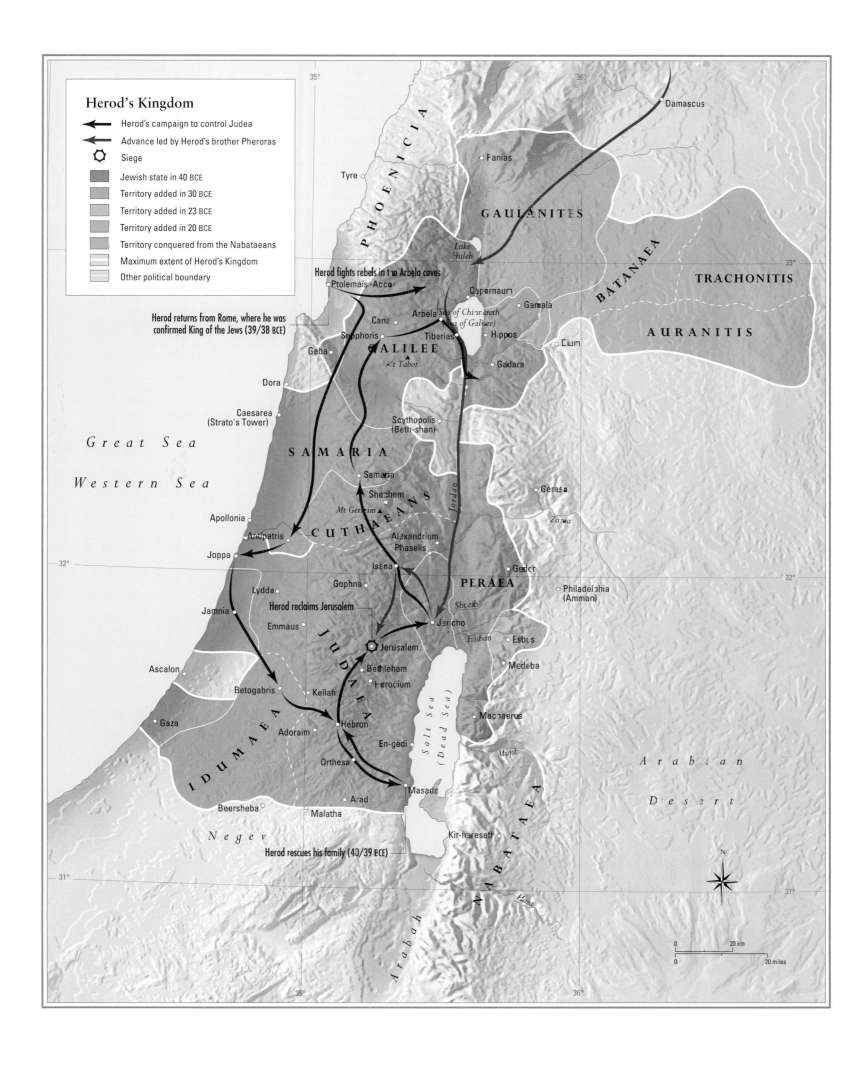

Herod's Kingdom

→ Herod's campaign to control Judea

→ Advance led by Herod's brother Pheroras

⬡ Siege

Jewish state in 40 BCE

Territory added in 30 BCE

Territory added in 23 BCE

Territory added in 20 BCE

Territory conquered from the Nabataeans

Maximum extent of Herod's Kingdom

Other political boundary

Herod fights rebels in the Arbela caves

Herod returns from Rome, where he was confirmed King of the Jews (39/38 BCE)

Herod reclaims Jerusalem

Herod rescues his family (40/39 BCE)

PHOENICIA

GAULANITES

BATANAEA

TRACHONITIS

AURANITIS

Damascus

Fanias

Tyre

Lake Huleh

Ptolemais Acco

Capernaum

Gamala

Cana

Arbela Sea of Chinnereth (Sea of Galilee)

Hippos

Sepphoris

GALILEE

Tiberias

Geba

Mt Tabor

Gadara

Dium

Dora

Caesarea (Strato's Tower)

Scythopolis (Beth-shan)

SAMARIA

Gerasa

Samaria

Shechem

Zaua

Mt Gerizim

CUTHAEANS

Great Sea

Western Sea

Apollonia

Antipatris

Alexandrium

Phaselis

Jordan

Joppa

Isana

Geder

PERAEA

Gophna

Philadelphia (Amman)

Lydda

Jericho

Jamnia

Emmaus

Shueib

Hisban

JUDAEA

Esbus

Jerusalem

Ascalon

Bethlehem

Herodium

Medeba

Betogabris

Kellah

Salt Sea (Dead Sea)

Gaza

Hebron

Macnaerus

Adoraim

En-gedi

IDUMAEA

Orthesa

Muji

Arabian

Masada

Arad

Desert

Beersheba

Malatha

Negev

Kir-hareseth

NABATAEA

Arabah

Pinah

N

0   20 km

0   20 miles

THE ESSENES

THE ESSENES WERE A JEWISH SECT ABOUT WHOM VIRTUALLY NOTHING WAS KNOWN UNTIL THE DISCOVERY OF THE DEAD SEA SCROLLS IN 1947.

The Scroll of Isaiah was found in Qumran near the north-eastern coast of the Dead Sea in 1947, one of the set of discoveries known as the Dead Sea Scrolls. This particular scroll represents the oldest complete book of the Bible and dates from around 100 BCE.

Jews interpreted the Torah and other sacred texts in various ways leading to schools of religious thought. Two groups have already been identified, the Pharisees and the Sadducees. The former stressed the Law and were concerned with its practical implementation. They were also narrowly nationalistic and their emotional messianic expectations eventually led to armed rebellion. The Sadducees were concerned with their social and political position within the nation and felt that the High Priest should be one of their own. They were extremely conservative and elitist.

A third group were the Essenes who are not mentioned in the New Testament, even though scholars have pointed out the similarity between their ideals and those of John the Baptist and Jesus. Christian scholars have focused on links between the Essenes and Christianity rather than locating them in Jewish religious thought and development.

The Essene community at Khirbet Qumran was excavated to reveal an extensive complex of buildings and caves occupied from c. 120 BCE to CE 68 with a gap in between, when the settlement was damaged by an earthquake. Biblical manuscripts and scrolls were found there and they shed light on religious attitudes of the time. Papyrus fragments discovered in 1947 in caves near the northern end of the Dead Sea, as well as a copper scroll, were unearthed over the next ten years. The Essene community buildings consisted of eight courtyards, a refectory, kitchen, assembly rooms, a laundry, two potteries, a toilet, a scriptorium, and eight water cisterns of various sizes, some of them with steps leading down into them. There is evidence of a dam in a large gully in the cliffs with channels to bring water from the dam to the cisterns.

The excavations revealed coins that indicate that Qumran commenced as a settlement in the early

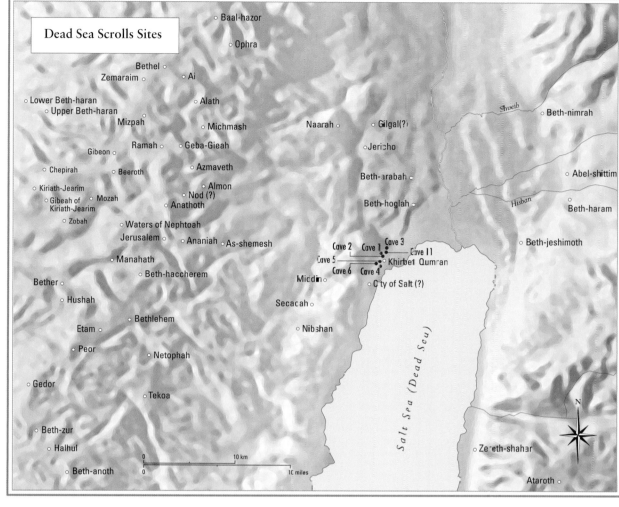

Dead Sea Scrolls Sites

The Essenes were a Jewish
sect who lived in the hills just
to the north west of the Dead
Sea. Little was known of them
until discovery of the Dead Sea
Scrolls in 1947.

part of the 1st century BCE but was abandoned after the earthquake in 31 BCE. A second occupation began after Herod's death, lasting until CE 68 when the Roman General Vespasian's forces destroyed most of the buildings during the first Jewish revolt. The manuscripts were hidden in caves when the inhabitants fled.

The writings include all the books of the Bible except Esther, plus other writings (a Commentary on Habbakuk and the Rule of War) including documents about the organization and its rules, such as Rule of the Community. Some writings differ in many respects from the version of the Bible that has come down to us; the Masoretic text.

The Essene community lived an austere life, involving joint ownership of all possessions, rituals of purification by water, plain clothing, public prayers, religious meals, and a novitiate. It kept a calendar of religious festivals differing from the official calendar of the Temple in Jerusalem. Apparently practising celibacy as a form of purity, the Essenes believed that the real meaning of the religious writings had been revealed by a "Teacher of Righteousness" at the beginning of the community's existence and that they had been chosen by God to be "Sons of Light" in conflict with the "Sons of Darkness" until God would finally send a Prophet and two Messiahs to bring victory and judgment. Meanwhile, the Essenes lived in the expectation of an apocalypse, so marriage made no sense. They strove to be prepared for the moment when God would establish his kingdom of righteousness. So, like the later Cathars, they looked for and found a lonely place where their asceticism would make ready for the messianic event.

THE FIRST JEWISH REVOLT AND THE SIEGE OF JERUSALEM

THE WORDS OF JOSEPH TRUMPELDOR: "IN BLOOD AND FIRE JUDAEA FELL ..." WERE CERTAINLY TRUE, IN THE DEFEAT OF THE JEWS AND THE UTTER DESTRUCTION OF JERUSALEM, AS COMMEMORATED ON THE ARCH OF TITUS IN ROME.

Head of the Emperor Nero
(37–68 CE).

Roman rule in Judaea was harsh and offended nationalist aspirations which were kept alive by Zealot violence. The Procurators Albinus (CE 62–64) and Gessius Florus (CE 64–66) added insult to injury with their corruption and brutality. The latter seized a large amount of money from the Temple when the Jews, led by Eleazar, son of the High Priest, refused to make offerings to the Emperor; an act the Romans considered to be treason. Other important incidents were the capture of Masada by rebels and the failure of Agrippa II to control the state by persuasion or force. Internecine fighting between Jews and the large gentile population added to the state's disintegration. There were outbreaks in Caesarea, Ptolemais, Gabe, Samaria, Ascalon and the Decapolis, as well as in Syria and Egypt.

Cestius Gallus, the Syrian legate (CE 63–66) failed to break the rebellion in Jerusalem. His second attempt was prevented by a Jewish victory at Beth-Horon in October, the rebel leaders being Pharisees and Sadducees. "*The Jewish War*" by Flavius Josephus provides key evidence about the division of the country into military districts, with Galilee and the area around Gamala in Gaulantis being handed to Josephus himself. He organised the fortification of major cities in Upper Galilee with village fortifications as obstacles to an enemy advance.

In December CE 66, the Emperor Nero sent Vespasian to pacify Judaea. He mustered his troops in Syria while his son, Titus, was sent to Egypt to find reinforcements. In spring, CE 67, Vespasian advanced into Galilee from Antioch via Ptolemais, where Titus and his Egyptian force joined him. The generals commanded some 60,000 legionaries and auxiliaries. Galilean resistance fell apart at this pressure, with Sepphoris joining the Romans immediately. Jotapata was besieged for two months before its

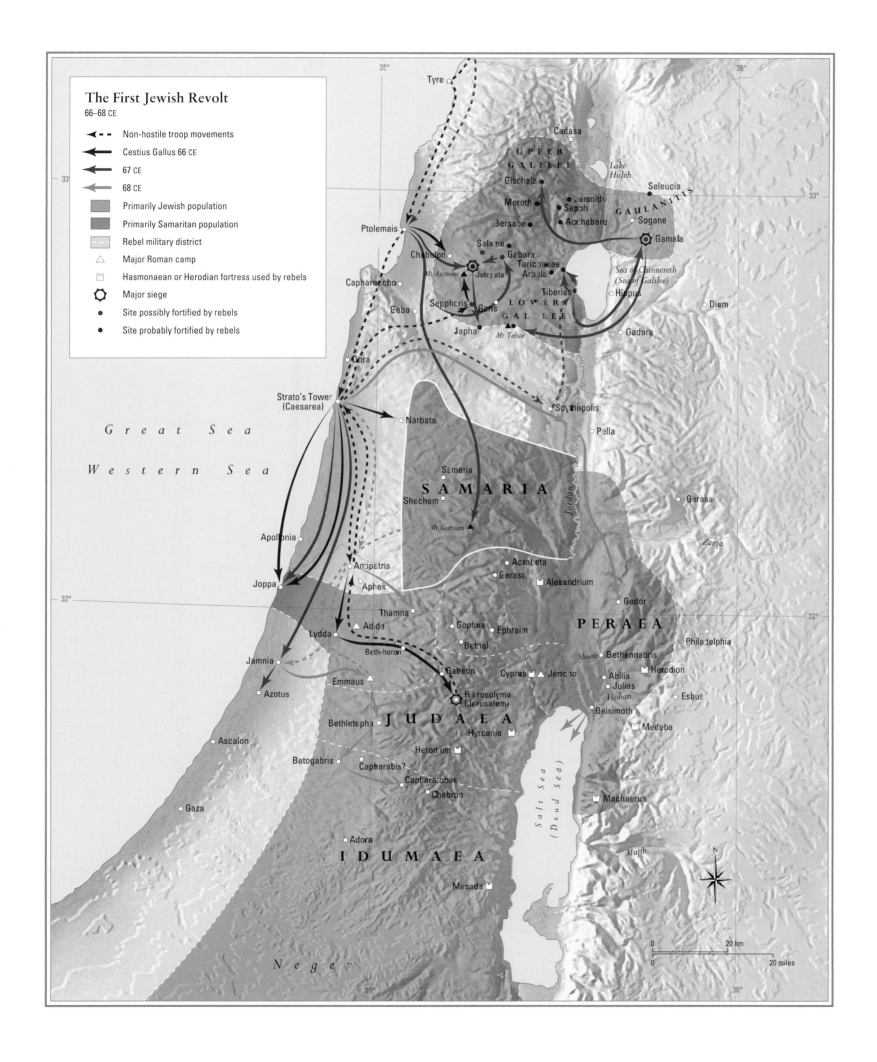

The First Jewish Revolt
66–68 CE

◄- - - Non-hostile troop movements

◄─── Cestius Gallus 66 CE

◄─── 67 CE

◄─── 68 CE

▢ Primarily Jewish population

▢ Primarily Samaritan population

▢ Rebel military district

△ Major Roman camp

⌂ Hasmonaean or Herodian fortress used by rebels

⬡ Major siege

• Site possibly fortified by rebels

● Site probably fortified by rebels

Tyre

Cadasa

UPPER GALILEE

Lake Huleh

Gischala

Seleucia

Meroth

Jamnith

Seph

GAULANITIS

Sogane

Bersabe

Acchabare

Gamala

Chabulon

Selame

Gabara

Taricheae

Ptolemais

Mt Ascmon

Jotepata

Arbela

Sea of Chinnereth
(Sea of Galilee)

Caphareccho

Tiberias

Hippus

Dium

Geba

Sepphoris

Gans

LOWER GALILEE

Japha

Mt Tabor

Gadara

Dora

Scythopolis

Strato's Tower
(Caesarea)

Narbata

Pella

Great Sea

Western Sea

Samaria

Gerasa

Shechem

SAMARIA

Jordan

Mt Gerizim

Zarqa

Apollonia

Acrabeta

Gerasa

Gedor

Antipatris

Alexandrium

Joppa

Aphek

PERAEA

Philadelphia

Thamna

Gophna

Ephraim

Lydda

Adida

Bethel

Shueib

Bethennabris

Beth-horon

Abilia

Herodion

Jamnia

Gabaon

Cyprus

Jericho

Julias

Esbus

Emmaus

Hierosolyma
(Jerusalem)

Hisban

Beisimoth

Azotus

Bethletepha

JUDAEA

Hyrcania

Medeba

Ascalon

Herodium

Betogabris

Capharabis?

*Salt Sea
(Dead Sea)*

Machaerus

Capharatobas

Chebron

Gaza

Adora

Mujib

IDUMAEA

N

Masada

Negev

0   20 km

0   20 miles

The instrument of Roman power – infantrymen of a Roman Legion, the best-trained, most disciplined and experienced army of the age. This re-enactment gives some idea of Roman infantry on the marsh.

garrison was annihilated. Josephus' force at Garis fled, leaving Lower Galilee open to the Romans. Josephus himself fled to Tiberias before surrendering. By the end of CE 67 the Roman legions had conquered northern Judaea and were sent to winter at Caesaria and Scythopolis (Bet Shean) thereby isolating Galilee isolated from other rebel areas. Vespasian chose to ignore Jerusalem for a while, knowing that the conflicts between the different factions would undermine its defense. Instead, he marched on Peraea where he rapidly subjugated the population as far south as Macherus. By late spring, he had taken Antipatris, Lydda and Jamnia. A legion was stationed outside Emmaus; after marching through Samaria, the Romans entered Jericho. As Vespasian was travelling to Caesaria to plan the siege of Jerusalem, Nero's suicide was announced, so he delayed operations until the political situation in Rome became clear. In the summer of CE 69, the armies of the Eastern Empire declared Vespasian emperor.

Confronted by the new rebel leader, Simon bar-Giora, Vespasian completed his conquest of Judaea, controlling Acrabeta, Bethel and Ephraim, together with Hebron in the south. Only Jerusalem, Macherus, Herodium and Masada remained defiant. Civil war raged in Jerusalem. A hill in the south-west of the city was held by aristocratic patriots while the Zealots under John of Giscala held the eastern city and most of the Temple Mount. The aristocrats asked Simon bar-Giora for help. He killed those amongst them who mentioned surrender. In Spring, CE 70, Titus marched on Jerusalem, pitched camp and attacked the north wall, one of three defense lines. The Jews attacked the siege towers but battering-rams were finally put in place, despite the defenders using catapults they had captured from Cestius years earlier. On 25 May, the first wall was breached. Roman soldiers entered and took Bezetha, north of the Temple Mount. Five days later, the second wall was breached, but the legionaries were repelled. The second wall was breached again, leaving the walls enclosing the Temple and the upper and lower parts of the city. The city was isolated by the Romans sealing off Jerusalem from the rest of the world. Sometimes as many as 500 were crucified daily by the Romans for trying to escape the city. The inhabitants died of starvation, with the dead stacked in houses and thousands thrown over the walls into the surrounding ravines. The Fortress of Antonia was breached by battering rams on 24 July. The Temple gates were set alight and soon the Temple was burned to ashes. The rebels made a final stand in Herod's palace but all were killed. Jerusalem was razed to the ground. Simon bar-Giora and John of Giscala were captives marching in Titus' triumphal procession in Rome in CE 71. Bar Giora was thrown to his death from the Tarpeian Rock.

Opposite: Between March and September 70 CE the Roman army besieged Jerusalem, first surrounding and cutting off the city from external support, they then battered their way through the city's defenses, destroying Jerusalem street by street.

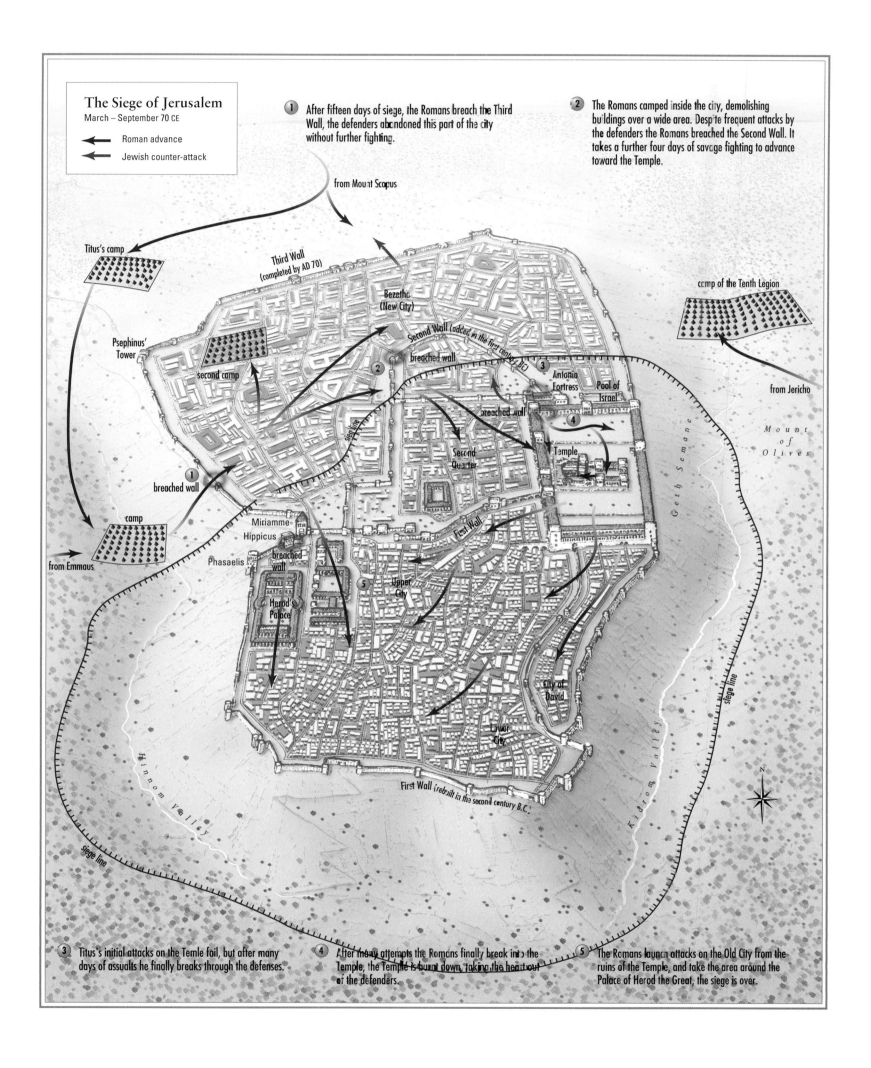

The Siege of Jerusalem
March – September 70 CE

→ Roman advance

→ Jewish counter-attack

① After fifteen days of siege, the Romans breach the Third Wall, the defenders abandoned this part of the city without further fighting.

② The Romans camped inside the city, demolishing buildings over a wide area. Despite frequent attacks by the defenders the Romans breached the Second Wall. It takes a further four days of savage fighting to advance toward the Temple.

from Mount Scopus

Titus's camp

Third Wall (completed by AD 70)

Bezetha (New City)

camp of the Tenth Legion

Psephinus' Tower

second camp

Second Wall (added in the first century BC)

breached wall

from Jericho

② breached wall

③ Antonia Fortress

Pool of Israel

Mount of Olives

breached wall

④

① breached wall

Second Quarter

Temple

Geth Semane

camp

from Emmaus

Miriamme
Hippicus

Phasaelis

breached wall

Herod's Palace

⑤

First Wall

Upper City

City of David

Kidron Valley

Hinnom Valley

Lower City

First Wall (rebuilt in the second century B.C.)

siege line

N

siege line

③ Titus's initial attacks on the Temple fail, but after many days of assaults he finally breaks through the defenses.

④ After many attempts the Romans finally break into the Temple, the Temple is burnt down, taking the heart out of the defenders.

⑤ The Romans launch attacks on the Old City from the ruins of the Temple, and take the area around the Palace of Herod the Great, the siege is over.

Masada

MASADA WAS THE FINAL STRONGHOLD DURING THE FIRST JEWISH REVOLT, DEFIANTLY HOLDING OUT AGAINST THE OVERWHELMING MIGHT OF THE ROMAN ARMY, ITS INHABITANTS PREFERRING DEATH TO CAPTURE.

Diagram of the Fortress of Masada as it would have looked before the siege.

Lucilius Bassus, governor of Judaea (CE 71–72) commenced the eradication of the remaining Zealot strongholds. Herodion, near Bethlehem, surrendered, and Macherus on the Dead Sea followed after some resistance. Masada, Herod's palace-stronghold on its high plateau remained defiant under the command of Eleazar, son of Jair, a descendant of the Zealot founder, Judah the Galilean. The new governor of Judaea, Flavius Silva (CE 73–81) began the siege after moving his troops there, using prisoners of war to carry provisions.

The fortress was built on a steep, craggy outcrop rising from the western shore of the Dead Sea. The main route to the top was a narrow trail, known as the "snake path" that zigzagged its way to the top for two miles. There was a shorter, much steeper route but it was too dangerous to use. The plateau's rim was circumscribed by an eighteen foot high wall, twelve feet broad with thirty seven towers. The plateau was cultivated and the water cisterns held some 200,000 gallons. The 1300-foot high rock was surrounded by Roman troops to prevent escape. The Romans then built a siege ramp and mound on the west side where a tower and battering-ram were brought into action. The wall collapsed but the defenders built another, made out of wooden beams and earth that could absorb the ram's blows, so the Romans set it alight. The rebels decided to commit suicide rather than face death or captivity. The men killed their wives and children and then drew lots to kill each other with the final man falling on his sword. A total of 960 died; only two women and five children escaped by hiding in the cisterns. '(The Romans) ... came within the palace, and so met with the multitude of the slain, but could take no pleasure in the fact, though it were done to their enemies. Nor could they do other than wonder at the courage of their resolution, and at the immovable contempt of death which so great a number of them had shown, when they went through with such an action as that was.' (Flavius Josephus, *The Jewish War*, Chapter 9).

Reconstruction of Herod's Palace at Masada, as it would have looked in Herod's time. Herod's Tomb was discovered at Herodion in 2007, but the grave had been desecrated probably by the fighters of the first Jewish Rebellion who blamed the Idumean king for their predicament.

THE SECOND JEWISH REVOLT

THE REVOLT LED BY SIMON BAR-KOKHBA WHOM RABBI AKIVA, HIS MENTOR, BELIEVED TO BE THE MESSIAH, ENDED IN EVEN GREATER DISASTER. A TEMPLE TO JUPITER WAS BUILT ON TEMPLE MOUNT. JEWS WERE ONLY ALLOWED TO VISIT JERUSALEM ON THE ANNIVERSARY OF THE DESTRUCTION OF THE TEMPLE, THE NINTH OF AV.

The second Jewish revolt commenced around CE 132 during the reign of the Emperor Trajan. There were two main reasons for this second rebellion. Firstly, Hadrian had attempted to ban circumcision in the Empire amongst all his subjects, irrespective of their faith. Secondly, he planned to construct a new city on Jerusalem's ruins, the pagan Aelia Capitolina. Hadrian happened to be present in Syria and Egypt between CE 129–131 and the revolt began as soon as he left. The rebel leader was Simeon bar Kokhba, as he was known to his friends, and Simeon bar Kosiba (son of a Lie) to his enemies. His name and title, as found in the caves of Wadi Murabba'at and Nahal Hever in the Judean desert, are recorded as Simeon bar Kosiba, Prince of Israel. The first name means 'son of the star' and this comes from rabbi Akiba ben Joseph (CE 40–c. 135), who sharpened up the school of Biblical interpretation known as Midrash. After he met Simeon bar Kokhba, Akiba was fascinated with his power and perceived a sense of destiny visualizing him as the promised messiah. Akiba was criticised for being wrong; there is no record of him taking part in the revolt.

Jerusalem was easily captured from the Roman governor Quintus Tineius Rufus and held out for two years. The rebels minted coins in the initial year of the rebellion bearing the words "liberation of Israel," "liberation of Jerusalem" and "the priest Eleazar," this last suggesting renaissance of the Temple cult. Hadrian then recalled his skilful general, Julius Severus, from Britain to command the Roman forces against the rebels. Severus had much experience of guerrilla warfare against the Celts in Britain and this proved valuable in Judaea. Rebel forces were mainly concentrated in the Judean desert around Herodion, Tekoa, Qiryat Arabayya, En-Gedi, and the unidentified Beth Mashko, the final three being centers of rebel administration. Guerrilla warfare ensued; the Roman soldiers inched their way into enemy territory, both sides losing many men. The rebels were flushed out of caves and armed posts intercepted supplies so many insurgents starved to death. CE 135 witnessed the final battle of the rebellion when the mountain fortress of Betar was captured and Simeon bar Kokhba killed. The siege of Betar lasted for one year, and the whole war three-and-a-half years. Roman losses had been severe but for the Jews the war was a disaster. Cassio Dio, the Roman historian, states that fifty important outposts and 985 villages were burned down, 580,000 men were killed and many others died from famine and disease. The Roman marketplaces were swamped with Jewish slaves; the price of a Jew in the Hebron market was less than that of a horse. Surplus slaves were sent to Gaza and Egypt. Hadrian celebrated by minting a Roman coin depicting an enslaved woman and bearing the words "Judaea Capta." Rabbi Akiva, Bar-Kokhba's spiritual mentor, was flayed alive.

Archaeological and papyri in Hebrew, Aramaic, Greek, and Latin concerning the revolt have been found in numerous caves in Wadi Murabba'at, Nahal Hever, Nahal Mishmar, and Nahal Ze'elim, along with many domestic items. The Cave of Horrors and the Cave of the Letters contained the bodies of men, women, and children who had starved to death. Jerusalem was then rebuilt as Colonia Aelia Capitolina, a pagan city, inhabited by Romans, Greeks and other gentiles. Jews were banned on pain of death. Only on the anniversary of the destruction of the Temple were they allowed in to grieve for its loss. The southern gate of the city facing Bethlehem was adorned with the image of a pig. On Temple Mount, a sanctuary was built to Jupiter Capitolinus and the province of Judaea was renamed Syria Palaestina. Jews were apparently eradicated in Judaea but some survived in Galilee which, like Samaria, seems not to have been involved in the rebellion. The law against the practice of Judaism in Galilee was rescinded in CE 138. The Mishnah, the Talmud, and other rabbinical texts were written there by Rabbis Simeon ben Gamaliel II, Simeon bar Yohai, and Rabbi Meir.

Among the hills and deserts of eastern Judaea lay the emotive ruins of the fortress of Masada, destroyed in the first Jewish revolt. Rebel forces again concentrated in this region in the second Jewish revolt. Above are the ruins of the synagogue at Masada with the hills of Judaea beyond.

THE JESUS MESSAGE

JESUS OF NAZARETH WAS A JEW WHO LIVED IN THE TROUBLED
TIMES OF ROMAN OCCUPATION. HIS INNOVATIVE IDEAS
AND CHARISMATIC PERSONALITY WON HIM A CONSIDERABLE
FOLLOWING DURING HIS LIFETIME. THE CHRISTIAN RELIGION
BECAME THE OFFICIAL RELIGION OF THE ROMAN EMPIRE.

Millstone at Capernaum (Kefar Nahum), beside the Sea of Galilee. The synagogue in which Jesus preached still stands.

It is often forgotten that Jesus was a Jew and a teacher who wrestled with alternative interpretations of religious life and spirituality. Like most teachers, he confronted orthodox thought and fell foul of religious leaders and the authorities. The first thirty years of his life will be ignored here as will his death. Instead, his ideas will be aired. It is noteworthy that Jesus did not seek to transgress Jewish Law but to uphold it by seeking its inner motive. In this, he followed the tradition of prophets and, later rabbis.

Jesus was baptized, a purification ritual, by John the Baptist who was later beheaded by Herod. Jesus went into the desert where he was twice tempted by the devil but resisted. He then began his ministry in Galilee, preaching and healing. He started to attract crowds who realised the special nature of this teacher. He commenced choosing a following and summoned twelve men to be particular disciples to accompany him everywhere. Some theologians suggest that the twelve represented the twelve tribes of Israel.

Jesus proclaimed his message, sometimes to individuals, sometimes to his disciples, as well as to congregations in synagogues, which suggests that his ideas did not preclude him from using Pharisaic institutions. He also preached in the open air, as in the Sermon on the Mount. The key themes of his teaching were the fatherhood and authority of God and the necessity for personal righteousness and selfless love. It was mainly with his disciples that he spoke of his role and used the term "the Son of God," predicting his own death and resurrection.

Undoubtedly, his most memorable sermon was the Sermon on the Mount, delivered both to his disciples and a large crowd. The sermon began with the Beatitudes, in which Jesus states that happiness lies, not in wealth, health or success, but in humility mercy, peace-making, and spiritual hunger. He proceeded by suggesting that anger was as great a sin as murder, and lustful thoughts as bad as adultery. He advocated love of one's enemies, disregard for money and possessions, and attention to one's own sins rather than condemnation of the sins of others. He admonished his listeners to avoid hypocritical, ostentatious worship and prayer, and taught the people the prayer that is now known as the Lord's Prayer, which is a shortened version of the Jewish prayer known as the Eighteen Benedictions.

A key aspect of Jesus' teachings was his use of parables, a not unusual teaching medium. His short allegorical tales of everyday life illustrated the spiritual points he wished to make. Of the parables, those of the Good Samaritan and the Prodigal Son are the best known. The former tells the story of a man who is attacked and robbed by thieves and left wounded on the road. First a priest and then a Levite come along the road and, seeing him, pass by on the other side. Then a Samaritan comes along and, although Jews and Samaritans were hostile toward each other, this Samaritan helps the injured man, binds his wounds, and pays for him to be cared for at an inn. The story illustrated the doctrine that people should love their neighbors, and that one's neighbor is anyone in need. Some commentators have made the point that Christian writers might have changed the original use of Israelite to Samaritan for polemical reasons. The parable of the prodigal son illustrates the paternal love and mercy of God. It is the tale of a young man who leaves home and squanders his inheritance on riotous living until he is reduced to poverty and humiliation. When he shamefully returns home, he is joyfully welcomed and forgiven by his father.

Jesus' three-year ministry witnessed numerous miracles, most of which were concerned with the healing of either physical or mental illness. He brought back sight to the blind, speech to the dumb, and hearing to the deaf (Matthew 9: 27–33; 12: 22; 20: 29–34). He healed people affected by leprosy, paralysis, and epilepsy (Matthew 8: 2–3; 9: 2–7; 17: 14–18). He exorcized demonic possession (Luke 4: 33–35; 8: 27–35; 11: 14) and proved capable of healing from a distance, without even seeing the sick person (John 4: 46–54). On three occasions he raised people from the dead: a widow's son, Jairus' young daughter (Luke 7: 11–15; 8: 41–42, 49–56),and Lazarus, Jesus' friend, who was raised after being dead and buried for four days (John 11: 1–44). Jesus also showed mastery over natural forces by walking on water (John 6: 19–21) and calming a storm (Matthew 8: 23–27). The multiplication of the five loaves and two small fishes to feed the 5000 (Matthew 14: 15–21) and transforming water into wine at the wedding feast at Cana (John 2: 1–11) are further examples of the miracles he performed.

Jesus broke with convention by his relationship with Mary Magdalene, Martha, and his conversation with a Samaritan woman. He certainly was unhappy in the company of the religious

Next pages: From its early centers in the Eastern Mediterranean, Christianity spread eastward towards Mesopotamia and Persia, and westward into Europe and North Africa.

leaders and teachers of his time, especially the strictly legalistic Pharisees, whom he admonished for their hypocrisy. The Pharisees constantly tried to catch him out. Typical of Jesus was his ability to turn the tables on his critics. The Pharisees had caught an adulteress and asked Jesus why she should not be stoned to death, as the Law demanded. His reply was to challenge the Pharisees by asking that anyone who had no sin should throw the first stone and the accusers drifted away.

Before Jesus was executed he conferred a task upon the disciples, the twelve Apostles, that they should rule and judge a perfected Israel when a New Age dawned after his death and resurrection. An interesting act by Jesus was his aggressive action in cleansing the Temple of money lenders and traders. Was he seeking to end corruption in the Temple? Was he reminded of Jeremiah?: 'Is this house, which is called by my name, become a den of robbers in your eyes? Behold, even I have seen it, saith the Lord.' (Jeremiah 7: 11) I Curious, too, are the Qumran texts alluding to the Temple as a seat of robbers.

The Spread of Christianity
45 CE–300 CE

- Christian by 45 CE
- Christian by 100 CE
- Christian by 185 CE
- Christian by 325 CE
- Roman Empire c. 300 CE

S A R M A T I A

Sinus
Oxianus

D A C I A

Maeotis
Palus

Mare Caspium
Caspian Sea

Caucasus Mountains

Pontus Euxinus
Black Sea

MOESIA

Sinope   Trapezus

ARMENIA

THRACIA

Artaxata

MACEDONIA
Byzantium

BITHYNIA AND PONTUS

Nieopolis

Apollonia   Thessalonica

ASSYRIA

CAPPADOCIA

PERSIAN EMPIRE

A S I A

GALATIA   CILICIA
Tarsus

MESOPOTAMIA

Athenae   Ephesus

Antiochia

LYCIA

SYRIA

Babylon

CYPRUS

Creta

Sinus
Persicus

M a r e   I n t e r n u m

Damascus

Tyre

Bostra

A r a b i a n

Cyrene

JUDAEA   Jerusalem
Gaza

Alexandria

ARABIA

D e s e r t

CYRENE

Heliopolis

Memphis

A E G Y P T U S

N

Antinopolis

S i n u s   A r a b i c u s

Thebes

0   500 km

0   500 miles

ROMAN TRADE ROUTES

TRADE FLOURISHED THROUGHOUT THE ROMAN EMPIRE AND
BEYOND. LUXURY GOODS CAME ALONG THE SILK ROAD AND
FROM INDIA AND THE SPICE ISLANDS. OYSTERS AND HERRINGS
WERE SENT IN TARRED BARRELS TO KEEP THEM FRESH FROM
NORTHERN GAUL AND FROM BRITAIN.

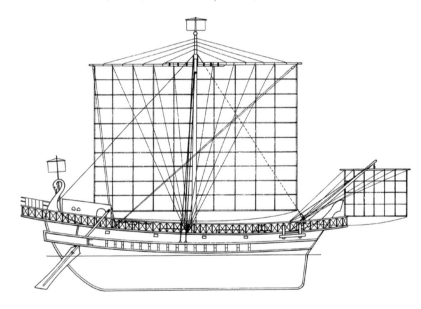

This example of a Roman
merchant ship is designed
to maximize its carrying
capacity. This type of vessel
plied between the wheat
growing regions of the near
east, especially Egypt, and the
granaries of the city of Rome.

The fact that the Mediterranean was a Roman-controlled lake and a Pax Romana existed throughout much of the ancient world meant that people, ideas and religions could move fairly easily and safely throughout the Empire. Commerce was an essential source of wealth to Rome and by CE 50, Italian traders were being replaced by Jewish, Egyptian, and Syrian merchants.

This Mediterranean world even had links with the Atlantic and the interior of continental Europe. Thanks to the powerful currents of the Indian Ocean, there was trade with India and beyond in the luxury goods market. Otherwise, the Empire was self-sufficient. Within the Empire certain inter-regional economic systems were centered on the large ports such as Carthage and Narbonne and towns situated at communication hubs, often built on former Celtic settlements. Examples of these are Lyon and London. Rome was the focus of four important sea routes with starting points at Alexandria, Cartage, southern Gaul at Marseilles, and the Iberian peninsula. A port such as Alexandria was a major exporting city that also funnelled in many of the luxury goods from the Red Sea and Arabia and reprocessed some of them, such as silk.

During the second century CE, other routes following river systems such as the Rhine and the Danube became important. Transit goods were surpluses from production in the Roman provinces or those imported from abroad. Some provinces became renowned for goods such as the pottery produced in

Gaul. Big cities such as Rome, with its huge population, needed regular provisions, maybe up to 200,000 tons of grain annually during the Antonine period.

External trade was located in four main areas. Firstly, the territories of northern Europe sent amber, slaves, hides, furs and dried fish while manufactured goods, gold and silver vessels, pottery, and glass were exported. The major staging post was Carnuntum, between Vienna and Bratislava on the Danube, with Aquileia, at the head of the Adriatic, as its Mediterranean destination. Trade with peoples north of the Black Sea was mainly in horses, slaves, and precious stones. Goods were moved via Olbi, at the mouth of the River Bug, and Tanais in the Don delta. There was also trade with sub-Saharan Africa. Some traffic came through Nubia and the Nile Valley and the rest crossed the deserts via Fazzan and Leptis Magna, bringing ivory, skins, and slaves. The Levant and southern Arabia sent goods via Antioch and Alexandria. Incense came from Arabia, spices from India, and silk from China. Goods were traded from the Red Sea, the Persian Gulf and via the Silk Road through Central Asia. Petra linked the Red Sea routes to western Asia. A Roman trading station existed near Pondicherry where archaeological digs have unearthed Roman pottery, beads, and glass. Hoards of Roman gold coins have been discovered in the Deccan. Pliny the Elder (CE 23–79) complained that India was draining Romes gold reserves.

The Roman Empire at its widest extent controlled territory from the northern parts of the British Isles to the Persian Gulf in the east, and from the forests of Germany to the entire coastline of North Africa in the south.

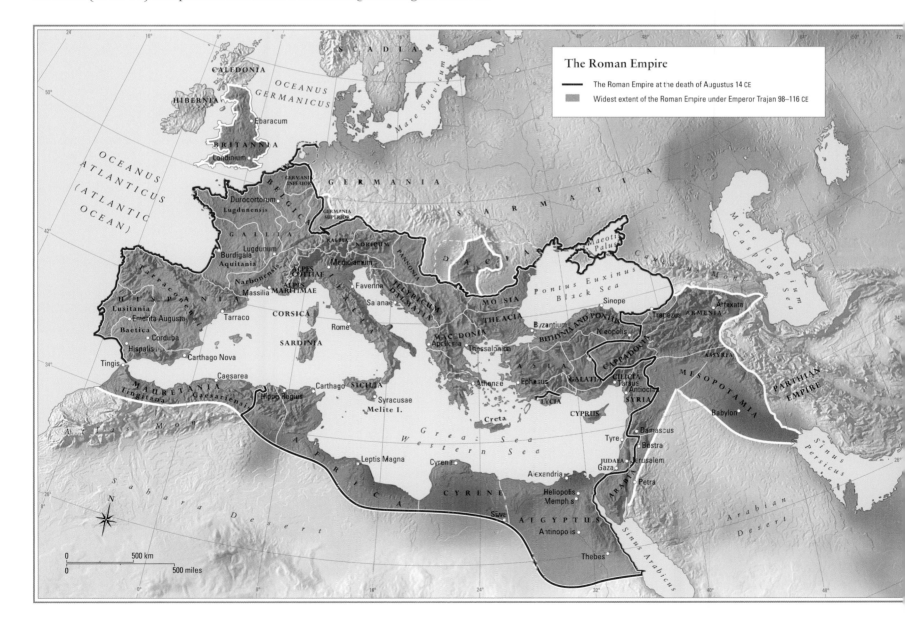

The Roman Empire

— The Roman Empire at the death of Augustus 14 CE

▢ Widest extent of the Roman Empire under Emperor Trajan 98–116 CE

Evangelising Christianity and the Diaspora

THE HELLENISED JEWS WHO LIVED UNDER THE HERODIAN DYNASTY WERE THE FIRST CHRISTIANS. THEY WERE DRAWN MAINLY FROM THE WEALTHIER, ASSIMILATED SECTIONS OF SOCIETY AND SPREAD THE RELIGION TO THE GENTILE WORLD.

Early Christianity spread widely, helped by several factors. In urban areas, a unifying language and culture existed from Italy to India. Alexander the Great's Empire and its successor states made Greek the main imperial language, in the form of demotic Greek or *koine*. The Pax Romana established by Augustus Caesar enabled missionaries to travel safely by sea and land, especially along the system of carefully engineered roads. A third key factor was the extent of the Jewish Diaspora which provided target audiences for the new Jewish message being spread by Jesus' supporters.

Large communities of Jews had existed outside the Promised Land since the Babylonian Exile. The Greek Empire enabled movement throughout the Fertile Crescent and trade played a major part in creating Jewish communities in many cities on the Mediterranean seaboard. Jewish populations swelled when Jewish captives were sold in the slave markets after the two Jewish revolts in Judaea in CE 66–70 and CE 132–135. The philosopher Philo of Alexandria claimed that there were a million Jews by birth or conversion in Egypt by CE 100.

The New Testament, notably the Acts of the Apostles, frequently mentions Jews, and often Christians, dwelling in Syria, Asia Minor, and Greece. Papyri and archaeological excavations of synagogues in Egypt attest to the Jewish presence. The exiles remained true to Judaism. Disputes sometimes occurred over interpretations of the Law. The Written and Oral Law (the Torah and the Talmud) were important to all Jews who observed the traditional dietary laws and the Sabbath. Remembering that Christianity began as a movement within Judaism, that Jesus and his Apostles were Jews, Jesus' adherents accepted him as the "Christ" sent to fulfil God's promise to Abraham,

Opposite: Medieval depiction of the Resurrection of Jesus.

Ruins of an early Christian church in Smyrna, Syria, third century CE.

Isaac, and Jacob. The gospel of God's reigning power was presented in an entirely Jewish context. However, a major issue emerged: should gentiles be allowed to accept Jesus' doctrines without accepting Judaic Law? The Jews pouring into Jerusalem for religious festivals were a captive audience for the Jesus message and they doubtless spread news of it when they returned home. Many of them formed the communities that St. Paul found on his journeys. However, some Jerusalem Christians were more radical and wanted to spread the new teachings beyond the Jewish community. Hellenised, assimilated Jews absorbed the ideas more rapidly. One of the deacons chosen to administer funds for what now may be called the Church, for convenience, was Stephen who thought his faith was for all people, not just orthodox Jews. He attacked the traditionalists and caused an ideological rift within Judaism. The High Priest had him seized and brought before the Jewish Supreme Court. He was accused of blasphemy, of disavowing the Temple cult, and the Jewish claim to be the sole authority in religious belief. He was condemned to death by stoning, later becoming a Christian martyr and eventually a saint.

The expansion of the early Christian Church was helped by the evangelism of Philip, Peter, and John. Their activities turned a movement within Judaism into something entirely different. The Hellenised Philip made mass conversions amongst the Samaritans. He also preached in Ashdod, Lydda, Joppa, Antipatris, and Caesarea Maritima. Peter acted unusually for a Jew when he stayed in the house of a tanner who was deemed unclean because he touched dead animal skins. Peter, therefore, flouted the Pharasaic laws. He even baptised a Roman officer named Cornelius and his entire household. This action shocked the disciples in Jerusalem. However, Peter defended his action in baptising this uncircumcised gentile and his views were accepted. It was recognized that observance of the Jewish Law was unnecessary for conversion, as was circumcision. This implied that belief in Jesus' message was no longer a continuation and extension of Judaism. The Jews who had shared Stephen's ideas had only preached to Jews. They had fled to Cyprus, Phoenicia and Antioch on his martyrdom. On hearing Peter's stand they began to evangelise among the gentiles.

The earliest congregations of the first century Christian church were concentrated in Judaea and Asia Minor. The Book of Revelation, allegedly written by St. John, addresses seven Churches in Asia— in Ephesus, Smyrna, Pergamon, Thyatira, Sardis, Philadelphia and Laodicea. Ignatius (c. 35–107), Bishop of Antioch-in-Syria, visited Asia, writing letters to various congregations there and also to the Christian community in Rome. Elsewhere, Christianity spread into Egypt into the native Egyptian communities and the Greek colonists. Papyri have been found at Oxyrrhynchus showing a Greek Christian presence which also spread to Nag Hamadi, where a complete collection of Jesus' sayings has been found dating from the 4th century AD, translated from their original Greek into Coptic. These are the Gnostic Gospels, the "Gospel of Thomas." Like so many other early Christian writings, as well as the Apocyrpha and Psudepigrapha, this gospel was some how not included in the New Testament.

Map indicating the spread of Christianity through the Mediterranean shortly after the death of Jesus, in the first and second centuries CE.

DIFFERENT RELIGIONS

CHRISTIANITY BECAME THE OFFICIAL RELIGION OF ROME UNDER CONSTANTINE BUT THIS DID NOT PREVENT THE SACK OF ROME IN 410 CE, AND THE SPLITTING OF THE ROMAN EMPIRE INTO TWO. THEN ANOTHER RELIGION EMERGED TO CHALLENGE CHRISTIANITY.

Solomon reading the Torah, from a late 13th-century Hebrew Bible and Prayer Book.

The early days of Christianity saw an apparently miraculous spread of the faith and the authors of the New Testament were certain of the divinity of Jesus. To them, the final stage of God's scheme to save the world must have commenced, evidenced by the numerous Christian groups growing and surviving in the towns of the eastern Mediterranean from Judaea, now renamed Syria Palaestina by the Romans, to Rome. Their faith was aided by the Pax Romana and good communications.

Christianity gained converts because it offered a feeling of equality and community which transcended all differences of race, social class and legal status. The destruction of Jerusalem by the Romans removed Christianity from its Jewish origins in order to generate a more universal appeal and meet the needs of gentile converts without the restrictions of Jewish religious law. It was not long before Christian writings commenced the demonisation of Jews as "Christ killers" to give anti-Jewish sentiment a renewed lease of life. The use of Greek as a lingua franca by all peoples, including the Jewish communities in the Near East, provided Christian missionaries with ready audiences. Syria, Asia Minor and Greece spawned Christian communities as did North Africa, particularly Alexandria and Cyrene. Until the end of the second century AD, all bishops of Rome were Greek-speakers and the New Testament was first written in Greek.

Eventually, Christianity moved into Mesopotamia where Syriac, eastern Aramaic, became the Christians' secular and liturgical language. The language spread into the Arab world, affecting Arabic, and was used to evangelize in India and China. In the west, in the Latin-speaking areas of the Roman Empire, by the third century CE, Christianity had made inroads into Gaul and Spain.

More than one hundred bishoprics were established in Italy alone. There were even three in Britain by the next century in London, York, and either Colchester or Lincoln. In around 432, St. Patrick began his mission to Ireland which resulted in Irish monasticism and a new remarkable Christian experiment.

Although Christianity was persecuted, as by the Emperor Nero after the great fire in Rome in CE 64, and the martyrdoms at Lyons in 177, there are records of just two universal persecutions. Emperor Decius (249–251) launched an anti-Christian campaign in 250 and in 303 Emperor Diocletian (284–305) decreed the destruction of all churches and Christian books together with the executions of many Christians. In 313, the Edict of Milan gave Christianity official recognition and Emperor Constantine made it the official religion of the Roman empire.

Christianity then faced a major issue. Although Constantine had hoped that all his subjects would be united in a common faith, this dream did not stop barbarian invasions and the sack of Rome. The capital was moved from Rome to Constantinople. The Latin section of the Empire collapsed, and differences emerged between the western and the Greek-speaking eastern Empire, resulting in the eventual division into Roman and Greek Orthodox Christianity. Further internecine strife developed in Alexandria where an argument grew about the exact status of Jesus Christ as God, and percolated throughout the Eastern churches. The Ecumenical Councils, held between 325 and 787, sought to resolve these differences. Monastic movements emerged in Arabia, Asia Minor, North Africa, Spain and Britain. Hermits, especially in Egypt and Armenia, withdrew into the deserts and formed organized communities. St. Columba took monasticism to Scotland, while St. Benedict established his Rule, which St. Augustine introduced into Britain at Canterbury in 597.

Ivory carving depicting Jesus with the disciples, eleventh century CE.

Eventually, the Eastern Roman Empire, or Byzantium as it is also known, also came under attack, this time from another religion that emerged in the Near East. The Arabian peninsula had been crossed by traders and nomads, though the peoples of the oases or the caravan routes worshipped many gods. This all changed after Mohammed commenced teaching and preaching in Mecca. Both Judaism and Christianity had penetrated Arabia and were known in the trading centers. Mohammed preached another form of monotheism which identified Allah, the chief god of Mecca, as the sole God of the universe who alone must be worshipped.

Believers were to accept the equality of all peoples before God, and had a duty to care for the less fortunate. Mohammed claimed to be the last in a line of prophets sent by God, which included Abraham, Moses, and Jesus, but to Mohammed God dictated a sacred book, the Qu'ran which lists five pillars of faith and life: belief in Allah as the only God, and Mohammed as his prophet; prayer five times a day; alms-giving; fasting during daylight hours in the month of Ramadan; and pilgrimage to Mecca.

War became a legitimate method of evangelism. Islam conquered Arabia, then turned its attention to Syria, the Levant, Mesopotamia, Egypt, and North Africa. By the middle of the eighth century Moslem invaders had captured most of Spain and parts of France, mostly within twenty years of Mohammed's death in 632. The mosque known as the Dome of the Rock was constructed in 691 over the place where Mohammed was taken up to heaven. Traditionally, this is also the place where Abraham prepared to sacrifice Isaac and the site of the Jewish Temple.

DIASPORA

DESPITE THE FALL OF JUDAEA AND THE DESTRUCTION OF THE TEMPLE, THE JEWS WERE DETERMINED TO CONTINUE THEIR WORSHIP OF GOD. THROUGH THE FORESIGHT OF INNOVATIVE RABBIS, CUSTOMS AND PRACTICES WERE CHANGED TO DEAL WITH THE NEW CIRCUMSTANCES.

The Fortress of Masada, the last stronghold of the Jews in their fight against the Romans. Israeli army recruits are now taken there for an induction ceremony.

The Emperor Hadrian (CE 76–138) brutally repressed non-pagans, including a ban on circumcision and religious instruction for the Jews. This provoked another armed rebellion, under the leader and statesman Simeon ben Koziba (bar Kochba). In 132 C.E., Simeon crushed the Roman legions in a surprise victory and re-established an independent Jewish state with himself at its head. Eleazar of Modi'in was appointed to the revived post of high priest. Rabbi Akiva, the great sponsor of the revolt, renamed Ben Koziba as Bar Kokhba (son of a star). But the success of this last Jewish revolt was shortlived. The Romans sent a mighty army to crush it and Bar Kokhba was finally defeated in battle after a two-year siege of the fortress of Bet Seir (Betar) southwest of Jerusalem, on the Hebrew date of 9 Av, 135, the anniversary of the fall of the First and Second Temples. The Romans massacred the inhabitants of the fortress. Rabbi Akiva, the spiritual leader who had supported Bar Kokhba and even claimed that he was the Messiah, was hideously tortured, flayed alive, and torn to death with metal combs.

The most lasting consequence of the Bar Kochba Revolt is one that must have seemed to have little significance at the time. The Romans banned the name "Judaea", derived from the Latin word for "Jewish"; henceforth, the Roman province was to be known as "Syria-Palaestina", the second part of the word being a reference to the hated Philistines, the Cretan invaders who had inhabited the coastal plane a thousand years earlier but who had long since disappeared. The name has been perpetuated as the negation of the very right of the Jews to live in their own land. Before his death, Hadrian also renamed Jerusalem "Colonia Aelia Capitolina" and dedicated the city to Jupiter. He removed all trace of the Second Temple, replacing it with a pagan temple on Temple Mount.

The next emperor, Antoninus Pius (86–161 CE), had a far more benign attitude to the Jews and this spirit of toleration was to last until the death of Alexander Severus in 235, reaching its apogee in the positively philo-Semitic Septimus Severus (reigned 193–211) who was of Semitic origin himself and spoke Aramaic, the lingua franca of the Eastern Mediterranean of the time. Jews were allowed back into Jerusalem but they now constituted only one tenth of the population.

The center of Jewish life moved to Galilee, where the Roman Emperor Vespasian permitted Rabban Yochanan ben Zakkai to set up his small academy at Yavneh, as the successor to the Jewish parliament, the Sanhedrin, in Jerusalem. Rabbi Gamaliel III, great-grandson of Hillel, continued the work of Jewish scholars by founding an academy at Usha. There were also academies in Lod (Lydda) and Bnei Brak, near the coast. In about the 100 CE, the scholars, known as the Tannaim, at the academies in the Holy Land and those of Nahardea in Babylonia, finalised the compilation of the third part of the Bible known as the Writings (ketuvim) or Hagiographia, consisting of the Psalms, Proverbs, Song of Songs, and the books of Job, Ruth, Lamentations, Ecclesiastes, Esther, Daniel Ezra, Nehemiah, and Chronicles I and II. They also created the concept of the synagogue and laid down a daily order or prayer, transferring the memory of the rituals and some of the rituals themselves that had been performed by the High Priest in the Temple. Small temples had existed previously in the time of the First Temple; they have been discovered in Tel Dan, Beersheba, and even in Elephantine, in Egypt. They were now replaced by synagogues, prayer-houses, in which the officiants were rabbis (teachers) but not priests. Rituals introduced into the synagogue from the Temple included the priestly blessing by the priests (kohanim), the blowing of the shofar (ram's horn) on the New Year and the Day of Atonement, which would become a fast day for the whole Jewish people, during which they would repent individually, instead of the high priest fasting and repenting on their behalf. Without the Temple, there could be no sacrifices, neither animal nor meal-offerings.

The scholars of the academies began to codify the so-called Oral Law, the laws that had to be introduced to perpetuate the religion in a changed world, in which the Jews were exiled from their land. The Mishna, the book that lies at the heart of the Talmud and is the foundation of the so-called Oral Law was first written down on the orders of Rabbi Judah Hanasi (c. 170–c. 219) who did not approve of the interpretation of the Scriptures in the light of the new circumstances of exile with which the Jews had to cope and the grafting of an Oral Law onto the Written Law, the law of the Torah. He therefore ordered that the Mishna now be written down, as opposed to passed down orally through generations of scholars. This, he thought, would terminate its development. In fact, it had the opposite effect, since Jewish scholars have never ceased to elaborate on it and comment on it, starting with the Gemarah, the commentaries of the Amoraim in Palestine and Babylonia, through later commentaries by medieval luminaries such as Rashi, the codifiers including Maimonides and

Joseph Caro (author of the Shulhan Arukh written in the mid-sixteenth century) and the subsequent responsa of rabbis to questions from their congregants. The tradition of commentary and discussion of the laws, begun as early as the days of Hillel (110 BCE–10 CE) and Shammai (50 BCE–30 CE), two rabbis and political leaders who held largely opposing views, was one that would last indefinitely.

The translations of the Bible into Aramaic and Greek, known as Targum, were early interpretations that began even before the destruction of the Second Temple, though work on them lasted into the Middle Ages. The various versions of the Targum (of which the best known are those of Yehonatan and Onkelos into Aramaic and Aquila into Greek) contained paraphrases and the first biblical commentaries, interspersed with the text itself. It became the custom to read these aloud to the people even in the time of the Second Temple and they are still read in public in synagogue today, in some communities, such as in the Yemen.

The center of Jewish scholarship gradually shifted to the Diaspora, more particularly to Nehardea in Babylonia. The large and powerful Jewish community had continued to live there since the Babylonian Exile in the sixth century BCE The work of the Tannaim continued here, as did that of their successors, the Amoraim who wrote their own commentaries on the Mishnah, a body of work that came to be known as the Gemarrah. The Mishnah and the Gemarrah together are known as the Talmud. Two versions of the Talmud emerged, the Palestinian, known as the Jerusalem Talmud, and the Babylonian, the latter being considered to be more authoritative.

In addition to the Talmud, many other writings were produced, such as the Pesikta de Rav Kahana and Bible commentaries such as Genesis Rabbah and Leviticus Rabbah. In addition to the twenty-four books of the Hebrew Bible, other books were written toward the end of the Second Temple period and after, known as the Apocrypha or Sefarim Hitzonim (external books) Archaeological excavations have revealed that the sect known as the Sadducees appear to have maintained an earlier and smaller number of texts as canonical. Other Jewish traditions held different books to be sacred, as in the case of the Falasha. These books, some of which are historical accounts, such as the Books of the Maccabees, others containing prophesies, are considered to be part of the enormous literary output that flourished from 200 BCE to 100 CE and beyond.

Jewish settlement outside the Holy Land had begun centuries earlier and by the time of the expulsion from

Jerusalem, there were substantial communities in Rome, Alexandria, Greece, Salamis in Cyprus and smaller communities all over the Roman Empire. The Sassanian monarchs who ruled Persia and Babyonia from 226, also encouraged Jewish immigration. It was the Sassanids who conferred the title of Resh Galuta or Exilarch on the head of the Jewish community.

The evolution of Judaism into a religion that did not depend on a priestly caste, one that allowed the people to play an active role, one that was constantly being interpreted and adapted to suit the situation is a process that began even while the Second Temple still stood. The Emperor Titus, destroyer of the Second Temple, who removed its holy vessels and paraded them through Rome, was convinced that once the Temple had been destroyed, Judaism would cease to exist. He had exterminated 25 percent of the Jewish population of Judaea, enslaved a further ten percent, and reduced the Jews to a minority in their own land, but he could not destroy Judaism.

Contrary to popular Christian belief, the Jewish Diaspora did not begin with the death of Jesus and the destruction of the Temple. Jews had founded colonies all over the Mediterranean for thirteen hundred years prior to that date.

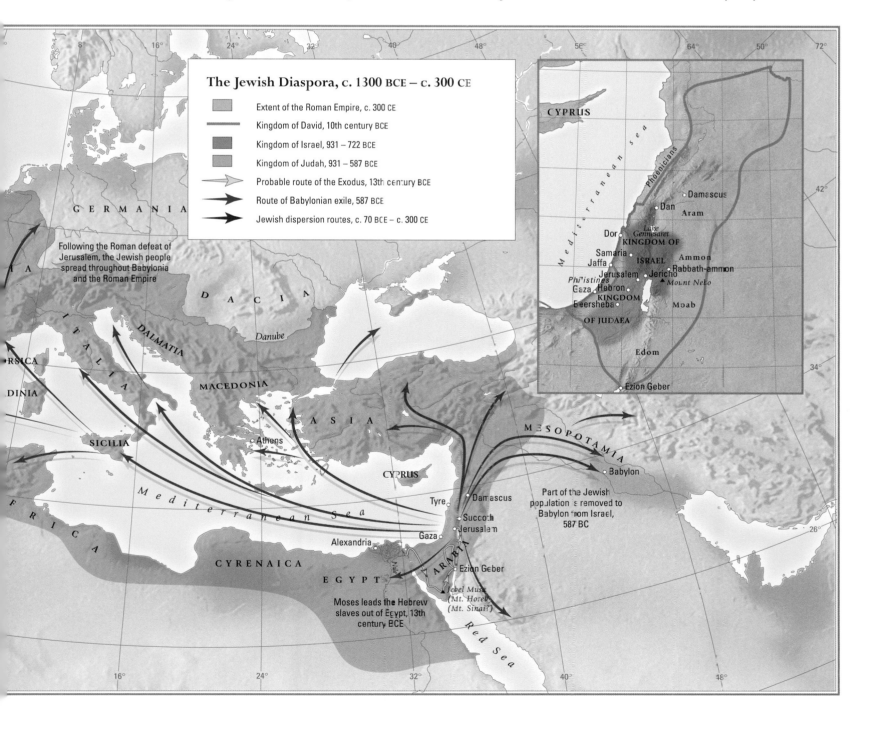

The Jewish Diaspora, c. 1300 BCE – c. 300 CE

- Extent of the Roman Empire, c. 300 CE
- Kingdom of David, 10th century BCE
- Kingdom of Israel, 931 – 722 BCE
- Kingdom of Judah, 931 – 587 BCE
- Probable route of the Exodus, 13th century BCE
- Route of Babylonian exile, 587 BCE
- Jewish dispersion routes, c. 70 BCE – c. 300 CE

Following the Roman defeat of Jerusalem, the Jewish people spread throughout Babylonia and the Roman Empire

Part of the Jewish population is removed to Babylon from Israel, 587 BC

Moses leads the Hebrew slaves out of Egypt, 13th century BCE

JEWS AND ISLAM

THE TOLERANCE OF JEWS THROUGHOUT MOST OF THE MUSLIM WORLD IN THE EARLY MIDDLE AGES PRODUCED MANY GREAT JEWISH SCHOLARS WHO COMBINED JEWISH LEARNING WITH SCIENCE. THE GREATEST IS MAIMONIDES, THE PHYSICIAN WHO LIVED MUCH OF HIS LIFE IN FOSTAT, BUT WHO IS BURIED IN TIBERIAS.

The colonnade in the church of Santa Maria La Blanca, in Toledo, Spain, a former synagogue.

The prophet Mohammed (570–632) came into conflict with the Jews of Arabia when they refused to accept the new faith he propagated. After his death, his followers moved northward, conquering their foes and spreading the Muslim faith. They brought an end to the Sassanian Empire in Persia and severely constricted the Byzantine Empire, the remains of the eastern Roman Empire, in both of which Jews had been persecuted. It took only a hundred years (632–732) for the Empire of Islam to stretch from the borders of China throughout central Asia, across northern India, the Middle East, North Africa, and the Iberian Peninsula.

The Jews found the new rulers more tolerant than their predecessors on the whole and Jews rose to prominent positions under the caliphs, and in particular, Caliph Omar (634–644 CE) and his successors, even rising to the rank of vizier (the equivalent of prime minister). The Ummayce Caliphate ruled the two main centers of Jewish learning at the time, the Holy Land and Babylonia. Jews and Christians, known as dhimmi, were granted exemption from military service, the right to maintain their own courts of law (a practice that has lasted to this day in modern Israel) and protection of property. Jews were now able to accumulate wealth and they began to trade, dealing in goods such as spices and perfumes and traveling the Silk Road to China via Central Asia. They were not allowed to make converts, however, or build houses higher than those of their Moslem neighbors. The special tax imposed on non-Moslems caused the Jews to abandon farming and congregate in the towns, where they tended to work as craftsmen. Until the Jews were driven out of Arab lands after World War II, they were the small tradesmen, shoe-menders, dyers, weavers, jewelers, carvers and musicians of the Moslem world, especially in Mesopotamia (Babylonia) and the Yemen.

With the Arab conquest, Jews were once again allowed to practice their religion freely and Jewish learning flourished. The position of Resh Galuta or Exilarch, head of the Jewish community, was reinstated in Babylonia. The two major academies of Sura and Pumbeditha had existed before the Islamic conquest. The academy at Sura was begun in 589 by Rav Ashi, also known as Rav, and lasted until 1038. Pumbeditha was founded by Ravina in around 550. The academies continued the work of the Tannaim and Amoraim in compiling the Babylonian Talmud which did not reach its final form until around 700 CE.

The head of an academy was known as the gaon (plural: geonim), which in modern Hebrew means "genius" but the word is an abbreviation for "Head of the Academy, the Pride of Jacob." Geonim were considered to be the greatest authorities on Jewish practice, now that the Temple and its priests no longer existed. Questions flooded into them from all over the Jewish world. These questions and their answers, known as responsa, have been preserved and provide an insight into enlightened Jewish life in the Diaspora at a time when Europe was in the Dark Ages. Three of the greatest of these sages were Yehudai ben Nahman, Saadia, known as Saadia Gaon, and Hai Gaon. Yehudai (c. 690–761), who was blind, made the very first attempt to codify the Talmud, entitled Halachot Pesukot (Decided Laws) explains the customs that had been practiced in the Diaspora since the destruction of the Second Temple. The text, which is organized in the same way as the tractates of the Babylonian Talmud, has been the subject of many rewrites and commentaries as is usually the case with important works of Jewish scholarship and law.

Saadia Gaon (882–946 CE), whose full name was Saadia ben Yosef ha-Gaon Fayyumi was born in the remote oasis of Fayyum in Egypt, identified with the city of Pithom, built for the Egyptians by Hebrew slaves. Saadia left Egypt at a young age to study in Tiberias in the Holy Land and wrote his first major work at the age of twenty, a Hebrew dictionary of linguistics that he entitled *Agron*. Saadia was a fierce opponent of the Karaites, a Jewish sect that repudiated the Talmud, writing many polemics against them and their leader, Anan ben David. In 922, Rabbi Aaron ben Meir, gaon of the leading Talmudic academy in Ramleh, in the Holy Land, attempted to change the dates of the Jewish festivals. Since the destruction of the Second Temple festivals had been held on fixed days, instead of being governed by the position of the moon. Saadia wrote "Sefer ha-Mo'adim" ('The Book of Festivals") to express his opposition to the change. For this great work, which averted a split in the Jewish community, the Exilarch, David ben Zakkai insisted in 928 on making Saadia the gaon of the Academy of Sura, although no "foreigner" had ever before been appointed to such high office. Under Saadia, the academy entered a golden age, marred only by Saadia's bitter dispute with David ben Zakkai the very Exilarch who had appointed him. Saadia translated the Bible into Arabic, to which he added a commentary, also in Arabic. In later, years, Saadia wrote a work in both Hebrew and Arabic entitled "Sefer ha-Galui"

Between the 7th and 8th Century BCE Islam spread rapidly across the Near East, North Africa and into Spain.

("Kitab al-á'arid" meaning "The Book of the Revealed") of which only a few fragments have survived.

Hai Gaon (939–1038), also known as Hai ben Sherira, was one of the last gaonim of the academy of Pumbedita. He is famous for his many responsa. Like Saadia, Hai was fluent in Arabic and wrote prolifically in that language. Questions reached him from Germany, France, Spain, Anatolia, the Maghreb and even India and Ethiopia. He also wrote many learned books dealing with commercial law such as mortgages and the sale of goods.

This is also the period, of the Golden Age of Spain. The cities of Toledo and Lucena are reputed to have been founded by Jews. Like their Arab contemporaries, the Jews of Spain helped to spread knowledge of Greek and Latin learning through translating the classics into Arabic and Hebrew and building on acquired knowledge. For instance, Avraham Ibn Daud (c. 1110–1180) was an astronomer and philosopher and Judah ben Samuel Ha-Levi (1075–1141), famous for his poetry, recorded the conversion of the Khazars to Judaism in the eighth or ninth century. He also wrote of his proto-Zionist longing for Jerusalem, "I am at the tip of the Western world, but my heart is in the East". Other poets and philosophers were Solomon Ibn Gabirol (c. 1021–c. 1058), Moses Ibn Ezra (c. 1055–c. 1155), and Judah Al-Harizi (1170–1235). Benjamin of Tudela was a medieval rabbi and explorer, about whom little is known, but he wrote a fascinating diary of his travels through Europe, Asia, and Africa between 1165 and 1173. Hasdai Crescas (1340–1410) was a later philosopher born in Barcelona, a precursor of Galileo, who refuted the more unreliable of Aristotle's theories through Talmudic reasoning. All of these great sages are perpetuated in street names in the district of Rehavia in modern Jerusalem.

Undoubtedly, the greatest scion of the Golden Age of Spain was Moses ben Maimon (known as Maimonides or Rambam) (1135–1204). By the time of his birth, in Cordoba, at the end of the Golden Age, the Moslems had become less tolerant. The Almohades conquered Cordoba in 1148, ordering the Jewish community to convert to Islam or face death or exile. Maimonides' family fled the city (where, ironically, he is commemorated with a statue) eventually settling in Fez, Morocco, where he studied at the University of Al-Karaouine. It was in Fez, between 1170 and 1180, that he wrote his two works of Jewish scholarship, the commentary on the Mishnah, *Mishneh Torah*, and his even more famous work, *Moreh Nevokhim*, that translates as "The Guide for the Perplexed". Maimonides lived briefly in the Holy Land, before settling in Fostat (now Cairo), where he became physician to the Grand Vizier Alfadhil and Sultan Saladdin of Egypt. He even treated the English King Richard the Lionheart during the Crusades. He was the leading physician of his day, combining medical skills with leadership of the Egyptian Jewish community and writing works of Jewish scholarship and medicine in Hebrew and Arabic.

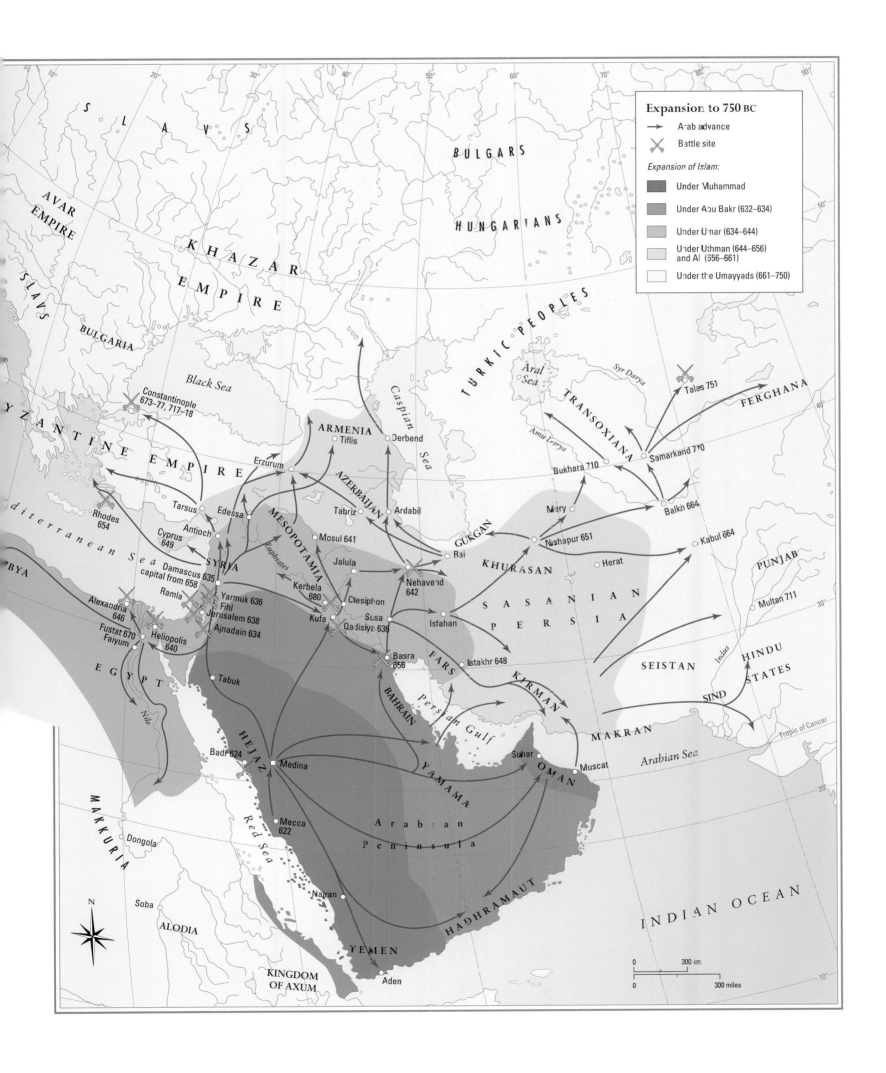

Expansion to 750 BC

→ Arab advance

⚔ Battle site

Expansion of Islam:

Under Muhammad

Under Abu Bakr (632–634)

Under Umar (634–644)

Under Uthman (644–656) and Ali (656–661)

Under the Umayyads (661–750)

SLAVS

AVAR EMPIRE

SLAVS

BULGARS

BYZANTINE EMPIRE

KHAZAR EMPIRE

BULGARIA

HUNGARIANS

Black Sea

TURKIC PEOPLES

Aral Sea

Syr Darya

Talas 751

TRANSOXIANA

FERGHANA

Constantinople 673–77, 717–18

ARMENIA

Tiflis

Derbend

Caspian Sea

Amu Darya

Samarkand 710

Bukhara 710

Mediterranean Sea

Rhodes 654

Cyprus 649

Tarsus

Antioch

Edessa

Erzurum

AZERBAIJAN

Tabriz

Ardabil

Mery

Nishapur 651

Balkh 664

Mosul 641

Euphrates

MESOPOTAMIA

GURGAN

Rai

KHURASAN

Herat

Kabul 664

PUNJAB

SYRIA

Damascus 635 capital from 658

Ramla

Jalula

Kerbela 680

Ctesiphon

Nehavend 642

Kufa

Susa

Qadisiya 636

Isfahan

SASANIAN PERSIA

Multan 711

Yarmuk 636

Fihl

Jerusalem 638

Ajnadain 634

Alexandria 646

Fustat 670

Faiyum

Heliopolis 640

Tabuk

Basra 656

FARS

Istakhr 648

KIRMAN

SEISTAN

Indus

SIND

HINDU STATES

LIBYA

EGYPT

Nile

BAHRAIN

Persian Gulf

MAKRAN

Tropic of Cancer

MAKKURIA

Badr 624

HEJAZ

Medina

YAMAMA

Suhar

Muscat

OMAN

Arabian Sea

Red Sea

Dongola

Mecca 622

Arabian Peninsula

Najran

HADHRAMAUT

INDIAN OCEAN

Soba

ALODIA

YEMEN

Aden

KINGDOM OF AXUM

N

0   300 km

0   300 miles

SAMARITANS AND KARAITES

SAMARITANS AND KARAITES ARE JEWISH SECTS WHOSE MEMBERS ARE ALLOWED TO MARRY JEWS. BOTH HAVE DWINDLED CONSIDERABLY IN NUMBERS BUT BOTH CAN CLAIM FLOURISHING COMMUNITIES IN MODERN ISRAEL.

There only two schisms or sects that have split away from Judaism, the Samaritans and the Karaites. Both claim to be the true religion of the Bible.

The Samaritans assert direct descent from the tribes of Ephraim and Manasseh and there is some reason to believe that they have lived continuously in the Holy Land since the time of the Kingdom of Israel. Jewish sources claim that they broke away from Judaism when the land they inhabited, Samaria (Shomron), was conquered by King Sargon II in 722/721 BCE, an event recorded in the Bible in II Kings: 17. At any event, the rift with mainstream Judaism appears to have occurred at this time.

The Samaritans accept only the Five Books of Moses and the Book of Joshua, rejecting the Prophets and the rest of the Scriptures and, of course, the Oral Law, the Mishnah and the Talmud. There is a Samaritan-Hebrew script in which their holy books are written and which they still use along with Samaritan-Aramaic. Some of the Samaritan community lives in Holon, just outside Tel-Aviv and they have integrated seamlessly into Israeli society, even serving in the Israel Defense Forces. In everyday life, the Samaritans speak Hebrew or Arabic, depending on which of the two communities they are from. They claim that their Temple on Mount Gerizim, near Shechem (Nablus) where the rest of the community still lives, is the true Temple. As a result, they still have a priestly caste and a High Priest. The main Samaritan festival is the Festival of the Sacrifice, their equivalent of Passover, when they sacrifice sheep on Mount Gerizim.

The Samaritans have suffered terrible religious persecutions down the ages, even from Jews but especially from the Byzantine Christians. Once numbering thousands, they have dwindled so that only just over 700 of them are left. They have helped to increase their numbers through the men marrying

Jewish women since the two communities, one on the West Bank and one in Israel, were reunited after 1967 and maintain close ties.

The Karaites are the other Jewish sect who, like the Samaritans, have denied any links to Judaism at various times, for strategic reasons. The movement was founded by Anan ben David between 780 and 800 CE when Anan was passed over for the post of Exilarch, head of the Jewish community of Mesopotamia, in favor of his younger brother, Hananiah. The rift with rabbinic Judaism finally came when Anan ben David was imprisoned on the orders of the rabbis for preaching heresy. The sages of the Talmudic Academies of Sura and Pumbeditha, most notably the great Saadia Fayyumi (892–942), head of the Academy of Pumbeditha, condemned Anan and his followers, originally known as Ananites, in particularly strong terms. While the Ananites rejected the Oral Law and solely to the Bible, this was an impracticality even as early as the Middle Ages. Anan claimed that no meat other than that of deer and pigeons could be eaten after the Exile, and that since the Lord proclaimed himself a healer, his followers were not allowed to consult physicians. He banned any lights on the Sabbath. The Karaites still do not allow any cooking on the Sabbath and festivals, even from a fire kindled beforehand. In fact, some authorities consider that the Jewish ritual lighting of candles just before the Sabbath and festivals has its origin in a negation by the Jews of the Karaite custom of spending the Sabbath and Festivals completely in the dark.

Karaitism reached its zenith between the tenth and eleventh centuries CE when much Karaitic literature was produced in the Muslim world. The Karaites followed the Jewish diaspora to Russia and Crimea, as well as to the Holy Land, and they have a synagogue in the Old City of Jerusalem. Nevertheless, in many of the countries in which they have settled, the Karaites claimed that they were not Jews and as a result they were exempt from many restrictive laws, such as those applied to Jews in the Muslim world and in nineteenth-century Czarist Russia. Although the numbers of the Karaites have dwindled to a few thousand, their remnants still survive. The Karaim are a distinct Karaite community from the Crimean peninsula of the Ukraine, who speak a Turkic language. There are several hundred Crimean Karaites in Lithuania who were invited to settle there by Grand Duke Vytautas in 1397. As a result, their houses are built with three windows, one dedicated to the family, one to God and one to the Grand Duke. Egypt also had a large Karaite population until the Karaites were expelled along with Jews and foreigners by General Neguib in 1956.

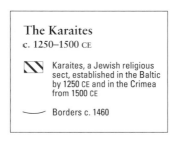

The Karaites
c. 1250–1500 CE

Karaites, a Jewish religious sect, established in the Baltic by 1250 CE and in the Crimea from 1500 CE

Borders c. 1460

The Karaites followed the Jewish Diaspora to Russia and the Crimea, where communities thrived for many generations. However, they have since declined though they still maintain a synagogue in Jerusalem.

Jews and Trade in the Early Medieval Era

ALTHOUGH JEWS HAD NOT BEEN IMPORTANT TRADERS IN THEIR OWN LAND, ONCE EXILED THEY BECAME TRAVELLERS. DESPITE THE RESTRICTIONS PLACED ON THEM, THEY BECAME SUCCESSFUL MERCHANTS.

Ruins of Gaochang on the Silk Road, at the edge of the Gobi Desert.

Jews had never engaged in trade and finance in their own land, it was only when they were dispersed in the Diaspora that they had to become merchants and traders, often against their will. This was partly because in so many places Jews were banned from owning land and so had to live in the towns. They were not allowed to join the Guilds and in most of Europe they were considered direct subjects of the king. This meant that the Jews of medieval Europe were "déclassé," having no place in the feudal system. Jews had other restrictions placed upon them by their religion. They needed to live in communities in which at least ten men could be found to gather for a prayer meeting, keep to the strict Jewish dietary laws, and other religious customs. In England, for instance, innkeepers would allow a traveling Jew who was a regular customer to store his eating utensils (which were kosher) in a special closet from which he could retrieve them whenever he patronised the establishment.

The first description of Poland came from a Jewish traveler, Ibrahim Ibn Ya'qub of Tortoba who visited Cracow in 966. He also claimed to have met Jewish travelling merchants in a number of towns in Austria and Germany. Two notable travellers of the period are the mysterious Eldad Ha-Dani, who lived in the ninth century and claimed to have travelled down the Nile to Ethiopia, and Benjamin of Tudela who visited Rome in 1173 and Jerusalem shortly thereafter.

The new rulers of what had once been the Roman Empire needed the skills of the Jews who became their money-lenders and bankers, also because the Catholics banned such activities among their own people. The Jews had passed down the Roman commercial practices and had other natural advantages when it came to trade. First of all, they could be sure of a welcome from their fellow countrymen when they travelled from home and they could communicate in a lingua franca—Hebrew and the early form of Yiddish. The Talmud contained detailed laws governing trade and these became the basis of English and even European commercial law.

The Frankish kings bought goods from the Jewish merchants of Narbonne and Marseilles, and they are mentioned as traders in Naples and Palermo (then under Moslem rule) and Genoa. They also had their own fleets of ships. Gregory of Tours (533–594) mentions a Jew who owned a sailing ship that plied between Nice and Marseilles.

Between the sixth and the tenth centuries, Jewish merchants known as Radhanites or Radanites travelled through Europe, the Middle East, and the Far East trading in spices, silks, coins, and jewels. The origin of the name is disputed, but it is believed to refer to a province of Mesopotamia (Iraq) known as Radhan. The trade routes all began in the Rhone Valley and ended in China. They acted as middlemen between the Christian and the Islamic world.

During the Early Middle Ages, the warring Islamic nations and the Christian kingdoms of Europe often banned each others' merchants from entering their ports. The Radhanites functioned as neutral go-betweens, keeping open the lines of communication and trade between the former Roman Empire and the Far East. This enabled Jewish merchants to enjoyed significant privileges under the early Carolingians in France and throughout the Muslim world.

While most trade between Europe and East Asia had been conducted via Persian and Central Asian intermediaries, the Radhanites were among the first to establish regular trading routes from Western Europe to Eastern Asia. More remarkably, they engaged in this trade centuries before they voyages of Marco Polo and ibn Battuta brought their tales of travel in the Orient to the Christians and the Muslims respectively.

Many historians believe that the art of Chinese paper-making was brought to Europe via Jewish merchants. Joseph of Spain, possibly a Radhanite, is credited by some sources with introducing the so-called Arabic numerals (which are not Arabic at all but Indian) from India to Europe. Certainly Abraham Ibn Ezra (c. 1093–1167) while visiting Verona in 1146, wrote *Sefer Ha-mispar* (*The Book of Numbers*), the earliest explanation in Europe of the new decimal system that introduced the concept of zero, which he called galgal, the Hebrew word for a wheel.

The system of letters or credit and bills of exchange that Jews could use to replace the heavy coins (paper money did not yet exist) was developed and put into force on an unprecedented scale by the Radhanites, making them the precursors of the merchant banks and discount houses that were first established during the late Middle Ages and the early modern period. Even the Hebrew word "star" (*shtar*) meaning a note or bill of exchange, was used throughout Europe for such financial contracts.

Some scholars believe that the Radhanites may have played a role in the conversion of the Khazars to Judaism. In addition, they may have helped establish Jewish communities at various points along their trade routes, and were probably involved in the early Jewish settlement of Eastern Europe, Central Asia, China and India. The Radhanites are mentioned by name only by a handful of sources. Ibn al-Faqih's early tenth century *Kitab al-Buldan* ("*Book of the Countries*") mentions them, but much of ibn al-Faqih's information was derived from ibn Khordadbeh's work. *Sefer ha-Dinim*, a Hebrew account of the travels of Yehuda ben Meir of Mainz, named the cities of Przemyl and Kiev as trading posts along the Radhanite route. In the early twelfth century, a French-Jewish trader named Yitzhak Dorbelo wrote that he traveled with Radhanite merchants to Poland.

Radhanite Jews founded a small colony in Kaifeng (now known as Hangchow) then a major stop on the Silk Road. It lasted until the Taiping Rebellion of the 1850s which caused the dispersal of the community, who later returned to Kaifeng. Three stones bearing Hebrew inscriptions have been found there, of which the oldest, dating from 1489, commemorates the construction of the synagogue in 1163. The inscription states that the Jews came to China from India during the Han Dynasty (2nd century BCE–2nd century CE). The names of seventy Jews are listed, stating that their religion was transmitted from Abraham down to the prophet Ezra. This is significant as Ezra is the prophet most closely associated with the Jews of Babylon (modern Iraq) who would have been among the first Jewish traders to settle in China. The second tablet, dating from 1512 (found in the

synagogue) details the religious practices. The third, dated 1663, commemorates the rebuilding of the Qingzhen Si synagogue. There are claims that Jews served as soldiers in the armies of Yue Fei.

Jewish merchants from Europe traveled to India in the medieval period but it is not clear whether they formed permanent settlements in south Asia. The first reliable evidence of Jews living in India comes from the early eleventh century. It is certain that the first Jewish settlements were centered along the western coast. The reference by Ibrahim ibn Daud (c. 1110 CE–1180 CE) to Jews in India is vague, and there are no references to Indian Jews until the seventeenth century.

Between the tenth and eleventh centuries, there were Jewish communities in every town of importance in France and Germany. Many had been welcomed in by Charlemagne (747–814) who needed their financial skills. A Jew named Isaac was a member of a delegation sent by the Holy Roman Emperor to the court of Haroun Al-Rashid (786–809); he was the sole survivor of the perilous journey,

Harun al-Rashid became the fifth caliph of the Abbasid dynasty in September 786 at the age of twenty. During his reign the power and prosperity of the dynasty was at its height, though it has also been argued that its decline began at that time.

returning with an elephant, the first ever seen in Europe.

Many of the Jews invited in by Charlemagne from Spain to encourage international relations settled in the Rhineland, where they came to dominate the wine trade and did so until driven out by the Nazis in the 1930s, nearly a thousand years later. The great Rashi, Rabbi Shlomo bar Yitzchak (1104–05), one of the most renowned of the Jewish scholars of medieval France is particularly remembered for his comprehensive commentaries on the Bible and the Talmud.

Rashi was born in Troyes, then the capital of the Champagne region of France, into a family of scholars. As a young man he gained experience in trade and agriculture, and then studied at the academies of Mainz and Worms. After returning to Troyes, he went into business as a wine merchant, and also set up his own rabbinical school. He was clearly a fluent French-speaker since occasionally in his commentaries he cannot find an appropriate Hebrew word and writes (a French word) "in the foreign tongue."

The First Crusade began during Rashi's lifetime and in 1099 followers of the Crusaders attacked the Jews of the Rhineland. Many of Rashi's friends and family were massacred and his grandson, Jacob ben Meir Tam, known as Rabbeinu Tam (c. 1100–c. 1171) was stabbed.

The pattern throughout Europe was the same. When it was expedient for rulers to allow the Jews to amass wealth, which could then be lent to them, they let them. When the debts became too big, or when Christians complained about competition from the Jews, fines and restrictions were imposed, and this could end in their expulsion from the land. Yet, however usurous the Jews had allegedly been, their Christian successors, usually the Germano-Italian Lombards, were worse. The cost of borrowing was so high in the Middle Ages because the risks were enormous and the chance of a return on the investment slight to remote. Paper money had not been invented so that large sums were only negotiated as bills of exchange.

Jewish communities scattered along the Mediterranean rim were linked by trade routes to other communities in central and northern Europe.

The Ties of Trade
c. 1300 CE

- Trading area of Hansa
- Hanseatic route
- Trading area of Genoa
- Genoese route
- Trading area of Venice
- Venecians route
- Town with commercial link with Antwerp
- Silk production
- Wool production
- Textile production

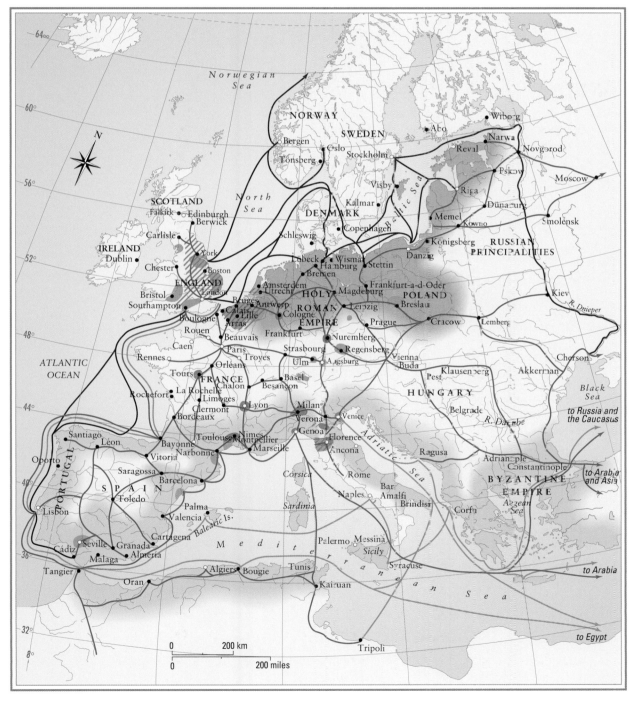

JEWS AND BYZANTIUM

THE CRUELTY OF THE FATHERS OF THE EARLY CHRISTIAN CHURCH
TOWARD THE JEWS WENT EVEN FURTHER THAN THE EXCESSES OF
THE ROMAN EMPERORS. NO WONDER THE JEWS OF BYZANTIUM
SOUGHT TO ESCAPE BY MOVING NORTH INTO CENTRAL EUROPE
AND FOUNDING THE ASHKENAZIC COMMUNITY.

Christianity became the official religion of the Roman Empire under Theodosius in 380 CE, after the Emperor Constantine converted to Christianity in 313. Theodosius was also the last Roman emperor to rule the whole Empire; after his death in 395 CE the Empire split in two for ever. The western or Latin empire, ruled from Rome, was unable to withstand the onslaught of the Visigoths in 410 CE and disintegrated. The last Roman emperor in the West was ousted by the Goths in 476 CE. Much of the Jewish population now lived under Byzantine rule.

Under Emperor Constantine and subsequently in the Byzantine Empire, whose capital was Byzantium (Constantinople), the Christians, hitherto a persecuted minority, became the ruling majority. They immediately began to persecute adherents of other religions, especially the Jews, through a series of repressive measures designed to isolate religious minorities, including Karaites and Armenians.

There had been a fashion for Judaism in the Roman Empire in the years between the death of Marcus Aurelius in 180 C.E. and the assassination of Alexander Severus in 235, the latter even installing a statue of Abraham in his private temple. Now Constantine and his successors banned proselytizing and conversion to Judaism and Jews were encouraged, and even commanded, to convert to Christianity. In 321, Constantine ordered that Sunday be observed as the Christian holy day, as opposed to Saturday, the Jewish Sabbath. For many hundreds of years, Christians continued to observe both days, however. There was a brief lull in the persecution of the Jews in 361 when the Julian the Apostate became emperor, but his rule lasted for only three years. Although he disliked Judaism, he hated Christianity even more and tried to reintroduce the old Roman pagan religion.

He even considered allowing the Jews to rebuild their Temple in Jerusalem, but when he died the plan was dropped.

His successors, Valentinian and then Theodosius, tried to prevent the destruction of synagogues and the attacks on the Jews and even offered Jews the protection of the law. Christian clerics were much harsher, however. St. Jerome claimed that despite the expulsions and dispersals leaving Jews a minority in what had once been their own land, they "grow like worms." St. Ambrose, Bishop of Milan, rebuked Theodosius in 388, when the Emperor insisted on rebuilding the burned out synagogue at Callinicum in Babylonia and punishing those responsible for attacking it. St. John Chrysostom, preaching from his pulpit in Antioch in 387, ascribed every imaginable evil to the Jews and forbade the Christians from fraternising with them. In 415, Cyril, patriarch of Alexandria, expelled all of the Jews from this ancient community, and the patriarchate of Judaea was abolished in 418. Theodosius II introduced a code in 438 which summarized all of the former anti-Jewish legislation, including a prohibition on the building of new synagogues. The legislation was a fullsome expression of the hatred and resentment felt by the Christians to their Jewish neighbors.

The Jews gradually withdrew, or were banned, from public life in the Empire. The abolition of the Jewish patriarchate in 425 caused leadership of the community to devolve on other prominent Jews, including laymen. In the economic sphere, Jews were ousted from the professions, including the practice of medicine; in 692 the Emperor Justinian II banned Jews and Christians from bathing together in public places. Jews were forced out of civic life and banned from residence in certain cities. The most prosperous parts of the Byzantine Empire for the Jews were the Balkans and southern Italy, where they could engage in agriculture and live in relative freedom.

Synagogues continued to be destroyed, although Theodoric the Great (454–526), King of the Ostrogoths and ruler of Italy from 493–526, offered the Jews his protection. Yet all this, and the fact that Jews had been banned from living in Jerusalem by the Emperor Hadrian, saw the gradual decline of Roman Syria Palaestina. In 614, Jerusalem fell to the Persian army (which included many Jews) and the Holy Land had a new conqueror. There was a brief re-conquest by Rome in 629, but the Arab armies finally captured Jerusalem in 641.

The Fourth Crusade, in 1204, disrupted the Byzantine Empire. The Jews of Pera, the Jewish district of Constantinople, briefly came under the rule of the Latin (or western) Patriarchate. Pera was burned and pillaged during the sack of the city by the Latins, but when Latin rule ended in 1261, Jews were allowed to live outside Pera. The Venetians, including Jews, as trading partners with Byzantium, were granted special privileges. The Byzantine Empire shrank after the Fourth Crusade. Local rulers, known as "despots" governed parts of Greece and the Balkans. When Constantinople finally fell to the Ottoman Turks in 1453, the Jews viewed this as the dawn of a new age of prosperity and freedom from persecution. It was the cruelty of the Byzantine Empire that caused Jews to move north and east into the center of Europe, and westward into Germany and establish what was to become the Ashkenazic branch of Jewry.

The Emperor Justinian I (483–565).
This detail from a contemporary mosaic shows the Emperor who recovered North Africa from the Vandals and southeast Spain from the Visigoths. Deploying the skills of his great general, Belisarius, he also recaptured Italy from the Ostrogoths.

ATLANTIC
OCEAN

FRANKISH KINGDOMS

- Colonia
  Agrippina
- Soissons
- Remi
- Lutetia
KINGDOM OF
THE LOMBAR
- Civitas
  Aurellanorum
Genava
Mediolanum   Verona
Augusta   *R. Po*
Taurinorum
Lemovicus   Lugdunum   Genoa   Bononia
Toulouse
Florentia
Dalmatia
Spalatum
Perusia
PREFECTURE OF ITA
Rome   Bari

Massilia

KINGDOM
OF THE
SUEVES

KINGDOM OF THE
VISIGOTHS

Corsica
Sardinia

Balearic Islands

536

Naples

Panormus

Sicily

Messana

CANTABRIANS   BASQUES
R. Ebro

Caesarea Augusta

Portus
Cale

Tarraco

Toletum

Valentia

549

Syracuse

Olisipo   *R. Tagus*

R. Guadiana

Hispalis

Corduba
Carthago Nova

P R E F E C T U R E

Septem

O F   A F R I C A

Hippo   Carthage

R. Moulouga

Leptis Magna

M
e

N

The Empire in the East

▓ the Empire at the accession of Justinian, 527	▪ Patriarchate
▒ Reconquered by Justinian to 565	● Metropolitan see
▨ Disputed territories	○ Major city or town
→ Justinian's campaigns	

0   200 km

0   200 miles

KINGDOM OF
THE GEPIDS

Drava

Viminacium

Ratiaria

R. Danube

M o e s i a

Marcianoplois

Justina
Prima

Serdica

Scodra

Philippopolis

Scupi

Adrianopole

Thracia

Stobi

Trajanopolis

Constantinople

Chalcedon

Thessalonica

Cyzicus

Nicomedia

Nicaea

PREFECTURE OF ILLYRICUM

Sardes

Corinth

Ephesus

Aphrodisias

Perga

Seleucia

Hierapolis

Crete

Laodicea

Gortyn

d i t e r r a n e a n   S e a

Cherson

Black   Sea

Sinope

Heraclea

P o n t i c a

Galatia

A s i a n a

Caesarea

Tyana

Anazarbus

Tarsus

Antioch

Cyprus

Citium

R. Dnieper

R. Dniester

R. Bug

R. Prut

R. Siret

R. Tisza

30∞

20∞

R. Donets

Sebastopolis

LAZICA

IBERIA

40∞

Kuma

R. Kuban

R. Laba

Trebizond

Sebastia

Cappadocia

ARMENIA

Melitene

Hierapolis

Beroea

Apamea

Syria

Emesa

Damascus

Busra

Jerusalem

Gaza

**PERSIAN
EMPIRE**

Amida

Dura

Nisibis

Edessa

Circesium

R. Euphrates

**LAKHMID
ARABS**

**GHASSANID
ARABS**

Alexandria

Heliopolis

Memphis

Aila

E G Y P T

R. Nile

Red   Sea

PREFECTURE OF ORIENS

KHAZAR JEWISH KINGDOM

THE KHAZAR KINGDOM WAS PRECEDED BY ANOTHER JEWISH KINGDOM, THAT OF ADIABENE. THE KHAZARS PRODUCED NO JEWISH SCHOLARSHIP OR SAGES AND VIRTUALLY NO TRACE OF THE KINGDOM HAS SURVIVED. IT IS POSSIBLE THAT THE KHAZAR PEOPLE DID NOT CONVERT WITH THEIR LEADER.

During the period following the destruction of the Second Temple and the forced expulsion of most of the Jewish population from the Holy Land, Jewish influence spread throughout the Middle East and to some parts of central Asia. This resulted in the conversion to Judaism by a number of rulers of small kingdoms that lay on the edge of vast empires, who no doubt wished to assert their independence from their larger neighbors.

A Jewish kingdom was founded in Arabia, in Himyar, present-day Yemen and Hadramaut, in 115 BCE. The Qatan tribe, half of whom converted to Judaism, claim to have ruled this Kingdom in Hadramaut, the fertile region of eastern Yemen, whose capital, Zafar, can still be seen. When the kingdom fell in 525 CE, the Jewish ruling class migrated northwards to Iraq where they remained until the great departure of the Iraqi Jews in the 1950s.

The Kingdom of Adiabene covered parts of present-day Kurdistan and Armenia, at the edge of the Assyrian Empire. It was a vassal state of the Persian Empire in the third century BCE but seems to have gained its short-lived independence during the first century CE. Queen Helena of Adiabene, wife of Monobaz I, converted to Judaism along with her son Izates II, before he became King, in about 30 CE. Helena, whose name indicates her Greek origin, sent her sons to be educated in Jerusalem. She is mentioned in the Talmud as an example of an exceptionally pious woman. She died about 56 C.E. and is buried in the catacombs known as the Tombs of the Kings on the outskirts of Jerusalem. Her tomb has been identified and can be visited.

The most famous of the Jewish kingdoms is Khazaria. It covered the land east of the Black Sea up to the Caspian Sea, between the Byzantine Empire, the Arab lands, and the Slavic lands

Khazar Empire
c. 700 CE

◼ Extent of the Khazar Empire

• Significant Jewish communities established before 1219

— Modern borders

of Crimea and Kievan Rus, covering much of the area of present-day Bulgaria and dominated the mouth of the Volga. The Khazars were a Turkic people who left Central Asia in the early seventh century CE. They were often attacked by their neighbors.

The exact date of the conversion to Judaism of the Khazars is unclear. The most reliable source, Judah Ha-Levi puts it at 740 CE. Arab sources place it some forty years later. According to legend, the Khazar King wished to choose a religion and summoned representatives of the three monotheistic religions. The one that most appealed to him was Judaism. Unusually for the time, this king allowed freedom of worship. As a result, many Jews fled from persecution in neighboring countries, particularly from the Byzantine Empire, until they outnumbered the native Khazars.

There is little evidence of Khazar Jewish scholarship of the period, although correspondence from Khazaria has been discovered in the Cairo Genizah, the treasure trove of documents discovered in the store-room of the Ezra Synagogue in Fostat (Cairo) in 1896 some of which date back to the time of the foundation of the synagogue in 882 C.E. This proves the existence of Jewish Khazars whom Jewish historians had sometimes believed to be mythical.

The Khazar kingdom fell in c. 960 and the population was scattered. This is said to be how the Jews dispersed throughout southern Russia and subsequently westward into Romania and Poland, a theory expounded by Arthur Koestler in *The Thirteenth Tribe*. Others claim this to be a myth because the Khazars spoke a Turkic language and Yiddish, the language of the Jews of Eastern Europe, is Germanic. Yet there are Turkic words in Yiddish, such as *daven*, the word for "to pray" (only for Jewish prayer, the word used for praying by a non-Jew is *oren*, from the Latin *orare*). The Khazars are believed to have been fair-haired and blue-eyed and Jews and Hungarians who have these features are said to be of Khazar origin. Writers who have tried to prove that no modern Jews are descended from the ancient Hebrews claim that all Jews of are of Khazar descent, which is patently not the case, as recent DNA evidence has shown.

The Byzantine Empire's intolerance towards Jews drove many to leave the empires heartlands in the eastern Mediterranean heading eastwards, westwards and northwards into Europe.

Next page: The ruler of the sprawling Khazar empire adopted Judaism, although to what extent its multi-ethnic subjects adopted the faith is unclear.

SLAUGHTER ON THE RHINE

THE CRUSADES WERE AN ATTEMPT BY SUCCESSIVE POPES TO REVIVE ENTHUSIASM FOR CHRISTIANITY THROUGHOUT EUROPE, ESPECIALLY AS SO MUCH OF THE FORMERLY CHRISTIAN WORLD HAD FALLEN INTO MUSLIM HANDS. THEY SPELLED DISASTER FOR THE JEWISH POPULATION OF EUROPE AND THE MIDDLE EAST.

Crac des Chevaliers, a medieval Crusader castle in what is now Syria.

The Crusades, the series of medieval European military expeditions to liberate the Holy Land from the Muslims, were a terrifying time for the Jews. The avowed aim of most of the leaders of the Crusades, and the only one that they achieved, was to attack and destroy any "infidels" they encountered on their way to the Holy Land.

Although the Muslims were also infidels, they were protected by the fact that they were so powerful in Spain, North Africa, and the Middle East; the Jews were a prime and easy target. The First Crusade was preached in 1095 by Pope Urban II at Clermont-Ferrand in central France. The Crusaders massed in the Rhineland, following the traditional route to the Middle East along the Rhine and the Danube rivers.

Godfrey of Bouillon, leader of the crusade, announced his determination to either convert or wipe out all Jews of Europe. He reached Cologne in April, 1096. Those Jews who refused to convert were murdered. A few brave Jewish women killed their children and themselves rather than surrender. The "Christ-killers" were massacred in their thousands in the three major Rhineland communities, known as SHUM (Hebrew initials for Speyer (Shpayer) Worms and Mainz (Magenda)). Count Emich of Leiningen, a Swabian and leader of the Knights Templar, attacked the Jews of Speyer, who first sheltered in their fortified synagogue, which for a time protected them from the mob, but they eventually succumbed. In May, 1096, he and his Knights swept through Worms. Emich and Godefroi justified their treatment of the

Jews by saying that: "Since they were the race responsible for the death and crucifixion of Jesus, they deserve nothing better than conversion or death."

The local clergy, and the nobility were worried that the massacres might lead to lawlessness against themselves and disapproved of the bloodshed, but they were mostly passive. The Bishop of Cologne was an exception, as he hid Jews in the surrounding villages, but the Crusaders eventually found them and killed them.

At Regensburg, the Jews were flung into the Danube in a sort of forced baptism and in Metz, Prague and throughout Bohemia, massacre followed massacre. The King of Germany and Holy Roman Emperor, Henry IV (1050–1106), allowed those Jews who had converted, and were practising their religion in secret, to revert to Judaism in 1097 for which he was roundly condemned by the Antipope Clement III.

The Crusaders did not manage to keep control of the Holy Land for long, and when Edessa was lost, Pope Eugene III preached a second Crusade. His successor, Innocent III, ordained in 1198 that any debts owed to Jews during the Crusaders' absence were not chargeable and any money owed was to be returned. This amounted to mass confiscation of Jewish assets especially as the term "Crusade" was extended to mean any conflict in which the Church took sides.

Crusader coin of John of Brienne (c. 1170–1237).

In 1146, Radulph, a Cistercian monk, again raised the spectre of "Christ-killing" and urged a massacre of the Jews, even though Bernard of Clairvaux, the spiritual leader of the Crusade, claimed that this was a theological error and tried to protect the Jews. This time, the Jews were better prepared in the Rhineland but there was terrible suffering in the communities in Germany especially in Halle, and in Carinthia in Austria. The great Rabbenu Tam was himself stabbed in five places, "in memory of the stabbing of Jesus" but he survived with the help of a knight. This time, the nobility and the bishops defended the Jews of the Rhineland against the mob, and one of the persecutors was even blinded for killing a Jew. In the Third Crusade, it was the Jews of England who suffered most. England had not been involved in the previous crusades, but Richard the Lionheart was an enthusiastic warrior. As a result, the Jews of Lynn, Norwich, and Stamford were massacred though they were saved in Lincoln, one of the most prosperous cities, by agents of the crown. Sixty-seven Jews died in Bury St. Edmunds, but the worst atrocity occurred in York, in 1190, where the nobles colluded with the mob to destroy the Jews who locked themselves for protection in Barnard's castle. Rather than perish at the hands of the violent mob that awaited them outside, many of the Jews took their own lives; others died in the flames they had lit, and those who finally surrendered were massacred. The fourteenth-century "Croisade des Pastoureaux" (the Shepherds' Crusade) in France consisted of a teenage mob of forty thousand who destroyed 1220 Jewish communities south of the Loire, even though the Pope had condemned and even excommunicated those who took part. Pope Calixtus II (1119–24) issued a bull entitled Sicut Judaeis, ordering that Jews were not to be harmed. In 1298, a rumor spread that the Jews of Röttingen had desecrated the host. After burning the Jews of Röttingen at the stake, under their leader Rindfleisch, a mob went from town to town, killing Jews. The community of Würzburg was annihilated. The Jews of Nuremberg sought refuge in the fortress but were butchered. The persecutions spread from Franconia and Bavaria to Austria, and within six months about 120 communities, numbering around 100,000 Jews, were destroyed.

CRUSADER MASSACRE IN JERUSALEM

DESCRIPTIONS OF THE CRUSADER CAPTURE OF JERUSALEM IN 1099 DESCRIBE THE INVADERS' HORSES BEING UP TO THEIR FETLOCKS IN THE BLOOD OF THE INHABITANTS.

The First Crusade eventually reached Jerusalem in 1099, and besieged it for five weeks. When Jerusalem fell, the crusaders entered through the Jewish Quarter, murdering anyone in their path. A contemporary Christian chronicler describes the blood of Jews and Muslims as flowing as high as the thighs of the crusaders' horses.

Jews fought side-by-side with Muslim soldiers to defend Jerusalem against the crusaders. According to the Muslim chronicler Ibn al-Qalanisi, "The Jews assembled in their synagogue, and the Franks burned it over their heads." A letter from a Jewish witness, dating from the late eleventh century and found as recently as 1975 by the historian S. D. Goitein, written only two weeks after the siege, refutes this claim. All sources agree that a synagogue was burned down during the siege, though it is not clear which one.

The crusader capture of Jerusalem radically changed the city's population. The few Jewish and Muslim inhabitants who survived were murdered or expelled, after first being made to clean the city of the dead. French became the language of everyday life and Latin the language of prayer. The Church of the Holy Sepulchre, the alleged site of the Crucifixion, was magnificently rebuilt in Romanesque fashion. The palace of the Patriarch of Jerusalem stood west of the church in what is still known as the Christian Quarter. To the south, on the road now known as Muristan, stood the huge hospice of the Knights Hospitalier of St. John, the ministering knights who subsequently defended the city. The sites holiest to Jews on the Temple Mount were declared Christian. The Knights Templar, another order of monastic knights, took their name from this site.

Elsewhere in the Holy Land, the Jews defended Haifa against the crusaders, holding out for a whole month (June–July, 1099). Even though it was over a thousand years since the fall of Judaea and the banishment of the Jews in 70 CE, Jewish communities continued to exist there. Apart from Jerusalem, the three other cities holy to Judaism—Hebron, Safed, and Tiberias—had sizeable communities, as did Ramleh, Ashkelon, Caesarea and Gaza. In Galilee, Peki'in survived and Acre had a Jewish academy in the thirteenth century. In the twelfth and thirteenth centuries, Jewish immigrants continued to arrive, many from other Islamic lands, especially North Africa.

Tancred (1072–1112), a leader of the First Crusade who became Prince of Galilee and regent of the Principality of Antioch, took Jews as prisoners-of-war and deported them by sea to Apuleia in Italy, though many were thrown overboard or beheaded on the way. Many Jews and their holy books (including the Aleppo Codex) were stolen for ransom by Raymond of Toulouse. The Karaites of Ashkelon asked the Jews of Alexandria for help and they were able to obtain the release of many Jews by the summer of 1100. The few who could not be rescued were either forced to convert to Christianity or murdered.

The crusaders were unsuccessful in their efforts to destroy the Jewish presence in the Holy Land. In 1165, Benjamin of Tudela, the renowned Spanish–Jewish traveler, found an "Academy of Jerusalem" in Damascus, only thirty miles from northern Galilee. By the fourteenth century Jews

This French illustration shows Godfrey of Bouillon, brother of the French King, leading his men in the attack and capture of Jerusalem in July 1099.

The Siege and Capture of Jerusalem June–July 1099

Deployment of Crusader forces

Crusader attacks on the city walls

Crusader advances within city

Muslim force and population retreat

After a siege of five weeks the crusaders broke into the city of Jerusalem, killing anyone in their path.

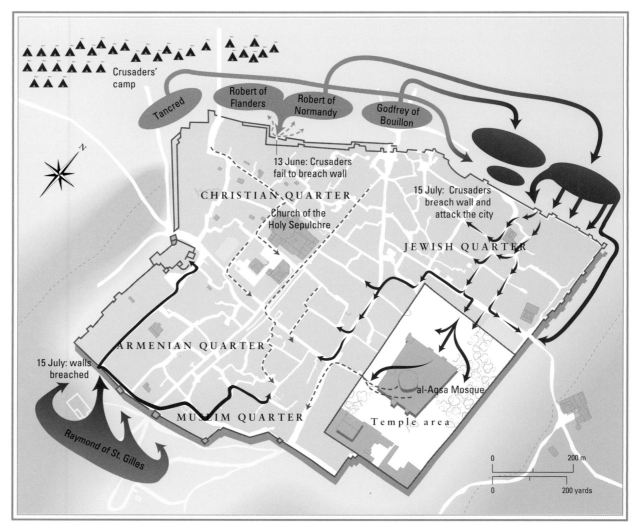

in Gaza, Ramle, and Safed were considered by Christian pilgrims to be the "ideal guides" to the Holy Land in the fourteenth century.

The Christian Kingdom of Jerusalem was not to last. The fall of Edessa, a city to the north and east of Galilee, in 1144, marked the beginning of the end. In 1187, Salah-ad-Din ibn Ayyub (Saladdin) captured Jerusalem, ushering in the Ayyubid period (1099–1250 CE).

The Christians had erected a cross on the Dome of the Rock, the golden-domed mosque on the site of the Temple, built from 685 to 691 to rival neighboring Christian places of worship in Jerusalem. This golden cross was toppled and shattered, to be replaced by the crescent moon, the symbol of Islam. The city was gradually rebuilt by Saladdin, who added massive fortifications and extended it to include Mount Zion. In 1212, Saladdin's nephew, Al-Mu'azim Issa, ruler of Damascus, who succeeded him, continued the building work, and added inscriptions in honor of Saladdin on the walls, though seven years later, in 1219 he tore them down, fearing the Crusaders might return and use them as protection. Jerusalem remained an unwalled city until Suleiman the Magnificent rebuilt its defenses, part of which can still be seen today.

Saladdin's conduct toward his Christian captives was exemplary, so unlike that of his Christian predecessors, and he permitted Jews to return to Jerusalem, where they were joined by many Jewish immigrants from the Maghreb (North Africa), France, and the Yemen. There was even a long-standing Jewish settlement at the foot of Mount Zion.

The Crusader states established themselves along the Levant coast with varying degrees of success. It was the Europe's first military expedition beyond the bounds of its own continent.

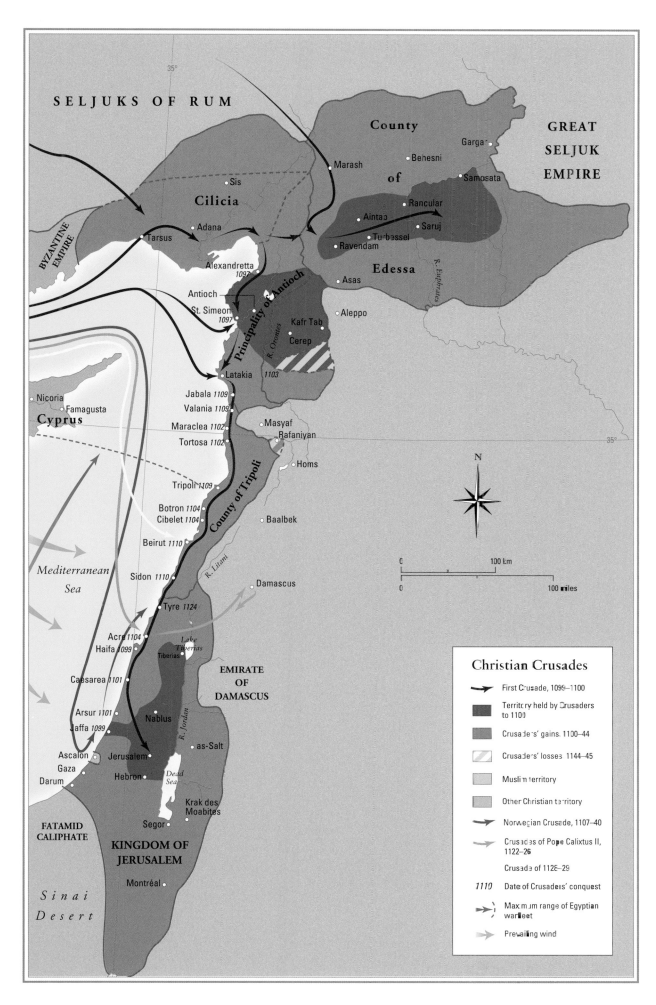

SELJUKS OF RUM

County of Edessa

GREAT SELJUK EMPIRE

Garga

Behesni

Marash

Samosata

Sis

Cilicia

Rancular

Adana

Aintab

Tarsus

Saruj

Turbessel

Ravendam

BYZANTINE EMPIRE

Alexandretta 1097

Asas

Antioch

St. Simeon 1097

Principality of Antioch

Kafr Tab

Aleppo

Cerep

R. Orontes

Latakia 1103

Jabala 1109

Valania 1109

Masyaf

Rafaniyan

Nicoria

Famagusta

Maraclea 1102

Cyprus

Tortosa 1102

Homs

Tripoli 1109

County of Tripoli

Baalbek

Botron 1104

Cibelet 1104

Beirut 1110

Mediterranean Sea

R. Litani

Sidon 1110

Damascus

Tyre 1124

Acre 1104

Lake Tiberias

Haifa 1099

Tiberias

Caesarea 1101

EMIRATE OF DAMASCUS

Arsur 1101

Nablus

Jaffa 1099

R. Jordan

as-Salt

Ascalon

Jerusalem

Gaza

Hebron

Dead Sea

Darum

Krak des Moabites

FATAMID CALIPHATE

Segor

KINGDOM OF JERUSALEM

Sinai Desert

Montréal

N

0   100 km
0   100 miles

Christian Crusades

First Crusade, 1099–1100

Territory held by Crusaders to 1100

Crusaders' gains 1100–44

Crusaders' losses 1144–45

Muslim territory

Other Christian territory

Norwegian Crusade, 1107–40

Crusades of Pope Calixtus II, 1122–26

Crusade of 1128–29

1110 Date of Crusaders' conquest

Maximum range of Egyptian war fleet

Prevailing wind

Medieval Italy

ITALY WAS THE FIRST COUNTRY TO HERD JEWS INTO GHETTOS.

Sign in the Ghetto Vecchio, the oldest ghetto, in Venice.

In the Middle Ages, Italy was a checker-board of small states. The south had been conquered by the Normans and Saracens, the north and center, almost up to Rome, consisted of states that owed allegiance to the Holy Roman Empire. The Pope issued edicts that affected political and religious life across Europe.

The spread of breakaway movements from the Catholic church, such as the Aryans and the Albigensians, in the late twelfth century, caused the church to embark on punitive actions against heretics, which were extended to include Jews. The Fourth Lateran Council convened in 1215 by Pope Innocent III issued a number of decrees affecting the Jews living in the Holy Roman Empire. No Jew was to be appointed to a position of authority, on pain of excommunication. Jews and Christians were not allowed to live together and the Jews had to wear a special pointed hat. The design of the hat may have been imported from Persia, and was already worn voluntarily by some Jews but now became compulsory. It was not necessarily seen as a badge of shame, since Jewish sources of the period, such as in the medieval Haggadot (orders of service for the Passover meal), depict Jews wearing it. No such hat has actually survived so it is not known exactly how it was made or what it was made of. This was not the first time distinctive clothing had been introduced. In 887, the Muslim ruler of Sicily, Ibrahim, had forced Jews to wear a yellow patch and this was customary all over the Islamic world for non-Muslims. Most of the Jewish communities of Italy had existed since Roman times and in Capua in 1000 a Jew was the chief tax collector and master of the mint. The decrees were not enacted universally or immediately but hung like the sword of Damocles over the heads of Jewish communities in Italy throughout the Middle Ages and beyond. Yet in many parts of northern Italy Jews remained relatively unmolested. In 1310, a conference was held in Foligno to discuss how to help the persecuted Jews of the Rhineland and Bavaria. In Italy, as elsewhere in Europe, Jews were blamed for the advent of the Black Death. It was in vain that Pope Clement IV published a bull in 1348 in which he reminded the populace that Jews were also dying from the Plague, it did not save them.

In Italy, many disputations were arranged between learned Jews and Christians to "prove" the veracity of the New Testament. If the Jews "lost," which was a virtual certainty, the Talmud would be burned. The most important such disputation in Italy was held in Rome in 1450, when Jewish holy books were again burned. In 1559, the Inquistor-General of Milan, Cardinal Ghsilieri, the future Pius V, ordered the Talmud to be burned in Cremona, the center of Jewish learning in Italy with its own Hebrew printing press. Some 12,000 copies of the Talmud and other Jewish books were burned.

In 1474, the townspeople of Monte San Giuliano or Erice, as it now known, attacked the Jewish inhabitants. On the eve of Assumption Day, encouraged by Catholic preachers, the mob slaughtered 360 Jews, shouting "Long live Mary! Death to the Jews!" (*Viva Maria! Morte ai Judey*)! They were later expelled from Sicily, under the Spanish Edict of Expulsion, in 1497. With them went many skills, such as iron-smelting and

Medieval Italy c. 1500

☐ Italian states

▨ Ottoman Empire

▨ Italian/Christian territories

☐ Other states and territories

▬ Border of the Holy Roman Empire

the island's sugar industry. They were expelled from the Kingdom of Naples in 1541. Marranos (converted Jews still secretly practicing their religion) found refuge in northern Italy. In Ferrara, a Hebrew printing press was set up as early as 1477. A new press was started there by a Marrano, Abraham Tsarfati, in 1553 and between 1553 and 1556, the presses began printing in Jewish books in Latin characters as well. The Renaissance did little to improve the lives of the Jews of Italy. In fact, the sixteenth century saw more burnings of the Talmud and in 1555 Pope Paul IV called for ghettos to be established throughout Catholic Europe. Gradually, every city in Italy that had not already expelled its Jews erected a ghetto, known as a Giudecca, to enclose them. Pius V (1566–72) ordered the expulsion of the Jews from the Papal states though they were readmitted after his death. Jews were allowed to remain in Ancona (where twenty-five Jews had been burned at the stake) and in Rome. The ghettos continued to exist in Italy until the nineteenth century, Rome's Trastevere being the last to go. It remains the Jewish quarter until today.

Medieval Italy was a patchwork of minor states. All vying for influence and power, though all owed allegiance to the city of Rome. From there the Pope, head of the Catholic Church, issued edicts which not only effected Italy but the rest of Catholic Europe.

York and Lincoln

ALTHOUGH JEWS PROSPERED IN ENGLAND, IT HAS THE
DISTINCTION OF PERPETRATING THE FIRST BLOOD LIBEL AND THE
FIRST EXPULSION OF THE JEWS. THE MYTH OF LITTLE ST. HUGH
ALLEGEDLY MURDERED BY JEWS SURVIVES. FOR MANY YEARS THE
SHRINE OF LITTLE ST. HUGH WAS A POPULAR PLACE OF PILGRIMAGE.

This three-story limestone building, known as Jews' Court (i.e. the synagogue) may have been the home of the wealthy financier, Aaron of Lincoln.

Under the Angevin kings (1215–1485), York was the second city of England and had a thriving Jewish community. It is recorded that a deputation of two of the leading Jews of York, Benedict and Joce, attended the coronation of Richard I in 1189. The festivities turned into anti-semitic rioting, during which Benedict was attacked and forced to convert to Christianity. He was released the next day and allowed to revert to his religion.

In the following year, Richard de Malbis, an aristocrat who was in debt to Aaron of Lincoln, the wealthiest Jew of his day, was about to join the Third Crusade, when a fire broke out in the city. De Malbis seized the opportunity to blame the Jews. The Jews fled to York Castle, where they took shelter in Clifford's Tower. The tower was then surrounded by a mob. A monk paced the castle walls and daily took the sacrament, as if Jew-baiting were a holy duty. A stone thrown by one of the Jewish captors dislodged him, inciting the mob to a frenzy.

When the Jews of York realised that there was no way out, their leader, Rabbi Yom Tov of Joigny, reminded them of the heroes of Massada and urged them to die rather than be captured. This they did, Joce cutting the throat of his own wife, Hannah, before he was killed by the Rabbi. The Rabbi, the last of them, committed suicide thus taking the crime upon himself.

The mob searched the castle for Jewish deeds of indebtedness but found none, so they ransacked York Minster, where they were kept. This indicates the real motive for the violence. William de Longchamp, who was regent in the absence of King Richard at the Crusades, was furious at this attack on the Jews who were under the King's protection. Most of the ringleaders were caught but not the arch-villain, de Malbis, who had fled to Scotland. His name is perpetuated in that of the Yorkshire village of Ancaster Malbis;

Bolton Percy is named for another of the ringleaders. Joce's son Aaron of York survived and became chief rabbi of England in 1237 under Henry III. York's medieval burial ground lay between St. Morris and the River Fosse, the synagogue was on the north side of the Jubbergate.

Medieval Lincoln ranked in importance alongside York. The Jews, of whom first mention is in 1159, settled on Steep Hill, just below the castle and the cathedral, where a couple of their stone houses can still be seen. One of them is known as "Jews' court" so it was probably the synagogue and beth din. During the anti-Jewish riots that broke out at the beginning of the Third Crusades, the Jews took refuge in the castle, where they were saved by the bishop, later canonised as St. Hugh of Lincoln, whose huge diocese extended from the River Humber to the Thames. Hugh's death in 1200 was deeply mourned by the Jewish community.

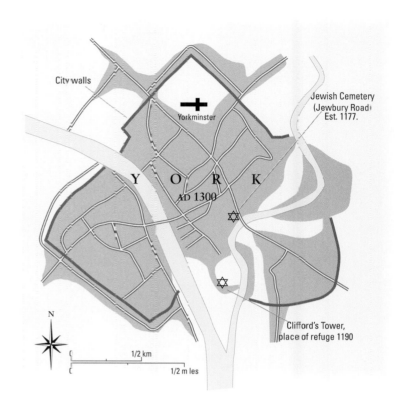

York c.1300 CE. A well established Jewish community lived in the second city of England and were influential in the financial undertakings of the English crown.

The most famous Jewish resident of Lincoln was Aaron (1123–1186) who was probably born in France. His vast wealth enabled him to contribute to the building of Lincoln Cathedral and York Minster, where he is said to have paid for some of the stained glass. In true English royal tradition, his estate was seized by King Henry II when he died.

Norwich, capital of East Anglia, also had a thriving Jewish community, until William, a 12-year old boy, was found dead in 1144. The Jews were blamed in the very first blood libel; the hideous calumny that Jews steal Christian children and kill them, mixing their blood with flour to make unleavened bread. William was alleged to have last been seen entering the home of a Jewish family. Jewish suspects were indicted before a grand jury, but the Sheriff intervened, claiming that the jury did not have authority to try Jews, as they were direct subjects of the King. They were released and the crime remains unsolved. *The Life and Miracles of St. William of Norwich*, a Latin work written nearly thirty years later by Thomas of Monmouth perpetrates the lie.

St. Hugh is not to be confused with the so-called Little St. Hugh of Lincoln whose disappearance in 1255, and the subsequent discovery of his body, provoked a second blood libel. In a confession under torture, a Jew named Copin was executed. In fact, six months earlier, King Henry III had sold his rights to tax the Jews to his brother, Richard, Earl of Cornwall. Having lost this source of income, he decided he could still seize Jewish money if a Jew was convicted of a crime. As a result, some 90 Jews were blamed for the ritual murder and held in the Tower of London. Eighteen were hanged—the first time a government had handed out a death sentence for ritual murder—so Henry was able to sequestrate their property. The remainder were pardoned and set free, probably due to Richard's intervention as it threatened his own source of income.

When the Jews returned to England in 1656, they did not settle in these cities, partly due to their economic decline in the interim, but also due to their history.

THE JEWS OF OXFORD

THE JEWISH CONTRIBUTION TO THE FOUNDING OF OXFORD UNIVERSITY IS NOT GENERALLY KNOWN. EVEN BEFORE OXFORD WAS A CENTRE OF CHRISTIAN LEARNING, IT WAS A CENTRE OF JEWISH LEARNING AND JEWS HAVE BEEN ASSOCIATED WITH THE CITY SINCE THE MIDDLE AGES.

Albert Einstein explaining some of his theories at the blackboard during his stay in Oxford.

It is little realized how deeply the Jewish community was involved with the founding of Oxford University. Soon after the Norman conquest, Jews settled in this city due to its strategic location, on the borders of the Anglo-Saxon kingdoms of Mercia and Wessex, and at an important crossing point of the River Thames. St. Aldates, a street at the very center of modern Oxford, was once known as The Great Jewry, and housed one of the most prosperous and learned Jewish communities of medieval Europe. Land was purchased for a Jewish cemetery, always one of the first acts of an organized Jewish community, which originally stood outside the East Gate to the city, where Magdalen Tower now stands. There is said to have been a Talmudic academy in Oxford, probably on the site of what is now 121 St. Aldates, then known as Jacob's Hall and the largest Jewish-owned building in medieval Oxford.

Wealthy Jews owned stone-built houses that lined the street, the synagogue standing opposite what is now St. Aldate's church. Several Jewish scholars lived in Oxford, including Magister Mosseus (d. 1268), later rabbi of London, and his father Rabbi Yom Tov. Their home stood on land later expropriated by the city, on which the present Oxford Town Hall was built. Benedict the Punctuator, another Oxford-Jewish scholar, wrote a number of works of ethics.

The Jewish cemetery was later transferred to the site of what is now the Botanic Garden. In one corner of the garden, the remains of a building has been found containing a flowing stream that may have been used as a Jewish ritual bath, or as a Bet Tehara for washing the dead. Deadman's Walk is a small path that is said to have been the route taken by Jewish funeral processions from the Jewry to the so-called "Jews' Garden"—the cemetery.

The first college established in Oxford by Bishop Walter de Merton was housed in a building acquired from Jacob of London, owner of Bek's Hall, in 1266–67. The deed of sale (known as a starr from the Hebrew shtar, most such commercial transactions in Normandy and England being founded on Talmudic law) survives and is written in Latin and Hebrew.

The first synagogue was founded c. 1228 by a wealthy Jewish benefactor named Copin of Worcester on part of what later became part of the site of Balliol College, founded in 1263. Jewish "halls"—large houses—were divided into rooms and rented to students.

Of course, the Jews were not left alone to prosper. Successive local sheriffs and reigning monarchs exacted huge tolls. Priories and churches were built on land compulsorily purchased from Jews in the middle of the Jewish district, with the specific aim of converting the local population. One of the most moving stories of all time of the conflict of religions is that of Robert of Reading, a deacon of the church, who met and fell in love with a Jewish woman. So desperate was he to win her affections that he converted to Judaism. A commemorative plaque at the entrance to the ruined Osney Abbey shows where, as Haggai of Oxford, he was "burned at the stake for his faith on Sunday April 17th, AD 1222, corresponding to 4 Iyyar, 4982."

When the Jews of England, subjected to constant taxation and expropriation, were finally expelled by a greedy Edward I in 1290, who used their wealth to pay his war debts, it marked the end for the medieval Jewish community in Oxford. Since the return of the Jews, Oxford has had many Jewish connections. In 1835, the architect George Basevi, a first cousin of Benjamin Disraeli, designed a building overlooking the West Front of Balliol College. Many Jews studied and researched at Oxford, including Albert Einstein (whose blackboard is displayed in the Hooke Museum of Science) and Boris Chain who shared the Nobel Prize with Alexander Fleming for the discovery of penicillin.

Two Jewish personalities associated with Oxford are Isaiah Berlin (1909–1997), one of the greatest modern liberal thinkers and the most distinguished Fellow of All Souls' College in his day and Cecil Roth (1899–1970). Roth, whose work as both a serious historian and researcher and a popularizer of

"The dreaming spires" of Oxford University in the sunset.

Jewish history, has never been equaled. He obtained his doctorate in 1924 and wrote over 600 books, including *The Jewish Contribution to Civilization* (1940) to refute Nazi claims of Jewish "racial inferiority." Roth never achieved the academic recognition he deserved from his beloved Oxford, as there was no chair or professorship available to him.

Professor Arthur Lehman Goodhart (1891–1978) was the first Jew to become head of house in Oxford when he became Master of University College in 1951.

1400 Years of Forced Conversions

IN THE PAST, JEWS HAVE BEEN FORCED INTO CONVERSIONS, PARTICULARLY DURING THE CRUSADES. IN FACT, IN JUDAISM THERE ARE THREE ABSOLUTE PROHIBITIONS, ONE OF WHICH IS CONVERTING TO ANOTHER FAITH.

Ferdinand and Isabella, known as "The Catholic Kings" whose zeal to ensure that Christian Spain, newly conquered from the Muslims, should be a hundred percent Christian, made them order Jews to convert or die.

Over the centuries, both Christianity and Islam have attempted forced conversions upon the Jews. Many Christians believed that at the End of Days, all Jews would automatically convert to Christianity but that the process needs to be hastened and most simply ascribe resistance to Jewish intransigence. In fact, in Judaism there are three absolute prohibitions, one of which is converting to another faith (murder and the cutting off parts of an animal which is still alive in order to eat them are the other two).

The Emperor Constantine made Christianity the official religion of the Roman Empire in 312 CE. Immediately, Jews were ordered to adopt the new religion. St. Augustine of Hippo was one of the early missionaries who preached against the Jews, calling them Christ-killers.

During the First Crusade in 1096, there were mass forced conversions of Jews, such as the involuntary baptism that occurred in Regensburg, where a mob of crusaders rounded up the Jewish community, forced them into the Danube, and performed a mass baptism. After the crusaders had left the region these Jews returned to practicing Judaism.

In 1190, a mob attacked Clifford's Tower, a part of York Castle, in England, in which Jews had taken refuge, demanding that the Jews convert to Christianity or die. The commemorative tablet placed there reads "On the night of Friday 16 March 1190 some 150 Jews and Jewesses of York having sought protection in the Royal Castle on this site from a mob incited by Richard Malebisse and others chose to die at each other's hands rather than renounce their faith". Benedict of York, the richest man in the

Jewish community, converted to save his family (who were later murdered after his death) but the King allowed him to renounce his conversion the next day. Having been badly beaten, he died of his wounds.

The "danger" of unconverted Jews was one of the major subjects for discussion at the Fourth Lateran Council convened in 1215 by Pope Innocent III and it was here that the Jews were ordered to wear distinctive clothing or a badge to mark themselves. In 1241, in Frankfurt, a Jewish boy preparing for baptism was persuaded by his parents to repent. As a result, local Christians attacked the Jews who fought back and a number of townspeople were killed. As the attack intensified, the Jews set fire to their own houses. The fire spread to the rest of the community, destroying nearly half the city. One hundred and eighty Jews died, and twenty-four were forced into baptism. Conrad IV, son of the Holy Roman Emperor, granted amnesty to the Christian attackers.

In 1253, King Henry III of England ordered the establishment of the Domus

A detail from Rembrandt's Jewish Bride.
As zealous european monarchs sought to promote the Christian faith in its various manifestations at the expense of its Jewish citizens, the Dutch republic was one of the first European nations to adopt polices of toleration and offer Jews legal emancipation.

Conversorum (House of Converts), a building in London in which to house Jews who had converted to Christianity could live and also be paid a small stipend, since on conversion all their property became the property of the king. When Edward I expelled the Jews in 1290, it was the only place in which Jews could remain in the country. At that time there were about eighty residents, the last one dying in 1356. All the expenses of the Domus were borne by the royal treasury, while some of the bishops left bequests to augment its funds. In addition to these sources of income a poll-tax, called the "chevage," was levied upon all Jews above the age of twelve in support of their converted brethren.

All over Europe, Jews were required to listen to conversion sermons. Two of the most prominent missionaries, St. Bernardino of Siena (1380–1444) and Bernardino de Feltre, Dominican and Franciscan friars preached both to the Jews and against them, especially the latter who encouraged the blood libel of the murder of the two-year-old Simon of Trentino, whose father accused the Jewish community of murdering him in 1475 to collect his blood for ritual purposes.

The Council of Basel (1431–49) imposed a number of decrees on Jews, but especially 'to provide measures whereby Jews ... may be converted to the orthodox faith and converts may remain steadfastly in it. It therefore decrees that all diocesan bishops should depute persons well trained in scripture, several times a year, in the places where Jews ... live, to preach and expound the truth of the Catholic faith in such a way that the infidels who hear it can recognize their errors". Catholic iconography of the time depicts early "missionaries" such as St. Stephen preaching to evil-looking Jews (shown wearing the conical Jewish hat).

In the late fourteenth century, Ferrand Martinez, Archdeacon of Ecija, began to incite mobs into attacking the Jewish quarter. The campaign soon spread throughout Spain, except for Granada. The Jewish quarter in Barcelona, the wealthiest in Spain, was totally destroyed. Over 10,000 Jews were killed, and many others chose conversion and became New Christians or conversos, referred to derogatorily as marranos (pigs). The Jews themselves refer to such converts as anusim "those who were forced to convert" from the Hebrew word for rape. Eventually, these mass forced conversions led to the establishment of the Inquisition, established in 1478 by Ferdinand II of Aragon and Isabella I of Castile to replace the medieval inquisition. It was not definitively abolished until 1834. Suspicions were especially raised against the large number of Jews who had recently been forced to convert to Christianity. In 1492, the Alhambra Decree ordered that all Jews remaining in Spain who would not convert to Christianity were to be expelled. The Auto da Fe (Act of Faith) combined the trial of the Inquisition with being forced to listen to sermons. The Inquisition accused converted Jews (and others), often through false witness of informers, of reverting to Judaism for actions such as not eating pork, washing the hands before prayer, and putting on clean clothes on the Jewish Sabbath. Over two thousand Auto da Fes are said to have taken place in the Iberian Peninsula and its colonies. The number of victims in Spain alone is estimated at 39,912, many of whom were burned alive. Approximately 340,000 people, most of them Jews, suffered at the hands of the Inquisition, although after the sixteenth century most were given lesser punishments.

Martin Luther (1483–1546), the German Reformation leader, is typical of those Christians who are convinced that as soon as some enlightened form of the religion emerges, the Jews will convert in droves. Early in Luther's career—until around 1536—he expressed concern for the Jewish plight in Europe and was enthusiastic at the prospect of converting them to Christianity through his evangelical reforms. When he discovered that this would not happen, he urged their harsh persecution. In his book *Von Den Juden und ihren Luegen* [*On the Jews and Their Lies*] he deplores Christendom's failure to exterminate them. Naturally, this was used by the Nazis as reinforcement for their own beliefs.

Forced conversions to Islam, though rare, occurred even in the nineteenth century. For instance, in 1839, the local community of Messhed in Persia (Iran) attacked the Jewish quarter. The synagogue was destroyed, over 30 Jews were killed. Moslem leaders offered to prevent further riots on the condition that the Jews convert, which they did. The Jews became known as Jadid al-Islam or New Moslems, thus ending the presence of a Jewish community in Meshed. In secret they continued to practice Judaism, taking whatever opportunities presented themselves to flee the city with their families.

It has been said that the nineteenth-century conversions to Christianity by prominent European Jews, such as composer Gustav Mahler, the poet Heinrich Heine, and even the British prime minister, Benjamin Disraeli, were a form of forced conversion as Jews were unable to advance in their careers if they remained loyal to their faith.

Benjim Disraeli, a Jew by ancestory, overcame political and social prejudice to become the British Prime Minister. Britain at the height of its power in the 1860s governed a vast global empire making Disraeli the most powerful and influential politician of his day.

FALSE MESSIAHS OF THE 16TH–17TH CENTURY

JUDAISM IS A MESSIANIC FAITH, BUT SINCE JEWS BELIEVE THAT THE MESSIAH WILL PUT AN END TO WAR AND SUFFERING, THEY STILL BELIEVE HE HAS YET TO COME. MANY JEWS BELIEVE THERE WILL NOT BE AN INDIVIDUAL, BUT A MESSIANIC AGE.

Judaism, like Christianity, is a messianic religion but Judaism claims that the Messiah is yet to come and many Jews believe the Messiah will not be an individual but a Messianic Age. At times when Jews suffer the worst persecutions, false messiahs have emerged, either proclaiming themselves to be the rescuers of the Jewish people or being seen as a the saviour by the people themselves. There is a Biblical promise that one day the throne of King David would be re-established. King Cyrus of Persia is referred to in the Bible as "the Anointed One" (Isaiah Ch. 45) and even Alexander the Great was considered by contemporary Jews as a possible messiah due to his conquest of the known world but Zachariah claimed that the "Prince of Peace" would arise not from the nobility but from the ranks of the oppressed and would ride into Jerusalem on an ass (Zachariah 19).

A series of false messiahs emerged around the time of Christ; they included leaders of the first and second Jewish Revolts against the Romans, such as the man known only as "The Egyptian" and Theudas who was proclaimed the Messiah in c. 42 CE but who was executed by the Romans with all his followers. Even Simon bar Kochba, who led the Second Revolt against the Romans in 132–35 CE was considered by his mentor, Rabbi Akiba, to be the Messiah.

With the Reformation and Counter-Reformation in Europe, Jews hoped that they too would be granted greater freedoms, like those among whom they lived—but this was not to be, in fact their suffering grew worse. Asher Lämmkin, who lived in Istria, in northern Italy in 1502, proclaimed himself herald of the Messiah and urged the Jews to do penance in anticipation of his coming. David Reubeni, the first of the latter-day false Messiahs, emerged in Venice in 1524, claiming to be a direct descendant of the lost tribe of Reuben. He accumulated many followers and persuaded

Pope Clement VII to grant him an audience. Even King João III of Portugal agreed to grant Reubeni a fleet of ships to conquer the Turks in the Holy Land. Like most messiahs, David Reubeni had his own "prophet", the former marrano (Jew forced to convert to Christianity by Spain) in the person of Shlomo Molcho. But Molcho's advocacy of the Reubeni messiah was not completely successful. He did not convince Josel von Rosheim, the great statesman and leader of the German Jews that he had indeed come to rescue the Jews. Josel warned Shlomo Molcho at the parliament of Augsburg not to approach Emperor Maximilian I but Molcho took no notice. The Emperor had him arrested and taken to Mantua where he was burned at the stake in 1530.

By far the most successful of the false messiahs was Sabbetai Zevi (Sabetai Sevi or Shabbetai Zvi, there are numerous spellings of his name), a Turkish Jew from Smyrna, born in 1626 CE. Zevi was a highly charismatic but rather erratic individual. He proclaimed himself the messiah in his home town of Smyrna at the age of twenty-two and subsequently traveled throughout the Jewish world making his messianic claims. Jews throughout Europe and the Near East gave away all their possessions, convinced that the end of the world had come. Others converted all that they owned into provisions for the journey to Jerusalem, where they would travel to await the day when Zevi would summon them to the Holy Land to await the End of Days. Prayers for Zevi were introduced into prayerbooks from Germany to Egypt and great rabbis of the day accepted him as their leader.

The upheaval was recorded by the diarist Glückl of Hameln (1646–1724) whose first father-in-law (she married twice) was caught up in the frenzy. In 1665, in the Holy Land, Sevi met a young kabbalistic scholar, Nathan of Gaza, who heard Zevi preach and was excited by his words. Nathan became Sabbetai Zevi's prophet, writing to Jewish communities all over the world, announcing that he would rescue them from persecution. In particular, he wrote to the Jews of Eastern Europe where the Cossacks, led by Bogdan Chmielnicki, had wiped out one-third of the Jewish population. In 1664, in Cairo, Sevi married Sarah, an orphaned victim of persecution and former prostitute, who believed that she herself was destined to marry the messiah.

The rabbis of the Holy Land were less than impressed by Zevi and even threatened to excommunicate him. So in 1666, he returned to minister to his enthusiastic followers in

Sabbatai Zevi, 1626–76, Jewish mystic and pseudo-Messiah, founder of the Sabbatean sect. After a period of study of the kabbalah, he became deeply influenced by its ideas of imminent redemption. In 1648, he proclaimed himself the Messiah, named the year 1666 as the millennium and gathered a host of followers.
He died in Albania, having chosen conversion to Islam rather than death.

Constantinople, but his ship was intercepted by the Turkish authorities and he was taken in chains to Adrianople. There, the Sultan gave Zevi the choice of being put to death for heresy or converting to Islam. Sevi immediately chose to convert as did many of his followers. He was banished to Dulcigno (Ulcinj) a remote town in Albania where he lived until he died, ten years later, in 1676.

Zevi's charisma was so great that he managed to retain a following even after his conversion. They practised their version of Judaism in secret while pretending to be Moslems. They even claimed that their leader never died, but had swum out to sea and was taken up to heaven by God. Sabbateans (also known as Dönme, the Turkish word for "convert") continue to survive as a secret sect, particularly in Turkey and in the city of Masshad in Iran. Like their leader, they practice a less rigorous form of Judaism in which women have equality with men. It is said that the views of the great leader of modern Turkey, Mustafa Kemal Attatürk (1881–1938), were heavily influenced by his contact with the Dönme and that he may even have become one of their number. There are several leading Turkish politicians who admit to being secret Sabbateans.

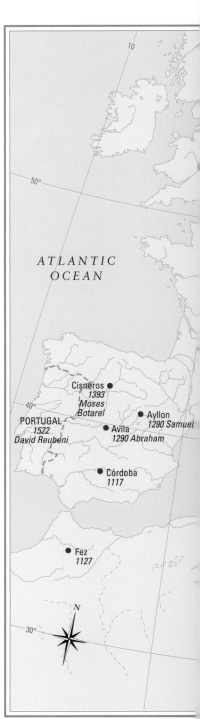

In 1755, Jacob Leibowitz (1726–1791) ("Jacob Frank") proclaimed himself to be the Messiah, a reincarnation of Sabbetai Zevi and also of King David. His "prophet" was a Polish Rabbi named Leib Krysa. Jacob Leibowitz, whose father was a Sabbatean, came from Podolia, where Jews suffered the worst of the eighteenth-century pogroms, but he traveled extensively through the Ottoman Empire and claimed to be of Sephardic origin. "Frank" is a name by which Sephardic Jews (those of Spanish origin) are known by Ashkenazim, and he was happy to be known as Jacob Frank, giving himself the aristocratic air of a Spanish Jew. Frank's unconventional doctrines involved acceptance of the New Testament and the "purification through transgression" (in other words, sexual orgies). Frank's followers, known as Frankists, eventually converted to Christianity.

The most recent manifestation of Jewish messianism is in the person of the Menahem Mendel Schneerson (1902–1994), known as the Lubavitcher Rebbe, who led the ultra-orthodox Chassidic sect known as Lubavitch or Chabad (initials for Intelligence, Wisdom, Knowledge). The Rebbe had been studying at the Sorbonne in Paris when called upon to succeed his father-in-law, Yosef Yitzchok Schneersohn. in 1950, becoming the seventh leader of the movement, a position he held until his death. The founder of the Lubavitch sect, Rabbi Schneor Zalman of Liady founded the movement in Russia in the late eighteenth century. During his lifetime, the Lubavitcher

Rebbe made Chabad into a hugely revitalised and forward-looking movement and he encouraged outreach programs into the remotest Jewish communities. As a result, the Chabad Movement now has 200,000 members and more than a million attend Chabad celebrations of the Sabbath and festivals. Even though Chabad has a strong presence in Israel and has never been anti-Zionist, the world headquarters of the movement are in Crown Heights, Brooklyn and it is here that the Rebbe is buried.

When the Rebbe died, the movement split, although many of his followers claimed that he would return as the Messiah. This view is not looked upon favourably by the religious authorities in Israel who have gone so far as rejecting Chabad converts to Judaism who proclaim "the Rebbe" to be the Messiah.

From Portugal in the west to Persia in the east, varying false messiahs arose to preach their interpretations of deliverance.

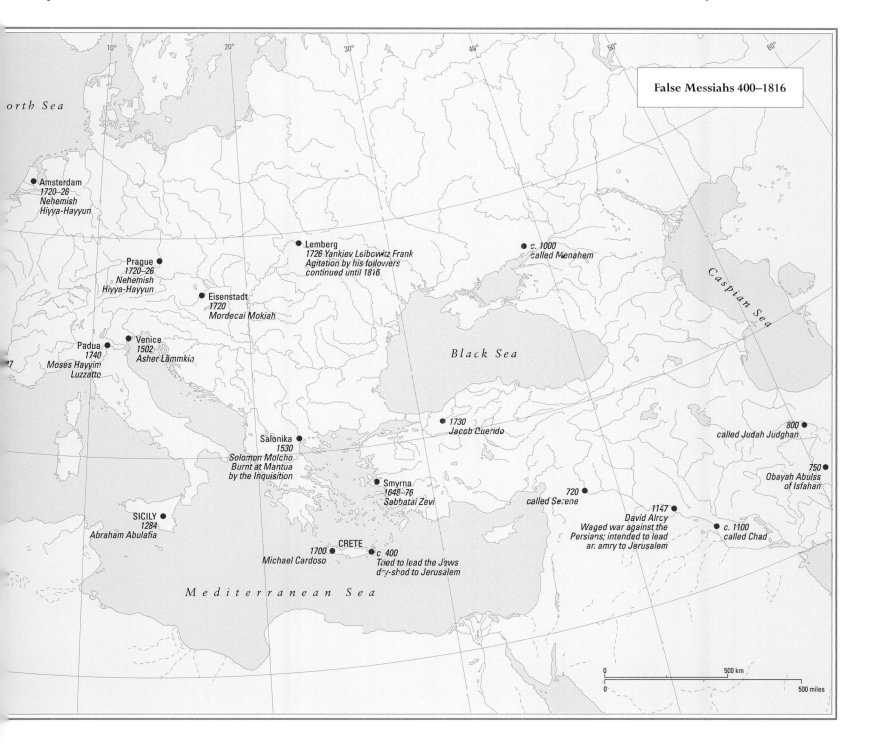

False Messiahs 400–1816

North Sea

Amsterdam
1720–26
Nehemish
Hiyya-Hayyun

Lemberg
1726 Yankiev Leibowitz Frank
Agitation by his followers
continued until 1816

c. 1000
called Menahem

Prague
1720–26
Nehemish
Hiyya-Hayyun

Eisenstadt
1720
Mordecai Mokiah

Padua
1740
Moses Hayyim
Luzzatto

Venice
1502
Asher Lämmkin

Caspian Sea

Black Sea

Salonika
1530
Solomon Molcho
Burnt at Mantua
by the Inquisition

1730
Jacob Querido

800
called Judah Judghan

750
Obayah Abulss
of Isfahan

Smyrna
1648–76
Sabbatai Zevi

720
called Serene

SICILY
1284
Abraham Abulafia

CRETE

1147
David Alroy
Waged war against the
Persians; intended to lead
an amry to Jerusalem

c. 1100
called Chad

1700
Michael Cardoso

c. 400
Tried to lead the Jews
dry-shod to Jerusalem

Mediterranean Sea

0   500 km
0   500 miles

FORCED INTO GHETTOES

IN ADDITION TO FORCING JEWS TO WEAR DISTINCTIVE CLOTHING, THE MIDDLE AGES SAW THEM HERDED INTO CONFINED DISTRICTS INTO WHICH THEY WERE LOCKED AT NIGHT. THE NAZIS ADOPTED THE SAME PLAN, COLLECTING JEWS IN CERTAIN CITIES FROM WHICH IT WOULD BE EASIER TO DEPORT THEM TO THE DEATH CAMPS.

The name "ghetto" dates from the year 1516, when the Venetian Republic locked Jews into a neighborhood known as "La Gheta" or The Foundry. Gradually, every city in Italy that had not expelled its Jews erected a ghetto in which to enclose them.

The Jews of Europe had been confined to districts behind high walls and strong gates from the early Middle Ages, as much for their own protection against a raging mob as to keep them out of sight. English cities had their Jewries, the French their Juiveries, and the Spanish their Juderías. In every major city in Europe today, vestiges of these quarters persist in names such as the Judengasse in Vienna, Jodenbreestraat in Amsterdam, and the Giudecca in Rome. A street near the cathedral in Rouen is called the rue des Juifs, there is Old Jewry in London, Market Jew Street in Penzance, Cornwall and in Poznan (Posen) Zydowska Ulica (Jews' Street) adjoins the main square, the Stary Rinek. Not all ghettos were entirely restricted to Jews, especially after the Reformation. In Cologne, for instance, as in Amsterdam, Christian homes, public buildings, and even churches were to be found in the ghetto just as they exist in Jewish neighborhoods today. Nor did they serve as headquarters for converting the Jews as they had in medieval London, for instance.

Long before the Church imposed segregation upon the Jews, Jewish communities found it expedient to live in groups. For one thing, Jews cannot hold a prayer meeting unless ten adult males are present. Since any form of travel on the Sabbath, except on foot, is prohibited, people had to live in close proximity for any form of organized worship to take place.

While the medieval church was busy burning heretics at the stake and any movement deviating from the Roman Catholic faith (such as the Aryans and Albigensians and later the Hussites) was ruthlessly suppressed, the Jews lived in relative safety in their overcrowded quarters. So long as the Jews' money was useful to the Christians and they could live their lives hidden from the gaze of their neighbors, they were secure.

The synagogue was the hub and focus of ghetto life and the rabbi its supreme leader. The thousands of rabbinical injunctions and edicts and their responsa (written answers to questions from congregants) issued in the Middle Ages are indicative of the restrictions placed on Jews.

The Jews of Europe were thus virtually self-governing. They had their own rabbinical courts (batei din) which ruled on religious matters such as food regulations, sumptuary laws (to ensure that Jews did not dress too ostentatiously and thus attract attention) and the minutiae of Jewish religious observance which extends to every sphere of life. The wealthier and more prominent members of the community, known as parnasim (from the Hebrew word "to supply, furnish") formed councils who organized the running of the ghetto. According to the Israeli statesman Abba Eban (1915–2002), the ghettos were "a training ground in self-government that prepared generations of Jews in the intricacies of civil government ..."

Eighteenth century painting of Frankfurt, showing the ghetto, the curved street in the center, of the city. After the ghetto was removed, the street was known as Ludwig Börne Strasse. Börne, (1786–1837) a political writer and satirist who converted to Christianity, had been born Leib Baruch in the ghetto.

The best-known of the medieval ghettos, because it has survived, is the Prague Ghetto. In its day, it was one of the most famous centers in the Diaspora, due to the great rabbis it produced. Located in the old city of Prague, the Stare Mesto, it had its own town hall, whose clockface has Hebrew letters (the letters of the alphabet are also used as numbers in Hebrew) and whose hands run "backwards", as well as the Jewish cemetery among whose crowded tombstones are those of two great luminaries of Judaism, David Gans (1541–1613) and the "miracle worker of Prague", Rabbi Judah Loeb ben Eezalel, known to Jews as the Maharal (c. 1525–c. 1609). The Maharal had been chief Rabbi of Moravia and did assume leadership in Prague until 1597. He was a brilliant mathematician, a friend of the astronomer Ticho Brahe, and founder of the Klaus Yeshiva. In 1594, Emperor Rudolf II invited him to an audience at his palace in Prague, allegedly because he wanted the Maharal to teach him about mysticism as it was alleged that he could perform kabbalistic wonders.

Among these wonders is the legend that has even passed into Czech folklore. Rabbi Loeb is supposed to have created a robotic monster, called the Golem, which roamed the streets preventing attacks on Jews. The Golem was "activated" by the placing of a piece of paper in its mouth that bore the sacred name of God. At sundown on Friday evening, the paper was removed, and replaced after the Sabbath so that the Golem would not desecrate the holy day by moving. The Golem is supposed to have helped the Jews to survive anti-Jewish measures and blood libel accusations but it eventually had be destroyed and returned to dust because it ran amok one Friday at the beginning of the Sabbath when the Rabbi forgot to remove the divine name from under its tongue. The remains of the Golem were allegedly sealed up in the attic of the Altneu Synagogue in Prague. Since 1917, the statue of Rabbi Loew has stood at the entrance to the City Hall of Prague. The Rabbi's first work Tikkun Ha'olam (Correction of the World) was first translated into English in 1995.

THE JEWS OF SPAIN

WHEREVER THEY WENT AFTER THE EXPULSION, THE JEWS NEVER FORGOT SPAIN AND THE SPANISH LANGUAGE, AND CONTINUE TO REMINISCE AND SING ABOUT THE GLORIOUS LAND THEY WERE FORCED TO LEAVE, EVEN THOUGH IT HAPPENED FIVE HUNDRED YEARS AGO.

The city of Toledo on the banks of the Tagus River in Spain. It is said to have been founded by Jews, the name being taken from the Hebrew word "toledot", generations.

During the latter days of Roman rule, when most of the population of Spain converted to Christianity, the many kingdoms of the Iberian peninsula imposed harsh restrictions on their Jewish minorities as well as on the Aryans, who were heretics in the eyes of the established church. Under the Visigoth rule of Toledo, for instance, Jews were forced to convert. This caused Jews to side with the invading Arabs, enraging the Christian rulers further. Under the Ummayad conquest (711–718), the Muslim kingdoms of southern Spain became a haven for Jews fleeing the Christian north. In the Battle of Jerez, fought in 711 CE, North African Jews, led by Kaula Al-Yahud, helped to defeat the last Gothic king, Rodrigo, and his knights. The invading Jews granted full religious liberty to their co-religionists living in Cordoba, Malaga, Seville, Toledo and Granada.

Muslim rule of southern Spain came to an end (with the exception of Granada) when the caliphate of Cordoba was split into twelve little kingdoms in 1013. The Muslims also changed their attitude to the Jews. In 1066, Jews of Granada were forced to flee, those that remained were butchered or forcibly converted. Shortly thereafter, in 1086, the fanatical Almoravids of North Africa invaded the peninsula and for ten years made the Jews of Lucena and Cordoba choose between conversion to Islam or death.

In the early days of Christian reconquest, the rulers were not unfriendly towards Jews. A number of Jews were given refuge in Castile where the tolerant Alfonso VII welcomed them. Despite the fact that Jews had fought against the Almohades in the Christian reconquest, the first counts of Castile and Kings of Leon showed no mercy to them though later Christian kings realised that they were valuable allies. Ferdinand I of Castile and Alfonso VI, who conquered Toledo in 1085, had many Jewish advisers, and the latter employed Jewish regiments of soldiers who fought for him, distinguished by their black-and-gold turbans. In the reign of Alfonso VIII of Castile (1155–1214) Jews gained even greater influence, partly through the King's Jewish mistress, Rachel of Toledo.

All this changed when the Crusaders began their "holy war" in Toledo in 1212 which soon turned into the familiar bloodbath. Under Ferdinand III, who united the kingdoms of Leon and Castile, the Jews were subjected to the ministrations of itinerant monks who harangued them and exhorted them to convert to "the true faith." Jews were now required to wear a yellow badge on their clothing. Pope Innocent IV exhorted Ferdinand to ensure that this rule was observed but the King and his successors allowed the badge-wearing to be relaxed in many of the cities in their realm.

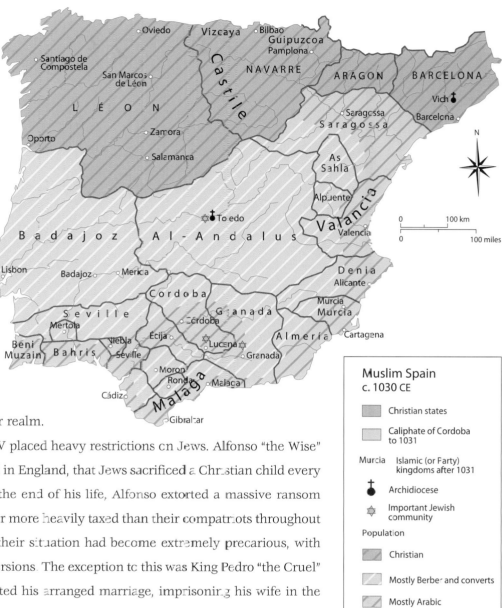

Muslim Spain proved to be a tolerant society where many Jews settled fleeing from Christian lands to the north.

In 1250, a papal bull issued by Pope Innocent IV placed heavy restrictions on Jews. Alfonso "the Wise" (1221–84) believed the story, originally perpetrated in England, that Jews sacrificed a Christian child every Good Friday in order to drink its blood. Towards the end of his life, Alfonso extorted a massive ransom from his Jewish subjects. Jews were, in any case, far more heavily taxed than their compatriots throughout Christian Spain; by the early fourteenth century their situation had become extremely precarious, with intermittent massacres and a series of forced conversions. The exception to this was King Pedro "the Cruel" (1333–69) of Castile (so-called because he repudiated his arranged marriage, imprisoning his wife in the fortress known as the Alcazar, and went to live with his mistress) who surrounded himself with Jewish ministers which enraged the populace even further.

In 1391, a massacre broke out in Seville, incited by Queen Leonora's confessor Archdeacon Ferrand Martinez. Juan I, her husband, had died in 1390 in a fall from his horse and had been succeeded by his 11-year-old son and a council of regents. As a result, Jews throughout the diocese were murdered and robbed. The unrest spread to Aragon, Catalonia, Toledo, and Valencia; in this last city, Vicente Ferrer, one of the wandering friars of Spain who considered it their duty to baptise the Jews, incited the mob to further atrocities. Rioting raged for many days in Barcelona and subsequently in Gerona and Lerida.

Thousands of Jews perished in that terrible year and many more suffered forced conversions while the agitators remained largely unpunished. This was the turning point for the Jews of Spain; never again were their Christian overlords to show them tolerance or mercy. It was the prelude to the Spanish Inquisition, ninety years later, when the "secret Jews' or "new Christians", who were referred to as maranos (pigs) or converses, were exposed, tortured, and burned at the stake in the ritual known as the auto da fé (act of faith).

Those Jews who survived the 1391 persecutions shut themselves into their juderías and created separate political institutions for themselves. The converts thrived, however, under the more liberal regimes of Enrico IV of Castile (1454–74) and Juan II of Aragon (1456–79). Practicing Jews abandoned the cities they had long ago founded, such as Toledo and Lucena and moved to Madrid, Estremadura and the cities of the kingdom of León.

In 1462, popular hatred of the Jews was stirred anew by two friars who had converted from Judaism, Alfonso de Spina and Paul de Burgos. The latter incited the population both against those who were overtly Jewish, the judíos publicos, and those he called the judíos ocultos, the New Christians. In Toledo in 1467 and in Cordoba in 1473 there were fresh outbreaks of rioting against the New Christians.

The culmination came with the ascent to the throne of Spain's beloved Catholic Kings. The marriage in 1469 of the royal cousins, Ferdinand of Aragon (1452–1516) and Isabella of Castile (1451–1504) united the two kingdoms. Ferdinand ruled Castile as the queen's consort until her death in 1504.

In 1477, the so-called Catholic kings requested Pope Sixtus IV for permission to institute the Inquisition to deal with the "new Christians." At the cortes (parliament) of Toledo in 1480, Jews were ordered to live in exclusively Jewish neighbourhoods or barrios. The Pope authorized the Inquisition throughout Castile and it began to operate in 1481. In 1483, the Pope agreed under pressure from the Spanish sovereigns to extend the Inquisition to Aragon, Catalonia, and Valencia. In that same year Tomás de Torquemada became head of the Inquisition. The torture and executions continued; in Guadalupe, the bodies of 48 people who had died of natural causes or under torture but who had been condemned to death, were dug up and executed, as were the effigies of 25 conversos who had managed to escape. Such exhumations and effigy burnings were another feature of the Inquisition.

During its first 12 years, the Inquisition condemned 13,000 Conversos to death for returning to their original faith. This was one of the factors that convinced the Catholic monarchs to order the expulsion of the Jews from Spain in 1492. By expelling those who had not converted, they hoped to remove Jewish influence from the New Christians.

Many Conversos had sought refuge in Portugal, but the Inquisition arrived there in 1497. Here it took on a new aspect. King Manoel I ordered the forced conversion of all the Jews in his realm but ordered that, to give them time to adjust to their new faith, they should not be persecuted for twenty years. There followed a strenuous conflict between the Portuguese clergy who petitioned Rome for permission to institute Spanish-style measures and those of the Conversos who just as strenuously exerted all of the influence they had, paying huge bribes to the prelates to leave them alone.

In Spain, the cruelties of the Inquisition persisted under Torquemada's successor Diego Dieza (1499–1507) who, like Torquemada, was of Jewish blood. From now on, unable to find enough genuine victims, the Inquisition decided to rely on rumor and hearsay and prosecute on the flimsiest of excuses. Nor were the victims restricted to New Christians, refugees from Portugal, Protestants and Alumbrados (a Christian movement of mystics) were all now fair game. In fact, having no Jewish or neo-Jewish victims left, the Inquisition had to make do with anyone else they could find who did not toe the Roman Catholic line.

It was not until the beginning of the eighteenth century and the accession of the Bourbons to the Spanish throne that the frenzy abated, with one major lapse in 1720, when the discovery of a secret synagogue led to a fresh outbreak of anti-Jewish hysteria.

The Jews and New Christians expelled from Spain in 1492 mainly fled to the Low Countries, North Africa, and the Ottoman Empire, with a few finding their way to central and Eastern Europe. Many were welcomed in, the Black Death having decimated the local population. Thanks to the efforts of another crypto-Jew, Christopher Columbus, they were also able to find refuge in the Americas. Wherever the Spanish Jews and conversos went, they took their own language, known as Ladino or Judezmo (Judaeo-Español) and their Sephardi (Spanish) traditions with them, and continued for centuries to write and sing of the glories of Spain.

When Spain became a republic in 1848, the edict of expulsion was lifted, but the cherem, the self-imposed ban on the return to Spain meant that few Jews of Spanish origin ever came back, even though it was lifted in the 1960s. Most of the Jews living in Spain today are Ashkenazi. Until as recently as the restoration of the Spanish monarchy in 1975, Jews were not allowed to worship publicly, but that has now changed. Many Jews from Western Europe have retired to southern Spain and the Balearic islands and set up small synagogues. The ancient synagogues of Portugal are being restored and re-opened though most of their congregants have long gone. In 1987, the then President Mário Soares, asked forgiveness of the Jewish communities of Portuguese origin for Portugal's responsibility in the Inquisition and all the past persecutions of Jews.

At present there are four synagogues in the country, in Lisbon, Porto, Ponta Delgada in the Azores and Belmonte. Kosher wine is produced in both Spain and Portugal.

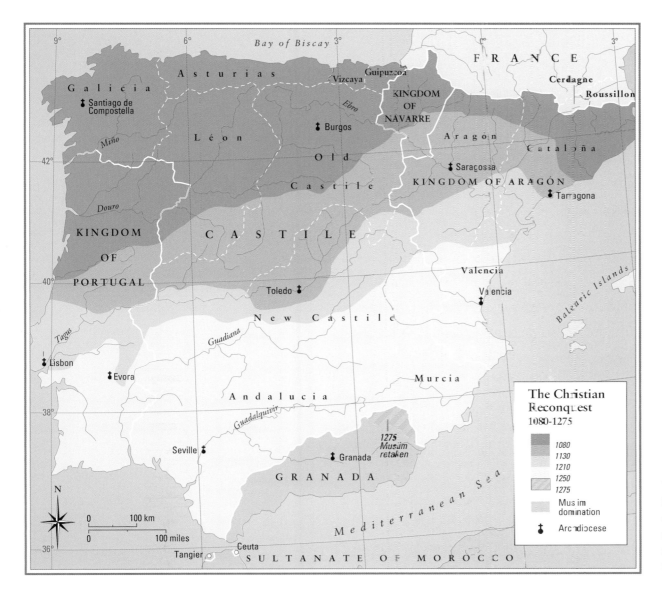

The Christian Re-conquest of Spain between 1080 and 1275 drove before it the Islamic faith, and the Jews under christian rule suffered forced conversion to their overlords religion.

JEWISH EXPULSIONS

THE FIRST COUNTRY TO EXPEL THE JEWS WAS ENGLAND IN 1290. JEWS WERE CONTINUALLY BEING EXPELLED FROM TOWNS AND CITIES THROUGHOUT EUROPE, THOUGH THEY WERE USUALLY ALLOWED BACK AGAIN, ESPECIALLY IF THEY PAID A RANSOM.

In the frenzy of religiosity that gripped early medieval Europe, England led the way in expelling its Jewish population. By the end of the thirteenth century, Jews had been expelled from England and large parts of France and what is now Germany.

The reason for the expulsions was that Jews were forced into an impossible situation. On the one hand, they were made to become money-lenders, as Christians were banned from doing so by the church (in fact, money-lending at interest is also forbidden in the Bible and the Talmud) and this often enabled them to acquire great wealth. It also meant that they had to become pawnbrokers to the peasantry, making them deeply unpopular. The medieval kings of Europe, who liked nothing better than to wage endless wars away from home, impoverishing their kingdoms, used the Jews as a money-box to be raided at will. When they money ran out, as it inevitably did, the King could make himself popular again by joining the mob in persecuting his erstwhile financiers.

During the Peasants' Revolt of 1262, Jews were attacked in many places, including London where 1,500 were killed. In 1278, Edward I decided to make coin-clipping a capital offence. He was convinced that Jews were involved, and had all those in London arrested and imprisoned in the Tower. After a show trial, 280 of them were executed. The King ordered the rest to leave the country by November 1, 1290. Their possessions were confiscated by the crown, of course. One month before the deadline, 16,000 left for France and Belgium. They were even persecuted in their flight, as when a sea captain, after taking their money and promising them a safe passage, dumped many on a sandbank in the Thames exposed by the low tide and left them there to drown.

Edward I was the first King to expel Jews from a whole country, but he was merely emulating

Opposite: As the political forms of Europe changed so did the attitude towards their Jewish subjects. Jews were expelled from cities and countries, forcing them to find new homes and livelihoods in nearby states.

Jews in Christian Europe

- Areas of Jewish communities
- → Expulsions, with date
- ○ Major centres of resettlement
- ● Main ghettoes, with date establishes
- ● Centres of disputaions between Jews and Christians

ATLANTIC

OCEAN

North

Sea

Baltic Sea

LITHUANIA

ENGLAND

WALES

1290

1290

Oxford 1222

Amsterdam

Hamburg

Hanover

Fosen pre-1532

POLAND

SILESIA

Grodno

Bialystok

Pinsk

FLANDERS

Antwerp

GERMANY

Cologne

Łódz

1012

Kalisz

Brest-Litovsk

1290

Frankfurt 1460-1864

1248

Radom

Lublin

Luck

Zhitomir

1182

Mainz 662

Paris

Prague 1473

Breslau 1266

1159

Kazimierz 1494

Lemberg

Sens

1306

Cracow

1348

Tarnopol

1306

FRANCE

1394

Alps

AUSTRIA

Vienna

1421

Carpathian mountains

Kishinev

1306

1420

Turin 1400

Mantua 1612

Verona

Udine

Venice 1517

HUNGARY

Buda

1349-1360

Burgos

1492

Pamplona

Pyrenees

Tarascon

1394

Genoa

Ferrara 1624

Florence 1571

Spalato

Nicopolis

PORTUGAL

Avila

SPAIN

NAVARRE

Madrid 1480

Barcelona

1492

Tortosa

CORSICA

ITALY

Livorno

Cattaro

Adrianople

Constantinople

Valencia 1390

1492

BALEARIC IS.

1490

Rome 1215, 1556-1870

Naples

OTTOMAN

Salonica

Granada

Murcia 1412

1492

Corfu

Smyrna

1492

Oran

Algiers

Mediterranean

1492

Palermo 1312

SARDINIA

Patras 1532

Modon pre-1481

Rhodes 1310-1522

Fez 1450

Tlemcen

Tunis

SICILY

MAGHREB

Tripoli

Sea

CRETE

N

0   300 km

0   300 miles

his predecessor, King Philippe-Auguste (1165–1223) of France. Jews had been living in France for over a thousand years, having arrived with the Romans. When Philippe-Auguste came to the throne in 1179 he immediately enriched himself by confiscating Jewish assets, then accused the Jews of committing ritual murder. He imprisoned all those in his realm, releasing them in 1180, after payment of a heavy ransom. The next year, he cancelled all loans made to Christians by Jews, and took twenty percent commission for himself on the deal. The year after, he confiscated all Jewish property and drove them out of his realm. Jews continued to live in parts of France not controlled by the French king, but when he conquered some of these lands, he re-issued the expulsion order. In 1306, Philippe le Bel expelled the Jews from France again but they were eventually allowed to return.

Jews were expelled from the German Rhineland after many were massacred there and throughout Europe, including Switzerland and Hungary, during the Black Death epidemic of 1348. Spain expelled the most prosperous and important Jewish community in the world, consisting of about 300,000 people, in 1492, many of whom fled to Portugal where at first they were offered sanctuary. In 1497, the Portuguese king, Manoel I (1469–1521), changed his mind under pressure from the church. In 1495, the Jews were expelled from Lithuania, but were allowed to return eight years later.

Expulsions of Jews from specific towns and regions occurred regularly. The first was probably the expulsion from Alexandria in 415 CE by Bishop Cyril. In 554, the Diocese of Clément expelled the Jews and the Bishop of Uzès followed suit in 561. The Visigothic kings were avid expellers of Jews as soon as they converted to Christianity. In 1012, Jews were expelled from Mayence (now Mainz, in Germany) but were allowed to return the following year. This was a familiar pattern, that included Graz in Austria in 1497, Naples 1510 and 1541, Prague in 1744, and Moscow in 1891. In 1547, Ivan the Terrible would not allow Jews to enter his kingdom because "they bring about great evil." In 1550, Dr. Joseph Hacohen was expelled from Genoa for practising medicine, and soon afterward all the other Jews were expelled. In 1727, Catherine I expelled the Jews from Russia and the Ukraine. Her successor, Elizabeth I expelled them from the entire Russian Empire. In 1744, the Archduchess of Austria, Maria Theresa ordered "no Jew is to be tolerated in … Bohemia". She changed her mind in 1748, requiring Jews to pay a fee for "readmission" every ten years.

In modern times, the Nazis first tried to rid themselves of the Jews by encouraging emigration between 1933 and 1939, but Jews were trapped in the Reich by the outbreak of World War II. Jews were subsequently deported from all of the Axis powers (including Italy in 1940) to concentration camps, mostly in Poland, where they were massacred, unless they were shot on home territory.

After 1948, most of the Arab countries with large Jewish populations, such as Iraq and Libya, forced their Jewish citizens to flee. In Egypt, this did not happen until 1952, when King Farouk was overthrown by General Neguib.

The tragic paradox is that Jewish suffering has been so immense that expulsion has often been the lesser of two evils—expulsion or death. In many places, Jews became accustomed to expulsion and rapid readmission. A poem written in 1692 by Elhanan Helin of Frankfurt reads: "We went in joy and in sorrow; because of the destruction and the disgrace, we grieved for our community and we rejoiced that we had escaped with so many survivors."

A Jewish cobbler goes about his rounds in the city of Vilna photographed toward the turn of the 19th century. His ancestors steadily settled in eastern europe from the 1500s moveing from less tolerant regimes. In his time he would again face expulsion from his place of birth.

Cossack Frenzy

IT IS AN IRONY THAT ONE OF THE WORST ENEMIES OF THE JEWS SHOULD BE THE UKRANIAN NATIONAL HERO. BOGDAN CHMIELNICKI EVEN HAS A STREET NAMED FOR HIM IN ODESSA THAT INTERSECTS WITH A STREET NAMED FOR SHOLEM ALEICHEM, THE GREAT YIDDISH WRITER.

Bogdan Chmielnicki, (c. 1595–1657) leader of the Polish Cossacks, known to the Jews as Chmiel Rasha (Chmiel the Wicked) massacred thousands of Jews.

By the start of the sixteenth century, the Cossacks numbers had swelled until they formed semi-autonomous states. They were deeply hostile to the Jews, whom they identified with the Polish rulers and in 1637, as a foretaste of the massacres, they killed about 2000 Jews in and around Pereyaslav. In 1648, their leader, Bogdan Chmielnicki (c. 1595–1657), known to the Jews as Chmiel Rasha (Chmiel the Wicked) led an uprising against Polish rule in the Ukraine, using the opportunity to massacre the Jews, telling the Ukranians that the Poles had sold them as slaves "into the hands of the accursed Jews."

The first large-scale massacres took place at Nemirov. After the massacre at Tulchin, the Poles agreed to surrender the Jews to the rebels in exchange for their own lives. Jews fled westwards into Poland to escape Chmielnicki's hordes who swept through Volhynia and towns bordering Byelorussia.

According to Jewish records, the death toll reached approximately 100,000, and nearly 300 Jewish communities were destroyed. Cossack cruelty was so great that many Jews preferred to flee to captivity under Crimean Tartars, to be sold as slaves.

Jewish settlement of the Ukraine, west of the Dnieper, nevertheless continued. The Polish King Sigismund III had died in 1648 and he was succeeded by his brother, Jan Casimir II. Jan quickly succeeded in defeating Chmielnicki and his Cossacks and allowed Jews who had been forcibly converted to return to their faith. The memory of the 1648–49 massacres, which is well-documented in contemporary Jewish sources, persisted, some calling it the 'Third Destruction', after the first and second destructions of the Temple. The Jewish self-government known as the Councils of the Lands redeemed hostages, and Jews actually began to return to Volhynia and even to the lands west of the Dnieper.

The Ukraine gained a short-lived independence, but in 1651, Chmielnicki was finally defeated at Beresteczko. In 1654, he persuaded the Cossacks to switch their allegiance to the Russian czars when Russia finally succeeded in annexing the Ukraine.

The second wave of Cossack attacks on the Jews was perpetrated in 1768 by the Haidamaky, (Haidamaks or in Russian and Ukrainian, Gaidamaki, from a Turkish word meaning "to pursue"). These paramilitary bands consisted of local Cossacks and peasantry who fought the

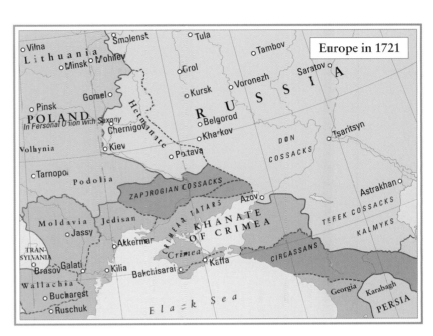

The Cossacks, occupying areas along the south Russian borderlands were a fiercely independent group of peoples, who were deeply hostile to the Jews.

Polish nobility and the Jews in the Ukraine. It centred on the city of Uman the scene of a terrible massacre known as "The Evil Decree," which was strongly supported by the Ukranian Orthodox Archimandrate Yavovsky.

The Haidamaks began their attacks in Lisyanka, Golta, Tulchin, Paulovich, Fastov, Zhivotov, Granov and then Teityev. Jews and Poles fled to the local fortified city of Uman for protection. The guards were under the command of Ivan Gonta who was suspected of sympathizing with the Haidamaks.

Gonta claimed that he had orders from the Tsarina Catherine II who allegedly had offered support to the Gaydamaks, to kill all the Jews of southern Poland. On the fifth of the Hebrew month of Tammuz (July), the Gaydamaks arrived at the outskirts of Uman. Gontas welcomed them in and horrific slaughter of both Jews and Poles ensued for six days.

After setting fire to the main synagogue, since they were unable to kill those within, the Gaydamaks ran through the streets in a frenzy, killing and looting Poles and Jews. Some Gaydamaks went to the city hall and informed the local Jewish merchants that, for a high price, they would be left alone. The Jews went to their homes and returned with funds for ransom, but were killed anyway. Following the massacre, as children who survived were roaming around in hunger searching for food, some Haidamaks took pity and aided children. They, too, were killed.

The estimates of the slaughter range from twelve thousand to thirty thousand, the figure cited in the above account. Following the attacks many Jews perished from disease and starvation as a result of the destruction.

The great Rabbi Nachman of Breslov (Bratzslav) (1772–1810) traveled to Uman to spend the last months of his life there, when he was dying from tuberculosis. He felt a special kinship with the martyrs of the massacre and wanted to be buried near them.

The Cossacks did not succeed in ridding the Ukraine of Jews. Despite the memory of the Cossack massacres, the region had among the densest Jewish population in the world in the eighteenth and nineteenth centuries. The Ukranians today refer to the Cossack rebellion of 1648–54 as a "war of liberation" and revere Bogdan Chmielnitzki and the Gaydamaks as heroes.

THE POGROMS

POGROMS ARE SOMETHING OF A TRADITION IN EASTERN EUROPE. THEY BEGAN IN THE SEVENTEENTH CENTURY WITH BOGDAN CHMIELNICKI AND OCCURRED SPORADICALLY THEREAFTER. IN POLAND THEY CONTINUED EVEN AFTER THE HOLOCAUST.

Polish chief rabbi Michael Schudrich and Polish Bishop Marian Florczyk attending a ceremony in Kielce to mark the sixtieth anniversary of the 1946 pogrom.

The Russian word "pogrom," is based on the word for "thunder," means a sudden attack. When, in 1791, Catherine the Great ordered that Jews in the vast Russian Empire be confined to a narrow strip of land, only 4 percent of the size of Imperial Russia, she turned the Jews into a sitting target.

The Pale of Settlement included most of the territory of present-day Poland, Latvia, Lithuania, the Ukraine and Belarus. More than 90 percent of Russian Jews were forced to live inside the Pale. The Jewish population of Russia nevertheless grew from 1.6 million in 1820 to 5.6 million in 1910.

Jews living in the Pale suffered further discrimination. They were taxed twice as heavily, forbidden to lease land, run taverns (this had been one of their main occupations in Poland), or to receive higher education. A few Jews had the opportunity for higher education and lived outside the Pale since they were from the wealthiest classes.

A liberalization period in the 1860s was reversed by Alexander III (1845–1894). The first pogroms broke out in 1881. While they were allegedly spontaneous attacks, they were in fact promoted, aided and encouraged by the authorities, either secretly or openly.

The first wave of pogroms had been confined to southern and eastern Ukraine—the first one occurred in Elizavetgrad and spread to surrounding villages, followed by a series of pogroms throughout the Pale. They culminated in the Kiev pogrom that lasted for three days while the governor-general and police stood by and watched. During this first wave of pogroms, there was much looting and burning of property but few deaths. In Warsaw, a pogrom broke out when a false alarm of fire affected worshippers at Holy Cross Church. The rumor was spread that it had been started by Jewish pickpockets, offering the excuse to loot, burn and murder the Jewish population.

The Russian authorities finally grew tired of the unrest (which they feared might spread to non-Jewish property) and took action to quell the rioting. Nevertheless, there were intermittent outbreaks of violence against Jews, even though Count Tolstoy, the Minister of the Interior, firmly blamed the governors of the provinces for the attacks. Alexander III's reaction was to enact the May Laws of 1882, which imposed even harsher conditions on the Jews in the Pale, in part for their alleged role in the assassination of Alexander II.

The second wave of pogroms lasted from 1903 to 1906, under the last Czar, Nicholas II, and was connected with the attempt by the secret police to quell the unrest surrounding 1905 Decembrist Revolution. The Russian press was allowed to inflame anti-Semitism by blaming the unrest on the Jews, rather than on the repressive government. Various reactionary, monarchist societies were formed which were known collectively as The Black Hundreds and these perpetrated hideous violence. The Kishinev, Bessarabia pogroms of 1903 and 1904 left 47 dead and hundreds injured. In 1905, some revolutionaries actually joined the government in supporting the attacks, hoping the unrest would turn into national revolt. The worst of the second wave of pogroms was perpetrated by the Black Hundreds in Zhitomir, in Odessa (over 300 dead and thousands wounded) and Ekaterinoslav (120 dead). There were 660 attacks in the Ukraine and Bessarabia, 624 of them in small towns and villages. Twenty-seven attacks even occurred outside the Pale of Settlement. In 1906 there were pogroms in Bialystok and Siedlce, in Poland. This time the police and military openly colluded with the mob, opening fire on the Jews. The pogroms in Czarist Russia were a turning point for the Jewish community who sought to escape from the tyranny, either through emigration to Palestine or to western Europe and the United States.

The third wave of pogroms between 1917 and 1921 far surpassed any of the previous violence, even though the Pale of Settlement had been officially abolished. Both the White and Red Armies wrought vengeance on the local Jewish population for the losses experienced by both sides during the fierce battles for the Ukraine, that declared its independence in 1918. In Titiev, 4000 Jews were murdered by retreating White Russians. Only when Russia regained a stable government after 1921 did the atrocities cease.

The attacks on Jews in Poland, continued after the Holocaust. The Kielce pogrom, another blood libel started by a Catholic priest, resulted in the murder of thirty-seven Polish Jews returning after the Holocaust. Jan Tomasz Gross, whose book *Fear—Anti-Semitism in Poland after Auschwitz*, documents anti-Semitism in Poland, revealed that 1,600 Jews in Jedwabne were massacred in 1941 by fellow-Poles, rather than by the Germans and there were other, similar instances.

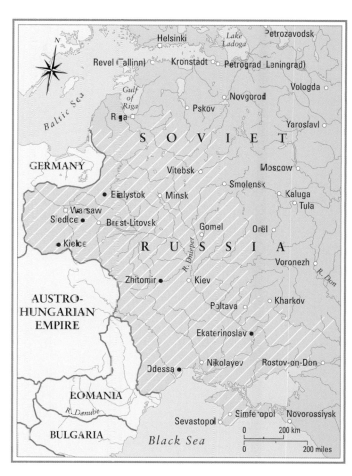

The Pogroms, Jewish Pale of Settlement, 19th century

Jewish Pale of settlement

• Major acts of violence against Jews

The map shows the Jewish Pale of Settlement in the nineteenth century. Pogroms were not confined to this region, however.

EMANCIPATION OF EUROPEAN JEWRY

WESTERN SOCIETIES BEGAN GRANTING JEWS EQUAL CITIZENSHIP
WITH THE ENLIGHTENMENT BUT THE PATH WAS NOT ALWAYS
SMOOTH, AS IN THE CASE OF THE DAMASCUS LIBEL.

Portrait of Moses Mendelssohn
as a young man.

A major liberalization movement occurred in Western European society starting in the late eighteenth century. The novel idea that "all men are created equal," promulgated by the philosophers of the Enlightenment and put into practice by the American and French Revolutions was to have major repercussions on Jewish life. Jews would finally be allowed to participate on equal terms with the citizens of the country in which they lived. Equality of opportunity, including secular learning, became available to Jews and, above all, they were allowed to dress like their fellow citizens and move out of the ghettoes to live among them.

In 1740, the American Colonies became the first country to grant Jews full citizenship, allowing them this right after seven years' residence. Jews fully supported the American Revolution, even though it might mean economic ruin for them. In 1791, France became the first European country to emancipate its Jewish population. By 1796, France, Britain and the Netherlands had granted Jews a measure of equal rights, though in Britain Jews were not allowed to sit in parliament for another fifty years. Napoleon gave the Jews of France their own representative council, the Consistoire, and freed the Jews living in the lands he conquered, as when he gave Polish Jews their own Sanhredrin. Jews did not become equal citizens in Russia until the 1917 Revolution.

The event that did much to encourage Jews to form secular, political liberation movements, including Zionism, was the Damascus Blood Libel. On February 5, 1840, a Franciscan friar in Damascus, Father Thomas, and his Greek servant, were reported missing. Their bodies were never found. The French consul, supported by the Turkish governor of Damascus, asserted that the Jews were responsible for ritual murder, claiming that deaths had occurred just before the Passover (the disappearance was three months earlier). A funeral procession was held for Father Thomas (without his body) in Damascus. His tombstone, in the Franciscan church in Damascus, still reads in Arabic "... assassinated by the Jews ..."

An investigation was launched. Solomon Negrin, a Jewish barber, "confessed" under torture and implicated other Jews. Two died under torture and one, Moses Abulafia, converted to Islam to escape torment. More arrests and atrocities followed, culminating in sixty-three Jewish children being held hostage and mob attacks on Jewish communities.

The affair was widely reported and the Austrian Consul in Aleppo, Eliahu Picotto, a Jew, made representations to Ibrahim Pasha (Egypt ruled Damascus at the time) who ordered an investigation. For the first time, Jewish and international opinion was mobilized. Fifteen thousand American Jews protested in six American cities on behalf of their Syrian brethren and the United States consul in Egypt made an official protest on behalf of U.S. President Martin Van Buren. Sir Moses Montefiore, the leader of the Board of Deputies of British Jews, backed by prominent Jews and non-Jews from all over the world led a delegation to the ruler of Syria, Mehmet Ali.

Negotiations in Alexandria eventually secured the unconditional release of the nine of the original 13 prisoners still alive. Later in Constantinople Montefiore persuaded Sultan Abdul Mecid to issue an edict intended to halt the spread of the blood libel in the Ottoman Empire, but it did not stop a wave of pogroms spreading through the Middle East that lasted 35 years.

Germany produced the most outstanding intellectuals of the Emancipation, in particular Moses Mendelssohn born in Dessau, the son of a poor scribe In childhood, Moses developed curvature of the spine and became a hunchback. He studied Jewish and secular subjects, including Latin and mathematics. In 1750, Isaac Bernhard, a wealthy merchant, appointed Mendelssohn to teach his children. In 1754, Mendelssohn met the playwright Gotthold Lessing (1729–1781) and became the role model for his Nathan the Wise (*Nathan der Weise*, 1779). This was Lessing's second play about Jews, the first was *Die Juden* (1749). Within a few months, the two became close friends. Mendelssohn owed his first introduction to the public to Lessing's admiration. Lessing published Mendelssohn's Philosophical Conversations (*Philosophische Gespräche*) anonymously in 1755. His Phaedon or the Soul's Immortality (*Phädon oder über die Unsterblichkeit der Seele* 1767), modeled on Plato's dialogue, earned Mendelssohn the nickname the "German Plato', or the "German Socrates." Royalty and aristocrats were eager to meet him and he was lionized by Berlin society.

Despite his fame in the secular world and unlike his descendants, all of whom converted to Christianity (including his grandson, the composer Felix Mendelssohn), Mendelssohn did not abandon Judaism. After his health broke down, he translated the Bible into English and added a commentary. This work was entitled "Clarification" (*Bi'ur*) (1783); only the Exodus commentary was written by Mendelssohn himself. His greatest contribution to Jewish thought is *Jerusalem* (1783; English trans. 1838 and 1852), the basic premise of which is that the state has no right to interfere in the religion of its citizens. The philosopher Immanuel Kant (1724–1804 called *Jerusalem* "the proclamation of a great reform, which, however, will be slow in manifestation and in progress, and which will affect not only your people but others as well." Mendelssohn is buried in the Jewish Cemetery in Berlin, where his grave has been restored.

Egypt, the Middle East and India

The Jews of the Middle East, North Africa and the three communities in India made a huge cultural contribution to the countries in which they lived. Most have left since 1948, expelled or through voluntary emigration.

The ruins or, Ur of the Chaldees, Mesopotamia (Iraq), where Judaism first emerged.

Resulting from their virtual annihilation since 1948, the culmination of growing nineteenth and twentieth-century anti-Semitism in the Arab world and Iran, and the result of Arab and Moslem nationalism that began long before the State of Israel, the history of the Jews in the Middle East has been largely forgotten. Yet these communities made an overwhelming contribution to scholarship throughout the Jewish and Islamic worlds, especially in poetry and music.

The history of the Alexandrian Jews dates from the foundation of the city by Alexander the Great in 332 BCE, an event witnessed by many Jews. Jews served in many Egyptian administrations as custodians of the Nile and even of Egyptian temples. Josephus claims that after Ptolemy I captured Judea, he led some 120,000 Jewish captives to Egypt, but many other Jews emigrated there of their own accord. An inscription recording the dedication of a synagogue to Ptolemy and Berenice was discovered near Alexandria.

The Ptolemies assigned the Jews two of the five districts of the city, to enable them to keep their own laws. The Alexandrian Jews enjoyed a greater degree of political independence than elsewhere, but the Jewish community of Alexandria was almost exterminated by Trajan's army during a revolt in 115–117 CE. Josephus puts the figure for Jews slaughtered by the Romans at 50,000.

There is evidence that at Oxyrynchus (modern Behneseh), on the east side of the Nile, there was a Jewish community of some importance which even had a Jews' street during the Roman period. The Arab invasion of Egypt in the seventh century was welcomed by the Jews who opposed the conversion policies of Patriarch Cyrus of Alexandria. Jews also reached Egypt from the Arabian peninsula. A copy of the letter sent by Muhammad to the Jew Banu Janba was found in the Cairo Genizah, the synagogue storeroom containing literary treasures, first discovered in 1896.

The Treaty of Alexandria in 641 expressly stipulated that the Jews were to be allowed to remain in the city. Of the fortunes of the Jews in Egypt under the Ommiad and Abbassid caliphs (641–868), little is known. Under the Tulunids (863–905) the Karaite community enjoyed robust growth alongside the Rabbanite (mainstream Jewish) community.

Under Saladdin (1169–1250) the Jews were shown the tolerance that was characteristic of the Kurdish ruler. At this time, Maimonides arrived and settled in Fostat (now Cairo) in 1166, where he wrote his two seminal works, *Mishneh Torah* (*Guide to the Torah*) and *Moreh Nevokhim* (*Guide for the Perplexed*). He became Saladdin's physician.

When the Mamelukes (1250–1517) ruled, there were outbreaks of anti-Jewish and anti-Christian hatred due to the fanaticism of the regime. Sultan Baybars (Al-Malik al-Thahir, 1260–77) doubled the tribute paid by to him by non-Moslems. At one time he had a ditch dug for the purpose of burning all the Jews but at the last moment he repented and instead exacted a heavy tribute, during the collection of which many were killed. Nevertheless, many Jews fleeing the Inquisition and persecution in Spain sought and found refuge in Egypt.

Under Ottoman rule (1517–1922), the Turkish sultans allowed Jews to rise to positions of prominence. When Abraham de Castro, a refugee from Spain, was made master of the Mint by Selim I, an event occurred that is referred to as "the Cairo Purim". The viceroy, Ahmed Shaitan, a Mameluke, wanted to seize power for himself from the Sultan and ordered Abraham de Castro to produce new coins stamped with his likeness. De Castro pretended to obey but left Egypt for Constantinople where he warned the Sultan of Ahmed's rebellion. Ahmed learned of the denunciation and seized 12 Jewish community leaders as hostages, throwing them in jail and pillaging the Jewish quarter. A delegation offered Ahmed what money they were able to collect. Ahmed had them locked up as well and told them they would be executed together with the rest of the community on that very day. But before the executions, Ahmed took a bath during which one of his vizirs, Mohammed Bey, tried to kill him. Ahmed survived but was seriously wounded. He fled the palace but was caught and beheaded. Mohammed Bey freed the imprisoned Jews. The Hebrew date was 28 Adar (only a week after the official Purim) and the Jews of Cairo celebrated the date for generations to come.

According to Manasseh ben Israel (1656), "The viceroy of Egypt has always at his side a Jew with the title zaraf bashi or 'chief treasurer', who collects the taxes." Shabbetai Zevi the false messiah, visited Cairo twice, the second time in 1660. It was there that he married Sarah who had been brought from Leghorn, Italy.

After the collapse of the Ottoman Empire, the British ruled Egypt through a puppet king, King Fuad. Egypt was friendly towards its Jewish population, though Egyptian nationality was usually denied to recent Jewish immigrants. Jews played an important role in the economy and the Jewish population climbed to nearly 80,000 as they came to Egypt to flee increasing persecution in Europe. Although there was a deep division traditionally between the Karaite and Rabbanite communities, they eventually began working together and the younger educated generation pressed for improving relations between the two.

Individual Jews played an important role in Egyptian nationalism. René Qattawi, leader of the Cairo Sephardic community, endorsed the creation in 1935 of the Association of Egyptian Jewish Youth, whose slogan was "Egypt is our homeland, Arabic is our language." Qattawi was a strong opponent of Zionism. The Zionist movement had much support in Egypt, however. The Karaite scholar, Murad Ben Farag (1866–1956), was both an Egyptian nationalist and a passionate Zionist, the most eloquent defender of Zionism in the Arabic language and one of the co-authors of Egypt's first Constitution in 1923. In 1937, the government annulled the Capitulations, by which traders from the permanent resident minorities, including the Jews, were granted immunity from taxation. Yaqub Sanu, was a patriotic Egyptian nationalist who advocated the expulsion of the British. He continued to edit the nationalist publication Abu Naddara 'Azra from exile. Henri Curiel founded The Egyptian Movement for National Liberation in 1943, an organization that was to form the core of the Egyptian Communist Party. Anti-Jewish, nationalistic organizations such as Young Egypt and the Muslim Brothers, however, expressed sympathy to the Axis Powers in Europe and were increasingly antagonistic to Jews. Sporadic anti-Jewish incidents occurred from 1942 onwards. As the Partition of Palestine and the founding of Israel drew closer, hostility to Jews increased and vast numbers of Egyptian Jews emigrated to the new Jewish State. When King Farouk was forced to abdicate and General Naguib seized power in 1952, followed by Gamal Abd-Al-Nasser, foreign nationals, including the large number of Jews who had never been given Egyptian nationality, were expelled. This, and subsequent wars with Israel, to say nothing of the Lavon Affair and other spying incidents, reduced the Egyptian-Jewish population to less than a hundred, who now maintain a low profile.

Iraqi Jews constitute one of the world's oldest and most historically significant Jewish communities. Their story began with the Babylonian captivity in about 800 BCE. The Jewish community of Babylon included Ezra the Scribe, whose return to Judea was associated with significant changes in Jewish ritual observance. The *Babylonian Talmud* was written during the period from 300 to 1000 CE when the centre of Jewish learning passed from Palestine to Babylon. From the Persian Sassanid period in the second century CE to the rise of the Islamic caliphate, the Jewish community of Babylon thrived as the centre of Jewish learning. The Mongol invasion and Islamic discrimination during the Middle Ages led to its decline.

The Umayyad caliph, Umar II (717–720), issued orders to his governors not to allow the building of new synagogues. Harun al-Rashid (786–809) was more tolerant and the delegation to Harun from the Emperor Charlemagne, included a Jew. Charles (possibly Charles the Bald) is said to have asked the "King of Babel" to send him a man of royal lineage; and in response the Caliph sent him a rabbi; this was the first step toward establishing communication between the Jews of Babylonia and European communities. Nevertheless, Harun forced Jews to wear a yellow badge on their clothing.

Under subsequent caliphs, synagogues were forcibly turned into mosques and Jews were excluded from public office. When the Ottoman Sultan Suleiman II retook Tabriz and Baghdad that had been captured by the Persians from the Mongols in 1534, this led to an improvement in the life of the Jews. The Persian reconquest in 1623, however, caused Jews to suffer again under the predominantly Shi-ite Persians. The Ottoman Turkish army that re-conquered Iraq in 1638 included as many as ten per cent of Jews. The day of the reconquest even became a Jewish holiday, known as "Yom Nes" (the Day of Miracle).

Over time, Ottoman rule declined and the situation of the Jews deteriorated, though the Jewish population continued to grow. By 1884 there were 30,000 Jews in Baghdad and by 1900, 50,000. The community also produced great rabbis, such as Joseph Hayyim ben Eliahu Mazal-Tov (1334–1909) and many powerful Jewish families, such as the Sassoons and the Kadoories. Many Jews left Iraq at this time, due to Moslem discrimination, especially when the British took control of Mesopotamia after World War I. A large number settled in India.

In the twentieth century, Iraqi Jews played an important role in the early days of the Iraq's independence, but in 1940, the so-called "Seven" or "Golden Square", extreme nationalists, announced a coup in Iraq and installed Nuri al-Sa'id as prime minister. Nuri remained close to the monarchy and Britain under King Ghazi who died in 1939 in a car accident and his successor Feisal II was only four years old at succession, under the regency of Prince 'Abd al-Ilah); and attempted to dissolve the Seven and re-establish civilian control.

In March, 1940, Nuri al-Sa'id was forced to resign and Rashid 'Ali, a pro-Nazi was installed as Prime Minister. Haj Amin Al-Husseini, the exiled Palestinian Mufti, agitated for a coup which he achieved in 1941 through "The Seven". Rashid 'Ali al-Kaylani was installed as head of "National Defence" government, causing Nuri al-Sa'id and King Feisal II to flee. In May, 1941, the British invaded Iraq to restore order. Rashid 'Ali fled to Teheran, then Germany and Saudi Arabia. Al-Husseini likewise escaped to Germany. In June 1941, a pro-Husseini and 'Ali mob attacked the Jews of Baghdad. The *farhud* (pogrom) against Jews claimed about 600 dead and 2,100 injured with much destruction of Jewish property by soldiers. The British ambassador, Kinahan Cornwallis, refused to allow British troops to enter the city until the pogrom was over. In 1948, the Iraqi-Jewish community, numbered at around 120,000 but almost all left the country in the two years following the Arab-Israeli war, in which Iraq participated. Today, fewer than a handful of Jews remain in Iraq.

The Jewish community of Persia, modern-day Iran, is one of the oldest in the Diaspora, with roots reaching back to the First Temple. Their history in the pre-Islamic period is intertwined with that of the Jews of neighbouring Babylon. Cyrus, the first Achaemid Emperor, conquered Babylon in 539 BCE and permitted the return of the Jewish exiles to the Land of Israel. The biblical books of Esther, Ezra, Nehemiah, and Daniel describe the close relationship of the Jews to the court of the Achaemids at Susa (Shushan in Hebrew).

Under the Sassanid dynasty (226–642 CE), the Jewish population of Persia grew considerably and spread throughout the region, yet Jews nevertheless suffered from intermittent oppression and persecution. The invasion by Arab Muslims in 642 CE ended the Persian Empire. Throughout the centuries in Iran, Jews have suffered sporadic persecution and discrimination. Sometimes whole communities have been forced to convert, as in Meshhed in 1839. During the nineteenth century, there was considerable emigration to the Land of Israel and the Zionist movement spread throughout the community.

Under the Pahlevi Dynasty, established in 1925, the country changed its name to Iran, when it became secularized and Western-orientated. This greatly benefited the Jews who were emancipated and played an important role in the economic and cultural life of the country. After 1948, Iran became the only Moslem country to maintain close (if somewhat clandestine) relations with Israel. On the eve of the Islamic Revolution in 1979, there were 80,000 Jews in Iran, mainly in Teheran (60,000), Shiraz (8,000),

Kermanshah (4,000), and Isfahan (3,000). As soon as the Ayatollah Khomeini came to power, tens of thousands of Jews, left the country, fleeing mainly to Israel and the United States (especially California). Since 1948, 76,244 Iranian Jews have emigrated to Israel.

The Council of the Jewish Community, established in Iran after World War II, is the representative body of the community. It is currently allowed one representative in the Iranian parliament who is forced by law to support Iranian foreign policy and its virulent anti-Zionism. The Jewish community has a measure of religious freedom but is faced with constant suspicion of cooperating with the "Zionist state" and the United States, both such activities being punishable by death. Similarly, Iranian-supported terrorists have been blamed for outrages against Jews and Israelis throughout the world, such as the explosion at the Jewish cultural centre in Buenos Aires in 1994. Most Jewish schools have been closed and in those that remain, Jewish principals have been replaced by Muslims. Saturday is no longer officially recognized as the Jewish sabbath, and Jewish pupils are compelled to attend school on that day. There are three synagogues in Teheran but, since 1994, there has been no rabbi in Iran and no Beth Din.

There are three major and separate Jewish communities in India. Most live in and around Bombay, particularly in Thane, a suburb 20 miles outside the city. These are the Bene Israel, who believe

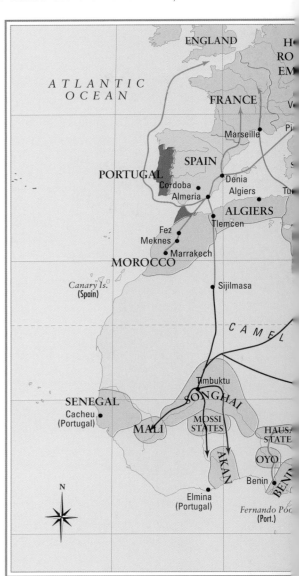

themselves to be the descendants of the original settlers who came to India as early as 2,000 years ago, probably from Aden; the Jews of Cochin (who divide themselves into two communities, Black Jews and White Jews), whose forefathers arrived in India from Europe and the Middle East a thousand years ago; and the Iraqi Jews, called "Baghdadis", who began settling in India at the end of the eighteenth century as soon as the British came to India. The Indian-Jewish community has shrunk considerably in recent years, primarily due to emigration, mostly to Israel.

The Bene Israel began to move to Bombay in the late eighteenth century where they built their first synagogue, Shaare Rahamim (Gates of Mercy), in 1796. In 1948, there were 20,000 Bene Israel in India.

The Cochin community is divided into three distinct groups, Paradesi or "White Jews", "Black Jews" and Meshukhrarim (Freedmen). These divisions were maintained until recent times by a rigid caste system. The Paradesi are descended from a mixture of Jewish merchants from Cranganore, a town on the Malabar coast from which they were expelled by the Moslem ruler who disliked their domination of the lucrative spice trade. They were joined by Jews from Spain, the Netherlands, Aleppo and Germany. Firm evidence of their presence dates back to around 1000 CE, when the local Hindu Rajah granted certain privileges to Joseph Rabban, the leader of the community and asylum in an area of town now famously known as "Jew Town". In 1568, the Jews of Cochin constructed the Paradesi Synagogue, which is still in use today. The Paradesi in Cochin still own the copper tablets on which these privileges are inscribed. The origins of the Black Jews are less clear but they are believed to have lived in Cochin before the Paradesi. The Meshukhrarim are descended from freed slaves, whose offspring were affiliated with either the Paradesi or the Black Jews.

The Baghdadi Jews first arrived from Iraq, Syria and Iran around 1796, fleeing persecution in their native lands. The most prominent Baghdadi Jew was David Sassoon, who established the Indian House of Sassoon in 1832 and paved the way for the arrival of many other Iraqi Jews in India. The central communal organization is the Council of Indian Jewry, which was established in 1978 in Bombay. There are a variety of other organizations, including the Zionist Association, B'nai B'rith, a Jewish Club in Bombay, *Bikkur Cholim* (a charity for the sick), and two women's associations. Despite the small number of Jews left, the Indian community thrives and has never suffered from government-sponsored discrimination. Since 1948, 26,641 Jews from India have emigrated to Israel. Since 1992, Israel and India have enjoyed full diplomatic and trade relations.

Jewish communities, stretching from Portugal in the west to India in the east, maintained trade and cultural links. These links extended beyond their area of settlement allowing imports of goods from as far east as the Mallacas and China and as far south as the Sahel of Africa.

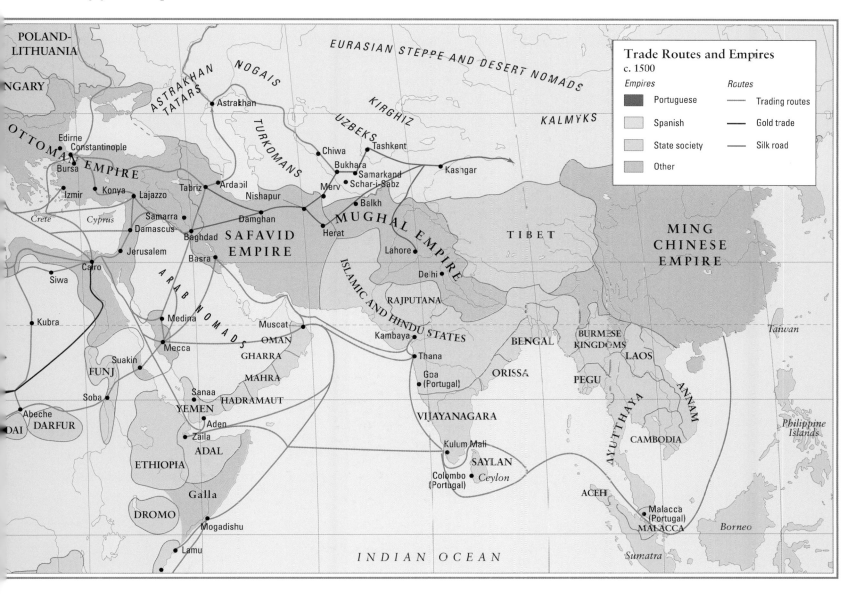

Jews in Poland and Eastern Europe

The largest and most vibrant Jewish community in the world before the Holocaust was that of Eastern Europe. Hitler's plans succeeded, in that this community can never be revived.

The synagogue at Jedwabne, accidentally destroyed by fire in 1913, was built in 1770. It was a typical example of the unique Polish Jewish architectural tradition of building large, domed, wooden synagogues. The layered, pitched roof conceals a series of massive trusses from which the great dome was suspended.

The first Jews are said to have arrived in what is now the territory of modern Poland in around the tenth century CE, but Jews almost certainly lived in the territory before this, having moved north from the Balkans and the Byzantine Empire. The trade routes travelled by Jewish merchants crossed Silesia toward Kiev and Bokhara, both cities that had sizeable Jewish populations in their heyday. The first mention of Jews in Polish chronicles occurs in the eleventh century when they were living in Gniezno, at that time the capital of the Polish kingdom of the Piast dynasty. The first permanent Jewish community is mentioned in 1085 by a Jewish scholar, Yehuda ha-Kohen, as living in the city of Przemysl.

The first wave of Jewish emigration from western Europe to Poland occurred during the First Crusade in 1098. Under Boleslaus III (1102–1139), the Jews were encouraged to settle throughout Poland and they moved into Lithuania and the Ukraine. Jews came to form the backbone of the medieval Polish economy and coins minted by Mieszko III even bear Hebrew letters. The Jews enjoyed prosperity in this region at a time when elsewhere they were being persecuted and banished. In Poland, they were the middle class in a country whose general population consisted of land-owners and peasants.

Pressure began to be exerted on the Polish monarchy by the Roman Catholic Church and by the neighbouring German states. Yet the Jews had some determined protectors including Boleslaus the Pious of Kalisz (c. 1221–1279) Prince of Greater Poland. In 1264 he issued the Statute of Kalisz which granted Jews the freedom of worship, trade and travel. In 1334, Casimir III the Great (1303–1370) amplified and expanded this former charter through the Wislicki Statute. Casimir was especially friendly to the Jews for most of his reign, no doubt due to his Jewish mistress by whom he had many children. In 1347, however, the first blood libel is recorded against Jews in Poland and, in 1367, the first pogrom in Poznan (Posen). There were subsequent massacres at Kalisz, Cracow, Głogów and other Polish cities along what was then the German frontier.

In 1386, Lithuania was united with the kingdom of Poland, but Jews were not given citizenship rights in the new kingdom until 1388. Under Wladislaus II and his successors, the first persecutions of the Jews in Poland began. Hysteria caused by the Black Death led to additional anti-Jewish riots supported by traders and craftsmen who feared Jews as their rivals. Casimir IV Jagiellonczyk (1447–1492) confirmed and extended Jewish charters, but he later issued the Statute of Nieszawa, abolishing ancient Jewish privileges. Casimir's successors were no more tolerant of the Jews and Alexander the Jagiellonian (1501–1506) expelled the Jews from Lithuania in 1495. Alexander reversed his position in 1503 and Jews were allowed to continue to enter Poland from Spain (after the Inquisition and Expulsion) and from Austria, Bohemia and Germany. With the expulsion of the Jews from Spain, Poland became the recognized haven for exiles from western Europe.

The most prosperous period for Polish Jews began with the reign of Zygmunt I (1506–1548). His son, Zygmunt II August (1548–1572), mainly followed in the tolerant policy of his father and granted autonomy to the Jews in the matter of communal administration, laying the foundation for the power of the Kahal, the autonomous Jewish community. By the mid-16th century, 80 per cent of the world's Jews lived in Poland. In 1503, the Polish monarchy appointed Rabbi Jacob Polak official Rabbi of Poland marking the start of a Chief Rabbinate. The Polish government permitted the Rabbinate to grow in power so that it could be used for tax collection purposes. Only 30 per cent of the money raised by the Rabbinate served Jewish causes, the rest went to the Crown. In this period Poland-Lithuania became the main centre for Ashkenazic Jewish learning and its yeshivot achieved fame from the early 1500s. Hebrew printing houses were established and many Talmudic academies flourished. One the great Talmudic scholars of the age was Moses ben Israel Isserles (1525–1572), the ReMA, best known as one of the authors of a major Talmudic commentary known as the *Shulkhan Arukh* (the Laid Table). Isserles founded a yeshiva and synagogue in Kazimierz, the Jewish quarter of Cracow founded by Casimir the Great as a special Jewish quarter (not a ghetto). Poland had, over the centuries, become "the new Jerusalem" a centre of Jewish scholarship that had no parallel elsewhere in the world. Although it had been the last to emerge, it was also the most long-lived (c. 1500–1929). With its yeshivot (religious academies) and Hebrew printing houses, by the early seventeenth century, Rabbi Nathan of Hanover was able to write "In every community, there is a yeshiva ... in all the lands of the Polish king, there is scarcely a family in which the Torah is not studied." Not only traditional Judaism but the more modern forms emerged in Poland. Positive-Historical Judaism, the intellectual forerunner to Conservative Judaism, was founded by Rabbi Zecharias Frankel, who became the head of the Jewish Theological Seminary in Breslau (now Wroclaw).

The founder of the town of Zamo, the chancellor Jan Zamoyski, was a wealthy aristocrat who turned his estate into a haven for Jews fleeing the inquisition and built many buildings for them, including a synagogue. The Jews from Spain and Portugal who settled in Poland brought many exotic plants and foods which crept into Jewish and later Polish cuisine, notably the onion (for which the Polish and Yiddish words are of Spanish origin), almonds and olive oil, now typical of Polish-Jewish cooking. The strip of gold or silver embroidery on the prayer-shawl (tallit) is known as *Spanishes werk* (Spanish work) in Yiddish.

The seventeenth century was a time of great unrest. In the Chmielnicki Uprising, the Cossacks massacred tens of thousands of Jews and Poles in the eastern and southern areas of the country in what is now the Ukraine. As many as 20 per cent of the Jewish population fled or was murdered. Subsequent incursions by the Russians, Crimean Tatars and Ottomans culminated in the defeat of Poland at the hands of Charles X of Sweden. The Jews were slaughtered by both sides. General Stefan Czarniecki, in his flight from the Swedes, massacred Jews as a revenge and the Plague returned to devastate the survivors.

Yet Polish Jewry survived and remained as the spiritual center of Judaism, even though with the accession to the throne of the Saxon dynasty the Jews completely lost the support of the government. The nobility and the townsfolk were increasingly hostile to the Jews. In the larger cities of Silesia, such as Poznan and Kraków, Jewish attacks by university student organizations, the Schüler-Gelauf, became everyday occurrences in the large cities and Jews were expelled from some towns.

It was during this difficult period for Jewish life that the Hassidic movement was born. The founder was Israel ben Eliezer (c. 1700–1760), a mysterious figure known as the Baal Shem Tov (Master of the Good Name) or Besht for short, who left no written records. He had been orphaned in the terrible massacres of the Jews but ordered that Jews should celebrate their lives with joy. His great disciple, Rabbi Dov Baer (1710–1772), known as the Maggid of Mezericz was a great preacher who spread the word through Poland, Byelorussia, and Lithuania. This also generated a huge volume of writings by the adherents of Hassidism. Once the Besht was dead, his followers fragmented into several sects headed by "rebbes" (rabbis). Most of these sects still exist but the most successful was Schneor Zalman of Lyady (1745–1813) who founded the Chabad Movement. Chabad is the initials for three words meaning "wisdom, understanding, knowledge". The greatest thinker of the movement was Rabbi Nachman of Bratzlav (Breslau, now Wroclaw).

There were also bitter opponents of the Hassidic movement, known as the Misnagdim (opponents), whose greatest leader was Elijah ben Solomon (1720–1797), commonly known by his epithet, the Vila Gaon (gaon means "genius"). The Vilna Gaon, who eventually settled in Jerusalem, went so far as to excommunicate the Hassidim.

Poland was divided successively in 1772, 1793 and 1795 between Russia, Prussia and Austria. Most of Poland's one million Jews fell under Russian rule. After the First Partition, in 1772, Catherine II, Empress of Russia, forced Jews out of the cities, confining them to the Pale of Settlement. Berek Joselewicz led a Jewish regiment to fight for Polish independence in the Kosciuszko Uprising in 1794, the year after the Second Partition. Following the unsuccessful revolt, the third and final partition of Poland took place in 1795. Jews also fought in the November Insurrection (1830–1831), the January Insurrection (1863), and in the 1905 Revolution. Many Polish Jews were enlisted in the Legions which fought for the Polish independence during World War I.

When Poland regained independence in 1918, anti-semitism re-emerged, though the dictator, Józef Piłsudski (1926–1935), opposed it. After Piłsudski's death in May 1935, which many Jews regarded as a tragedy, the situation deteriorated, and the Endecja party's growing anti-Semitism gathered new momentum. Jews were still allowed to attend university but had to sit in special sections of the hall and Jewish quotas (*numerus clausus*) were introduced in 1937 to halve the number of Jews in higher education. Jews were also excluded from the civil service and from receiving welfare benefits. In 1937, a series of professional and trade unions, including those for lawyers and physicians, enacted "Aryan clauses" expelling Polish Jews from their ranks. This discrimination was accompanied by physical violence: in the years between 1935 and 1937 79 Jews were killed and 500 injured in anti-Jewish incidents, there were also victims among anti-semites. Like the Nazis, the Endecja Party promoted a national boycott of Jewish merchants. The term 'Christian shop' was introduced and, in the late 1930s, some carriage drivers bore the inscription "Christian carriages" on their caps. No wonder, then, that the Nazis considered Poland the most suitable site for their concentration and extermination camps.

On the eve of the German invasion (for which the pretext was staged by dressing dead Jews, murdered in concentration camp, in Polish uniforms and pretending they had "invaded" the Reich) there were 3,474,000 Jews in Poland, of whom 130,000 soldiers served in the Polish Army. It is estimated that as many as 32,216 Polish-Jewish officers and men died (some murdered by the Russians in Katyn). The 61,000 who were taken prisoner by the Germans suffered the same fate as other Jews. Jews served in the

Poland's Jewish population was inevitably caught up in the varying fortunes of Poland itself. By the close of the eighteenth century, the state of Poland, once a might multi-ethnic empire, had disappeared. It re-emerged under the Napoleonic rule in 1812, as the Grand Duchy of Warsaw, to disappear once again in 1815. After World War I, the Poles seized their opportunity to re-establish an independent state and between 1919 and 1921 this was achieved. Spread across its territory were 3.3 million Jews, including large communities, long-settled in cities like Warsaw, Cracow and Lvov.

Polish People's Army in the Soviet Union, as well as in civilian resistance movements and as partisans.

In the partition of Poland created by the Molotov-Ribbentrop Pact, over 60 per cent of Polish Jews found themselves under German occupation. Those who were now Russian citizens had their property confiscated. Zionism was banned as counter-revolutionary. All Jewish and Polish newspapers were shut down within a day of the Soviet occupation and anti-religious propaganda was conducted mainly through the Soviet press which attacked religion in general and the Jewish faith in particular. At least Jews were now entitled to become civil servants which many did to avoid starvation. The general feeling amongst Polish Jews was a sense of relief in having escaped the dangers of falling under Nazi rule, as well as from the overt policies of discrimination against Jews which existed in the Polish state, including discrimination in education, employment and commerce, as well as anti-Semitic violence that in some cases reached pogrom levels.

About 6,000 Polish Jews were able to leave the Soviet Union in 1942 with the Wladyslaw Anders' Free Polish army, among them the future Prime Minister of Israel Menachem Begin. During the Polish army's II Corps' stay in the British Mandate of Palestine, 67 per cent (2,972) of the Jewish soldiers deserted, many to join the Irgun, the secret Zionist army. General Anders decided not to prosecute the deserters though anti-Semitism was also rife in his army. Anders' Jewish soldiers also fought in Italy and the Polish section of the cemetery for the dead of the Battle of Monte Cassino contains many headstones bearing a Star of David.

Under the Nazis, most of the Jewish population of Poland was exterminated in the extermination camps of Auschwitz, Treblinka, Majdanek, Belzec, Sobibór and Chelmno or died of starvation in

Jewish sugar peddlars in the market place of the ghetto of Warsaw. Poland at this time was part of the Russian Empire and was included in the Pale of Settlement.

the ghettos. In 1939 several hundred synagogues were blown up or burned by the Germans who sometimes forced the Jews to do it themselves. Other synagogues were turned into factories or places of entertainment such as swimming pools (one synagogue in Poznan is still a swimming pool). Jews were banned from public places and forced to wear a blue-and-white badge. The Warsaw Ghetto Uprising of 1943 was the most notable incident of resistance, though there was Jewish resistance in many other places.

Some of the German massacres of Jews in Eastern Poland were carried out with help from, or the active participation of, the Poles themselves.

Poland Moves West
1945–46

▨ Poland 1920–39

▓ Poland from 1945

This included the massacre at Jedwabne, in which about a thousand Jews perished. The Polish Institute for National Remembrance has identified 22 other towns in which such pogroms took place.

Emanuel Ringelblum, the historian of the Warsaw Ghetto, wrote in 1944 in his *"Polish-Jewish Relations during the Second World War"* of the indifference and sometimes joyful responses in Christian Warsaw to the destruction of the Warsaw Ghetto. Another historian, Gunnar S. Paulsson, has shown that the citizens of Warsaw managed to support and hide the same percentage of Jews as did the citizens of cities in western Europe. Despite the draconian measures imposed by the Nazis for assisting Jews, Poland has the highest number of Righteous Among The Nations awards at the Yad Vashem Museum in Jerusalem.

After World War II, Soviet-style Communism was imposed and the boundaries of Poland were moved west. The attitude of Christian Poles toward Jews remained hostile and there were even anti-Jewish riots. The massacre at Kielce was a turning point in the attempt to rebuild a Jewish community and convinced most survivors that they had no future in Poland. Between 1945 and 1948, 100,000–120,000 Jews were helped to leave Poland through the organization known as *Berihah* ("Flight" in Hebrew) which also organized emigration from Romania, Hungary, Czechoslovakia and Yugoslavia. Stalin's death in 1953 eased the situation for the Jews, who were allowed to re-establish connections with Jewish organizations abroad and began producing Jewish literature. In this 1958–59 period, 50,000 Jews emigrated to Israel, the only country to which Jews were able to migrate to under Polish law.

Another wave of Jewish emigration (50,000) took place during the liberalisation of the Communist regime between 1957 and 1959. The last mass migration of Jews from Poland took place in 1968–69, after Israel's 1967 Six-day War, due to the anti-Jewish and anti-Israel policy adopted by Polish Communist Party.

In 1977, Communist Poland began to try to improve its image regarding Jewish matters. Partial diplomatic relations with Israel were restored in 1986 – Poland was the first of the communist bloc countries to do so but full diplomatic relations were not restored until the end of its communist rule. In 2000, Poland's Jewish population was estimated to be anywhere between 8,000 and 12,000, most of whom live in Warsaw, Wrocław, Cracow and Bielsko-Biala. Most conceal their Jewish identity.

Jews in the U.S.A. and Canada 1650–1865

THE LARGEST JEWISH COMMUNITY OUTSIDE OF ISRAEL IS CURRENTLY THAT OF NORTH AMERICA. THE THIRTEEN COLONIES WERE THE FIRST TO EMANCIPATE THE JEWS.

This photograph depicts the market in New York City's Hester Street, on the Lower East Side, where the city's poorer Jews lived.

Christopher Columbus, who is strongly suspected of being a "New Christian", sailed westward in 1492, looking for a passage to Asia, with four Jews on board, two of them also being "New Chrisstians". One of them, Luis de Torres, remained behind on Hispaniola when Columbus returned to Spain and can therefore claim to be the very first Jewish settler in the western hemisphere.

When the Dutch rebelled against the harsh rule of Philip II of Spain (1527–1598), Recife in Brazil became Dutch and thus a safe haven for Jews but the Spanish reconquered it and gave the Jews three months in which to either convert or be put to death.

In 1654, a contingent of 23 Jews, including families, sailed from Recife northward to the colony of New Amsterdam and after a terrible journey, including capture by pirates in Cuba, they landed in Manhattan. The governor, Peter Stuyvesant, was deeply hostile to Jews and tried to have them removed but without success, as they had support from the Dutch authorities back in Europe. These few settlers were supplemented by many more, all of Sephardic origin, most of whom prospered as merchants and traders as well as vigorously campaigning for their right to serve in the army along with Christian citizens. All of these "Portuguese" colonists had to fight hard for their rights, as Jews have had to do down the ages in North America, where discrimination against Jews lasted well into the 1960s, extending to private clubs and hotels, even in Hollywood. When the embassy of the new state of Israel was seeking a home for its embassy in Washington D.C. in 1948, Israeli diplomats discovered that the building they had selected was "zoned", i.e. there was a covenant in the lease to deny Jews and Blacks the right to live there.

In 1656, the Jews of New Amsterdam, who had formed themselves into a congregation even though they were not permitted a synagogue, purchased land for a cemetery. The congregation which called itself Shearith Israel (the Remnant of Israel) did not build their own house of worship until 1729. The Touro Synagogue in Newport, Rhode Island, a colony founded by the judophile Roger Williams in 1658, was built in 1763, and is a national historic landmark. It is the oldest synagogue still standing in the United States.

Jews did not fare as well in the parts of what is now the United States that remained under Spanish control. The Spanish Inquisition was exported to the Spanish colonies, among them the Territory of New Mexico, where its first victim in the New World, in 1661, was the governor Bernardo Lopez de Mendizabel.

The first Jews to settle in the South reached Georgia in 1733, only five months after the colony was founded. They were impecunious Ashkenazic Jews from Germany, and had been sent by the wealthy Sephardic community of London, where they had originally sought refuge, no doubt as a ploy to be rid of them. They were soon followed by more Sephardic Jews. Governor James Olgethorpe granted land to the Jews even though he was pressured not to do so. In the Thirteen Colonies, Jews were allowed freedom of worship at a time when the only religious group to whom this was denied were Catholics. The Naturalization Act passed by the British parliament in 1740 gave Jews the right to citizenship in British colonies.

In the American Revolution, the Jews mainly supported independence. Jewish financiers, such as Haym Solomon and Barnard Gratz, helped fund the purchase of weapons and there were many Jewish foot soldiers. Colonel Solomon Bush of the Pennsylvania State Militia was badly wounded, captured, then freed in a prisoner exchange; he was cited for his bravery in the winter of 1776. Eighteen

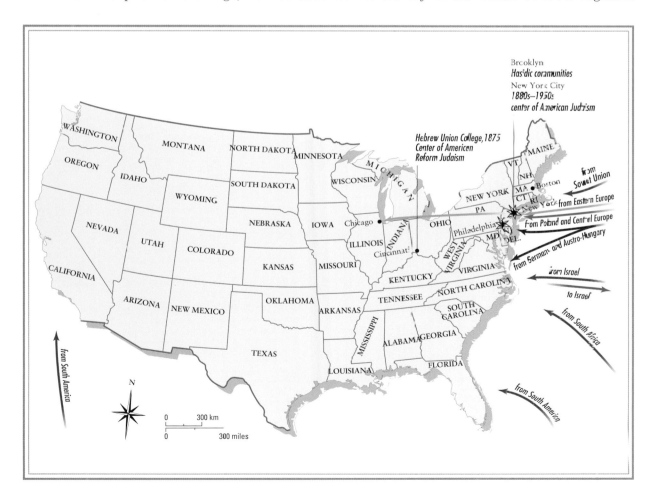

Jews have been part of the European settlement of what became the United States from the 1650s, notably in the city of New Amsterdam, later New York.

Judaism

→ German and Austro-Hungarian immigration, 1820–60 Reform Judaism

→ Eastern European (Russian, Lithuanian, Polish, Ukrainian, Rumanian) immigration, 1880–1924 Orthodox Judaism

→ Hasidic immigration from Poland and Central Europe, 1930s and 1940s

→ Recent Jewish immigration from South Africa, South America, and Israel, 1960s and 1970s

→ American Jewish emigration to Israel, 1960s–

✡ Early Sephardic/Ashkenazic tensions

★ Early Ashkenazic congregations

Jews have largely moved away from what were once the poorer neighbourhoods. This magnificent synagogue, on Eldridge Street in the Lower East Side, was abandoned but was restored in 2007. It was originally built in 1887.

Jewish soldiers who gave their lives for the Revolution are buried in the old Jewish cemetery in New York City. Yet in some states, such as Maryland, Jews were not granted equal citizenship with Christians until well into the nineteenth century.

The death of Lincoln was a terrible shock to the Jews and he was the first non-Jew for whom prayers were said in synagogue. During the Civil War, about 7,000 Jews fought for Union and 1,500 for the Confederacy, though Major Alfred Mordecai of North Carolina resigned his commission rather than serve the Confederacy. He purchased only one slave in his life and only for the purpose of setting her free. Judah P. Benjamin, on the other hand, became Jefferson Davis' right-hand man. This New Orleans lawyer and senator became Attorney-General in the Confederate government, then in 18621, acting Secretary of State for war. When the Confederacy fell, he fled to England where he successfully continued his legal career.

By now, many Ashkenazic Jews were reaching North America from Germany in the aftermath of the unrest that swept through Europe in the post-Napoleonic era, culminating in the revolutions of 1848. Between 1840 and 1860, the Jewish population rose to 150,000, most of them immigrants from Bavaria and Alsace. One example is that of Adolphus Sterne, who settled in Nacogdoches, East Texas, fighting for Texas in its successive wars of liberation and eventually being elected a state senator.

Jews helped develop the West. Adolf Sutro (1830–1898), owner of the Sutro Metallurgical Works, in East Dayton, Nevada was responsible for the Sutro Tunnel that made it possible to drain and ventilate the mines in the Comstock Lode. In 1879, Sutro sold his tunnel and returned to San Francisco. In 1894, he was elected mayor and served a two-year term. At one time, Sutro owned one-twelfth of the acreage of San Francisco. He purchased the Cliff House in the early 1880s, and one thousand acres of land facing the ocean, now called Sutro heights. He owned the finest private libary in America, much of which was destroyed in the Great Earthquake of 1906.

Bret Harte (1836–1902) was an early writer of short stories about Wild West themes and Louis Moreau Gottschalk (1829–1869) from New Orleans was the first Americn virtuoso pianist, followed by so many other great musicians, including Isaac Stern (1920–1901) and Yehudi Menuhin (1916–1999). Another well-known westerner, a convert to Judaism through his second marriage, was Wyatt Earp (1848–1929), who is buried in the Jewish cemetery in Palo Alto, California. While the Sephardic and German Jewish elite prospered in the late nineteenth century, millions of destitute Jews were pouring into America due to the persecutions in Eastern Europe. It was they who were to change the face of the New World.

The Jewish cultural contribution to American life is too vast to list. They were among the founders of Hollywood and there have been Jews in every branch of the movie industry and show business ever since. Another major Jewish contribution to American life has been its department stores. Although the first department store, founded in Chicago, was not Jewish-owned; May Company, Macy's, Wannamaker's, Sears Roebuck, Neiman Marcus and Bloomingdales were all founded by Jews; and where would American fashion be without Levis, the denim jeans with riveted pockets invented by the German immigrant Levi Strauss, who supplied them to Californian miners during the Gold Rush?

Canada currently has the world's fourth-largest Jewish population of around 351,000 Jews, yet they came late to the country because they were banned from New France. There were four Sephardic Jewish officers in General Amherst's army who won Canada for the British one of whom, Aaron Hart had a son, Ezekiel, who became the first Jew to be elected to the legislature of Lower Canada, in 1807. In 1831, Canada was the first colony to grant male Jews full political and religious rights. Most early Jewish settlers were fur traders or soldiers. The first synagogue, Shearith Israel, was built in Montreal, yet there were only 450 Jews in Canada in 1850. A cemetery was acquired in Quebec City in 1853 but there was no synagogue until 1892. Yet, thanks to the massive emigration to Jews to the New World, between 1880 and 1930, the Jewish population grew to over 155,000. In 1872, Henry Nathan (1842–1914) was the first Jewish member of Parliament. By 1911, all of Canada's major cities had Jewish communities. In the late 1800s and early 1900s, the Jewish Colonization Association established 15 Jewish farms on the prairies. One community that prospered was Yid'n Bridge, Saskatchewan, started by South African Jews. The settlement grew into a town, whose name was later anglicised to Edenbridge.

For most of its subsequent history, Canada had a restrictive immigration policy, accepting the fewest number of refugees from Germany before and during World War II. After the war 40 000 survivors were admitted. In the 1950s, tens of thousands of French-speaking Jews arrived from North Africa, settling in French-speaking Montreal and Quebec City.

The Jews of the United States and Canada currently face demographic challenges from factors such as the aging of the Jewish population, increased rates of intermarriage and a relatively low percentage of children of mixed marriages identifying themselves as Jewish.

Most Jewish immigrants had settled in the big cities of the north east, later moving to California and the west. For retirees, Florida was a favourite destination.

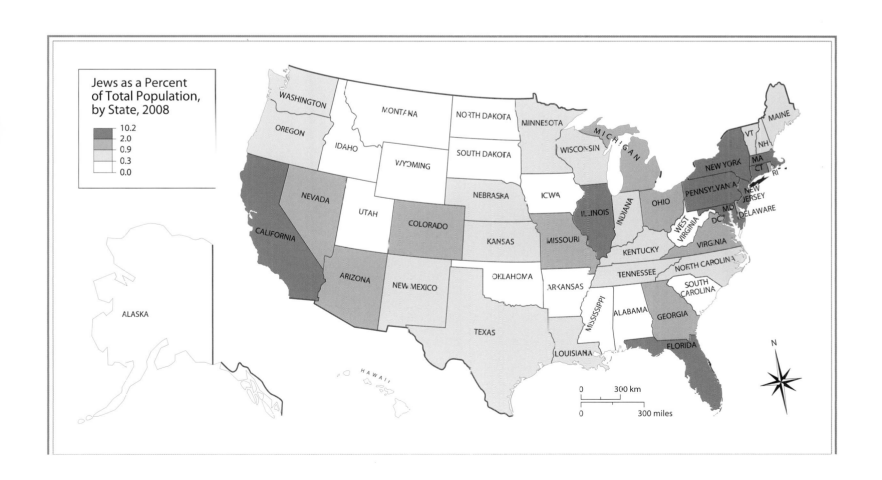

Jews as a Percent of Total Population, by State, 2008

- 10.2
- 2.0
- 0.9
- 0.3
- 0.0

JEWS IN THE WORLD

THE JEWISH POPULATION SUFFERS FROM THE SAME PROBLEMS
AS THE REST OF THE DEVELOPED WORLD, A FALLING BIRTH RATE
AND INCREASING NUMBERS OF THE AGED, ALTHOUGH ISRAEL
BUCKS THE TREND WITH A HEALTHY BIRTH RATE EVEN AMONG
THE NON-ORTHODOX JEWISH COMMUNITY.

There are currently some 13 million Jews in the world, though Jewish demographics can never be totally accurate, partly because of the age-old question of "who is a Jew?" There are people who consider themselves Jewish even though orthodox communities might not consider them to be because their father, not their mother, is Jewish, others who do not consider themselves Jewish even though they are considered so under Israeli law. In countries where anti-semitism is rife, such as in the former Soviet Union and Eastern Europe, many Jews continue to feel uneasy about revealing their identity.

Jews have all but disappeared from the Arab countries where the Jewish communities date back to biblical times. It is a fallacy that Arab anti-Semitism began with the return of Jews to Palestine or with establishment of the State of Israel in 1948. The seeds were sown by the Nazis whose ideology was willingly embraced by leaders such as the Mufti of Jerusalem, Haj Amin al-Husseini, his Iraqi ally Rashid Ali and many others in the Arab world who thought Germany would free them from French and British domination. The Iraqi farhud (pogrom) in 1941, preceded by persecutions in Libya and Egypt in 1940, are examples of this. The partition of Palestine merely exacerbated the situation. In 1947, the Egyptian delegate to the United Nations openly threatened the Jewish population of Egypt with a massacre when Partition was on the agenda. The immediate aftermath of the establishment of the State of Israel in 1948, caused 900,000 Jews to flee from Arab lands, from Lebanon in the north to Libya in the south. Two-thirds went to Israel, the rest settled in western Europe and the Americas. The small Jewish population that remains in the Yemen is being exhorted to leave for anywhere but Israel by the anti-Zionist, ultra-orthodox communities of Britain and America.

In Iran, with the fall of the Shah, most Jews left, though 10,000 remain; the refugees settled mainly in California and Israel. Today, very few Jews remain in Egypt, Libya, Eritrea Somalia and Algeria. Elsewhere in the Arab world they number between ten and twenty per country. The only Jewish populations of any size are in Tunisia and Morocco and these have shrunk considerably through emigration to Israel and France.

Israel has finally overtaken the United States in numbers, with just over 5.5 million Jews. The United States comes next with 5.25 million, so together they account for more than 80 per cent of world Jewry. Over a 1.5 million Jews live in Europe – two-thirds in Western Europe, one third in Eastern Europe and the Balkans. The Jewish population is aging in Europe, resulting in more deaths than births. This, together with intermarriage, constitute the main demographic threats to the Jews of western Europe. France now has the third-largest Jewish population, estimated at nearly 500,000. The loss of France's North African colonies saw a huge influx of Sephardic Jews from Algeria, Morocco and Tunisia in the 1950s and 1960s, and they now outnumber the Ashkenazic (European-descended) community which traces its roots back to Roman times. In addition to the depradations of intermarriage and an aging community, French Jewry has suffered numerous anti-Semitic incidents, including bombings and vandalism. Support for both the extreme-right Front National and Islamic extremists is a continued source of concern, encouraging French Jews to emigrate to Israel.

The United Kingdom has the next-largest Jewish population in Europe, accounting for just over 2.25 per cent of world Jewry. British Jews are well integrated but have suffered from the same type of anti-Semitic incidents as in France.

Poland and Czechoslovakia have experienced a reawakening of Jewish consciousness, with young Jewish people joining the community and seeking a to learn more about their faith which was suppressed for so long. The biggest European Jewish revival has been in Germany, which now accounts for almost 1 per cent of world Jewry. Although a few Jews trickled back after World War II, the main influx has been from the former Soviet Union who have revived the synagogues and improved the demographics with their relatively high birth rate.

By far the largest Jewish population in Africa is in South Africa. The Jewish community is well-organized, with a wide network of welfare, educational, political and Zionist institutions. Intermarriage rates are low, support for Israel is strong and religious identity has intensified. The community is experiencing continued emigration, mainly to Australia, the United Kingdom, and Israel stemming from the high crime rate and fears for the future. There are also native Jewish populations in Uganda and Kenya.

Small Jewish communities exist throughout Asia. China has a Jewish population of 1,000, the same number as Japan. Though relics of the ancient Chinese-Jewish population can still be found in Hangchow and Harabin on the Russian border harboured Jews during the World War II period, the only active community is Shanghai, first settled by Jews in the 1860s. The authorities recently permitted the only synagogue, Ohel Rachel, to be used for festivals.

The Jews of India, living mostly around Bombay, currently number 5,300. The community consists of three distinct groups: Bnei Israel, descendants of shipwrecked Yemenites who settled in India in the second century BCE; the two groups of Cochin Jews ("black" and "white"), whose ancestors arrived in

India from Europe and the Middle East 1,000 years ago; and the "Baghdadis", Iraqis who began moving to India in the late 18th century under British rule.

In Latin America, Argentina is home to some 200,000 Jews, mostly in Buenos Aires. The new regime has enabled the Jewish community to overcome the emotional trauma of the 1994 bombing of the Buenos

Jewish migrations worldwide had developed settled Jewish communities in all the continents: North America, Central and South America, Europe, Africa, Asia and the Australia/ Pacific.

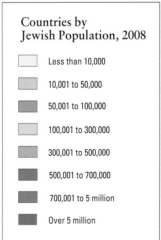

Countries by Jewish Population, 2008

- Less than 10,000
- 10,001 to 50,000
- 50,001 to 100,000
- 100,001 to 300,000
- 300,001 to 500,000
- 500,001 to 700,000
- 700,001 to 5 million
- Over 5 million

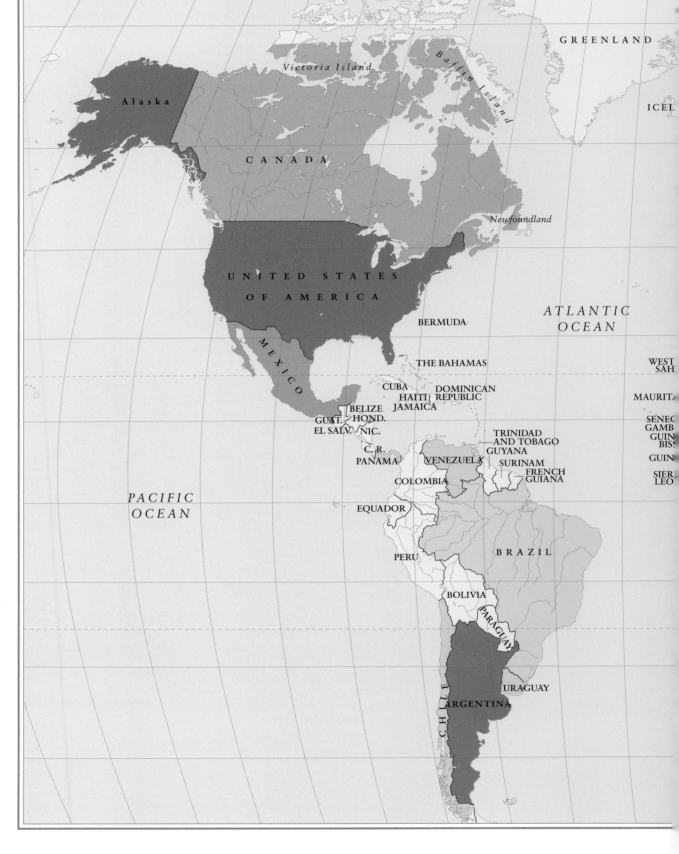

Aires Jewish Community Centre, attributed to Iranian extremists though no one was ever prosecuted.
There is a thriving Jewish population in Mexico, half of them post-World War II immigrants from Eastern
Europe. The Jewish community of Brazil, currently numbering over 100,000, is concentrated mainly in
Saõ Paulo. South America is the only continent on which Yiddish still flourishes.

EUROPEAN ANTI-SEMITISM

OVER THE CENTURIES EXPULSIONS FROM EUROPEAN CITIES
HAVE TAKEN PLACE THROUGHOUT EUROPE. THIS INCLUDES THE
EXODUS OF FRANKFURT IN 1614, PERSECUTIONS DURING THE
REFORMATION, AND EXPULSIONS FROM PRAGUE AND VIENNA
DURING THE EIGHTEENTH CENTURY.

Etching depicting the so-called
Hep! Hep! Riots against the
Jews, this one in Frankfurt,
that took place in Germany
in 1819 amidst a climate of
anti-Semitism fuelled by various
anti-Jewish publications. The
rallying cry, "Hepp Hepp" may
have been an acronym for
"Hierosolyma est perdita,"
meaning "Jerusalem is lost."

The term "anti-Semitic" (*antisemitisch* in German) appears to have been first used in 1860 by the Austrian-Jewish writer, Moritz Steinschneider when he described the racist ideas of Ernest Renan as "anti-semitic prejudices." Pseudo-scientific theories of racial superiority and inferiority were first promulgated in late 19th-century Germany. In 1873, German journalist Wilhelm Marr published a pamphlet entitled "The Victory of the Jewish Spirit over the Germanic Spirit. Observed from a non-religious perspective." (*Der Sieg des Judenthums über das Germanenthum. Vom nicht confessionellen Standpunkt aus betrachtet*) in which he used the word Semitismus. This hugely successful work was reprinted 12 times between 1873 and 1879. Thus although "semitic" is a term applicable to all Semitic races, including Arabs, it is aimed specifically at Jews.

The Oxford Dictionary definition of anti-Semitism is "hostility to Jews". This can cover a multitude of actions from refusal to accept a hotel reservation or allow membership of a club from someone who is, or appears to be, Jewish (as in the United States) to hurling insults at children attending Jewish schools and throwing stones at a person dressed in traditional orthodox Jewish garb. This form of anti-semitism, and other attacks on Jews such as the desecration of Jewish gravestones, have been frequent occurrences in France, England and other western European countries. It also covers restrictive laws applied specifically to Jews, expulsions, executions, pogroms and the Holocaust. Modern anti-Semitism has been defined by the Council of Europe to include blanket condemnation of Israel and Israel's policies, so claiming to be "anti-Zionist" is no

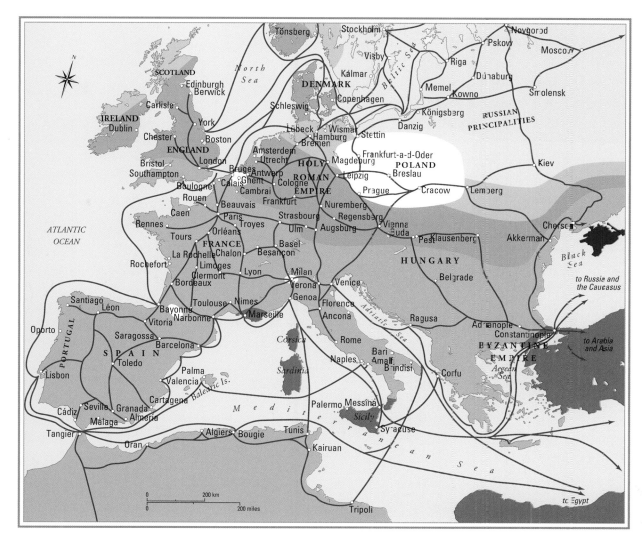

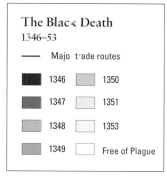

The Black Death, a plague that swept across Europe after 1346, was in many communities blamed upon the Jews. People faced with devastation had no scientific answer, therefore frequently chose minorities in their midst.

longer an excuse for anti-Semitism. Recent German case law has determined that the fact that a person is Jewish does give them immunity from the charge of anti-Semitism. There have been many examples of Jews or persons of Jewish origin who were anti-Semitic, including leading Nazis, such as Reinhard Heydrich who had Jewish blood on both sides of his family and yet who chaired the Wansee Conference in 1942 that devised the Final Solution for European Jewry.

The origins of anti-Semitism lie in the rivalry of Judaism and Christianity. When Christianity ceased being a minor Jewish sect and became a universal religion, Jews were blamed for the death of the Messiah, starting a long tradition of religious persecution which lasted from Byzantine times to the Holocaust and beyond. Much hostility stemmed from the fact that Christian clerics could not believe that even if Jews were forced to listen to sermons and bullied into conversion to Christianity, they still refused to "see the light" and accept Christ. This was the rationale for the decision of the Council of Nicaea in 325 to ban the celebration of Passover earlier than Easter; it was the reason for banning Jewish prayers, such as the priestly blessing and "Holy, holy, holy" because they are also used in the Christian order of service; it was the reason for banning the reading aloud of the Old Testament in Aramaic, Greek or the vernacular, a Jewish custom since the fourth century BCE.

It was also the reason for the numerous burnings of the Talmud. In 1240, the Jews of northern France were compelled to attend the Disputation of Paris, at the end of which Louis IX ordered

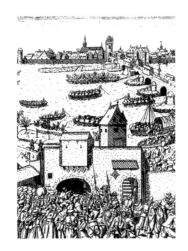

The exodus of Jews from Frankfurt, from which they were banned in 1614. These expulsions took place throughout European cities on a regular basis. The Jews were usually allowed to return for a huge bribe.

that all copies of the Talmud be confiscated and burned. Twenty-four cartloads of Jewish holy books were consigned to the flames in 1242. Successive popes continued to advocate burning the Talmud; in 1552, Pope Julian III had the Talmud burned publicly in Rome, followed by many other burnings in Italy and Spain on the instructions of the Inquisition. In Venice over a thousand copies of the Talmud and other sacred Jewish literature were burned. The last such public burning was held in 1757, in Kamieniec-Podolsk, Poland.

In 1243, a new libel against the Jews, the alleged stealing and desecration of the Host – the sacramental wafer distributed during the Eucharist – was the cause of a massacre in Beilitz near Berlin, in which the Jewish population was burned to death. The same excuse was used for the Rindfleisch Massacres in Austria and Germany (1298). In Acquitaine, in 1321, the story was spread that in revenge for their ill-treatment by the Shepherds' Crusade, the Jews had poisoned the wells. For this, 160 Jews were burned in Chinon.

In 1347–50, Europe was ravaged by a series of disastrous harvests, due to bad weather, followed by the Black Death that killed up to half the population in some places. It was in vain that Pope Clement VI published a papal bull in 1348 in which he reminded the faithful that Jews were also dying of the Plague and that there had been outbreaks in places where there were no Jews at all. This was yet another excuse for massacres of the Jews in the Rhineland and Alsace.

Jews were forced to wear distinctive clothing so they could be recognized. The Fourth Lateran Council (1215) decreed that Jews should wear a badge in the form of a yellow circle. The strange conical hat, the cornutus pileus, which was green in Bohemia, yellow in other places, the badge of a Jewish male, is believed to have been adapted from a headdress worn by the Jews in Babylonia. Since religious Jews have to cover their heads, the hat was originally worn voluntarily but soon its wearing was decreed by the authorities, including Pope Paul IV, who also ordered the burning of the Talmud in Cremona, a centre of Jewish learning.

There was no improvement during the Reformation. Martin Luther, like so many before him, assumed that his new version of Christianity would prove irresistible to the Jews. When they did not convert en masse, he turned violently against them, writing a pamphlet entitled *Letter against the Sabbathists*, followed by *The Jews and their Lies* in 1538. The latter repeated all of the calumnies levelled against the Jews throughout their history, including the poisoning of wells and ritual murder of children to use their blood for baking the Passover unleavened bread (*matzo*), and the desecration of the host.

In 1613, Vincenz Fettmilch, a Frankfurt baker, led a mob to murder and pillage the ghetto, forcibly expelling the remaining Jews, naked, from the city. A similar incident occurred in Worms in 1615. However, this was an unfortunate move for Fettmilch and his friends. The Thirty Years War (1618–1648) was looming and Archduke Ferdinand needed the Jews to raise money for his war-chest. Fettmilch and his horde were arrested and executed. In 1703, the Court Jew Josef Süss Oppenheimer was arrested and executed, after first being hung in cage. His story was twisted into an anti-semitic film made by the Nazi Propaganda Ministry and entitled *Jüd Süss* (1940).

The eighteenth century was marked by expulsions of the Jews from central Europe. During the reign of Charles VI of Austria, the Jews were driven out of Vienna and under his daughter, the Empress Maria Theresa, they fared even worse, when the Jews of Prague were accused of siding with Frederick II of Prussia who had briefly captured the city. As a result of allegations of disloyalty the Empress banned them from Bohemia and subsequently Moravia. The kings of Prussia were no better, only allowing the wealthiest Jews to live in Berlin. Frederick the Great ordered the expulsion of "excessive, unnecessary Jews" from his newly conquered city of Breslau (Wroclaw) allowing only 12 families to remain and he did the same in Posen (Poznan). Frederick the Great also ordered Veitel Ephraim, the Jew who owned the only mint in Prussia, to issue debased coinage to swell the royal coffers. The resulting economic crisis was, of course, blamed on the Jews.

As literacy spread in the allegedly more enlightened eighteenth and nineteenth, the tradition of anti-Semitic literature was born. Johannes Eisenmenger (1654–1704), a Protestant theologian from Frankfurt and a professor at Heidelberg University, scoured the Talmud for anything that could be construed as anti-Christian. The result was a book whose lengthy title begins *Judaism Unmasked...* First published in 1699, it became a best-seller, a forerunner of the *Procotols of the Elders of Zion*, a fiction first published in 1903 in St. Petersburg by Pavel Krushevan in his ultra-conservative Russian orthodox newspaper *Znamya*. It is written in the first person and is alleged to be a Jewish plot to take over the world. The text was enthusiastically circulated by the Nazis and today it is widely available wherever there is hostility to Jews, particularly in the Arab world as is the equally anti-Semitic two-volume *Mein Kampf* written by Adolf Hitler in his prison cell and published in 1925 and 1926. In 1850, the composer Richard Wagner (1813–1883) published *Das Judenthum in der Musik* (Jews in Music) attacking his Jewish contemporaries Felix Mendelssohn and Giacomo Meyerbeer in particular, and accusing Jews of being alien in German culture.

The early nineteenth century saw an outpouring of works by respected German scholars attacking the Jews. A highly influential pamphlet was the essay by the academic, Johann Gottlieb Fichte, who became rector of the New Berlin University in 1810. His 1793 essay on the French Revolution contains vicious attacks on the Jews. Inspired by this kind of anti-semitic literature, and by the return of the reactionary regimes after Napoleon's defeat at Waterloo, a new wave of German riots broke out, known as the Hep! Hep! Riots for the war cries of the rioters "Hep, hep, Jüde verrecke." Hep is believed to stand for "Hierusclyma est perdita", Latin for "Jerusalem is lost". The unrest started in Würzburg and spread to Bamberg, Darmstadt, Baden-Baden, Mannheim, Bayreuth, Karlsruhe, Hamburg and Frankfurt. The authorities finally intervened when the Rothschild house in the Frankfurt Ghetto was attacked, since the house contained large government funds!

German anti-Semitic outbursts continued long after they had ended in the rest of Europe. The 1873 financial crisis was blamed on the Jews as, of course, was the soaring inflation of the immediate post-war years. All this was happening in Hitler's formative years and formed the prelude to the Holocaust. After the post-war revelations and consequent condemnations of racism in all its forms, it was assumed that like other forms of racism, anti-Semitism would die out. In fact, it has experienced a post-war resurgence, fueled by Israel's enemies, Islamic extremism and the far-right political parties of Europe.

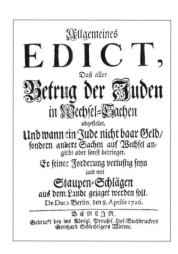

The title page of an edict against the Jews, issued by Frederick William I of Prussia in 1726. The Jews, under his rule, could only escape forcible exile by handing over their wealth to the Prussian crown.

Global Migrations

BEGINNING IN THE NINETEENTH CENTURY WITH IMPROVED
TRAVEL AND COMMUNICATIONS, MANY OF THE JEWS OF EASTERN
EUROPE EMIGRATED TO WESTERN EUROPE AND THE NEW WORLD
IN SEARCH OF A BETTER LIFE.

The centuries of persecutions suffered by Jews throughout Europe culminated in the mid-
to late-nineteenth century with the grinding poverty of the Jewish masses, combined with
the pogroms and the Black Hundreds. Even the more affluent Jews of central and western
Europe suffered from discrimination. All of this made many Jews decide that enough was enough,
it was time to leave. Many contributing factors helped them on their way. The invention of the
telegraph in 1844, followed by photography and the telephone, enabled newspapers to expand and
flourish and news to travel, news of a far better world beyond the Pale of Settlement.

As has recently been pointed out by modern historians, it was not just the persecutions that Jews
wanted to leave behind. They learned of a new world, a world in which personal freedoms were
important, and this included freedom of worship – or the freedom not to worship. The stories of Isaac
Bashevis Singer (1902–1991) illustrate how the whole world was changing and the Jewish world with
it, even in the shtetls of Poland, where reactionary, narrow-minded rabbis ruled their congregations
with a rod of iron. The most important of the new inventions was transport. All over the world,
people who had never ventured outside their native village were starting to enjoy the benefits of
mass transit. The unrest that travelled in waves through Europe due to the 1848 revolutions were the
most worrying times for ethnic minorities.

Small ships, precursors of the ocean liners, began taking emigrants all over the world. Most
Jews wanted to go to America, *der goldene medine* (the golden state). Not all of them made it; many,
speaking nothing but Yiddish, ended up in France, the Netherlands or Great Britain and it might take
them days to discover that they were not where they wanted to be. In those days, many ships would

ferry their passengers to Hull on the east coast of England, from whence they had to travel overland to Liverpool and take a big ship across the Atlantic.

Two million Jews left eastern Europe between 1881 and 1914, of whom some 150,000 settled in England, mostly in London's East End, near the docks where they had arrived. Between 1841 and 1846, By 1910, 125,000 Jews lived in less than two square miles around Whitechapel and Spitalfields, often in conditions of extreme overcrowding. The same was true of New York's Lower East Side, the pletzel (the Paris ghetto), and the many other districts of capital cities into which the Jews huddled together for safety as much as for reasons of religious worship.

Of all the shipping lines that brought the emigrants to what was a New World in every sense, none was as successful as the Hamburg Amerikanische Packetfahrt Aktien Gesellschaft (or HAPAG, the Hamburg-America Line). The company was established in Hamburg, Germany in 1847 to run a shipping across the Atlantic Ocean. It soon developed into the largest German and, at times, the world's largest shipping company. In those days, the majority of the emigrants streaming across the Atlantic (most of them non-Jewish) left from Bremen; the shipowners of Hamburg were determined to change that.

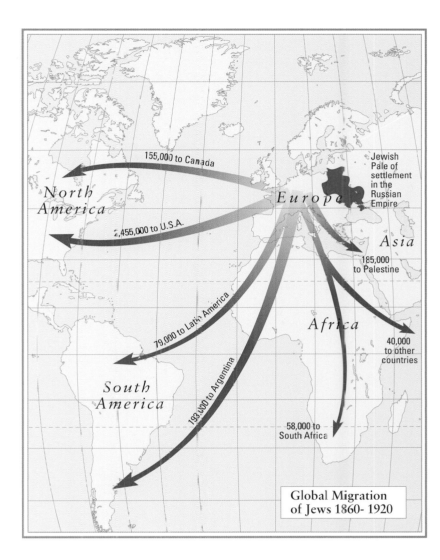

Global Migration of Jews 1860- 1920

This map shows the routes taken by Jews fleeing eastern Europe and Russia in the late nineteenth and early twentieth centuries. As can be seen, many migrants made for South America and the British colonies.

When 18-year-old Albert Ballin took over his father's emigration bureau in 1874, the business was doing moderately well. Six years later, the assassination of Czar Alexander II and the resulting wave of pogroms sent Jews scurrying westward to seek a way out of their misery and Albert was swamped with clients. He went into partnership with a cargo ship-owner named Edward Carr, persuading him to convert his tramp steamers to carry passengers. The first of these left Hamburg on June 7, 1881 with 800 passengers aboard. Over the next two years, the company carried 16,500 emigrants. In 1886, HAPAG bought into Ballin's business, making him a director. Six years later, Ballin owned the company, now the largest and most successful shipping company in the world. Under Ballin's direction, in 1901 HAPAG opened a huge complex for the emigrants, who had to spend 14 days' quarantine in Hamburg before they were allowed to board a ship. It had every facility, including kosher kitchens. Ballin remained a Jew, though he took a non-Jewish wife. Despite being a personal friend of the Kaiser, he was shunned by the Imperial German court for being Jewish. He tried to use his own diplomacy to avert the 1914–18 war. In the aftermath, with German businesses ruined, Albert Ballin committed suicide in 1918. The avenue leading to HAPAG's main office is now called Ballindamm. Thanks to this mass emigration, a considerable proportion of the world's Jews were saved from the wrath to come.

The Rothschilds

THE ROTHSCHILDS ARE AMONG THE WORLD'S MOST POWERFUL AND WEALTHY DYNASTIES IN THEIR LONG PROSPERITY AND BOUNDLESS PHILANTHROPY. THEIR STORY, BEGINNING IN THE HARSH CONDITIONS OF THE FRANKFURT GHETTO, IS ONE THAT IS EXTRAORDINARY.

Mayer Anselm Rothchild (1836–1905), a member of the Austrian branch of the family and head of the Rothschild Bank in Vienna.

The rise and rise of the Rothschilds is a tale that has fascinated Jews and non-Jews over the centuries. In the early to mid-nineteenth century, less than a hundred years after leaving the Frankfurt Ghetto, they were estimated to be the wealthiest and most influential bankers in the world. While their notoriety has waned, their power and influence continues, even if behind the scenes.

The story began in the overcrowded and squalid Frankfurt ghetto in the late eighteenth century, where Amschel Moses Rothschild (1736–1794) lived in a house that was distinguished from the rest by the red shield over the door. Moses was a general merchant but he inherited a money-changing business from his father. Amschel decided to concentrate on this lucrative profession, one which was vitally necessary for trade between the 235 principalities of which Germany then consisted. He built up his trade through contacts with the various rulers, and at the same time began a collection of coins and trinkets that was to be the nucleus of the massive collections of art works and valuables amassed by Rothschilds throughout Europe.

Amschel Moses' eldest son, Meyer Amschel, followed in his father's footsteps, selling coins to Prince William of Hesse, Count of Hanau, with whom he developed a close business relationship. Through the trade in Hessian mercenaries supplied to King George III of England to quell the rebellion American colonists, Meyer Amschel came to control the discounting of bills of large sums, the first of a new breed of international businessman.

Meyer Amschel's five sons were sent all over Europe to found branches of the House of Rothschild in England, France, Germany and Austria. As partners in his counting house, they constituted the original

Five Arrows, the symbol of the House of Rothschild.

The story of Meyer Amschel's son, Nathan, who opened the firm's branch in England and was first with the news of Napoleon's escape from Elba, then of the outcome of the Battle of Waterloo in 1815, thus making a huge killing for himself on the Stock Exchange, is well known. It was Nathan's money that paid the British troops' wages on the battlefield. The founder of the firm of N.M. Rothschild was a highly respected figure and having himself contributed massively to England's prosperity in the early nineteenth century, was sorely missed when he died. A cartoon was published showing a black silhouette beside the pillar "on'Change" which was Nathan's pitch. Today, the Rothschild Bank is run 200 years after its foundation, by Evelyn de Rothschild. The French branch of the Rothschilds were hardly affected by the vagaries of French revolutions and other political upsets. James de Rothschild, head of the French house, besides heading the bank, became a railway magnate and began the French Rothschild tradition of racehorse breeding.

Two of the outstanding features of the Rothschilds is that, however wealthy and influential they became, they never abandoned their religion and, above all, the needs of their co-religionists. Whenever heads of state and even the Vatican, came cap-in-hand to the Rothschilds for loans, the conditions included the easing or lifting of constraints on Jews. That is why the Jews of nineteenth-century eastern Europe came to regard the Rothschilds as "fairy godparents" of the poor and oppressed.

The Rothschilds were among the earliest of the Jewish "nobility" to embrance Zionism. Baron Edmond James de Rothschild of the French branch, started the Carmel-Mizrahi Winery in 1886, where David Ben-Gurion, Israel's first prime minister, headed the workers' union. Israel's other leading winery, Zichron Yaacov, is named for the Baron, as is Be'er Yaakov. The Balfour Declaration (1917), in which the British government claimed to "view with favour the establishment in Palestine of a national home for the Jewish people" is, in fact, a private letter from Arthur Balfour to Walter Rothschild, then member of parliament for Aylesbury.

In 1853, Nathan Rothschild, of the English branch of the family, bought the Château Brane Mouton vineyards in Pauillac, Bordeaux, having tried in vain to buy the even more prestigious Lafite vineyards next door. Baron James Mayer finally acquired Lafite for the family in 1868, for the incredible sum of 4.4 million francs, and the estate became Château Lafite Rothschild. Baron James died only three months later and Lafite was inherited by his three sons Alphonse, Gustave and Edmond. Subsequent Rothschilds have made wines from these premier cru vineyards into finest and most costly in France. The Rothschilds are famous for their art collections, their stately homes, and their lavish entertaining, as well as their charitable donations to Jews and non-Jews alike. Typical of his generation was Baron Guy Edouard Alphonse Paul de Rothschild (1909–2007) owner of Château Lafite and Château Mouton, who chaired the Rothschild Frères Bank in Paris until it was nationalized by the French government in 1979. Guy, who bred horses, grew up in his parents' mansion in Paris, once home of the Prince de Talleyrand. His country estate, the Château de Ferrières, was built in the 1850s to a design by Joseph Paxton based on the architect's earlier design of Mentmore Towers for Baron Mayer de Rothschild of the English branch of the Rothschild family.

This is but a cursory glance at the enormous influence and contribution made by what must be one of the world's most powerful dynasties.

JEWISH SUPPORT GROUPS 1750–1918

THE FOUNDATIONS FOR THE MODERN JEWISH PHILANTHROPIC SOCIETIES WERE LAID IN THE EIGHTEENTH CENTURY AND EARLIER. THERE IS A STRONG TRADITION OF CHARITY AMONG JEWS, FOR WHOM IT IS A SACRED DUTY TO HELP THE LESS FORTUNATE.

The Jews' Free School after its relocation to Bell Lane in the East End of London in 1822.

Jewish society has always been highly organized into groups and associations. Until the Enlightenment, these had always been centred around the synagogue. The so-called kehilla was an organization in each synagogue whose purpose was to help the poor and destitute of the congregation. The *hevra kaddisha* (holy society), known in English as the burial society, was a group of congregants who organized and arranged funerals (something that had to be done at very short notice, as Jewish burials must take place within 72 hours) and the 30-day memorial ceremony at which the headstone was set.

After the Emancipation and the emigration of Jews to western Europe and the New World, the ghetto was left behind and Jewish organizations needed to look beyond the synagogue if they were to cater for the community as a whole. It was no longer enough to have a plethora of rabbis or ad hoc advocates, such as Manassah ben Israel, speaking for the community in dealings with the authorities, there needed to be proper representation. The body representing British Jewry, the Board of Deputies, was founded in May, 1761. The word "deputy" is a literal translation of the Spanish/Portuguese "deputado" or representative, these being elected by synagogues and other Jewish organizations.

Charitable and educational institutions were founded in the countries in which Jews were newly emancipated. In England, for instance, the organization founded as the Jewish Board of Guardians (1859), and now known as Jewish Care, is the largest private welfare organization in Europe. It runs a network of old people's homes and cares for the physically and mentally disabled throughout the country. The Manchester Jewish Board of Guardians was founded in 1867.

The Jews' Free School opened on April 13, 1732 in Ebenezer Square, London and in 1822 it relocated to Bell Lane in the East End of London, where it remained until bombed in World War II. It has since moved twice in the London suburbs. The JFS currently has around 2,000 students and is the largest Jewish school in Europe. Its alumni are diverse: diamond millionaire and African pioneer Barney Barnato (1852–1897), the writer, Israel Zangwill (1864–1926), members of parliament, and two musicians in the Jamiroquai acid/ funk band. In Manchester, England, the Jews' School

The Second Canadian Jewish Congress which met on January 24 1934.

was established in 1842, through Abraham Franklin and his brother Jacob (subsequently editor of the *Voice of Jacob*, an early Jewish newspaper), (1904) has 2,300 scholars (800 in the boys' and girls' classes respectively, and 700 infants). The head master, Ephraim Harris, M.A., has occupied that position since 1869. Both these schools have striven to inculcate British as well as Jewish values and turn the pupils into model British citizens. In their early days, the use of Yiddish, the language spoken by most of the children at home, was frowned upon and Yiddish forenames were anglicised upon the orders of the head teacher.

Jewish philanthropists in Canada established Hebrew or Jewish Philanthropic Societies in Montreal (1848) and Quebec where there was a Hebrew Relief Association for Immigrants and the Hebrew Philanthropic Society in Toronto. The Canadian Jewish Congress (CJC), established in 1919, merged with several of these smaller organizations. Similar bodies were funded in the United Kingdom, in Manchester (1804), Birmingham, England (1829) there developed a wide range of communal organizations and groups. Recently arrived immigrant Jews in England and North America also founded the *landsmanschaft*, guilds of people who originating from the same town or shtetl.

In the United States, the Jewish relief and welfare groups struggled in the big cities into which thousands of refugees from eastern Europe poured, starting in the 1870s. They had to feed the hungry, shelter the homeless, find employment for those fit to work and help the sick and elderly. In 1895, the Jews of Boston created a central organization later known as the Combined Jewish Philanthropies, the first combined welfare body in North America. Each agency maintained independence and was represented on the CJP board of trustees. Jews in other cities quickly copied the Boston federation. Today there are nearly 200 federations across North America – one in every city with a Jewish population of more than 1,000

The Alliance Israélite Universelle was founded in Paris in 1860 by the French-Jewish statesman Adolphe Crémieux (1796–1880), with aim of protecting the rights of Jews as citizens of countries where they live and to educate them, especially in countries under French colonial rule where education might be denied to women. In 1870, Charles Netter of the AIU received a tract of land from the Ottoman Empire as a gift and started Mikveh Israel, the first Jewish agricultural settlement in Palestine to grow oranges. The school is still going strong.

JEWISH POLITICIANS IN EUROPE

SINCE THEIR EMANCIPATION, JEWS HAVE PLAYED A PROMINENT PART IN THE POLITICAL LIFE OF THEIR COUNTRIES, ACROSS THE RANGE OF AFFILIATIONS. THEY HAVE ALSO BEEN ACTIVE IN TRADES UNIONS AND CAMPAIGNS FOR WORKERS' RIGHTS.

Léon Blum, led the Popular Front, a coalition of left-wing political parties to power in France during the 1930s.

Although there is scarcely a country in Europe that does not have a Jew at least in a ministerial position if not in the cabinet, three European Jewish politicians made an outstanding contribution their country prior to World War II.

One of the earliest Jewish statesman was Isaac Moïse Crémieux (1796–February 10, 1880), later known as Adolphe Crémieux, who came from a wealthy Jewish family in Nîmes. After the Revolution of 1830, he practised law in Paris, defending liberal ideas in the courts and in the press. An example of his writing is his plea for the political rehabilitation of Marshal Ney (1833), Napoleon's leading general who had been tried and executed after the fall of Napoleon. Crémieux was elected a deputy to the French parliament in 1842.

From 1834 until his death, Crémieux served as vice-president of the Representative Committee of French Jewry founded by Napoleon. In 1848, he was elected as a Republican member of the provisional government, becoming Minister of Justice. His ministry was an exceptionally progressive one, abolishing the death penalty for political offences and abolishing slavery in the French colonies. In December, 1851, Crémieux was arrested and imprisoned due to his opposition to Napoleon III's imperial ambitions. He was re-elected a Republican deputy in 1869 and again became Minister of Justice in 1870. With his colleagues, he resigned on February 14, 1871 after France's defeat in the Franco-Prussian war. Eight months later he was again elected a deputy, then senator for life in 1875.

Crémieux did much to improve the lot of the Jews in France. In 1827, he advocated the repeal of the More Judaico, anti-Jewish legislation that had survived from pre-revolutionary France. He founded the Alliance Israelite Universelle in 1860, becoming its president four years later. The organization is dedicated to defending Jews and fostering Jewish education, especially in the Sephardic world. In 1866, Crémieux travelled to Saint Petersburg to defend Jews of Saratov in Russia who had been accused in a blood libel. While in government, he secured full French citizenship for Jews in the French colony of Algeria, through the 1870 Décret Crémieux.

Walther Rathenau (1867–1922) was a German industrialist, politician, writer and statesman. He was born in Berlin, son of the founder of the Allgemeine Elektrizitäts-Gesellschaft (AEG), a company that still exists. Rathenau studied physics, chemistry and philosophy in Berlin and Strasbourg. He joined the AEG board in 1899, becoming a leading industrialist. During World War I Rathenau held senior posts in the Raw Materials Department of the German War Ministry, and became chairman of AEG upon his father's death in 1915. He played a leading role in enabling wartime Germany to continue fighting for years despite shortages of labour and raw materials. After World War I, Rathenau became a founder of the German Democratic Party. In 1921, he was appointed Minister of Reconstruction, and in 1922 he became Foreign Minister. His insistence that Germany should fulfil its obligations under the Treaty of Versailles, and the treaty he negotiated with Soviet Russia made him deeply unpopular with the Right who claimed he was part of a "Jewish-Communist conspiracy". Rathenau advocated assimilation for German Jews, opposing Zionism. He was assassinated in 1922 in an anti-semitic plot. A memorial stone in the Koenigsallee in Berlin-Grunewald marks the spot.

Léon Blum (1872–1950), France's first Jewish prime minister (unless one counts Nicholas Sarkozy) is one France's great heroes of the Left. Blum took little interest in politics until the Dreyfus Affair of 1894, when he joined the Socialist Party. In 1920, Blum worked to prevent a split between supporters and opponents of the Russian Revolution but the radicals formed the French Communist Party taking L'Humanité with them. Blum led the Socialist Party through the 1920s and 1930s. When Adolf Hitler came to power, the Left in France formed a strategic alliance. In 1935, they created the Front Populaire which won a sweeping victory in the 1936 elections. In February, 1936, shortly before becoming Prime Minister, Blum was dragged from a car and almost beaten to death by a group of anti-Semites and royalists.

Blum resigned in June 1937 due to internal wrangling in the Front Populaire. He was briefly Prime Minister again in March and April 1938. When the Germans occupied France in June 1940, Blum made no effort to leave the country, despite the extreme danger he was in as a Jew and a Socialist leader. He was arrested in September and held until 1942, when he was tried on charges of treason, for having "weakened France's defences". He used the courtroom to make a brilliant indictment of the French military and collaborators such as Pierre Laval.

In April 1943, Blum was deported to Germany and imprisoned in Buchenwald and later in other camps. In the last weeks of the war, the Nazi regime gave orders for him to be executed but the local authorities decided to ignore the order. Blum was liberated in May 1945. While in prison he wrote the essay "À l'échelle Humaine" ("For all Mankind"). After the war, Léon Blum returned to politics, and served again briefly as Prime Minister in the post-war coalition government. He also served as an ambassador on a government loan mission to the United States, and as head of the French mission to UNESCO. He died in 1950

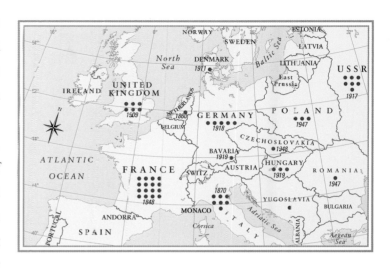

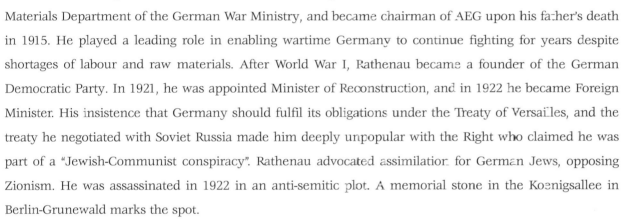

Jewish Government Ministers in Europe 1848–1948

- Jewish cabinet ministers and leading political figures with year of entry into office

With Jewish emancipation came the right to represent their respective nations in political office. Jewish citizens rose to important governmental posts across Europe.

New York's Jews

THE JEWS OF NEW YORK, WHO MAKE UP ONE-FOURTH OF THE POPULATION, ARE AMONG THE MOST VIBRANT AND ACTIVE IN THE WORLD. ARRIVING IN THE SEVENTEENTH CENTURY, JEWS HAVE PROSPERED IN NEW YORK, ESTABLISHING ONE OF THE MOST INFLUENTIAL COMMUNITIES OF JEWS IN THE WORLD.

Klezmer musicians playing to celebrate the reopening of the Eldridge Street synagogue in New York's Lower East Side in 2007. Klezmer is a Jewish music style from eastern Europe, most popular at weddings, that has enjoyed a recent revival.

When a small group of Jews sailed up the Atlantic coast taking refuge from Recife in Brazil, determined to settle in New Amsterdam in 1654, despite the determination of governor Peter Stuyvesant to expel them, they could not have realized that they would be founding the largest, strongest and most influential Jewish community in the world.

The little Sephardic community of New Amsterdam, consisting at first of refugees from the Inquisition, supplemented by those from the Low Countries who had recently thrown off the Spanish yoke and later by Sephardic Jews from England had a precarious existence for ten years, but it prospered when the British recaptured the city. The synagogue was not opened until 1729 though a burial ground had been purchased in 1656, and another in 1682. In those early days, New York played second fiddle to Philadelphia as the main east coast port; it was not to come into its own until the mid-nineteenth century.

As New York grew, so its settled Jewish population prospered, as did the institutions they founded. In 1848, German Jews in New York, established the first major secular Jewish organization, the Bnai Brith, whose structure was based on the lodges of the Masonic Order; by 1860, it had 50,000 members. It is now has branches all over the free world.

While the Civil War put a curb on immigration, between the 1830 and the 1880s, growing numbers of middle class German Jews reached New York, escaping from discrimination and seeking fame and fortune. Many of them made it and made it big. They include the bankers, August Belmont (1813–1890), Joseph Seligman (1819–1880) and Henry Schiff (1847–1920).

New York Jews were among the founders of the new progressive form of Judaism that emerged with the Enlightenment. The father of Reform Judaism in the United States was Isaac Mayer Wise (1819–1900) and its leading synagogue, the vast Temple Emmanu-El, was opened in 1870. Although the Conservative movement originated in nineteenth-century Breslau, the movement's current headquarters is the Jewish Theological Seminary (JTS) founded in New York in 1886 through the efforts of two Sephardic rabbis, Dr. Sabato Morais and Dr. H. Pereira. Orthodoxy is represented in New York by the Yeshiva University founded in 1886. Its philosophy is that of Modern Orthodox Judaism, Torah Umadda "Torah learning combined with secular studies."

While the wealthy Jews of New York visited each other in their Fifth Avenue Mansions, their less fortunate fellow-Jews were toiling in the Lower East Side. The massive influx began in 1870; by the early 1900s, the Jews had made this district their own. Contemporary photographs show the streets thronged with Jews in Russian caps and kaftans, women in headscarves and voluminous skirts, peddlers hawking their wares, amid a host of shop signs in English, Yiddish and Hebrew. The Museum of the Lower East Side is housed in a building in Orchard Street (so-called because it led to British Lieutenant-governor James Delancey's apple orchard) built by a German-Jewish tailor in 1863. It is a graphic illustration of how the "greeners", the recent immigrants, used to live since the building has been untouched since the 1930s (except for the storefront below).

Authors such as Jerome Weidmann depict the struggle to make it from these humble beginnings. Those who did include Al Jolson (1886–1950), Irving Berlin (1888–1989) and Sophie Tucker (1884–1966) to name but a few Jewish performers. None were born in the U.S.A. and they performed all over the country but they always considered themselves New Yorkers, as did the next, American-born, generation, including Tony Curtis (1925–), Stephen Sondheim (1930–) and Brooklyn's Barbra Streisand (1942–). While Jews have mostly left the Lower East Side and Brooklyn, just across the Hudson, for the greener pastures, inner city neighbourhoods such as Williamsburg and Crown Heights, are home to communities of ultra-orthodox Jews and it is here that the world headquarters of Chabad, the Lubavitch Movement, are located.

Jews have made many contributions to the New York diet, including the bagel (now a world-wide export), the bialy (short for bialystoker roll, a flattened round bread roll sprinkled with salt and fried onion) and, above all the knish, a pastry filled with mashed potato and onion or kasha (buckwheat grits). The soft drinks known as egg cream (which contains no egg and no cream!) and lime rickey (a shot of lime cordial with seltzer) are also Jewish inventions.

New York has had three Jewish mayors – Abraham Beame (1906–2001), Ed Koch (1924–), and the current incumbent, Michael Bloomberg (1942–) – and a fourth, often thought of as Jewish, the most popular mayor in New York's history. Fiorello LaGuardia (1882–1947) had an Italian-Jewish mother, a non-practicing Catholic father, but was raised an Episcopalian.

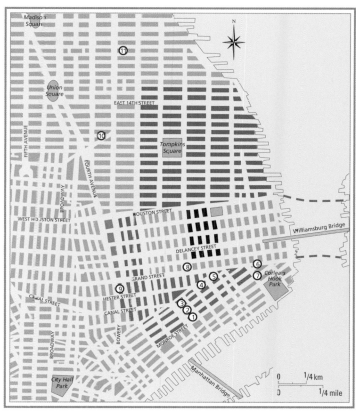

East European Jewish Settlements on New York's Lower East Side, c. 1900

- Hungarians
- Rumanians
- Russians
- Galicians
- Rumanians and Levantines

① Beth Israel Hospital
② Israel Elchanan Yeshiva
③ Forward Building on Yiddish Newspaper Row
④ Machzike Talmud Torah
⑤ Hebrew Sheltering House
⑥ Hebrew Technical School for Girls
⑦ Jewish Maternity Hospital
⑧ Beth Hamedrash Hagadol
⑨ Yiddish Rialto
⑩ Hebrew Technical School for Boys
⑪ Hebrew Charities Building

Jewish immigrants from many eastern European countries settled particularly in New York's Lower East Side, forming vibrant and successful communities.

LONDON'S EAST END

THE HEYDAY OF THE JEWISH EAST END IS LONG GONE BUT IT
WAS ONCE THE EQUIVALENT OF NEW YORK'S LOWER EAST SIDE,
WITH JEWISH STREET MARKETS, YIDDISH THEATRE AND CULTURAL
EVENTS, AND NIGHTLY MEETINGS OF EVERY SHADE OF LEFT-WING
POLITICAL AND TRADE UNION ACTIVISTS.

The East End of London can be defined as the area from the Thames northwards, stretching about one mile east of the boundary of the City of London and including the districts of Aldgate, Whitechapel, Bethnal Green and Stepney Green. It has always been the first stop for immigrants landing in the Port of London and as such has been favoured by successive waves of newcomers, Jews among them.

The first plot of land to be used for a cemetery was purchased by the newly-admitted Jewish community of London in Mile End in 1657 and Jewish merchants settled in the more affluent parts of the East End, such as Bow. Beginning in the mid-nineteenth century, when thousands fled from the unrest and persecution in Europe, Jews from Eastern Europe flocked to the East End. Despite the fact that the Sephardic and Ashkenazic Jews who had been in England for so much longer disapproved of their rowdier (and left-wing) co-religionists, a number of philanthropic organizations sprang up to help the newcomers. They included the Jewish Soup Kitchen for the Jewish Poor (founded 1902), whose façade still stands in Brune Street and the Poor Jews Shelter (founded 1896; renovated 1906) a hostel for destitute newcomers.

From 1870 until well after World War II, the area from Aldgate at the edge of the City to Mile End, via Whitechapel, was largely Jewish territory. It was dominated by the huge market centred in Middlesex Street, known as Petticoat Lane for the second-hand clothing it sold, that straggled into the adjoining streets such as Wentworth Street and Goulston Street. There were also markets in Hessel Street (famous for its meat and the chickens that could be bought live then ritually slaughtered at the other end of the street) and Brick Lane. The shops were all Jewish-owned, including the famous Barnett's Restaurant where they served the finest hot salt beef in the country and there were Jewish street vendors of pickled herrings and cucumbers in barrels and bagels on strings. On cold winter days, there were hot blackcurrant and hot sarsparilla drinks served. The food in this part of London was unlike anything else that could be found in the metropolis. On Friday nights, the streets were deserted but a strong smell of fried fish filled the air, the traditional Jewish Friday night meal. It is here that fried fish (Jewish) and chips (Irish) met and married.

The Jews of the East End, like most Jewish communities, were highly organized. There were three large community organizations that incorporated youth clubs for boys and girls of all ages, women's organizations and those for old people. These "settlements" were modelled on the non-Jewish Toynbee Hall (founded 1884), the first of its kind. The Brady Clubs and Settlement, The Bernhard Baron settlement (founded 1929 and also known as Oxford and St. Georges) and the Stepney Jewish Clubs and Settlement catered for different parts of the borough. For the politically active, there were all kinds of Zionist, Socialist and radical organizations, seething with discontent at the appalling conditions of the sweat-shops, the filthy streets, lack of sanitation and cramped living conditions.

The non-Jewish but Yiddish-speaking Rudolf Rocker (1873–1958) was a committed anarcho-syndicalist who published the anarchist newspaper "*Arbeiter Freint*' (The Worker's Friend) from 1904. The anarchists were a powerful movement in the East End, but their decline was inevitable after the Siege of Sidney Street in January 1911, where a gang of anarchists, most of them Jewish, who

The ark of the Fieldgate Street synagogue with some of the scrolls of the Law arranged outside it.

had earlier tried to rob a jewellery store, barricaded themselves in at 100 Sidney Street and shot any police who came near. The Home Secretary, a certain Winston Churchill, visited the premises which eventually caught fire. Churchill ordered that the flames should not be put out, so that those trapped inside perished.

Rocker's newspaper, published daily during the nine-day General Strike in 1926, was by no means the only Yiddish publication; by the 1920s, the East End was publishing no fewer than three newspapers in Yiddish and a range of Zionist, Socialist and Marxist literature. There were Jewish trades unions – the Furniture-makers Union, the Bakers Union and the Garment-workers Union, who proudly took their elaborate banners to rallies.

Entertainment was here aplenty, in the form of Yiddish music hall and Yiddish theatres, including the largest, the Grand Palais in Whitechapel Road. It is here that the play *Der Kenig fun Lampeduse* (The King of Lampedusa), based on a true story, premiered in December, 1943.

The Jewish East End lasted for around a hundred years, declining gradually as Jews became more affluent and moved to the healthier suburbs of London, to Stamford Hill, Golders Green, Ilford and Redbridge. Perhaps the only such "Jewish" neighbourhood, anywhere in the world, to survive into modern times is the Fairfax district of Los Angeles.

THE DREYFUS AFFAIR

THE DREYFUS AFFAIR, IN WHICH A FRENCH ARMY OFFICER WAS
ACCUSED OF BETRAYING FRANCE TO THE HATED GERMANS,
ROCKED NOT ONLY FRANCE BUT THE FREE WORLD, AND HAD
IMPLICATIONS FAR BEYOND THE ACTUAL CASE.

Alfred Dreyfus was tried in
1894 on charges of espionage
and found guilty. He was
sentenced to life in prison on
Devil's Island in French Guyana,
where he spent five years.

Although the French Revolution emancipated the Jews and in the decree of 11 December, 1808 Napoleon had granted French jewry a measure of self-rule in the shape of the Consistoire, major pockets of anti-semitism remained. The protagonists were the usual suspects – reactionaries, royalists, the established church and conservatives. Feelings reached fever pitch in the year 1894, when Alfred Dreyfus, a rather unprepossessing and unpopular captain in the French army, who happened to be Jewish, was tried and convicted of treason and sentenced to life imprisonment on Devil's Island in French Guyana. He was first publicly humiliated in a "drumming out" ceremony. The Dreyfus case was to split France into deeply divided factions for the next ten years.

Dreyfus was accused of having passed information to the Germans, who were hated as a result of the humiliating defeat suffered by France in the Franco-Prussian War of 1870–1871. Dreyfus' own family had left Alsace for France when the French province was ceded to the Germans as the result of the war. The incriminating evidence was known as *le bordereau*, an unsigned note taken by a cleaning-woman from a waste basket in the German Embassy. There was no proof at all that the note was in Dreyfus' handwriting or that he had anything to do with it.

Édouard Drumont's newspaper *La Libre Parole* (Free Speech) intensified its attacks on Jews, portraying this incident as further evidence of Jewish treachery. The political right and the Catholic Church – both of which were openly hostile to the Republic – declared the Dreyfus case to be a conspiracy of Jews and Freemasons designed to damage the prestige of the army and thereby destroy France. The pro-Dreyfus camp, which included many influential left-leaning politicians, laboured hard to prove his innocence. In 1896, the real wrongdoer was exposed when a second piece of incriminating evidence appeared that had been written while Dreyfus was serving his sentence of Devil's Island. French counter-intelligence, realizing its error in convicting Dreyfus, tried to conceal this new document. The real culprit, a Major Ferdinand Esterhazy, had sold intelligence information to the Germans in order to cover his gambling debts. The French military dismissed or ignored this new evidence, anti-Semitism being rife in the army. Esterhazy underwent a token court martial in January 1898 but two days after the trial began the judges halted it and unanimously acquitted Esterhazy. French military counter-intelligence then proceeded to fabricate additional evidence against Dreyfus.

Public opinion was aroused, in large part due to the long article by Emile Zola in the form of a letter to the President of France and entitled *J'accuse* (I Accuse). The article, claimed to be the most influential in the history of journalism, was published by the progressive newspaper *L'Aurore* on January 13, 1898. Dreyfus also had the support of the leading statesman Georges Clémenceau (1841–1929) who was twice elected prime minister.

The case was finally re-opened in 1899; Dreyfus was brought back from Guiana to be tried again. Despite overwhelming evidence of his innocence, he was yet again found guilty, though his sentence was reduced to ten years "due to extenuating circumstances".

The scandal outraged Europe and divided French society between those who supported Dreyfus (the Dreyfusards) and those who condemned him (the anti-Dreyfusards). The new President of the Republic hastily pardoned Dreyfus but it was not until 1906 that he was finally exonerated and re-instated in the French army with the rank of major. He served in World War I, ending with the rank of Lieutenant-Colonel. The Dreyfus case had another significant side effect. Among the journalists sent from all over Europe to cover the first trial in 1894 was the Hungarian-Jewish journalist Theodor Herzl, representing the Viennese paper *Neue Freie Presse*, had been assigned to cover the trial. Herzl claimed in his memoirs that the Dreyfus case had inspired him to write *Der Judenstaat* (The Jewish State,1896). Having witnessed the howling mob outside the courthouse during the trial, screaming "Death to the Jews!" all because of one alleged traitor, Herzl realised that if Jews could not feel safe in France, the country that first offered them emancipation, they could not feel safe anywhere until they had their own country.

In fact, most French people were disgusted at the prejudice exhibited in the Dreyfus case and went on to elect a series of left-wing presidents and prime ministers. The effect of the trial was to smash the power of the Catholic Church in France and lead to a rigorous separation of Church and state in the *laïcité* (secularism) movement, enshrined in the law of 1905, amended in 2004 to ban the wearing of religious symbols in state schools. On the 100th anniversary of the exoneration of Dreyfus on July 12, 1906, President Jacques Chirac attended a ceremony at the military school where Captain Dreyfus had been stripped of his rank amid calls for his death and that of all Jews.

EARLY ZIONISM AND HERZL

EVENTS SUCH AS THE DREYFUS AFFAIR AND THE DAMASCUS LIBEL, OCCURRING AFTER THE JEWS BELIEVED THEY WERE FINALLY BEING ACCEPTED INTO MAINSTREAM SOCIETY, LED MANY TO BELIEVE THAT JEWS WOULD NEVER BE FREE UNTIL THEY HAD THEIR OWN STATE.

Jews had imagined that as they became part of the world around them, instead of being herded into ghettos and the Pale of Settlement, that this would do much to combat anti-Semitism. This proved to be far from the case. As the Enlightenment Movement emerged in the late eighteenth century, so Jewish and non-Jewish thinkers considered that if Jews had their own country, attitudes toward them would be completely different. The thinkers covered the spectrum from the Yugoslav Sephardic Rabbi Yehudah Alkalai (1798–1878) to the German orthodox Rabbi Tzvi Hirsch Kalischer (1795–1874). They included the writer Moses Hess (1812–1875), whose book *Rome and Jerusalem* (1862) is an advocacy of Labour-Zionism. classic Zionist book, in which he writes of his return to "his" people. The future Jewish state, he wrote, should be based on national land acquisition, creation of legal conditions to encourage work and founding Jewish societies for agriculture, industry and trade.

An other early Zionist was Leon Pinsker (1821–1891), a medical doctor and originally leader of the assimilationist movement among Russian Jewry. As a witness to the Odessa pogrom of 1871, Pinsker became convinced that Jews would never be safe in Russia. He traveleld to Germany where he lived for two years, trying unsuccessfully to popularize the idea that Jews need to organize a nationalist movement. He returned to Odessa, where he wrote a pamphlet entitled *Selbstemanzipation* (Auto-Emancipation) 1882 in German. Pinsker was willing to settle for a Jewish homeland in a country other than Palestine but the book was well received and Pinsker was subsequently chosen to head the *Hovevei Zion* (Lovers of Zion) movement that had been organized in Russia to unite a network of underground Zionist study circles.

The most influential of the early Zionists, generally credited with being the founder of the Jewish nationalist movement, was Theodor Herzl (1860–1904), an Austrian-Jewish journalist, born in Hungary.

Herzl studied law at university but afterward he devoted himself almost exclusively to journalism and literature and working as Paris correspondent for the Viennese newspaper *Neue Freie Presse*. It was in Paris that Herzl had his first taste of virulent anti-Semitism when sent to report on the Dreyfus Affair (q.v.). This, coupled with his grandfather's enthusiastic devotion to the nationalist ideas of Rabbi Alkali, influenced Herzl's thinking. In 1896, Herzl produced his seminal work, *Der Judenstaat* (the Jewish State), published in Vienna and Leipzig. In April, 1896, the book appeared in an English translation and Herzl immediately became the leading

Artefacts relating to Herzl in the Jewish Museum in Budapest. Herzl was born in Hungary in 1860.

world spokesman for Zionism. Herzl travelled extensively to promote Zionism to Jewish communities and he was feted wherever he went by the poorer Jewish communities and by statesmen. He visited Istanbul in April, 1896, and the Jews of Sofia, Bulgaria referred to him as their "fuehrer"! In June 1896, Herzl met the Sultan of Turkey but the Sultan refused to cede Palestine to the Zionists. This was a disappointment and sowed the first seeds of doubt in Herzl's mind as to the practicality of setting up the new Jewish state on the ancient land of Palestine.

At the first Zionist Congress in Basel in 1897 Herzl was elected president of the World Zionist Federation, a post he held until his death. He continued his diplomatic initiatives to build support for a Jewish state and was received by the German Kaiser on several occasions, and granted an audience by the Ottoman emperor in Jerusalem. In 1902–03 Herzl was invited to give evidence before the British Royal Commission on Alien Immigration. This brought him into close contact with members of the British government, particularly Joseph Chamberlain, Secretary of State for the Colonies, through whom he negotiated with the Egyptian government for a charter for the settlement of the Jews in Al 'Arish, in the Gaza Strip. The scheme failed however, but in August 1903, the British government offered to facilitate Jewish settlement, in Uganda, East Africa. The Zionist movement was threatened by the deeply hostile Russian government. Herzl visited St. Petersburg and was received by Sergei Witte, then Finance Minister and the notoriously anti-semitic Minister of the Interior Viacheslav Plehve. Herzl used the opportunity to plead for the improvements of the Jewish situation in Russia.

In 1902, Herzl published his extraordinarily prescient novel, *Altneuland*, in which he describes the then-mythical Jewish state. It was translated into Hebrew by a leading Labour-Zionist, Nahum Sokolov, under the title *Tel-Aviv*. At the Sixth Zionist Congress, in Basel in August 1903, Herzl pleaded eloquently for the "Uganda Project," which was finally approved, though the Russian delegation stormed out in protest, firmly believing the Jewish National Home could not exist anywhere but Palestine. Herzl died in 1904 so he did not live to see the ultimate rejection of the Uganda plan. Yet his will states "I wish to be buried in the vault beside my father, and to lie there till the Jewish people shall take my remains to Palestine." In 1949, his remains were removed from Vienna to be reburied on a hill in Jerusalem that was renamed Mount Herzl. Next to the grave is a museum dedicated to his story.

Palestine under Turkish Rule

In the late nineteenth century, Zionist movements brought settlers to Palestine. Many sought to support the British in their military aims at taking over the land as the Ottoman Empire declined.

In 1516, the Ottoman Turks conquered Palestine and the country was incorporated into the Ottoman Empire. Local governors were appointed from Constantinople, to which annual revenues were sent. The only significant works from the period were the rebuilding of the walls of Jerusalem by Suleiman the Magnificent in 1537. Toward the close of the eighteenth century Napoleon undertook a campaign in Palestine, capturing Jaffa, Ramle, Lydda, Nazareth and Tiberias in 1798, but his siege of Acre was unsuccessful. In 1831, Egypt invaded Palestine, capturing Acre, but by 1840 Ottoman authority had been fully re-established. The territory of Palestine under Ottoman rule consisted of two districts (*sanjaks*). The sanjak of Jerusalem was directly subject to the Sultan and extended from Jaffa to the River Jordan in the east and from the Jordan south to the borders of Egypt. Northward, including Galilee, lay the *wilaya* or *vilayet* (province) of Beirut, consisting of the sanjak of Nablus from Jaffa to Jenin, and the sanjak of Acre, from Jenin to Naqura (now Rosh Hanikra). In the reorganization of 1873, which established the administrative boundaries that remained in place until 1914, Palestine was split into three major administrative districts. The north, above a line connecting Jaffa to north of Jericho and the Jordan, was assigned to the wilaya of Beirut, subdivided into the sanjaks of Acre, Beirut and Nablus. South of Jaffa was part of the district of Jerusalem. The southern boundaries of Palestine were unclear but petered out in the eastern Sinai Peninsula and northern Negev Desert an area that was inhabited exclusively by Bedouins which was totally undeveloped. Most of the central and southern Negev was assigned to the wilayet of Hijaz, which included the Sinai Peninsula and western Arabia.

Ottoman rule over the eastern Mediterranean lasted until World War I when the Ottomans sided with Germany and the Austro-Hungarian Empire and were defeated, causing them to lose their empire.

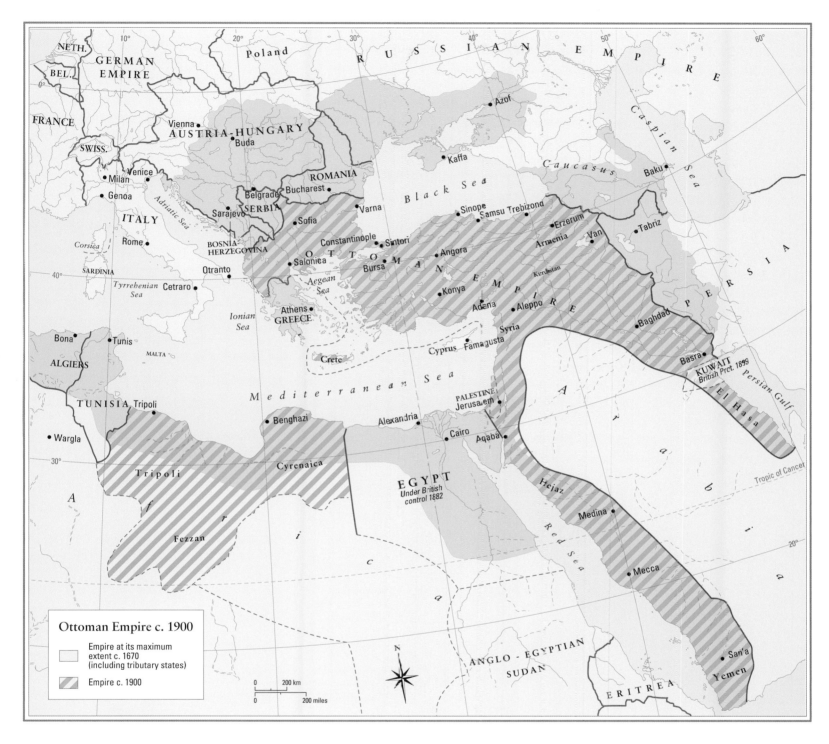

The defeat had been very much expected, mainly due to the upheavals in the empire, due to the Young Turks movement which had begun as early as 1889 and eventually led to the overthrow of the sultanate and the founding of the Turkish Republic in 1923. French and British ambitions for the region had been planned in the Sykes-Picot Agreement of 1916, a secret pact whereby the two powers intended to divide the Middle East between them.

Under Ottoman rule, most of the Arab landowners of Palestine, lived outside the country, enjoying life in Cairo or Istanbul while the peasants and tenant farmers earned a subsistence living from the soil. There was no development, no new roads or public buildings. Mark Twain, in his book, "*Innocents Abroad*", depicts the desolation of Palestine under Ottoman rule.

"Palestine is desolate and unlovely ... Of all the lands there are for dismal scenery, I think Palestine

The Ottoman Empire, a multi-ethnic state, had ruled over Jewish communities for over 500 years. By 1900 many Jews of North Africa, the Near East and Europe, remained under Turkish rule.

must be the prince … Every outline is harsh … it is a hopeless, dreary, heart-broken land." Nevertheless, under Ottoman rule, the Jewish population of Palestine which, until the start of the Zionist immigration in the 1880s, was confined largely to the holy cities of Jerusalem, Hebron, Tiberias and Safed, was left in peace, though like all the non-Muslim citizens of the Empire, Jews had the status of *dhimmi*. This meant paying a special tax and there were other restrictions on dress and housing.

　　As the Jewish population of Ottoman Palestine increased, the newcomers with their progressive ideas, rejected the stultifying conservatism and bureaucracy of Ottoman rule. A group known as the Nili Spies, set up in Zikhron Yaakov by Aaron Aharonson, the famous agronomist, his sister Sarah and their friend, Avshalom Feinberg, was motivated to assist the British in their ambitions to conquer Palestine after Sarah had witnessed the genocide perpetrated upon Armenians by the Ottoman Turks in 1915. From March to October 1915, a plague of locusts stripped Palestine of almost all crops and the Turkish authorities, worried about feeding their troops, turned to world-famous botanist and the region's leading agronomist, Aaron Aaronsohn. This enabled Aaronsohn and his team fighting the locust invasion to move around the country and collect information about Ottoman troop deployments.

　　Attempts by Alex Aaronsohn and Avshalom Feinberg to establish communication channels with the

Opposite: Between 1914–18 British and French armies fought a series of campaigns which culminated in the end of the Ottoman Empire.

Rabbi Yehuda Chai Alkalai, an early Zionist who emigrated to Ottoman Palestine with his wife in 1873.

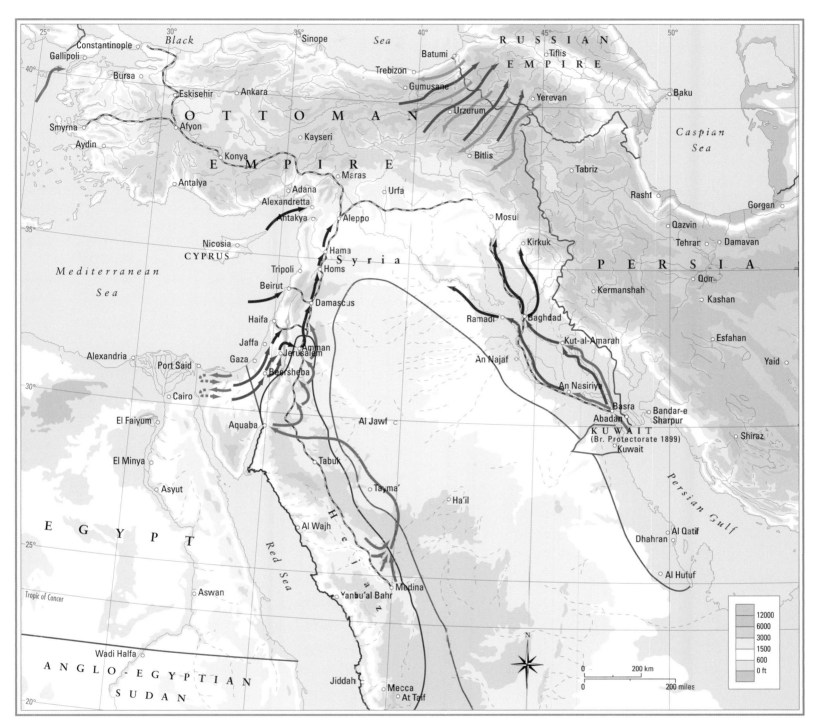

British in Egypt failed but Feinberg eventually made contact with the British diplomat Sir Mark Sykes. Feinberg was killed while attempting to reach Port Said on foot but Yosef Lishansky, managed to reach British lines. In autumn, 1917, one of the homing pigeons used by Nili was caught by the Turks, who deciphered the Nili code and destroyed the network. The Turks surrounded Zichron Yaakov and arrested many of the Nili Spies, including Sarah Aaronsohn, who committed suicide after four days of torture. Others were imprisoned in Damascus where Lishansky and Naaman Belkind were sentenced to death. Aaron Aaronsohn died in an air accident on May 1919. It has been claimed by military experts that the Nili intelligence passed to General Allenby was of enormous value to the British conquest of Palestine. In November 1967, Avshalom Feinberg's remains were reinterred on Mount Herzl with full military honors. The Aaronsohn home in Zikhron Ya'akov has been preserved as a memorial to Nili

The Middle East 1914–18

➔ British attacks 1914–15

➔ British attacks 1916–17

➔ British attacks 1918

➔ Turkish attacks 1915

➔ Turkish attacks 1917–18

➔ Russian attacks 1915–16

➔ French landing 1918

— Main area of Arab revolt 1916–18

PALESTINE UNDER THE BRITISH MANDATE

DESPITE THE INITIAL PROMISES MADE BY BRITAIN, SUBSEQUENT EVENTS TURNED THE BRITISH GOVERNMENT AGAINST THE JEWS, AND IN FAVOUR OF THE ARABS WHO WERE GROWING INCREASINGLY RESENTFUL OF THE NEW JEWISH POPULATION OF PALESTINE.

In 1920, following the collapse of the Ottoman Empire and the post World War I peace conference, the League of Nations handed over a Mandate for Palestine to the British government. The Mandate was originally designed to offer international recognition for the stated purpose of "establishing in Palestine a national home for the Jewish people", as laid down in the Balfour Declaration, the letter written to Lord Rothschild by the then Prime Minister, Arthur Balfour, in 1917. The British, however, had also promised Palestine to the Arabs in 1915. In that year, the British launched a massive naval invasion of Turkey at Gallipoli, but they suffered an unexpected defeat. The British had expected a rapid victory, to be followed by an overland march to Istanbul and the collapse of the Turkish Empire. The British government therefore adopted an alternative strategy for carving up the Middle East after World War I, recruiting Arab assistance from Palestine and Syria to help defeat the Turkish Empire. Accordingly, Henry McMahon, High Commissioner in Egypt, opened a correspondence with the Sharif of Mecca, of the Hashemite dynasty that ruled the Hejaz in Western Arabia. The British government promised military support for an Arab revolt against the Turks and British recognition of Arab independence after an uprising. The area of Arab rule was not defined by McMahon, though it appeared to include Lebanon and Palestine. In the 1922 White Paper, however, the British Government interpreted the McMahon Letter as denying any promise that Arab independence would extend west of the River Jordan.

In 1920, the British Mandate covered about 45,000 square miles but in 1921, it was extended to cover an area east of the Jordan River, creating Trans-Jordan (the area that is now the Kingdom of Jordan). Jews were forbidden by law from living in or owning property east of the Jordan River.

In 1923, Britain ceded the Golan Heights to the French Mandate of Syria. Jews who were living there were expelled and forced to abandon their homes and move into the British Mandate. The southern part of the Mandate – the Negev Desert – was also barred by the British to Jewish settlement. The desert population at the time consisted exclusively of nomadic Bedouins.

Due to Arab hostility, which took the form of pogroms regularly conducted against the Jewish population, Jewish immigration was ever more severely restricted by the

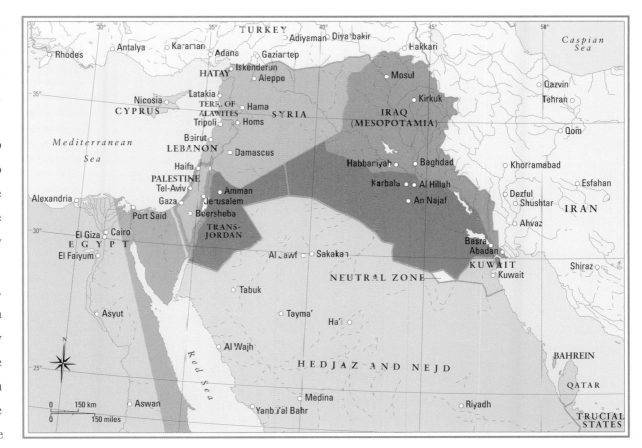

British, especially after the publication of the White Paper in 1939. Arab immigration was not restricted or even recorded, though Arabs continued to enter the country from elsewhere in the Middle East, attracted by the flourishing economy created by the Zionists.

Under the British Mandate, the Jewish population continued to grow and organized itself into a "state within a state." The Yishuv, as it was called, ran its own bus services (the Egged co-operative, now one of the biggest bus lines in the world, was founded in 1933), operating between the towns and cities and the Jewish settlements such as Petah Tiqvah and Rishon LeZion. The Yishuv had its own postal service, medical services and other co-operatives, such as the construction company Solel Boneh (Paving Building), founded by the Jewish trades union federation, the Histadrut, in 1921. Solel Boneh, which is now an international concern, took its current name in 1924, though it collapsed in the economic crisis of 1927, starting up again in 1935. During the period of Arab-Jewish unrest in 1936–39, Solel Boneh built several stockade and watchtower settlements, as well as fortifications and security roads. Through the Histadrut, it also organized Jewish labour for the ports of Haifa and Jaffa. In one generation, the Zionists transformed a barren, underpopulated land of mosquito-infested swamp in the north and arid desert in the south into a thriving mixed economy of farmers and fishermen, mechanics and factory workers. Three Jewish institutions of higher learning were founded under the Palestine Mandate, the Technion in Haifa (1924), the Hebrew University of Jerusalem (1925), and the Weizmann Institute of Science in Rehovot (1934).

All of this was against a background of Arab and British hostility to Jewish settlement. The British government heavily favoured the Arabs, since then, as now, the West needed Arab oil and Arab support in its plans for the Middle East. Eventually, realizing that it was powerless to get rid of the Jews and assuage Arab hostility, and on the verge of bankruptcy after World War II, Britain dumped the problem of Partition in the lap of the United Nations and ignominiously withdrew from Palestine in May, 1948.

League of Nations Mandate 1921

French Mandate, 1921, (areas formally under Ottoman rule)

Arab areas helped by Britain in their revolt against Ottoman rule, then becoming independent

British Mandate, 1921, (areas formally under Ottoman rule)

Areas under British rule or control in 1914

Palestine in 1922

After World War I, Britain and France, under the terms of the peace treaties, were granted significant regions of the Near East.

RISE OF THE NAZI EUROPE

RIGHT-WING POLITICS WERE A FEATURE OF THE INTERWAR YEARS THROUGHOUT EUROPE. IN THOSE DAYS, RACISM, IN THE FORM OF RACIAL THEORIES AND EUGENICS, WERE PERFECTLY ACCEPTABLE. PERHAPS NO ONE FORESAW WHERE THESE DESTRUCTIVE THEORIES MIGHT LEAD.

A German poster from 1938 celebrating the Pact between Hitler and Mussolini.

The armistice negotiations following World War I, in which the French insisted on massive reparations from Germany, resulted in galloping inflation in Germany in the 1920s. Then came the Wall Street Crash of 1929 which affected most of the world's economies and produced economic depression in Europe and the United States. At a time when overt racism was considered perfectly socially acceptable, the Jews became the inevitable scapegoats. Anti-semitism could be described as a "fashionable prejudice" and right-wing politics were in vogue. The early thirties, when the world was beginning to climb out of the slump, were hailed as a new era, with an emphasis on "fitness" and the doctrine of eugenics (racial engineering) and racial stereotyping were considered perfectly acceptable. This combined with an anti-democratic movement. The German Nazi Party decried the Weimar Regime as part of its platform, considering it to be "soft" and "unmanly" – and, of course, influenced by Jews.

The aftermath of the World War I was a time of widespread political instability. Communist leaders such as Bela Kun in Hungary and Rosa Luxemburg in Berlin were overthrown and replaced by fascist dictators. All over Eastern Europe, tyrants flourished. Benito Mussolini, founder of the Fascists, was invited by King Victor Emmanuel to form a government in 1922, and in 1925, he made himself dictator of Italy. In Hungary, the right-wing Admiral Miklos Horthy, seized power in 1920 and eventually joined the Axis; in Romania, General Ion Antonescu assumed supreme power in 1940, after forcing the King to abdicate. Once Hitler had come to power in Germany in 1930, Nazi agents and sympathizers were to be found all over the world, stirring up anti-semitic hatred.

Western Europe and the United States were also affected. The rise of extremist parties in Germany, Italy, Spain and Portugal also had its reverberations in France, nurtured by L'Action française, led by Charles Maurras, which targeted Jews, freemasons and Protestants, the ancient French conflict between clericalism and anti-clericalism. In Great Britain, influential writers such as Hilaire Belloc, G. K. Chesterton and the American-born poet T. S. Eliot did much to promote anti-Semitism. In 1932, Sir Oswald Mosely formed the British Union of Fascists. Four years later, he and his Blackshirts organized a march through the Jewish East End. The marchers were met with missiles and barricades and forced to retreat in what became known as "The Battle of Cable Street", defeated despite the protection they received from the Metropolitan Police. "They Shall Not Pass", the slogan of the anti-fascist Jewish and other Eastenders, was to become a war-cry of many subsequent encounters with the racist right including in the Spanish Civil War. Moseley, whose wife, Diana, was an aristocrat, had the support of a section of the British aristocracy known as the "Cliveden Set", Cliveden being the stately home inhabited by Nancy Visccuntess Astor, the arch-anti-semite who had been the first woman member of parliament.

Nancy Astor was an American who shared the deeply racist views of many of her contemporaries in the United States, whose attitude to Jews was similar to their attitude to blacks. It was not until the Civil Rights Acts of the 1960s that Jews were admitted to country clubs and upmarket hotels and an end was put to "zoning", whereby houses in certain expensive neighbourhoods were barred to anyone who was not a white Protestant. In the 1920s, the Ku Klux Klan extended their attacks from blacks to Jews and Catholics and staged marches demanding a "White America". The preacher, Father Charles Coughlin (1891–1979) was one of the radio evangelists; more than forty million Americans tuned to his weekly broadcasts during the 1930s. He admired the policies of Adolf Hitler and Benito Mussolini, especially in regard to the Jews. His broadcasts have been called "a variation of the Fascist agenda applied to American culture." Father Coughlin's contemporary, the aviator and national hero Charles Lindbergh (1902–1974) was an isolationist active in the "America First" Committee, a group of Fascist fellow-travellers. He had considerable influence, though not as much as the automobile millionaire Henry Ford (1863–1947) who spent much of his fortune promoting anti-semitism through his newspaper, *The Dearborn Independent*. He financed the translation, publication, and sale of the *Protocols of the Elders of Zion* and other anti-Semitic literature. Support for Nazism in Germany came from the usual coalition of the aristocracy and the uneducated working class. The aristocrats imagined they could control Hitler him but found themselves the victims of his homicidal ambitions.

By 1938/39 Britain and France had become involved in guaranteeing the security of Poland, sandwiched between the growing military might of Nazi Germany and Soviet Russia.

Political Agreements
1938–39

British and French guarantees for Poland, Greece, Romania and Turkey, 1939

Copenhagen declaration of neutrality, July 1938

Axis, May 1939

German-Soviet Non-Aggression Pact, 23 August 1939

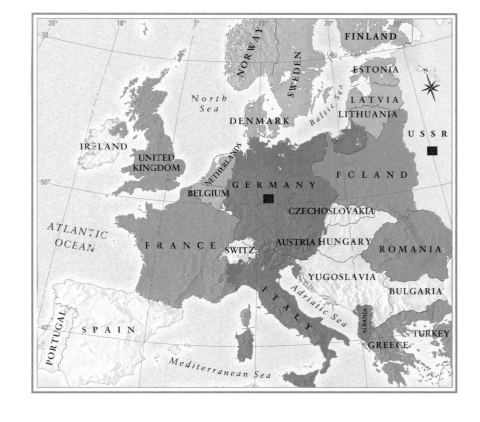

Isle of Barbed Wire

THE ISLE OF MAN, MIDWAY BETWEEN IRELAND AND ENGLAND IN THE IRISH SEA, WAS USED BY THE BRITISH DURING WORLD WAR II AS AN INTERNMENT CAMP FOR 'ENEMY ALIENS' FLEEING NAZI PERSECUTION, MOST OF WHOM WERE JEWISH.

By the end of 1940, 14,000 'enemy aliens' were interned on the Isle of Man.

The trickle of Jewish refugees from Germany who had begun leaving as soon as the Nazis came to power in 1933 increased in subsequent years until it reached a flood after *Kristallnacht* (the Night of the Broken Glass) in November, 1938. Many wanted to come to Great Britain, but the island was in the throes of the Depression and feared that there were not enough jobs to go round for its own citizens. Visas were only granted to those prepared to do the hardest manual labour or work as servants.

As soon as war with Germany was declared in September, 1939, the gates clanged shut. During the lull that followed the declaration of war, the period known as the "phony war", all kinds of hysterical rumours were spread. Germans dressed as nuns were being parachuted into the country, there were spies everywhere, etc. Posters exhorting discretion and stating "Walls have ears" and "Be like dad – keep mum" were displayed in all government offices. After the fall of France in 1940, a decision had to be taken about the large numbers of refugees who had come to Britain, not all of whom could be relied upon to be anti-Nazi. They were classified into three categories, Class A (high security risk) – 596, Class B (doubtful cases) – 6782, and Class C (no risk) – 66,002. Class A aliens were rounded up and put in internment camps immediately war broke out but most Class B and C aliens were imprisoned by the summer of 1940.

Against this background that the British Government decided to intern the 28,000 "enemy aliens", most of whom were Jewish. These refugees, having suffered so much already, were appalled to find themselves imprisoned as potential Nazi spies. At first, it was decided to send them abroad to Canada and Australia. The first ship to be torpedoed was the *Arandora Star* sunk by a German submarine on July 2, 1940. A total of 805 people were lost, including many Jews. Only eight days later, the *Dunera* left Liverpool for Australia, carrying at least double her standard passenger load, including 2,036 Jewish refugees from Austria and Germany. Incredibly, the survivors of the *Arandora Star* disaster had been added to the transportees. The ship normally had a maximum capacity of 1,500 – including crew – and the resulting conditions were described as "inhumane." The transportees were also subjected to ill-treatment and theft by the 309 British guards on board, many of whom were violently and openly anti-Semitic. The voyage took 57 days. When

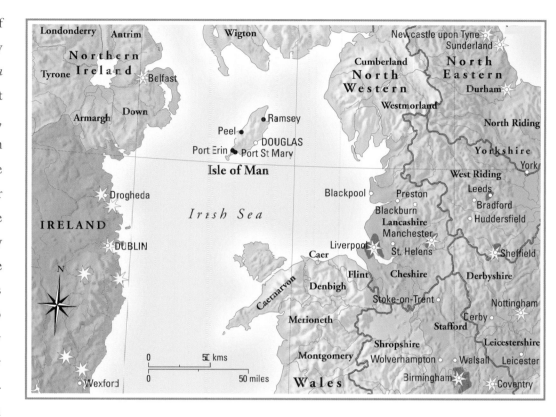

the ship arrived in Sydney, the first Australian on board was medical army officer Alan Frost who was appalled at the conditions. His report led to the court martial of the officer-in-charge, Lieutenant-Colonel William Scott. The passengers included Franz Stampfl, later athletics coach to the four-minute-mile runner Roger Bannister. The internees were dispersed to camps in Australia where their treatment was generally good. When the Japanese attacked Pearl Harbor in 1941, they were reclassified as "friendly aliens" and hundreds joined the Australian Army. One thousand "Dunera boys" settled in Australia after the war.

The British government subsequently decided to stop sending refugees abroad and decided to intern them in camps on the Isle of Man, the island in the Irish Sea which had been used by the British Government for the internment of enemy aliens in World War I. The camps were located in the Douglas area, Peel, Port Erin/Port St Mary and Ramsey, each holding several hundreds of prisoners. The same camps were also used to house Nazi sympathizers in the British Union of Fascists and the IRA, who were sometimes only separated from the Jewish refugees by a few strands of barbed wire. By the end of 1940, 14,000 "enemy aliens" were interned on the Isle of Man including the architect Sir Nikolaus Pevsner, the publisher Lord Weidenfeld, the artist Kurt Schwitters and the concert pianists Rawicz and Landauer. The men were segregated from their wives and families. Sometimes only the men were interned, the women and children being left to fend for themselves on the mainland. The spiritual and material welfare of the refugees was taken care of by the Chief Rabbi's Religious Emergency Council. Rabbi Dr. Solomon Schonfeld was a frequent visitor who inspected the makeshift synagogues on behalf of the Council. The Jewish Chronicle reported in November 1940, "In ordinary camps on a weekday there are more worshippers than in the Great Synagogue, London, on a Sabbath." The community was served by two kosher boarding houses that had been there before the war. After the panic ended, restrictions were lifted and most internees were allowed to return home.

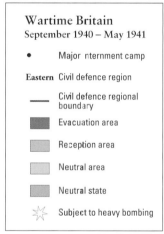

Wartime Britain
September 1940 – May 1941

•   Major internment camp

Eastern   Civil defence region

───   Civil defence regional boundary

▓   Evacuation area

▒   Reception area

░   Neutral area

▒   Neutral state

✳   Subject to heavy bombing

Britain chose to place what it called "Enemy Aliens" in special camps created within the towns of the Isle of Man. Many of the people sent there were of Jewish origin escaping Nazi persecution in Europe.

THE HOLOCAUST 1937–45

EVEN THE GRADUAL ELIMINATION OF JEWS FROM GERMAN, THEN AUSTRIAN, SOCIETY AND THEIR SYSTEMATIC PERSECUTION DID NOT PREPARE THE WORLD FOR THE MOST BARBARIC CRIME OF THE PAST MILLENNIUM, THE ATTEMPT TO EXTERMINATE A PEACEFUL POPULATION PERPETRATED BY A SUPPOSEDLY CIVILIZED SOCIETY.

There was nothing new about the anti-Jewish measures of the Holocaust – first demonization and incitement, removal of citizenship followed by all other rights, book-burning, imprisonment and eventually mass slaughter. All had been practiced before. The difference in this case was that the Nazis made it official government policy. The combined effect of these measures, perpetrated on a massive scale, brought about the destruction of European Jewry. The Nazis were extremely successful. Most of the Jewish communities of central and eastern Europe have disappeared forever.

The seeds of the Holocaust were sown in nineteenth-century Germany and Austria where Jews were denied access to many jobs and were not allowed to work in the civil service, for instance. As Adolf Hitler gradually rose from down-and-out veteran of World War I to up-and-coming politician of an anti-democratic, reactionary, right-wing political party, he realised that anti-Semitism would be a hugely popular vote-winner. The fact that he was anyway anti-Semitic by nature is borne out in his last will and testament, discovered after his suicide, in which he has the effrontery to claim that he never wanted war and blamed the Jews for World War II.

In discovering the benefits of anti-Semitism for fueling his political ambitions, Hitler was influenced by two sources. The first was the German racist nationalism propagated by such advocates as the politician Georg von Schönerer and others, by no means all of them pro-Nazi; some of them in later years would claim that Hitler looked Jewish. It must be admitted that eugenics, the "science" of racial characteristics, was fashionable at the time throughout Europe. The second key influence was that of Karl Lüger, Mayor of Vienna from 1897 until his death in

1910. Hitler lived in Vienna from 1907 to 1913 and attended many of the rallies addressed by Lüger whose populist demagoguery won him many fans. Hitler and the party ideologue, Alfred Rosenberg, were inspired by Schönerer-type racists, but Hitler's strategy and tactics, and those of his propaganda minister, Josef Göbbels, were heavily inspired by Lüger.

Hitler first attempted to seize power in 1923, in an abortive coup known as the "Beer Hall Putsch", staged in the Munich Beer Hall in which his National Socialist German Workers' Party comrades held their meetings. He was prosecuted and sentenced to five years' imprisonment, during which he wrote his famous "confession of faith' *Mein Kampf* (My Struggle). This hysterical and sometimes incomprehensible rant is full of anti-Semitic ravings.

In 1928, thanks largely to the post-war crisis suffered by Germany involving galloping inflation and the assertion purveyed by several political parties that democracy, in the form of the Weimar Republic, was "bad" for Germany, the Nazis gained many adherents and polled 810,000 votes. Hitler was now courted by German big business so he conveniently dropped the "socialist" element of his platform. In 1930, he did even better with six million votes and in 1932, the party reached its electoral zenith, polling 14 million votes and gaining 230 seats in the German parliament, the Reichstag. This was only 43 per cent of the vote and, in a proportional representation system, not enough for unilateral power but Hitler did a deal with former chancellor Von Papen and the president, 85-year-old Field Marshall Paul von Hindenberg, appointed Hitler as Chancellor. This enabled him to pass laws turning Germany into a dictatorship, Hitler held new elections in November that year, not surprisingly gaining 92 per cent of the vote. When Hindenberg died in 1934, Hitler elevated himself to the position of *Führer* (leader) of what he described as the "Thousand Year Reich."

Hitler acted cautiously at first, setting up the earliest concentration camps to house his political enemies, mainly socialists and communists, and those such as the (non-Jewish) comedian, Karl Valentin, who mocked him. On April 1, 1933, the paramilitary force known as the stormtroopers (*Sturmabteilung*) organized a national boycott of Jewish businesses and daubed swastikas and stars of David on Jewish shops, writing slogans such as "*kauf nicht bei Juden*". Less than a week later, Jews were barred from working as civil servants. A succession of petty anti-Jewish measures followed, culminating in the Nuremberg Laws passed in 1935 which took away most of the Jews' rights as citizens. They could not visit cafés and places of entertainment, frequent public baths or swimming pools, swim in rivers or enter public parks. Marriages between Jews and non-Jews were banned and some women were paraded in the streets wearing placards proclaiming "I slept with a Jew". The vote was taken away from them and they could not hold public office Josef Göbbels instituted a series of public book burnings, such as had not been held since the Middle Ages, the books being by and about Jews as well as other literature of which the Nazis disapproved. Goebbels screamed at the flames, "The soul of the German people can once again express itself! These flames light up a new age!" Soon, Jews were barred from the liberal professions and dismissed from their posts in universities.

Jews were excluded from competitive sports although, ironically, there were Jews among Germany's outstanding athletes. They included the high-jumper Gretel Bergmann, expelled from

Georg von Schönerer a landowner and politician. From 1879 leader of the deutschnationale Bewegung (the Pan-German Party) in Austria; fierce enemy of Austrian patriotism, the Catholic Church, and liberalism. He was a radical anti-Semite, advocating close connections between Austria and the German Reich, His ideas strongly influenced the young Adolf Hitler..

her athletics club in 1933 and several champion Jewish swimmers. The German Boxing Association expelled amateur champion Erich Seelig in April 1933. He later resumed his boxing career in the United States. Daniel Prenn, Germany's top-ranked tennis player, was removed from Germany's Davis Cup Team. In the 1936 Olympic Games, hosted by Germany, the authorities allowed the half-Jewish fencer Helene Mayer to compete, after much protest, and she won a silver medal. Like all the other German winners, she gave the Nazi salute on the podium. After the Olympics, Mayer returned to the United States. No fully Jewish athlete competed for Germany but eight other Jews, including five Hungarians, won medals. At that stage, even the Jews outside were not aware of the true depth of government-initiated antisemitism. In any case, such was the climate of anti-Semitism that pervaded Europe (including Britain and the United States) that many foreign correspondents found the anti-Semitic jokes and displays of posters to be mildly amusing.

In March of that year, the Germans re-occupied the Rhineland that had been demilitarized under the Treaty of Versailles after World War I. The British Prime Minister, Neville Chamberlain, then signed a pact with Hitler, allowing him to march into the Sudetenland, the German-speaking area of Czechoslovakia. This reassured Hitler that he could pursue his conquests with impunity. On March 11, 1938, the Germans marched into Austria to great acclaim from the crowds thronging the streets. The Anschluss (annexation) was wildly popular. Antisemitic actions were immediately introduced. Jews of all classes were rounded up and made to scrub the streets with corrosives that damaged their skin. Jewish shops were looted and synagogues stoned and burned. Mass arrests of Jews were initiated.

Attempts by Jews to escape from Nazi-occupied territory were inevitable. By 1938, 118,000 had fled, some to places, such as France and Holland, where they were eventually captured by the invading Germans; others, more fortunate, managed to get into the United Kingdom and the United States. Approximately 47,000 went to Palestine, then under the British Mandate. The Nazis fostered and encouraged emigration, as long as the refugees took no valuables with them.

The "refugee problem" now began to preoccupy the western powers and in July, 1938, U.S. President Roosevelt convened a conference on the subject at Evian-les-Bains, France. Most countries were unwilling to take more than a trickle of refugees. The United States would only agree to take 27,000 although it was subsequently discovered that there were 248,000 applications pending, 98 per cent of them from Jews. Britain attempted to stop any immigration to Palestine; it hoped thereby to win Arab support throughout the Middle East. This was a vain hope; the Mufti of Jerusalem was a fervent Nazi ally who did all he could to persuade the Arabs of Palestine and the Iraqis to side with Hitler. The Peel Commission, which had first met in 1937 to discuss Jewish immigration to Palestine, took over a year to reach its decision and limited immigration to 12,000 a year, to be increased "in case of an emergency" to a further 25,000 certificates, which of course never materialized.

In November, 1936, following Mussolini and Hitler's proclamation of the Rome-Berlin axis, Nuremberg-style laws were promulgated in Italy, followed on May 29, 1938, by Hungary under the dictator, Admiral Horthy, who had seized power in a coup d'etat. In October, 1938, Jews of Polish origin were expelled from the Reich. Many were Austrian nationals who had lived in the country since the Austrians had ruled Poland after the partitions in the eighteenth century. Five thousand of these Jews were stranded on the Polish border since the Poles, equally unfriendly to Jews, refused to admit them. A young man named Herschel Grynszpan who was living in Paris at the time, learned of the terrible plight of his parents who were among these Jews and rushed into the German Embassy where he shot a minor diplomat named Ernst von Rath.

This was just the excuse that the Nazis needed. The night of November 9–10 will always be known as *Krystalnacht* (Crystal Night or "the Night of the Broken Glass"). Well-organized looting and damage was perpetrated on Jewish property, conducted by German civilians in an orderly fashion. People were encouraged to loot and burn synagogues; more than 40 were destroyed in Austria alone. Some 35,000 Jews were rounded up and sent to concentration camps. Several thousand died there, though the survivors were released in 1939. Jews who tried to emigrate had to give everything they owned to the Nazis, instead of just paying a huge ransom as before. The Nazis even considered extorting money from world Jewry for the release of German Jews but were forced to abandon the project on the outbreak of war. Trapped in this hostile environment, with no countries willing to accept them, eight thousand Jews committed suicide.

Poster depicting the Holocaust from the Museum of War World II, Nattick, Massachussets.

On March 15 1939, Hitler invaded Czechoslovakia, the first time he had taken over a non-German nation, making Bohemia and Moravia into an integral part of the Reich and turning Slovakia into a puppet state ruled by the pro-Nazi priest, Father Tiso. When Germany invaded Poland on September 1 1939, Great Britain and France finally declared war on the Reich.

As soon as Poland, with its huge Jewish population, had been conquered, there were mass executions of Polish Jews. In fact, the alleged "invasion" by Polish soldiers which had been Germany's excuse for going to war to combat Polish 'aggression" had consisted of Jewish concentration camp victims, murdered and then dressed in Polish uniforms. Those who escaped death were herded into small ghettos in the major cities, where overcrowding and starvation prevailed, followed by disease and death.

The Nazis now controlled most of the Jewish population of Europe. For the first time since the eighteenth century, Jews were forced to wear a distinguishing mark the yellow star with

The German Empire
Late 1942

- Germany
- Allied to Germany
- German/Axis occupied
- Allied states or under Allied control
- Neutral states

N

North Cape

Murmansk

Narvik

FINLAND

L. Onega

Arkhangelsk

Norwegian Sea

Arctic Circle

Luleå

L. Ladoga

SOVIET UNION

Helsinki

Leningrad

Oslo

Stockholm

Estonia

Moscow

Edinburgh

North Sea

Baltic Sea

Latvia

Lithuania

REICHKOMMISSARIAT OSTLAND

Denmark
Copenhagen

Königberg

East Prussia

Dublin

IRELAND

UNITED KINGDOM

Amsterdam

Neth.

Hamburg

Berlin

Warsaw

Gen. Gov. of Poland

REICHKOMMISSARIAT UKRAINE

Kiev

London

Brussels

Belgium

GERMAN EMPIRE

Frankfurt

Prague

Prot. of Bohemia-Moravia

SLOVAKIA

Paris

Munich

Vienna

ATLANTIC OCEAN

France

Bern

SWITZ.

Geneva

Austria

Budapest

HUNGARY

ROMANIA

Crimea

Sebastopol

Milan

Banat

Bucharest

Danube

Black Sea

Genoa

Venice

CROATIA

Belgrade

Serbia

Marseille

Adriatic Sea

Mont.

Sofia

BULGARIA

Istanbul

PORTUGAL

SPAIN

Corsica

ITALY

Rome

ALBANIA

TURKEY

Lisbon

Madrid

Sardinia

Taranto

Greece

Aegean Sea

to Italy

Cyprus

Balearic Is.

Athens

Gibraltar
to Britain

Mediterranean

Algiers

Bone

Tunis

Sicily

Crete

LEBANON

Sea

Malta
to Britain

ISRAEL

French North Africa

Tripoli

Libya *to Italy*

Benghazi

Libya

EGYPT

the word "Jew" in the appropriate language written in the centre. Between 1939 and 1941, they continued to deport German and Austrian Jews to the ghettos they had created all over Poland and subsequently in Lithuania and Latvia.

The Germans were now faced with a dilemma. Thanks to the war they had started they could no longer get rid of their Jews through emigration and their numbers in German lands were increasing due to conquests in eastern Europe. Mass shootings of Jews began in 1941, mostly in the parts of the Soviet Union that had been conquered by the Germans. In Babi Yar, a ravine on the outskirts of Kiev, on September 29 and 30, a special squad of the SS supported by other German units, collaborators and the Ukranian police, murdered 33,771 Jewish civilians, the largest single massacre of the Holocaust. The Nazis always had willing collaborators, eager to help them murder Jews wherever they went. Local Romanians in the southern Ukranian city of Odessa were handed machine-guns by the Nazis which were used to massacre 25,000 Jews and this pattern was repeated in Poland, Latvia, Lithuania and Byelorussia.

The decision to embark on the "Final solution to the Jewish question" was taken at the Wannsee conference held on January 20 1942. The plan consisted of deporting the entire Jewish population of Europe to German-occupied areas of the Soviet Union. Jews who could work would labour on road-building projects, in the course of which they would die, the remnant being annihilated after completion of the projects. This aspect of the plan was never fully implemented since it depended on Germany winning its war against the Soviet Union. Instead, labour camps/extermination camps (such as Auschwitz-Birkenau) or pure death camps (such as Chelmno, Treblinka, Maidanek, Sobibór and Belzec) were set up to exterminate the Jews. Between 1941 and 1944, more than two million Jews were murdered in the gas chambers of Auschwitz alone; a further two million were killed at the other death camps. In the labour camps in Germany, France and Austria, Jews and non-Jews were worked, starved and tortured to death. News of the camps finally leaked to the incredulous West through escapees. The fate of the Jews being "relocated to the East" was something of which the inhabitants of the ghettos were becoming well aware. On July 22 1942, the order came from Hans Frank, Governor-General of Poland, to liquidate the 500,000 Jews of the Warsaw Ghetto, a daily quota of 4500. Nine months later, those who were left determined to fight to the death. Battle commenced on April 18 and the astonished Nazis retreated, setting fire to the ghetto.

After the war, when the Allies realized that the stories of atrocities were no exaggeration, they determined to put the perpetrators on trial as war criminals. The Nuremberg Trials were later followed by prosecutions in the German Federal Republic. The Communist countries executed many such criminals, including Hans Frank. Nevertheless, many escaped the net, through sympathizers who hid them.

The Nazi Empire, at its peak, controlled most of western Europe and large regions of eastern Europe. Within this area lay the killing grounds and death camps, specifically designed for enemies of the Nazi state.

JEWISH RESISTANCE

THE JEWS HAD ALWAYS BEEN PORTRAYED AS COWARDLY AND UNRESISTING BUT THE NAZIS WERE OFTEN SURPRISED TO DISCOVER THAT THIS WAS NOT THE CASE. THERE HAVE BEEN MANY JEWISH RESISTANCE MOVEMENTS TO PERSECUTION AND OPPRESSION OVER THE CENTURIES.

Jews have done what they could to ward off their oppressors throughout the ages, from the siege of Masada in 73 CE to the attack at Clifford's Tower in York in 1190, both of which ended in mass suicide. Since the narrative of wars is always told by the victors, many such battles have gone unrecorded. Simeon Bar Kochba, who led Jewish resistance and crushed the forces of the Roman Emperor Hadrian in a surprise victory in 132 CE, had his exploits recorded by his mentor Rabbi Akiba and by the historian Josephus.

During the Crusades, some of the attacks on Jews in the Rhineland were defended. In Mainz, for instance, according to Solomon bar Shimshon, a chronicler of the atrocities writing 50 years later in 1096 "young and old put on their armour ... At their head was Rabbi Kalonymos ben Meshullam, head of the community."

During World War II, Jews joined the resistance and the partisans in large numbers where this was possible, some partisan groups being as anti-Semitic as the Germans, particularly in the Ukraine and Poland. In Soviet Russia, Jewish resistance movements were part of the general Soviet resistance. Of the partisans, the best known groups are the Tobias Belski division and the Vilna Avengers. By the end of the war, the forests of Belarus had become a haven for escaping Jews. There are estimated to have been 120,000 Jewish partisans in the USSR and 33,000 in Poland. In France, as many as 30 per cent of Jews were involved in the resistance and in occupied Algiers, a Jewish fighter, José Aboulker, organized the resistance enabling the American landing on November 8 1942.

The Nazis kept their plans as secret as possible so that their victims could not know the fate that awaited them, and the outside world was incredulous that in the modern day and age, something as horrifying as the "Final Solution" could be perpetrated. But in the ghettos, where *aktionen*, round-ups of Jews to be "resettled" in the East were taking place regularly, the truth could not be hidden. This was especially true in the Warsaw Ghetto. When the Germans came to finally "liquidate" the ghetto in July, 1942, to their utter amazement they were met with armed resistance and had to retreat twice. Jews had managed to smuggle arms in from the outside and improvised other weapons such as Molotov cocktails. The Jewish fighters were under no illusions; they could never overcome the German forces but were determined to die in battle. On April 19 1943, the ghetto was besieged. Hand-to-hand combat ensued. Buildings were set on fire and the bunkers and sewers in which the fighters hid were blown up. On the 28th and last day of the fighting the ghetto synagogue was dynamited. Many Jews also succeeded in infiltrating the German forces and doing damage from within.

In the Vilna ghetto, the battle of the barricades in September 1943, was fought by a Jewish resistance group calling itself The Vilna Avengers. Even though unsuccessful, it was still the preferred course of action for those still fit enough to resist. Dr. Elhanan Elkes, chair of the "Council of Elders" in the Kovno ghetto, exhorted Jews to fight. "This is the honourable road that we should choose. I will bear all the responsibility – it is for the good of the remnant of Lithuanian Jewry and the Jewish people as a whole."

The Warsaw Ghetto fighters and their leader, Mordecai Anilewicz, were immortalized in Emmanuel Ringelblum's diaries hidden in milk churns and buried, being discovered accidentally after the war. Sobibor, near Lublin, was one of the earliest and smallest of the extermination camps, built in March, 1942. It was built in March 1942, and killed around 260,000 Jews, mostly from Poland and the occupied Soviet Union but some from Western Europe, including transports of children. On October 14 1943, some 300 Jewish inmates rebelled, killing several of their SS supervisors and the Ukrainian guards. Several inmates were killed during the rebellion or during the escape attempt. All who stayed behind were executed the next day and the camp was liquidated. There was an uprising in Treblinka, the camp to which the Warsaw Ghetto victims were brought, on August 2 1943. Treblinka II, like the first such camp, Kulmhof (Chelmno) and Sobibor, was a camp the sole purpose of which was extermination. The memory of the ghetto fighters and other Jewish resistance groups is perpetuated in Kibbutz Lohamei Hagettaot (the Ghetto Fighters' Kibbutz) in western Gallilee, founded by survivors from the ghettos, which has its own holocaust museum dedicated to the fighters.

Jewish Resistance in East Europe
1940–44

- ● Concentration camps
- ● Ghettoes where Jews organise uprisings against Germans
- ▬ Partisan groups in German-occupied territories

Many Jews, escaping the Nazi death squads, flee into the forests of eastern Europe where they formed resistance units, usually as part of the Soviet sponsored partisans.

JEWISH SERVICEMEN 1939–45

DESPITE ANTI-SEMITIC SLURS TO THE CONTRARY, JEWS HAVE ALWAYS "DONE THEIR BIT" FIGHTING FOR THEIR COUNTRIES AND IN WARS OF INDEPENDENCE AND MANY HAVE BEEN DECORATED FOR BRAVERY. JEWS STILL SERVE IN THE MILITARY IN THEIR HOME COUNTRIES, EVEN OUTSIDE ISRAEL.

The Star of David, one of many on Allied graves of the fallen in World War II. This one is in the Arlington National Cemetery, Virginia, U.S.A.

Jews usually avoided military service under the feudal system due to their privileged position as direct servants of the crown. This was not the case in Tsarist Russia, where conscription was introduced for Jews in 1827. It was not universal which was just as well as a Jew had to serve for 25 years. Jewish communities had to fulfil a quota of men, some of whom were sent off as young as 12 years of age. Despite the hardships and, in most cases, being cut off from any kind of Jewish life, a Jewish order of service has been discovered that includes a prayer for the welfare of the Tsar.

In the free world, Jews had joined the armed forces ever since their emancipation in the eighteenth century, and there are many records of Jewish service at every level, from private to general, in the British and American armies.

One such conscript was Joseph Trumpeldor (1880–1920). Trumpeldor was born in a small town in the northern Caucasus and witnessed the model of collective communal life at a nearby farming commune established by followers of the writer Leo Tolstoy. Trumpeldor realized that this was the perfect model for settling the land of Israel which, at the time, was mostly swampland in the north and desert in the south. Trumpeldor lost an arm while fighting in the Russo-Japanese war. He reached the Holy Land in 1912 and worked for a while at the first kibbutz, Deganya, and helped to defend the Jewish settlements in the lower Galilee against Arab marauders. He was deported to Egypt in 1914, due to his refusal to join the Turkish army or take Turkish citizenship. In Alexandria, he initiated the formation of a legion of volunteers drawn from the other Jewish deportees to help the British to liberate the country from the Turks.

The British allowed the formation of this first Jewish brigade, known as the "Zion Mule Corps", of which Trumpeldor became the deputy commander and which participated in the Gallipoli campaign of 1915. Between 1915 and 1919 Trumpeldor travelled widely, spending time in England and Russia, promoting the organization of Jewish regiments to fight the Turks and Jewish self-defense units to protect Jewish settlements in Palestine. He was a founder of the He-Halutz movement whose aim was the training of young Jews for settling in Erez Israel.

In January 1920 he helped organize settlements in the northern Galilee to which were being increasingly attacked by the Arabs. He was mortally wounded at Tel Hai where a monument to him was erected in 1934. His dying words were "Ein davar, tov lamut be'ad arzenu" (Never mind, it is good to die for our country.)

Another such fighter for Jewish rights in Palestine was Sander Hadad (Aleksander Krinkin), born in Russia in 1859, who came to Palestine in 1872. He was the lead defender of the Jewish settlement of Petah Tiqva. He died in 1899, weakened from skirmishes with Bedouin attackers.

Some Jewish men joining the British Army in World War II.

During World War II, Jews were eager to serve in the Allied armies. There were 60,000 British Jews on active service, of whom 1,150 were killed. It is estimated that a fifth of the soldiers fighting for the USSR were Jewish. More than half a million American and Canadian Jews donned uniforms, some of them enlisting in Canada before the United States joined the war at the end of 1941. Five thousand fought for the partisans in Yugoslavia and eight thousand in Greece. In Palestine, 26,000 Jews volunteered, many fighting in the Jewish Brigade. In 1944, the British parachuted a handful of young Palestinian Jews into occupied Europe to establish contact with the Jewish underground. Hannah Szenes was parachuted with fellow soldiers, Yoel Palgi and Peretz Goldstein, into occupied Yugoslavia. They were all captured almost immediately, tortured and executed. Enzo Sereni was captured by the Germans and executed in Dachau in 1940.

The most extraordinary aspect of Jewish military involvement in World War II is the number of Jews who served in Hitler's army. Research on the subject was first embarked upon by Bryan Mark Rigg in the 1990s. Rigg's ten-year research involved interviewing more than 400 of these ex-servicemen. Those who could get away with it – many of them only a half- or quarter-Jewish – joined up to escape discrimination, some even reaching the rank of colonel. Rigg concluded that over 100,000 soldiers in Hitler's army would have been considered Jewish under German racial laws. Even stranger, a handsome soldier with a typically "Aryan" face, wearing the typical German metal helmet, was used on a recruiting poster; his name was Hermann Goldberg.

Jews continue to serve in the armed forces of the free world. Although figures are kept confidential, at least nine Jews serving in the U.S. forces have been killed in the Iraq war.

Voyage of St Louis and the Exodus

The episodes of the ships full of Jews escaping the Holocaust who tried to land in United States and Palestine but which were sent back to Europe are among the most shameful in the West's history.

The Nazis had been trying to rid Germany of its Jews since they came to power in 1933. The Central Office for Jewish Emigration, headed by Adolf Eichmann, was established in Vienna in 1938 and it introduced quotas for the number of Jews it demanded leave the country. This was also another way of extorting money. Rich Jews were to finance the emigration of poorer ones and no one could take anything of value with them. In early 1939, the Reich Central Office for Jewish Emigration was established with the same motive.

The Evian Conference was convened on the initiative of U.S. President Franklin D. Roosevelt in July 1938 to discuss the problem of Jewish refugees. Delegates from 32 countries deliberated for nine days in Evian-les-Bains in France, close to the Swiss border. The conference was, in fact, a smokescreen for doing nothing. Roosevelt refrained from suggesting Palestine as a possible haven for Jews and, in exchange, the British did not condemn the United States' for refusing to accept refugees. The conference did not even pass a resolution condemning the German treatment of Jews. This delighted Hitler and was widely used in Nazi propaganda.

The Hamburg–America Line, now run by Nazi sympathisers, was the owner of the *St. Louis*, a ship chartered in 1939 to sail to Cuba. The majority of the 936 passengers were Jewish. The U.S. State Department, and some Jewish welfare organizations became aware eight days before the ship was due to sail that its passengers would probably not be allowed to land in Cuba. Although most passengers held landing certificates issued by the Cuban Director General of Immigration they were not told that Cuban President Federico Laredo Bru had revoked the certificates due to an internal power struggle, involving the corrupt Director-general of the Immigration Office Manuel Benitez Gonzalez. Pro-Fascist elements in Cuba, encouraged by Nazi agents, also bitterly opposed the admission of Jewish refugees.

When the St. Louis arrived in Havana harbour on May 27, only 28 passengers were allowed to land, six of whom were not Jewish. An additional passenger ended up in a Havana hospital after a suicide attempt. The ship sailed on to Miami but was not allowed to dock. Eventually,

Approximately 4,500 Jews aboard the refugee ship *Exodus* were barred from landing in British-controlled Palestine in 1947.

it was forced to return to Europe. The American Jewish Joint Distribution Committee negotiated with European governments to allow the passengers to be admitted to Great Britain, the Netherlands, Belgium and France. Many of those who ended up in continental Europe subsequently perished in the concentration camps. The voyage of the *St. Louis* attracted a great deal of media attention but no newspapers suggested that the refugees be admitted into the United States.

Two smaller ships also made for Cuba in May, 1939 carrying Jewish refugees. The French ship, *Le Flandre*, carried 104 passengers and the *Orduña*, a British vessel, 72 passengers. Like the *St. Louis*, these ships were not permitted to dock. *Le Flandre* returned to its home port in France; the *Orduña* sailed on to central America where its passengers were eventually admitted to the U.S.-controlled Panama Canal Zone. Most were later allowed in to the United States, despite massive hostility to admitting Jewish refugees. For instance, the Wagner-Rogers bill, which would have permitted the admission of 20,000 Jewish children from Germany in addition to the existing meagre quota, was allowed to fail with President Roosevelt's tacit approval.

Even after the war began, emigrant ships still sailed from Germany. In September 1940, the Committee for Sending Jews Overseas chartered three ships, the *Milos*, the *Pacific*, and the *Atlantic*, to transport 3,600 Jews from Vienna, Danzig and Prague to Palestine, sailing from the Romanian port of Tulcea. The Pacific reached Palestinian waters on November 1 1940, followed by the *Milos* a few days later. The ships were intercepted by the British Royal Navy and taken to Haifa. British High Commissioner for Palestine, Sir Harold MacMichael, ordered the refugees be sent to the British colonies of Mauritius and Trinidad. The refugees from the three ships were transferred to another ship, the *Patria*,for the journey to Mauritius. It only had enough lifeboats for half the passengers and crew. The deportation was opposed by the Haganah who planted a bomb on board to disable the ship and prevent it from leaving Haifa. The effects of the explosion were miscalculated and the bomb caused the ship to sink in under 15 minutes, trapping hundreds in the hold; 260 were killed. The survivors were subsequently permitted to remain in Palestine, the only such example of compassion shown by the British during the War.

Opposite: Jews attempting to escape persecution in Nazi Europe or find a new home in Israel took to the sea. Their denial of landing rights was a sad episode in the history of the West.

The fate of the *Struma* was even worse. It was chartered in 1942 by the Zionist Betar movement to carry Jewish refugees from Romania to Palestine. The ship was unseaworthy; the engine had been rescued from a sunken vessel and broke down as the ship moved through the Black Sea, towed from Istanbul, where its passengers were refused entry, through the Bosporus out to the Black Sea, where it was left adrift. Within hours, it was torpedoed and sunk by Soviet submarine SC 213 on February 24, killing 768 men, women and children, with only one survivor, one of the largest losses of life at sea during World War II. On July 11 1947, the renamed *Exodus 1947*, a former U.S. tramp steamer, left France to take camp survivors to Palestine where the passengers were not allowed to land. Following a hunger strike and wide media coverage, the Royal Navy seized the ship, boarded it using brute force and killing several of the crew. Media coverage of the human ordeal even came to the attention of the United Nations Special Committee on Palestine (UNSCOP). After three weeks of stand-off, during which the prisoners on the ships held fast under difficult conditions, rejecting offers of alternative destinations, the ships were sailed to Hamburg. There they were transported to DP camps, behind barbed wire, guarded by Germans. Within a year, over half the original *Exodus 1947* passengers had attempted to emigrate illegally to Palestine and were held in prison camps on Cyprus where they remained until January 1949 when Great Britain formally recognized the State of Israel.

On September 8 1947, British troops forcibly disembarked Jewish immigrants from the British troop-carrier "*Ocean Vigour*" at Hamburg. These were some of those who had tried to sail to Palestine on the "*Exodus 1947*."

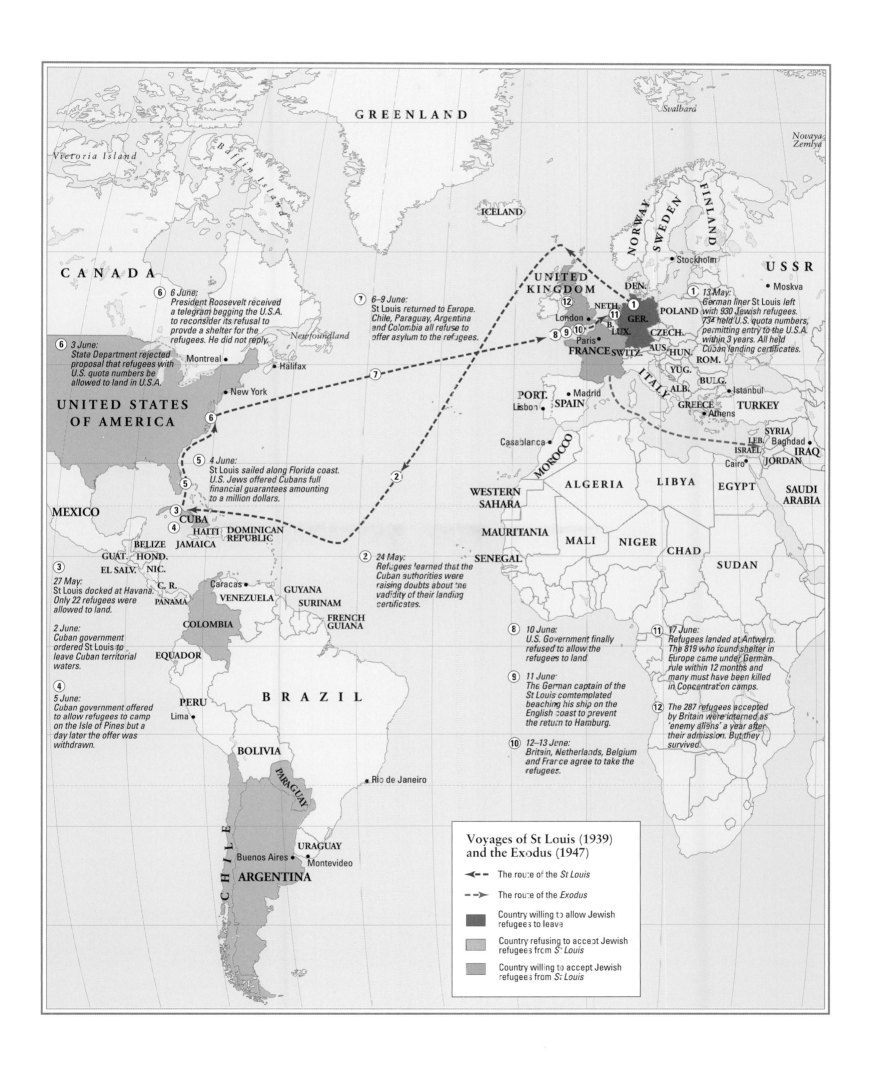

GREENLAND

Svalbard

Victoria Island

Baffin Island

ICELAND

Novaya Zemlya

NORWAY

SWEDEN

FINLAND

• Stockholm

USSR

UNITED KINGDOM

DEN.

• Moskva

CANADA

⑥ 6 June:
President Roosevelt received a telegram begging the U.S.A. to reconsider its refusal to provide a shelter for the refugees. He did not reply.

⑦ 6–9 June:
St Louis returned to Europe. Chile, Paraguay, Argentina and Colombia all refuse to offer asylum to the refugees.

NETH.

① **① 13 May:**
German liner St Louis left with 930 Jewish refugees. 734 held U.S. quota numbers, permitting entry to the U.S.A. within 3 years. All held Cuban landing certificates.

London •
⑪
B.
⑫
GER.
POLAND

⑧ ⑨ ⑩
Paris •
LUX.
CZECH.

⑥ 3 June:
State Department rejected proposal that refugees with U.S. quota numbers be allowed to land in U.S.A.

Newfoundland

FRANCE
SWITZ.
AUS.
HUN.
ROM.

Montreal •
• Halifax

⑦

PORT.
SPAIN
• Madrid
Lisbon •

YUG.
BULG.
ITALY
ALB.
• Istanbul
GREECE
TURKEY
• Athens

UNITED STATES OF AMERICA

• New York

SYRIA
LEB. Baghdad
ISRAEL
IRAQ
JORDAN
Cairo •

⑥

Casablanca •
MOROCCO

⑤ 4 June:
St Louis sailed along Florida coast. U.S. Jews offered Cubans full financial guarantees amounting to a million dollars.

⑤

②

WESTERN SAHARA

ALGERIA

LIBYA

EGYPT

SAUDI ARABIA

MEXICO

⑤
③
CUBA
④ HAITI DOMINICAN
REPUBLIC

MAURITANIA

MALI

NIGER

CHAD

BELIZE HOND.
GUAT.
JAMAICA
EL SALV. NIC.

SENEGAL

SUDAN

② 24 May:
Refugees learned that the Cuban authorities were raising doubts about the validity of their landing certificates.

③
27 May:
St Louis docked at Havana. Only 22 refugees were allowed to land.

C. R.
Caracas •
PANAMA
VENEZUELA
GUYANA
SURINAM

2 June:
Cuban government ordered St Louis to leave Cuban territorial waters.

COLOMBIA

FRENCH GUIANA

⑧ 10 June:
U.S. Government finally refused to allow the refugees to land.

⑪ 17 June:
Refugees landed at Antwerp. The 819 who found shelter in Europe came under German rule within 12 months and many must have been killed in Concentration camps.

EQUADOR

④
5 June:
Cuban government offered to allow refugees to camp on the Isle of Pines but a day later the offer was withdrawn.

PERU

BRAZIL

⑨ 11 June:
The German captain of the St Louis contemplated beaching his ship on the English coast to prevent the return to Hamburg.

⑫ The 287 refugees accepted by Britain were interned as 'enemy aliens' a year after their admission. But they survived.

Lima •

BOLIVIA

⑩ 12–13 June:
Britain, Netherlands, Belgium and France agree to take the refugees.

PARAGUAY

• Rio de Janeiro

CHILE

URAGUAY
Buenos Aires •
• Montevideo
ARGENTINA

Voyages of St Louis (1939) and the Exodus (1947)

◄--- The route of the *St Louis*

--➤ The route of the *Exodus*

■ Country willing to allow Jewish refugees to leave

■ Country refusing to accept Jewish refugees from *St Louis*

■ Country willing to accept Jewish refugees from *St Louis*

JEWS IN BRITAIN

JEWS HAVE FLOURISHED IN BRITAIN IN EVERY SPHERE OF LIFE,
FROM THE HUMBLEST TO THE MOST EXHALTED. THEY HAVE
ALSO CONTRIBUTED GENEROUS FINANCIAL SUPPORT TO BRITISH
INSTITUTIONS, FROM MUSEUMS TO CHARITABLE FOUNDATIONS.

The Lord Mayor of London elected in 2008, Alderman Ian Luder at his inaugural banquet at the Guildhall on November 10. He is one of a number of Jewish Lords Mayor of the capital city.

Most of the remaining restrictions on Jews in Britain were lifted under the first Jewish Disabilities Bill, passed in 1831. Subsequent Jewish Disabilities Bills had a rough ride through the Houses of Parliament. The first Jewish M.P. to be elected was Lionel de Rothschild, M.P. who was elected in 1847 by the City of London but it took another 11 years for him to be able to take his seat, during which time he was re-elected several times, the House of Lords repeatedly refusing to allow the wording of the oath of allegiance, "upon the true faith of a Christian" to be changed. The first Jew to be admitted to the bar was Francis Henry Goldsmid (1808–1878) who was also the first Jewish judge. This member of the Goldsmid banking family entered parliament in 1860 as Member of Parliament for Reading which he represented until his death. Francis Goldsmid was the founder of the Jews Free School and made generous endowments to University College London, the only British university at the time that was avowedly secular.

Goldsmid's nephew, Sir David Salomons (1797–1873), was the first Jewish Sheriff of the City of London. He served two terms as Lord Mayor of London and was another early Jewish member of parliament. His father was a founder of what is now the NatWest Bank and a member of the London Stock Exchange. In 1839, he became High Sheriff of Kent, the county in which his Broomhill estate was located near Tunbridge Wells. In 1851, David Salomons stood as a Liberal candidate at a by-election in the Greenwich constituency. When asked to take the oath he did so but omitted the Christian phrases. He was asked to withdraw, and did so on the second request, but he returned three days later, on July 21, 1851. In the debate that followed, Salomons defended his presence but was removed by the Sergeant-at-Arms and fined £500 for having voted illegally in three divisions of the House. When the law was changed in 1858, Lionel de Rothschild became the first Jewish M.P. to legally take his seat, having been elected in 1857. In the 1859 General Election, David Salomons was re-elected for Greenwich and served as the constituency's M.P. until his death in 1873.

Since then, Jewish members of parliament have represented all of the British political parties and have served as ministers in many governments. They include Emmanuel (Manny) Shinwell (1884–1986) and Leslie Hore-Belisha (1893–1957) both of whom served in various posts in the wartime

London c. 1900

Cities in Britain have served as the focal point of Jewish life, perhaps no more so than the city of London. Many Jews escaping persecution in Europe settled in London's East End.

coalition government and the post-World War II Labour Government, Michael Howard (1941–, Home Secretary, 1993–1997), Malcolm Rifkind (1946–, various posts and Foreign Secretary 1995–1997), and the Foreign Secretary at the time of writing, David Miliband. The most famous "Jewish" politician, however, is Disraeli who was not Jewish, in fact, because his father had him converted to Christianity at the age of 13, due to a dispute with Bevis Marks synagogue. Benjamin Disraeli, 1st Earl of Beaconsfield, KG, PC, FRS (1804–1881). Disraeli had a brilliant political career, serving in the Conservative Government for 30 years and twice becoming Prime Minister. He was also an extremely popular novelist, his novels containing many sympathetic portraits of Jews. Disraeli's close relationship with Queen Victoria, who preferred him to all her other ministers, is well-known. Disraeli's two greatest achievements were the creation of the modern Conservative Party after the Corn Laws schism of 1846 and his involvement in the creation of the Suez Canal.

Since Disraeli's time, despite occasional hostility, Jews have prospered in the United Kingdom and distinguished themselves in every sphere of public life. The contribution made by the refugees from Nazi Europe is particularly noteworthy. Four of the most important are the Nobel prize-winner in 1946, the chemist Sir Ernst Boris Chain (1906–1979) who did crucial work on the development of penicillin, Professor Sir Herman Bondi (1919–2005), the pure mathematician, Fellow of the Royal Society, and "father" of the Thames Barrier, Professor Nicholas Kurti (1908–1998), an expert on low-temperature physics and Professor Sir Joseph Rotblat (1908–2005) a chemist. Both Kurti and Rotblat worked on Britain's atom bomb. The Jewish contribution to the performing and plastic arts in Britain is so immense that there is no room here to list all of the writers, painters, sculptors, actors, movie-makers and musicians of every generation. Much information about the history of prominent Jews can be found in the Jewish Museums in London and Manchester, containing collections of Jewish ceremonial art and recording Jewish history since the Norman conquest.

JEWS IN THE SOVIET UNION

JEWS WERE SO PERSECUTED UNDER THE TSARIST REGIME THAT IT IS NOT SURPRISING THAT THEY WELCOMED THE DISSIDENT MOVEMENTS OF THE EARLY TWENTIETH CENTURY. THEY WERE ACTIVE IN ALL LEFT-WING MOVEMENTS, INCLUDING COMMUNISM, DESPITE STALIN'S PERSECUTIONS.

Lev Davidovich Bronstein (Leon Trotsky) was born on October 26, 1879, son of a Jewish farmer, in southern Ukraine.

Opposite: Jewish intellectuals played a leading role in radical groups under the Tsarist regime and were an important part of the Russian revolution

The Jewish Labour Movement swept through eastern Europe in the late nineteenth century, its various divisions and branches embracing all forms of socialism, including bolshevism – though rarely anarchism – in short, any ideology that might free them from the restrictions of the Pale of Settlement and the persecutions of the pogroms and the Black Hundreds. One of the earliest such movements, the General Jewish Labour Union, known as the Bund, was founded in 1897. It was in direct opposition to the Zionist movements, such as Hibbat Zion, which emerged after the pogroms of 1881–83. This was to become the trend in Jewish political movements worldwide, which were to be split henceforth between Zionists and anti-Zionists, the Zionists generally being the most popular among the Jewish population.

From the outset, Jews led the revolutionary parties, Yuli Martov and Leon Trotsky headed the Social Democrats and G. Gershuni was one of the founders of the Socialist Revolutionary Party. During the Russia Civil War of 1917 to 1921, atrocities were committed by both the Red and the White armies. Units of the Red Army retreating before the Germans in northern Ukraine in 1918 and before the Poles in 1920 terrorized the Jews they encountered. Symon Petlyura (1879–1926), a Ukranian nationalist, led a peasant's army that attacked the Jews of the Ukraine, for which he was assassinated by a Jew when visiting Paris. One of the slogans of the White Army was "Fight the Jews and save Russia". As a result, able-bodied Jewish men formed themselves into self-defense bands to save their communities from attack, notably in Odessa and elsewhere in the Ukraine and Byelorussia (today's Belarus).

The founder of the Red Army, Leon Trotsky (Lev Davidovitch Bronstein, 1879–1940) was a key figure in the Bolshevik seizure of power, second only to Lenin in the early stages of Soviet communist rule. He

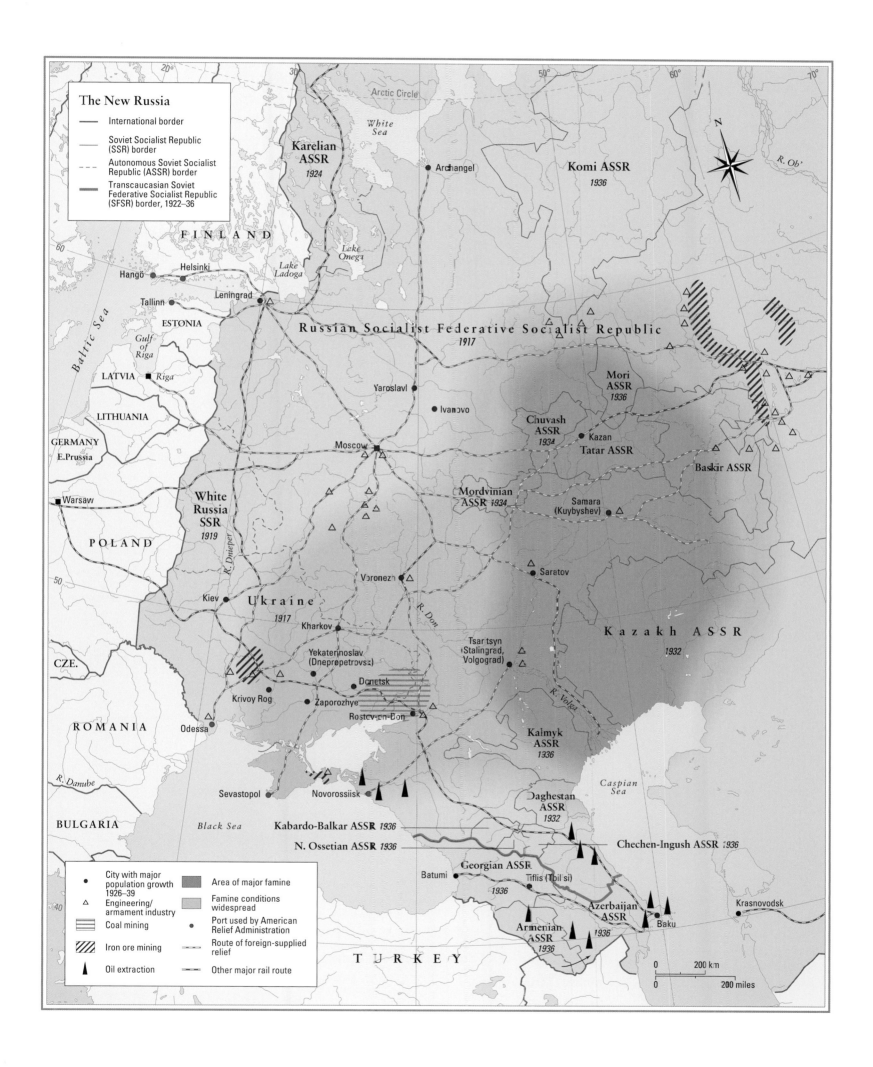

The New Russia

— International border

— Soviet Socialist Republic (SSR) border

- - - Autonomous Soviet Socialist Republic (ASSR) border

━━ Transcaucasian Soviet Federative Socialist Republic (SFSR) border, 1922–36

● City with major population growth 1926–39

△ Engineering/ armament industry

▤ Coal mining

▨ Iron ore mining

◣ Oil extraction

▨ Area of major famine

▨ Famine conditions widespread

● Port used by American Relief Administration

⋯ Route of foreign-supplied relief

═ Other major rail route

Karelian ASSR *1924*

Komi ASSR *1936*

Arctic Circle

White Sea

Archangel

FINLAND

Lake Onega

Lake Ladoga

Hangö   Helsinki

Leningrad

Tallinn

ESTONIA

Baltic Sea

Gulf of Riga

LATVIA   ■ Riga

LITHUANIA

GERMANY

E.Prussia

■ Warsaw

POLAND

CZE.

ROMANIA

BULGARIA

R. Danube

Russian Socialist Federative Socialist Republic *1917*

Yaroslavl

● Ivanovo

Mori ASSR *1936*

Chuvash ASSR *1934*

Kazan
Tatar ASSR

Baskir ASSR

Moscow

Mordvinian ASSR *1934*

Samara (Kuybyshev)

White Russia SSR *1919*

R. Dnieper

Kiev

Ukraine *1917*

Kharkov

Yekaterinoslav (Dnepropetrovsk)

Krivoy Rog   Zaporozhye

Donetsk

Rostov-on-Don

Odessa

Sevastopol   Novorossiisk

Black Sea

Voronezh

R. Don

Saratov

R. Volga

Kazakh ASSR *1932*

Tsaritsyn (Stalingrad, Volgograd)

Kalmyk ASSR *1936*

Caspian Sea

Daghestan ASSR *1932*

Kabardo-Balkar ASSR *1936*

N. Ossetian ASSR *1936*

Chechen-Ingush ASSR *1936*

Georgian ASSR *1936*

Batumi

Tiflis (Tbilisi)

Azerbaijan ASSR *1936*

Baku

Krasnovodsk

Armenian ASSR *1936*

TURKEY

N

R. Ob'

0   200 km

0   200 miles

lost out to Stalin in the power struggle that followed Lenin's death and was assassinated while in exile in Mexico on Stalin's orders. Other prominent Jewish Bolsheviks included Lev Kamenev (1883–1936), briefly nominal head of the Soviet state in 1917 and later chairman of the Politburo and Grigori Zinoviev (1883–1936). Zinoviev lived in political exile for much of the pre-revolutionary period, and travelled with Lenin on the sealed train that brought him back to Russia in 1917.

Zinoviev, Lenin and Kamenev joined Leon Trotsky and others in 1917 in plotting against the government led by Alexander Kerensky. Zinoviev became the new editor of Pravda, reaching the height of his power in 1923 when, with Stalin and Kamenev, he became one of the triumvirate that planned to take over from Lenin. After Lenin's death in 1924, Zinoviev joined with Kamenev and Stalin to keep out Leon Trotsky. When Stalin got rid of Trotsky he felt strong enough to plot the downfall of Zinoviev and Kamenev, claiming they were creating disunity in the party. He had them expelled from the Central Committee and in 1936, Zinoviev and Kamenev were charged with forming a terrorist organization to kill Joseph Stalin and other leaders of the government. They were found guilty and executed in Moscow in 1936.

The Bolsheviks at first granted equal status to the Jews and through its war on anti-Semitism, the new regime gained the sympathy of the Jewish masses but they, like everyone else, were to suffer economic ruin as a result of the devastation wrought by the Revolution, the privatization of property, collectivization and the Western powers' boycotts of the Bolshevik regime. This was then followed by the famine that swept the Ukraine and Byelorussia in the 1920s.

Bolshevism was determined to eradicate any vestige of religion among the entire Russian population. As a result, a special Jewish Section of the Bolshevik regime, known as Yevsektsia, was set up to "impose the proletarian dictatorship upon the Jews". Its first action, in 1919, was to dissolve all Jewish national and religious organizations and confiscate their property. Religious instruction was banned and synagogues were turned into storehouses, workshops or – as in Kiev – theatres. Hebrew was also banned, the most appropriate language for the emergent secular Jewish nation being Yiddish. The Yiddish language was even distorted so as to break the link with Hebrew, the language of prayer and of Zionism. From the outset the regime was hostile to Zionism and subsequently to Israel. Zionist organizations, including Labor Zionists such as Poale Zion, were banned in the late 1920s. In 1921, a group of Jewish writers, including Hayyim Nahman Bialik (1873–1934), were allowed to emigrate, first settling in Germany and later moving to Palestine. The Soviet Habimah Jewish theater, founded in 1917, left the Soviet Union in 1926. For a short time, Yiddish schools were opened, and many Yiddish publications and the Yiddish theater existed until the outbreak of hostilities in World War II.

With the introduction of the Five-year Plan (1927–32), the authorities attempted to liquidate the class of self-employed Jews by forcing them to migrate to the interior from which they had been banned under the Tsars, enabling them to settle the land and moving them to the industrial heartlands of the Don and Byelorussia. In 1928, the Soviet government decided to direct Jewish internal migration into Birobidzhan, a bleak swamp in the Soviet Far East. In 1934, the region was proclaimed an Autonomous Jewish Region whose official language would be Yiddish. Today, few Jews remain in the region and Yiddish has almost died out; by the time the Soviet Union ended, less than five per cent of the population was Jewish.

During World War II, the Jewish population of the Soviet Union was swelled to over five million by the Russian annexation of territories under the Ribbentrop Pact with Hitler in 1939, but when Germany invaded the Soviet Union, at least three million of these Jews were murdered. In the post-war period, Soviet-Jewish artists were "liquidated" including the actor Solomon Mikhoels (1809–1948) and Isaac Babel (1894–1940) the writer. After Stalin's death, official (though not unofficial) anti-Semitism declined though figures such as the dancer, Maya Plisetskaya (1925–) russified their names and did what they could to hide their origins. Hostility to Zionism, and subsequently Israel, was not merely a feature of Bolshevik, then Soviet policy. Russia had always had ambitions in the Middle East even before the Soviets. Although the Soviet Union and its satellites had supported the establishment of the

In this photograph of members of the Politburo, the Communist Party's political bureau, the real rulers of Russia in 1924, there are two Jewish members, Kaganovitch (second from the left) and Gomberg (in the foreground).

State of Israel in the United Nations and helped the Jews of Palestine fight the British, supplying them with Czech armaments, this was merely to rid the area of yet another imperial power. Almost as soon as Israel had gained its independence, it became another "running-dog of imperialism" in the eyes of Pravda and Izvestia. In the late 1950s and early 1960s, blood libels were even spread in official publications in parts of the USSR. The worst anti-Semitic excesses were Stalin's allegation of the "Doctors' plot" of 1952, and the Slansky Trials in Czechoslovakia, show-trials of Jews. Fortunately, Stalin died before all of those accused could be executed and those who were still alive were released.

All of this fuelled the desire of the Jewish population to emigrate, whether to Israel or elsewhere. When Golda Meir, later Israel's Prime Minister, was appointed Israel's ambassador to the Soviet Union in 1949, she attended high holiday services at the one remaining synagogue in Moscow, where she was mobbed by thousands of Russian Jews, showing the strength of feeling in the Jewish community. The event was commemorated in Israel's 10,000-shekel banknote issued in 1984 showing a portrait of Golda on one side and the crowd that turned out to cheer her in Moscow on the other. The Soviet Union seized the opportunity of the 1967 Six-Day War to break off diplomatic relations with Israel but this did not stop Jews trying to emigrate to Israel. The "prisoners of conscience" also known as Refuseniks, included Anatoly Shcharansky (1948–), later an Israeli government minister, were Jews who applied to emigrate to Israel. They lost their jobs and were often imprisoned, though a trickle were allowed out of the country, because they could claim Polish or other nationality of a Soviet satellite. All of this changed with the coming to power of Mikhail Gorbachev (1931–) in 1985, and subsequently with the demise of Communism. Jews flooded out, some two million to Israel, the rest to the United States and Europe. Surprisingly, many chose to settle in Germany, where conditions were especially favourable to immigrants thanks to Germany's past. The effects of this immigration on Israel has also been considerable. The Russians have formed their own political parties, mostly on the right of the political spectrum. Since Israel's Law of Return permits people with one Jewish grandparent to immigrate, many are not Jewish according to orthodox Judaism rules and even attend church. In fact the Christian congregations of Israel have seen a swelling of their numbers as have the synagogues. Many young Russians have also been killed in terror attacks and fighting in the Israel Defense Forces, including in the Second Lebanon War (2006).

THE BIRTH OF ISRAEL

THE CULMINATION OF THE ZIONIST DREAM, THE BIRTH OF ISRAEL, WAS A DIFFICULT ONE, FULFILLING THE PROPHESY OF THE POET YITZHAK KAHAN, "IN BLOOD AND FIRE JUDAEA FELL, IN BLOOD AND FIRE JUDAEA WILL ARISE."

Zionism has been by far the most important Jewish political movement of the modern age. In the nineteenth century, so many other ethnic minorities were calling for their own nationhood, it was more than reasonable for the Jews, the only landless nation, to join in. An early advocate of a Jewish state was Moses Hess, (1812–75) a German-Jewish socialist who also believed in assimilation. The primary advocate of Zionism in Russia was Peretz Smolenskin (1842–85) the Hebrew novelist and journalist who also edited and published the Hebrew newspaper *Ha-Shahar* ("The Dawn") in Vienna.

While throughout history Jews – such as those who came to Jerusalem with the Vilna Gaon – had been immigrating to the Holy Land, and by the early nineteenth century constituted half the population of Jerusalem, they did not have a secular, nationalist goal. It was realized from the outset that if Jews wanted their own land, they would have to learn once more to be farmers. In 1870, the Alliance Israelite founded the Mikve Yisrael Agricultural College north-east of Jaffa. Petah-Tiqva, north of Jaffa, was the first farming community, founded in 1878 by a group of religious settlers from Jerusalem. The original settlement failed but in 1888, Baron Edmund de Rothschild began to support it through the purchase of additional land. Petah-Tiqva became a training ground for thousands of pioneers, who learned to be farmers there before venturing out to establish other settlements. The settlers in Petah Tiqva were soon joined by the pioneers of the First Aliyah (*aliyah* is the Hebrew word specifically reserved for emigration to Israel; it means "rising up") a mass movement which began in 1881–82, lasted until 1903 and involved an estimated 25,000–35,000 Jews from the Pale of Settlement and the Yemen (the Yemenite Jews reached the Holy Land on foot). Settlements founded during the

Opposite: As Zionism was founded in the nineteenth century, the Hebrew lands of history were now under the control of the Ottoman Empire and would remain so until after the peace accords of World War I.

First Aliyah included Rishon LeZion, Rosh Pina, Zikhron Ya'akov, Yesud Hama'alah and Gedera. The first neighbourhoods of Tel Aviv, Neve Shalom and Neve Tzedek, were also built by these pioneers, although Tel Aviv was officially founded until 1909.

The First Aliyah included two movements, BILU (an acronym for "beit Ya'akov lechu venelekha" (House of Jacob let us arise and go) founded in 1882, and the Hibbat Tziyon (Love of Zion) and Hovevei Tziyon (Lovers of Zion) groups that were established at around the same time. Hibbat Tziyon began as a network of independent underground study groups, eventually forming larger groups called Hovevei Tziyon. The outstanding First Aliyah pioneer was Eliezer ben-Yehuda (1858–1922), founder of the modern Hebrew language who arrived from Lithuania in 1881. With the help of Nissim Béchar, principal of a school operated by the Alliance Israelite Universelle, Ben Yehuda began teaching Hebrew. Later he founded and published *Ha-Zvi* ("The Deer") newspaper, set up a linguistic council and published dictionaries, inventing as many as four thousand new words.

In 1907, a young economist named Arthur Ruppin (1876–1943) was sent to Palestine to study the conditions of the Yishuv (Jewish settlement). He became one of the founders of *Tel-Aviv*. Arthur Ruppin's report and ideas formed the basis for the Zionist action programme in the coming years and shaped the Second Aliyah. Ruppin understood that it was impossible to continue with the colony settlement model of the First Aliyah programme. The only way this barren land could be farmed was communally and collectively. He backed a small group of socialist settlers who wanted to found a commune at Sejera (one of whose members was David Ben-Gurion, Israel's first Prime Minister),

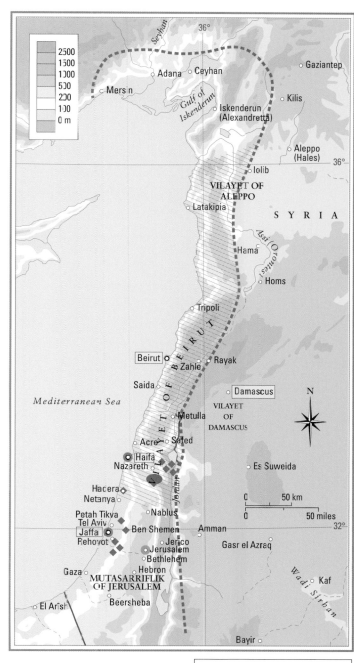

which became Kibbutz Degania in 1909. Degania was soon followed by Kinneret, Merchavia and other kibbutzim. The Kibbutz movement was to become the backbone of Labour Zionism and provided the political and military leadership of what was to become the State of Israel.

A fresh wave of pogroms in Russia provided the impetus for a second wave of immigration, the Second Aliyah, beginning about 1904. The Jewish population of Palestine increased to approximately 100,000 on the eve of World War I. New Labour Zionist movements sprung up such as Hapoel Hatzair ("the Young Worker"), founded by Aaron David Gordon (1856–1922). Poalei Zion ("Workers of Zion") and later Hashomer Hatzair ("the Young Guard") were inspired by Ber Borochov (1881–1917). The new immigrants, however, who had no training in agriculture, were unable to compete on the labour market with Arab peasants. Arab labour was also preferred by the farmers of the First Aliya. They therefore formed their own collective farms, the kibbutz and the moshav, on which resources were shared.

It was during the early years of the twentieth century that various alternatives were sought to

The Last Years of Turkish Rule 1882–1916

- ⊚ Official attempts to prevent Jewish immigrants landing
- ◆ Jewish settlements subject to Arab attacks 1886–1914
- ● Anti-Jewish societies established (also in Cairo and Constantinople (Istanbul))
- ● Zionists purchase 2400 acres of land 1310–11
- Haifa — Anti-Jewish newspapers published 1908–14 protesting Jewish land purchase from Arabs
- --- Line west of which should be excluded from future Arab State (McMahon, 25 October 1915)
- Areas declared by Sherif of Mecca to be part of a purely Arab Kingdom (5 November 1915)

Jewish settlement in Palestine, such as the Uganda project, favoured by Herzl. Fortunately, it was the settlers themselves who insisted that the Holy Land, which the Jews had lost two thousand years previously, must be reclaimed.

The father of Cultural Zionism, Ahad Ha'am (a nom de plume of Asher Hirsch Ginsberg (1856–1927); the name means "One of the People") had an extraordinarily prescient view of the situation of the Jews in Palestine. He foresaw that no colonial ruler would support mass Jewish immigration and the local Arab population would also fight against it. Ahad Ha'am, as a cultural Zionist, who eventually settled in Tel-Aviv where he died, attacked traditional Judaism and advocated reforms in the education system, including the revival of Hebrew as the language of everyday life.

As the network of Jewish collective settlements grew, so did the hostility of the authorities, first Ottoman then British, to the influx of Jewish immigrants and the problem of Arab labor became more serious. Ben-Gurion and the other Labour-Zionist leaders insisted that only Jewish workers could be used by the Jewish settlements. As he told the Arab leader, Musa Alami, in 1934, "If we become merely landlords, then this will not be our homeland."

Disease, poverty and Ottoman persecution threatened the Second Aliyah. Jews from countries at war with Turkey were viewed as enemy aliens and were expelled during World War I and a wave of epidemics swept the country to which many fell victim.

The Balfour Declaration of 1917, the promise by Britain to support a Jewish national home in Palestine and the League Nations Mandate awarded to Britain on the condition that it was to be used as a Jewish homeland, marked a turning point. In 1920, Chaim Weizmann ((1874–1952), subsequently the first president of the State of Israel, became head of the World Zionist Organization, that had been founded in 1897.

The creation of the British Mandate, which began so promisingly, soon became a bitter disappointment. The British split Transjordan from the Palestine Mandate, infuriating Jabotinsky's revisionist Zionists, who eventually left the Zionist movement over this and other issues. In 1923, the British also split off the Golan Heights which had a crucially strategic position overlooking the early kibbutzim around the Sea of Galilee, handing it over to French-controlled Syria.

The third Aliyah lasted from 1919–1923. During this period, about 35,000–40,000 Jews came to Palestine from eastern Europe. The fourth Aliyah lasted from 1924–1929 or 1932 and consisted mainly of Polish Jews who were motivated to come to Palestine by the Polish anti-democratic regime and the new immigration quotas imposed in the United States. The fourth Aliyah is generally considered to have ended in 1929, when Arab riots in Hebron and Jerusalem left many Jews dead, or in 1932, the eve of Nazi control of Germany. About 60,000–70,000 Jewish immigrants came during this period.

The Jewish Agency, an institution to facilitate immigration, was set up in 1929, in accordance with the stipulation of the League of Nations Mandate that an agency comprised of representatives of world Jewry should assist in the establishment of the Jewish National Home.

The fifth Aliyah lasted until 1939, when those who had the foresight to escape from Nazi-controlled Europe did so, until the British White Paper closed the gates to Jewish immigration due to internal Arab opposition and international Arab pressure on Great Britain. About 200,000–250,000 Jews arrived in this period, 174,000 of them between 1933 and 1936, when strict quotas were first introduced.

In the face of fierce Arab opposition to Jewish immigration, the revisionist leader Ze'ev (Vladimir) Jabotinsky (1880–1940) wanted the British authorities to allow the Jews to form a separate defensive force under British supervision, to combat attacks such as the riots of 1920 and 1921. The British refused, but Jabotinsky went ahead with the formation of the Haganah defensive underground, though it did not fall under the wing of mainstream Zionism until after the riots of 1930.

The Arabs refused to participate in a Palestinian local government which gave equal representation to the Jewish minority. The few services provided by the British Mandate government were paid for from taxes raised from the local inhabitants. Meanwhile, the Yishuv grew apace in self-sufficiency, founding educational networks for religious, secular and labour-Zionist schools all using Hebrew as the language of instruction. The first medical healthcare network, the Kupat Cholim Klalit, had been founded in 1911 and was taken over by the Histadrut Labour federation upon its foundation in 1920, providing Hebrew education, medical care, worker-owned enterprises and cultural facilities, as well as union representation. There was an attempt to organize Arab labour beginning in 1927, and the Palestine Communist party attempted to represent both Jewish and Arab labour. The Egged bus co-operative was founded in 1933, creating a Jewish public transport system.

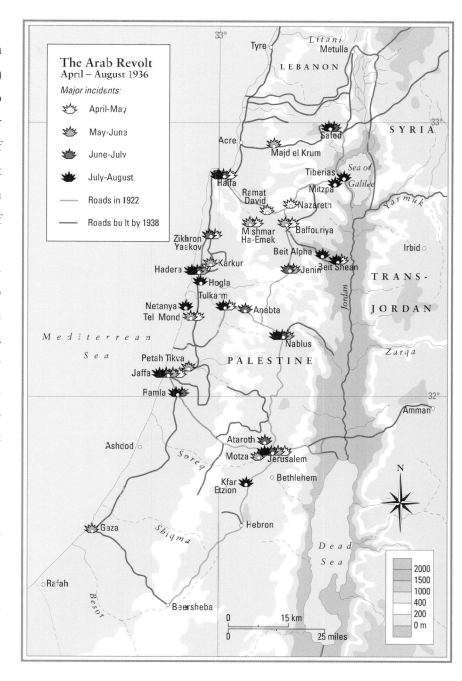

The scale of Jewish settlement triggered off a series of riots which left many Jews dead.

During the 1920s, riots were instigated by local Arab leaders, led by the Grand Mufti of Jerusalem. The British government increasingly abandoned its promise of a Jewish homeland. The Passfield White Paper, issued in 1930, which proposed to limit Jewish immigration was withdrawn under pressure from British public opinion and the League of Nations but Britain remained frightened of Arab pressure. In 1933, the Revisionist Movement, Herut, which was deeply hostile to the British, split off from the Zionist movement.

In 1936, in response to increased Jewish immigration from Europe due to the Nazis, there was an Arab rebellion, resulting in hundreds of Jewish casualties and an estimated 4,500 Arabs were killed, many by the Mufti's own forces. Although the British expelled the Mufti, they decided to partition Palestine, a plan mooted in the Peel Report. This caused a split in the Zionist movement, some members favouring a bi-national Jewish-Arab state, while the revisionists and religious Zionists refused to give up any part of Palestine. The British went on to issue the notorious 1939 White Paper, almost completely banning Jewish immigration. The Revisionists formed the Irgun Zva'i Leumi (National Army Organization) which attacked British soldiers and administrators and perpetrated terror attacks against Arabs in retaliation for Arab attacks on Jews.

When the Yishuv eventually learned of the Holocaust, attempts were made to ransom Jews from Nazi Germany in return for economic concessions. The World Zionist Organization managed to save over 200,000 European Jews before the outbreak of World War II. Between 1939 and 1942, illegal immigration (known as Aliyah Bet) was organized by the Jewish Agency when a tightened British blockade and stricter controls in occupied Europe made it impractical but it resumed between 1945 and 1948. Despite the many setbacks, the lives of tens of thousands of Jews were saved by illegal immigration and 67 ships reached the Promised Land.

About 26,000 Jews out of a population of about 500,000, and 6,000 Arabs out of a population of over a million, volunteered to fight in the British army during World War II. The Jews pleaded for combat duty in Europe in a special Jewish Brigade which the British finally permitted, though not until November, 1944. In 1942, the World Zionist leadership met in the Biltmore Hotel in New York City in 1942 and declared that it supported the establishment of Palestine as a "Jewish Commonwealth." On November 6 1944, members of the Lehi, a left-wing underground movement, known to the British as the Stern Gang, assassinated the anti-Zionist Lord Moyne in Cairo. Then on July 22 1946, the Irgun and Lehi joined forces to blow up an entire wing of the King David Hotel in Jerusalem that house the British High Command. Despite the fact that a warning had been issued, as revealed in a subsequent inquiry, it was not acted upon and 28 Britons, 41 Arabs, 17 Jews and five others were killed. The Haganah, the "official" Zionist army, fearing that these acts of terrorism would arouse world opinion against the Zionist cause, attacked Lehi and the Irgun in a campaign known in Hebrew as *Ha-sezon* ("Open Season"). When the leaders of the two organizations were caught by the Haganah, they were interrogated and about a thousand were turned over to the British.

Following World War II, the Zionist factions united to fight an underground war against British restrictions on immigration. In February 1947, the British announced that they were returning their mandate to the UN. The UNSCOP commission set up to recommend a solution to the UN and it recommended partition. The Arabs were opposed to both partition and a bi-national state but the United States and the USSR both supported the partition of Palestine and carried a large bloc of votes with them. On November 29 1947, the United Nations, with Britain abstaining, voted to partition Palestine into Jewish and Arab states in General Assembly Resolution 181.

Almost as soon as the UN decided on partition of Palestine, Arabs began attacking Jews, beginning with lethal riots in Jerusalem and attacks on Jewish transport. The Arab League immediately declared war on the Jewish community even while the British were still in Palestine, with the declared aim of "driving the Jews into the sea." The British allowed a volunteer army under Fawzi Al-Kawukji to enter Palestine in January, 1948. During the fighting, with Jewish Jerusalem still under seige, the state of Israel was declared by David Ben-Gurion in Tel-Aviv on May 15, 1948. The Arab countries – Egypt, Syria, Jordan, and Iraq – invaded almost immediately.

Thus was Israel born. In the words of the poet Yitzhak Kahan "In blood and fire Judaea fell; in blood and fire Judaea will arise again."

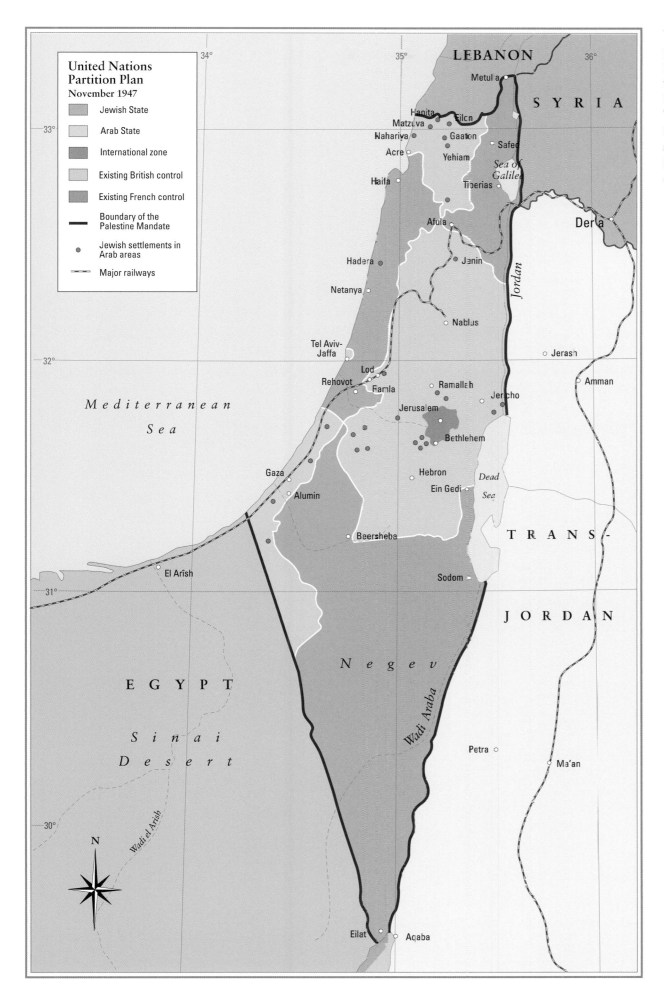

United Nations
Partition Plan
November 1947

- Jewish State
- Arab State
- International zone
- Existing British control
- Existing French control
- Boundary of the Palestine Mandate
- Jewish settlements in Arab areas
- Major railways

The United Nation's plan partitioned Palestine in an ill-fated attempt to allow for the diverse claims on a limited amount of territory. The plan also called for the internationalization of Jerusalem and its surrounds, a city important to Judaism, Islam and Christianity.

LEBANON

SYRIA

Metul a

Hanita
Matzuva   Eilon
Nahariya   Gaaton
Acre   Yehiam   Safed
Haifa   Sea of Galilee

Afula   Tiberias   Der a

Hadera   Jenin

Netanya

Nablus   Jordan

Tel Aviv-Jaffa   Jerash

Lod   Ramallah   Amman
Rehovot   Ramla   Jericho
Jerusalem

Bethlehem

Mediterranean Sea

Gaza   Hebron   Dead
Alumin   Ein Gedi   Sea

Beersheba   TRANS-

Sodom

El Arîsh   JORDAN

Negev

E G Y P T

S i n a i
D e s e r t   Wadi Araba   Petra

Ma'an

Wadi el Arish

N

Eilat   Aqaba

THE WAR OF INDEPENDENCE

ISRAEL'S WAR OF INDEPENDENCE CLAIMED SO MANY YOUNG LIVES THAT THE FIGURES FOR THE LOSSES WERE KEPT SECRET FOR MANY YEARS. DESPITE THE OVERWHELMING ODDS, ISRAEL RETAINED MUCH OF THE LAND CEDED TO IT UNDER THE UN RESOLUTION AND EVEN GAINED MORE, BUT IT LOST JERUSALEM.

The Israel War of Independence or 1948 War is divided into the pre-independence and post-independence periods. The pre-Independence war began shortly after the passage of UN General Assembly Resolution 181 to partition Palestine into a Jewish state and an Arab State, with an area around Jerusalem being internationalized. The Jews were to gain about 55 per cent of the country, including the Negev, a barren, empty desert. The plan could only have worked if both sides had co-operated fully but all parties, including the United Nations, were fully aware that the local Arabs and surrounding Arab countries utterly rejected partition and were intent on a war to "drive the Jews into the sea" in the words of the representative of the Arab League. The outgoing British sabotaged the efforts of the UN to internationalize Jerusalem and tried to hasten the Arab victory which they believed to be certain by providing large quantities of arms to the Arab Legion. The United States government, on the advice of the Central Intelligence Agency, was equally convinced that the Jews were doomed.

Riots and terror attacks began as soon as the partition plan was announced and gradually escalated. In Jerusalem, the Arabs blew up the Jewish Agency and subsequently killed about 60 people in the Ben-Yehuda Street bombing in February, 1947. In Jerusalem, Arab riots broke out on November 30 1947, and Palestinian Arab irregulars cut off the supply of food, water and fuel to Jewish Jerusalem. Riots broke out in Haifa around the oil refinery on November 30 and on April 13, a convoy was ambushed as it was bringing supplies to the Hadassah Hospital on Mount Scopus, Jerusalem, which was surrounded by Arab territory, killing about 80 medical personnel.

Although the state of Israel was not declared until May 15 1948, even before the withdrawal of British troops, attacks began by Arab volunteer irregulars. In late March 1948, forces commanded by the Palestinian Abd al-Qadir al-Husseini, a nephew of the Grand Mufti, were able to prevent supply convoys from reaching Jewish Jerusalem which was under siege. Operation Nahshon was named for the Biblical figure Nahshon Ben Aminadav, who was the first to wade into the Red Sea when the Hebrews escaped from slavery in Egypt.

Operation Nahshon lasted from April 5–20, 1948. It was the first major Haganah operation and the first step in Plan D (Tokhnit Dalet), the Jewish government's plan to hold on to the area allotted to the Jews by the 1947 UN Partition Plan. The operation was carried out by the Givati and Harel Brigades of the Haganah, with the Irgun and Lehi participating in the capture of Deir Yassin which was not originally included in the plan.

The operation was a military success. All the Arab villages that blocked the route were either captured or destroyed and the Jewish forces were victorious in all their engagements, though only 1,800 tons of the 3,000 planned got through, as the Arabs gained control of the road again. The Arab village of Abu Ghosh had decided to side with the Jews and still dominates a strategic section of the Jerusalem–Tel-Aviv road. During the fighting, Al-Husayri was killed in the battle for the Qastel, the highest strategic point on the route. His successor, Emil Ghuri, changed tactics. Instead of constructing a series of ambushes along the route, he had a huge road block erected at Sha'ar Ha-Gai (Bab-al-Wad) and Jerusalem was once again cut off from the rest of the Yishuv. The major problem for the Tel-Aviv–Jerusalem road was the section of the main road at the foot of the Judean Hills around the monastery of Latrun. Several Israeli attempts to take the Arab Legion's positions in Latrun failed, even though most the road was cleared of snipers by the end of May. Passage of 150 troops on foot from Hulda to Harel Brigade headquarters at Kiryat Anavim showed it might be possible to turn this by-pass section of narrow track, which

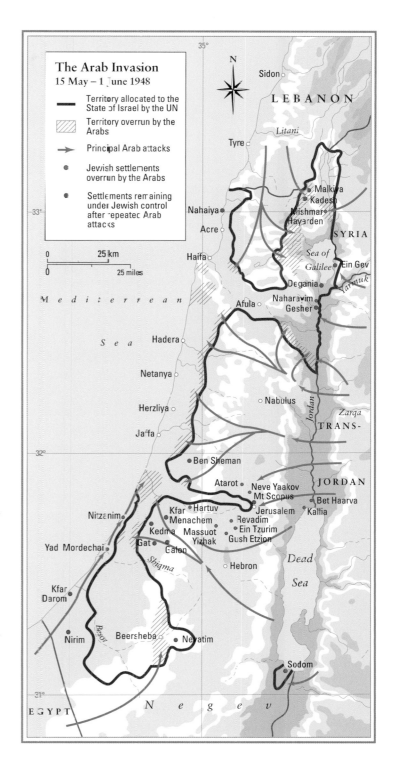

was hidden from the firing range of the British 25-pound cannon in Latrun, so that it could take vehicular traffic. Frantic work began to widen this new section of road which was nicknamed "The Burma Road" after the roads that the Allied prisoners of war of the Japanese had been forced to build during World War II. On the night of May 30–31 1948, an attempt to use the new section failed when the lead jeep overturned. A second attempt on the following night succeeded. On the night of June 1–2 the vehicles returned, with three jeeps from Jerusalem that went on to Tel-Aviv to organize a supply convoy for Jerusalem, that returned that night. The new road was still really impassable, vehicles having to be pushed by hand through sections. Porters and donkeys were used to bring supplies to Jerusalem while bulldozers and road workers worked frantically to

As British forces withdrew Arab attacks began on lands ceded to it by the United Nations resolution.

Opposite: Israel counter-attacked immediately its only hope for survival. Every effort was made to smuggle in arms and men to support the battle front

build critical parts of the road out of the line-of-sight of Jordanian artillery. The Legion spotted the activity and shelled the road but because they could not see the road, they did not hit anyone. Arab snipers killed several road workers and an attack on June 9 left eight Israelis dead. One convoy finally got through unscathed on June 10, in time for the UN-imposed cease fire but new potholes had been opened up. The road was finally completed on June 14, and water and fuel pipes were laid along side it. Latrun remained in Jordanian territory until 1967. The Arab Higher Committee asked the High Commissioner for Palestine, Sir Alan Cunningham, to allow the return of the Mufti who actually gave his permission. Fortunately, the Mufti did not make it back and command of the local Arab forces in the Jerusalem area was assumed by Fawzi al-Kawukji. The first period of fighting after the State of Israel was declared on May 15 lasted from that day until June 10, 1948. The second period of fighting, the "ten days" lasted approximately from July 9 to July 18. The final period lasted from October 15 1948, until January 7 1949. During the "truce" periods, not a day passed without one or more deaths. The regular armies of Jordan, Syria, Iraq and Egypt more or less obeyed the truces, at least outside Jerusalem, but the Arab irregulars, including Fawzi al-Kawukji's troops, took no notice.

For the Jews, the principle determining factor was the ability to transform the Haganah and the secret armies of the Irgun and Lehi into a regular army capable of withstanding the onslaught of the combined invading forces from the Arab countries. Furthermore, the Arabs generally held the high ground while the Jews were in the plains, having neither territory nor strategic depth. At first, the Haganah also had very few arms in contrast to the state-of-the-art weapons of the Arab armies, much of them supplied by the British. At one point, the Egyptians were easily able to cut off the Negev and the Iraqis were only a few miles from the Mediterranean. The Syrians and the ALA could well have reached Haifa. Jerusalem, with its 100,000 Jews, many living in the Old City which was entirely surrounded by Arab territory, was cut off. It was captured by the Arab Legion (led by the British soldier, Sir John Glubb) on May 14 together with the Etzion Block of settlements on the eastern side of Jerusalem. By the first ceasefire of June 10, Israel was not very far from collapse.

Though the Israel Defense Force was officially created on May 28 1948, most of its soldiers had little or no training. Many were new immigrants straight from the ships, unable even speak Hebrew and understand commands. The total arms available to the Haganah in 1947 consisted of 900 rifles, 700 light machine guns and 200 medium machine guns, and only enough ammunition to last three days. The Haganah had 11 single-engine light civilian aircraft and about 40 pilots, 20 of whom had RAF combat experience. There were about 350 sailors but as yet no ships. The Irgun and Lehi numbered between 2,000 and 4,000 troops.

A critical part in the war was played by volunteers from abroad known by the Hebrew acronym Makhal (*mitnadvim hutz-la'aretz*). They provided trained fighting manpower, including officers and helped to smuggle in arms, air crew and aircraft.

The Arab Higher Committee made various strategic mistakes by encouraging Arab Palestinians to leave their homes to escape the fighting, promising they could return after victory. The exodus of Arabs grew from a trickle to a torrent.

By February 1948, the Haganah had six brigades ranging from about 800 to 3,000 troops, Golani in eastern Galilee, Carmeli in western Galilee, Givati in the southern coast and lowlands, Alexandroni in the Sharon area, Etzioni in Jerusalem and Qiryati in Tel Aviv. Three Palmach battalions were converted into brigades, the Negev brigade in the Northern Negev, Yiftach in Galilee, and Harel in the Jerusalem corridor and Jerusalem. Clandestine arms shipments, especially from Czechoslovakia, meant that by April, 1948, the Haganah had a total of about 20,000 guns, including Sten guns of its own manufacture. There were no tanks or artillery. "Armoured cars" were pick-up trucks covered with sheet iron and plywood.

Operation Hametz conquered Arab villages east of Tel-Aviv and Jaffa, controlled by Iraqi volunteers. The Haganah did not attack Jaffa initially because it was meant to be part of the Arab state but Arab forces in Jaffa attacked Tel Aviv, and the Irgun launched its own attack on the nearby village of Manshiyeh. Gush Etzion, four settlements east of Jerusalem, was again the centre of conflict in May of 1948, when, for a period of three days, the residents were able to hold off a large Arab army headed for Jerusalem. Eventually, despite surrendering, 240 residents of kibbutz Kfar Etzion were massacred, another 260 captured and the settlement razed to the ground. It was the first settlement to be re-established by Israel after the 1967 Six-Day War.

By 1949, the Israelis had won the whole of the territory allotted to the Jews under the United Nations Partition Plan and even gained more, but at a heavy price. More than 4,000 Jewish soldiers and 2,000 civilians, out of a population of 600,000 or so, had been killed. The Old City and the Western Wall of the Temple, so crucial to orthodox Jews, had been lost to Jordan. Israel, only six miles wide at its centre and southern tip, was still very vulnerable to attack as subsequent years proved—but it had survived.

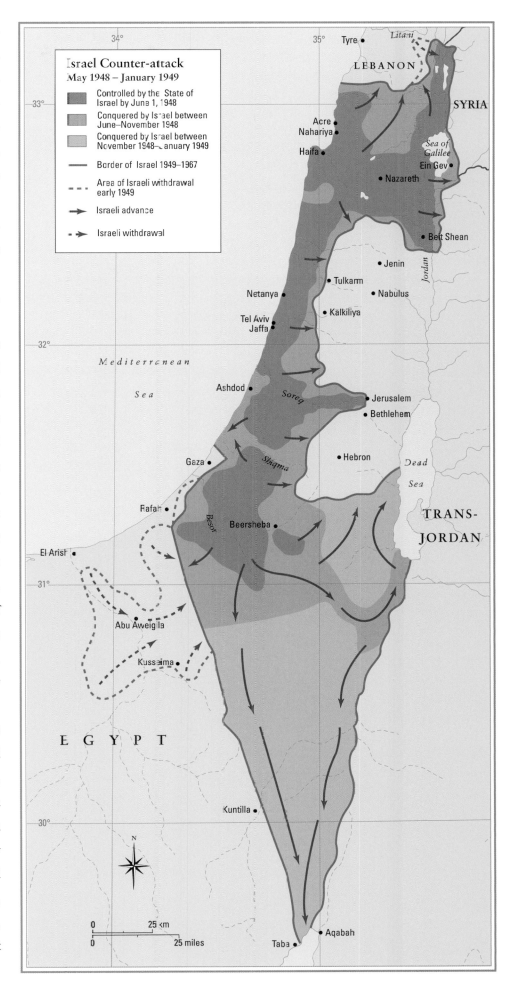

Israel Counter-attack
May 1948 – January 1949

Controlled by the State of Israel by June 1, 1948
Conquered by Israel between June–November 1948
Conquered by Israel between November 1948–January 1949
Border of Israel 1949–1967
Area of Israeli withdrawal early 1949
Israeli advance
Israeli withdrawal

THE SIX-DAY WAR

THE WORLD HELD ITS BREATH WHEN GAMAL ABD AL-NASSER OF EGYPT DECLARED WAR ON ISRAEL IN JUNE, 1967. DESPITE ALL PREDICTIONS, THE COMBINED ARAB FORCES, WITH VOLUNTEERS FROM OTHER MUSLIM COUNTRIES, WERE OVERWHELMINGLY DEFEATED AND ISRAEL WAS ABLE TO REUNITE JERUSALEM.

Burnt-out Syrian tank on the Golan Heights. The Israelis halted their advance only 40 miles from Damascus.

The Six-day War, fought from 5 to 10 June, 1967 was triggered by the demand of Gamal Abd Al-Nasser (1918–1970), ruler of Egypt from 1956 until his death, to the United Nations to withdraw all the UN Emergency Forces from Gaza and Sinai. They had been positioned there as part of the UN-negotiated deal for the Israeli withdrawal from Gaza and Sinai after the 1956 war with Egypt. While the UN Secretary-General, U Thant, was on his way to Cairo, Nasser announced a blockade of the Straits of Tiran, at the southern entrance to the Red Sea. This would have prevented shipping from using Israel's only Red Sea port – Eilat. At the time, Israel warned Egypt through the United Nations that blockading the port was a *casus belli*, a reason for going to war. Yet on arriving in Cairo, U Thant readily agreed to withdraw the United Nations Emergency Forces forces, effectively forcing Nasser – who was probably calling the UN's bluff – into war with Israel.

Nasser hoped to draw the whole Arab world into the conflict but he managed to persuade Syria and Jordan to fight alongside Egypt. As Israel's soldiers waited on the various fronts and the country was fully mobilised, it waited in vain for the world to rescue it from potential annihilation. The economy ground to a halt. Army Chief of Staff Yitzhak Rabin, later to be hailed as a war hero, had a nervous breakdown due to the unbearable tension of waiting with the life of his country in the balance, knowing that if the Israelis delayed too long, the armies of 100 million Arabs would strike his country of three million. Foreign Minister Golda Meir later admitted "the public parks in each city were being consecrated for possible use as mass cemeteries and hotels emptied of tourists to be used as first-aid posts."

As Cairo Radio's *Saut Al-Arab* (Voice of the Arabs) put it on May 18, 1967: "Every one of the hundred million Arabs has been living ... to see the day Israel is liquidated." Nasser proclaimed, "The armies of Egypt, Jordan, Syria and Lebanon are poised on the borders of Israel ... to face the challenge, while standing behind us are the armies of Iraq, Algeria, Kuwait, Sudan and the whole Arab nation. This act will astound the world."

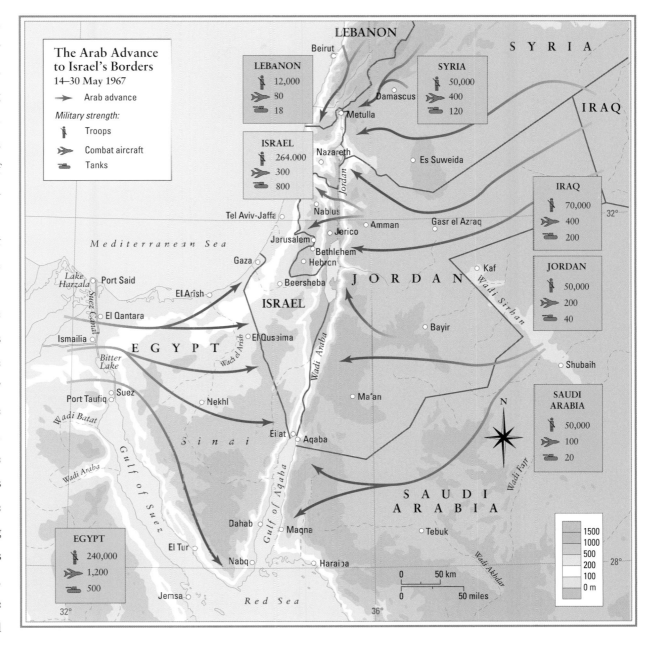

The Arab states attacked Israel after Egypt's declaration of war in June 1967.

U.S. President Lyndon Johnson and Secretary of State Dean Rusk continued to negotiate with the Egyptians but Israel knew that the longer the delay, the better prepared the Arabs would be for battle. On June 5, Israel pre-empted a lethal Egyptian air strike by attacking the Egyptian planes in their airfield, bombing and strafing the planes and the runways. At 11.00 a.m. that day, Jordan entered the war by shelling Netanya, only nine miles from its border and Jewish Jerusalem which was surrounded at the time on three sides.

On the eve of the war, Egypt massed around 100,000 of its 160,000 troops in the Sinai peninsula, including all of its seven divisions, as well as four infantry and four armoured brigades. These forces possessed 950 tanks, 1,100 armoured personnel carriers and more than 1,000 artillery pieces. Syria had an army of 75,000. Jordan had 55,000 troops, including 300 tanks, a new battalion of mechanized infantry and a paratrooper battalion, 12 battalions of artillery and six batteries of mortars. The Iraqis had readied 100 tanks near their border with Jordan and had the finest air force in the Middle East.

The Israeli army had a total strength, including reservists, of 264,000, though this number could

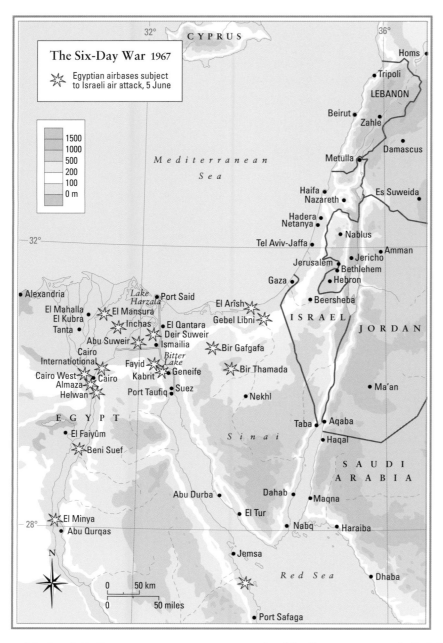

The Israeli Air Force counter-attacked the Arab offensive by successful bombing of Egyptian airfields, enabling Israel to seize air superiority.

not be sustained for long, as the reservists were vital to civilian life. On June 1, Moshe Dayan was appointed Minister of Defense and immediately began discussing the battle plan with his generals.

On the first day of the war, the Jordanian, Syrian and Iraqi air forces attacked Israel but responses by the Israeli Air Force against secondary Egyptian airfields as well as Jordanian, Syrian and Iraqi fields wiped out most of the Arab aircraft. By the evening of the first day, the Jordanian Air Force had lost over 20 fighter planes, six transport aircraft and two helicopters. The Syrian Air Force lost some 32 Russian Mig-21s, 23 Mig-15s and Mig-17s and two Illyushin-28 bombers. A number of Iraqi Air Force aircraft were destroyed at H3 base in western Iraq by an Israeli air strike. A lone Iraqi Russian TU-16 bomber was shot down later that day by Israeli anti-aircraft fire while it was attempting to bomb Tel-Aviv. On the morning of June 6 1967, a Lebanese Hunter, one of 12, was shot down over the Lebanese border by an Israeli Mirage jet. By nightfall, Israel claimed to have destroyed 416 Arab aircraft, while losing 26 of their own, a claim which most Western correspondents covering the war refused to believe.

Still on the first day, at the very moment the Egyptian planes were being destroyed on the ground, Israeli forces massed on the Egyptian border at Gaza, north and central Sinai, planning to surprise the Egyptians with their 70,000 men, organized in three armoured divisions. The central and southern divisions entered the heavily defended Abu-Ageila-Kusseima region. The battle of Abu-Ageila lasted for nearly four days. Ariel Sharon initiated the attack, backed up by helicopter-borne paratroops to the rear of Egypt's defensive positions. Some Egyptian units remained intact and could have prevented the Israelis from reaching the Suez Canal but when the Egyptian Minister of Defense, Field Marshal Abdel Hakim Amer heard about the fall of Abu-Ageila, he panicked and ordered all units in Sinai to retreat. The Israelis decided not to pursue the Egyptian units but to bypass them and trap them in the mountain passes of western Sinai. So Sharon's division made a dash for the Mitla Pass, while other units blocked the Gidi Pass and a third section entrenched itself along the Suez Canal.

Only the Gidi Pass was captured before the Egyptians approached it. A fierce battle was fought at the Mitla Pass but elsewhere a few Egyptian units managed to filter through and cross the Suez Canal to safety. Nevertheless, in four days, Israel had defeated the largest and most heavily equipped of the Arab armies. By June 8, Israel had completed the capture of the Sinai by sending infantry units to Ras-Sudar. Sharm El-Sheikh, at the southern tip, had fallen on June 7, to the Israeli Navy.

Jordan's Arab Legion was a professional, well-equipped force, trained by the British. The Royal Jordanian Air Force consisted of 24 British-made Hawker Hunters, the equal of the Israeli Air Force's French-built Dassault Mirage III.

Even though Israel had sent a message promising not to initiate action against Jordan if it stayed out of the war, Hussein replied that it was too late. The Israeli army intended to remain on the defensive along the Jordanian front, so as to concentrate on the campaign against Egypt. The Royal Jordanian Air Force attacked Israeli airfields though the attacks caused little damage. The Israelis only went into action after Jordanian forces occupied the strategically placed Government House in no-man's land, which was used as the headquarters for the UN truce observers, a threat to the security of Jewish Jerusalem.

On June 6, Israeli units were scrambled to attack Jordanian forces in the West Bank and that afternoon, the Israeli Air Force destroyed the Royal Jordanian Air Force. That evening, the Yerushalmi infantry brigade moved over the border into south Jerusalem, while tanks and paratroopers encircled the Old City from the north, engaging in the fierce Battle of Ammunition Hill. Fearing damage to the Holy Places and having to fight in built-up areas, Dayan ordered the troops not to enter the Old City.

The West Bank 1967

- - - Jordanian forces

Israeli attacks:
→ 5th June
→ 6th June
→ 7th June

After tough fighting, Israel captured not only Jerusalem, but all of the West Bank Jordanian state.

On 7 June, Israeli infantry attacked the fortress of Latrun on the old Jaffa Road, which had remained unconquerable during the War of Independence. This enabled the Israelis to advance toward Ramallah, reaching it by evening. The Israelis detected and destroyed the 60th Jordanian Brigade on its way from Jericho to reinforce Jerusalem. On the northern front, one battalion was sent to destroy Jordanian defences in the Jordan Valley. One brigade captured Jenin and the third engaged Jordanian tanks to the east.

Even though Dayan had ordered his troops not to enter Jerusalem, upon hearing that the UN was about to achieve a ceasefire, he changed his mind and decided to take the city, despite not having authorization from the cabinet. Motta Gur's paratroopers entered the Old City via the Lion Gate, and captured the Western Wall and the Temple Mount. The Jerusalem brigade then continued to the south, capturing the rest of Judea. The Harel brigade proceeded eastward to the Jordan River. Israeli combat engineers blew up the Abdullah and Hussein bridges across the Jordan River.

False Egyptian reports of victory influenced Syria's willingness to enter the war. The Syrian leadership was cautious, however, and only attacked northern Israel with shells. When the Israeli Air Force had completed its mission in Egypt, on the evening of June 5, it destroyed two-thirds of the Syrian Air Force. The rest retreated to bases far from the battleground. Several Syrian tanks sank in the Jordan River and others were captured in the Israeli farmland around the Sea of Galilee. The Syrian command abandoned hopes of a ground attack and began a massive shelling of Israeli towns in the Hula Valley instead.

The Sinai Front
6–7 June 1967

🚂 Tank battles

➜ Israeli attacks

Israeli armoured attacks, backed up with infantry and under the cover of air superiority, seized the Sinai region from Egypt up to the line of the Suez Canal.

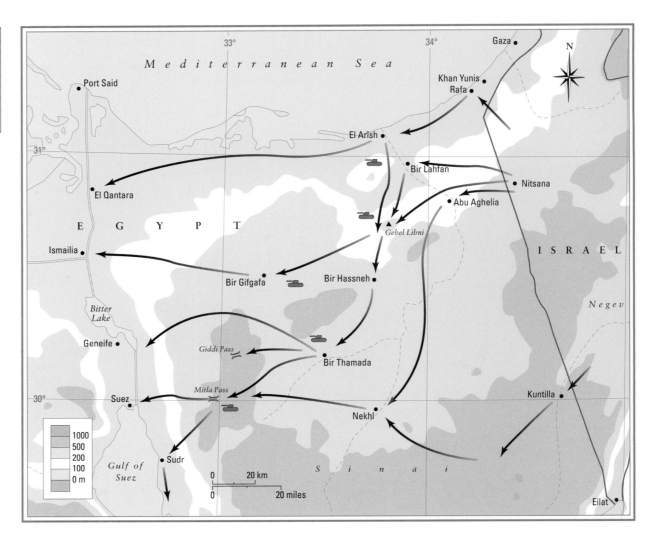

The Israelis decided to capture the Golan Heights, from which the Syrians had shelled Israel for decades. Israeli forces consisted of two brigades in the northern front, and another two in the centre. Thanks to air support, by the evening of June 9, the Israeli brigades broke through to the plateau. The next day, the central and northern forces joined in a pincer movement on the plateau but found the Syrian forces had fled, including their Soviet "advisors."

On June 8, the USS *Liberty*, a U.S. Navy electronic intelligence vessel was attacked near El-Arish by Israeli forces, nearly sinking the ship and causing heavy casualties. Israel apologized, and paid restitution. By June 10, Israel had completed its final offensive in the Golan Heights and a ceasefire was signed the next day. Israel had captured the Gaza Strip, the Sinai Peninsula, the entire West Bank of the Jordan River – including the Old City of Jerusalem – and the Golan Heights. On June 19 1967, the Israeli government voted to return the Sinai to Egypt and the Golan Heights to Syria in exchange for peace agreements. Since then, Egypt and Jordan have made their peace with Israel, only the Syrians have refused.

About 600,000 Palestinians remained in the West Bank. Only the inhabitants of east Jerusalem and the Golan Heights were allowed to receive full Israeli citizenship, when Israel annexed these territories in 1981. Many Israelis have since settled in what they call Judea and Samaria (the West Bank), an integral part of biblical Israel, though Jewish settlements in the Gaza Strip, some of which had been there since 1930, were evacuated in August 2005 as a part of Israel's unilateral disengagement.

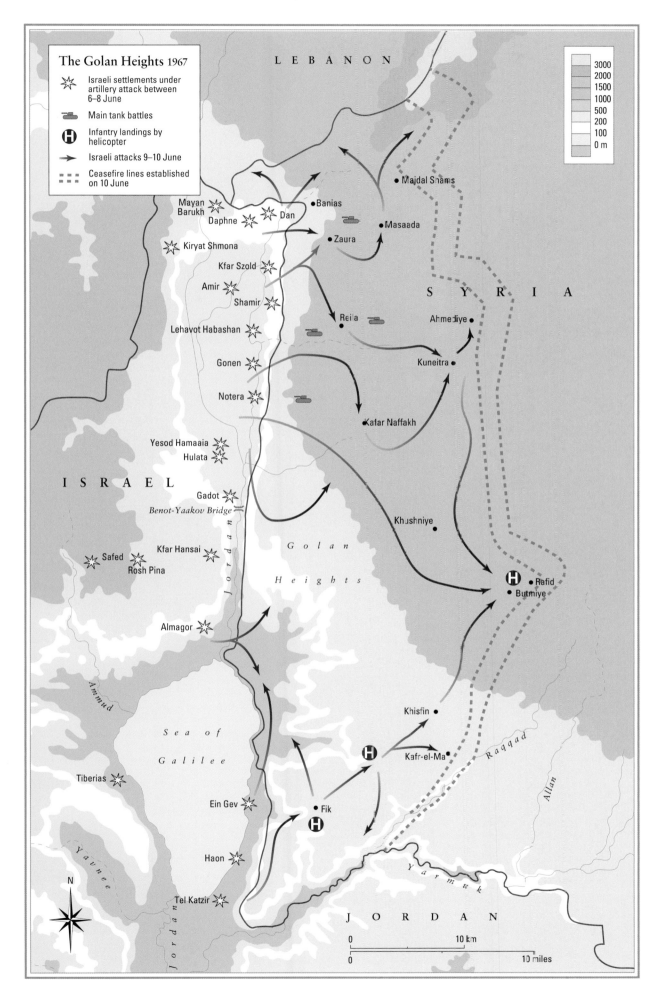

The Golan Heights 1967

- ✳ Israeli settlements under artillery attack between 6–8 June
- Main tank battles
- Ⓗ Infantry landings by helicopter
- → Israeli attacks 9–10 June
- ┄┄ Ceasefire lines established on 10 June

3000
2000
1500
1000
500
200
100
0 m

LEBANON

SYRIA

ISRAEL

Majdal Shams

Mayan Barukh
Daphne
Dan
Banias
Masaada
Zaura
Kiryat Shmona
Kfar Szold
Amir
Shamir
Reila
Ahmediye
Lehavot Habashan
Kuneitra
Gonen
Notera
Kafar Naffakh
Yesod Hamaaia
Hulata

Gadot
Benot-Yaakov Bridge

Khushniye

Golan

Heights

Safed
Kfar Hansai
Rosh Pina

Ⓗ Rafid
Butmiye

Almagor

Ammud

Sea of

Galilee

Khisfin

Ⓗ

Raqqad

Tiberias

Kafr-el-Ma

Ein Gev
Ⓗ Fik

Allan

Haon

Yavnee

Tel Katzir

Yarmuk

Jordan

N

JORDAN

0   10 km

0   10 miles

Fighting along the heights of the Golan, Israel eventually secured the plateau overlooking the settlements of northern Israel.

THE YOM KIPPUR WAR

THIS WAR WAS A SHOCK TO THE ISRAELIS WHO WERE
UNPREPARED FOR IT DESPITE INTELLIGENCE WARNINGS. THE
ARAB OFFENSIVE, LAUNCHED ON OCTOBER 6 1973, GAVE LITTLE
TIME FOR THE ISRAELI ARMY TO MOBILIZE.

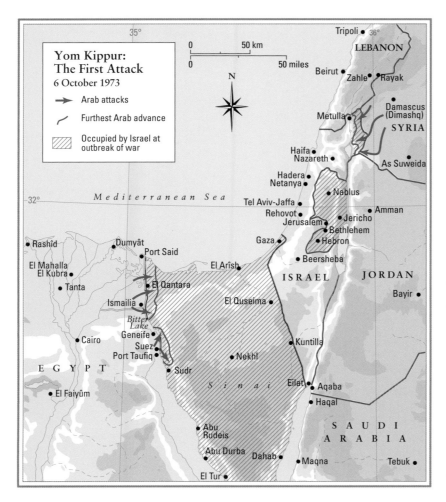

The Yom Kippur War can be said to be round two of the Six-Day War in which the Israelis had captured Egypt's Sinai peninsula all the way up to the Suez Canal and about half of the Golan Heights, previously owned by Syria.

In 1971, Israel spent $500 million fortifying its positions along the Suez Canal, which became known as the Bar Lev Line, named for Israeli General Chaim Bar-Lev. As is so often the case with such fortifications, they provided a false sense of security and were totally useless when tested.

When Nasser died in September, 1970, he was succeeded by Anwar Sadat, who resolved to win back the territory lost to Israel. In 1971, Sadat, in response to an initiative by UN intermediary Gunnar Jarring, declared that if Israel committed itself to "withdrawal of its armed forces from Sinai and the Gaza Strip," Egypt would enter into a peace agreement with Israel.

Hafiz al-Assad, the Syrian dictator, refused to negotiate, intending to retake the Golan Heights by force. Assad had built up Syria's forces again, with Soviet help and hoped to make Syria the dominant power in the Middle East.

Sadat also had other reasons for wanting war. In the years following the Six-Day War, the Egyptians were utterly demoralized. Nasser's expansionism and aspirations to pan-Arabism had ruined the economy so that, for the first time, Egypt was a net importer of grain. Sadat wanted to introduce reforms but only a military victory would give him the popularity he needed to make changes. He promised the Palestine Liberation Organization (PLO) that it would be given control of the West Bank and Gaza in the event of an Egyptian victory. King Hussein of Jordan, however, still saw the West Bank as part of Jordan, especially as during the Black September crisis of 1970, civil war had almost broken out between the PLO and the Jordanian government.

Relations were also strained between Iraq and Syria, and this time, the Iraqis refused to join in the initial offensive. Lebanon was not expected to join the war effort due to its small army and instability. Sadat managed to get the backing of more than a hundred countries in the Arab League, the Non-Aligned Movement, and the Organization of African Unity. For the first time, Britain and France actually sided with the Arab powers against Israel in the United Nations Security Council.

The Soviets, however, did not want another war between the Arabs and Israelis as it might mean confrontation with the United States. When the Soviets learnt that the Egyptians were planning a push across the Suez Canal, they tried to stop it. As a result, in July 1972, Sadat expelled almost all of his 20,000 Soviet military advisers and changed Egypt's foreign policy to be more favourable to the United States. The Syrians remained close to the Soviet Union.

Egyptian forces conducted large-scale exercises several times in early 1973, putting Israel on a high level of alert, costing its economy millions. The war itself was planned in absolute secrecy. The plan to attack Israel in concert with Syria was code-named Operation Badr (the Arabic word for "full moon"), for the Battle of Badr, in which Muhammad defeated the Quraishi tribe of Mecca.

The real reason for Egypt's initial military successes is that Israeli Intelligence did not believe until the last moment that Egypt and Syria really meant to go to war. Even King Hussein tried to warn Foreign Minister Golda Meir, but she failed to believe him. In fact, Egypt struck on the Day of Atonement, the most solemn Jewish festival, Yom Kippur, when the country comes to a complete

Yom Kippur: Israeli Counter-attacks
24 October 1973

➔ Initial Arab attacks

▨ Occupied by Israel during the Six-Day War of June 1967

▨ Occupied by Israel during the October War and held at the time of the ceasefire

▨ Retaken from the Israelis and held by the Egyptians at the time of the ceasefire

➔ Israeli counter offensive to 24 October

Israeli counter-attacks held the Egyptian army, and in a daring manoeuvre Israeli forces crossed Suez, turning south, surrounding Egyptian units east of Suez.

standstill. Even secular Jews fast and soldiers go home, leaving Israel at its most vulnerable. The war also coincided with the Muslim holiday of Ramadan, meaning that many of the Muslim soldiers were also fasting, at least during the day.

When the warnings were finally heeded, it was almost too late. Only hours before the attack began, orders went out for a partial call-up of the Israeli reserves. Ironically, calling up the reserves proved to be easier than usual, as almost all the reservists were attending synagogue or at home for the festival.

The Israelis were forced by the United States not to launch the sort of pre-emptive strike that had proved so successful at the start of the Six-Day War. A message had arrived from Henry Kissinger stating baldly "Don't preempt".

In the first wave of the Egyptian attack at the Canal, Egyptian soldiers were armed with unprecedented numbers of portable anti-tank weapons. In addition, the ramp on the Egyptian side of the canal had been increased to twice the height of the Israeli ramp, so they could fire down on the Israelis and any approaching tanks. The scale and effectiveness of the Egyptian strategy coupled with the Israelis' inability to provide its forces with air support, due to the SAM shield, greatly contributed to Israeli losses.

The Egyptian forces cleverly used water-cannon with water from the Suez Canal to blast away parts of Bar Lev Line which had been built of sand. They then crossed the Suez Canal in dinghies and rafts, capturing or destroying all but one of the Bar-Lev forts. The Egyptian forces advanced approximately ten miles into the Sinai Desert. The Israeli garrison in the Bar-Lev forts was vastly outnumbered and overwhelmed. Only one fortification remained in Israeli control through the end of the war. On October 8, an Israeli counter-attack was ordered at Hizayon but the Israeli tanks were easily destroyed. Toward nightfall, a counter-attack by the Egyptians was finally stopped by Ariel Sharon's 143rd Armoured Division, the first Egyptian reversal in the war. On October 15, in a change of tactics, the Israelis launched an infantry counter-attack, infiltrating the Egyptian SAM and anti-tank batteries north of the Great Bitter Lake, near Ismailiya, breaching the Egyptian line and reaching the Suez Canal. A small force crossed the canal and created a bridgehead on the other side. For over 24 hours, Israeli troops were ferried across the canal, even though they had no armoured support. Once the anti-aircraft and anti-tank defences of the Egyptians had been neutralized, the infantry could again rely on tank and air support. Deploying an Israeli-made pontoon bridge on the night of October 16–17, Israel's 162nd Division crossed the Canal and raced south. By October 19 the Israelis had managed to construct four separate bridgeheads north of the Great Bitter Lake under heavy Egyptian bombardment. By the end of the War, the Israelis had got to within 60 miles from Cairo.

In the Golan Heights, the Israelis were outnumbered nine to one, with 180 tanks as against about 1,300 Syrian tanks. Syrian commandos dropped by helicopter captured the most important Israeli stronghold on Mount Hermon. Fighting in the Golan Heights was given priority by the Israeli High Command, since it was so much closer than Sinai to the Israeli population centres. Reservists were assigned to tanks and sent to the front as soon as they arrived at army depots. The Syrians had expected it would take at least 24 hours for Israeli reserves to reach the front lines, but it took them only 15. The Syrians on the Golan Heights were also protected by their SAM batteries and used Soviet anti-tank weapons.

By the end of the first day, the Syrians had achieved moderate successes. That night, Lieutenant Zvika Greengold, who had just arrived at the front and was not yet attached to a unit, confronted the Syrians alone in his tank until help arrived. For the next 20 hours, "Zvika Force", as he came to be known, fought running battles with Syrian tanks – sometimes alone, sometimes as part of a larger unit, swapping tanks half a dozen times as his vehicles were knocked out. Wounded and suffering from burns, he remained in action.

During the four days of fighting, the Israeli 7th Armoured Brigade managed to hold the northern flank of their headquarters in Nafah. They suffered heavy casualties, their brigade commander being killed on the second day as the Syrians tried to break through toward the Sea of Galilee. The tide in the Golan began to turn on October 8 when the Israelis were able to contain the Syrian advance. By October 10, the last Syrian unit had been pushed back across the pre-war border.

The Israelis had to decide whether to pursue the Syrians further. Some favoured disengagement, to allow soldiers to be redeployed to Sinai; others favoured pushing on to Damascus. Prime Minister Meir realized that "It would take four days to shift a division to the Sinai. If the war ended during this period, it would be with a territorial loss for Israel in Sinai and no gain in the north – an unmitigated defeat." So from October 11 to 14, Israeli forces advanced into Syria, even shelling the outskirts of Damascus.

Iraq finally sent an expeditionary force to the Golan, consisting of some 30,000 men, 500 tanks and 700 APCs. The Iraqis attacked the southern flank of the advancing Israeli armour, forcing its advance units to retreat to prevent encirclement. Combined Syrian, Iraqi and Jordanian counter-attacks prevented further Israeli gains. On October 22, Israeli commandos recaptured the outpost on Mount Hermon, after sustaining heavy casualties.

The naval battle of Latakia took place on October 7. This was the first battle between launches equipped with surface-to-surface missiles and it resulted in a resounding Israeli victory. Many Arab states and even Cuba, financed the Yom Kippur War but they could not defeat Israel.

Egypt's initial success had given the country back some of its pride and this contributed to the eventual official peace deal between Egypt and Israel.

Once again the Golan Heights were the setting of a vicious struggle to control this vital area, by the time of the cease fire, Syrian forces had been driven back and an Israeli defence line established.

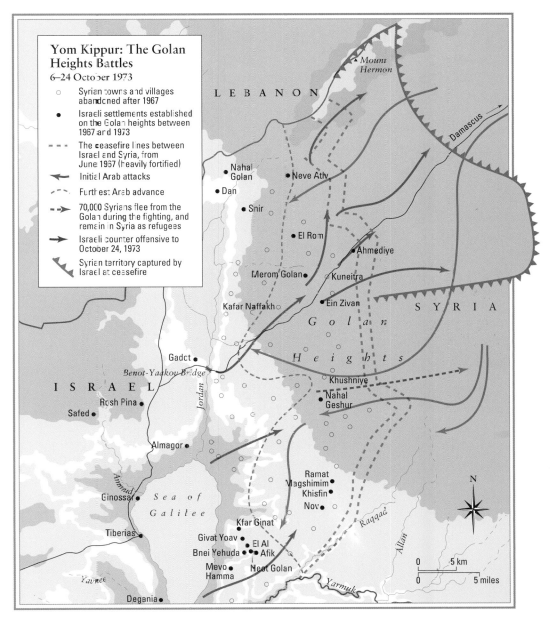

Yom Kippur: The Golan Heights Battles
6–24 October 1973

○ Syrian towns and villages abandoned after 1967

● Israeli settlements established on the Golan heights between 1967 and 1973

- - - The ceasefire lines between Israel and Syria, from June 1967 (heavily fortified)

← Initial Arab attacks

↽-- Furthest Arab advance

- -➤ 70,000 Syrians flee from the Golan during the fighting, and remain in Syria as refugees

→ Israeli counter offensive to October 24, 1973

⇜ Syrian territory captured by Israel at ceasefire

Israel and the Territories

THE TERRITORIES CAPTURED IN THE SIX-DAY WAR HAVE BEEN DIFFICULT TO ADMINISTER. SINCE 1995, THE WEST BANK HAS HAD SOME AUTONOMY.

Israeli flags flying over Hebron in the West Bank, 1967.

Certain historians have claimed that when the War of Independence ended in 1949, Israel was in such a strong position, having repulsed the armies of the neighbouring Arab countries and Iraq, as well as various groups of local Arab insurgents, that it could have retaken the Old City of Jerusalem and even the West Bank and Gaza. It is said that David Ben-Gurion, Israel's first prime minister, quashed the whole project for demographic reasons, since it would have turned the Jews into a minority in their own land.

The 1949 Armistice left Israel in a much better strategic position than it would have had if the United Nations Partition Plan had been implemented, but there was still a large bulge of land cut out of the centre of the country. This meant that there was a narrow "waist" right opposite the city of Natanya, at which the country was only six miles away from Jordan a country with which Israel was still technically at war. In fact, the cease-fire line left part of the Haifa-Jerusalem railway line in Jordanian territory, which had to be settled subsequently by an exchange of land, still leaving the line running within yards of the border at some points. Due to this geographical configuration and the largely uninhabited areas south of Beer Sheba, there were constant incursions by Arab guerrillas.

Tensions between Israel and Egypt began to escalate in 1954, when the Egyptians uncovered an Israeli spy ring that was plotting to blow up US installations in Egypt in order to embarrass the Egyptian government (known in Israel as "the Lavon affair"). A series of border incursions by Palestinians and by Egyptians from Gaza evoked increasingly severe Israeli reprisals, triggering larger raids. Israeli generals concluded that Israel needed to wage a preventive war. The October, 1956, the Franco-British attack on the Suez Canal gave Israel the opportunity to invade Sinai via the Gaza Strip, to prevent attacks on its territory from Egypt by the fedayeen, insurgents trained and equipped by the Egyptian army to engage in hostile action on the border and infiltrate Israel to commit acts of sabotage and murder. The escalation continued with the Egyptian blockade of the Straits of Tiran, and President Nasser's nationalization of the Suez Canal (to which he had always denied access by Israeli shipping or ships bound for Israel) in July 1956. President Eisenhower, furious at not being made a party to the plans of the allies and the Israelis, sided with the Soviet Union in the United Nations in forcing Great Britain, France and Israel to withdraw only a month later. He even threatened to discontinue all U.S. assistance to Israel, UN sanctions and Israel's expulsion from the UN.

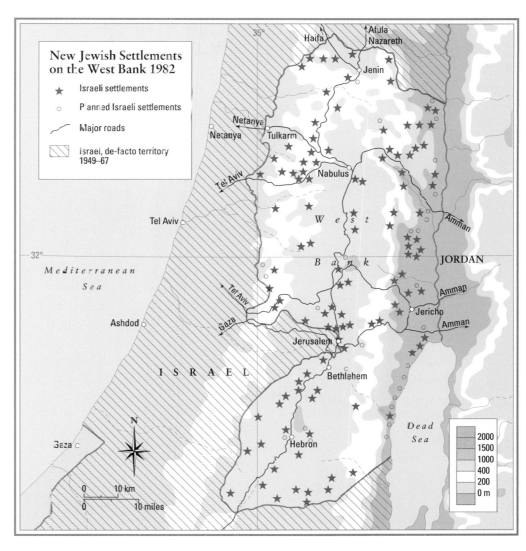

New Jewish Settlements on the West Bank 1982

★ Israeli settlements
○ Planned Israeli settlements
— Major roads
▨ Israel, de-facto territory 1949–67

As a result, Israel was forced to withdraw from the areas it conquered without obtaining any concessions from the Egyptians.

It was this U.S. action that was one of the factors that gave President Nasser of Egypt the confidence to attack in the 1967 war and it was the crushing Arab defeat in that war that gave Israel control over the Sinai Peninsula (which it subsequently returned to Egypt in the peace treaty of 1979), the Gaza Strip, originally captured by Egypt from Palestine in 1948, as well as Judaea and Samaria, usually referred to as the West Bank.

After an initial period of peace and reconciliation after 1967, when families separated since 1948 were once again reunited – to say nothing of the reunification of Jerusalem – and important trade and employment links were established between Israel and these newly acquired territories, hostilities broke out again. The post-1967 lands, with the exception of Jerusalem which was annexed by Israel, were placed under military government which naturally aroused hostility. Furthermore, the memory of the Etzion Bloc still rankled with the Israelis. These were four settlements, east of Jerusalem, between Bethlehem and Hebron which was the only important territory lost in the War of Independence. Hebron itself, a city holy to Jews and Arabs alike as it contains the tombs of Abraham and the Patriarchs. The Etzion Bloc has been rebuilt and contains 18 communities with nearly 40,000 residents. These together with other Jewish settlers in the West Bank (almost all either orthodox or very right-wing and unlikely to forge links with their Arab neighbours) have been a thorn in the side of the local Arab population. Other

In the years that followed the Six-Day War, Jewish communities were established across the West Bank.

Israeli soldiers stand next to the Western Wall after capturing the Old City of Jerusalem, in June 1967. Very quickly these same soldiers would have to face security tasks in administering the newly-acquired territories.

Jewish settlements have been built in Judaea and Samaria since 1967, which was part of the historic homeland of the Jewish people as much as Jerusalem and more so than the coastal plain (the Tel-Aviv region). Hebron, in particular, has been settled by orthodox families since 1967, for the first time since Jews were driven out by the massacre and riots of 1929.

The years since 1967 have not been peaceful ones in the relationship between the Palestinians of the West Bank and Gaza and Israel. This has been largely due to the PLO leadership, both inside the territories and abroad which have incited hatred and aggression. The attacks from the West Bank have been too numerous to mention, culminating in the First Intifada which broke out in December 1987. Intifada means "shaking off" in Arabic. It quickly developed into a well-organised rebellion orchestrated by the PLO from its headquarters in Tunis. Masses of civilians attacked Israeli troops in the West Bank and Gaza with stones, axes, Molotov cocktails, hand grenades and firearms supplied by Fatah, killing and wounding soldiers and civilians. Israeli soldiers were unprepared for this type of guerrilla warfare. The signal for this uprising began when an Israeli was stabbed to death while shopping in Gaza and on the following day, four residents of the Jabalya refugee camp in Gaza were killed in a traffic accident. Rumours spread that the four had been killed by Israelis as a deliberate act of revenge. Mass rioting broke out in Jabalya on the morning of December 9, during which a youth threw a Molotov cocktail at an army patrol and was killed by a soldier. His death became the trigger for large-scale riots that engulfed the West Bank, Gaza and Jerusalem. As the intifada ran its course from 1987 to 1993, the level of violence and the degree to which it was organised and coordinated by the PLO only increased. The first intifada, which ended in 1993 with the Oslo Agreement, when Israel granted a large measure of autonomy to the West Bank and Gaza, resulted in the deaths of 1,100 Palestinians and 160 Israelis. Another 1,000 Palestinians were killed by their own people as alleged collaborators, often by putting tires around their necks and setting them alight.

The second intifada was also triggered on a pretext. On the morning of September 28, 2000, a six-member Knesset delegation led by the then-leader of the Israeli opposition, Ariel Sharon, paid a brief visit to the Temple Mount in Jerusalem, avoiding the mosques. This was the excuse that the PLO had been waiting for, and this is why the second intifada is known as the Al Aqsa Intifada. As soon as the visit ended about 1,000 Palestinians led by Israeli Arab Knesset members hurled stones at Israeli policemen. Within hours, the Voice of Palestine was accusing Sharon of desecrating the Muslim holy places. Following Friday morning prayers in the mosques on the Temple Mount, hundreds of Palestinians threw down rocks on the Jewish worshippers at the Western Wall.

The second Intifada brought fear to the streets of Israeli towns in the form of suicide bombers blowing themselves up on buses and in restaurants as well as rocket attacks and shootings, all in the Israeli heartland. It dealt a grievous blow to the entire Israeli political left, which had supported the Oslo Peace Process but worse still, but the effect on the Palestinian economy was far worse. The Second Intifada has resulted in the deaths of more than 5,300 Palestinians, over 1,000 Israelis and 64 foreign nationals.

The creation of a physical barrier between the Israeli and Palestinian populations was first proposed by Prime Minister Yitzhak Rabin in 1992, following the murder of an Israeli teenage girl in Jerusalem. The Israeli government built the Gaza Strip barrier in 1994. In 2002, Israel began the construction of a fence to separate most of the West Bank from areas inside Israel. The fence is transparent along most of its length with a high wall at the point outside Jerusalem where the Jewish neighbourhood of Giloh came under heavy fire in 2000 from the West Bank village of Bet Jallah. The barrier was greeted with immense joy by the Israeli right and fear and loathing by the Palestinians but it has stopped 90 percent of atrocities such as the murder of Passover celebrants in Netanya in 2002 and the Sbarro café attack in Jerusalem in 2004.

Israeli Prime Minister Ariel Sharon proposed a unilateral withdrawal from the Gaza Strip in 2004 which was enacted in August 2005. The operation was completed by September 12, 2005. As soon as Hamas was elected in 2006, it conducted a campaign of rocket attacks into Israeli territory, most of which have fallen on the town of Sderot. Since Hamas declared a truce in early 2008, and there have been fewer rockets but the situation remains tense.

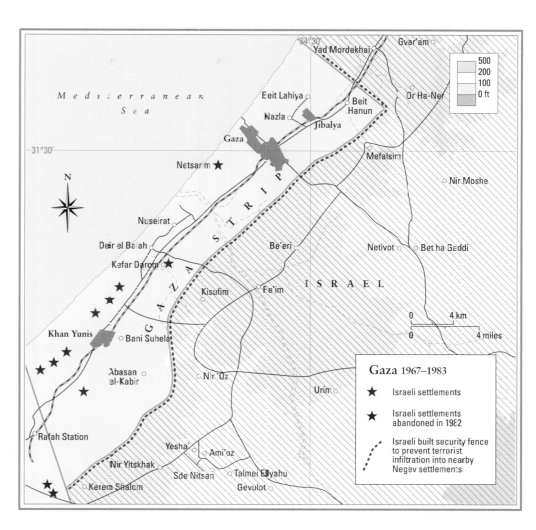

Gaza 1967–1983

★ Israeli settlements

★ Israeli settlements abandoned in 1982

┅ Israeli built security fence to prevent terrorist infiltration into nearby Negev settlements

In the years after 1967, Jewish settlers attempted to create communities in the densely populated Gaza Strip, these would ultimately prove unsuccessful.

Next page: The Israeli state after the war of independence still remained under threat with many of its settled areas within artillery range of its enemies. After the Six-Day War, West Bank, Gaza and Sinai fell under Israeli control. The new borders now included millions of non-Israeli citizens, what had been an external trans-border threat to security now became an internal one. New borders meant new problems.

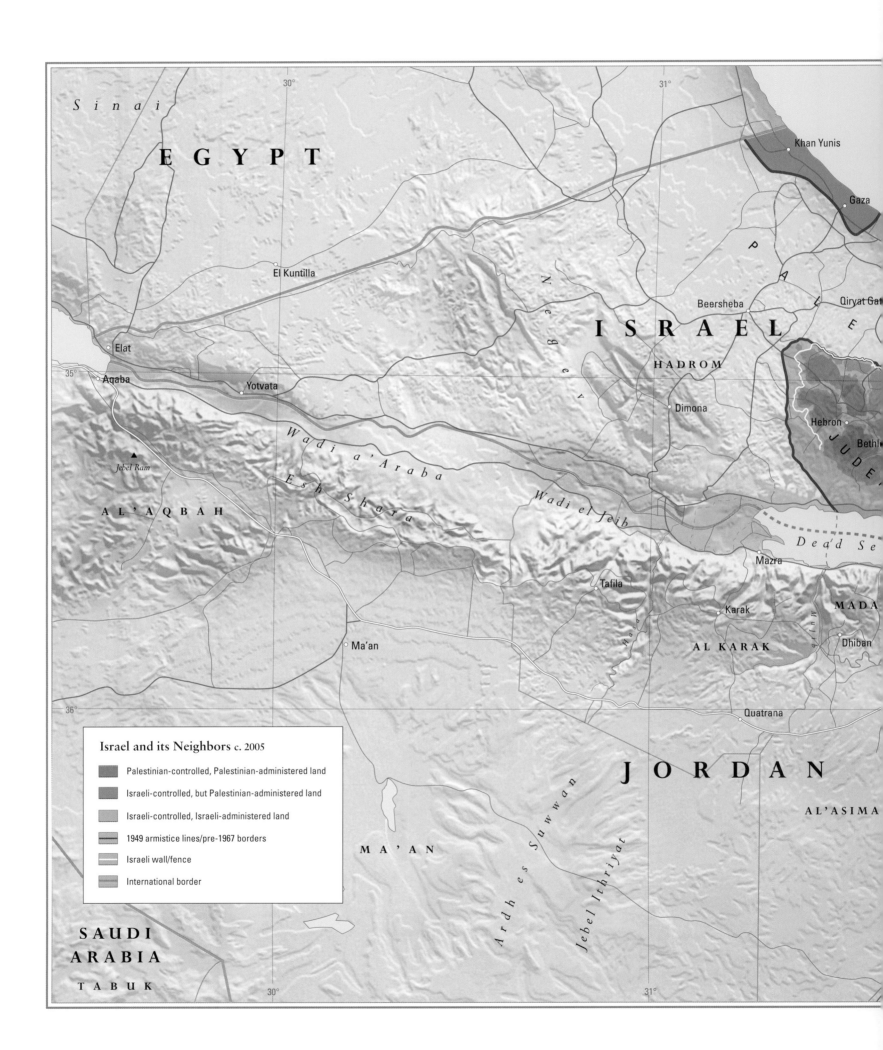

EGYPT

Sinai

El Kuntilla

Elat

Aqaba

Yotvata

Wadi a'Araba

Esh Shara

▲ _Jebel Ram_

AL'AQBAH

Wadi el Jeib

Ma'an

JORDAN

Ardh es Suwwan

Jebel Ithriyat

MA'AN

SAUDI
ARABIA

TABUK

Khan Yunis

Gaza

P A L E

Beersheba

Qiryat Gat

ISRAEL

HADROM

Dimona

Hebron

JUDE

Bethl

Dead Se

Mazra

Tafila

Karak

MADA

AL KARAK

Dhiban

Quatrana

AL'ASIMA

Israel and its Neighbors c. 2005

- Palestinian-controlled, Palestinian-administered land
- Israeli-controlled, but Palestinian-administered land
- Israeli-controlled, Israeli-administered land
- 1949 armistice lines/pre-1967 borders
- Israeli wall/fence
- International border

Mediterranean Sea

0   20 km
0   20 miles

N

elon
Ashdod
Rehovot
Rishon   Tel Aviv
le Zion   TEL AVIV
        Herzliyya
        Netanya
HAMERKAZ   Hadera
        HEFA   Ha fa   Nahariyya
        Tulkarm   Tyre
WEST   LIBAN-SUD
    SAMARIA   Afula   HAZAFON   Sayda
Ramallah   Nablus   Nazareth
Ba'al Hazor   Jenin   Beirut
BANK   NABATIYE   MONT-
Jericho   Tiberias   Qiryat Shemona   LIBAN
                Lake Tiberias   LEBANON
            Jordan   (Sea of Galilee)   El Quanytirah
AL BALQA   Yarmuk   AL
    A'JLÜN   QUNAYTIRAH   AL BEQAA
Salt   Ajlun   IRBID
    Jebel Um ed Daraj   Irbid
JARASH
Amman
                            Damascus
ZARQA'   AL MAFRAQ   Dar'a   Al Kiswah
    Mafráq
            Shaykh Miskin
                SYRIA
            Suwa·da
Z ZARQA'   AS SUWAYDA'   DIMASHQ

The Kibbutz and Moshav Movements in Israel

COLLECTIVE FARMING ON A GRAND SCALE IS ANOTHER OF ISRAEL'S SUCCESS STORIES. ALTHOUGH THE KIBBUTZ MOVEMENT IS CURRENTLY EXPERIENCING DIFFICULTIES, IT WAS THE ONLY WAY IN WHICH SUCH UNFORGIVING TERRAIN COULD BE FARMED.

The word "kibbutz" literally means "gathering" or "cluster." It is a form of collective based on Labour-Zionist principles that is unique to Israel. There is no question that without this form of collective endeavour, it would have been impossible to turn the Land of Israel from a mixture of mosquito-infested swamp and parched desert into the fertile and highly productive farmland it has today. The various types of collective farm kick-started the dormant economy of Palestine and has played a dominant role in the development of the Israeli economy.

The first kibbutz, Degania, was founded in 1909, in the Jordan Valley. Those that followed were established in the low-lying, regions of the country such as the upper Jordan Valley, the Jezreel Valley and the Plain of Sharon. The land was highly fertile but was available for purchase because it was infested with malaria and thus unproductive. Most of the pioneering kibbutzniks, including David Ben-Gurion, caught malaria which was not eradicated from Israel until the mid-1950s.

The early kibbutzniks wanted to create a new type of society in which men and women would be equal and free from exploitation. For this reason, there were bitter disputes in the early years about whether it was ethical to use hired labour and particularly Arab workers. Like other early Zionists, the founders of the kibbutz movement never envisaged the possibility of conflict between Jews and Arabs over Palestine. They believed that the Arab peasant (falah) would be grateful for the economic benefits that the Jews brought and that the Arab labourers would realize that their true enemies were the absentee Arab landowners (the effendis). But by the late 1930s, as Arab unrest grew in Palestine, the kibbutzim came under repeated attack from their Arab neighbours. In the 1930s and 1940s, kibbutzim were founded on the "tower and stockade" (Homa Umigdal) model. Under an old Ottoman law, if a tower and a stockade could be built to enclose the land between sundown and the following sunrise, the land was owned by the settlers and the British could not remove them. Many kibbutzim were first settled in this manner, as strongholds to withstand Arab attacks during the British Mandate period.

In the early kibbutzim, all property was collectively owned, even clothing. Until the 1970s, anyone could go to the kibbutz store and take what they needed without paying money. All meals were and still are eaten in the communal dining room, though dwelling units have facilities for making light meals and many kibbutzniks now breakfast at home. The kibbutz is run by its members and weekly meetings are held to discuss every kind of problem from the installation of new latrines to the prices received for the crops. Kibbutz memoirs from the twenties and thirties report that these meetings varied from heated arguments to free-flowing philosophical discussions, but by the 1950s and 1960s they had already become businesslike and less well attended.

It is the practice in kibbutzim to rotate people into different jobs, except in the case of certain highly skilled and specialized workers or those who work outside the kibbutz, as in both cases their financial contribution is valuable. One week a person might work in planting, the next with livestock, the week after, in the kibbutz factory and the following week in the laundry or dining-room.

The most revolutionary feature of kibbutz life—and the one on which the most sociological studies have been performed—is the way in which the children are raised. They spend all their time together, sleeping in the children's house, their parents spending two hours a day with them at most, typically after work. In kibbutzim belonging to the Kibbutz Artzi movement of the far left, at one time parents were explicitly forbidden to put their children to bed at night. As their children grew older, parents might go for days on end without seeing them, other than through chance encounters. Boys and girls lived and slept in the same dormitories. Children's reactions to this lifestyle have been mixed. Nowadays, many kibbutzim have "taken their children home" and they live in a family unit. It has been discovered that children born and raised on kibbutz tend to regard those of the opposite sex with whom they have been raised as their siblings, feeling no sexual attraction for them and seeking partners outside the kibbutz.

There are three major kibbutz movements currently, the Kibbutz Hameuhad (secular Labor-Zionists), Kibbutz Artzi (left-wing Labor Zionists, formerly belonging to the Mapam party),and Hakibbutz Ha-dati movement, belonging to the Labour wing of the Mizrahi religious Zionist movement.

Although less than five per cent of Israelis currently live on kibbutzim, the members have a high social status and are disproportionately represented in government and other senior positions. In the early years of the Yishuv (Jewish settlement in Palestine) and of the State of Israel, all of its leaders without exception had been or were currently kibbutz members. They include David Ben-Gurion, a member of the first kibbutz, Degania, who retired to the Negev kibbutz of Sde Boker, and Golda Meir who spent time on Revivim in the northern Negev.

Israel has also spawned two other types of collective settlements, the Moshav (full name, Moshav Ovdim) and the Moshav Shitufi. A moshav is like a village except that the land is leased from the Jewish National Fund. Although families live in single homes, earn their own money, and farm the plots of land, farm machinery and other resources are communally owned. The Moshav Shitufi, of which there are forty, is a cross between a kibbutz and a moshav. Children live with their parents in family units but the land and resources are owned and worked communally. Income earned outside the Moshav is pooled, the families being allocated a sum of money to live on. There are a number of religious moshavim-shitufiim, of both the Mizrahi (modern orthodox) and Aguda (strictly orthodox) movements, as this is a lifestyle that suits religious Jews better than the kibbutz. Other moshavim shitufiim have other affiliations, including to the right-wing Beitar movement.

The Moshav Ovdim is a more individualistic type of cooperative agricultural community, though it was also pioneered by the Labour Zionists of the Second Aliyah, the wave of Jewish immigration in the 1920s and early 1930s. The first moshav, Nahalal, was established in the Jezreel Valley (also known as the Valley of Esdraelon) on September 11 1921, on land donated by the Jewish National Fund. The founders had come to Palestine from Eastern Europe in what is known as the Second Aliyah and Third Aliyah between 1904 and 1914. Some, including the parents of Moshe Dayan, had been members of the first kibbutz, Degania. They wanted to establish a collective farming community similar to a kibbutz, but they wanted to retain the individual family unit.

The village layout in Nahalal, devised by architect Richard Kauffman, became the pattern for many moshavim established before the State of Israel, and is based, for safety, on concentric circles, with the public buildings (school, administrative and cultural offices, cooperative shops and warehouses) in the center, the dwellings in the innermost circle, the farm buildings in the next, and beyond those, ever-widening circles of gardens and fields, initially into 80 equal parts, 75 parts for the members and 5 parts for the agricultural school at the moshav. This equal parcelling of the land became the trademark geometric shape of Nahalal. There are now 405 moshavim, affiliated to eight federations, which themselves belong to the major political groupings, from the far left to the far right, and including the two streams of orthodox Jewish settlement. Because the moshav retains the family as the center of social life, it has also been much more attractive to immigrants from traditional backgrounds, such as observant Ashkenazim and the so-called Oriental Jews from the Middle East and North Africa. Many so-called immigrant moshavim (moshav olim) were set up during the mass immigration of the 1950s. It was a very difficult transition for Jews who had previously been town-dwelling small traders and craftsmen, since they now had to learn agricultural techniques, but farming allowed them to prosper in a way that was not possible in most of the development towns. Their lack of previous knowledge was even an advantage, as they were willing to take instructions and happy to adopt progressive farming and husbandry techniques.

Like the kibbutzim, the moshavim were hit by financial instability in the early 1980s, caused partly by the problem of absorbing all the children born into the community who might wish to remain and for whom there was not enough land. By the late 1980s, increasing numbers of kibbutz and moshav members were employed in non-agricultural sectors outside the community, so that some moshavim, especially those on the edge of large towns and cities, have come to resemble suburbs or dormitory towns whose residents commute to work. As on the kibbutzim, serious ethical problems have arisen in the case of members who have been awarded large sums in reparations from Germany due to their sufferings in World War II, as this has created serious inequalities and much soul-searching.

A communal levy known as the Mas Va'ad, which is the same for all members of the community is collected on moshavim, to support communal institutions. Moshavim, like kibbutzim, are run by a committee elected by the members and there are regular meetings. In general, moshav residents have never enjoyed the elite status afforded to the kibbutzniks, but their prestige increased in 1970s and 1980s with the increasing value of their properties.

By 2005, 717 kibbutzim and moshavim had a combined population of 347,200. Although many of those in the centre of the country experienced severe financial difficulties in the 1990s, others, such as Yotvata in the Arava, which supplies most of the milk and dairy products consumed in Eilat and has a milk-bar in Tel-Aviv, are thriving. The bare huts have been replaced by air-conditioned, solar-heated dwelling units and every kibbutz and moshav has a swimming-pool. Whether the kibbutz model will survive permanently, unlike the collective farming institutions of other countries, remains to be seen.

David Ben-Gurion (1886–1973), first Prime Minister of Israel, was one of the first settlers at Sejera, then Degania in the early 1900s. When he retired from politics in 1970, he went to live on kibbutz Sde Boker in the Negev.

MUNICH AND TERRORISM

ISRAEL HAS SUFFERED FROM VARIOUS ACTS OF TERRORISM, INCLUDING THE CAMPAIGN OF SUICIDE BOMBINGS LAUNCHED DURING THE SECOND INTIFADA. ONE OF THE MOST NOTORIOUS ATTACKS, ON THE ISRAELI ATHLETES AT THE MUNICH OLYMPICS, TOOK PLACE IN 1972.

It is not always easy to define terrorism. Organised Arab attacks on the Jewish population of Palestine began in 1920 but they could best be described as riots or pogroms rather than terrorism, although they claimed Jewish lives. After the establishment of the State of Israel, armed insurgents who belonged to a number of anti-Israel organisations, ranging from the Egyptian-sponsored fedayeen to the PLO-sponsored Black September, carried out raids into Israel, during which they randomly killed soldiers and civilians alike.

The litany of terrorist attacks by Arabs on Israelis, starting almost as soon as the State of Israel was established reads like an endless horror story. The first such attack that killed more than ten people occurred in 1954, with the ambush of a bus travelling between Eilat and Tel-Aviv. In 1968, there was the first of two bombings of the central Jerusalem market in Mahane Yehuda; 12 people were killed, 52 injured (in the subsequent bombing in 1997, 16 people were killed and 178 injured). In May, 1970, bazookas were fired from Lebanon on a school bus travelling near the border. Twelve children were killed and 19 were injured.

May 15, 1974, the 26th anniversary of Israel's independence, was the date chosen for the incident known as the Ma'a lot Massacre. A group of terrorists infiltrated from the Lebanese border, shooting at anyone in their path including a van driven by a Druze who was taking Druze women from their work. They eventually reached the development town of Ma'alot, six miles from the Lebanese border, taking children in a school hostage. The attackers were three members of the Popular Democratic Front for the Liberation of Palestine (PDFLP), Ahmed Lini, Ahmed Harbi and Ziad Rachim. Most of the 27 people who died, including the perpetrators, were killed in the rescue attempt.

On March 6 1975, a gang of terrorists landed from boats on a Tel-Aviv beach, firing at cars and soldiers. They then seized a hotel, seizing hostages and attempting to negotiate. The hotel was stormed by Israeli troops, but one hostage was killed, as was one soldier and six terrorists.

The wave of airplane hijackings, which reached a peak throughout the world in the 1970s, as a favourite way to attack Israel abroad since it would attract international media attention. The first such attack occurred on July 23 1968, with the only successful hijacking of an El Al plane. Three members of Popular Front for the Liberation of Palestine (PFLP) hijacked El Al Flight 426 on its way from Rome to Tel Aviv. The plane was diverted to Algiers. Negotiations lasted for more than 40 days after which all of the hijackers and hostages were released. The hijackers were never caught. In September 1970, Arab hijackers attempted to capture four planes, one of them an El Al plane. Three of the planes were flown to Jordan and blown up; on the fourth, the El Al plane, the hijackers were overpowered.

The last time a hijacking was attempted on a plane flying to Israel was in 1976. On June 27 of that year Air France Flight 139 from Paris to Tel-Aviv, carrying 246 passengers made a stopover in Athens, an airport at which security was notoriously lax. There it was hijacked and ordered to divert to Benghazi, Libya where one passenger, a young, pregnant woman, was allowed to leave the plane. The plane then took off again and flew south to Entebbe, Uganda, where it landed in the early hours of June 28.

The hijacking was a collaboration between the Popular Front for the Liberation of Palestine (PFLP) and the Ugandan dictator Idi Amin. Once at Entebbe, the passengers were moved to the old terminal building, where they were guarded by Ugandan soldiers and local PFLP terrorists as well as by the hijackers themselves. The Israeli passengers were then separated from the rest, and the non-Israelis were allowed to leave. Threats were made to kill the Israelis if Arab prisoners were not released from Israeli jails. This ominous move caused the Israeli government to undertake an extraordinary and unprecedented act of daring. On the night of July 3–4, the Israel Defense Forces dispatched planes to collect the hostages. One of the planes contained a black Mercedes car of the kind used by the Ugandan dictator and his cohorts and this was used inside the airport to fool the guards allowing the Israeli commando squads inside to gain entry and rescue the hostages. In the ensuing gun battle with the captors, all of the terrorists were killed as well as three hostages and five Israeli commandos, including Lieutenant-Colonel Yehonatan Netanyahu, elder brother of the Israeli statesman Binyamin Netanyahu. The hostages were flown back to Israel in the rescue planes. An old lady who had been taken ill previously and removed to hospital was murdered by the Ugandans in her hospital bed.

It was during the 1970s that a wave of shootings and bombing was unleashed on Israelis abroad as well as on Jewish institutions, giving the lie to the fact that the terrorists were merely anti-Israel not anti-Jewish.

The first such attack has become known as the Munich Massacre. During the 1972 Summer Olympics, terrorists of the Black September organisation, an offshoot of the PLO, entered the apartment occupied by the Israeli Olympics team, and took the athletes hostage. The negotiations were poorly conducted by the German police when then staged a botched rescue attempt in which all 11 Israeli athlete hostages, as well as one German police officer and five of the terrorists, were killed. Since then, a ceremony to commemorate the victims is held by the Israeli embassy in the host country at each Olympics since then.

Also in 1972, on May 30, three Japanese Red Army terrorists arrived at the Lod Airport, Israel, via Air France Flight 132. The operation had been planned and funded by the General Command of the Popular Front for the Liberation of Palestine (PFLP-GC). The terrorists opened fire with sub-machine guns, killing 26 and injuring 78. Sixteen of the dead were Puerto Ricans on a pilgrimage to Israel. The plan was masterminded by a woman, Fusako Shigenobu, who was only caught and arrested in Osaka, Japan, in November 2000.

In 1975, Ahmed Jbarra, planted a booby-trapped refrigerator in Jerusalem's Zion Square, killing 13 people, including an English tourist. He was caught and sentenced to 75 years in prison but released after 27, making him the longest serving prisoner in Israel. Immediately upon his release he was feted in the West Bank and appointed a special advisor to Palestinian Authority Chairman Yasser Arafat. Senior PA officials said the decision to appoint Jbarra to the new post was a "natural" one, taking into consideration his "great contribution to the Palestinian cause."

In October 1980, a bomb was planted on a motorcycle parked outside the Liberal synagogue in the rue Copernic, Paris. Three Frenchmen and a young Israeli woman who happened to be passing by were killed. In 2007, the perpetrator, a member of the PFLP, was traced to Canada where he is living at the time of writing.

The result is that since the 1970s, Jewish communities all over the world have had to take extreme precautions whenever they gather together for social occasions and even for prayer. In many countries, Jewish organizations outside Israel such as the United Kingdom's Community Services Trust, provide guards at synagogues and other venues to ensure the safety of the worshippers or attendees.

This did not prevent the virtually fatal shooting of the Israeli ambassador in London in 1982. The ambassador, Shlomo Argov, was just leaving a diplomatic function at the Dorchester Hotel in Mayfair when a young man shot him in the head with a machine pistol. Argov survived the attack but was left permanently paralysed and requiring constant medical attention. He lived for another 21 years. Two Jordanians and an Iraqi with links to a Palestinian extremist organisation were convicted of the attempted murder of the envoy in March 1983. It was the incident that Israeli Prime Minister Menachem Begin was seeking to launch "Operation Peace for Galilee", the first Lebanese war.

On July 18, 1994, a huge bomb exploded in the community center of the Asociación Mutual Israelita Argentina (AMIA, the Argentine Israelite Mutual Association) in Buenos Aires, killing 85 people and injuring hundreds. Argentina has the largest Jewish community in Latin America. No one has ever been prosecuted for the attack which occurred under the presidency of Carlos Menem, himself of Arab origin. Every local suspect, including many members of the Buenos Aires Provincial Police Force were exonerated in a trial in September 2004. In August 2005, Federal Judge Juan José Galeano, who was in charge of the case, was impeached and removed from his post on charge of "serious" irregularities and of mishandling of the investigation.

In October, 2006, Argentinian prosecutors Alberto Nisman and Marcelo Martínez Burgos officially accused the Iranian Government of having orchestrated the bombing, and Hezbollah of carrying it out. Argentina had allegedly been targeted by Iran after Buenos Aires' decision to suspend a nuclear technology transfer contract to Tehran but this is unlikely. The bombing is commemorated nationwide in exhibitions and ceremonies, radio and television stations and police cars all across Argentina sounded sirens at 9:53 am, the time of the bombing.

From the outbreak of the period of Arab unrest in the Occupied Territories, in 2000, wave of terror was unleashed against Jewish civilians in Israel and anywhere else in the world. There were attacks on Jewish schools, cemeteries, and synagogues in Paris, London and Berlin where a petrol bomb was thrown at a synagogue in Berlin's Kreuzberg district late on Sunday. The synagogue had also been targeted in October 2000, when paving stones were thrown at the windows. In April, a north London synagogue was desecrated with swastikas, windows were smashed and excrement left.

Also in April, a suicide bomber driving a truck filled with natural gas bottles entered the compound of the historic Al-Greiba synagogue on the island of Djerba in Tunisia. The truck detonated at the front of the synagogue, killing 14 German tourists, six Tunisians and one Frenchman. More than 30 others were wounded. Nizar Nawar, aged 24, was the suicide bomber, carrying out the attack with the aid of a relative. In March 2003, five people were arrested in Spain who were believed to have financed this attack. In April 2003, Christian Ganczarski, a German convert to Islam and allegedly one of the Al-Qaida leaders in Europe, was arrested in Paris in connection with the bombing. He remains in custody.

Again in 2002, suicide bombers in a vehicle struck at an Israeli-owned hotel in Mombasa, Kenya, just as two missiles were fired at an Israeli holiday jet that had taken off from the city's airport.

The missiles narrowly missed the Arkia Airlines plane carrying 261 passengers, but a large part of the Paradise Hotel was reduced to rubble. Sixteen people, including the bombers, died, three suicide bombers, nine Kenyans, and three Israelis, two of whom were children. About 80 people, most of them Kenyans, were injured in the attack.

In June, 2005, three men accused of conspiracy in the case of the 2002 suicide bombing of the Israeli-owned hotel in Mombasa were cleared of all charges. On March 27 2002, a suicide bomber managed to enter an hotel in Natanya, a point at which Israel is only six miles wide, and blow himself up at the guests for the Seder, the ritual Passover meal. Twenty-seven people were killed. This is one of the very few sites that have been preserved as they were after the bombing to try to explain to tourists the horror of what Israel suffered during those years, when people hardly dared travel by bus or congregate in public places.

There followed a series of horrific attacks on civilian targets including the Sbarro pizza restaurant in Jerusalem (15 killed), two bombings of Haifa restaurants, one in March 31 2002 (15 killed, over 40 injured), the second on October 4, 2003 (21 killed, 60 injured) and 16 were killed and over 80 wounded in two suicide bombings which took place within the space of six hours on September 9 2003. The bombers both came from the village of Rantis in the West Bank. The first blew himself up at the main entrance to the Tsrifin army base and Assaf Rofeh Hospital near Rishon Lezion. Nine soldiers were killed and 30 people wounded. The other went to Jerusalem, where he entered a café. Seven people were killed and over 50 wounded. Hamas claimed responsibility for the attack. In view of the fact that the terrorists were able to enter Israel proper through the West Bank, the Israeli government decided in 2001 to erect a security fence along the entire border with the Occupied Territories. Along 97 per cent of its length, it consists of an electrified fence that is not designed to kill, or even hurt, but when touched sends back a signal to a control point. There is a sanded path on either side of the fence to clearly show footprints. Arab extremists complain that it has seriously hampered their operations reduced terrorist attacks within Israel by as much as 90 per cent.

The terrorist attacks continue, though thanks to the fence, the checkpoints in the West Bank, and

The twenty-first century has witnessed new forms of terror across the globe, particularly the appearance of the suicide bomber. Terrorism has been a part of human society for centuries. However, with modern media, incidence can now reach a world stage within hours. The perpetrators hope to influence world events.

a variety of other security measures in Israel and abroad, they are on a much reduced scale. In 2008, there were three attempts by Arabs driving heavy machinery and trucks in central Jerusalem to mow down as many people as possible, resulting in many casualties and the deaths of the perpetrators.

World Terrorism 2003

Countries where terrorists or terrorist groups operate

Attack by suicide bomber

THE TWO LEBANESE WARS

LEBANON HAS BEEN AN INTRACTABLE PROBLEM FOR ISRAEL.

DUE TO THE WEAKNESS OF THE LEBANESE POLITICAL SYSTEM,

EXTREMISTS HAVE BEEN ALLOWED TO TAKE OVER ITS SOUTHERN

HALF FROM WHENCE THEY HAVE CONTINUALLY ATTACKED ISRAEL.

THE RESULT HAS BEEN TWO INCONCLUSIVE FULL-SCALE WARS.

Israel has been involved in one major raid and two protracted wars with her northern neighbour, Lebanon. In all cases Israel invaded as a result of intense provocation and acts of war from the northern border. In order to understand why this is, it is necessary to understand the make-up of Lebanon. Lebanon is a country that has been riven by deep divisions ever since it first gained its independence from the French in 1943. Prior to this, it had been the Ottoman province of Greater Syria, and becoming a French mandated territory in 1918. It was granted independence from Syria by France in 1926 when it became a republic, and was then granted full autonomy under the Vichy Government in 1943 but the last French troops did not withdraw until 1946. Lebanon is the only country in the Arab world that has a substantial Christian minority, consisting mostly of Maronites (a local form of Roman Catholicism) with some Greek Orthodox and Greek Catholics and both Sunni and Shi'ite Muslims as well as Druzes. As a result, the Lebanese constitution of 1943 determines that the president shall always be a Christian and the prime minister a Sunni Muslim.

Lebanon was historically the one Arab state with which there was no direct confrontation after the ceasefire with the new state of Israel in 1949. It was often said that the first of Israel's neighbours to make peace would be followed by Lebanon. However, Lebanon was also the refuge of more than 100,000 Palestinian refugees who fled north from Galilee between 1947 and 1950. As was the case in other Arab countries, the Lebanese government discouraged the integration of Palestinians into Lebanon's own population. This is because all the Arab states have maintained a tacit agreement that Palestinian refugees are politically more useful than Palestinian citizens incorporated into their countries of refuge and, because the Christian population feared a sizable increase in the Muslim population. Lebanon, imposed harsher conditions for the refugees than other Arab countries. As "non-nationals," Palestinians were barred from employment in the government and the military, and their children were generally excluded from Lebanese schools.

As the refugee camp population grew during the 1950's, so did the resistance movement. The original Palestine National Assembly, formed in Gaza in 1948, gradually gave way to more active groups. In October 1954, a secret resistance group known as Fatah was formed by Yasser Arafat. Another group, the Palestinian Liberation Organisation (PLO), was established in early 1964. It was organised into an Executive Committee, a national council of elected representatives, and a military wing, the Palestinian Liberation Army (PLA).

When the Palestine Liberation Organisation was expelled from Jordan in 1970, it moved its entire operation to Lebanon. It proceeded to occupy the southern half of the country

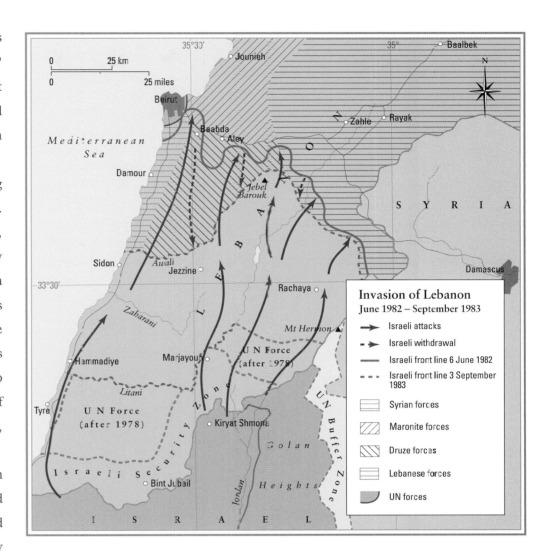

(referred to familiarly as "Fatahland") up to the border with Israel. From here it was able to organise continuous rocket attacks and raids into Israel. The Israeli border settlements, including the city of Kiryat Shemona in Upper Galilee were under constant threat and many lives were lost, to say nothing of the disruption to daily life and economic activities. A major Israeli incursion in 1978 put a temporary end to the attacks, but they were revived with renewed force in the early 1980s.

Israel's borders with Lebanon have been a base from which the state could be attacked for decades. The 1982 invasion was an attempt to consolidate Israeli security.

At the same time, there was an escalation of terrorist attacks on Israelis and other Jews outside Israel, culminating in the shooting of the Israeli ambassador to the United Kingdom in 1982. This was used by Israel's Prime Minister Menahem Begin as a trigger to launch the war which Israel termed "Operation Peace for Galilee". Although the campaign was initially perceived as limited in purpose and duration, it was to become the longest and most controversial military action in Israel's history, lasting for three years. The aims were to eliminate the PLO threat to Israel's northern border, destroy its infrastructure in Lebanon and remove the Syrian military presence in the Bekaa Valley in southern Lebanon.

There was an initial eight-day offensive which destroyed the PLO and damaged the Syrian occupation forces, but in its attempt to push back the PLO to north of the Litani River, Israeli planes bombed and strafed West Beirut, where the anti-Israel forces had their stronghold.

The Israeli Defense Force (IDF) conducted a successful combined arms offensive which achieved every military objective assigned to it. Yet although the strategic goals were initially met – the evacuation of much of the PLO from Beirut and the defeat of the Syrian forces in the Bekaa Valley – in the long term,

One of the largest protests in Israeli history was seen at a rally in Tel Aviv in September 1982, opposing the war in Lebanon.

the militants returned to power in Lebanon. The Palestine Liberation Organisation was replaced in the south by the militant Shi'ite fundamentalists of Hezbollah ("Army of God") under Sheikh Nasrallah who were, if anything, even more of a threat to Israel than the PLO. The almost total collapse of the Lebanese power structure soon brought back the Syrian presence, resulting in the assassinations of several Lebanese politicians who opposed the Syrian presence, including the Sunni Muslim former prime minister Rafiq Hariri in 2005 and Pierre Gemayel, a Lebanese politician and Maronite Christian leader, in 2006. In Israel, opposition to this protracted war mounted, causing deep political divisions and resulting in the increase in political violence and outbreak of the First Intifada (1987–1992) in the West Bank.

The Second Lebanese War was a 33-day military conflict in Lebanon and northern Israel which began on July 12 2006, and continued until a United Nations-brokered ceasefire went into effect on August 14 2006, though it formally ended on September 8, 2006 when Israel lifted its naval blockade of Lebanon.

The conflict began when Hezbollah, which had replaced the PLO, opened fire with rockets on mortars on the Israeli border towns of Zar'it and Shtula, wounding several civilians. This was a diversion for an anti-tank missile attack on two armored cars patrolling the Israeli side of the border fence. Of the seven Israeli soldiers in the two jeeps, two were wounded, three were killed, and two were captured and taken to Lebanon. Five more were killed in a failed Israeli rescue attempt. Israel responded with massive airstrikes and artillery fire on targets in Lebanon, including the International Airport which was being used for the import of weapons and supplies for Hezbollah. Hezbollah launched a huge fusillade of rockets into northern Israel and engaged the IDF in guerrilla warfare from entrenched positions. The conflict killed about 1,200 Lebanese, of whom about 500–700 were estimated by Israel or the UN to have been Hezbollah guerrillas. About 149 Israeli soldiers and 44 civilians were killed. More than 4,000 civilians on each side were injured, and hundreds of thousands of Israelis and Lebanese were displaced from their homes temporarily or permanently. The conflict killed over a thousand people, severely damaged

Lebanese infrastructure, and displaced approximately one million Lebanese and 300,000–500,000 Israelis. Hezbollah rockets reached as far as Haifa, and did considerable damage. After the ceasefire, some parts of Southern Lebanon remained uninhabitable due to unexploded cluster bombs.

On August 11 2006, the United Nations Security Council unanimously approved UN Resolution 1701 in an effort to end the hostilities. The resolution, which was approved the next day by both Lebanese and Israeli governments, called for the disarmament of Hezbollah (which, unsurprisingly, has not happened) the withdrawal of Israel from Lebanon, and the deployment of Lebanese soldiers and an enlarged United Nations Interim Force in Lebanon (UNIFIL) force in southern Lebanon. On October 1 2006, most Israeli troops withdrew from Lebanon. In the time since the enactment of Resolution 1701 both

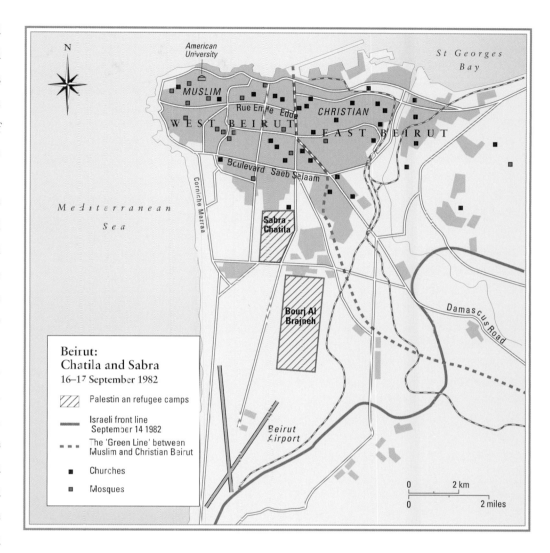

Beirut:
Chatila and Sabra
16–17 September 1982

▨ Palestinian refugee camps

— Israeli front line
September 14 1982

- - - The 'Green Line' between
Muslim and Christian Beirut

■ Churches

▪ Mosques

Map showing the position of the Sabra and Chatila refugee camps outside Beirut. Lebanese Phalangist allies of the Israelis entered the camp in 1982 with the tacit approval of the Israeli commander. Ariel Sharon, in and murdered many residents.

the Lebanese government and UNIFIL have announced that they will not disarm Hezbollah. The dead bodies of the two captured Israeli soldiers, Ehud Goldwasser and Eldad Regev, who were probably alive when captured, were returned to Israel on July 16 2008, in exchange for a number of prisoners including Samir Kuntar, who was sentenced to 29 years in prison (Israel has no death penalty) for the random killings of an Israeli man, his four-year old daughter, and a policeman when he raided a village during an attack. Kuntar was hailed as a hero on his return to Lebanon.

The result of the Second Lebanon War was a stalemate, both sides claiming to have won. The goal of the summer 2006 war was to defeat Hizballah, and prevent it from regaining its strategic capability by destroying the arms route from Iran and Syria. To win such a war Israel would have had to inflict such a massive defeat on Hizballah that the Lebanese army could have completed the task and destroyed it. This did not happen, due to Israeli military failures. After the war ended, Hizballah was still strong enough to continue to launch its rockets.

UN Resolution 1701 did nothing to prevent Hizballah from regaining its strategic capabilities and only mentioned Israel's kidnapped soldiers in the preamble, with no linkage and no sanctions. Politically, Hizballah has become even stronger in Lebanon. It is therefore highly likely that the conflict with Hezbollah, as Iran's closest ally to Israel (although Hamas is funded by Iran, the relationship is problematic for religious reasons, the Gazans being Sunni Muslims and Iran being Shi'ite) will continue and the Second Lebanese War was only the first round.

Extremist Behaviour

THE TWIN TOWERS WERE A WAKE-UP CALL TO THE WEST TO TAKE ARAB TERRORISM SERIOUSLY. SINCE THEN, INNOCENT CIVILIANS HAVE BEEN SERIOUSLY INCONVENIENCED BY ALL OF THE SECURITY MEASURES THAT ARE NECESSARY, ESPECIALLY AT AIRPORTS.

"Five Jews were arrested after they were seen dancing on a rooftop, filming and cheering as the planes crashed into our world trade centers." This is an excerpt from a statement published on the Internet by the American Nazi Party. On September 11 2001, Al-Qaida agents captured four airplanes on routine internal flights and deliberately flew two of them into the World Trade Center and crashed two others, one of them on the Pentagon in Washington. The notorious David Duke posted a video clip on 'YouTube' claiming that no Jews died in the World Trade Center and there was only one Jew on any of the planes.

The facts are that of the several thousand victims of these incidents, religious affiliation was not something that was recorded so there is no way of proving the ridiculousness of the claims. Suffice to say, there have been hundreds of funerals of Jews who were caught up in the terrorist horror of which far too few people had an inkling. The absence of Jews in the Twin Towers belongs in the litany of anti-Semitic myths, such as the Blood Libel and the Protocols of the Elders of Zion. Despite all the laws promulgated to combat race hatred, especially in Europe, no one has been prosecuted for spreading any of these anti-Semitic myths or publishing new versions of the *Protocols of the Elders of Zion* or Hitler's anti-semitic diatribe *Mein Kampf*, the texts of both being freely available on the Internet.

The destruction of the Twin Towers may have marked a turning point in the world's attitude to Jews and the Israel-Palestine conflict. It was finally realized that the Islamic extremism is not merely directed against Israel but has a much wider range. In fact, the primary target of Al-Qaeda was never Israel but rather the West as a whole, including Christianity, democracy, and the West's

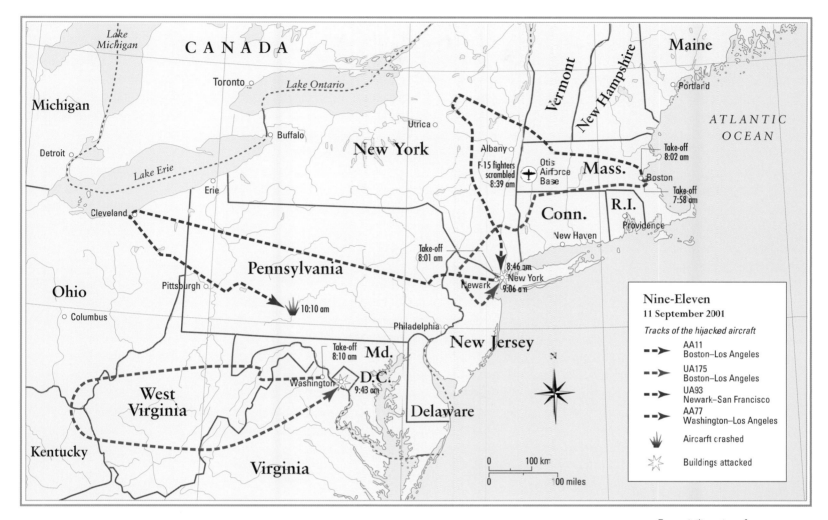

Map labels (clockwise/by region):

Lake Michigan · CANADA · Maine · Toronto · Lake Ontario · Portland · ATLANTIC OCEAN · Michigan · Utrica · Vermont · New Hampshire · Buffalo · New York · Albany · Take-off 8:02 am · Detroit · Lake Erie · F-15 fighters scrambled 8:39 am · Otis Airforce Base · Mass. · Boston · Erie · Take-off 7:58 am · Cleveland · Conn. · R.I. · New Haven · Providence · Pennsylvania · Take-off 8:01 am · 8:46 am New York · Ohio · Pittsburgh · Newark 9:06 am · Columbus · 10:10 am · Philadelphia · New Jersey · Take-off 8:10 am Md. · D.C. · West Virginia · Washington 9:43 am · Delaware · Kentucky · Virginia

Nine-Eleven
11 September 2001
Tracks of the hijacked aircraft

- - ➤ AA11 Boston–Los Angeles
- - ➤ UA175 Boston–Los Angeles
- - ➤ UA93 Newark–San Francisco
- - ➤ AA77 Washington–Los Angeles
🌿 Aircarft crashed
✳ Buildings attacked

0   100 km
0   100 miles

support for the despotic oil-fuelled regimes of the Middle East.

In practical terms, the Jewish ethical problems of the victims of terrorism were never more clearly demonstrated than in the Twin Towers attack. For Jews, every part of the body is sacred and every fragment must be gathered, identified and given a suitable burial. The huge assistance given by Jewish and Israeli organisations, such as the Hevra Kadisha (Jewish Burial Society) which has so much experience in these devastating attacks has been acknowledged by Shiya Ribowsky, former director of special projects at the New York City Medical Examiner's Office and one of America's most experienced medico-legal investigators, who has written a book about his experiences. In the case of the Twin Towers, so many of the bodies were blown into pieces and so were totally untraceable. Nevertheless, he and his team were able to find body parts, such as those of the husband of a young Jewish widow that had been blown from where he had been sitting at his desk to the rooftop of a neighbouring building.

The subsequent attack in London on July 7, 2005 (also known as the 7/7 bombings) consisted of a series of co-ordinated bomb blasts timed to explode in the London subway system during the morning rush hour. At 8:50 am, three bombs exploded within 50 seconds of each other on three subway trains travelling through central London. The fourth bomb could not be planted in the subway because the stations had been closed due to the blasts, so the bomber, carrying the bomb in his rucksack, boarded a diverted bus. The bomb exploded at 9:47 am in London's Tavistock Square. Fortunately, this occurred right outside the British Medical Association and close to hotels

Four civilian aircraft were seized in a well planned suicide plot, the aircraft, fully loaded with fuel became flying bombs aimed at unprepared civilian targets.

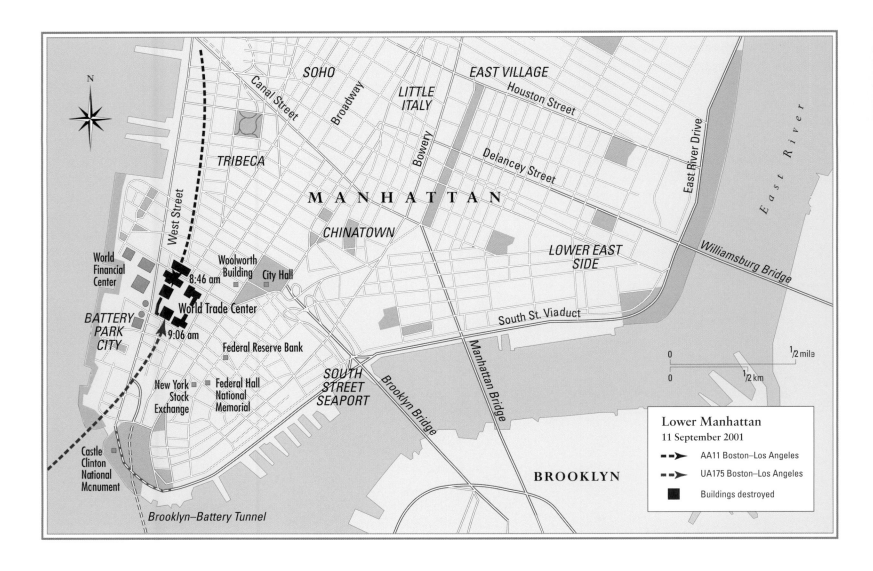

Two aircraft flying from Boston to Los Angeles were seized in flight, their targets were the famous Twin Towers of the World Trade Center.

and a major hospital so assistance could be provided quickly and this probably saved many lives. The bombings killed fifty-two commuters and the four suicide bombers, including the terrorists themselves, several young Jews on their way to work, an Israeli woman, and a Moslem bank clerk. Seven hundred people were injured. The series of suicide-bomb explosions constituted the worst terrorist attack ever on London's public transport system. Perhaps the most horrific aspect as far as the British public were concerned was that this attack, and several subsequent – though fortunately abortive – acts, such as attacks on London buses on July 7 2005, and the attempt to blow up Glasgow Airport on June 30, 2007, were perpetrated not by foreigners from the Middle East as in the 9/11 attacks, but by British nationals.

This was a wake-up call to the United Kingdom authorities who had taken no action against extremist groups with a Middle Eastern agenda, even after it had become known that the two terrorists who blew up the Mike's Place nightclub in Tel Aviv on April 30, 2003 had come from the United Kingdom and were British citizens. In that attack, three Israeli civilians were murdered, and over fifty wounded. The terrorists were Asif Muhammad Hanif and Omar Khan Sharif. Khan Sharif's bomb failed to explode but he may have been injured by the detonator blast. He fled the scene; his body was washed ashore on the Tel Aviv beachfront on 12 days later. Both men were given assistance by anti-Israel organisations in the United Kingdom.

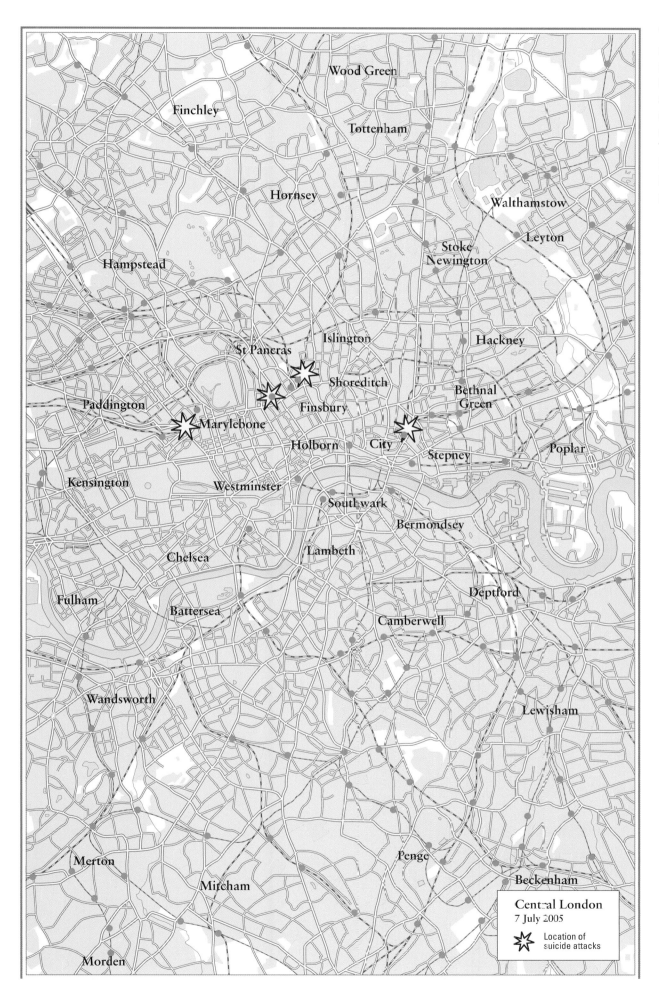

The sprawling, multi-cultural metropolis of London was attacked on 7 July 2005. At 8.50 am, three bombs exploded almost simultaneously. Almost an hour later, a fourth bomb exploded in Tavistock Square. These attacks, aimed at London's transport system, killed 52 and wounded 700 people.

Central London
7 July 2005

Location of suicide attacks

Palestinian Insurgency

PALESTINIAN INSURGENCY HAS NOT ONLY HARMED PALESTINE-
ISRAEL RELATIONS BUT HAS DONE IRREPARABLE HARM TO THE
PALESTINIAN ECONOMY. RELATIONS WHICH WERE SO GOOD JUST
AFTER THE SIX-DAY WAR HAVE NOW DETERIORATED BADLY, AND
FEW ISRAELIS VENTURE INTO THE WEST BANK, LET ALONE GAZA.

E ver since the Jewish population of Palestine began to increase substantially, in the time of the Second Aliyah (1900–20), Arab leaders, both inside and outside Palestine, as well as other powers, have realised the political capital that can be made out of this situation. The Jews of Palestine, and later Israel, have been made the scapegoats for all of the Arab misfortunes by Arab politicians as well as by the Communist Bloc and the West, both of whom have used the situation to deflect attention from their own exploitation of the oil wealth of the Middle East for their own ends.

The first Arab leader to foment major rioting between Arabs and Jews was Mohammed Amin al-Husseini, known as Haj Amin al-Husseini (1893–1975), son of the Mufti of Jerusalem. The Husseinis were and still are, one of the wealthiest clans in the Holy Land. Amin al-Husseini studied at al-Azhar University, Cairo, and attended the Istanbul School of Administration. He volunteered for the Ottoman Turkish army in World War I but returned to Jerusalem in 1917 and expediently switched sides to that of the victorious British. He acquired the reputation as a violent, fanatical anti-Zionist zealot and was jailed by the British in 1920 for instigating an attack on Jews praying at the Western Wall.

When Husseini's father died in 1921, Sir Herbert Samuel, the British High Commissioner who, as a Jew himself, was frightened of being accused of being pro-Zionist, pardoned al-Husseini and, in January 1922, appointed him the new Mufti, even inventing the new title of Grand Mufti. Al-Husseini was simultaneously made President of the newly created Supreme Muslim Council, thus becoming religious and political leader of the Arabs of Palestine.

Husseini was typical of the emergent militant, Palestinian Arab nationalism, a previously unknown concept. Once in power, he began a campaign of terror and intimidation against anyone, including

Opposite: Major incidents of the Palestinian insurgency, the Intifada, have taken place not only in the West Bank and Gaza, but in Israel itself.

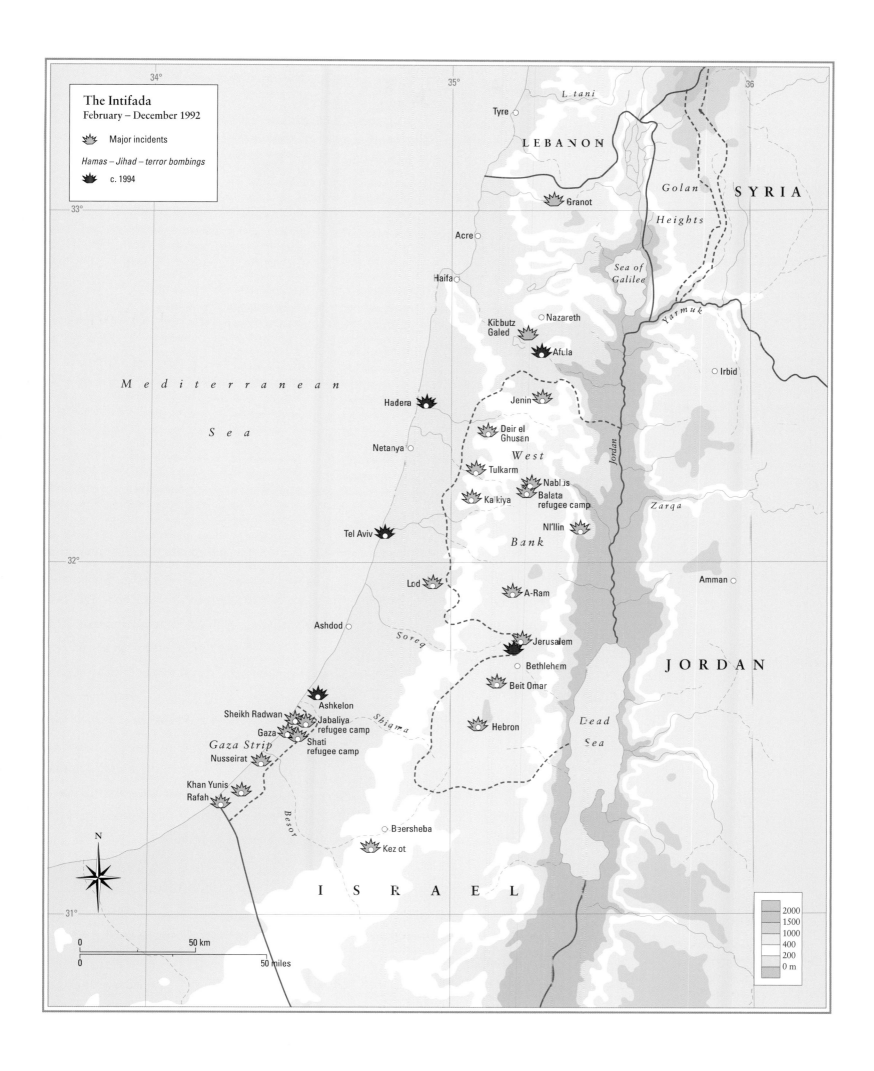

The Intifada
February – December 1992

Major incidents

Hamas – Jihad – terror bombings

c. 1994

L. tani

Tyre

LEBANON

Golan

Heights

SYRIA

Granot

Acre

Sea of
Galilee

Haifa

Yarmuk

Nazareth

Kibbutz
Galed

Afula

Irbid

Mediterranean

Jenin

Sea

Hadera

Deir el
Ghusen

Netanya

West

Tulkarm

Nablus
Balata
refugee camp

Kalkiya

Zarqa

Ni'llin

Jordan

Bank

Tel Aviv

Lod

A-Ram

Amman

Ashdod

Soreq

Jerusalem

Bethlehem

JORDAN

Beit Omar

Dead

Ashkelon

Sheikh Radwan

Shiqma

Sea

Jabaliya
refugee camp

Hebron

Gaza

Gaza Strip

Shati
refugee camp

Nusseirat

Besor

Khan Yunis

Rafah

Beersheba

N

Kez ot

ISRAEL

0   50 km

0   50 miles

2000
1500
1000
400
200
0 m

moderate Arabs, opposed to his rule and policies. In 1929, he falsely accused Jews of defiling and endangering local mosques, including al-Aqsa. After the massacre of Jews in Hebron, the Mufti disseminated photographs of the slaughtered Jews claiming they showed Arabs killed by Jews. By the time the massacres ended, 67 Jews lay dead and the survivors were removed to Jerusalem, leaving Hebron, the second-holiest city for Jews, devoid of Jews for the first time in hundreds of years and playing into Husseini's hands.

In April, 1936, six prominent Arab leaders formed the Arab Higher Committee, with Husseini at its head. It immediately instigated riots in Jaffa commencing a three-year period of violence and civil strife against Jewish and British targets that is known as the Arab Revolt. Husseini consolidated his control over the Palestinian Arabs with a campaign of violence against Jews and non-compliant Arabs. Funds flowed to him from all over the Muslim world. In 1937, he changed sides again, throwing in his lot with Nazi Germany. He begged the Nazis to oppose establishment of a Jewish state, stop Jewish immigration to Palestine, and provide arms to the Arab population. Finally, in 1937, following an assassination attempt on the British Inspector-General of the Palestine Police Force and the murder by Arab extremists of Jews and moderate Arabs, the Arab Higher Committee was declared illegal by the British and Husseini was forced into exile in Syria. The British deported the Arab mayor of Jerusalem and the rest of the Arab Higher Committee.

There is ample documentation to prove that the SS helped finance Al-Husseini's efforts in the 1936–39 revolt in Palestine. Adolf Eichmann actually visited Palestine and met with Al-Husseini at the time and subsequently maintained regular contact with him later in Berlin. It emerged at the Nuremberg and the Eichmann trials that Al-Husseini visited the death camps in Germany in order to plan how these could be installed in Palestine to exterminate the Jews. Al-Husseini moved to Baghdad, aiding the pro-Nazi revolt and pogrom (farhud) against the Jews in 1941. He spent the rest of World War II as Hitler's special guest in Berlin, advocating the extermination of Jews in radio broadcasts to the Middle East and recruiting Bosnian Muslims for the infamous SS "mountain divisions" that tried to exterminate the Jewish communities of the Balkans.

With the collapse of Nazi Germany in 1945, the Mufti moved to Egypt where he was received as a national hero. After the war Al-Husseini was indicted by Yugoslavia for war crimes, but was never tried out of fear of the reaction of the Arab world. Haj Amin al-Husseini arranged King Abdullah's assassination in 1951, while still living in exile in Egypt. When he died, his place as leader of the radical, nationalist Palestinian Arabs was taken by two of his nephews, Abd Al-Qadir Al-Husseini, leader with Hasan Salama of the Army of the Holy War, and Yasser Arafat (1929–2004) who founded the Fatah (Palestine Liberation Organization) in 1959. In August 2002, Arafat gave an interview in which he referred to "our hero al-Husseini" as a symbol of Palestinian Arab resistance.

Yasser Arafat was born in Cairo, and had never set foot in Palestine until the Israelis permitted the Palestine Liberation Organization to set up its headquarters in Ramallah on the West Bank in 1994. In 1964, a coalition of the insurgent factions was established, known as the Palestine Liberation Organisation (PLO), under the auspices of the Arab League. It had its headquarters in Jordan. After the 1967 Six-Day War, Fatah emerged as the most powerful and best organized of the groups of which the PLO consisted and in 1969, Arafat became its chairman. King Hussein feared the growing power of the PLO and its "state within a state" and after several battles with the Jordanian army amounting to an incipient civil war, King Hussein expelled the PLO from Jordan in 1970.

During the 1970s, the PLO began to engage in overtly terrorist activities, a strategy that won notoriety and sympathy for the Palestinian cause in the international arena. The various constituent groups and factions, especially Black September, were responsible for a number of terrorist attacks, including the assassination of Jordan's prime minister in Cairo in 1971 and the murder of 11 Israeli athletes at the Olympic Games in Munich in 1972. In October, 1974, a year after the Yom Kippur War, the heads of the Arab states, meeting in Rabat, Morocco, formally affirmed the "right of the Palestinian people to

Israeli Prime Minister Yitzak Rabin, President Clinton and the PLO chairman Yaser Arafat prepare to shake hands at the signing of the Israeli-Palestinian Peace Agreement in September 1993.

return to its homeland" and named the PLO as the Palestinians' "sole legitimate representative." Despite the PLO's success in bringing the Palestinian issue to world attention, Israel refused to deal with it, preferring, with limited success, to try to develop an independent Palestinian leadership in the West Bank and Gaza. A 1980 Israeli law made it a crime for Israeli citizens to have contact with the PLO.

After expulsion from Jordan, the organization moved to Beirut, where it had more success. In Lebanon, the organization again used its host country's Palestinian refugee population to establish a quasi-independent entity ("Fatahland") as a base for launching attacks against Israel. These included bloody incursions into the northern Israeli towns of Ma'alot and Kiryat Shemona designed to kill civilians indiscriminately. The PLO was eventually driven out of Lebanon in the war launched by Israel in 1982. Arafat then moved the PLO headquarters to Tunis, from which, starting in 1991, he began in a series of peace negotiations with Israel. These included the Madrid Conference of 1991, the 1993 Oslo Accords, and the 2000 Camp David Summit. In 1994, Arafat was awarded the Nobel Peace Prize, together with Yitzhak Rabin and Shimon Peres, for the negotiations at Oslo.

The 1987 uprising in the West Bank and Gaza Strip, known as the First Intifada (literally, "shaking") had been instigated by the indigenous leadership, but it deferred to the PLO as its political representative. During the First Intifada, Jordan officially renounced its claims to East Jerusalem and the West Bank, paving the way for the PLO to announce the establishment of a "state of Palestine," which claimed Jerusalem as its capital though it refrained from defining the borders. With this step, the PLO became a sort of government-in-exile that was recognized by some 70 countries.

Israel and the PLO signed a series of agreements between 1993 and 1998 that transferred almost all Palestinian towns and cities and most of the Arab population in the West Bank and the Gaza Strip to Palestinian administration. The agreements created an interim body, the Palestinian National Authority (PNA), to administer these Palestinian areas until their final status was determined. The following year, the Palestine National Council, the PLO's governing body, named Arafat president of the new "state." During this period, the PLO also formally accepted UN resolutions 242 and 338 (the basis of the "land for peace" formula), thereby implicitly acknowledging Israel's right to exist. Two weeks later,

Yasser Arafat, with a revolver strapped to his hip in a dramatic breach of UN protocol, addressed the UN General Assembly with the words, "I have come bearing an olive branch and a freedom fighter's gun. Do not let the olive branch fall from my hand." In response, the UN affirmed the "inalienable rights" of Palestinians to national independence and the following year awarded the PLO observer status in the General Assembly and many UN organizations. In 1976, the PLO was admitted to full membership of the Arab League.

During this time, Hamas rose to power and shook the foundations of the authority of the PLO. In late 2004, after effectively being confined within his Ramallah compound for over two years by the Israeli army, Arafat became ill and died at the age of 75.

Fatah is one of several groups that make up the Palestine Liberation Organisation. The second-largest is the Popular Front for the Liberation of Palestine (PFLP), a Marxist-Leninist, secular Palestinian political and military organization, founded in 1967 by Dr. Georges Habash (1926–2008) a Christian Arab originally from Lydda (Lod). The PFLP opposed the Oslo Accords and was long opposed to the idea of a two-state solution to the Israeli-Palestinian conflict, but in 1999 came to an agreement with the PLO leadership regarding negotiations with Israel. It has been designated as a terrorist organisation by most western countries. After the Six Day War, the armed wing of the PFLP merged with two other groups, Youth for Revenge and Ahmed Jibril's Syrian-backed Palestine Liberation Front, to form the PFLP, with Habash as leader.

The PFLP had the financial backing of Syria, and was headquartered in Damascus though it had a training camp in as-Salt, Jordan. In 1968, Ahmed Jibril broke away from the PFLP to form the Syrian-backed Popular Front for the Liberation of Palestine—General Command (PFLP-GC). In 1969, the Democratic Front for the Liberation of Palestine (DFLP) formed as a separate organization under Nayef Hawatmeh and Yasser Abd Rabbo, initially as the PDFLP. In 1972, the Popular Revolutionary Front for the Liberation of Palestine was formed following a split in PFLP. In 1974, the PFLP withdrew from the PLO's executive committee, accusing the PLO of abandoning the goal of destroying Israel outright in favor of a bi-national solution. It rejoined the executive committee in 1981. The PFLP boycotted the 1996 elections in the West Bank and Gaza, and this caused its decline in favor of Hamas.

Following the death of Yasser Arafat in November 2004, the PFLP decided to support the independent Palestinian National Initiative's candidate Mustafa Barghouti. In the municipal elections of December 2005 it had greater success, winning the mayoralty of Bir Zeit. The PFLP is powerful politically in the Ramallah area, the eastern districts and suburbs of Jerusalem and Bethlehem, and the primarily Christian Refidyeh district of Nablus, but is little or no threat to the established Hamas movement in Gaza.

The PFLP participated in the Palestinian legislative elections of 2006 as the "Martyr Abu Ali Mustafa List." It won only 4.2 percent of the popular vote and took three of the 132 seats in the Palestinian Legislative Council. It did best in Bethlehem but even there it gained less than ten percent of the vote.

Hamas, the faction that now controls the Gaza Strip, was created in 1987 by Sheikh Ahmed Yassin and Mohammad Taha of the Palestinian wing of the Muslim Brotherhood at the beginning of the First Intifada. Notorious for its numerous suicide bombings and other attacks on Israeli civilians and security forces, Hamas was at first supported by the Israeli government, due to its social programs to establish medical clinics, hospitals, schools, libraries and other services throughout the West Bank and Gaza Strip.

The Hamas charter calls for the destruction of the State of Israel and its replacement with a Palestinian Islamic state in Palestine. Hamas describes its conflict with Israel as political but its founding charter, writings, and many of its public statements are full of anti-Semitic conspiracy theories.

During the period 1993–96, Hamas enjoyed increasing popularity in the wake of its successful strategy of suicide bombings devised by Yahya Ayyash (known as "the Engineer") who was killed in 1996 by a booby-trapped cellphone. In January 2006, Hamas won the Palestinian parliamentary elections, taking 76 of the 132 seats in the chamber, while the ruling Fatah party took 43. The result was seen largely as a protest against the corruption of the Fatah leadership, particularly in Gaza. Since Hamas's election victory, there has been bitter infighting between Hamas and Fatah in Gaza, leading to the deaths of many Fatah supporters. In June 18, 2007, Palestinian President Mahmoud Abbas (Fatah) issued a decree outlawing the Hamas militia and executive force.

Since Israel withdrew from the Gaza Strip in 2005, Hamas has largely been funded by Iran, to the displeasure of neighbouring Egypt. Egypt has always been wary of Hamas power since it is part of the Muslim Brotherhood, an organisation that has long been outlawed in Egypt. Egypt is the channel through which Iranian aid reaches Gaza but if Egypt feels too threatened it could move against Hamas. Since the establishment of the Hamas government, Jordan has strongly opposed Hamas in part because of the impact this relationship is likely to have in strengthening what Jordan perceives as the Shi'ite influence in the Middle East.

Hezbollah is a political and paramilitary organisation based in Lebanon, and has become dominant in Lebanese politics. Hezbollah operates numerous schools, hospitals, and agricultural services for Lebanese Shia muslims. Hezbollah first emerged as a Shi'a extremist group in response to the Israeli invasion of Lebanon in 1982. Its leaders were inspired by Iran's Ayatollah Khomeini, and its forces trained and organized by Iran's Revolutionary Guards. Hezbollah leaders have also made numerous statements calling for the destruction of Israel. The terrorist group calling itself Islamic Jihad is, in fact, believed to be a branch of Hezbollah.

Under Hassan Nasrallah, who became its secretary-general in 1992, Hezbollah instigated the 2006 Lebanon War against Israel. Hezbollah receives its financial support from the Iranian and Syrian regimes. It now has seats in the Lebanese government and a radio and a satellite television-station. In August, 2008 Lebanon's cabinet unanimously approved a draft policy statement which secures Hezbollah's existence as an armed organisation and guarantees its right to 'liberate or recover occupied lands."

Relations between Hezbollah and the Palestinians are problematic, largely due to their source of funding. Hamas and Hezbollah compete over the same Iranian purse. Both realize that Iranian interests and their own do not always coincide and that this gap is greater for the Hamas than it is for Hezbollah. The change in the balance of power in the Palestinian insurgency, with Shi'ite influence gaining over the native Suni version of Islam and the decline of the non-Muslim factions, has had some interesting repercussions. The Gulf States which have significant Shi'ite minorities—Bahrain, Kuwait, and Qatar— are wary of Hamas after the second Lebanese war. An International Monetary Fund study on aid and transfers to the PA in the past year reveals that all Arab state finances have gone to President Abbas of the Palestine National Authority and away from Hamas and Hezbollah.

THE STRUGGLE FOR WATER

MANY BELIEVE THAT WHAT LIES AT THE HEART OF THE MIDDLE

EAST CONFLICT IS NOT OIL BUT WATER. CERTAINLY THE ISRAELIS

GUARD THEIR WATER SUPPLIES JEALOUSLY, AS THEY CONSUME FAR

MORE WATER THAN THEIR NEIGHBOURS BOTH FOR PERSONAL

USE AND FOR INDUSTRY.

Opposite: In an arid region where rainfall is only seasonal a secure supply of water is a critical asset to Israel's survival

Water shortage has been a problem in the Middle East throughout history. The Bible is full of episodes of drought and famine which were matters of life and death to the Israelites in the Holy Land and the surrounding lands. Then, as now, a year of plentiful rainfall meant good harvests and prosperity. The most important prayer in Jewish ritual, for which the High Priest entered the Holy of Holies in the Temple once a year on the Day of Atonement, was the prayer for rain. The reason why the New Year and subsequent cluster of festivals known as the High Holidays are in the autumn when the year actually begins in spring, is because this is the beginning of the yearly cycle, the start of the rainy season.

Many water conservation methods were developed by ancient peoples in the Land of Israel. The Israelites are said to have been the first to terrace the land to prevent run-off and the Nabateans, the desert-dwellers who ruled the Negev and much of the Arabian desert from ca. 300 B.C.E. until ca. the fourth century C.E. from their capital, Petra, developed ingenious techniques for conserving water and using it for irrigation. These have been carefully studied by Israeli scientists and water engineers. One strategy used by the Nabateans was to contour an area of land into a shallow funnel and to plant a single fruit tree in the middle. Just before the rains came, which might consist of only one or two showers all season, the area around the tree was broken up. When it rained, all the water which collected in the funnel would flow toward the fruit tree and sink into the ground. The sandy soil would clog into a seal when wetted and retain the water. It has been shown that such systems concentrate water from an area that is five times larger than that in which the water actually drains. Other studies have shown that the system causes the accumulation of fertile silt in the wadis, making them more suitable for cultivation. The practice of collecting and conserving water in large cisterns beneath houses has been used since ancient times Jews and Arabs in Palestine and lasted until the advent of piped, running water.

Drip-feed irrigation is another ancient technique that has been modernized. The modern technology of drip-feed irrigation was invented in Israel, but instead of releasing the water through tiny holes, that can easily get blocked by particles, it flows through wider, longer flattened plastic pipes, in which friction is used to slow flow, emerging from a plastic emitter. The method has now been adopted all over the world in arid regions.

Israel continues to suffer from a chronic water shortage and the drought of recent years has produced a cumulative deficit in the renewable water resources of approximately 2 billion cubic meters, an amount equal to the annual consumption of the State. The main natural reservoirs, the River Jordan, the Dead Sea and the Sea of Galilee, have dropped to record low levels.

The increase in demand for water for domestic use, caused by population growth (Israel currently has a population of 7.3 million, compared with about 1.3 million in Palestine in 1947) and the rising standard of living, together with the need to supply water to the West Bank and Gaza as a result of international undertakings, have led to a crisis in renewable water sources. Israel's complex political system of coalition governments has mired the development of a long-term water strategy in complications, although Israel has been in the forefront of the technology and has pioneered it in other countries. The agricultural sector has suffered most. Due

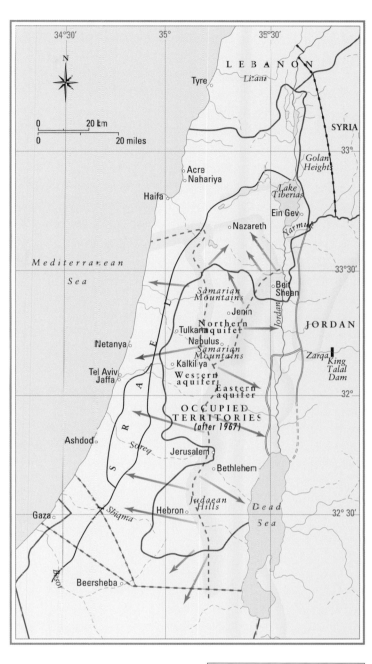

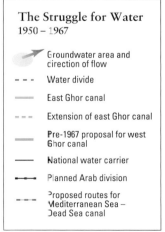

The Struggle for Water
1950 – 1967

→ Groundwater area and direction of flow

--- Water divide

— East Ghor canal

--- Extension of east Ghor canal

— Pre-1967 proposal for west Ghor canal

— National water carrier

•—•—• Planned Arab division

--- Proposed routes for Mediterranean Sea – Dead Sea canal

to the shortage, water allocations to the sector have been reduced, causing a reduction in the agricultural productivity. The current crisis has led to the realization that a master plan for policy, institutional and operational changes is required to stabilize the situation and to improve Israel's water situation in the long-term while ensuring supplies to the West Bank and Gaza.

Israel's main freshwater resources are the Sea of Galilee (Kinneret), the Coastal Aquifer the coastal plain of the Mediterranean Sea, and the Mountain Aquifer under the central north-south (Carmel) mountain range. Additional smaller regional resources are located in the Upper Galilee, Western Galilee, Beit Shean Valley, Jordan Valley, the Dead Sea Rift, the Negev. and the Arava (southern Negev). The long-term average quantity of replenishable water from major water resources amounts to about 1,800 million cubic meters a year.

Non-conventional water sources include reclaimed waste-water (used mainly for watering decorative and landscape plantings) intercepted run-off, and artificially recharge; artificially-induced rain-cloud seeding, and desalination. Public parks have been placed under a conservation regime, including the planting of drought-resistant plants and watering at night.

Another problem is that even the freshwater sources, such as the Sea of Galilee contain brackish water and tough measures are needed to prevent seawater contaminating the water table. This has already occurred in many wells.

The most advanced technology and practices are now being applied to protect and minimize the pollution of water resources. Water conservation maps, restricting land use activities above groundwater resources, have been produced to protect the underlying resources. Regular monitoring of water resources, including water recharge, water table levels, abstraction, salinity (chlorides) and pollution (nitrates) data are regularly monitored and reported.

In 1959, a comprehensive water law was passed, making water resources public property and regulating the exploitation and allocation of water resources, as well as pollution prevention and water conservation. Under the law, all available water resources are made available for use by consumers as directed by the Water Commissioner. The Water Commissioner is responsible for implementing government policy, ensuring sufficient water supply of the required quality and reliability, while conserving and preserving water resources. Mekorot Water Company Ltd. is a government-owned company that is responsible for managing the country's water resources, developing new sources, and ensuring a regular supply of piped water to all localities for every purpose. Mekorot is in charge of the wholesale supply of water to urban communities, industry and agricultural users. Mekorot produces and supplies about two-thirds of the total amount of water used in Israel. The remainder is provided through privately-owned facilities. In 1997, Mekorot supplied 1,380 million cubic meters of water, of which 745 million cubic meters were supplied for irrigation, 540 million cubic meters for domestic use, 94 million cubic meters for industry and 27 million cubic meters to replenish over-pumped aquifers.

The shortage of water in the southern, semi-arid region of Israel required the construction of an extensive water-delivery system that supplies water to this region from resources in the north. Thus, most of the country's fresh water resources were connected to the National Water Carrier, commissioned in 1964. The National Water Carrier, a gigantic pipeline, supplies a blend of surface and groundwater. Water not required by consumers is returned to the aquifer through spreading basins and dual-purpose wells. Recharging of aquifers helps to prevent evaporation loss and the intrusion of seawater in coastal areas. The National Water Carrier supplies a total of 1,000 major consumers, including 18 municipalities and 80 local authorities.

Israel's future plans for making more water available are as follows:

* The construction of desalination plants with an installed annual capacity of 400 million cubic meters for seawater and with an annual capacity of processing 50 million cubic meters of brackish water.
* The rehabilitation of polluted and depleted wells with an annual total yield of up to 50 million cubic meters.
* The importation from Turkey of 50 million cubic meters of fresh water annually.
* Increasing the amounts of treated effluent suitable for irrigation purposes to 500 million cubic meters annually.

The amount of additional water thus produced and/or imported will hopefully restore Israel's water balance that has been caused by overexploitation and depletion of natural water sources on the one hand and increased demand on the other.

The problem of allocation of water resources has been a major sticking point in the peace process, especially as Israel uses vastly more water proportionately than its Arab neighbors. Israel is afraid of allowing the West Bank and Gaza to have any control of water resources that might affect Israel, both for security reasons and because Israel fears misappropriation of the water. Water continues to be supplied to Jordan and the Palestinian Authority, under the various peace agreements.

Table I

LONG-TERM POTENTIAL OF RENEWABLE WATER

Resource	Replenishable Quantities (million cubic meters per year)
The Coastal Aquifer	320
The Mountain Aquifer	370
Lake Kinneret	700
Additional Regional Resources	410
Total Average	1,800

Table II

WATER DEMAND/WATER SOURCES

Year	Urban	Sector	Natural Effluents	Brackish	Wastewater	Total
1998	800	920	120	260	1300	2100
2005	980	750	95	380	1225	2430
2010	1060	680	75	490	1245	2680
2020	1330	600	60	640	1300	2680

Source: Israel Water Commission, 1998

Water Distribution

It has often been said that water is to the Israel-Palestine conflict as oil is to the rest of the Middle East. Peace negotiations with the Palestinians have certainly placed water in the center of the discussions and Israel's reluctance to allow the Palestinians control over water resources has caused a stalemate.

JEWS IN AMERICAN POLITICS

JEWS HAVE BEEN PROMINENT IN BOTH THE BACKGROUND AND
FOREGROUND OF POLITICAL LIFE OF NORTHERN AMERICA, EVEN
BEFORE THE AMERICAN REVOLUTION. JEWS ARE ACTIVE IN BOTH
POLITICAL PARTIES, BUT HAVE TENDED HISTORICALLY TO FAVOUR
THE DEMOCRATS.

American Jewry has been shown to follow a very similar voting pattern to that of other white populations. This consists of support for the Democrats among the urban poor and middle-class voters, due to the party's perceived support for the wage-earner and more liberal attitude to supporting the underprivileged, and to vote Republican when becoming more affluent. This was very much the case in the past, though Jews overwhelmingly supported Franklin D. Roosevelt and his strategies for extricating the United States from the crash and slump of the late 1920s and the 1930s. His Secretary of the Treasury throughout his term of office was Henry Morgenthau, Jr.

A survey of Jews prominent in American public life shows that they have been prominent in every field of American political life and in both political parties, as well as in all parts of the United States, giving the lie to the accusations of "a Jewish lobby" and "the Jewish vote". They have been active in politics even in states with few Jews, as in the case of Simon Bamberger, who was a member of Utah State Senate, 1903–1907 and Governor of Utah, 1917–1921. In the South, David Emanuel, was a member of the Georgia State Senate and Governor of Georgia in 1801. Judah Benjamin was a United States Senator from 1853–1861, then in the Confederacy, he was Attorney General, Secretary of War and Secretary of State, 1861–1865. An early pioneer of the West, Edward Saloman, was Governor of Washington Territory, 1870–1872.

Since in the United States, judges are elected, this includes the judiciary. The most famous American-Jewish is Judge Louis Brandeis (1856–1941), the first Jewish Supreme Court Justice and leader of the American Zionist movement. Justice Brandeis, a leading Democrat, was appointed by

President Woodrow Wilson to the Supreme Court of the United States in 1916, and served until 1939. Brandeis University, founded in 1948 and located in Waltham, Massachusetts, is named for him as is the University of Louisville's law school, where Brandeis is buried. Among the many Jewish associate Supreme Court justices, one of the most outstanding is Arthur Goldberg, who served in the supreme court from 1962 through 1965, when he was appointed ambassador to the United Nations where he served until 1968; before that he had been Secretary of Labor, 1961–1962.

Samuel Gompers (1850–1924) has been described as a key figure in American labor history, as founder of the American Federation of Labor (AFL) in 1886 of which he served as president until his death. Gompers was born in London into a prominent Jewish family (who also spell their name Gompertz) and immigrated to the U.S. at an early age, where he lived in New York's Lower East Side. He was always a pragmatist, concentrating on higher wages and collective bargaining for the workers, rather than engaging in ideology, though after 1907, he encouraged the AFL to take political action to "elect their friends" and "defeat their enemies." Gompers supported American entry into World War I. Another left-wing activist, Daniel De Leon, was a Socialist leader who in 1905 founded the Industrial Workers of the World (IWW, known as "the Wobblies), the only truly militant trade union movement the United States has ever known. David Dubinsky was President of the International Ladies Garment Workers Union from 1932 to 1966.

Many Jews have been active in New York politics. They include Jacob Javits, a United States Senator 1957-1981, member of Congress 1947–1954 and Attorney General of New York 1954–1956. The New York Convention Center is named for him. Abraham Beame was Comptroller of New York, 1962–965 and 1969–1973 and the first Jewish Mayor of New York from 1974–1978. He was followed by Ed Koch and David Bloomberg (2002–). Dianne Feinstein, a Democrat and now a United States Senator since 1992 was Mayor of San Francisco from 1978 through 1988. Of the leading figures in Republican politics the two best-known Jews are Henry Kissinger and Paul Wolfowitz. Wolfowitz was U.S. Ambassador to Indonesia, 1986–1989, Undersecretary of Defense, 1989–1993 and Deputy Secretary of Defense, 2001-present. Henry Kissinger, an immigrant from Germany with a strong foreign accent, was President Nixon's right-hand man, serving as Secretary of State from 1973 through 1977 before which he had been Assistant to the President for National Security Affairs from 1969 through 1975. Ari Fleischer has held several posts in Republican regimes, including White House Press Secretary, 2001–2008.

The German born Henry Kissinger rose to the highest ranks of American diplomacy, winning the Nobel Peace Prize in 1973.

JEWS IN NORTH AFRICA

ALGERIA, MOROCCO, AND TUNISIA, KNOWN COLLECTIVELY AS
THE MAGHREB, SHARE A COMMON HISTORY, AT LEAST AS FAR AS
JEWISH SETTLEMENT IS CONCERNED.

Jews have been present in North Africa since before the Common Era but their numbers swelled during the Spanish Inquisition and subsequent expulsions. When the French occupied the Maghreb in 1830, Jews enthusiastically adopted French culture and were granted French citizenship under the Crémieux Decree in 1870. On the eve of the civil war that gripped the country in the late 1950s, there were some 130,000 Jews in Algeria, approximately 30,000 of whom lived in the capital. Nearly all Algerian Jews fled the country shortly after it gained independence from France in 1962. Most of the remaining Jews live in Algiers, but there are individual Jews in Oran and Blida. A single synagogue functions in Algiers, although there is no resident rabbi. All other synagogues have been taken over for use as mosques.

The first documented evidence of Jews in Tunisia dates back to 200 CE, when there was a community in Latin Carthage under Roman rule. Several sages mentioned in the Talmud lived in this area from the second to the fourth centuries CE.

The Jews of North Africa suffered under the Byzantines. An edict issued by Justinian in 535 excluded Jews from public office, prohibited Jewish practice, and forced the conversion of synagogues into churches. Many Jews fled to the bled, the hinterland where they mingled with Berber communities in the mountains and the desert. After the Arab conquest of Tunisia in the seventh century, Jews lived under satisfactory conditions, despite the usual discriminatory measures meted out to the dhimmi (non-Moslems).

The Spanish invaded Tunisia in 1535–1574, resulting in the flight of Jews from the coastal areas, but situation of the community improved once Ottoman rule had been established. During

The Ghriba synagogue on the island of Djerba in Tunisia. There has been a synagogue on this site since the 6th century BC. Legend has it that Jewish settlers arrived on Djerba after the destruction of the First Temple and refused to return even when Ezra arrived to announce the Temple's reconstruction.

this period, the community also split, due to strong cultural differences between the Touransa (native Tunisians) and the Grana (those adhering to Spanish or Italian customs). Improvements in the condition of the community occurred under beginning in 1837. A large number of Jews rose to positions of political power during this reign.

Under French rule, Jews were gradually emancipated. However, in November 1940, the country fell under the Vichy authorities, who imposed Nazi racial laws against the Jews. From November 1942 until May 1943, the country was occupied by German forces. During this time, the condition of the Jews deteriorated further, and many were deported to labor camps and had their property seized. Tunisia achieved independence in 1956, and this resulted in nationalist attacks on Jews. The rabbinical courts were abolished in 1957, and a year later, Jewish community councils were dissolved. The Jewish quarter of Tunis was demolished by the government. Anti-Jewish rioting followed the outbreak of the Six-Day War in 1967, when Moslems burned down the Great Synagogue of Tunis. While the community was compensated for the damage, these events increased the steady stream of emigration.

Since 1948, 53,068 Jews from Tunisia have immigrated to Israel.

El Ghirba Synagogue in the village of Hara Sghira on the island of Djerba is still a tourist attraction. Although the present structure was built in 1929, the site has been used as a synagogue for the past 1,900 years. In 2002, a suicide bomber drove a truck at the synagogue resulting in nineteen deaths, mostly of tourists.

The Jewish community of present-day Morocco dates back more than 2,000 years and Jews lived in the country before it became a Roman province. The Jews of Morocco are generally descended from three different groups: Sephardim, Berbers, and Ashkenazim. In 1391, a wave of Jewish refugees expelled from Spain brought new life to the community, as did new arrivals from Spain and Portugal in 1492 and 1497. From 1438, the Jews of Fez were forced to live in special quarters called mellah, a name derived from the Arabic word for salt because the Jews in Morocco were forced to salt the heads of executed prisoners prior to their being put on public display.

With the establishment of the French Protectorate in 1912, Jews were given equality and religious autonomy. During World War II, when France was ruled by the anti-Semitic Vichy government which also controlled Morocco, King Muhammed V prevented the deportation of Jews. By 1948, there were some 270,000 Jews in Morocco, but many Jews chose to leave for Israel, France, the United States, and Canada.

The Jews no longer reside in the Jewish mellahs and are now among the most affluent members of Moroccan society. In 1992, most of the Jewish schools were closed down and only those in Casablanca have remained. Nevertheless, the full range of Jewish services is available in Casablanca, Fez, Marrakesh, Mogador, Rabat, Tetuan and Tangier. The Moroccan-Jewish community has a great tradition of rituals and pilgrimages to the tombs of holy sages. Every year on special dates, crowds of Moroccan Jews from around the world, including Israel, throng to these graves. A unique Moroccan festival, the Mimunah, is celebrated in Morocco and in Israel. Israel and Morocco maintain close ties, symbolized by the official visit of Prime Minister Yitzhak

Rabin to Morocco after signing the agreement with the Palestine Liberation Organisation in 1993. Since 1948, 295,900 Moroccan Jews have emigrated to Israel.

In addition to the Jewish communities, the major sites of pilgrimage for the Jewish traveler

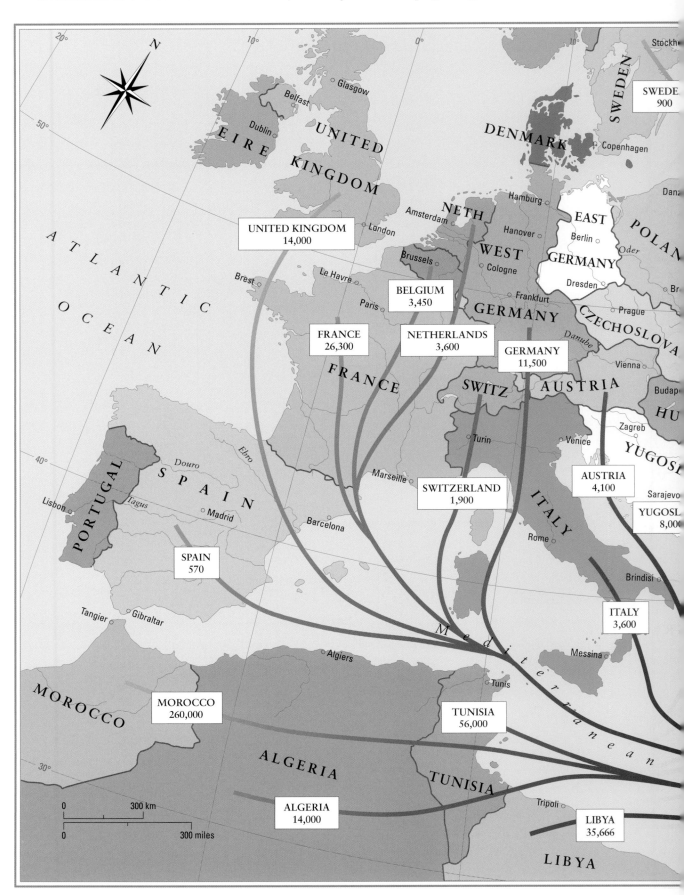

SWEDE 900	
UNITED KINGDOM 14,000	
BELGIUM 3,450	
FRANCE 26,300	NETHERLANDS 3,600
	GERMANY 11,500
SPAIN 570	AUSTRIA 4,100
	SWITZERLAND 1,900
	YUGOSL 8,00
	ITALY 3,600
MOROCCO 260,000	
	TUNISIA 56,000
ALGERIA 14,000	LIBYA 35,666

are the tombs of the holy sages, scattered around the country. The most popular are Rabbi Yehouda Benatar (Fez), Rabbi Hayyim Pinto (Mogador), Rabbi Amram Ben Diwane (Ouezzan), and Rabbi Yahia Lakhdar (Beni-Ahmed).

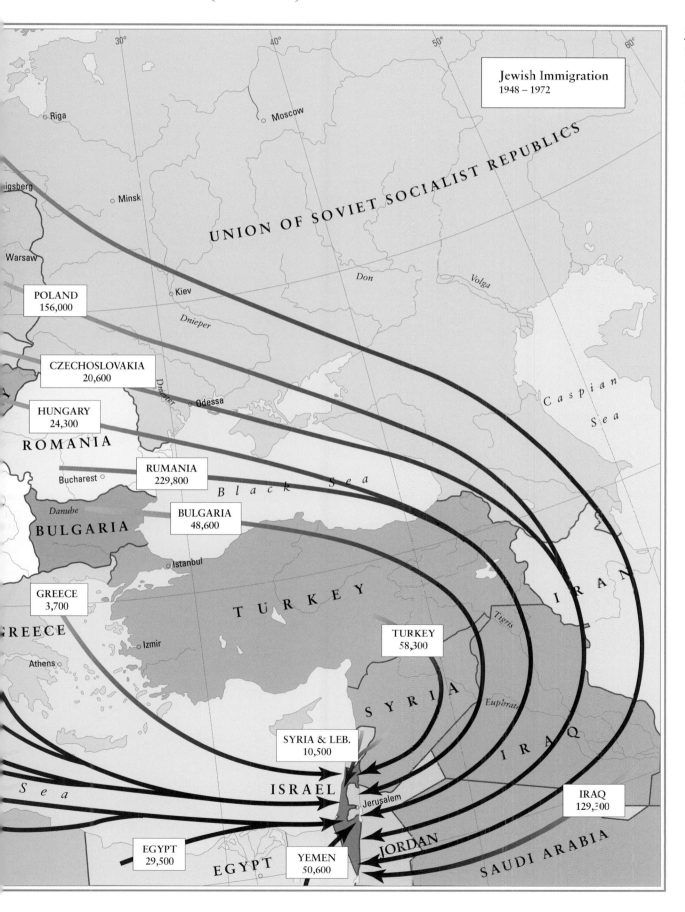

Jewish Immigration
1948 – 1972

POLAND
156,000

CZECHOSLOVAKIA
20,600

HUNGARY
24,300

RUMANIA
229,800

BULGARIA
48,600

GREECE
3,700

TURKEY
58,300

SYRIA & LEB.
10,500

IRAQ
129,300

EGYPT
29,500

YEMEN
50,600

Jews from North Africa and the Middle East were well represented among the thousands who found a new home in Israel.

FALASHAS

THE INGATHERING OF THE EXILES IS A FUNDAMENTAL ASPIRATION
OF ZIONISM AND THE STATE OF ISRAEL. THE LAW OF RETURN
(1950), GRANTS EVERY JEW THE RIGHT TO SETTLE IN THE JEWISH
HOMELAND. MANY HAVE BEEN RESCUED SINCE 1948 FROM
PERSECUTION OR, AS IN THE CASE OF THE FALASHAS, FROM FAMINE.

A Falasha woman inspects the memorial erected in Israel to those who died while trying to reach the Holy Land, many of them on foot.

Tiny pockets of practicing Jews have been found in many parts of the world since the various dispersals that began with the Babylonian Exile (ca. 538 BCE). The origins of many such communities—in Uganda and Cochin, Southern India, for instance—is obscure. The largest such community was in Ethiopia where it was known to the Ethiopians as "falasha" which means "stranger" in Amharic, the national language. The community calls itself Beta Israel, the house of Israel.

The origin of the Jewish community of Ethiopia is obscure. Some Falashas claim to be direct descendants of Abraham who came from the Chaldees. The Chaldeans were said to be Kushite tribes in Mesopotamia and, in the Bible, Kushite refers to Blacks. Certainly, the Falashas are indistinguishable from their fellow Ethiopians. Other Falashas assert their origin to be the result of the union between King Solomon and the Queen of Sheba. Some scholars claim that they are descended from the Jewish community, founded as a military outpost in ca. 650 BCE, on the island of Elephantine in the Nile, close to the border of Nubia. Certainly, the Falashas can date their origins back a long way because they are not familiar with either the Babylonian or Palestinian Talmud and they do not have rabbis, only priests and assistant priests.

The Bible of the Falashas is written in Geez, the same Semitic language as the Ethiopian Christian holy books. They do not know Hebrew. In addition to the Biblical canon, the Beta Israel hold sacred the Apocryphal books of Enoch, Jubilees (Yovel), Baruch, and the Book of Ezra. These Biblical writings appear to have been passed down through translations such as the Septuagint, the Bible translated into Greek in Alexandria some time between the third and first centuries BCE, which indeed incorporates some of the Apocrypha.

The Beta Israel possess several other holy books, including the Acts of Moses, Apocalypse of Gorgorios, Meddrash Abba Elija, and biographies of the nation's forebears, Gadla Adam, Gadla Avraham, Gadla Ishak, Gadla Ya'akov, Gadla Moshe, Gadla Aaron, Nagara Musye and Mota Musye. Another important book, known as the Abu Shaker, was written around 1257 CE and lists civil and lunar dates for Jewish feasts, including Matqeh (New Year), Soma Ayhud or Badr (Yom Kippur), Masallat (Sucot), Fesh (Passover), and Soma Dehnat (Fast of Salvation) or Soma Aster (Fast of Esther Purim).

Falasha synagogue or masjid in a village in Ethiopia.

The Falashas still practice animal sacrifice. They celebrate feasts that are mentioned in the Bible as well as others, such as the Commemoration of Abraham, that are not. One important holiday, known as Sigd, is celebrated on 29 Heshvan (November) in the Hebrew calendar. Sigd or Seged is derived from a Semitic root and means "to bow or prostrate oneself." These actions are known as mehella. Sigd celebrates the giving of the Torah and the return from exile in Babylonia to Jerusalem under Ezra and Nehemiah. It is also held to commemorate Ezra's proclamation against the Babylonian wives (Ezra 10: 10–12). In Ethiopia, the Sigd was celebrated on hilltops outside villages.

The Sabbath regulations of the Falash are stringent. They observe biblical dietary laws, but not the post-biblical rabbinic regulations, such as those separating milk and meat. Marriage outside the religious community is forbidden. The Falasha are monogamous, although the Bible permits a Jewish man to take four wives and polygamy is practiced in other isolated Jewish communities such as that of the Yemen. This may indicate that the Falasha are not, as some claim, descendants of Yemenite-Jewish migrants to Ethiopia.

The center of Falasha religious life is the masjid, the synagogue. The Falashas have monks who live alone or in monasteries, a practice unique to their form of Judaism. The Falashas of Ethiopia lived mainly north of Lake Tana. Under Emperor Haile Selassie, some Falashas rose to positions of power in education and government, but the community was persecuted when the Emperor was overthrown in 1974.

More than 12,000 Falashas were secretly airlifted to Israel in 1984–1985, but news leaked out and the Ethiopian government stopped the emigration for fear of Arab pressure. The airlift resumed in 1989, and about 3,500 Falashas immigrated in 1990. Nearly all of the remaining Falashas in Ethiopia were evacuated by the Israeli government in May 1991 to escape the famine. In 2008. Some 50,000 Ethiopian Jews—a quarter of them Israeli-born—were living in Israel.

The situation is different for the Falashmura or Falash Mura, Falashas who were forcibly converted to Christianity at various times in the past. In 2005, the Israeli government agreed to allow some 17,000 of them into Israel, but when this quota was filled, thousands more were still waiting in transit camps in Gondar.

The Falashas have generally integrated well into Israel, though they still tend to work in menial jobs. Sadly, they have mostly abandoned their beautiful traditional white robes edged with a thin strip of blue and red embroidery, in favor of western dress.

THE NEW ANTI-SEMITISM

ANTI-JEWISH PROPAGANDA, FUELLED BY HUGE FUNDS FROM THE OIL-RICH ARAB STATES, RANGES FROM OVERTLY ANTISEMITIC LITERATURE AND INTERNET POLEMICS TO INDIRECT ATTACKS ON JEWS, AND PARTICULARLY ON ISRAEL.

The revulsion that filled the civilized world when the extent of Nazi atrocities was known ought to have marked the end of anti-Semitism, but sadly this has been far from the case. In the Soviet sphere of influence, the Holocaust was played down as had Jewish ethnicity, the communist line being that certain ethnicities (Tartars and Jews) had no right to claim a separate identity. Memorials to the dead of World War II, such as at Babi Yar, outside Kiev in the Ukraine, where one of the worst massacres of Jews occurred, even have Yiddish inscriptions but there is nothing else to indicate that the victims were Jewish. Consequently, the "street-level" anti-Semitism that prevailed before the war continued thereafter, and Jews continue to face discrimination in employment and are subjected to insulting remarks in the street.

Many former collaborators with the Nazis were horrified to discover that some Jews had survived, come home and wanted to reclaim their homes. The worst incidents occurred in Poland, a country in which anti-Semitism was deeply ingrained. In Rzeszów and Cracow in 1945 and especially in Kielce in 1946, the blood libel was revived. The Kielce pogrom began when a child claimed to have been kidnapped and held in the cellar of the Jewish Committee building, even though the building had no cellar. Most of the victims, including women and children, were beaten to death indiscriminately with stones, planks, and metal bars by a mob, with the collusion of local police and militia. Trains at the main railway station were searched for Jews; the forty-two victims identified as such, were thrown from the trains and killed. Only when troops arrived from Warsaw did the mob scatter and the pogrom end. In the following months, virtually the whole remnant of Polish Jewry fled the country, mostly to Palestine. Once Lithuania had become an independent state in 1991, Jewish partisans have been accused of war crimes for killing their enemies.

Activists of the extreme right in Western Europe and the United States have continued with their campaign aimed at Jews in all walks of life. One of the new strategies has been Holocaust denial which has been made a crime in Germany and Austria. Neo-fascists even claim that Hitler knew nothing about the death camps or the Final Solution, yet anyone reading Mein Kampf (freely available, like all anti-Semitic literature, throughout the Arab world in many translations, and even through internet-based bookshops) or his Testament written just before his death has ample evidence of his rabid anti-Semitism, and if his minions never informed him of the plan to exterminate the Jews he would have been very disappointed. Anti-semitism is rife in the Arab world, as in the case of the Mufti of Jerusalem who had even planned the site of the extermination camp he would use to murder the Jews of Palestine. When it was revealed in 1986 that Kurt Waldheim, the former UN secretary-general, had been a senior officer in the German army and witnessed, if not participated, in the murder of Jews in Greece and Yugoslavia, he suddenly became an honored guest throughout the Arab world. The desecrations of Jewish graveyards that are particularly

Between 1989 and 1991 many Jews settled in Israel, particularly from Russia. Of this new wave of settlers some chose to begin their new lives in the West Bank.

This kind of anti-Israel propaganda is based on the kind of propaganda that brands all antisemitic attacks as legitimate because of "what Israeli is doing to the Palestinians." The far left has been so heavily influenced by such propaganda that some of its members have even aided and abetted terrorism that has claimed innocent lives, not all of them Jewish.

prevalent in France and England are normally perpetrated by youthful anti-semites. In 1990, four young Nazis desecrated Jewish graves in Carpentras, southern France, even digging up a corpse.

Since the establishment of the State of Israel, a new strain of anti-Semitism has emerged, especially among marxists in Europe and the United States, calling itself anti-Zionism. It includes a very small minority of Jews, most from the extreme left. Prior to the existence of Israel, there were Jewish organisations, such as the Bund in late nineteenth-century Russia and the Jewish Fellowship in England, founded in 1942, that believed a Jewish state was not the answer. These and similar organisations collapsed from lack of Jewish support. They were not anti-semitic in any way, but the German courts have judged that the virulent anti-Zionism expressed by left-wing activists is, in fact, anti-Semitic, as in the case of Evelyn Hecht-Galinski, in September, 2008.

It is no coincidence that anti-Israel hostility became fiercer after the peace treaties had been signed between Israel and Egypt (1979) and Israel and Jordan (1994). The Arab League, conscious that Israel cannot be exterminated in battle, supports and funds anyone—including Jews—who expresses hostility to the Jewish state per se. Hostility to Israel in the non-Jewish world has never been stronger in the English-speaking world than it is today. In Britain, it permeates the national and local press, the broadcast media, the universities and, of course, the Internet. And clearly this manifests itself not merely in hostility to Israel but to Jews in general.

The old canard of the Jewish lobby and Jews "controlling" the media was recently revived in a book written by two Harvard professors, John Mears and Stephen Waltheimer in 2007, entitled *The Israel Lobby and U.S. Foreign Policy*. The Internationalen finanzjudentum (international finance Jewry) a phrase beloved of Adolf Hitler is recognizable in the phrase "International Zionism," Conspiracy theories formerly based around the Jews or the "Elders of Zion" are now transferred to "Zionists." Former President Jimmy Carter even used the vicious smear of anti-Zionists that Israel is an "Apartheid State" in his book entitled *Palestine: Peace not Apartheid* published in 2006. Then there are those who claim that they advocate a "one-state solution", the state in question being one, in which Jews do not predominate and that it is "politically correct" to abolish Israel as a Jewish homeland since Jews are the only ethnic minority in the world who have no right to self-determination. The doctrines of "progressive" anti-Zionism are so indistinguishable from racism that a left-wing British "Boycott Israel" activist saw no problem in recommending an article that had been posted on the website of American extreme right-winger David Duke.

The imagery of anti-Zionist cartoons and graphics in the Arab world and even in European countries such as Great Britain (an example is the cartoon that appeared in the national daily The Independent showing Ariel Sharon devouring Arab babies, for which the cartoonist won an award) is indistinguishable from Nazi stereotypes used in anti-Semitic cartoons and propaganda themes.

The United Nations has made anti-Zionism respectable. Beginning in the late 1960s, the full weight of the UN has gradually been turned against one of its smallest members, the very country conceived by General Assembly resolution a mere two decades earlier. The campaign to demonize and delegitimize Israel in every UN and international forum was initiated by the Arab states together with the Soviet Union, and supported by the so-called non-aligned states, most of which are dictatorships.

The campaign reached new heights during the Arab oil embargo of 1973, when many African states were pressured into severing ties with Israel. In 1975, following a stream of anti-Israel declarations at UN-sponsored international conferences, the General Assembly adopted a "Zionism is Racism" resolution. At the same time, it instituted a series of related measures that together installed an infrastructure of anti-Israel propaganda throughout the UN. It was not until 15 years later, after strenuous efforts by democratic forces, that the infamous resolution was repealed. Nevertheless, UN committees, annual UN resolutions, an entire UN bureaucratic division, permanent UN exhibits in New York and Geneva headquarters remain dedicated to a relentless and virulent propaganda war against the Jewish state. Paradoxically, one of the greatest violators of the UN Charter's equality guarantee has been the UN body charged with establishing and enforcing international human rights, the Human Rights Council. The UN's discrimination against Israel is not a minor infraction, nor a parochial nuisance of interest solely to those concerned with equal rights of the Jewish people and the Jewish state. Instead, the world body's obsession with censuring Israel at every turn directly affects all citizens of the world, for it constitutes (a) a severe violation of the equality principles guaranteed by the UN Charter and underlying the Universal Declaration of Human Rights, and (b) a significant obstacle to the UN's ability to carry out its proper mandate. UN bias against Israel is overt in bodies such as the General Assembly, which each year passes some nineteen resolutions against Israel and none against the world's most repressive regimes. The World Health Organisation, meeting at its annual assembly in Geneva in 2005, passed but one resolution against a specific country: Israel was charged with violating Palestinian rights to health. Similarly, the International Labor Organisation, at its annual 2005 conference in Geneva, carried only one major country-specific report on its annual agenda—a lengthy document charging Israel with violating the rights of Palestinian workers.

In the summer of 2004, the UN's International Court of Justice at The Hague issued an advisory opinion ruling the Separation Fence (which has reduced suicide bombings by ninety percent, saving thousands of Israeli lives) that followed the script of a political campaign orchestrated by the PLO representative at the UN, Nasser al-Kidwa. In 1975, the General Assembly added the Committee on the Exercise of the Inalienable Rights of the Palestinian People. Supporting its work is the Division for Palestinian Rights. Lodged within the UN Secretariat, the Division boasts a sixteen-member staff and a budget of millions, which it devotes to the constant promotion of anti-Israel propaganda throughout the world.

Shadows of World War II

THE HOLOCAUST WAS ONE OF THE MOST HORRIFIC EVENTS OF THE TWENTIETH CENTURY. IT DESCRIBES THE GENOCIDE OF SIX MILLION JEWS DURING WORLD WAR II, PERPETRATED BY THE GERMAN NAZI PARTY. THE DANGEROUS ANTI-SEMITISM LIVES ON IN HOLOCAUST DENIAL.

An extraordinary and unique manifestation of "post-modern" anti-Semitism is Holocaust Denial. It is the claim that an event that occurred within living memory, to which there are hundreds and thousands of survivors and eye-witnesses, never happened.

These self-styled historians claim variously that: a) Hitler was not as anti-Semitic as claimed; b) that far fewer Jews were killed by the Nazis; c) that there was no deliberate policy of genocide and that; d) the gas chambers and other means of mass destruction never existed. Another claim is that Jews have spread this "myth" to enable the creation of a Jewish homeland in Palestine and win support for the state of Israel.

Holocaust denial, despite the claims of many of its proponents to be objective and unbiaised, is generally considered to be an anti-Semitic conspiracy theory. Although there are professed Jews, including Noam Chomsky and Norman Finkelstein, who assert that the deniers have a right to their views, most historians of World War II claim that Holocaust Denial is a dangerous distortion of the truth.

The Holocaust was so carefully documented by the Nazis, that people trying to trace dead relatives have been able to reconstruct the train transports of Jews to the death camps through the paperwork that survived. This huge exercise could not fail to have produced vast amounts of paperwork. Indeed, orders for the shipment of crematorium ovens, canisters of poison gas, train movements, the design of the gas chambers, have all been found and documented.

The aftermath of the Holocaust was witnessed by the Allied forces who entered Germany and its associated Axis states toward the end of World War II and liberated the camps. The Nazis attempted to destroy the evidence when they faced defeat; much incriminating evidence, such as the interrogations of leading Nazis.

One of the first to publish a denial of the Holocaust was Robert Faurisson (1929–) then a professor of literature at the University of Lyon. Faurisson claims to have studied the Holocaust extensively, and to have come to the conclusion in the late 1970s that it was a hoax. Since then he has written numerous letters to newspapers, published several books, and written articles for Holocaust denial journals.

Faurisson has claimed that the gas chambers were a hoax as they could not have worked as described. Zündel also states that the level of cyanide found in the walls of the surviving gas chambers at Auschwitz is too low, and that if they had been

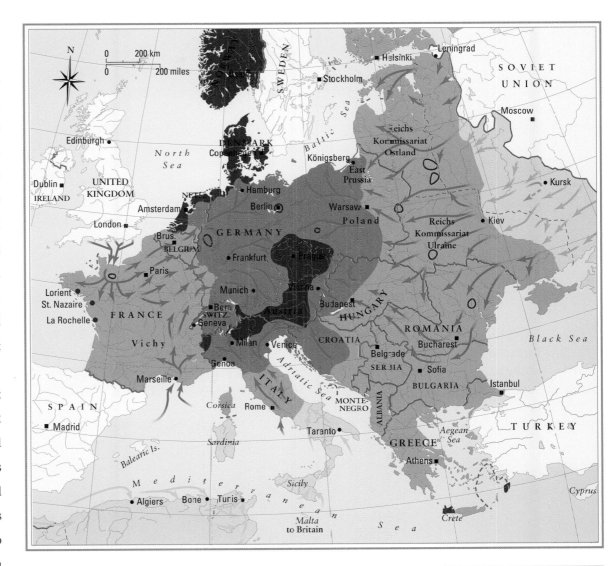

used as claimed, they would still be impregnated with the gas. These arguments were refuted by a former Faurisson supporter, Jean-Claude Pressac. Henri Roques, another French Holocaust denier, was actually awarded a doctoral degree by the University of Nantes in 1986 on the strength of his claim that allegations of mass gassings of Jews in 1942 made by SS officer Kurt Gerstein were untrue. The degree was subsequently revoked through by a decree of French education minister Alain Devaquet. In 1991, Faurisson was removed from his university chair under the Gayssot Act, a French statute passed in 1990 that prohibited Holocaust denial.

Ernst Christof Friedrich Zündel (1939–) is a German neo-Nazi, Holocaust denier and pamphleteer who has been jailed several times in Canada for publishing literature which "is likely to incite hatred against an identifiable group." He lived in Canada from 1958 to 2000 when he returned to Germany. His Samizdat publishing house has produced *"Did Six Million Really Die?"* (1974) by Richard Harwood (also known as Richard Verrall, prominent in the British National Front).

David Irving (1938–) is a British Holocaust-denier and author of thirty books, including *"Hitler's War"* (1977) and *"Goebbels—Mastermind of the Third Reich"* (1996). In 1998, he brought an unsuccessful libel case against American historian Deborah Lipstadt and Penguin Books. On a visit to Austria, Irving was apprehended, tried and convicted of "glorifying and identifying with the German Nazi Party", which is a crime in Austria. He served a prison sentence from February to December 2006 on these charges.

The Destruction of Nazi Europe

→ Western Allies advance, late 1942–Oct. 1943

- → German withdrawal

→ Soviet advance to Oct. 1943

→ Allied advance, 1943–45

◯ Isolated German pocket

▢ Retaken by Allies, Oct. 1942–Oct. 1943

▢ Retaken by Allies, Dec. 1944

▢ Retaken by Allies, end of hostilities

▢ Still held by German armies, 9 May, 1945

The destruction of Nazi Germany left Europe in ruins, with some 43,000,000 of its people dead. Amongst this dreadful total were 6,000,000 Jews.

JERUSALEM, CITY OF RELIGIONS

THE NAME JERUSALEM CONJURES UP SO MANY ASSOCIATIONS CONNECTED WITH PEACE AND AN APOCALYPTIC VISION. YET THIS CITY, HOLY TO THREE RELIGIONS, HAS BEEN DISPUTED FOR THOUSANDS OF YEARS.

It is the Jewish misfortune that Jerusalem, the capital city of Israel, is also holy to two other religions. While the Christians have Rome and the Moslems have Mecca, the Jews have only Jerusalem and subordinately, another three cities Hebron–also claimed by the Moslems—Tiberias and Safed. In the course of its history, Jerusalem has been completely destroyed twice, besieged 23 times, attacked 52 times, and captured and recaptured 44 times.

The city of Jerusalem, was first settled in c. 3800 BCE is one of the oldest continuously inhabited cities in the world and sadly one of the most fought over. It became Jewish when King David purchased a threshing-floor on which to set up an altar from Araunah the Jebusite (II Samuel, 21–23). David established Jerusalem as a mountain stronghold, choosing a site that was not within the territory of any of the tribes of Israel. The City of David was located outside the present walls close to the Dung Gate at the Ophel, above the Gihon spring; it has recently been excavated and has yielded some amazing finds, including the seals (bullae) of two of the ministers of King Zedekiah (597–586 BCE), and many relics from the days of David and his son, King Solomon, builder of the First Temple on Mount Moriah. The Temple was constructed to replace the portable shrine, the Ark of the Covenant, first made on the orders of Moses. This was to signify that the nomadic existence of the Israelites was over, they must now live in permanent settlements.

The First Temple was a relatively small building, surrounded by a huge courtyard which contained the King's palace. It was paneled in the cedarwood which King Solomon's ships had brought from Lebanon and there were other rich decorations from distant lands. Pagan visitors to the Temple were astonished to realize that the Holy of Holies, which only the High Priest could enter and then only on certain days was, in fact, an empty chamber. They also marvelled at the absence of statues. Temple ritual required that the priests and worshippers perform sacrifices. These took various forms for different purposes, including animal sacrifices, meal offerings, the show-bread, and the first fruits.

The City of David can be visited today, starting from the vantage point of the Ophel and moving underground to some of the newest archaeological excavations at the site. Visitors can wade through the 2,700-year-old tunnel built by King Hezekiah to bring water to the city, one of the wonders of early

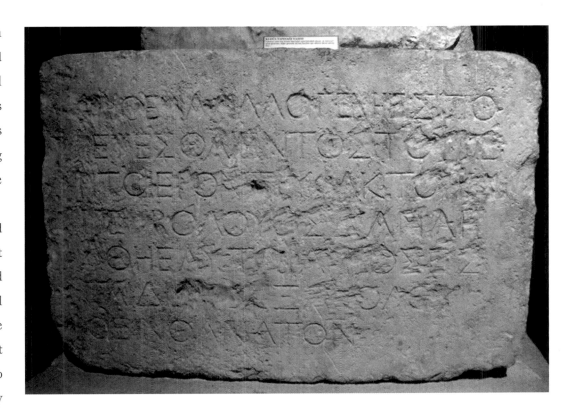

Greek inscription on a stone found in the Temple Mount warning pagans that parts of the Temple precinct were forbidden to them. It dates from the time of the Second Temple.

engineering. One of the most significant finds from the Old Testament period in what is today known as the Jewish Quarter of the Old City is the Broad Wall built by King Hezekiah before the invasion in 701 BCE by the Assyrian King Sennacherib to enclose the Western Hill. This expanded the walled city of Jerusalem fivefold.

The Second Temple was built after the return from the Babylonian Captivity. It was begun in about 536 BCE and completed on March 12 (Adar 3), 515 BCE. It stood on the site of the First Temple. Sacrifices were first resumed on the first day of Tishrei, 538 CE, the day of the Feast of Trumpets, the festival now known as Jewish New Year. Again, cedarwood was brought from Lebanon to line the walls. The pagan population of what was now the Persian province of Yahud, including the Idumeans, who later converted to Judaism (of whom King Herod was one), bitterly opposed the rebuilding of the Second Temple. They complained to Cambyses, the Persian king, who halted the work. During the next nine years, the Jews resettled the areas surrounding Jerusalem, including the Kidron Valley, at the foot of Temple Mount, but they allowed the city walls to fall into disrepair.

Herod's Temple, started around 19 BCE, was a massive expansion of the Second Temple, including renovation of the entire Temple Mount. It is never referred to as the "Third Temple," since Herod was so deeply unpopular with the Jewish people. He was a tyrant who had destroyed Antigonus and his Sanhedrin, the Jewish parliament, at the beginning of his reign. The new Temple extension was a massive project, typical of this megalomaniac who murdered his own sons and his wife Mariamne. The Second Temple and Herod's work, as well as the neighboring Fortress of Antonia were attacked by Roman troops under Titus in 70 CE and the buildings were razed to the ground and replaced by a temple to Jupiter under the Emperor Hadrian in 135 CE. Archaeologists are convinced that the Romans sliced off the top of the Temple Mount, so that nothing will more ever be found at the site of the Temple itself, though many artifacts and remains of buildings have been found around the site, including the row of shops where stone "vouchers" were sold for bird and animal sacrifices, as well

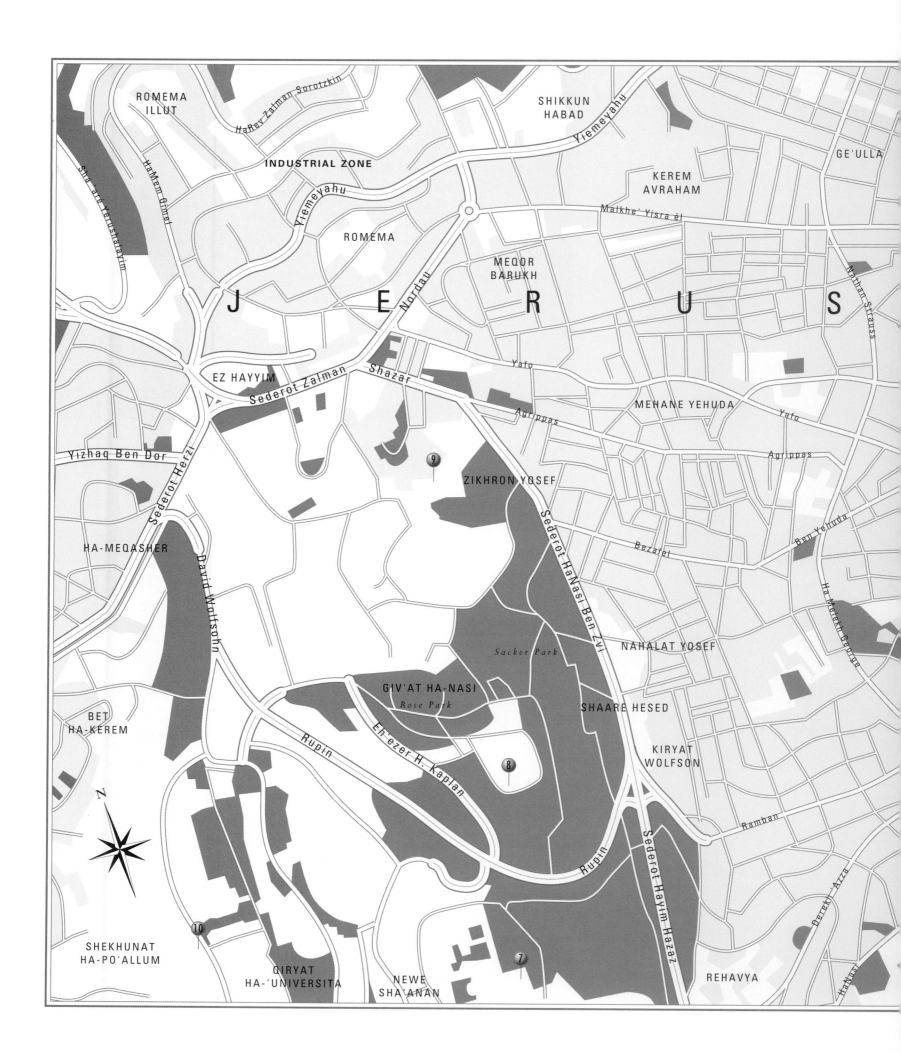

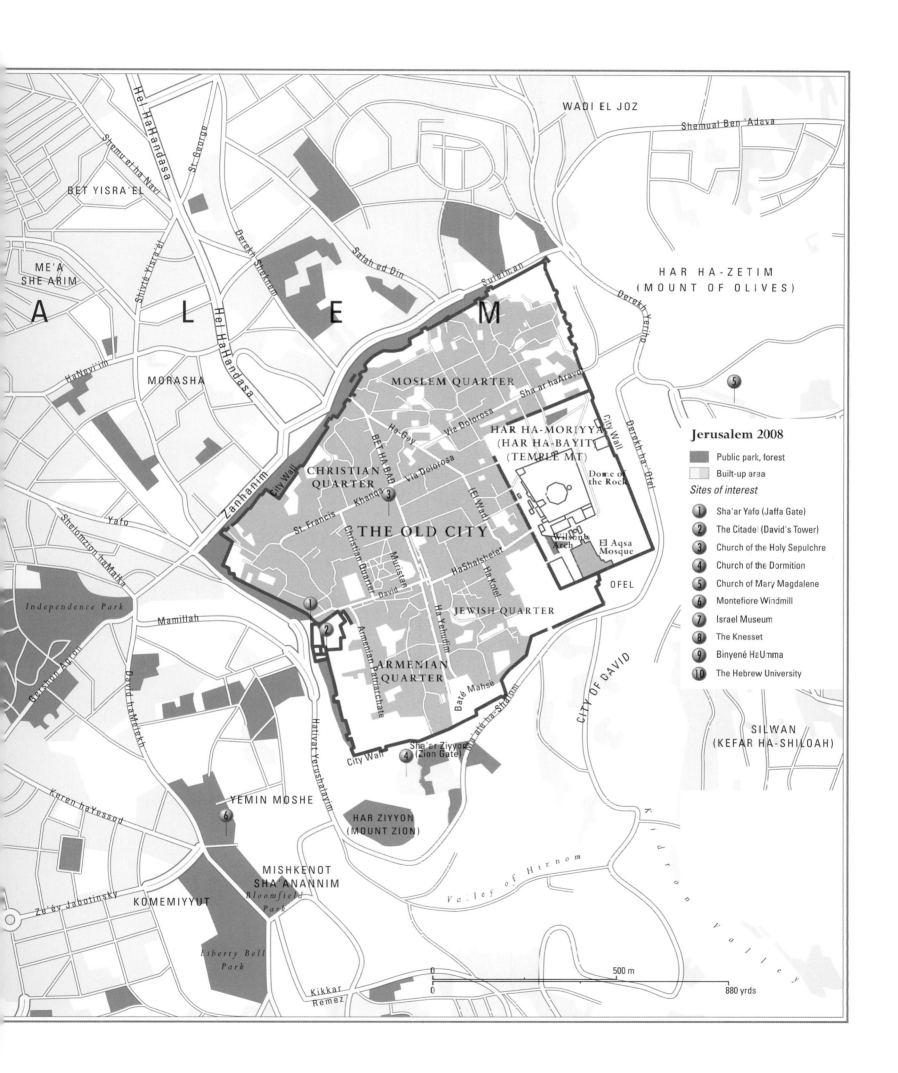

WADI EL JOZ

Shemuel Ben 'Adaya

BET YISRA'EL

Hei HaHandasa

Shemuel ha-Navi

St. George

Derekh Shekhem

Salah ed Din

ME'A
SHE'ARIM

HaNevi'im

MORASHA

Shivte Yisra'el

Hei HaHandasa

A   L   E   M

Suleiman

HAR HA-ZETIM
(MOUNT OF OLIVES)

Derekh Yeriho

MOSLEM QUARTER

Sha'ar haAravot

City Wall

Zanhanim

Yafo

Shelomzion ha-Malka

Ha-Gay

Via Dolorosa

HAR HA-MORIYYA
(HAR HA-BAYIT)
(TEMPLE MT)

City Wall

CHRISTIAN
QUARTER

BET HA-BAD

Via Dolorosa

Dome of
the Rock

Derekh ha-Ofel

Khanda

③

El Wadi

St. Francis

Christian Quarter

Independence Park

Gershon Agron

Mamillah

Muristan

David

HaShalshelet

Ha-Kotel

THE OLD CITY

Wilson's
Arch

El Aqsa
Mosque

OFEL

①

HaYehudim

JEWISH QUARTER

②

David haMelekh

Armenian Patriarchate

ARMENIAN
QUARTER

HaShalom

CITY OF DAVID

Keren haYessod

Hativat Yerushalayim

Bate Mahse

Sha'ar ha-Shalom

Ze'ev Jabotinsky

KOMEMIYYUT

YEMIN MOSHE

⑥

MISHKENOT
SHA'ANANNIM
Bloomfield
Park

④ Sha'ar Ziyyon
(Zion Gate)

HAR ZIYYON
(MOUNT ZION)

Valley of Hinnom

⑤

SILWAN
(KEFAR HA-SHILOAH)

Kidron Valley

Liberty Bell
Park

Kikkar
Remez

500 m

0

880 yrds

Jerusalem 2008

Public park, forest

Built-up area

Sites of interest

① Sha'ar Yafo (Jaffa Gate)
② The Citadel (David's Tower)
③ Church of the Holy Sepulchre
④ Church of the Dormition
⑤ Church of Mary Magdalene
⑥ Montefiore Windmill
⑦ Israel Museum
⑧ The Knesset
⑨ Binyené HaUmma
⑩ The Hebrew University

Previous pages: Beyond the walls of the old city, modern Jerusalem has continued to expand and is now the capital of the state of Israel.

as the booths of money-changers. These are the merchants whom Jesus Christ reviled, as reported in all four Gospels.

The Church of the Holy Sepulchre, now inside the city walls built by Suleiman the Magnificent in 1538–40, is built over Golgotha, the spot at which Christ was crucified and where he was buried (certain Protestant sects believe that he was buried at the site known as the Garden Tomb, outside the city walls almost opposite the Rockefeller Museum, but this is thought to be unlikely). The original building was a magnificent basilica built in 335 C.E. on the orders of the Emperor Constantine, after his mother, Queen Helena, visited Jerusalem and determined the locations of events associated with the last days of Christ. The Church, along with all of Jerusalem's other churches and synagogues, was destroyed in 1010 on the orders of the Fatimid Caliph Al-Hakim bi-Amr Allah but agreements were reached between the Christians and later Caliphs to build a new church. This handsome Romanesque construction was finally completed in 1048 by Constantine IX Monomachos and Patriarch Nicephorus of Constantinople. It was badly damaged in an earthquake in 1927 but still stands.

The Church is the headquarters of the Greek Orthodox Patriarchate in Jerusalem, who were the original custodians. The Armenian Apostolic and Roman Catholics also have a place in the church. In the nineteenth century, the Egyptian, Ethiopian and Syrian Copts acquired lesser responsibilities, which include shrines and other structures within and around the building. Times and places of worship for each community have to be strictly regulated to prevent disputes. Two Arab families were given the key to the main door in 1245 and guard it to this very day.

Jerusalem has another thirty or so important churches inside and outside the present city walls, which belong to every Christian denomination from Anglican to Ethiopian Copt. Two of the most spectacular churches are Russian Orthodox, the Church of St. Mary Magdalene at the foot of the Mount of Olives and the Alexander Nevsky Church in the Old City. The Franciscan Abbey of the Dormition on Mount Zion is where the Virgin Mary is said to have fallen into a deep sleep and been transported up to heaven.

The Persians conquered Jerusalem in 614, destroying most of the churches and again expelling the Jews who had been readmitted by the Empress Eudoxia in 438, but in 629 the city was recaptured by Byzantines. In 638, only six years after the death of Mohammed, Caliph Omar entered Jerusalem as a conqueror, and he allowed the Jews to return. In 691, Caliph Abd al-Malik completed the construction of the Dome of the Rock, built on the site of Temple Mount, the place where the Sacrifice of Isaac is said to have taken place and where the Muslims believe the Prophet ascended into heaven on his horse, Al-Buraq. It is a shrine for pilgrims, rather than a mosque. In 701, the construction of the Al-Aqsa mosque, at one end of the compound, was completed by Caliph al-Walid. This is the second-oldest mosque in the Islamic world and third in importance only after the two mosques in Mecca.

The destruction of the churches of Jerusalem and the killing of Christian pilgrims were the excuse for the First Crusade. In July, 1099, Christian soldiers captured Jerusalem after a month-long siege. The Jews had been among the most vigorous defenders of Jerusalem against the Crusaders and when the city fell, the Crusaders placed as many Jews as they could find inside a synagogue and burned it down.

Jerusalem became the capital of the Kingdom of Jerusalem. Godfrey of Bouillon was elected Lord of Jerusalem in 1099, but died a year later. The Barons offered the lordship of Jerusalem to Godfrey's brother Baldwin, Count of Edessa, who had himself crowned by Patriarch Daimbert on Christmas Day, 1100 in the basilica at Bethlehem, only five miles south-east of the city.

The Crusaders set about rebuilding the principal shrines associated with the life of Christ. The Church of the Holy Sepulchre was rebuilt in Romanesque style and the Muslim shrines on the Temple Mount (the Dome of the Rock and the al-Aqsa Mosque) were used as churches. The Knights Hospitalier and the Knights Templar were founded at this time to protect the pilgrims traveling to Jerusalem. Ironically, the best guides to the city for the pilgrims were those Jews who had survived the slaughter. The Kingdom of Jerusalem lasted until 1291 though Jerusalem was recaptured by the tolerant Saladin in 1187, who allowed all religions freedom of worship. At this time, there were both Sephardic and Ashkenazic Jewish communities in the city.

In 1219, the walls of Jerusalem were demolished on the orders of the Sultan of Damascus, rendering it defenseless and damaging its status. In 1229, through a treaty with the Egyptian ruler Al-Kamil, it fell to Frederick II of Germany. In 1239, after a ten-year truce expired, he began to rebuild the walls but they were demolished by the Emir of Kerak, in the same year. In 1243, Jerusalem was recaptured by the Christians, and the walls were repaired. The Khwarezmian Tatars took the city in 1244, but were driven out by the Egyptians in 1247.

In 1267, Rabbi Moses ben Nahman of Catalonia (1194–1270), also known as Nahmanides, travelled to Jerusalem where he established the oldest synagogue still active in the city, the Ramban Synagogue. In the mid-thirteenth century, Jerusalem was captured by the Egyptian Mameluks. In 1517, it was captured by the Ottoman Turks. Under Suleiman the Magnificent who rebuilt the walls that can be seen to this day, the city enjoyed peace and religious toleration. In 1700, Judah He-Hasid led the largest group of Jewish immigrants to the Land of Israel that had arrived for centuries. They began building the Hurva Synagogue in the Jewish Quarter, but the failure of the Ashkenazic community to pay the debts incurred by the half-built synagogue led to riots that resulted in their expulsion from Jerusalem in 1720. Construction did not resume until 1836 and was finally completed in 1856. The Hurva was one of the largest buildings in the Old City, but was utterly destroyed by the Jordanian Arab Legion during Israel's War of Independence. The conservation of the ruins began in 1977 with the building of an arch from the synagogue's dome. At the time of writing, the synagogue is being rebuilt to the original design and is expected to re-open in 2009. Jerusalem remained a remote corner of the declining Ottoman Empire. In the early nineteenth century, the mixed population numbered only 8,000. The four major non-Muslim communities—Jewish, Christian (Latin and Greek Orthodox), Muslim, and Armenian—each had their own districts, a division that can still be seen today. In the mid-nineteenth century, more Jewish immigrants began making the arduous journey from all over the Jewish world, so that they could die in the Holy City and be buried on the Mount of Olives. More yeshivot (Jewish academies) were founded which attracted students. At the same time, European colonial powers hoped to expand their influence and the Christian religious revival encouraged churches to send missionaries, believing that the Second Coming would only happen if the Jews converted to Christianity. The new science of archaeology began to result in

Archaeological excavations by the walls of the old city of Jerusalem reveal cultural and religious influences over the city's long history.

spectacular finds, bringing the Bible to life.

By the 1860s, the Old City was overcrowded to bursting point. The Jewish philanthopist Sir Moses Montefiore, who had visited the city in 1832, financed the construction of a new district in 1861, a row of houses known as Mishkenot Shaananim. The Russian Orthodox Church began constructing a complex, now known as the Russian Compound, near the Jaffa Gate. More and more Jewish neighborhoods, such as Rehavia and Talpiot, and middle-class Moslem and Christian neighbourhoods, such as Talbieh and the German and Greek Colonies, sprang up west of the Old City in the late nineteenth and early twentieth centuries.

The British defeated the Ottomans during World War I and General Allenby, Commander-in-Chief of the Egyptian Expeditionary Force, entered Jerusalem on foot, out of respect for the Holy City, on December 11, 1917, marking the start of the British Mandate. One of the British bequests to Jerusalem was the ordinance passed by Sir Ronald Storrs, part of a master plan for the city drawn up in 1918 by Sir William McLean, requiring new buildings in the city to be faced with the local pink dolomite or with white limestone, a requirement that has continued. During the 1930s, the Hadassah Medical Center and the Hebrew University were founded on Mount Scopus in the north of the city. The cornerstone for Hadassah Hospital was laid in 1934 and the complex, designed by Erich Mendelsohn, opened in 1939. The dream of establishing a University had been part of the Zionist vision. The cornerstone for the university was laid in 1918, and seven years later, on April 1, 1925, the Hebrew University of Jerusalem was opened at a ceremony attended by Jewish leaders and British dignitaries including Lord Balfour, Viscount Allenby, and Sir Herbert Samuel.

By 1920, however, British rule was resented by the Arabs who blamed it for the influx of Jewish immigrants (by 1948 one in six Jews in Palestine lived in Jerusalem). They staged anti-Jewish riots in Jerusalem in 1920, 1929, and 1930. The Jewish community organized self-defense forces in response. In response to British complicity with the Arabs to prevent Jewish immigration, manifested in the White Paper of 1939, other Zionist groups fought the British. The level of violence escalated with the outbreak of World War II. In July, 1946 members of the Irgun Tsva'i Leumi, an underground Zionist group, blew up a wing of the King David Hotel which housed the British administration, causing the deaths of many civilians. In its 1947 plan, the United Nations proposed that Jerusalem become a city under international control although it would have been completely surrounded by the "Arab State" with only a road connecting it to the "Jewish State". By the end of March, 1948, just before the British withdrawal, and with the British increasingly reluctant to intervene, the roads to Jerusalem were cut off by Arab irregulars, placing the Jewish population of the city under siege. The siege was eventually broken, even before the start of the 1948 Arab-Israeli War which began with the end of the British Mandate in May 1948, but there were heavy losses of life especially among the convoys who were trying to break the siege. The Jordanian invasion and the apathy of the United Nations in the face of Israeli protests, ended the international city project. In 1948, the Old City was surrounded on three sides by the Arab Legion. The western part, became the capital of the state of Israel, surrounded on three sides by Jordanian territory, including the Old City. The Jordanians, under their British leader General Sir John Glubb ("Glubb Pasha"), expelled the Jews or exchanged them for Arab prisoners of war. They destroyed 57 synagogues, as well as libraries and centers of learning. The few buildings that remained standing were defaced, some used as stables. The Jewish gravestones from the Mount of Olives were used for building barracks and latrines by the Jordanian army. When Israel regained the Old City after the Six Day War in 1967, work began to reconstruct the ancient Jewish Quarter which occupies about 15 acres facing the Western Wall, all that survives of the Second Temple. The Cardo, the Roman shopping street, excavated in the 1970s, now runs through its heart. The most prominent synagogue in the Old City, the Hurvah Synagogue, was blown up by the Jordanians.

In 1967, Jerusalem was once more reunited. The fire-walls and sandbags were removed and the ugly ruins of Nomansland between the new Jewish city and the Jaffa Gate were cleared and rebuilt. The city, with a population of about 650,000, is the now the largest in Israel. Yet the status of Jerusalem remains at the heart of the Israel-Palestine conflict, both sides regarding it as their future capital.

View of Jerusalem with Temple Mount in the foreground, seen from the Mount of Olives Jewish cemetery.

Jewish Dietary Laws

THE DIETARY LAWS ARE SAID TO HAVE BEEN A FUNDAMENTAL
BINDING FORCE IN JEWISH COMMUNITIES WORLDWIDE. THEY ARE
STRICTLY ENFORCED AMONG ORTHODOX JEWS, THOUGH THE
PROGRESSIVE JEWISH MOVEMENTS TEND TO IGNORE THEM.

Food plays a very large part in Jewish ritual, having been part of Moses' exhortation to the Children of Israel to cleanliness and purity. The laws of food purity are called kashrut from the word kosher meaning "whole." The Bible is extraordinarily "modern" in many of its hygiene precepts and in the days before refrigeration, koshering was a good way of preserving meat from deterioration.

To summarize the Jewish dietary laws, they involve a ban on eating certain foods perceived to be "unclean" and the separation of milk and milk products from meat and meat products. The foods that are utterly prohibited are listed in the Bible in Leviticus XI. The pig, being mentioned twice, is the most prohibited animal; the only meat that is permitted from a mammal must come from an animal that chews the cud and has a cloven hoof. This means that beef, lamb, and venison are permitted but not rabbit. There is also a strong prohibition on drinking the blood of an animal, since blood was used in pagan sacrifice. As a result, meat (with the exception of liver) must be drained of excess blood before it can be cooked. This so-called koshering is done by first rinsing the meat in lukewarm water to remove any signs of blood; the meat is then soaked in water for thirty minutes. After this, it is sprinkled with coarse (often called kosher) salt. The salt must not be laid on in a thick crust, as the blood must be allowed to drain through it. The salted meat is left to drain for one hour on a perforated, slanting board kept especially for the purpose. Liver is koshered by being held over a naked flame to congeal the blood.

As for fish, only fish with fins and scales are permitted. No doubt the ancients recognized the similarity between crustaceans and insects and banned them for this reason. However, this also

Bagels in a variety of flavors stacked up in the store. New York City even celebrates St. Patrick Day with green bagels! The bagel, a ring-shaped bread roll that is first boiled before baking, was originally made in Poland by Jewish bakers to celebrate the victory of the Polish King Jan III Sobieski over the Turks at the gates of Vienna in 1683.

means that the more primitive fish, such as shark, sturgeon, and dogfish, which do not have scales, are not permitted. It has been mooted that fish with fins and scales are somehow "cleaner," yet carp, a bottom-feeder, is perfectly kosher because it has scales. Indeed, carp was a favorite meal, whole or chopped, for the Sabbath in eastern Europe.

Insects are banned, which is why ultra-orthodox Jews minutely examine salad greens before eating them, even after thorough washing, to ensure that no insect has remained. The exception is locusts, which are eaten by Yemenite Jews but only if there is a family tradition for them to do so. Honey is also permitted. No birds of prey, reptiles, or any crawling thing may eaten and no vermin (such as rabbits, called coneys, in the King James Bible).

The prohibition on separating milk and meat, which comes from a biblical injunction against animal cruelty, does not apply to fish, another reason why fish is such a popular food. It applies to chicken, however, because in the view of the rabbis, poultry might be mistaken for red meat.

Foods that do not fall into either the dairy or the meat category are known as pareve or parveh. The origin of this word is obscure, some believe it is a Yiddish word derived, as is much of early Yiddish, from French, in this case, from the French word "pauvre" (poor) meaning that people who ate pareve were too poor to buy meat or dairy foods.

The time that must elapse between eating a meal containing any milk product (butter, cheese, yogurt, etc.) and one containing meat varies between Jewish communities from between one and six hours. The time that must elapse between eating meat and eating milk is much shorter, usually half an hour to one hour.

There are exceptions to the rule of mixing milk and meat. Rennet, made from a cow's stomach, is used to curdle milk and make cheese. Gelatin is usually made from animal bones, usually calf. There is also a principle known as ehad beshishim (one in sixty) whereby if the meat component is one sixtieth or less than the milk component, and vice versa, it is permitted. Nowadays, however, orthodox Jews eat cheese made with a vegetarian rennet substitute and gelatin sold in Israel is made from the bones of kosher fish or a vegetable alternative, such as agar, is used. If flatware and dishes used for milk and meat are accidentally mixed, they can be made "kosher" again by if they are buried in the ground. Glassware is considered neither dairy nor meat and can be used for both types of foods.

The other restriction on meat concerns tradition and ritual. Hindquarter meat is not permitted unless it has been porged, i.e. the veins and sinews removed, in memory of Jacob's wrestling bout with an angel who damaged his sinews. In some countries, such as the United Kingdom, it is alleged that the kashrut authorities no longer have anyone expert enough to porge meat, so no hindquarter meat is sold as kosher. Suet, the fat of the kidney is also not eaten since this, the finest fat, was reserved for sacrifice in the Temple in Jerusalem.

At Passover, the rules change again. No leaven, whether natural or artificial, is permitted, so no bread. Beer is not allowed although wines and spirits are permitted. The Ashkenazic Jews also prohibit the eating of rice and legumes (peas, beans, chick-peas), although Sephardim eat them. Matzo, the unleavened bread that can be said to be the only truly and uniquely Jewish food, replaces bread for the eight days of the festival.

Food can thus be seen to play an extremely important part in Jewish life. Certain dishes are associated with the festivals and important Jewish occasions. For instance, at funerals, beans and chick-peas are served, as they are rounded to symbolize the life cycle. The same is true of eggs, served at Passover, a spring festival, along with other traditional dishes, symbols of the life cycle and rebirth.

The Jewish calendar is based on the Canaanite pastoral calendar and includes three harvest festivals. It begins in early spring, in the month of Nissan. The Jewish New Year, however, is celebrated in the seventh month, Tishrei, in the fall, along with a cluster of other solemn occasions including the Day of Atonement. Traditional foods for the New Year are honey cake and apple dipped in honey, symbolizing a sweet New Year. Polish Jews also eat fish heads and carrot (because the head is buried in the ground) to symbolize the "head" of the year, since that is the literal translation of "Rosh". The Seven Kinds (sheva minim) of foods that are harvested in the Holy

Land at this time of year are celebrated. They are: wheat, barley, dates, figs, grapes, olives, and pomegranates. At the Feast of Tabernacles, soon after the Day of Atonement, the Four Kinds (arba minim) are carried by worshippers and waved in the synagogue. They consist of the lulav, a closed date-palm branch, the hadass or myrtle, the willow, and the yellow, lemon-like fruit known as a citron, etrog. The citron is often eaten afterward candied or in a dessert.

Shavuot, the Feast of Weeks, is the festival of the First Fruits, and celebrates the giving of the Torah. It is celebrated by Ashkenazic Jews with milk dishes, as this is the season when animals are giving their best milk. They consist of cheesecakes, soft cheeses, and blintzes—pancakes filled with sour cream and cream cheese. The Sephardic communities bake a cake known as Seite Sielos (Seventh Heaven) for this festival. At Hannukah, the midwinter festival, the Ashkenazic Jews eat fried foods, especially potato pancakes (latkas) and donuts, to commemorate the miracle of the oil that lasted for eight days. Sephardic Jews eat milk dishes at Hannukah and eat fried foods at Purim (based on the biblical story of Esther) when Ashkenazim eat three-cornered pastries known as Haman's hats or Haman's pockets filled with plum or poppyseed preserves.

Celebrating the Passover meal, known as the Seder. There is a plate on the table with the five items required for the seder: the shankbone of a lamb, a roasted egg, bitter herbs (maror), green herbs (karpas), haroseth (a sweet mixture to symbolize the mortar used for brick-laying by the Hebrew slaves), and there is matzo, unleavened bread. Jews must not eat any leaven during the eight days of Passover, so matzo must be substituted for bread.

BIBLIOGRAPHY

Abrahams, Beth-Zion (ed.), *The Life of Glückel of Hameln 1646–1724*, written by herself. Translated from the original Yiddish, Yoselof, 1963. Horovitz Publ. Co., London, 1962.

Ackerman, Susan, *Warrior, Dancer, Seductress, Queen. Women in Judges and Biblical Israel*, New York: Bantam, Doubleday, Dell Publishing Group Inc., 1998

Alimi, Eitan, *Israeli Politics and the First Palestinian Intifada*. Routledge, London, 2006.

Anderson, Bernard, *Living World of the Old Testament*, London: Prentice Hall, 1998

Aronson, Geoffrey, *Israel, Palestinians, and the Intifada: Creating Facts on the West Bank*. Kegan Paul International. London, 1990.

Bar-Kochva, B., *Judas Maccabaeus: the Jewish Struggle against the Romans*, Cambridge: Cambridge University Press, 2002

Bein, Alex (trans. Maurice Samuel), *Theodore Herzl: A Biography of the Founder of the Modern Zionism*, 1941.

Beinin, Joel and Zachary Lockman, *Intifada: The Palestinian Uprising Against Israeli Occupation*. South End Press, Boston, 1989.

Black, Jeremy (ed), *The Literature of Ancient Sumer*, Oxford: Oxford University Press, 2006

Blum, Léon, *For All Mankind*, Left Book Club, London, 1946.

Bosworth, A.B., *The Legacy of Alexander: Politics, Warfare and Propaganda under the Successors*, Oxford: Oxford University Press, 2005

Bregman, A. and El-Tahri, *The Fifty Years' War: Israel and the Arabs*, BBC, London, 1998.

Brettler, Marc Zvi, *The Book of Judges*, London: Routledge, 2001

Bright, John, *A History of Israel*, London: SCM Press, 1972

Brook, Kevin Alan, *The Jews of Khazaria*, Jason Aaronson, New Jersey, 1999.

Bryce, Trevor, The Kingdom of the Hittites, Oxford: Oxford University Press, 2005

Burns, M., *France and the Dreyfys Affair*, Macmillan, London, 1999.

Caplan, Neil, *Palestine Jewry and the Palestine Question, 1917–1925*, Frank Cass, 1978.

Chavalas, Mark. W., *The Ancient Near East. Historical Sources in Translation*, Oxford: Blackwell Publishing, 2006

Chazan, Robert, *European Jewry and the First Crusade*, University of California Press, Stanford, 1987.

Collins, Larry and Lapierre, *Dominique, O Jerusalem!*, Pan Books 1973.

Conder, Clause Reigner, *The Tell Amarna Tablets*, Athena University Press, 2004

Curtis, J.E. and Tallis, Nigel, *Forgotten Empire: the World of Ancient Persia*, London: British Museum Press, 2005

Dicks, Brian, *The Ancient Persians. How They Lived and Worked*, London: David and Charles, 1979

Dunlop, D.M., *History of the Jewish Khazars*, New York, 1967.

Elon, Amos, *Herzl, Holt, Rinehart, Winston*. New York, 1975.

Elon, Amos, *The Israelis: Founders and Sons*, Holt, Rinehart, Winston. New York, 1971.

Elon, Amos, *Jerusalem: City of Mirrors*, Weidenfeld and Nicolson, London, 1989.

Encyclopedia of the Holocaust, Tel-Aviv, 1990.

Falk, Avner, *Herzl, King of the Jews: A Psychoanalytic Biography of Theodor Herzl*, University Press of America, 1975, 1993.

Fairbairn, Donald, *Grace and Christology in the Early Church*, Oxford: Oxford University Press, 2006

Falk, Avner, *Herzl, King of the Jews: A Psychoanalytic Biography of Theodor Herzl*, University Press of America, 1975, 1993.

Finkelstein, Israel and Silberman, Neil Asher, *The Bible Unearthed: Archaeology's New Vision of Ancient Israel*, New York: Simon and Schuster, 2002

Fohrer, Georg, *Introduction to the Old Testament*, London: SPCK, 1976

Fox, Robin Lane, *Alexander the Great*, London: Penguin Books Ltd., 2004

Frankel, Jonathan, *The Damascus affair : "ritual murder," politics, and the Jews in 1840 Cambridge*, Cambridge and New York, 1997.

Fuchs, Daniel and Sevener, Harald A., *From Bondage to Freedom: A Survey of Jewish History from the Babylonian Captivity to the Coming of the Messiah*, New York: Loiseaux Brothers, 1996

George, A. R., *The Babylonian Gilgamesh Epic*, Oxford: Oxford University Press, 2003

Gilbert, Martin, *Auschwitz and the Allies*, New York, 1981.

Gilbert, M., *The Routledge Atlas of Jewish History*, London: Routledge, 1993

Golden, Jonathan M., *Ancient Canaan and Israel: New Perspectives*, Oxford: ABC-Clio, 2004

Grottanelli, Christiano, *Kings and Prophets, Monarchic Power, Inspired Leadership and Sacred Text in Biblical Narrative*, Oxford: Oxford University Press, 1999

Gruen, Erich S., *Diaspora*, London: Harvard University Press, 2004

Habicht, Christian, *Hellenistic Monarchies. Selected Papers*, Chicago: University of Michigan Press, 2006

Hamilton, V., *Handbook on the Historical Books: Joshua, Judges, Ruth, Samuel, Kings, Chronicles, Ezra-Nehemiah, Esther*, Baker Book House Company, 2001

Hawks, J., *The First Great Civilizations: Life in Mesopotamia, the Indus Valley, and Egypt*, London: Penguin, 1977

Hayes, John H. and Mandell, Sara R., *The Jewish People in Classical Antiquity from Alexander to Bar Kochba*, Louisville, Kentucky, USA: Westminster John Knox Press, 1998

Hoess, Rudolf, *Commandant of Auschwitz*, Cleveland, 1959.

Josephus, *Complete Works*, London: Pickering and Inglis Ltd., 1960

Kent, Charles Foster, *A History of the Hebrew People from the Settlement in Canaan to the Division of the Kingdom*, Kessinger Publishing LLC, 2004

Kenyon, Kathleen, *Amorites and Canaanites*, Oxford: Oxford University Press, 2004

King, Leonard William, *Babylonian Religion and Mythology*, USA: Fredonia Books, 2003

Klarsfeld, Serge (ed.), *The Auschwitz Album. Lilly Jacob's Album*, New York, 1980.

Knoblet, Jerry, *Herod the Great*, Lanham, Maryland, USA: University Press of America Inc., 2005

Killebrew, Ann E., *Biblical Peoples and Ethnicity: An Archaeological Study of Egyptians, Canaanites, Philistines, and Early Israel, 1300–1100 BC*, The Netherlands, Leiden: Brill, 2006

Koestler, Arthur, *The Thirteenth Tribe*, Random House, New York, 1976.

Korobkin, Daniel (trans.), *The Kuzari: In Defense of the Despised Faith*, a new translation of Kuzari by Yehuda HaLevi, Jason Aronson, New Jersey, 1998.

Kramer, S.N., *Sumerian Mythology*, Philadelphia: University of Pennsylvania Press, 1998

Kriwaczek, Paul, *Yiddish Civilisation: The Rise and Fall of a Forgotten Nation*, Weidenfeld and Nicolson, London, 2005; Knopf, New York, 2005.

Kuhrt, Amelie, *The Ancient Near East, c. 3000–330 BC*, London: Routledge, 1997

Lacqueur, Walter, *The History of Zionism*, I.B. Tauris, London, 2003.

Le Glay, Marcel, Voisin, Jean-Louis, Le Bohec, Yann, *A History of Rome*, Oxford: Blackwell Publishing, 1996

Lowenstein, Steven M., *The Jewish Cultural Tapestry*, OUP, Oxford, 2000.

Ma, John, *Antiochus III and the Cities of Western Asia*, Oxford: Oxford University Press, 2002

Mandel, Neville, *The Arabs and Palestine*, UCLA, 1976.

Mascarenhas, Theodore, *The Missionary Function of Israel in Psalms 67, 96 and 117*, Oxford: Rowman and Littlefield Publishing, 2005

Miller, J. Maxwell and Hayes, John H., *A History of Ancient Israel and Judah*, London: SCM Press, 1986

Moscato, Sabatino, *The Phoenicians*, London: I. B. Tauris, 2001

Murphy-O'Connor, Jerome, *Paul: A Critical Life*, Oxford: Oxford University Press, 1998

Nakhai, Beth Alpert, *Archaeology and Religions of Canaan*, American Schools of Oriental Research, 2002

Niditch, Susan, *Ancient Israelite Religion*, USA: Oxford University Press, Inc., 1988

Peretz, Don, *Intifada: The Palestinian Uprising*. Westview Press, Boulder, Colorado, 1990, ISBN 0-8133-0860-7.

Pinches, Theophilus Goldridge, *The Old Testament in the Light of the Historical Records and Legends of Assyria and Babylon*, Chestnut Hill, Massachussetts: Adamant Media Corporation, 2005

Reitlinger, Gerald, *The Final Solution*, Beechhurst Press, New York, 1953.

Rhodes, P.J., *A History of the Classical Greek World, 478–323 BC*, Oxford: Blackwell Publishing, 2006

Rogerson, John and Davies, Philip, *The Old Testament World*, London: Continuum International Publishing Group, 2005

Ross, Aubrey, *The Messiah of Turkey: A 21st Century View*, i2i, London, 2007.

Schürer, E., *The History of the Jewish People in the Age of Jesus Christ (175 BC–AD 135)*, revised edition, 3 vols. Trans. T. A. Burkill et al., Edinburgh, 1973–87

Shalev, Aryeh, *The Intifada: Causes and Effects*. Jerusalem Post & Westview Press, Jerusalem, 1990, ISBN 0-8133-8303-X.

Shimoni, Gideon and Wistrich, Robert S. (eds.), *Theodor Herzl, Visionary of the Jewish State*, Magnes Press, Jerusalem and New York, 1999.

Shirer, William, *The Rise and Fall of the Third Reich*, 1960.

Sievers, Joseph, *The Hasmoneans and their Supporters: From Mattathias to the Death of John Hyrcanus I*, Cambridge: Scholars Press, 1990

Soggin, J. Alberto, *An Introduction to the History of Israel and Judah*, London: SCM Press, 1993

Spalinger, Anthony J., *War in Ancient Egypt. The New Kingdom*, Oxford: Blackwell Publishing, 2004

Sweeney, Marvin A., *King Josiah of Judah*, Oxford: Oxford University Press, 2001

Terry, Michael, *Reader's Guide to Judaism*, London: Routledge, 2000

Teveth, Shabtai, *Ben-Gurion and the Palestinian Arabs: From Peace to War*, Oxford University Press, London, 1985.

Thompson, Thomas L., *The Historicity of the Patriarchal Narratives: The Quest for the Historical Abraham*, London: Continuum International Publishing Group

Tyldesley, Joyce, *Ramesses: Egypt's Greatest Pharaoh*, London: Penguin Books Ltd., 2001

White, Ellen G., *The Acts of the Apostles in the Proclamation of the Gospel of Jesus Christ*, Kessinger Publishing Company, 2005

Wilson, Derek, *Rothschild: A Story of Wealth and Power*, André Deutsch, London, 1988.

Wiseman, D.J., *Nebuchadnezzar and Babylon*, Oxford: Oxford University Press, 1991

Yadin, Yigael, *Hazor*, Oxford: Oxford University Press, 2005

Yadin, Yigael, *Masada. Herod's Fortress and the Zealot's Last Stand*, London: Weidenfeld and Nicolson, 1966

Ze'ev Schiff, Ehud Ya'ari. *Intifada: The Palestinian Uprising: Israel's Third Front*. Simon & Schuster, New York, 1989.

INDEX

JEWISH POPULATION BY STATE

COUNTRY	JEWISH POPULATION	PERCENTAGE OF TOTAL POPULATION	PERCENTAGE OF TOTAL WORLD JEWISH POPULATION
U.S.A.	7,000,000	2	38.2
Israel	5,600,000	76.1	35.7
Russia	800,000	0.57	4.91
France	606,561	1	4.15
Canada	393,660	1.2	2.695
United Kingdom	350,000	0.6	1.97
Argentina	250,000	0.67	1.335
Germany	118,000	0.25	1.51
Ukraine	142,276	0.3	0.97
Australia	120,000	0.55	0.82
South Africa	88,688	0.04	0.61
Brazil	94,000	0.1	0.6
Belarus	72,103	0.7	<0.5
Hungary	49,000	0.47	<0.5
Mexico	53,101	0.05	<0.5
Belgium	51,821	0.5	<0.5
Spain	48,409	0.12	<0.5
Netherlands	32,814	0.2	<0.5
Moldova	31,187	0.7	<0.5
Uruguay	30,743	0.9	<0.5
Italy	30,213	0.052	<0.5
Chile	25,375	0.131	<0.5
Poland	24,999	0.065	<0.5
Venezuela	20,900	0.1	<0.5
Iran	20,405	0.03	<0.5
Ethiopia	20,000	0.027	<0.5
Sweden	18,003	0.2	<0.5
Uzbelistan	17,453	0.065	<0.5
Turkey	17,415	0.025	<0.5
India	15,405	0.005	<0.5
Switzerland	14,649	0.2	<0.5
Panama	10,029	0.33	<0.5
Latvia	9,092	0.397	<0.5
Austria	8,184	0.17	<0.5
Georgia	7,951	0.17	<0.5
Azerbaijan	7,911	0.1	<0.5
Denmark	7,062	0.13	<0.5
Romania	6,029	0.027	<0.5
New Zealand	5,447	0.135	<0.5
Greece	5,334	0.05	<0.5
Morocco	5,236	0.016	<0.5
Kazakhstan	4,100	0.027	<0.5
Lithuania	3,596	0.1	<0.5
Colombia	7,436	0.008	<0.5
Czech Republic	3,072	0.03	<0.5
Slovakia	3,041	0.056	<0.5
Peru	2,800	0.01	<0.5
Costa Rica	2,409	0.06	<0.5
Bulgaria	2,300	0.031	<0.5
Ireland	1,930	0.045	<0.5

ACKNOWLEDGMENTS

For Cartographica Press
Design, Maps and Typesetting: Jeanne Radford, Alexander Swanston, Malcolm Swanston and Jonathan Young

The publishers would like to thank the following picture libraries for their kind permission to use their pictures and illustrations:

Archiv Gerstenberg   258, 259
Associated Press   379
Bibliotheque National, Paris   203
Bridgeman Art Library   213
C. M. Dixon 118,   176
Corbis   29, 30, 33, 68, 146, 180, 184, 190, 200, 211, 236, 275
David Rubinger   328
et Archive   175, 195, 282
Getty   9, 43, 48, 52, 55, 56, 64, 66, 77, 78, 80, 82, 87, 88, 95, 99, 109, 111, 112, 120, 124, 128, 136, ,142, 160, 168, 192, 201, 206, 210, 212, 221, 222, 223, 233, 234, 242, 250, 262, 266, 278, 298, 300, 305, 316, 326, 335, 336, 349, 362, 366, 383, 385
Israeli Press and Photo Agency   337. 334
J. Catling Allen   20, 221
Josephine Bacon   375.
Klause Otto Hunde   10
National Archives, Washington DC   248
New York Times   297
Peter Newark Historical Pictures   133
Popperphoto   229, 246
Private collection   68, 71, 76, 106, 107, 154, 162, 208, 217, 231, 256, 264, 265, 271, 272, 284, 287, 295, 302, 353, 360, 361, 366, 367, 370, 375, 381
Quarto Publishing Limited   12, 14, 46, 51, 61, 113, 130, 156, 164, 165
RHPL/ F.L. Kennet   36
RLR&R   23, 26, 59, 72, 85, 89, 90, 103, 140, 158, 150, 172, 179289, 294
Roland Dean   101
Staatliche Museum Berlin   24
The Mansell Collection   138, 215
Warburg Institute, University of London   35
Werner Braun, Jerusalem   167

Every effort had been made to contact the copyright holders for images reproduced in this book.
The publishers would welcome any errors or omissions being brought to their attention.